THE OFFICIAL RED BOOK®

A GUIDE BOOK OF

UNITED STATES COINS

R. S. YEOMAN

SENIOR EDITOR
KENNETH BRESSETT

RESEARCH EDITOR
Q. DAVID BOWERS

VALUATIONS EDITOR
JEFF GARRETT

67th Edition

Fully Illustrated Catalog and
Retail Valuation List—1616 to Date

A Guide Book of United States Coins™
THE OFFICIAL RED BOOK OF UNITED STATES COINS™

THE OFFICIAL RED BOOK and THE OFFICIAL RED BOOK OF UNITED STATES COINS
are trademarks of Whitman Publishing, LLC. Library of Congress Catalog Card No.: 47-22284

www.whitman.com

Printed in the United States of America.
The WCG™ pricing grid used throughout this publication is patent pending.

© 2013 Whitman Publishing, LLC
3101 Clairmont Road • Suite G • Atlanta GA 30329

OCG™ Collecting Guide   Whitman®

For a complete listing of numismatic reference books,
supplies, and storage products, visit us at
www.whitman.com

Scan this QR code to browse
Whitman Publishing's full catalog
of coin-related books, supplies,
storage and display products.

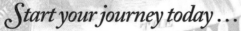

CONTENTS

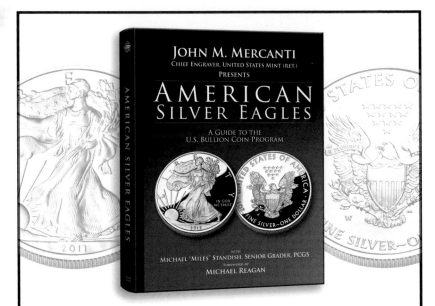

Senior Editor: Kenneth Bressett. Research Editor: Q. David Bowers. Valuations Editor: Jeff Garrett. Special Consultants: Philip Bressett, Robert Rhue, and Ben Todd.

Gary Adkins
John Albanese
Mark Albarian
Dominic Albert
Buddy Alleva
Richard S. Appel
Richard M. August
Mitchell A. Battino
Lee J. Bellisario
Mark Borckardt
Larry Briggs
H. Robert Campbell
Jason Carter
J.H. Cline
Elizabeth Coggan
Alan Cohen
Gary Cohen
James H. Cohen
Stephen M. Cohen
Steve Contursi
Adam Crum
Raymond Czahor

Sheridan Downey
Ken Duncan
Mike Fuljenz
John Gervasoni
Dennis M. Gillio
Ronald J. Gillio
Ira M. Goldberg
Lawrence Goldberg
Kenneth M. Goldman
J.R. Grellman
Tom Hallenbeck
James Halperin
Ash Harrison
Steven Hayden
Brian Hendelson
Gene L. Henry
JohnW. Highfill
Karl Hirtzinger
Brian Hodge
Jesse Iskowitz
Steve Ivy
James J. Jelinski

Larry Johnson
Donald H. Kagin
Bradley S. Karoleff
Jim Koenings
John Kraljevich
Richard A. Lecce
Julian M. Leidman
Stuart Levine
Kevin Lipton
Denis W. Loring
Dwight Manley
David McCarthy
Chris McCawley
Robert T. McIntire
Harry Miller
Lee S. Minshull
Scott P. Mitchell
Michael C. Moline
Charles Morgan
Casey Noxon
Paul Nugget
Mike Orlando

Joseph Parrella
Robert M. Paul
William P. Paul
Joel Rettew Jr.
Joel Rettew Sr.
Greg Rohan
Maurice Rosen
Gerald R. Scherer Jr.
Roger Siboni
James Simek
Rick Snow
David M. Sundman
Anthony J. Swiatek
Anthony Terranova
Troy Thoreson
Frank Van Valen
Douglas Winter
David Wnuck
Mark S. Yaffe

Special credit is due to the following for service and data in this book: Stewart Blay, Roger W. Burdette, John Burns, Frank J. Colletti, Columbus–Amcrica Discovery Group, Charles Davis, Tom DeLorey, Steven Ellsworth, David Fanning, George B. Fitzgerald, Bill Fivaz, George Fuld, Chuck Furjanic, James C. Gray, Charles Hoskins, R.W. Julian, Richard Kelly, George F. Kolbe, David W. Lange, G.J. Lawson, Andy Lustig, J.P. Martin, Syd Martin, Paul Montgomery, Eric P. Newman, John M. Pack, Ken Potter, P. Scott Rubin, Paul Rynearson, Mark Salzberg, Mary Sauvain, Cherie Schoeps, Richard J. Schwary, Neil Shafer, Robert W. Shippee, Craig Smith, Jerry Treglia, Mark R.Vitunic, Holland Wallace, Fred Weinberg, Weimar White, John Whitney, Raymond Williams, and John Wright.

Special credit is due to the following for service in past editions: David Akers, Lyman Allen, Jeff Ambio, Michael Aron, Philip E. Benedetti, Richard A. Bagg, Jack Beymer, George Blenker, Walter Breen, James H. Cohen, Silvano DiGenova, Ken Duncan, Bob Entlich, John Feigenbaum, Dennis Forgue, Harry Forman, Henry Garrett, William Gay, John Gervasoni, Harry Gittelson, Ron Guth, John Hamrick, Karl D. Hirtzinger, Michael Hodder, Robert Jacobs, A.M. Kagin, Stanley Kesselman, Jerry Kimmel, Mike Kliman, Paul Koppenhaver, John Kraljevich, Robert B. Lecce, Ed Leventhal, Dwight N. Manley, Arnold Margolis, Glenn Miller, Richard Nachbar, Thomas Payne, Beth Piper, Doug Plasencia, Andrew Pollock III, John Porter, Mike Ringo, J.S. Schreiber, Hugh Sconyers, Robert Shaw, Arlie Slabaugh, Thomas Smith, William Spencer, Paul Spiegel, Lawrence R. Stack, Maurice Storck Sr., Charles Surasky, Steve Tanenbaum, Mark Van Winkle, and Russell Vaughn.

Special photo credits are due to the following: Al Adams, the American Numismatic Association, Douglas F. Bird, Steve Contursi, Bill Fivaz, Ira & Larry Goldberg Coins & Collectibles, Tom Mulvaney, Numismatic Guaranty Corporation of America (NGC), PCGS, Brent Pogue, Sarasota Rare Coin Gallery, the Smithsonian Institution, Spectrum, Stack's Bowers Galleries, Superior Galleries, and the U.S. Mint.

Coin values shown in this book are retail prices figured from data from the listed contributors approximately two months prior to publication. The coin market is so active in some categories that values can easily change during that period. Values are shown as a guide and are not intended to serve as a price list for any dealer's stock. A dash appearing in a price column indicates that coins in that grade exist even though there are no current sales or auction records for them. The dash does not necessarily mean that such coins are exceedingly rare. Italicized prices indicate unsettled or speculative values. A number of listings of rare coins lack prices or dashes in certain grades, indicating that they are not available or not believed to exist in those grades.

Prices rise when (1) the economic trend is inflationary and speculators turn to tangible assets as a hedge, or when the number of collectors increases, while coin supplies remain stationary or decrease through attrition or melting; (2) dealers replace their stocks of coins only from collectors or other dealers, who expect a profit over what they originally paid; (3) speculators attempt to influence the market through selective buying; or (4) bullion (gold and silver) prices rise.

Prices decline when (1) changes in collecting habits or economic conditions alter demand for certain coins; (2) speculators sell in large quantities; (3) hoards or large holdings are suddenly released and cannot be quickly absorbed by the normal market; or (4) bullion (gold and silver) prices decline.

Those who edit, contribute to, and publish this book advocate the collecting of coins for pleasure and educational benefits. A secondary consideration is that of investment, the profits from which are usually realized over the long term based on careful purchases.

The *Handbook of United States Coins* (commonly called the Blue Book), by R.S. Yeoman, Whitman Publishing, Atlanta, GA, contains average prices dealers will pay for these coins, and is obtainable through most coin dealers, hobby shops, bookstores, and the Internet.

ABBREVIATIONS USED IN THIS BOOK

Abbreviation	Meaning	Abbreviation	Meaning	Abbreviation	Meaning
Arr	Arrows	Inv	Inverted	Pf	Proof
BM	Branch Mint	Knbd	Knobbed	Pl	Plain
Cap	Capped	Leg	Legend	Pt	Partial
Cl	Close	Lg	Large	Rev	Reverse
CN	Copper-Nickel	Lib	Liberty	Rt	Right
DblDie	Doubled-Die	Ltrs	Letters	SE	Small Eagle
Drap	Drapery	Med	Medium	Sm	Small
Drpd	Draped	NM	No Motto	Sq	Square
Dt	Date	Nml	Normal	Std	Seated
HE	Heraldic Eagle	NS	No Stars		
Horiz	Horizontal	Obv	Obverse		

A slash between words or letters represents an overdate or overmintmark: "3/2" is an abbreviation of "3 Over 2," "D/S" is "D Over S," etc.

Photographs in This Book

Collectors should be aware that unofficial copies of certain American issues were made after 1850 to provide facsimiles of rarer issues that would otherwise have been unobtainable. Many crude imitations have also been made in recent years, as well as forgeries intended to deceive collectors. All photos herein, however, are of genuine specimens.

CONDITIONS OF COINS

Essential Elements of the American Numismatic Association Grading Standards

Proof—A specially made coin distinguished by sharpness of detail and usually with a brilliant, mirrorlike surface. *Proof* refers to the method of manufacture and is not a grade. The term implies superior condition unless otherwise noted. See page 343 for details.

> **Gem Proof (PF-65)**—Surfaces are brilliant, with no noticeable blemishes or flaws. A few scattered, barely noticeable marks or hairlines.

> **Choice Proof (PF-63)**—Surfaces are reflective, with only a few blemishes in secondary focal places. No major flaws.

> **Proof (PF-60)**—Surfaces may have several contact marks, hairlines, or light rubs. Luster may be dull and eye appeal lacking.

Mint State—The terms *Mint State (MS)* and *Uncirculated (Unc.)* are interchangeable and refer to coins showing no trace of wear. Such coins may vary slightly due to minor surface imperfections, as described in the following subdivisions:

> **Perfect Uncirculated (MS-70)**—Perfect new condition, showing no trace of wear. The finest quality possible, with no evidence of scratches, handling, or contact with other coins. Very few circulation-issue coins are ever found in this condition.

> **Gem Uncirculated (MS-65)**—An above-average Uncirculated coin that may be brilliant or lightly toned and that has very few contact marks on the surface or rim.

> **Choice Uncirculated (MS-63)**—A coin with some distracting contact marks or blemishes in prime focal areas. Luster may be impaired.

> **Uncirculated (MS-60)**—A coin that has no trace of wear, but which may show a number of contact marks, and whose surface may be spotted or lack some luster.

Choice About Uncirculated (AU-55)—Evidence of friction on high points of design. Most of the mint luster remains.

About Uncirculated (AU-50)—Traces of light wear on many of the high points. At least half of the mint luster is still present.

Choice Extremely Fine (EF-45)—Light overall wear on the highest points. All design details are very sharp. Some of the mint luster is evident.

Extremely Fine (EF-40)—Light wear on the design throughout, but all features are sharp and well defined. Traces of luster may show.

Choice Very Fine (VF-30)—Light, even wear on the surface and highest parts of the design. All lettering and major features are sharp.

Very Fine (VF-20)—Moderate wear on design high points. All major details are clear.

Fine (F-12)—Moderate to considerable even wear. The entire design is bold with an overall pleasing appearance.

Very Good (VG-8)—Well worn with main features clear and bold, although rather flat.

Good (G-4)—Heavily worn, with the design visible but faint in areas. Many details are flat.

About Good (AG-3)—Very heavily worn with portions of the lettering, date, and legend worn smooth. The date may be barely readable.

A star (★) in the grade on a slab means "exceptional quality."

Important: Undamaged coins are worth more than bent, corroded, scratched, holed, nicked, stained, or mutilated ones. Flawless Uncirculated coins are generally worth more than values quoted in this book. Slightly worn coins ("sliders") that have been cleaned and conditioned ("buffed") to simulate Uncirculated luster are worth considerably less than perfect pieces.

Unlike damage inflicted after striking, manufacturing defects do not always lessen values. Examples include colonial coins with planchet flaws or weakly struck designs; early silver and gold coins with weight-adjustment "file marks" (parallel cuts made on the planchet prior to striking); and coins with "lint marks" (surface marks due to the presence of dust or other foreign matter during striking).

Brief guides to grading are placed before each major coin type. While grading *standards* strive to be precise, interpretations are subjective and often vary among collectors, dealers, and certification services.

THIRD-PARTY GRADING AND AUTHENTICATION

In this guide book values from under $1 up to several hundred dollars are for "raw" coins—that is, coins that have *not* been graded and encapsulated by a professional third-party grading service. Coins valued near or above $500 are assumed to be third-party-graded. A high-value coin that has not been professionally certified as authentic, graded, and encapsulated by an independent firm is apt to be valued lower than the prices indicated.

What *is* third-party grading? This is a service providing, for a fee, an impartial, independent opinion of a coin's grade and its authenticity. The grader is neither buyer nor seller, and has no biased interest in the coin's market value. Third-party grading started in the late 1970s with ANACS (then a service of the American Numismatic Association; now privately owned and operated). ANACS graders would examine a coin and, after determining its authenticity, would assign separate grades to its obverse and reverse (such as MS-63/65) and return it to the sender, along with a certificate and photograph.

In 1986 a group of coin dealers launched the Professional Coin Grading Service (PCGS), which grades coins for a fee and hermetically seals them in plastic holders with interior labels. This "slabbing" helps guarantee that a coin and its grade certificate cannot be separated. In 1987 Numismatic Guaranty Corporation of America (NGC) was started, offering a similar encapsulation service. Both companies guarantee the authenticity and grades of the coins they certify. Coins are judged by consensus, with the graders having no knowledge of who submitted them.

From the 1970s to the present there have been more than 100 different commercial grading companies. Readers are cautioned to investigate the background of a TPG (third-party grader) before trusting in its services.

Today the hobby's leading third-party grading firms are NGC (Sarasota, Florida) and PCGS (Newport Beach, California).

Professional grading strives to be completely objective, but coins are graded by humans and not computers. This introduces a subjective element of *art* as opposed to *science.* A coin's grade, even if certified by a leading TPG, can be questioned by any collector or dealer—or even by the service that graded it, if resubmitted for a second look. Furthermore, within a given grade, a keen observer will find coins that are low-quality, average, and high-quality for that grade. Such factors as luster, color, strength of strike, and overall eye appeal can make, for example, one MS-65 1891 Morgan dollar more visually attractive than another with the same grade. This gives the smart collector the opportunity to "cherrypick," or examine multiple slabbed coins and select the highest-quality coin for the desired grade. This process builds a better collection than simply accepting a TPG's assigned grades, and is summed up in the guidance of "Buy the coin, not the slab." (Also note that a coin certified as, for example, MS-64 might have greater eye appeal—and therefore be more desirable to a greater number of collectors—than a less attractive coin graded MS-65.)

Over the years, collectors have observed a trend nicknamed "gradeflation": the reinterpretation, in practice, of the standards applied to a given grade over time. For example, a coin evaluated by a leading TPG in 1992 as MS-64 might be graded today as MS-65 or even MS-66.

The general effect of third-party grading and authentication has been to increase buyers' and sellers' comfort levels with the perceived quality of rare coins in the marketplace. And, as mentioned, there still exists the potential for keen-eyed collectors to cherrypick coins that are "exceptional for their grade."

AN INTRODUCTION TO UNITED STATES COINS
The Spanish Milled Dollar

The Spanish milled dollar, valued at 8 reales, and otherwise known as the *Pillar dollar* or *piece of eight,* has been given a place in romantic fiction unequaled by any other coin.

This time-honored piece and its fractional parts (one-half, one, two, and four reales) were the principal coins of the American colonists, and were the forerunners of our own silver dollar and its fractional divisions. Thomas Jefferson even recommended to the Continental Congress on September 2, 1776, that the new country adopt the silver Spanish milled dollar as its monetary unit of value.

The coin shown above bears the M̊ mintmark for Mexico City. Similar pieces with other mintmarks were struck in Bolivia, Chile, Colombia, Guatemala, and Peru. Average value for an 8 reales Pillar dollar of common date and mint is about $225 in Fine to Very Fine condition. Dates range from 1732 to 1772. Bust-type 8 reales dollars, made from 1772 to 1825, also circulated widely. These are valued at $85 to $110 in Very Fine conditon. *Note that many modern copies of the 8 reales exist. These are produced mostly as souvenirs and have little or no value.*

Money of the Early Americans

The saga of American money covers a period of nearly four centuries, from 1620 to the present. It began when the early European settlers in New England started trading with Native Americans for furs and commodities that could be exported to Britain. The furs, tobacco, and lumber exports were used to purchase needed items that could not be produced locally. Trade was carried on with the Indians through the use of barter and strings of wampum, which were fashioned from mussel shells in the form of beads. Beaver skins, wampum, and, in Virginia, tobacco, soon became the commonly accepted local media of exchange for all other available commodities that were not bartered. The immigrants, in fact, had little use for coined money at first; but when merchandise arrived from Europe, coins were usually demanded in payment for goods.

Nearly all foreign coins were accepted for purchases. The most popular were French louis, English guineas, German thalers, Dutch ducats, and various Spanish coins, including gold doubloons and, particularly, the Spanish milled dollar, or piece of eight. The piece of eight continued to be a standard money unit throughout the entire colonial period. Even after the Revolutionary War ended (in 1783) and the United States Mint was established (in 1792), the Spanish dollar and its fractional parts circulated in this country with official sanction, until 1857. One real equaled 12-1/2 cents and was known as a *bit.* A quarter of the dollar thus became known as *two bits,* a term that is still understood to mean 25 cents.

Because of the shortage of small change, large coins were sometimes cut into smaller pieces for convenience. Spanish-American milled dollars were often chopped into halves, quarters, or eighths. Fraudulent cutting into five or six "quarters" caused many to distrust these cut pieces.

Early Americans cut Spanish-American silver coins into pieces to make small change.

England consistently ignored the plight of its American colonists and made no effort to provide gold or silver coins, or small change in any form, for their convenience. The English mercantile system relied on exports from the colonies, and sought to control trade by limiting the amount of "hard" money paid to them. Under these constraints, the colonists were able to trade for most necessities only with England, and were left with very little coinage for trade with other countries. The foreign coins that were sometimes available were a valuable commodity for purchases outside the normal English trade.

As a remedy for the dearth of circulating coinage, a wide assortment of foreign coins and tokens was pressed into use. Only a very few were made in America prior to 1783. Copper coins known as *Hogge Money* (from their design; see page 36) were privately made for the Sommer Islands, now known as Bermuda, about the year 1616. The first coins minted for the colonies in America were made by John Hull in Boston for the Massachusetts Bay Colony. The General Court of the colony granted him authority to begin coinage, despite the possibility of objection and recrimination by the king of England. Starting in 1652 the Massachusetts minter began producing the famous NE, Willow, Oak, and Pine Tree shillings, with their fractional parts, for the convenience of the colonists. This venture, which defied English law and lasted from 1652 to 1682, was in a sense the first declaration of independence for the colonies.

As time passed, coins and tokens of many types were introduced and employed by the colonists to supplement their use of barter. Lord Baltimore was responsible for a small issue of silver pieces struck in England in 1659 and sent to Maryland for use there. Mark Newby imported from Ireland coins known as *St. Patrick's halfpence,* for use in the province of New Jersey in 1682. Coins dated 1722 to 1724, known as *Rosa Americana* issues, were produced by William Wood in England and were widely circulated in America. In addition, many British and other European coppers circulated there.

Enterprising Americans were responsible for some of the other copper and brass pieces that circulated during the 18th century. The Gloucester token, about which little is known, was one of these. Samuel and John Higley of Granby, Connecticut, made an interesting series of threepence pieces during the period from 1737 to 1739. John Chalmers, a silversmith in Annapolis, Maryland, issued silver shillings, sixpence, and threepence pieces in 1783. In 1786 and 1787 Ephraim Brasher, a New York goldsmith, struck gold coins of the value of a doubloon (about $15 in New York currency). Standish Barry of Baltimore, Maryland, made a curious silver threepence token in 1790.

Still other tokens, struck in Britain, reached our shores in early times and were for the most part speculative ventures. These much-needed, small-denomination coppers were readily circulated because of the great scarcity of fractional coins. Included in this category were the Nova Constellatio coppers and various English merchants' tokens.

During the period of turmoil following America's War of Independence, from about 1781 to 1795, still more English- and American-made copper pieces were added to the great variety of coins and tokens employed in the new nation. It was a time when Americans were suffering from postwar economic depression, a shortage of currency, high taxes, and foreclosures from bankruptcies. In the 1780s the Nova Eborac pieces (known as *New York coppers*), the Georgivs Triumpho coppers, and the Auctori Plebis tokens found their way into circulation as small change, despite their unofficial nature.

Collectors of colonial coins also include other pieces that are interesting because of their close association with early America and its first president. These consist of the Kentucky, Myddelton, and Franklin Press tokens, and those pieces bearing the portrait of George Washington. Although most of these pieces are dated from 1783 to 1795, many of them were made in England around the turn of the 19th century. Few of them actually circulated in the United States.

Coinage of the States

The Articles of Confederation, adopted March 1, 1781, provided that Congress should have the sole right to regulate the alloy and value of coin struck by its own authority or by that of the respective states. Each state, therefore, had the right to coin money, with Congress serving as a regulating authority. New Hampshire was the first state to consider coinage, but few if any of its copper coins were placed into circulation. The only specimens known bear the date 1776.

In the period from 1785 to 1788, Vermont, Connecticut, and New Jersey granted coining privileges to companies and individuals. Massachusetts erected its own mint in Boston, where copper coins were produced in 1787 and 1788. A number of interesting types and varieties of these state issues, most of which were struck in fairly large quantities, are still extant, and form the basis for many present-day collections and museum exhibits of early American coins.

The Beginnings of United States Coinage

Throughout the years from 1620 to 1776, colonists were forced to rely on numerous European coins and denominations that had to be converted to some common value to facilitate transactions. Further compounding this mathematical obstacle was the variation of values from one colony to another. Merchants became accustomed to using the Spanish dollar and its fractional parts, the real, the medio (half-real), and other, similar denominations. In time, those coins became more familiar to them than the old English coins, which were always scarce. It was only natural, therefore, that when a national coinage was under consideration a dollar-size coin was the first choice.

Contracts, currency statutes, and prices in the colonies were usually quoted in English pounds or Spanish dollars. In 1767 Maryland took the lead and produced paper money that was denominated in dollars. Connecticut, Massachusetts, and Virginia soon passed laws making Spanish coins legal tender. The first issue of Continental paper money, May 10, 1775, offers further evidence that the dollar was to be the basic American money unit, for it provided that the notes should be payable in "Spanish Milled Dollars or the value thereof in gold or silver."

The assistant financier of the Confederation, Gouverneur Morris, proposed a decimal coinage ratio designed to make conversion of various foreign currencies easier to compute in terms of a dollar-size unit. His plan was incorporated into a report presented by Robert Morris, superintendent of finance, to the Congress, January 15, 1782. Plans for a mint were advanced, and a uniform national currency to relieve the confused money conditions was outlined. Morris's unit, 1/1,440 of a dollar, was calculated to agree without a fraction with all the different valuations of the Spanish milled dollar in the various states. Although a government mint was approved on February 21, 1782, no immediate action was taken. During 1784, Thomas Jefferson, then a member of the House of Representatives, brought in a report concerning the plan and expressed disagreement with Morris's complicated money unit. He advocated the simple dollar unit because he believed the dollar was already as familiar and convenient a unit of value as the British pound. He favored the decimal system, and remarked, "The most easy ratio of multiplication and division is that of ten. George Washington referred to it as 'a measure, which in my opinion, has become indispensably necessary.'"

The Grand Committee in May 1785 recommended a gold five-dollar piece; a dollar of silver with fractional coins of the same metal (in denominations of half, quarter, 10th, and 20th parts of a dollar); and copper pieces valued at 1/100 and 1/200 of a dollar.

In 1783 Robert Morris submitted a series of pattern pieces in silver that were designed by Benjamin Dudley to carry out the decimal idea for United States money. These are known as the Nova Constellatio patterns and consist of the "mark," or 1,000 units; the "quint," or 500 units; the "bit," or 100 units; and a copper "five." The unit was to be a quarter grain of silver. This was not the first attempt at a dollar coin, for the Continental Currency piece of dollar size, dated 1776, had been struck in such metals as brass, pewter, and silver. The reason is unknown for making a very limited number of pieces in silver. The more-common pewter pieces were most likely intended as a substitute for the paper dollar, and saw considerable circulation.

Congress gave formal approval to the basic dollar unit and decimal coinage ratio in its resolution of July 1785 but other, more pressing matters delayed further action. Not until the Constitutional Convention of 1787 had placed the country on firm ground and the new nation had elected George Washington president did the Congress again turn attention to the subjects of currency, a mint, and a coinage system.

The Massachusetts cents and half cents struck in 1787 and 1788 were the first official coins in the United States to bear stated values in terms of decimal parts of the dollar unit. The cent represented a hundredth part of a Spanish dollar.

The first federally authorized coin for which we have extensive documentation was the Fugio copper (sometimes called the Franklin cent, as Benjamin Franklin is believed to have supplied the design and composed the legends). This piece, similar in design to the Continental Currency dollar of 1776, was privately struck in 1787 by contract with the government.

Alexander Hamilton, then secretary of the Treasury, reported his views on monetary matters on January 21, 1791. He concurred in all essentials with the decimal subdivisions and multiples of the dollar contained in the earlier resolutions, and urged the use of both gold and silver in U.S. standard money.

Congress passed a resolution on March 3, 1791, that a mint be established, and authorized President Washington to engage artists and procure machinery for the making of coins. No immediate steps were taken, but when Washington delivered his third annual address, he recommended immediate establishment of a mint.

On April 2, 1792, a bill was finally passed providing "that the money of account of the United States should be expressed in dollars or units, dismes or tenths, cents or hundredths, and milles or thousandths; a disme being the tenth part of a dollar, a cent the hundredth part of a dollar, a mille the thousandth part of a dollar. . . ."

In the early 1790s Congress and President George Washington worked on starting a mint for the new nation.

Denominations specified in the act were as follows:

	Value	Grains Pure	Grains Standard
Gold eagle	$10.00	247-4/8	270
Gold half eagle	5.00	123-6/8	135
Gold quarter eagle	2.50	61-7/8	67-4/8
Silver dollar	1.00	371-4/16	416
Silver half dollar	.50	185-10/16	208
Silver quarter dollar	.25	92-13/16	104
Silver disme (dime)	.10	37-2/16	41-3/5
Silver half disme	.05	18-9/16	20-4/5
Copper cent	.01	11 pennyweights	
Copper half cent	.005	5-1/2 pennyweights	

The word *pure* meant unalloyed metal; *standard* meant, in the case of gold, 11/12 fine, or 11 parts pure metal to one part alloy, which was mixed with the pure metal to improve the wearing qualities of the coins. The fineness for silver coins was 1,485/1,664, or approximately 892.43 thousandths, in contrast with the gold coins' fineness of 22 carats, or 916-2/3 thousandths.

The law also provided for free coinage of gold and silver coins at the fixed ratio of 15 to 1, and a token coinage of copper cents and half cents. Under the free-coinage provision no charge was to be made for converting gold or silver bullion into coins "weight for weight." At the depositor's option, however, he could demand an immediate exchange of coins for his bullion, for which privilege a deduction of one-half of 1% was to be imposed.

President Washington appointed David Rittenhouse, a well-known scientist, as the first director of the Mint. Construction began on a mint building nearly four months after the passage of the Act of April 2, 1792. The building was located on Seventh Street near Arch in Philadelphia.

The first coin struck by the government was the half disme. Fifteen hundred of these pieces were produced during the month of July 1792 before the mint was completed. George Washington supplied some of his own silver in the form of bullion or tableware, in the value of about $100, to make those first coins. A few dismes were also struck at this time or a short while later. Silver and gold for coinage were to be supplied by the public, but copper for cents and half cents had to be provided by the government. This was accomplished by the Act of May 8, 1792, when the purchase of not more than 150 tons was authorized. On September 11, 1792, six pounds of old copper was purchased, and probably used for the striking of patterns. Thereafter, planchets with upset rims for cents and half cents were purchased from Boulton and Watt of Birmingham, England, from 1798 to 1838.

Several pattern coins were prepared in 1792 before regular mint operations commenced. *Patterns* are test or trial pieces intended to show the size, form, and design of proposed coins. These included Henry Voigt's silver center cent, a piece smaller than that of regular issue. The small plug of silver, worth about three-quarters of a cent, was evidently intended to bring the intrinsic value of the coin up to the value of 1¢ and to permit production of a coin of more convenient size. Alexander Hamilton had mentioned a year before that the proposed "intrinsic value" cent would be too large, and suggested that the amount of copper could be reduced and a trace of silver added. The pattern cent with a silver center may have been designed to conform to this recommendation.

The cents by Robert Birch are equally interesting. These patterns are identified by their legends, which read LIBERTY PARENT OF SCIENCE AND INDUSTRY and TO BE ESTEEMED BE USEFUL. The quarter with an eagle on the reverse side, by Joseph Wright, belongs among the 1792 patterns devised before regular issues were struck.

The Bank of Maryland deposited the first silver, sending $80,715.73-1/2 in French coins to the mint on July 18, 1794. Moses Brown, a Boston merchant, deposited the first gold in the form of ingots (February 12, 1795) amounting to $2,276.22, receiving silver coin in payment. The first coins transferred to the treasurer consisted of 11,178 cents on March 1, 1793. The first return of coined silver was made on October 15, 1794, and the first gold coins (744 half eagles) were delivered July 31, 1795. The early Mint was constantly vigilant to see that the weights of these coins were standard. Overweight blank planchets were filed and adjusted prior to striking, and many of the coins made prior to 1836 show file marks and blemishes from these adjustments.

Regular Mint Issues

Cents and half cents, exclusively, were coined during the year 1793, and by 1799 approximately $50,000 in these coins had been placed into circulation. This amount proved insufficient for the requirements of commerce, and small-denomination coins of the states and of foreign countries continued in use well into the 19th century.

One of the most serious problems confronting commercial interests prior to 1857 was the failure of the government to provide a sufficient volume of circulating coins. The fault, contrary to popular opinion at the time, did not lie with any lack of effort on the part of the Mint. Other circumstances tended to interfere with the expected steady flow of new coinage into the channels of trade.

Free circulation of United States gold and silver coins was greatly hindered by speculators. For example, worn Spanish dollars of reduced weight and value were easily exchanged for U.S. silver dollars, which meant the export of most of the new dollars as fast as they were minted, and a complete loss to American trade channels.

Gold coins failed to circulate for similar reasons. The ratio of 15 to 1 between gold and silver was close to the world ratio when Alexander Hamilton recommended it in 1791, but by 1799 the ratio in European commercial centers had reached 15-3/4 to 1. At this rate, the undervalued gold coins tended to flow out of the country, or were melted for bullion. After 1800, therefore, United States gold coins were rarely seen in general circulation. As no remedy could be found, coinage of the gold eagle and the silver dollar was suspended by President Jefferson in 1804. It is generally held that the silver dollar was discontinued in 1804, although the last coins minted for the period were dated 1803.

With the lack of gold coins and silver dollars, the half dollar became America's desirable coin for large transactions and bank reserves. Until 1834, in fact, half dollars circulated very little as they were mainly transferred from bank to bank. This accounts for the relatively good supply of higher-condition half dollars of this period that is still available to collectors. A Senate committee

David Rittenhouse—surveyor, astronomer, mathematician, and inventor—was named the first director of the U.S. Mint.

of 1830 reported that United States silver coins were considered so much bullion and were accordingly "lost to the community as coins."

There was only a negligible coinage of quarters, dimes, and half dimes from 1794 to 1834. It has been estimated that there was less than one piece for each person in the country in the year 1830. This period has been described as one of chaotic currency made up of bank notes, underweight foreign gold coins, foreign silver coins of many varieties, and domestic fractional silver coins. Paper money of that time was equally bothersome. Privately issued bank notes sometimes had no little or no backing and were apt to be worthless at the time of redemption. In this period, before national paper money commenced in 1861, notes of the state-chartered banks flooded the country and were much more common than silver coins.

On June 28, 1834, a new law was passed reducing the weight of standard gold, which had the effect of placing American money on a gold standard. Trade and finance greatly benefited from this act, which also proved a boon to the gold mines of Georgia and North Carolina. Branch mints in Dahlonega, Georgia; New Orleans; and Charlotte, North Carolina, began operations in 1838 to handle the newly mined gold near the source. The various issues of private gold coins were struck in these areas.

The law of January 18, 1837, completely revised and standardized the Mint and coinage laws. Legal standards, Mint charges, legal tender, Mint procedure, tolerance in coin weights, accounting methods, a bullion fund, standardization of gold and silver coins to 900 thousandths fineness, and other desirable regulations were covered by the new legislation. Results of importance to the collector were the changes in type for the various coin denominations and the resumption of coinage of the eagle in 1838 and larger quantities of silver dollars in 1840.

Prior to Andrew Jackson's election as president in 1828, the Second Bank of the United States had considerable control over the nation's currency. In 1832 Jackson vetoed a bill rechartering the bank, and transferred government deposits to state banks. The action took away some stability from the economy and eventually led to a national financial collapse. By 1837 the country was so deprived of circulating coinage that merchants resorted to making their own "hard times tokens" to facilitate trade. The few available government coins were hoarded or traded at a premium for private paper money, which was often unreliable.

The California gold discovery in 1848 was responsible for an interesting series of private, state, and territorial gold issues in the western region, culminating in the establishment of a branch mint at San Francisco in 1854.

Two new regular gold issues were introduced in 1849. In that year the double eagle and gold dollar joined the American family of coins. The California gold fields greatly influenced the world gold market, making the exportation of silver profitable. For example, the silver in two half dollars was worth $1.03-1/2 in gold. The newly introduced gold dollars soon took over the burden and hastened the disappearance of silver coins from trade channels. This was the situation when the

The California Gold Rush had a great influence on American coinage.

new 3¢ postage rate brought about the bill authorized by Congress on March 3, 1851, calling for the coinage of a silver three-cent piece in 1851. This was the United States' first subsidiary coin in precious metals, for its silver value was intrinsically 86% of its face value, as an expedient designed to prevent its withdrawal from circulation.

The $3 gold piece was authorized by the Act of February 21, 1853. It was never a popular or necessary coin because of the existing $2.50 and $5 coins; it nevertheless was issued regularly from 1854 until 1889.

On February 21, 1853, fractional silver coins were made subsidiary by reduction of their weights. As the coins' face value now exceeded their bullion value, free coinage of silver was prohibited except for dollars, and the Mint was authorized to purchase its silver requirements on its own account using the bullion fund of the Mint, and, according to law, "the profit of said coinage shall be . . . transferred to the account of the treasury of the United States."

To identify the new lightweight pieces, arrows were placed at the date on all silver coins except three-cent pieces, for which arrows were added to the reverse. Dollars, which were not reduced in weight, were not marked in any way. On the quarters and half dollars of 1853, rays were added on the reverse to denote the change of weight. In 1854, the rays were removed, and in 1856, the arrows disappeared from all but the silver three-cent coins. Large-scale production of silver coins during this period greatly relieved the demands on gold dollars and three-cent pieces, and for the first time in U.S. history, enough fractional coins were in general circulation to facilitate commerce.

The Coinage Act of February 21, 1857, was designed primarily to reform the copper coinage. Although large cents and half cents are interesting and valuable in the eyes of the modern collector, they were unpopular with the American public in the 1850s because of their size. They also cost the Mint too much to produce.

The new law abolished the half cent, and reduced the size and changed the design of the cent. The new Flying Eagle cent contained 88% copper and 12% nickel. Nearly 1,000 pattern cents were stamped from dies bearing the date 1856, although no authority for the issue existed before 1857. Other important effects of the law were the retirement of Spanish silver coins from circulation, and dispersal of the new cents in such excessive quantities as to create a nuisance to business houses, particularly in the eastern cities. The Indian Head design replaced the Flying Eagle in 1859, and in 1864 the weight of the cent was further reduced and its composition changed to a proportion of 95% copper and 5% tin and zinc. (This bronze composition was the standard for the cent except for the years 1943 and 1944–1946. In 1962 the alloy was changed to 95% copper and 5% zinc. In 1982 the composition was changed to a core of 99.2% zinc and 0.8% copper, covered with an outer layer of pure copper.)

An abundance of coins turned to scarcity following the outbreak of the Civil War. Anticipation of a scarcity of hard money, and uncertainty as to the outcome of the war, induced hoarding. The large volume of greenbacks in circulation caused a premium for gold. Subsidiary silver coins, as a result of the sudden depreciation, quickly vanished from circulation. As an expediency, some people made use of postage stamps for small change. Merchants, banks, individuals, and even some towns and cities produced a wide array of small-denomination paper scrip and promissory notes to meet their needs. In 1862 the government released its first issue of "Postage Currency" and subsequent fractional notes. In 1863 many privately issued copper tokens appeared to help fill the void. They are of two general classes: tradesmen's tokens and imitations of official cents. Many of the latter were political or patriotic in character and carried slogans typical of the times. They not only served as a medium of exchange, but also often advertised merchants or products, and were usually produced at a profit.

The Coinage Act of April 22, 1864, which effected changes in the cent, provided also for the new bronze two-cent piece. The act, moreover, provided legal tender status for these two coins up to 10 times their face value. The two-cent piece was the first coin to bear the motto IN GOD WE TRUST. The new coin at first was readily accepted by the public, but it proved an unnecessary denomination because of the competing three-cent coins, and production was halted after only nine years. The secretary of the Treasury had issued a great many currency notes of the three-cent denomination early in 1865. American nickel interests seized upon this circumstance to fight for a new three-cent coin for redemption of the paper money. A law was quickly passed and signed by President Abraham Lincoln on March 3, 1865, providing for a three-cent coin of 75%-25% copper-nickel composition. The United States then possessed two types of three-cent pieces, although neither was seriously needed. The nickel three-cent piece was struck continuously until 1889, the silver three-cent piece until 1873.

The Civil War brought dramatic changes to our nation's coins.

The new copper-nickel alloy ratio was selected for the five-cent coin, adopted May 16, 1866, and thereafter known as a *nickel.* Again, the people had a coin denomination available to them in two forms. The silver half dime, like the three-cent piece, was retired from service in 1873 to curb the use of silver.

The great influx of silver from the Comstock Lode in Nevada, mainly in the 1860s and '70s, increased the nation's supply of silver for coins and taxed the Philadelphia Mint's capacity for production. Pressure from silver-mine interests in Nevada influenced the opening of a special mint in Carson City to assay and mint silver locally, rather than having it shipped to Philadelphia or San Francisco. Production was inefficient, costly, and slow. By 1893 the lode was virtually depleted, and minting activities at Carson City ceased.

The Law of March 3, 1871, was a redemption measure and was passed to provide the United States Treasury with means for the disposal of millions of minor coins, which had accumulated in the hands of postmasters, merchants, and others. Small-denomination coins, because of this new law, were placed on an equal footing with silver and could be redeemed when presented in lots of $20.

There was a general revision of the coinage laws in 1873. Several years of study and debate preceded the final enactment. The legislative history of the bill occupies hundreds of pages of the *Congressional Globe,* and the result was considered by many a clumsy attempt and a failure. The law has sometimes been referred to as the "Crime of '73." One consequence of the bill, which achieved final enactment on February 12, 1873, was the elimination of the silver dollar. In its stead, the trade dollar of greater weight was provided for use in commerce with the Orient in competition with the Mexican dollar. The legal tender provision, which gave the trade dollar currency within U.S. borders, was repealed in 1876 to avoid profiteers' buying them at a reduced rate. The trade dollar was thus the only United States coin ever demonetized. (Through an oversight, the legal tender status was reinstated under the Coinage Act of 1965.)

It may be a surprise to some collectors to learn that silver dollars did not circulate to any great extent after 1803 (except in the 1840s). The coin was turned out steadily since 1840, but for various reasons (such as exportation, melting, and holding in bank vaults), the dollar was virtually an unknown coin. The Act of February 21, 1853, in effect demonetized silver and committed the country to gold as a single standard. The silver-mining interests came to realize what had occurred in the 1870s, and the ensuing quarter century of political and monetary history was filled with their voluble protests. There was a constant bitter struggle for the return to bimetallism.

From an economic point of view the abundant supply of gold was responsible for a steady decline in gold prices worldwide. This brought about a gradual business depression in the United States, particularly in the South and Midwest. Private silver interests influenced great sections of the West for bimetallism as a remedy for the failing price level. Worldwide adoption of bimetallism might have improved economic conditions; but, had the United States alone proceeded to place its money on a double standard at the old 16-to-1 ratio, the situation would only have worsened.

Of particular importance to collectors were those features of the Law of 1873 that affected the statuses and physical properties of the individual coins. The weights of the half dollar, quarter, and dime were slightly changed, and arrows were placed at the date for the ensuing two years to indicate the differences in weight. Silver three-cent pieces, half dimes, and two-cent pieces were abolished by the act, and the manufacture of minor coins was restricted to the Philadelphia Mint.

The short-lived twenty-cent piece was authorized March 3, 1875. It was created for the Western states, where the Spanish "bit" had become equivalent to a U.S. dime. The five-cent piece did not circulate there, so when a quarter was offered for a "bit" purchase, only a dime was returned in change. The so-called double dime was frequently confused with the quarter dollar and was issued for circulation only in 1875 and 1876.

On February 28, 1878, Congress passed the Bland-Allison Act, which restored coinage of silver dollars. It required the Treasury to purchase at market price two to four million dollars' worth of silver each month and to coin it into silver dollars at a ratio to gold of 16 to 1. Proponents of "free silver" contended that with more money in circulation, workers would receive higher wages. Business leaders argued for the gold standard and against free silver because they believed that inflation would cheapen the value of money. The act was called by some "a wretched compromise."

The North and East so avoided the silver dollars that the coins did not actively circulate there and eventually found their way back to the Treasury, mostly through tax payments. Treasury Secretary Daniel Manning transferred ownership to the people and the coins were specifically earmarked as backing for Silver Certificates.

The silver dollar struck from 1878 to 1921 is named for its designer, U.S. Mint engraver George T. Morgan.

The Bland-Allison Act was repealed in 1890 and the Sherman Silver Purchase Act took its place. Under this new law, 4,500,000 ounces of silver per month could be paid for with Treasury Notes that were to be legal tender, and redeemable in gold or silver dollars coined from the bullion purchased. Important in this case was the fact that the notes were constantly being redeemed for gold that mainly was exported. The measure was actually a government subsidy for a few influential silver miners, and as such it was marked for failure. It was hastily repealed. The Bland-Allison Act and the Sherman Act added a total of 570 million silver dollars to the nation's monetary stocks.

The Gold Standard Act of 1900 again gave the country a single standard, but reaffirmed the fiction that the silver dollar was a standard coin. It still enjoyed unlimited legal tender, but was as much a subsidiary coin, practically speaking, as the dime, for its value in terms of standard gold, even before the gold-surrender executive order several decades later, was far below its face value.

The lapse in silver dollar coinage after 1904 and until 1921 was due to lack of silver. Legislation authorizing further metal supplies for silver dollars was not forthcoming until 1918, when the Pittman Act provided silver for more dollars.

Prior to March 1933, the metallic worth of U.S. gold coins was equal to their face value. In order to encourage a steady flow of gold to the mints, the government (with the exception of the period 1853–1873) had adopted a policy of gratuitous coinage. The cost of converting gold into coin had generally been considered an expense chargeable to the government.

In practice, the Mint made fine bars for commercial use, or mint bars for coinage, at its discretion. The bars in later years were stored in vaults and Gold or Silver Certificates issued in place of the coins.

On April 5, 1933, President Franklin Roosevelt issued an order prohibiting banks from paying out gold and Gold Certificates without permission, and gold coins were thus kept for reserve purposes. The law was intended to stabilize the value of gold. In effect, it removed all gold from circulation and prevented it from being hoarded. Gold imports and newly mined domestic gold could be sold only to the government. Today, gold bullion and coins may be collected and saved by anyone, as all restrictions were removed on December 31, 1974.

Under the Coinage Act of 1965, the compositions of dimes, quarters, and half dollars were changed to eliminate or reduce the silver content of these coins because the value of silver had risen above their face values. The replacement "clad" dimes and quarters were composed of an outer layer of copper-nickel (75%-25%) bonded to an inner core of pure copper. Beginning in 1971 the half dollar and dollar compositions were changed to that of the dime and quarter. All silver clad coins have an outer layer of 80% silver bonded to an inner core of 21% silver, for a total content of 40% silver.

By the Law of September 26, 1890, changes in designs of United States coins cannot be made more often than once every 25 years without congressional approval. Since that date, there have been design changes in all denominations, and there have been many gold and silver bullion and commemorative issues. In 1999, programs were started to honor each of the individual states and territories, and various national parks, by using special designs on the reverse of the quarter. The one-cent, five-cent, and dollar coins have also undergone several design changes. These factors, and a growing awareness of the value and historical importance of older coins, are largely responsible for the ever-increasing interest in coin collecting in the United States.

MINTS AND MINTMARKS

Mintmarks are small letters designating where coins were made. Coins struck at Philadelphia before 1979 (except 1942–1945 five-cent pieces) do not have mint-marks. Starting in 1979, a letter P was used on the dollar, and thereafter on all other denominations except the cent. Mintmark position is on the reverse of nearly all coins prior to 1965 (the cent is an exception), and on the obverse after 1967.

C—Charlotte, North Carolina (gold coins only; 1838–1861)
CC—Carson City, Nevada (gold and silver coins only; 1870–1893)
D—Dahlonega, Georgia (gold coins only; 1838–1861)
D—Denver, Colorado (1906 to date)
O—New Orleans, Louisiana (gold and silver coins only; 1838–1861; 1879–1909)
P—Philadelphia, Pennsylvania (1793 to date; P not used in early years)
S—San Francisco, California (1854 to date)
W—West Point, New York (1984 to date)

Prior to 1996 all dies for United States coins were made at the Philadelphia Mint. Some dies are now made at the Denver Mint. Dies for use at other mints are made with the appropriate mintmarks before they are shipped to those mints. Because this was a hand operation prior to 1985, the exact positioning and size of the mintmarks may vary slightly, depending on where and how deeply the punches were impressed. This also accounts for double-punched and superimposed mintmarks such as the 1938 D Over D, and D Over S, Buffalo nickels. Polishing of dies may also alter the apparent size of fine details. Occasionally the mintmark is inadvertently left off a die sent to a branch mint, as was the case with some recent Proof cents, nickels, and dimes. Similarly, some 1982 dimes without mintmarks were made as circulation strikes. The mintmark M was used on coins made in Manila for the Philippines from 1925 through 1941.

Prior to 1900, punches for mintmarks varied greatly in size. This is particularly noticeable in the 1850 to 1880 period, in which the letters range from very small to very large. An attempt to standardize sizes started in 1892 with the Barber series, but exceptions are seen in the 1892-O half dollar and 1905-O dime, both of which have normal and "microscopic" mintmarks. A more or less standard-size, small mintmark was used on all minor coins starting in 1909, and on all dimes, quarters, and halves after the Barber series was replaced in 1916. Slight variations in mintmark size occur through 1945, with notable differences in 1928, when small and large S mintmarks were used.

In recent years a single D or S punch has been used to mark all branch-mint dies. The change to the larger D for Denver coins occurred in 1933. Nickels, dimes, quarter dollars, half dollars, and dollars of 1934 exist with either the old, smaller-size mintmark or the new, larger-size D. All other denominations of 1934 and after are standard. The San Francisco mintmark was changed to a larger size during 1941 and, with the exception of the half dollar, all 1941-S coins are known with either small or large mintmarks. Halves were not changed until 1942, and the 1942-S and 1943-S pieces exist both ways. The 1945-S dime with "microscopic" S is an unexplained use of a punch originally intended for Philippine coins of 1907 through 1920. In 1979, the punches were replaced. Varieties of some 1979 coins appear with either the old- or new-shaped S or D. The S punch was again replaced in 1981 with a punch that yielded a more distinct letter.

The mintmark application technique for Proof coins was changed in 1985, and for circulation-strike production in 1990 and 1991, when the letter was applied directly to the master die rather than being hand punched on each working die. At the same time, all the mintmark letters were made much larger and clearer than those of previous years.

QUANTITIES OF COINS STRUCK, AND MINT DATA

Collectors are cautioned that Mint reports are not always reliable for estimating the rarities of coins. In the early years of the Mint, dies of previous years were often used until they became worn or broken. It should also be emphasized that certain quantities reported, particularly for gold and silver, cover the number of coins struck and have no reference to the quantity that actually reached circulation. Many issues were deposited in the Treasury as backing for paper currency and were later melted.

Gold coins struck before August 1, 1834, are rare today, because from 1821 onward (and at times before 1821), the gold in the coins was worth more than their face values, so they were struck as bullion and traded at a premium above face value.

The quantities reported by the Mint of three-dollar gold pieces from 1873 to 1877 and half cents from 1832 to 1835 are subject to doubt.

Coinage figures shown for 1964 through 1966 are for coins bearing those dates. Some of them were struck in more than one year and at various mints, both with and without mintmarks. In recent years, mintage figures reported by the Mint have been revised several times and remain uncertain as to precise amounts.

Mintage quantities are shown adjacent to each date throughout this book. Figures shown in italic are estimates based on the most accurate information available. Exact mintage figures for most pre-1878 Proof minor coins, and most pre-1860 silver and gold coins, are not known. Listed figures are occasionally revised when new information becomes available. Proof totals are shown in parentheses, and are not included with coins made for circulation.

TODAY'S RARE-COIN MARKET

Investing in rare coins can be a rewarding experience for anyone who approaches the calling armed with the right attitude and background knowledge about this exciting field. It can just as easily become a costly mistake for anyone who attempts to profit from coins without giving serious thought to the idiosyncrasies of this unique market.

For hundreds of years, rare coins and precious metals have proven themselves to be an excellent hedge against inflation and a source of ready money in times of crisis, provided that purchases are carefully made. There is little reason to think that this will change in the future. Gone are the days when coin collecting was only a passive hobby mainly for those who would study the history and artistry of these enjoyable objects. The activity has grown to the point that speculation on the future demand for rare coins has made them a part of many investment portfolios. Some people describe it as an "industry," no longer mainly a hobby. With this change in attitude about collecting has come a measure of concern for those who purchase coins without the background or experience necessary to avoid costly mistakes.

The best advice for investing in rare coins is to use common sense. No thinking person would expect to buy a genuine diamond ring from a street peddler, or an art masterpiece at a garage sale. It is just the same with rare coins, and the more careful you are in selecting a qualified dealer and making an educated evaluation of the coins you purchase, the greater will be your chance of making a profitable investment. If you have access to the Internet, visit the sites of the Professional Numismatists Guild (the leading nationwide association of rare coin dealers, at PNGdealers.com). Many of these dealers have web sites or issue catalogs. Reviewing them will give you much basic information that can be useful.

At any given time there are many advertisements, talks given by "experts," and the like on television, in magazines, and elsewhere stating that investment in gold, silver, rare coins, and related items is the best way to preserve and increase assets. Some of these promotions are by firms that are not part of established professional numismatics. Collectors and investors should investigate the background of a potential seller before making any significant purchases.

Take your time and go slowly. As is the case with art, securities, and other investments, coins can be bought instantly, but selling them at a profit may be another thing entirely. That said, for the careful buyer the opportunities for successful collecting and investing in quality numismatic items are as great today as at any time in the past. Inexperienced buyers can purchase coins that have been graded and authenticated by third-party services (see "Third-Party Grading and Authentication" on page 10), and services such as CAC (Certified Acceptance Corporation) offer additional professional opinions as to a coin's grade. There is also more written and digitized information available for beginners than ever before. And the pricing of rare coins is very competitive in today's widespread market.

The shift in emphasis from collecting to investing on the part of many buyers in recent decades has created a dynamic market and demand for coins, resulting in more stringent grading methods and in pricing geared to the perceived rarity of coins in various levels of Mint State or Proof perfection. Coins in high grades that have been certified (professionally graded and guaranteed authentic) and encapsulated ("slabbed") may be valued significantly higher than similar coins that have not been so treated. In this book, values above several hundred dollars are generally for coins certified by a reputable grading service. In today's marketplace, "raw" or non-certified coins, or coins certified by other services, are usually valued at less, except for modern U.S. Mint and bullion products. Some television promotions, investment pitches, and offers to sell coins to the general public are priced above what a knowledgeable collector would pay. Moreover, it is important to remember that popular coin magazines and newspapers give no guarantee that items advertised in certain grades will merit those grades if submitted to a reputable grading service. "Bargains" are often anything but. A bargain offering might actually be a loss leader designed to gather collector names for future offerings. On the Internet, auction sites do not examine coins offered for sale—and countless offerings range from overgraded to counterfeit.

Always buy from an established professional dealer or firm—as you would do if you were buying a valuable painting or antique.

The editors of the Guide Book reiterate and emphasize that buyers must beware of overpriced or overgraded coins that simply are not worth what is charged for them. This is especially true of coins that are offered for sale online or at electronic auctions, where it often is not possible to examine the items carefully enough to determine authenticity or grade. Extreme caution is advised for anyone considering an investment in expensive coins. Investigate the person or firm with whom you are dealing. Seek professional, unbiased help with grading determinations. Satisfy yourself that the coins you select are authentic and are not priced considerably higher than is being charged by other dealers. This takes time. Do not be in a hurry. Most coins that are available today will also be available next month. Take time to track the price history and trends of coins you are most interested in purchasing.

Protecting valuable coins from deterioration and theft is another important part of investing. The best protection for keeping coins pristine is to store them in inert, airtight plastic holders (the encapsulation slabs of third-party grading services are a good example), and away from paper products, cigarette smoke, wood, natural rubber, paint, and textiles such as wool and felt. Humidity greater than 75% can also be harmful and should be avoided. When you buy coins, take physical possession of them. They should be insured and kept in a secure place such as a bank safe deposit box. There have been many frauds in which sellers of gold, rare coins, and the like have offered to hold them for the buyer and later it was found that the coins did not exist or were other than described.

It is important to keep invoices and to maintain a listing of your purchases for identification and tax purposes. Digitally capturing the coins is easily enough done with an inexpensive camera or scanner and provides proof of identification should any become lost or stolen. Note that bank storage boxes are not automatically insured. Insurance costs very little and is highly recommended.

Beyond the financial aspect, collectors and investors alike can profit by investigating the background and history of the coins they buy. Coins are a mirror of history and art, telling the story of mankind over the past 2,600 years and reflecting the economic struggles, wars, prosperity, and creativity of every major nation on earth. Most traditional numismatists acquire coins for their historical, artistic, and similar appeals—as tangible links with early America, ancient Rome and Greece, the British Empire, and other connections. Today, the investigation of the motifs, issuance, and other aspects of a coin can be done easily on the Internet. The lives of presidents, monarchs, and other figures depicted on a coin are interesting to study. Often, a single coin can lead to a pleasant hour or two of research. Building a working library is also strongly recommended. Most popular series such as Morgan and Peace silver dollars, various denominations of gold coins, commemoratives, and the like can be studied and enjoyed by reading books, with the Whitman Publishing list of titles being a fine place to start.

Purchased with care and over a period of time, nearly all specialized collections have proved to be good financial investments as well—an instance of having your cake and eating it too. More than just a few enthusiasts have called it the world's greatest hobby.

We are but the custodians of these historical relics; we must appreciate and care for them while they are in our possession. Those who treat rare coins with the consideration and respect they deserve will profit in many ways, not the least of which can be in the form of a sound financial return on their investments of time and money.

Enjoy the experience!

CHECKING YOUR COINS FOR AUTHENTICITY

Coin collectors occasionally encounter counterfeit coins, or coins that have been altered so that they appear to be something other than what they really are. Any coin that does not seem to fit the description of similar pieces listed in this guide book should be looked upon with suspicion. Experienced coin dealers can usually tell quickly whether a coin is genuine, and would never knowingly sell spurious coins to a collector. Coins found in circulation or bought from a nonprofessional source should be examined carefully.

The risk of purchasing a spurious coin can be minimized through the use of common sense and an elementary knowledge of the techniques used by counterfeiters. It is well to keep in mind that the more popular a coin is among collectors and the public, the more likely it is that counterfeits and replicas will abound. Until recently, collector coins valued at under $100 were rarely replicated because of the high cost of making such items. The same was true of counterfeits made to deceive the public. Few counterfeit coins were made because it was more profitable for the fakers to print paper money. Today, however, counterfeiters in Asia and elsewhere create fakes of a suprising variety of coins, most notably silver dollar types, but also smaller denominations.

Replicas

Reproductions of famous and historical coins have been distributed for decades by marketing firms and souvenir vendors. These pieces are often tucked away by the original recipients as curios, and later are found in old furniture by others who believe they have discovered objects of great value. Most replicas are poorly made by the casting method, and are virtually worthless. They can sometimes be identified by a seam that runs around the edge of the piece where the two halves of the casting mold were joined together. Genuine specimens of extremely rare or valuable coins are almost never found in unlikely places.

Counterfeits

For many centuries, counterfeiters have produced base-metal forgeries of gold and silver coins to deceive the public in the normal course of trade. These pieces are usually crudely made and easily detected on close examination. Crudely cast counterfeit copies of older coins are the most prevalent. These can usually be detected by the casting bubbles or pimples that can be seen with low-power magnification. Pieces struck from handmade dies are more deceptive, but the engravings do not match those of genuine Mint products.

More recently, as coin collecting has gained popularity and rare coin prices have risen, "numismatic" counterfeits have become more common. The majority of these are die-struck gold coin counterfeits that have been mass produced overseas since 1950. Forgeries exist of most U.S. gold coins dated between 1870 and 1933, as well as all issues of the gold dollar and three-dollar gold piece. Most of these are very well made, as they were intended to pass the close scrutiny of collectors. Few gold coins of earlier dates have been counterfeited, but false 1799 ten-dollar gold pieces and 1811 five-dollar coins have been made. Gold coins in less than Extremely Fine condition are seldom counterfeited.

Silver dollars dated 1804, Lafayette dollars, several of the low-mintage commemorative half dollars, and the 1795 half dimes have been forged in quantity. Minor-coin forgeries made in recent years are the 1909-S V.D.B., 1914-D and 1955 doubled-die Lincoln cents, 1877 Indian Head cents, 1856 Flying Eagle cents, and, on a much smaller scale, a variety of dates of half cents and large cents. Nineteenth-century copies of colonial coins are also sometimes encountered.

Alterations

Coins are occasionally altered by the addition, removal, or change of a design feature (such as a mintmark or date digit) or by the polishing, sandblasting, acid etching, toning, or plating of the surface of a genuine piece. Changes of this sort are usually done to deceive collectors. Among U.S. gold coins, only the 1927-D double eagle is commonly found with an added mintmark. On $2.50 and $5 gold coins, 1839 through 1856, New Orleans O mintmarks have been altered to C (for Charlotte, North Carolina) in a few instances.

Over a century ago, five-dollar gold pieces were imitated by gold plating 1883 Liberty Head five-cent coins without the word CENTS on the reverse. Other coins commonly created fraudulently through alteration include the 1799 large cent and the 1909-S, 1909-S V.D.B., 1914-D, 1922 "plain," and 1943 "copper" cents. The 1913 Liberty Head nickel has been extensively replicated by alteration of 1903 and 1912 nickels. Scarce, high-grade Denver and San Francisco Buffalo nickels of the 1920s; 1916-D and 1942 Over 1941 dimes; 1918 Over 1917-S quarters; 1932-D and -S quarters; and 1804 silver dollars have all been made by the alteration of genuine coins of other dates or mints.

Detection

The best way to detect counterfeit coins is to compare suspected pieces with others of the same issue. Carefully check size, color, luster, weight, edge devices, and design details. Replicas generally have less detail than their genuine counterparts when studied under magnification. Modern struck counterfeits made to deceive collectors are an exception to this rule. Any questionable gold coin should be referred to an expert for verification.

Cast forgeries are usually poorly made and of incorrect weight. Base metal is often used in place of gold or silver, and the coins are lightweight and often incorrect in color and luster. Deceptive cast pieces have been made using real metal content and modern dental techniques, but these too usually vary in quality and color.

Detection of alterations sometimes involves comparative examination of the suspected areas of a coin (usually mintmarks and date digits) at magnification ranging from 10x to 40x.

Coins of exceptional rarity or value should never be purchased without a written guarantee of authenticity. Professional authentication of rare coins for a fee is available with the services offered by commercial grading services, and by some coin dealers.

COINS FROM TREASURES AND HOARDS: A KEY TO UNDERSTANDING RARITY AND VALUE

by Q. David Bowers

Elements of Rarity

In many instances, the mintage of a coin can be a determinant of its present-day rarity and value. However, across American numismatics there are many important exceptions, some very dramatic. Some of these situations are well known, others less so. As an introduction and example, if you peruse this issue of the *Guide Book* you will find many listings of Morgan silver dollars of 1878 through 1921 for which the mintage figure does not seem to correlate with a coin's price. For example, among such coins the 1901, of which 6,962,000 were made for circulation, is valued at $450,000 in MS-65. In the same series the 1884-CC, of which only 1,136,000 were struck, is listed at $475, or only a tiny fraction of the value of a 1901.

Why the difference? The explanation is that nearly all of the 6,962,000 dollars of 1901 were either placed into circulation at the time, and became worn, or were melted generations ago. Very few were saved by collectors, and today MS-65 coins are extreme rarities. On the other hand, of the 1,166,000 1884-CC silver dollars minted, relatively few went into circulation. Vast quantities were sealed in 1,000-coin cloth bags and put into government storage. Generations later, as coin collecting became popular, thousands were paid out by the Treasury Department. Years after that, in the early 1960s, when silver metal rose in value, there was a "run" on long-stored silver dollars, and it was learned in March 1964 that 962,638 1884-CC dollars—84.7% of the original mintage—were still in the hands of the Treasury Department!

With this information, the price disparities become understandable. Even though the 1901 had a high mintage, few were saved, and although worn coins are common, gem MS-65 coins are rarities. In contrast, nearly all of the low-mintage 1884-CC dollars were stored by the government, and today most of them still exist, including some in MS-65 grade.

There are many other situations in which mintages are not particularly relevant to the availability and prices of coins today. Often a special circumstance will lead to certain coins' being saved in especially large quantities, later dramatically affecting the availability and value of such pieces. The following are some of those circumstances.

Excitement of a New Design

In the panorama of American coinage, some new designs have captured the fancy of the public, who saved them in large quantities when they were released. In many other instances new designs were ignored, and coins slipped into circulation unnoticed.

In 1909, much publicity was given to the new Lincoln portrait to be used on the one-cent piece, replacing the familiar Indian Head motif. On the reverse in tiny letters were the initials, V.D.B., of the coin's designer, Victor David Brenner. The occasion was the 100th anniversary of Lincoln's birth. Coinage commenced at the Philadelphia and San Francisco mints. In total, 27,995,000 1909 V.D.B. cents were struck and 484,000 of the 1909-S V.D.B.

On August 2, 1909, the new cents were released to the public. A mad scramble ensued, and soon, banks had to ration the number paid out to any single individual, this being particularly true in the East. Interest in the West was less intense, and fewer coins were saved. A controversy arose as to the V.D.B. initials, and some newspaper notices complained that as Brenner had been paid for his work, there was no point in giving his initials a prominent place on the coins. Never mind that artists' initials had been used on other coins for a long time. As examples, the M initial of George T. Morgan appeared on both the obverse and reverse of silver dollars from 1878 onward; Chief Engraver Charles E. Barber was memorialized by a B on the neck of Miss Liberty on dimes, quarters, and half dollars from 1892 onward; and the recent (1907 onward) double eagles bore the monogram of Augustus Saint-Gaudens prominently on the obverse. In spite of these precedents, the offending V.D.B. initials were removed, and later 1909 and 1909-S cents were made without them.

Word spread that the cents with V.D.B. would be rare, and even more were saved. Today, the 1909 V.D.B. cents are readily available in Mint State. The 1909-S V.D.B., of lower mintage and of which far fewer were saved, lists for $2,000 in MS-63.

A few years later, at the Denver Mint, 1,193,000 1914-D cents were struck. Not much attention was paid to them, and today examples are rare, with an MS-63 listing for $3,300. Years later, only 866,000 1931-S cents were made. However, at this time there was a strong and growing interest in the numismatic hobby, and the low mintage figure was widely publicized; and although the mintage of the 1931-S is lower than for the 1914-D, an MS-63 1931-S is valued at just $195.

Other Popular First-Year Coins

Among other United States coins struck since 1792, these first-year-of-issue varieties (a partial list) were saved in large numbers and are especially plentiful today:

- **1943 zinc-coated steel cent.** The novel appearance of this coin resulted in many being saved as curiosities.
- **1883 Liberty Head nickel without cents.** The Mint expressed the value of this new design simply as "V," without mention of cents—not particularly unusual, as three-cent pieces of the era were simply denominated as "III." Certain people gold-plated the new nickels and passed them off as five-dollar gold coins of similar diameter. Soon, the Mint added CENTS. News accounts were printed that the "mistake" coins without CENTS would be recalled and would become very rare. So many were saved that today this variety is the most plentiful in Mint State of any Liberty Head nickel in the entire series from 1883 to 1913.

- **1913 Buffalo nickel.** These were saved in large quantities, and today there are more Mint State coins of this year in existence than for any other issue of the next 15 years.

- **1837 Liberty Seated, No Stars half dime.** Several thousand or more were saved, a large number for a half dime of the era. Apparently, their cameo-like appearance made them attractive curiosities at the time, the same being true of the dimes of the same year.

- **1837 Liberty Seated, No Stars dime.** Somewhat over a thousand were saved, a large number for a dime of the era.

- **1916 "Mercury" dime.** Quantities were saved of the 1916 and 1916-S, the first year of issue. However, for some reason the low-mintage 1916-D was generally overlooked and today is very rare in Mint State.

- **1932 Washington quarter.** At the Philadelphia Mint, 5,504,000 were minted, and it is likely that several hundred thousand were saved, making them plentiful today. The 1932-D quarter was struck to the extent of 436,800, but for some reason was overlooked by the public, with the result that Mint State coins are rare today. On the other hand, of the 408,000 1932-S quarters struck, thousands were saved. Today, Mint State 1932-S quarters are at least 10 to 20 times more readily available than are equivalent examples of the higher-mintage 1932-D.

- **1999–2008, state quarters.** From 1999 to 2008, five different quarter dollar designs were produced each year, with motifs observing the states in the order that they joined the Union. These coins were highly publicized, and many were, and still are, saved as souvenirs.

- **1964 Kennedy half dollar.** The popularity of the assassinated president was such that although hundreds of millions were minted, it is likely that many were saved as souvenirs both at home and abroad. This was also the last year of the 90% silver-content half dollar made for circulation, further increasing its popularity.

- **2000 Sacagawea "golden dollar."** These coins, intended to be a popular substitute for paper dollars and to last much longer in circulation, were launched with much fanfare in 2000, and more than just a few were saved by the public. However, the coin did not catch on for general use in commerce. Later issues have been made for sale to collectors, not for circulation.

- **MCMVII (1907) High-Relief gold twenty-dollar coin.** Although only about 12,000 were minted, at least 6,000 survive today, mostly in Mint State. Released in December 1907, the coin, by famous sculptor Augustus Saint-Gaudens, created a sensation, and soon the coins were selling for $30 each. Today, Mint State coins are plentiful, but as the demand for them is extremely strong, choice specimens sell for strong prices. An MS-63 coin lists for $24,000.

- **1892 and 1893 World's Columbian Exposition commemorative half dollars.** These, the first U.S. commemorative half dollars, were widely publicized, and hundreds of thousands were saved. Today they are very common in used condition.

Coins Few People Noticed

In contrast to the above, most coins of new designs attracted no particular notice, and examples were not saved in unusual quantities. In sharp contrast to the ultra-popular Kennedy half dollar of 1964, its predecessor design, the Franklin half dollar (launched in 1948), generated very little interest, and even numismatists generally ignored them—perhaps preferring the old Liberty Walking design that had been a favorite.

Although a long list could be made, here are some first-year-of-issue coins that were not noticed in their own time. Consequently, specimens range from scarce to rare in Mint State today:

- **1793 cent and half cent.** As popular as these may be today, there is no known instance in which a numismatist or museum in 1793 deliberately saved pieces as souvenirs.

- **1794–1795 half dime, half dollar, and silver dollar.** The Flowing Hair coins, highly desired today, seem to have attracted little notice in their time, and again there is no record of any having been deliberately saved.

- **1807 and related Capped Bust coinages.** The Capped Bust and related coins of John Reich, assistant engraver at the Mint, were first used in 1807 on the silver half dollar and gold five-dollar piece, and later on certain other denominations. Today these are extremely popular with collectors, but in their time they were not noticed, and few were saved in Mint State.

- **1840 Liberty Seated dollar.** Specimens are very scarce in Mint State today and are virtually unknown in gem preservation.

- **1892 Barber dime, quarter dollar, and half dollar.** In 1892 the new Liberty Head design by Charles E. Barber replaced the long-lived Liberty Seated motif. The new coins received bad press notices. Another factor detracting from public interest was the wide attention focused on the forthcoming commemorative half dollars of the World's Columbian Exposition. Not many of the new Barber coins were saved.

- **1938 Jefferson nickel.** Although the numismatic hobby was dynamic at the time, the new nickel design attracted little notice, and no unusual quantities were saved. The market was still reeling from the burst bubble of the 1935 through 1936 commemorative craze, and there was little incentive to save coins for investment.

The 1962–1964 Treasury Release

The Bland-Allison Act of February 28, 1878, a political boondoggle passed to accommodate silver-mining interests in the West, mandated that the Treasury Department buy millions of ounces of silver each year and convert it to silver dollars. At the time, the world price of silver bullion was dropping, and there were economic difficulties in the mining states. From 1878 to 1904 and again in 1921, silver dollars of the Morgan design were minted under this legislation and subsequent acts, to the extent of 656,989,387 pieces. From 1921 to 1928, and 1934–1935, silver dollars of the Peace design were produced in the amount of 190,577,279 pieces.

Although silver dollars were used in commerce in certain areas of the West, paper currency by and large served the needs of trade and exchange. As these hundreds of millions of newly minted dollars were not needed, most were put up in 1,000-coin canvas bags and stored in Treasury vaults. In 1918, under terms of the Pittman Act, 270,232,722 Morgan dollars were melted. At the time, the market for silver was temporarily strong, and there was a call for bullion to ship to India to shore up confidence in Britain's wartime government. No accounting was kept of the dates and mints involved in the destruction. Just the quantities were recorded (this procedure being typical when the Treasury melted old coins). However, hundreds of millions remained.

Now and again there was a call for silver dollars for circulation, especially in the West; and in the East and Midwest there was a modest demand for pieces for use as holiday and other gifts; in such instances many were paid out. The earlier example of the high-mintage 1901 dollar being rare in Mint State, as most were circulated, is reflective of this. Other coins were stored, such as the aforementioned low-mintage

1884-CC, of which 84.7% were still in the hands of the Treasury as late as 1964! At this time the Treasury decided to hold back bags that were marked as having Carson City dollars, although in records of storage no account was made of them earlier.

Beginning in a significant way in the 1950s, silver dollars became very popular with numismatists. The rarest of all Morgan silver dollars by 1962 was considered to be the 1903-O. In the *Guide Book,* an Uncirculated coin listed for $1,500, the highest price for any variety. Experts estimated that fewer than a dozen Mint State coins existed in all of numismatics. It was presumed that most had been melted in 1918 under the Pittman Act.

Then this—in November 1962, during the normal payout of silver dollars as gifts for the holiday season, some long-sealed bags of coins were taken from a Philadelphia Mint vault that had remained under seal since 1929. It was soon found that brilliant 1903-O dollars were among these! A treasure hunt ensued, and hundreds of thousands of these former rarities were found. The rush was on!

From then until March 1964, hundreds of millions of Morgan and Peace dollars were emptied from government and bank storage. At one time a long line of people, some with wheelbarrows, formed outside of the Treasury Building in Washington, D.C., to obtain bags of dollars. Finally, only about three million coins remained, mostly the aforementioned Carson City issues, which the Treasury decided to hold back. These were later sold at strong premiums in a series of auctions held by the General Services Administration.

In the meantime, Morgan and Peace dollars became very large and important sections of the coin hobby, as they remain today. However, as can be seen, the combined elements of some coins' having been melted in 1918, others having been placed into circulation generations ago, and still others existing in Mint State from long-stored hoards, results in silver dollar prices that often bear little relation to mintage figures.

Other Famous Hoards

While the great Treasury release of 1962 through 1964 is the most famous of all hoards, quite a few others have attracted interest and attention over the years.

- **Castine Hoard of Early Silver Coins (discovered in the 1840s).** From November 1840 through April 1841, Captain Stephen Grindle and his son Samuel unearthed many silver coins on their farm on the Bagaduce River about six miles from the harbor of Castine, Maine. The number of pieces found was not recorded, but is believed to have been between 500 and 2,000, buried in 1690 (the latest date observed) or soon afterward. Most pieces were foreign silver coins, but dozens of Massachusetts Pine Tree shillings and related silver coins were found. This hoard stands today as one of the most famous in American history.

- **Bank of New York Hoard (1856).** Circa 1856, a keg containing several thousand 1787 Fugio copper cents was found at the Bank of New York at 44 Wall Street. Each was in Mint State, most with brown toning. For many years these were given out as souvenirs and keepsakes to clients. By 1948, when numismatist Damon G. Douglas examined them, there were 1,641 remaining. Today, many remain at the bank and are appreciated for their history and value.

- **Nichols Find of Copper Cents (by 1859).** In the annals of American numismatics, one of the most famous hoards is the so-called Nichols Find, consisting of 1796 and 1797 copper cents, Mint State, perhaps about 1,000 in total. These were distributed in the late 1850s by David Nichols. All were gone as of 1863, by which time they were worth $3 to $4 each, or less than a thousandth of their present-day value.

- **Randall Hoard of Copper Cents (1860s).** Sometime soon after the Civil War, a wooden keg filled with as-new copper cents was located, said to have been beneath an old railroad platform in Georgia. Revealed were thousands of coins dated 1816 to 1820, with the 1818 and 1820 being the most numerous. Today, the Randall hoard accounts for most known Mint State examples of these particular dates.

- **Colonel Cohen Hoard of 1773 Virginia Halfpennies (by the 1870s).** Sometime in the 1870s or earlier, Colonel Mendes I. Cohen, a Baltimore numismatist, obtained a cache of at least 2,200 Uncirculated specimens of the 1773 Virginia halfpenny. These passed through several hands, and many pieces were dispersed along the way. As a result, today these are the only colonial (pre-1776) American coins that can be easily obtained in Mint State.

- **Exeter Hoard of Massachusetts Silver (1876).** During the excavation of a cellar near the railroad station in Exeter, New Hampshire, a group of 30 to 40 Massachusetts silver shillings was found in the sand, amid the remains of what seemed to be a wooden box. All bore the date 1652 and were of the Pine Tree and Oak Tree types, plus, possibly, a rare Willow Tree shilling.

- **Economite Treasure (1878).** In 1878 a remarkable hoard of silver coins was found in a subterranean storage area at Economy, Pennsylvania, in a building erected years earlier by the Harmony Society, a utopian work-share community. The March 1881 issue of the Coin Collector's Journal gave this inventory: Quarter dollars: 1818 through 1828, 400 pieces. Half dollars: 1794, 150; 1795, 650; 1796, 2; 1797, 1; 1801, 300; 1802, 200; 1803, 300; 1805 Over 04, 25; 1805, 600; 1806, 1,500; 1807, 2,000; 1815, 100. Common half dollars: 1808 through 1836, 111,356. Silver dollars: 1794, 1; 1795, 800; 1796, 125; 1797, 80; 1798 Small Eagle reverse, 30; 1798 Large Eagle reverse, 560; 1799 5 stars facing, 12; 1799, 1,250; 1800, 250; 1801, 1802, and 1803, 600. Foreign silver (French, Spanish, and Spanish-American), total face value: $12,600. Total face value of the hoard: $75,000.00. Other information indicates that most of the coins had been taken from circulation and showed different degrees of wear.

- **Hoard of Miser Aaron White (before 1888).** Aaron White, a Connecticut attorney, distrusted paper money and even went so far as to issue his own token, inscribed NEVER KEEP A PAPER DOLLAR IN YOUR POCKET TILL TOMORROW. He had a passion for saving coins and accumulated more than 100,000 pieces. After his death the coins were removed to a warehouse. Later, they were placed in the hands of dealer Édouard Frossard, who sold most of them privately and others by auction on July 20, 1888, billing them as "18,000 American and foreign copper coins and tokens selected from the Aaron White hoard." An overall estimate of the White hoard, as it existed before it was given to Frossard, was made by Benjamin P. Wright, and included these: "250 colonial and state copper coins, 60,000 copper large cents (which were mainly 'rusted' and spotted; 5,000 of the nicest ones were picked out and sold for 2¢ each), 60,000 copper-nickel Flying Eagle and Indian cents (apparently most dated 1862 and 1863), 5,000 bronze two-cent pieces, 200 half dollars, 100 silver dollars, 350 gold dollars, and 20,000 to 30,000 foreign copper coins."

- **Collins Find of 1828 Half Cents (1894).** Circa 1894, Benjamin H. Collins, a Washington, DC, numismatist, acquired a bag of half cents dated 1828, of the 13-stars variety. It is believed that about 1,000 coins were involved, all bright Uncirculated. By the early 1950s all but a few hundred had been distributed in the marketplace, and by now it is likely that all have individual owners.

- **Chapman Hoard of 1806 Half Cents (1906).** About 1906, Philadelphia dealer Henry Chapman acquired a hoard of 1806 half cents. Although no figure was given at the time, it is estimated that a couple hundred or so coins were involved. Most or all had much of their original mint red color, with toning to brown, and with light striking at the upper part of the wreath.

- **Baltimore Find (1934).** One of the most storied hoards in American numismatics is the Baltimore Find, a cache of at least 3,558 gold coins, all dated before 1857. On August 31, 1934, two young boys were playing in the cellar of a rented house at 132 South Eden Street, Baltimore, and found these coins hidden in a wall. Later, more were found in the same location. On May 2, 1935, many of the coins were sold at auction, by which time others had been sold quietly, some unofficially. This hoard included many choice and gem coins dated in the 1850s.

- **New Orleans Bank Find (1982).** A few minutes past noon, on October 29, 1982, a bulldozer unearthed a cache of long-hidden silver coins, believed to have been stored in three wooden boxes in the early 1840s. The pieces were mostly Spanish-American issues, but hundreds of United States coins, including 1840-O and 1841-O Liberty Seated quarters, were also found. A scrabble in the dirt and mud ensued, and men in business suits, ladies in dresses, and others scrambled to find treasure. The latest coin found was from 1842. This must have been a secret reserve of some long-forgotten merchant or bank.

- **Wells-Fargo Hoard of 1908 $20 (1990s).** In the 1990s, dealer Ron Gillio purchased a hoard of 19,900 examples of the 1908 No Motto double eagle. For a time these were stored in a Wells Fargo Bank branch, giving the name to the cache. All were Mint State, and many were of choice and gem quality. Offered in the market, these were dispersed over a period of several years.

- **Gold coins from abroad (turn of the 21st century).** In the late 20th and early 21st centuries, some exciting finds of Mint State double eagles were located in foreign banks. Involved were high-grade examples of some Carson City issues in the Liberty Head series and hundreds of scarce-mintmark varieties dated after 1923. As is often the case when hoards are discovered, pieces were filtered into the market without any publicity or an accounting of varieties found.

Sunken Treasure

Throughout American history, tens of thousands of ships have been lost at sea and on inland waters. Only a handful of these vessels were reported as having had significant quantities of coins aboard. In recent decades, numismatists have been front-row center as wrecks from several sidewheel steamers lost in the 1850s and 1860s have yielded rare coins.

The SS *New York* was launched in 1837, carrying passengers between New York City and Charleston, South Carolina. The steamer was carrying $30,000 or more in money when she encountered an unexpected hurricane in the Gulf of Mexico on September 5, 1846. Captain John D. Phillips ordered the anchor dropped, hoping to ride out the storm. The wind and waves increased, however, and for two days those aboard watched as the rigging and other parts of the ship were torn apart. On September 7 the storm prevailed and the *New York* was overwhelmed, sinking into water 60 feet deep. An estimated 17 people—about one third of the passengers and crew—lost their lives. Decades later, in 2006 and 2007, treasure seekers recovered more than 2,000 silver coins and several hundred gold coins from the shipwreck. Most of the silver was heavily etched from exposure to the salt water, but certain of the gold coins were in high grades, including some of the finest known examples of their date and mint.

Eight years after the loss of the *New York*, the SS *Yankee Blade* was off the coast of Santa Barbara, California, steaming at full speed in a heavy fog. Captain Henry T.

Randall believed the ship was in deep water far out to sea, and he was trying to establish a speed record—certain to be beneficial in advertising. In fact the steamer was amid the rockbound Channel Islands, and in the fog she smashed onto a rock and got hung up. The date was October 1, 1854. On board was some $152,000 in coins consigned by a banking house, plus other gold, and about 900 passengers and crew. Most of them escaped, but in the ensuing confusion before the *Yankee Blade* sank, between 17 and 50 lost their lives. Over the years most of the coins appear to have been recovered, under circumstances largely unknown. In 1948 the hull was found again and divers visited the wreck. Circa 1977 more recoveries were yielded, including 200 to 250 1854-S double eagles. All showed microscopic granularity, possibly from the action of sea-bottom sand, and all had die cracks on the reverse. Little in the way of facts has ever reached print.

The wreck and recovery of the SS *Central America* was much better documented. The steamer was lost on September 12, 1857, carrying about $2,600,000 in gold treasure, heading from Havana, Cuba, to New York City. A monster hurricane engulfed the ship on the 10th and 11th; Captain William Lewis Herndon enlisted the aid of male passengers to form a bucket brigade to bail water, but their efforts proved futile. The ship was swamped, and the captain ordered the American flag be flown upside-down, a signal of distress. The nearby brig *Marine* approached and nearly all of the *Central America*'s women and children were transferred over, along with some crew members, before the *Central America* was overwhelmed by the waves and went down, with Captain Herndon standing on the paddle box. The steamer ultimately settled 7,200 feet deep, and some 435 lives were lost. The wreck was found in 1987 and over time more than $100 million worth of treasure was brought to the surface. This included more than 5,400 mint-fresh 1857-S double eagles, hundreds of gold ingots (including one weighing 80 pounds), and other coins.

In the 1990s another sidewheel steamer was found: the SS *Brother Jonathan*, lost with few survivors as she attempted to return to safe harbor in Crescent City, California, after hitting stormy weather on her way north to Oregon (January 30, 1865). More than 1,000 gold coins were recovered from the wreck, including many Mint State 1865-S double eagles. Detailed files and photographs recorded every step of the recovery.

In 2003 another 1865 shipwreck was located: that of the SS *Republic*, lost off the coast of Georgia while en route from New York City to New Orleans, October 25, just months after the Civil War ended. The steamer sank in a hurricane along with a reported $400,000 in silver and gold. Recovery efforts brought up 51,000 coins and 14,000 other artifacts (bottles, ceramics, personal items, etc.). The coins included 1,400 double eagles dating from 1838 to 1858, and thousands from the 1850s and 1860s; plus more than 180 different examples of Liberty Seated half dollars, including five 1861-O die combinations attributed to Confederate control of the New Orleans mint. The most valuable single coin was a Mint State 1854-O $20 then valued at more than $500,000.

Shipwrecks continue to be found even today, and the hobby community eagerly awaits news of coins and treasure found amidst their watery resting places.

Money had a rich history in America prior to the advent of the United States' national coinage in 1793. When coins tumbled off the presses from the first U.S. Mint the country was much more accustomed to coins from other countries. People were content to use currency, both old and new, whose value was based more on the metal content than on the issuer's reliability. Foreign money in America during the colonial period had become so embedded that it continued to be accepted as legal tender until discontinued by law in 1857. Coins of this era are so fundamental to American numismatics that every collection should include at least a sampling.

Many of the foreign coins from England, Spain, Portugal, France, and the Netherlands have names, sizes, and expressions whose usage has continued to the present day. Not only did the popular Spanish-American silver 8 reales, Pillar dollar, or piece of eight become a model for the American silver dollar, but its fractional parts morphed into the half-dollar and quarter-dollar coins that are now considered decimal fractions of the dollar. The American quarter dollar, which was similar in size and value to the Spanish 2-real coin, took on the nickname *two bits*—a moniker that remains today. It was not until 1997 that stock-market prices ceased being quoted in the Spanish-real system of eighths of a dollar. Similarly, the American one-cent coin has never totally lost its association with the English penny, and continues to be called that by anyone indifferent to numismatic accuracy.

The use of foreign coins was so prevalent in colonial times that the dollar sign and the very term *dollar,* as we know them today, did not come into general use until 1767. The paper dollars printed by Maryland and issued that year were the first to include the term to indicate the Spanish-American piece of eight, which was a radical departure from denominations in terms of English pounds, shillings, and pence. Distinguishing between the relative values of the multitude of different foreign currencies was not a simple task. The English, Portuguese, Spanish, German, Dutch, and other currencies all had to be calculated in terms that related to their values in various colonies and states. To facilitate conversions, books and tables showed comparison prices for each currency. In mid-1750, for instance, the Spanish dollar was quoted as being worth eight shillings in New York, but sixpence less in New Jersey, and only four shillings, eightpence in Georgia.

Coins, tokens, paper money, and promissory notes were not the only media of exchange used during the early formation of the country. Many day-to-day transactions were carried on by barter and credit. Mixed into this financial morass were local trade items such as native wampum, hides, household goods, and tools.

Beyond these pre-federal considerations are the many kinds of private and state issues of coins and tokens that permeate the colonial period from 1616 to 1776, and that are the true essence of collectible money of that era. These are items that catch the attention and imagination of everyone interested in the history and development of early America. Yet, despite their enormous historical importance, forming a basic collection of such items is not nearly as daunting as one might expect.

The coins and tokens described in this book are fundamentally a major-type listing of the metallic money used throughout the pre-federal period. Many collectors use this as a guide to forming a comprehensive set of these pieces. It is not encyclopedic in its scope. Beyond the basic types are numerous sub-varieties of some of the issues, and a wide range of European coins. Collectors attempt to accumulate as many of those as time and finances will permit. Some aim for the finest possible condition, while others find great enjoyment in pieces that saw actual circulation and use during the formative days of the country. There are no rules about how or what to collect other than to enjoy owning a genuine piece of early American history.

BRITISH NEW WORLD ISSUES
Sommer Islands (Bermuda)

This coinage, the first struck for the English colonies in the New World, was issued circa 1616. The coins were known as *Hogge Money* or *Hoggies.*

The pieces were made of brass or copper, lightly silvered, in four denominations: shilling, sixpence, threepence, and twopence, each indicated by Roman numerals. The hog is the main device and appears on the obverse side of each. SOMMER ISLANDS is inscribed within beaded circles on the larger denominations. The reverse shows a full-rigged galleon with the flag of St. George on each of four masts.

The islands were named for Sir George Sommers, who was shipwrecked there in 1609 while en route to the Virginia plantations. Shakespeare's *Tempest* was possibly based on this incident.

The Bermuda Islands, as they are known today, were named for Juan de Bermúdez, who is believed to have stopped there in 1515. A few hogs that he carried for delivery to the West Indies were left behind. When Sommers and his party arrived, the islands were overrun with the animals, which served as a welcome source of food for the expedition.

Twopence Threepence

Sixpence Obverse Large Portholes Reverse Small Portholes Reverse

Shilling Obverse Small Sail Reverse Large Sail Reverse

	AG	G	VG	F	VF	EF
Twopence, Large Star Between Legs	$4,250	$6,500	$9,000	$18,000	$45,000	$75,000
Twopence, Small Star Between Legs	4,250	6,500	9,000	18,000	45,000	75,000
Threepence.	—	—	75,000	125,000	175,000	—
Sixpence, Small Portholes.	3,250	4,250	7,500	15,000	50,000	70,000
Sixpence, Large Portholes	3,750	4,750	7,500	16,000	60,000	90,000
Shilling, Small Sail	4,750	6,500	11,000	35,000	65,000	95,000
Shilling, Large Sail	6,000	10,000	35,000	65,000	90,000	—

Massachusetts
"New England" Coinage (1652)

The earliest authorized medium of exchange in the New England settlements was wampum. The General Court of Massachusetts in 1637 ordered "that wampamege should passe at 6 a penny for any sume under 12 d." Wampum consisted of shells of various colors, ground to the size of kernels of corn. A hole was drilled through each piece so it could be strung on a leather thong for convenience and adornment.

Corn, pelts, and bullets were frequently used in lieu of coins, which were rarely available. Silver and gold coins brought over from England, Holland, and other countries tended to flow back across the Atlantic to purchase needed supplies. The colonists, thus left to their own resources, traded with the friendly Native Americans in kind. In 1661 the law making wampum legal tender was repealed.

Agitation for a standard coinage reached its height in 1651. England, recovering from a civil war between the Puritans and Royalists, ignored the colonists, who took matters into their own hands in 1652.

The Massachusetts General Court in 1652 ordered the first metallic currency—the New England silver threepence, sixpence, and shilling—to be struck in the English Americas (the Spaniards had established a mint in Mexico City in 1535). Silver bullion was procured principally from the West Indies. The mint was located in Boston, and John Hull was appointed mintmaster; his assistant was Robert Sanderson (or Saunderson). At first, Hull received as compensation one shilling threepence for every 20 shillings coined. This fee was adjusted several times during his term as mintmaster.

NE Threepence

NE Sixpence   NE Shilling

Early American coins in conditions better than those listed are rare and are consequently valued much higher.

	G	VG	F	VF	EF	AU
NE Threepence *(unique)*			—			
NE Sixpence *(8 known)*	$45,000	$90,000	$150,000	$275,000		
NE Shilling	55,000	100,000	190,000	300,000	$350,000	$450,000
$416,875, AU-50, Heritage auction, August 2010						

Willow Tree Coinage (1653–1660)

The simplicity of the designs on the NE coins invited counterfeiting and clipping of the edges. Therefore, they were soon replaced by the Willow, Oak, and Pine Tree series. The Willow Tree coins were struck from 1653 to 1660, the Oak Trees from 1660 to 1667, and the Pine Trees from 1667 to 1682. All of them (with the exception of the Oak Tree twopence) bore the date 1652, which gives them the appearance of having been struck when Cromwell was in power, after the English civil war. The coinage was abandoned in 1682; a proposal to renew coinage in 1686 was rejected by the General Court.

These pieces, like all early American coins, were produced from handmade dies that are often individually distinctive. The great number of die varieties that can be found and identified are of interest to collectors who value each according to individual rarity. Values shown for type coins in this guide are for the most common die variety.

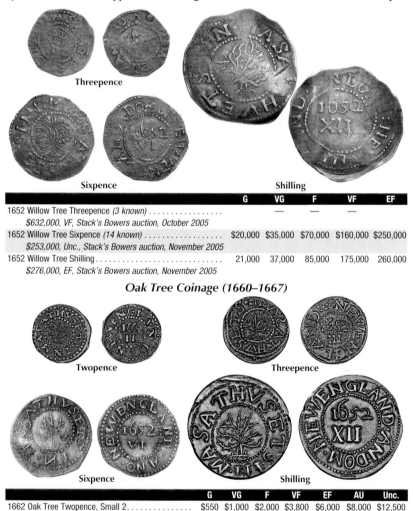

Threepence

Sixpence

Shilling

	G	VG	F	VF	EF
1652 Willow Tree Threepence *(3 known)*	—	—	—		
$632,000, VF, Stack's Bowers auction, October 2005					
1652 Willow Tree Sixpence *(14 known)*	$20,000	$35,000	$70,000	$160,000	$250,000
$253,000, Unc., Stack's Bowers auction, November 2005					
1652 Willow Tree Shilling	21,000	37,000	85,000	175,000	260,000
$276,000, EF, Stack's Bowers auction, November 2005					

Oak Tree Coinage (1660–1667)

Twopence

Threepence

Sixpence

Shilling

	G	VG	F	VF	EF	AU	Unc.
1662 Oak Tree Twopence, Small 2	$550	$1,000	$2,000	$3,800	$6,000	$8,000	$12,500
1662 Oak Tree Twopence, Large 2	550	1,000	2,000	3,800	6,000	8,000	12,500
1652 Oak Tree Threepence, No IN on Obverse	675	1,250	3,000	6,500	11,000	17,000	—
1652 Oak Tree Threepence, IN on Obverse	675	1,350	3,250	7,000	13,000	21,000	50,000

	G	VG	F	VF	EF	AU	Unc.
1652 Oak Tree Sixpence, IN on Reverse..	$750	$1,300	$3,200	$7,500	$16,000	$21,000	$40,000
1652 Oak Tree Sixpence, IN on Obverse..	750	1,300	3,200	7,500	14,000	19,000	35,000
1652 Oak Tree Shilling, IN at Left.......	750	1,250	3,000	7,000	10,500	16,000	28,000
1652 Oak Tree Shilling, IN at Bottom	750	1,250	3,000	6,500	10,000	14,500	26,000
1652 Oak Tree Shilling, ANDO	900	1,900	4,000	8,500	15,000	20,000	34,000
1652 Oak Tree Shilling, Spiny Tree......	750	1,250	3,250	7,000	12,000	17,000	31,000

Pine Tree Coinage (1667–1682)

The first Pine Tree coins were minted on the same size planchets as the Oak Tree pieces. Subsequent issues of the shilling were narrower and thicker to conform to the style of English coins. Large Planchet shillings ranged from 27 to 31 mm in diameter; Small Planchet shillings ranged from 22 to 26 mm in diameter.

Threepence   Sixpence

Shilling, Large Planchet (1667–1674)   Shilling, Small Planchet (1675–1682)

	G	VG	F	VF	EF	AU	Unc.
1652 Threepence, Pellets at Trunk......	$550	$800	$1,600	$3,200	$6,000	$9,000	$19,000
1652 Threepence, Without Pellets	550	800	1,600	3,250	6,000	9,000	19,000
1652 Sixpence, Pellets at Trunk........	600	925	1,800	3,600	6,250	10,000	20,000
1652 Sixpence, Without Pellets.........	600	950	1,900	3,800	6,750	11,000	21,000
1652 Shilling, Large Planchet (27–31 mm)							
Pellets at Trunk	700	1,100	2,200	5,000	8,750	13,000	24,000
Without Pellets at Trunk.............	700	1,000	2,100	4,750	8,500	13,000	23,000
No H in MASATUSETS...............	800	1,400	2,800	7,500	13,500	20,000	—
Ligatured NE in Legend	700	1,100	2,200	5,000	8,750	13,000	23,500
1652 Shilling, Small Planchet (22–26 mm)	600	925	2,000	4,000	6,800	11,000	25,000

Maryland
Lord Baltimore Coinage

Cecil Calvert, the second Lord Baltimore, inherited from his father nearly absolute control over Maryland. Calvert believed he had the right to coin money for the colony, and in 1659 he ordered shillings, sixpences, and groats (four-penny pieces) from the Royal Mint in London and shipped samples to Maryland, to his brother Philip, who was then his secretary for the colony. Calvert's right to strike coins was upheld by Cromwell's government. The whole issue was small, and while his coins did circulate in Maryland at first, by 1700 they had largely disappeared from commerce.

Calvert's coins bear his portrait on the obverse, with a Latin legend calling him "Lord of Mary's Land." The reverses of the larger denominations bear his family coat of arms and the denomination in Roman numerals. There are several die varieties of each. Many of these coins are found holed and repaired. The copper penny, or denarium, is the rarest denomination, with only nine reported specimens.

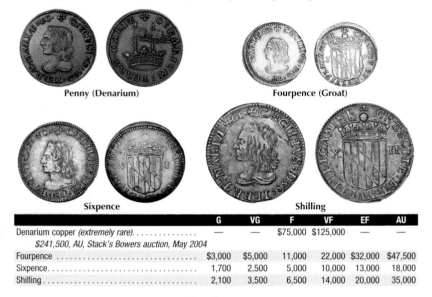

Penny (Denarium)   Fourpence (Groat)

Sixpence   Shilling

	G	VG	F	VF	EF	AU
Denarium copper *(extremely rare)*.	—	—	$75,000	$125,000	—	—
$241,500, AU, Stack's Bowers auction, May 2004						
Fourpence	$3,000	$5,000	11,000	22,000	$32,000	$47,500
Sixpence.	1,700	2,500	5,000	10,000	13,000	18,000
Shilling	2,100	3,500	6,500	14,000	20,000	35,000

New Jersey
St. Patrick or Mark Newby Coinage

Mark Newby, who came to America from Dublin, Ireland, in November 1681, brought copper pieces believed by numismatists to have been struck in Dublin circa 1663 to 1672. These are called *St. Patrick coppers*.

The coinage was made legal tender by the General Assembly of New Jersey in May 1682. The legislature did not specify which size piece could circulate, only that the coin was to be worth a halfpenny in trade. Most numismatists believe the larger-size coin was intended. However, as many more farthing-size pieces are known than halfpennies, some believe that the smaller-size piece was meant. Copper coins often circulated in the colonies at twice what they would have been worth in England.

The obverses show a crowned king kneeling and playing a harp. The legend FLOREAT REX ("May the King Prosper") is separated by a crown. The reverse side of the halfpence shows St. Patrick with a crozier in his left hand and a trefoil in his right, and surrounded by people. At his left side is a shield. The legend is ECCE GREX ("Behold the Flock"). The farthing reverse shows St. Patrick driving away reptiles and serpents as he holds a metropolitan cross in his left hand. The legend reads QUIESCAT PLEBS ("May the People Be at Ease").

The large-size piece, called by collectors a *halfpenny,* bears the arms of the City of Dublin on the shield on the reverse; the smaller-size piece, called a *farthing,* does not. Both denominations have a reeded edge.

The decorative brass insert found on the coinage, usually over the crown on the obverse, was put there to make counterfeiting more difficult. On some pieces this decoration has been removed or does not show. Numerous die variations exist.

St. Patrick "Farthing"   St. Patrick "Halfpenny"

	G	VG	F	VF	EF	AU
St. Patrick "Farthing"	$125	$300	$800	$3,000	$7,500	$17,000
Similar, Halo Around Saint's Head	500	1,500	7,000	17,000	40,000	—
Similar, No C in QUIESCAT	800	3,750	11,000	22,000	—	—
St. Patrick "Farthing," silver	1,800	3,500	10,000	20,000	30,000	50,000
St. Patrick "Farthing," gold *(unique)* *$184,000, AU, Stack's Bowers auction, January 2005*						—
St. Patrick "Halfpenny"	350	800	1,200	3,500	12,000	20,000

COINAGE AUTHORIZED BY BRITISH ROYAL PATENT
American Plantations Coins

These tokens, struck in nearly pure tin, were the first royally authorized coinage for the British colonies in America. They were made under a franchise granted in 1688 to Richard Holt. Most examples show black oxidation of the tin. Bright, unblemished specimens are more valuable. Restrikes were made about 1828 from original dies.

	G	VG	F	VF	EF	AU	Unc.
(1688) James II Plantation 1/24 Real coinage							
1/24 Part Real	$225	$300	$500	$1,000	$1,500	$2,100	$6,000
1/24 Part Real, ET. HB. REX	275	400	900	2,000	3,200	8,500	12,000
1/24 Part Real, Sidewise 4 in 24	425	1,000	1,900	4,250	6,500	10,000	20,000
1/24 Part Real, Arms Transposed	650	1,500	2,500	6,500	8,500	12,000	—
1/24 Part Real, Restrike	100	150	250	450	600	900	2,200

Coinage of William Wood
Rosa Americana Coins

William Wood, an Englishman, obtained a patent from King George I to make tokens for Ireland and the American colonies.

The first pieces struck were undated; others bear the dates 1722, 1723, 1724, and 1733. The Rosa Americana pieces were issued in three denominations—half penny, penny, and twopence—and were intended for America. This type had a fully bloomed rose on the reverse with the words ROSA AMERICANA UTILE DULCI ("American Rose—Useful and Pleasant").

The obverse, common to both Rosa Americana and Hibernia pieces, shows the head of George I and the legend GEORGIUS D:G MAG: BRI: FRA: ET. HIB: REX ("George, by the Grace of God, King of Great Britain, France, and Ireland") or abbreviations thereof. Rosa Americana tokens, however, were rejected by the American colonists. The coins are made of a brass composition of copper and zinc (sometimes mistakenly referred to as *Bath metal*). Planchet quality is often rough and porous.

	VG	F	VF	EF	AU	Unc.
(No date) Twopence, Motto in Ribbon *(illustrated)*...	$200	$400	$700	$1,300	$3,200	$6,000
(No date) Twopence, Motto Without Ribbon *(3 known)*	—	—	—			

	VG	F	VF	EF	AU	Unc.
1722 Halfpenny, VTILE DVLCI..................	$925	$2,250	$3,800	$6,750	$9,750	
1722 Halfpenny, D.G.REX ROSA AMERI. UTILE DULCI	150	200	400	950	1,500	$3,500
1722 Halfpenny, DEI GRATIA REX UTILE DULCI......	150	200	400	950	1,500	3,200

	VG	F	VF	EF	AU	Unc.
1722 Penny, GEORGIVS			$12,000	$17,500	$28,000	$40,000
1722 Penny, VTILE DVLCI....................	$170	$300	700	1,300	2,750	6,000
1722 Penny, UTILE DULCI....................	150	200	400	700	1,300	3,200

	VG	F	VF	EF	AU	Unc.
1722 Twopence, Period After REX	$150	$275	$600	$1,200	$2,500	$4,500
1722 Twopence, No Period After REX	150	275	600	1,200	2,500	4,500

	VG	F	VF	EF	AU	Unc.
1723 Halfpenny, Uncrowned Rose	$900	$1,750	$3,500	$5,000	$8,000	$10,000
1723 Halfpenny, Crowned Rose	110	170	350	750	1,600	3,900

	VG	F	VF	EF	AU	Unc.
1723 Penny *(illustrated)*	$100	$150	$350	$600	$1,000	$2,500
1723 Twopence	150	275	400	800	1,300	2,700

	EF	AU	Unc.
1724, 4 Over 3 Penny (pattern), DEI GRATIA.	$7,500	$15,000	$22,000
1724, 4 Over 3 Penny (pattern), D GRATIA	8,750	20,000	34,000
(Undated) (1724) Penny, ROSA: SINE: SPINA. *(5 known)*	35,000	45,000	—
$21,850, VF, Stack's Bowers auction, May 2005			

43

1724 Twopence (pattern) *$25,300, Choice AU, Stack's Bowers auction, May 2005.* . . . .

The 1733 twopence is a pattern piece and bears the bust of George II facing to the left. It was issued by the successors to the coinage patent, as William Wood had died in 1730.

1733 Twopence (pattern), Proof *$63,250, Gem PF, Stack's Bowers auction, May 2005* . . . .

Wood's Hibernia Coinage

The type intended for Ireland had a seated figure with a harp on the reverse side and the word HIBERNIA. Denominations struck were farthing and halfpenny, with dates 1722, 1723, and 1724. Hibernia coins were unpopular in Ireland, so some of them were sent to the American colonies. Numerous varieties exist.

| | **First Type** | **Second Type** | | **1723, 3 Over 2** |

	VG	F	VF	EF	AU	Unc.
1722 Farthing, D: G: REX	$500	$750	$2,200	$3,500	$7,500	$14,000
1722 Halfpenny, D: G: REX, Rocks at Right (pattern)	—	—	8,000	12,000	20,000	40,000
1722 Halfpenny, First Type, Harp at Left.	100	150	300	600	900	1,600
1722 Halfpenny, Second Type, Harp at Right	70	100	200	550	1,100	2,000
1722 Halfpenny, Second Type, DEII (blunder)	150	350	800	1,500	2,000	3,200
1723 Farthing, D.G.REX	100	125	250	400	550	1,000
1723 Farthing, DEI. GRATIA. REX	50	80	125	225	400	600
1723 Farthing (silver pattern)	1,800	2,500	4,500	6,000	8,500	15,000

1724, Hibernia Farthing			**1724, Hibernia Halfpenny**			

	G	VG	F	VF	EF	AU	Unc.
1723 Halfpenny, 3 Over 2 (varieties exist)	$45	$75	$150	$450	$850	$1,300	$2,400
1723 Halfpenny	30	45	75	125	275	400	775
1723 Halfpenny (silver pattern)			—	—	—	—	—
1724 Farthing	55	125	225	750	1,600	2,250	4,000
1724 Halfpenny	50	100	150	350	700	1,100	2,200
1724 Halfpenny, DEI Above Head					—	—	

Virginia Halfpennies

In 1773, coinage of a copper halfpenny for Virginia was authorized by the Crown. The pattern, in Proof struck on a large planchet with a wide milled border, is often referred to as a penny. Most Mint State pieces are from the Colonel Cohen Hoard discussed on page 32.

The silver piece dated 1774 is referred to as a shilling, but may have been a pattern or trial for a halfpenny or a guinea.

Red uncirculated pieces without spots are worth considerably more.

	G	VG	F	VF	EF	AU	Unc.
1773 Halfpenny, Period After GEORGIVS	$25	$50	$100	$150	$350	$500	$900
1773 Halfpenny, No Period After GEORGIVS	35	75	140	200	400	600	1,200

1773, "Penny"	**1774, "Shilling"**	

	PF
1773 "Penny"	$25,000
1774 "Shilling" *(6 known)*	130,000

EARLY AMERICAN AND RELATED TOKENS
Elephant Tokens
London Elephant Tokens

The London Elephant tokens were struck circa 1672 to 1694. Although they were undated, two examples are known to have been struck over 1672 British halfpennies. Most were struck in copper, but one was made of brass. The legend on this piece, GOD PRESERVE LONDON, is probably just a general plea for divine aid and not a specific reference to the outbreak of plague in 1665 or the great fire of 1666.

These pieces were not struck for the colonies, and probably did not circulate widely in America, although a few may have been carried there by colonists. They are associated with the 1694 Carolina and New England Elephant tokens, through a shared obverse die.

	VG	F	VF	EF	AU	Unc.
(1694) Halfpenny, GOD PRESERVE LONDON, Thick Planchet	$300	$550	$900	$1,500	$2,500	$4,200
(1694) Halfpenny, GOD PRESERVE LONDON, Thin Planchet	500	1,000	3,250	4,750	7,250	12,000
Similar, brass *(unique)*					—	
(1694) Halfpenny, GOD PRESERVE LONDON, Diagonals in Center of Shield	700	2,500	7,000	9,500	17,000	38,000
(1694) Halfpenny, Similar, Sword in Second Quarter of Shield	—	—	20,000	—	—	—
(1694) Halfpenny, LON DON	1,100	2,500	5,000	8,500	15,000	24,000

Carolina Elephant Tokens

Although no law is known authorizing coinage for Carolina, two very interesting pieces known as Elephant tokens were made with the date 1694. These copper tokens were of halfpenny denomination. The reverse reads GOD PRESERVE CAROLINA AND THE LORDS PROPRIETERS 1694.

The second and more readily available variety has the last word spelled PROPRI-ETORS. The correction was made on the original die, for the E shows plainly beneath the O. The elephant's tusks nearly touch the milling on the second variety.

The Carolina pieces were probably struck in England and perhaps intended as advertising to heighten interest in the Carolina Plantation.

	VG	F	VF	EF	AU	Unc.
1694 PROPRIETERS	$4,500	$6,000	$13,000	$22,000	$38,000	$60,000
1694 PROPRIETERS, O Over E	4,250	5,800	12,500	20,000	30,000	57,500

New England Elephant Tokens

Like the Carolina tokens, the New England Elephant tokens are believed to have been struck in England as promotional pieces to increase interest in the American colonies.

	VG	F	VF	EF	AU
1694 NEW ENGLAND		$100,000	$120,000	$150,000	—

New Yorke in America Token

The New Yorke in America token is a farthing or halfpenny token intended for New York, issued by Francis Lovelace, who was governor from 1668 until 1673. The token uses the older spelling with a final "e" (YORKE), which predominated before 1710. The obverse shows Cupid pursuing the butterfly-winged Psyche—a rebus on the name Lovelace. The reverse shows a heraldic eagle, identical to the one displayed in fesse, raguly (i.e., on a crenellated bar) on the Lovelace coat of arms. In weight, fabric, and die axis the tokens are similar to the 1670 farthing tokens of Bristol, England, where they may have been struck. There is no evidence that any of these pieces ever circulated in America.

	VG	F	VF	EF
(Undated) Brass or Copper	$7,500	$18,000	$27,500	$57,500
(Undated) Pewter	7,000	23,000	33,000	72,500

Gloucester Tokens

S.S. Crosby, in his book *The Early Coins of America,* stated that this coin appears to have been intended as a pattern for a shilling—a private coinage by Richard Dawson of Gloucester (county), Virginia. The only specimens known are struck in brass, although the denomination XII indicates that a silver coinage (one shilling) may have been planned. The building may represent some public building, possibly the courthouse.

Although neither of the two known examples shows the full legends, combining the pieces shows GLOVCESTER COVRTHOVSE VIRGINIA / RIGHAVLT DAWSON. ANNO.DOM. 1714. This recent discovery has provided a new interpretation of the legends, as a Righault family once owned land near the Gloucester courthouse. A similar, but somewhat smaller, piece possibly dated 1715 exists. The condition of this unique piece is too poor for positive attribution.

	F
1714 Shilling, brass *(2 known)*	$120,000

Higley or Granby Coppers

Dr. Samuel Higley owned a private copper mine near Granby, Connecticut. He worked the mine as an individual, smelting his own ore and making his own dies for the coins that he issued. After his death in 1737 his brother John continued the coinage.

The Higley coppers were never officially authorized. All the tokens were made of pure copper. There were seven obverse and four reverse dies. The first issue, in 1737, bore the legend THE VALUE OF THREEPENCE. After a time, the quantity exceeded the local demand, and a protest arose against the stated value of the piece. Higley, a resourceful individual, promptly created a new design, still with the Roman III, but with the inscription VALUE ME AS YOU PLEASE. On the reverse appeared the words I AM GOOD COPPER. Electrotypes and casts exist.

	AG	G	VG	F	VF
1737 THE VALVE OF THREE PENCE, CONNECTICVT, 3 Hammers	$5,800	$11,000	$20,000	$38,000	$84,000
1737 THE VALVE OF THREE PENCE, I AM GOOD COPPER, 3 Hammers *(3 known)*	6,300	12,500	25,000	50,000	100,000
1737 VALUE ME AS YOU PLEASE, I AM GOOD COPPER, 3 Hammers	5,800	11,000	20,000	38,000	88,000

	AG	G	VG	F	VF
1737 VALVE • ME • AS • YOU • PLEASE, I • AM • GOOD • COPPER, 3 Hammers *(3 known)*			—		
(1737) VALUE • ME • AS • YOU • PLEASE, J • CUT • MY • WAY • THROUGH, Broad Axe	$5,500	$10,000	$19,000	$37,000	$82,000
(1737) THE • WHEELE • GOES • ROUND, Reverse as Above *(unique)*			*150,000*		
1739 VALUE • ME • AS • YOU • PLEASE, J • CUT • MY • WAY • THROUGH, Broad Axe	8,000	20,000	27,500	50,000	135,000

Hibernia–Voce Populi Coins

These coins, struck in the year 1760, were prepared by Roche, of King Street, Dublin, who was at that time engaged in the manufacture of buttons for the army. Like other Irish tokens, some could have found their way to colonial America and possibly circulated in the colonies with numerous other counterfeit halfpence and "bungtown tokens."

There are two distinct issues. Coins from the first, with a "short bust" on the obverse, range in weight from 87 to 120 grains. Those from the second, with a "long bust" on the obverse, range in weight from 129 to 154 grains. Most of the "long bust" varieties have the letter P on the obverse. None of the "short bust" varieties bear the letter P, and judging from their weight, may have been contemporary counterfeits.

Large-Letter Variety Farthing

Halfpenny

Halfpenny, "P" Before Face

VOOE POPULI

	G	VG	F	VF	EF	AU	Unc.
1760 Farthing, Large Letters	$235	$400	$600	$1,750	$3,000	$5,750	$10,000
1760 Farthing, Small Letters			6,000	22,000	60,000	—	—
1760 Halfpenny	70	100	170	300	525	850	1,700
1760 Halfpenny, VOOE POPULI	100	150	225	500	650	1,250	3,750
1760 Halfpenny, P Below Bust	125	200	300	700	1,100	2,400	6,500
1760 Halfpenny, P in Front of Face......	100	175	250	600	1,000	1,800	5,500

Pitt Tokens

William Pitt, the British politician who endeared himself to America, is the subject of these pieces, probably intended as commemorative medalets. The so-called halfpenny served as currency during a shortage of regular coinage. The reverse legend (THANKS TO THE FRIENDS OF LIBERTY AND TRADE) refers to Pitt's efforts to have the Stamp Act repealed. The Pitt farthing-size tokens, struck in brass or copper, are rare.

Farthing

Halfpenny

	G	VG	F	VF	EF	AU	Unc.
1766 Farthing	$3,500	$6,000	$12,000	$30,000	$42,000	—	
1766 Halfpenny		500	600	1,350	2,500	$3,600	$9,500
1766 Halfpenny, silvered				2,000	4,250	6,000	13,000

Rhode Island Ship Medals

The obverse shows the flagship of British admiral Lord Richard Howe at anchor, while the reverse depicts the retreat of American forces from Rhode Island in 1778. The inscriptions show that the coin was meant for a Dutch-speaking audience. It is believed the medal was struck in England circa 1779 or 1780 for the Dutch market, as propaganda to persuade the Dutch to sign the Treaty of Armed Neutrality (December 1780). Specimens are known in brass, copper, and pewter.

Rhode Island Ship Medal (1778–1779)

Wreath Below Ship

	VF	EF	AU	Unc.
With "vlugtende" (fleeing) Below Ship, brass or copper		—		
Wreath Below Ship, brass or copper	$1,100	$1,900	$3,500	$6,000
Without Wreath Below Ship, brass or copper	1,000	1,800	2,900	5,200
Similar, pewter	4,500	7,500	11,500	17,000

John Chalmers Issues

John Chalmers, a silversmith, struck a series of silver tokens at Annapolis in 1783. The shortage of change and the refusal of the people to use underweight cut Spanish coins, or "bits," prompted the issuance of these pieces.

On the Chalmers threepence and shilling obverses, two clasped hands are shown, symbolizing unity of the several states; the reverse of the threepence has a branch encircled by a wreath. A star within a wreath is on the obverse of the sixpence, with hands clasped upon a cross utilized as the reverse type. On this denomination, the designer's initials TS (for Thomas Sparrow, a fellow silversmith of Chalmers's) can be found in the crescents that terminate the horizontal arms of the cross. The reverse of the more common shilling varieties displays two doves competing for a worm underneath a hedge and a snake. There are only a few known examples of the shilling type with 13 interlinked rings, from which a liberty cap on a pole arises.

	VG	F	VF	EF	AU
1783 Threepence	$2,200	$4,400	$9,000	$20,000	$37,500
1783 Sixpence, Small Date	3,200	7,000	18,000	30,000	47,000
1783 Sixpence, Large Date	2,600	6,000	15,000	30,000	47,000

	VG	F	VF	EF	AU
1783 Shilling, Birds, Long Worm *(illustrated)*	$1,250	$2,500	$7,500	$14,000	$25,000
1783 Shilling, Birds, Short Worm	1,200	2,200	6,500	12,000	22,500
1783 Shilling, Rings *(5 known)*	—	—	*175,000*	—	—

FRENCH NEW WORLD ISSUES

None of the coins of the French regime relate to territories that later became part of the United States. They were all general issues for the French colonies of the New World. The coinage of 1670 was authorized by an edict of King Louis XIV dated February 19, 1670, for use in New France, Acadia, the French settlements in Newfoundland, and the French West Indies. The copper coinage of 1717 to 1722 was authorized by edicts of 1716 and 1721 for use in New France, Louisiana, and the French West Indies.

Coinage of 1670

The coinage of 1670 consisted of silver 5 and 15 sols and copper 2 deniers (or "doubles"). A total of 200,000 of the 5 sols and 40,000 of the 15 sols was struck at Paris. Nantes was to have coined the copper, but did not; the reasons for this may never be known, since the archives of the Nantes Mint before 1700 were destroyed. The only known specimen is a pattern struck at Paris. The silver coins were raised in value by a third in 1672 to keep them circulating, but in vain. They rapidly disappeared, and by 1680 none were to be seen. Later they were restored to their original values. This rare issue should not be confused with the common 1670-A 1/12 ecu with reverse legend SIT. NOMEN. DOMINI. BENEDICTUM.

The 1670-A double de l'Amerique Françoise was struck at the Paris Mint along with the 5- and 15-sols denominations of the same date. All three were intended to circulate in France's North American colonies. Probably due to an engraving error, very few 1670-A doubles were actually struck. Today, only one is known to survive.

Copper Double　　　　　　　　　　　**Silver 5 Sols**

	VG	F	VF	EF	Unc.
1670-A Copper Double *(unique)*			$225,000		
1670-A 5 Sols	$600	$1,000	2,250	$4,000	$12,500
1670-A 15 Sols	12,000	32,000	75,000	125,000	—

Coinage of 1717–1720

The copper 6 and 12 deniers of 1717 were authorized by an edict of King Louis XV dated December 1716, to be struck at Perpignan (mintmark Q). The order could not be carried out, for the supply of copper was too brassy. A second attempt in 1720 also failed, probably for the same reason.

1720 6 Deniers　　　　　　　　　　　**1720 20 Sols**

	F	VF	EF
1717-Q 6 Deniers, No Crowned Arms on Reverse *(extremely rare)*			—
1717-Q 12 Deniers, No Crowned Arms on Reverse			$45,000
1720 6 Deniers, Crowned Arms on Reverse, copper	$600	$950	1,750
1720 20 Sols, silver	375	700	1,500

Billon Coinage of 1709–1760

The piece of 30 deniers was called a *mousquetaire,* and was coined at Metz and Lyon. The 15 deniers was coined only at Metz. The sou marque and the half sou were coined at almost every French mint, those of Paris being most common. The half sou of 1740 is the only commonly available date. Specimens of the sou marque dated after 1760 were not used in North America. A unique specimen of the 1712-AA 30 deniers is known in the size and weight of the 15-denier coins.

30 Deniers "Mousquetaire"　　　　　　　**Sou Marque (24 Deniers)**

	VG	F	VF	EF	AU	Unc
1711–1713-AA 15 Deniers...................	$150	$300	$500	$1,000	$1,750	$4,000
1709–1713-AA 30 Deniers...................	75	100	250	400	675	1,500
1709–1713-D 30 Deniers...................	75	100	250	400	675	1,500
1738–1748 Half Sou Marque, various mints.......	60	100	200	350	575	1,200
1738–1760 Sou Marque, various mints	50	80	125	175	300	500

Coinage of 1721–1722

The copper coinage of 1721 and 1722 was authorized by an edict of King Louis XV dated June 1721. The coins were struck on copper blanks imported from Sweden. Rouen and La Rochelle struck pieces of nine deniers in 1721 and 1722. New France received 534,000 pieces, mostly from the mint of La Rochelle, but only 8,180 were successfully put into circulation, as the colonists disliked copper. In 1726 the rest of the issue was sent back to France.

Copper Sou or Nine Deniers

	VG	F	VF	EF
1721-B (Rouen)	$500	$1,000	$4,000	$12,000
1721-H (La Rochelle)	100	150	900	2,500
1722-H..	100	150	900	2,500
1722-H, 2 Over 1	175	250	1,000	3,250

French Colonies in General

These were coined for use in the French colonies and only unofficially circulated in Louisiana along with other foreign coins and tokens. Most were counterstamped RF (République Française) for use in the West Indies. The mintmark A signifies the Paris Mint.

	VG	VF	EF	AU
1767 French Colonies, Sou....................................	$120	$250	$800	$1,600
1767 French Colonies, Sou, counterstamped RF....................	100	200	300	600

SPECULATIVE ISSUES, TOKENS, AND PATTERNS
Nova Constellatio Coppers

The Nova Constellatio coppers, dated 1783 and 1785 and without denomination, were struck in fairly large quantities in Birmingham, England, beginning in 1785, and were shipped to New York where they entered circulation. Apparently they resulted from a private coinage venture undertaken by Constable, Rucker & Co., a trading business formed by William Constable, John Rucker, Robert Morris, and Gouverneur Morris as equal partners. The designs and legends were copied from the denominated patterns dated 1783 made in Philadelphia (see page 86). A few additional coppers dated 1786 were made by an inferior diesinker.

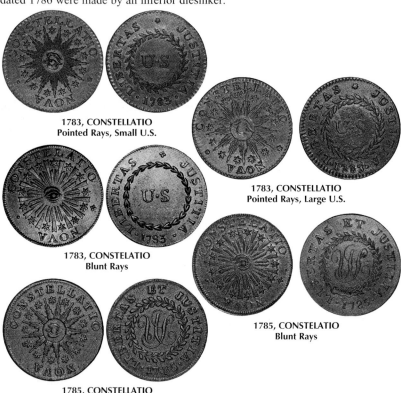

1783, CONSTELLATIO
Pointed Rays, Small U.S.

1783, CONSTELLATIO
Pointed Rays, Large U.S.

1783, CONSTELATIO
Blunt Rays

1785, CONSTELATIO
Blunt Rays

1785, CONSTELATIO
Pointed Rays

	VG	F	VF	EF	AU	Unc.
1783, CONSTELLATIO, Pointed Rays, Small U.S.....	$100	$200	$350	$700	$1,250	$2,750
1783, CONSTELLATIO, Pointed Rays, Large U.S.....	100	225	650	1,100	2,500	6,750
1783, CONSTELATIO, Blunt Rays	100	225	550	1,050	1,800	5,750
1785, CONSTELATIO, Blunt Rays	100	225	550	1,200	3,000	7,200
1785, CONSTELATIO, Pointed Rays.............	100	200	375	750	1,200	2,750
1785, Similar, Small, Close Date	300	600	2,500	4,500	6,500	15,000
1786, Similar, Small Date....................	4,000	6,000	8,000	15,000		

Immune Columbia Pieces

These are considered private or unofficial pieces. No laws describing them are known. There are several types bearing the seated figure of Justice. The Immune Columbia device with liberty cap and scale replaced the LIBERTAS and JUSTITIA on the Nova Constellatio coppers.

1785, Silver, 13 Stars

1785, Pointed Rays, CONSTELLATIO

	F	VF	EF
1785, Copper, 13 Stars	$15,000	$27,000	$40,000
1785, Silver, 13 Stars	22,000	45,000	60,000
1785, Pointed Rays, CONSTELLATIO, Extra Star in Reverse Legend, copper	15,000	27,000	40,000
1785, Blunt Rays, CONSTELLATIO, copper *(2 known)*		—	—
1785, Blunt Rays, CONSTELATIO, gold *(unique)*			—

Note: A gold specimen in the National Numismatic Collection (now in the Smithsonian) was acquired in 1843 from collector Matthew A. Stickney in exchange for an 1804 dollar.

1785, George III Obverse

	G	VG	F	VF
1785, George III Obverse	$5,500	$8,500	$11,000	$16,000
1785, VERMON AUCTORI Obverse, IMMUNE COLUMBIA	6,250	10,000	14,000	35,000

1787, IMMUNIS COLUMBIA, Eagle Reverse

	VG	F	VF	EF	AU	Unc
1787, IMMUNIS COLUMBIA, Eagle Reverse	$600	$1,000	$3,000	$4,500	$6,500	$11,000

Note: Believed to be a prototype for federal coinage; some were coined after 1787.

Confederatio Coppers

The Confederatio coppers are experimental or pattern pieces. This explains why the die with the CONFEDERATIO legend was combined with other designs, such as the bust of George Washington, Libertas et Justitia of 1785, Immunis Columbia of 1786, the New York "Excelsiors," Inimica Tyrannis Americana, and others. In all, 13 dies were struck in 14 combinations. Some of the dies may have been made by George Wyon of Birmingham, England.

There are two types of the Confederatio reverse. In one instance the stars are contained in a small circle; in the other, larger stars are in a larger circle.

Typical Obverse

Small Circle Reverse

Large Circle Reverse

	VF
1785, Stars in Small Circle, Various Obverses	$65,000
1785, Stars in Small Circle, Silver.	—
1785, Stars in Large Circle, Various Obverses	60,000

Speculative Patterns

The motto-and-shield design used on some of these patterns was later adopted for use on the New Jersey copper coins (see pages 68 and 69).

1786, IMMUNIS COLUMBIA

Eagle Reverse

Shield Reverse

	VF	EF
1786, IMMUNIS COLUMBIA, Eagle Reverse.		$80,000
1786, IMMUNIS COLUMBIA, Shield Reverse	$40,000	60,000

Washington Obverse

Eagle Reverse

Shield Reverse

(No date) (1786) Washington Obverse, Shield Reverse . . . .   —
$253,000, AU, Stack's Bowers auction, October 2003
1786, Eagle Obverse, Shield Reverse *(unique) $37,500, Unc., B&R auction, 1980.* . . . .   —
1786, Washington Obverse, Eagle Reverse *(2 known)* . . . .   —

COINAGE OF THE STATES
New Hampshire

New Hampshire was the first of the states to consider the subject of coinage following the Declaration of Independence.

William Moulton was empowered to make a limited quantity of coins of pure copper authorized by the State House of Representatives in 1776. Although cast patterns were prepared, it is believed that they were not approved. Little of the proposed coinage was ever actually circulated.

Other purported patterns are of doubtful origin. These include a unique engraved piece and a rare struck piece with large initials WM on the reverse.

VG

1776 New Hampshire Copper *$172,500, VG-10, Stack's Bowers auction, March 2012.* . . . .   —

Massachusetts
Massachusetts Unofficial Coppers

Nothing is known regarding the origin of the Pine Tree piece dated 1776. The obverse has a crude pine tree with "1d LM" at its base and the inscription MASSACHU-SETTS STATE. The reverse has a figure probably intended to represent the Goddess of Liberty, seated on a globe and holding a liberty cap and staff. A dog sits at her feet. The legend LIBERTY AND VIRTUE surrounds the figure.

VF

1776 Pine Tree Copper *(unique, in Massachusetts Historical Society collection)*.   —

A similar piece, probably from the same source, has a Native American with a bow on the obverse, and a seated figure on the reverse.

VG

1776 Indian Copper *(unique)*. . . . .   —

This piece is sometimes called the *Janus copper.* On the obverse are three heads, facing left, front, and right, with the inscription STATE OF MASSA. 1/2 D. The reverse shows the Goddess of Liberty facing right, resting against a globe. The legend is GODDESS LIBERTY 1776.

F

1776 Halfpenny, 3 Heads on Obverse *(unique)* $40,000, Fine, B&R auction, November 1979 . . . .   —

Massachusetts Authorized Issues

An "Act for establishing a mint for the coinage of gold, silver and copper" was passed by the Massachusetts General Court on October 17, 1786. The next year, the council directed that the design should incorporate "the figure of an Indian with a bow and arrow and a star at one side, with the word 'Commonwealth,' the reverse, a spread eagle with the words 'of Massachusetts A.D. 1787.' "

The coinage of Massachusetts copper cents and half cents in 1787 and 1788 was under the direction of Joshua Witherle. These were the first coins bearing the denomination *cent* as established by Congress. Many varieties exist, the most valuable being that with arrows in the eagle's right talon.

Most of the dies for these coppers were made by Joseph Callender. Jacob Perkins of Newburyport also engraved some of the 1788 dies.

The mint was abandoned early in 1789, in compliance with the newly ratified Constitution, and because its production was unprofitable.

1787 Half Cent

1787 Cent, Obverse

Arrows in Right Talon

Arrows in Left Talon

	G	VG	F	VF	EF	AU	Unc.
1787 Half Cent	$100	$125	$225	$500	$750	$1,200	$2,800
1787 Cent, Arrows in Right Talon	10,000	16,000	25,000	50,000	75,000	100,000	180,000
1787 Cent, Arrows in Left Talon	100	110	200	600	1,250	2,500	6,000
1787 Cent, "Horned Eagle" (die break) . . .	110	120	225	650	1,300	2,800	7,000

1788 Half Cent

1788 Cent, Period After MASSACHUSETTS

	G	VG	F	VF	EF	AU	Unc.
1788 Half Cent	$100	$125	$215	$550	$1,000	$1,500	$3,200
1788 Cent, Period After MASSACHUSETTS	100	110	200	500	800	1,750	4,750
1788 Cent, No Period After MASSACHUSETTS	115	120	250	675	1,500	2,800	6,000

Early American coins were produced from handmade dies, which are often individually distinctive. The great number of die varieties that can be found and identified are of interest to collectors who value each according to individual rarity. Values shown for type coins in this book are for the most common die variety of each.

Connecticut

Authority for establishing a mint near New Haven was granted by the state to Samuel Bishop, Joseph Hopkins, James Hillhouse, and John Goodrich in 1785.

Available records indicate that most of the Connecticut coppers were coined under a subcontract, by Samuel Broome and Jeremiah Platt, former New York merchants. Abel Buell was probably the principal diesinker.

1785 Copper,
Bust Facing Left

1785 Copper,
Bust Facing Right

1785 Copper,
African Head

1786 Copper,
ETLIB INDE

1786 Copper,
Large Head
Facing Right

1786 Copper,
Mailed Bust
Facing Left

1786 Copper,
Draped Bust

1786 Copper, Mailed Bust
Facing Left, Hercules Head

	G	VG	F	VF	EF	AU
1785 Copper, Bust Facing Left	$150	$250	$500	$1,500	$3,600	$8,000
1785 Copper, Bust Facing Right	40	70	150	500	1,400	3,500
1785 Copper, African Head	70	120	400	1,250	3,500	8,000
1786 Copper, ETLIB INDE	75	140	325	850	2,500	7,000
1786 Copper, Large Head Facing Right	250	500	1,500	4,600	10,000	
1786 Copper, Mailed Bust Facing Left	45	75	140	450	1,100	2,800
1786 Copper, Draped Bust	80	150	400	1,100	2,750	6,700
1786 Copper, Mailed Bust Facing Left, Hercules Head	110	200	500	2,000	4,750	

The Connecticut coppers were often crudely struck and on imperfect planchets.

1787 Copper, Small Head Facing Right, ETLIB INDE

1787 Copper, Muttonhead Variety

	G	VG	F	VF	EF	AU
1787 Copper, Small Head Facing Right, ETLIB INDE	$100	$170	$300	$1,600	$4,200	$8,500
1787 Copper, Liberty Seated Facing Right *(2 known)*	—					
1787, Mailed Bust Facing Right, INDE ET LIB	100	180	400	2,200	5,000	
1787 Copper, Muttonhead	100	180	400	2,200	5,000	9,000

1787 Copper, Mailed Bust Facing Left

1787 Copper, Horned Bust

1787 Copper, Laughing Head

1787 Copper, Reverse

	G	VG	F	VF	EF	AU
1787 Copper, Mailed Bust Facing Left	$45	$70	$120	$400	$1,100	$2,800
1787 Copper, Mailed Bust Facing Left, Laughing Head	55	100	200	500	1,100	2,300
1787 Copper, Mailed Bust Facing Left, Horned Bust	45	70	125	400	750	1,800
1787 Copper, Mailed Bust Facing Left, Hercules Head *(see 1786 for illustration)*	400	800	2,000	4,250	8,000	—
1787 Copper, Mailed Bust Facing Left, Dated 1787 Over 1877	90	180	600	1,600	4,750	—
1787 Copper, Mailed Bust Facing Left, 1787 Over 88	180	235	700	1,800	5,000	—
1787 Copper, Mailed Bust Facing Left, CONNECT, INDE	55	125	200	600	1,500	3,000
1787 Copper, Mailed Bust Facing Left, CONNECT, INDL	375	700	1,500	3,200	7,000	

1787 Copper, Draped Bust Facing Left

	G	VG	F	VF	EF	AU
1787 Copper, Draped Bust Facing Left	$35	$60	$90	$250	$600	$1,050
1787 Copper, Draped Bust Facing Left, AUCIORI	45	70	100	350	900	1,500
1787 Copper, Draped Bust Facing Left, AUCTOPI . . .	50	75	140	500	1,200	2,200
1787 Copper, Draped Bust Facing Left, AUCTOBI . . .	50	75	140	500	1,200	2,000
1787 Copper, Draped Bust Facing Left, CONNFC . . .	45	65	110	400	900	1,500
1787 Copper, Draped Bust Facing Left, CONNLC . . .	75	150	250	800	3,000	—
1787 Copper, Draped Bust Facing Left, FNDE	45	70	150	400	1,300	2,400
1787 Copper, Draped Bust Facing Left, ETLIR	45	65	125	350	1,000	1,700
1787 Copper, Draped Bust Facing Left, ETIIB	45	65	125	350	1,000	1,800
1787 Copper, GEORGIVS III Obv, INDE•ET Rev	1,500	3,250	3,500	—	—	—

1788 Copper, Mailed Bust Facing Right   **1788 Copper, Mailed Bust Facing Left**   **1788 Copper, Draped Bust Facing Left**

	G	VG	F	VF	EF	AU
1788 Copper, Mailed Bust Facing Right	$45	$80	$150	$500	$1,300	$2,500
1788 Copper, GEORGIVS III Obv (Reverse as Above)	110	210	550	1,550	3,250	—
1788 Copper, Small Head *(see 1787 for illustration)*	1,750	4,000	5,000	12,000	22,000	—
1788 Copper, Mailed Bust Facing Left	45	75	150	400	1,100	2,200
1788 Copper, Mailed Bust Facing Left, CONNLC	60	130	250	600	1,800	3,200
1788 Copper, Draped Bust Facing Left	50	75	200	400	1,100	2,200
1788 Copper, Draped Bust Facing Left, CONNLC . . .	85	200	450	1,100	2,500	4,000
1788 Copper, Draped Bust Facing Left, INDL ET LIB	80	140	300	800	2,000	3,800

New York and Related Issues
Brasher Doubloons

Among the most famous pieces coined before establishment of the U.S. Mint at Phila-delphia were those produced by the well-known New York goldsmith and jeweler Ephraim Brasher, who was a neighbor and friend of George Washington.

The gold pieces Brasher made weighed about 408 grains and were valued at $15 in New York currency. They were approximately equal to the Spanish doubloon, which was equal to 16 Spanish dollars.

Pieces known as *Lima Style doubloons* were dated 1742, but it is almost certain that they were produced in 1786, and were the first efforts of Brasher to make a circulating coin for local use. Neither of the two known specimens shows the full legends; but weight, gold content, and punchmark are all identical to those for the other Brasher coins. An analogous cast imitation Lima style doubloon dated 1735 bears a hallmark attributed to Standish Barry of Baltimore, Maryland, circa 1787.

An original design was used on the 1787 Brasher doubloon with an eagle on one side and the arms of New York on the other. In addition to his impressed hallmark, Brasher's name appears in small letters on each of his coins. The unique 1787 gold half doubloon is struck from doubloon dies on an undersized planchet that weighs half as much as the larger coins.

It is uncertain why Brasher produced these pieces. He was later commissioned to test and verify other gold coins then in circulation. His hallmark EB was punched on each coin as evidence of his testing and its value. In some cases the foreign coins have been weight-adjusted by clipping.

"1742" (1786) Lima Style gold doubloon *(2 known)* $700,000
　$690,000, EF-40, Heritage auction, January 2005

	EF
1787 New York gold doubloon, EB on Breast *$2,990,000, EF-45, Heritage auction, January 2005* . .	$7,000,000
1787 New York gold doubloon, EB on Wing *$2,415,000, AU-55, Heritage auction, January 2005* . . .	6,000,000
1787 New York gold half doubloon *(unique, in Smithsonian Collection)*	—
Various foreign gold coins with Brasher's EB hallmark	5,000–16,000

Copper Coinage

Several individuals petitioned the New York legislature in early 1787 for the right to coin copper for the state, but a coinage was never authorized. Instead, a law was passed to regulate the copper coins already in use. Nevertheless, various unauthorized copper pieces were issued within the state, principally by two private mints.

One firm, known as Machin's Mills, was organized by Thomas Machin and situated near Newburgh. Shortly after this mint was formed, on April 18, 1787, it was merged with the Rupert, Vermont, mint operated by Reuben Harmon Jr. Harmon held a coinage grant from the Republic of Vermont. The combined partnership agreed to conduct their business in New York, Vermont, Connecticut, or elsewhere if they could benefit by it.

The operations at Machin's Mills were conducted in secret and were looked upon with suspicion by the local residents. They minted several varieties of imitation George III halfpence, as well as coppers of Connecticut, Vermont, and New Jersey.

The other mints, located in or near New York City, were operated by John Bailey and Ephraim Brasher. They had petitioned the legislature on February 12, 1787, for a franchise to coin copper. The extent of their partnership, if any, and details of their operation are unknown. Studies of the state coinage show that they produced primarily the EXCELSIOR and NOVA EBORAC pieces of New York, and possibly the "running fox" New Jersey coppers.

Believed to be the bust of George Washington.

	G	VG	F	VF	EF	AU
1786, NON VI VIRTUTE VICI.	$6,000	$10,000	$20,000	$40,000	$60,000	$90,000

1787
EXCELSIOR
Copper,
Eagle on Globe
Facing Left

1787
EXCELSIOR
Copper,
Large Eagle
on Obverse

	G	VG	F	VF	EF
1787 EXCELSIOR Copper, Eagle on Globe Facing Right.	$2,750	$4,000	$8,500	$22,000	$40,000
1787 EXCELSIOR Copper, Eagle on Globe Facing Left.	2,750	3,500	8,000	18,000	37,500
1787 EXCELSIOR Copper, Large Eagle on Obverse, Arrows and Branch Transposed	4,000	6,500	16,000	33,000	55,000

1787, George Clinton

1787, Indian and New York Arms

1787, Indian and Eagle on Globe

1787, Indian and George III Reverse

	G	VG	F	VF	EF
1787, George Clinton	$9,000	$18,000	$45,000	$75,000	$200,000
1787, Indian and New York Arms	7,500	14,000	40,000	80,000	175,000
1787, Indian and Eagle on Globe	12,000	20,000	50,000	85,000	150,000
1787, Indian and George III Reverse *(3 known)*	—				

British Copper Coins and Their Imitations
(Including Machin's Mills, and Other Underweight Coinage of 1786–1789)

The most common coin used for small transactions in early America was the British copper halfpenny. Wide acceptance and the non–legal tender status of these copper coins made them a prime choice for unauthorized reproduction by private individuals. Many such counterfeits were created in America by striking from locally made dies, or by casting or other crude methods. Some were made in England and imported into this country. Pieces dated 1781 and 1785 seem to have been made specifically for this purpose, while others were circulated in both countries.

Regal British halfpence and farthings dated 1749 are of special interest to collectors because they were specifically sent to the North American Colonies as reimbursement for participation in the expedition against Cape Breton, and circulated extensively throughout New England.

Genuine British halfpenny coppers of both George II (1729–1754) and George III (1770–1775) show finely detailed features within a border of close dentils; the 1 in the date looks like a J. They are boldly struck on good-quality planchets. Their weight is approximately 9.5 grams; their diameter, 29 mm.

British-made lightweight imitation halfpence are generally smaller in diameter and thickness, and weigh less than genuine pieces. Details are crudely engraved or sometimes incomplete. Planchet quality may be poor.

	G	F	VF	EF	AU
1749, George II British farthing	$15	$30	$65	$125	$200
1749, George II British halfpenny	20	35	80	150	275
1770–1775, George III British halfpenny **(a)**	10	20	50	100	250
1770–1775, British imitation halfpenny **(a)**	8	15	20	100	250

a. Values shown are for the most common variety. Rare pieces are sometimes worth significantly more.

During the era of American state coinage, James F. Atlee and/or other coiners minted unauthorized, lightweight, imitation British halfpence. These American-made false coins have the same devices, legends, and, in some cases, dates as genuine regal halfpence, but contain less copper. Overall quality of these pieces is similar to that of the British-made imitations, but details are more often poorly rendered or missing. Identification of American-made imitations has been confirmed through association of punch links to known engravers.

There are four distinct groups of these halfpence, all linked to the regular state coinage. The first group was probably struck in New York City prior to 1786. The second group was minted in New York City in association with John Bailey and Ephraim Brasher during the first half of 1787. The third group was struck at Machin's Mills during the second half of 1787 and into 1788 or later. A fourth group, made by the Machin's coiners, consists of pieces made from dies that were muled with those of the state coinages of Connecticut, Vermont, and New York. Pieces with very crude designs and other dates are believed to have been struck elsewhere in New England.

Georgivs/Britannia
"Machin's Mills" Copper Halfpennies Made in America

Dates used on these pieces were often evasive, and are as follows: 1771, 1772, and 1774 through 1776 for the first group; 1747 and 1787 for the second group; and 1776, 1778, 1787, and 1788 for the third group. Pieces generally attributed to Atlee can be identified by a single outline in the crosses (British Union) of Britannia's shield and large triangular dentils along the coin circumference. The more-valuable American-made pieces are not to be confused with the similar English-made George III counterfeits (some of which have identical dates), or with genuine British halfpence dated 1770 to 1775.

*Group I coins dated 1771, 1772, and 1774 through 1776
have distinctive bold designs but lack the fine details of the
original coins. Planchets are generally of high quality.*

*Group II coins dated 1747 and
1787 are generally poorly made. The 1 in the date is
not J-shaped, and the dentils are of various sizes. There
are no outlines to the stripes in the shield.*

*Group III coins dated 1776,
1778, 1787, and 1788, struck at
Machin's Mills in Newberg, New York, are similar to
coins of Group II, with their triangular-shaped dentils.
Most have large dates and berries in obverse wreath.*

	AG	G	VG	F	VF	EF	AU
1747, GEORGIVS II. Group II	$150	$325	$450	$1,000	$4,500	$10,000	$20,000
1771, GEORGIVS III. Group I	70	110	250	400	1,500	3,300	6,000
1772, GEORGIVS III. Group I	80	150	275	600	2,000	3,750	8,000
1772, GEORGIUS III. Group I	85	200	375	900	2,800	5,500	—
1774, GEORGIVS III. Group I	40	80	125	300	900	2,750	5,000
1774, GEORGIUS III. Group I	80	150	250	500	2,000	4,500	—
1775, GEORGIVS III. Group I	35	75	125	300	800	2,200	4,750
1776, GEORGIVS III. Group III	175	325	500	1,000	3,000	7,000	—
1776, GEORCIVS III, Small Date	1,000	2,000	4,500	9,000	18,000	—	—
1778, GEORGIVS III. Group III	40	90	150	350	900	2,500	4,000
1784, GEORGIVS III	200	400	900	1,750	3,500	5,000	7,500
1787, GEORGIVS III. Group II	30	75	125	250	750	1,500	3,250
1787, GEORGIVS III. Group III	30	75	125	250	750	1,500	3,250
1788, GEORGIVS III. Group III	35	80	150	300	800	1,750	3,500

*Note: Values shown are for the most common varieties in each category. Rare pieces can be worth significantly more.
Also see related George III combinations under Connecticut, Vermont, and New York.*

The muled coins of Group IV are listed separately with the Immune Columbia
pieces and with the state coins of Connecticut, Vermont, and New York. Other
imitation coppers made by unidentified American makers are generally very crude
and excessively rare. Cast copies of British coins probably circulated along with the
imitations without being questioned. Counterfeit copies of silver Spanish-American
coins and Massachusetts tree coins may have also been coined by American minters.

Nova Eborac Coinage for New York

**1787, NOVA EBORAC,
Reverse: Seated Figure
Facing Right**

**1787, NOVA EBORAC,
Reverse: Seated Figure
Facing Left**

**1787, NOVA EBORAC,
Small Head**

**1787, NOVA EBORAC,
Large Head**

	AG	G	F	VF	EF	AU
1787, NOVA EBORAC, Seated Figure Facing Right ..	$50	$110	$225	$800	$1,500	$3,250
1787, NOVA EBORAC, Seated Figure Facing Left ...	50	90	200	600	1,000	2,000
1787, NOVA EBORAC, Small Head	1,700	4,000	9,000	18,000		
1787, NOVA EBORAC, Large Head	500	900	2,000	5,000		

New Jersey

On June 1, 1786, the New Jersey General Assembly granted to Thomas Goadsby,
Albion Cox, and Walter Mould authority to coin three million coppers weighing
six pennyweight and six grains (150 grains total, or 9.72 grams) apiece, to be completed by June 1788, on condition that they deliver to the state treasurer "one Tenth
Part of the full Sum they shall strike." These coppers were to pass current at 15 to
the shilling. Matthias Ogden also played a significant financial and political role in
the operation.

In an undertaking of this kind, the contractors purchased the metal and assumed all
expenses of coining. The difference between these expenses and the total face value
of the coins issued represented the profit.

Later, Goadsby and Cox asked authority to coin two-thirds of the total independently of Mould. Their petition was granted November 22, 1786. Mould was known to
have produced his coins at Morristown, while Cox and Goadsby operated in Rahway.
Coins with a diameter of 30 mm or more are generally considered Morristown products. Coins were also minted in Elizabethtown by Ogden and by others in New York.

The obverse shows design elements of the state seal, a horse's head with plow, and
the legend NOVA CÆSAREA (New Jersey). The reverse has a United States shield
and, for the first time on a coin, the legend E PLURIBUS UNUM (One Composed

of Many). More than 140 varieties exist. The majority have the horse's head facing to the right; however, three show the head facing left. Other variations have a sprig beneath the head, branches below the shield, stars, cinquefoils, and other ornaments.

1786, Date Under Plow Beam	1786 and 1787, Pattern Shield	1786, Date Under Plow, No Coulter

	AG	G	F	VF	EF
1786, Date Under Plow Beam.........................			$85,000	$125,000	$200,000
1786, Date Under Plow, No Coulter	$500	$900	3,000	7,000	10,000
1787, Pattern Shield **(a)**	400	700	1,750	3,000	5,000

a. The so-called Pattern Shield reverse was also used on several speculative patterns. See pages 56 and 57.

1786, Straight Plow Beam, Protruding Tongue	1786, Wide Shield	1786, Curved Plow Beam, Bridle Variety

	AG	G	F	VF	EF	AU
1786, Straight Plow Beam (several varieties)	$25	$55	$200	$575	$1,400	$2,500
1786, Curved Plow Beam (several varieties).......	25	55	200	575	1,400	2,500
1786, Protruding Tongue	30	70	235	600	1,850	4,500
1786, Wide Shield	30	75	240	650	2,000	5,000
1786, Bridle variety	30	75	240	650	2,000	5,000

1787, U Over S in PLURIBUS

1787, PLURIBS Error	1787, PLURIRUS Error

	AG	G	F	VF	EF	AU
1786, PLUKIBUS error........................	$30	$75	$250	$450	$1,700	$4,500
1787, PLURIBS error.........................	40	125	500	1,600	3,500	7,500
1787, Second U Over S in PLURIBUS	40	160	470	1,100	3,200	5,000
1787, PLURIRUS error........................	40	160	470	1,100	3,200	5,500

1787, Sprig Above Plow   1787, WM Above Plow   1787, Hidden WM

	AG	G	F	VF	EF	AU
1787, Sprig Above Plow (several varieties)	$25	$65	$220	$550	$1,200	$3,000
1787, No Sprig Above Plow (several varieties)	35	75	225	675	1,500	3,200
1787, WM Above Plow *(unique)*				—		
1787, Hidden WM in Sprig	35	75	225	675	1,500	3,200

1787 Over 1887   1787, Camel Head   1787, Serpent Head

	AG	G	F	VF	EF	AU
1787, Date Over 1887	$200	$600	$3,000	$6,000	$15,000	—
1787, Camel Head (snout in high relief)	30	60	200	650	900	$1,750
1787, Serpent Head	35	85	400	1,700	4,000	6,500
1787, Goiter Variety	40	75	250	700	2,500	5,000

1788, Fox Before Legend   1788, Indistinct Coulter   1788, Fox After Legend

1788, Braided Mane   1788, Head Facing Left

	AG	G	VG	F	VF	AU
1788, Horse's Head Facing Right, several varieties.........	$25	$60	$175	$550	$900	$1,600
1788, Horse's Head Facing Right, Running Fox Before Legend	75	150	550	2,000	4,500	9,000
1788, Similar, Indistinct Coulter.......................	150	650	2,500	6,500	15,000	—
1788, Horse's Head Facing Right, Running Fox After Legend	9,000	25,000	75,000	100,000	—	
1788, Braided Mane...............................	50	300	1,200	3,500	6,000	12,000
1788, Horse's Head Facing Left......................	175	450	1,750	4,750	12,000	—

Vermont

Reuben Harmon Jr., of Rupert, Vermont, was granted permission to coin copper pieces for a period of two years beginning July 1, 1785. The well-known Vermont "Landscape" coppers were first produced in that year. The franchise was extended for eight years in 1786.

Harmon's mint was located in the northeast corner of Rupert near a stream known as Millbrook. Colonel William Coley, a New York goldsmith, made the first dies. Some of the late issues were made near Newburgh, New York, by the Machin's Mills coiners.

Most Vermont coppers were struck on poor and defective planchets. Well-struck coins on smooth, full planchets command higher prices.

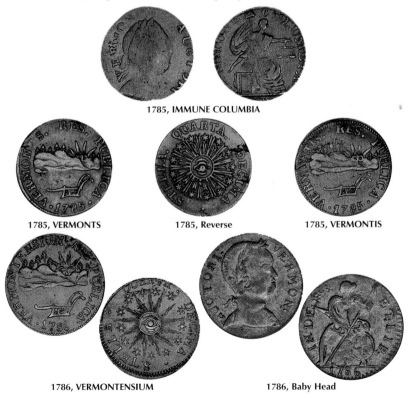

1785, IMMUNE COLUMBIA

1785, VERMONTS

1785, Reverse

1785, VERMONTIS

1786, VERMONTENSIUM

1786, Baby Head

Entry continued on next page.

Bust Left	**1786, Reverse**	**1787, Reverse**

	AG	G	VG	F	VF	EF	AU
1785, IMMUNE COLUMBIA	$4,250	$6,250	$10,000	$14,000	$35,000	—	—
1785, VERMONTS.	150	275	500	750	2,500	$4,250	$9,000
1785, VERMONTIS	175	325	650	1,400	4,250	10,000	19,500
1786, VERMONTENSIUM.	110	200	350	550	1,350	3,000	5,500
1786, Baby Head	200	275	400	1,250	4,000	10,500	—
1786, Bust Left.	80	125	250	650	2,400	4,000	—
1787, Bust Left.	3,000	4,500	10,500	27,000	42,000	—	

1787, BRITANNIA

	AG	G	VG	F	VF	EF	AU
1787, BRITANNIA	$45	$90	$120	$200	$450	$1,000	$2,200

Note: The reverse of this coin is always weak.

1787, 1788, Bust Right (Several Varieties)

	AG	G	VG	F	VF	EF	AU
1787, Bust Right (several varieties)	$60	$110	$150	$250	$900	$2,250	$4,000
1788, Bust Right (several varieties)	50	90	120	225	600	1,400	3,250
1788, Backward C in AUCTORI	3,000	4,500	7,500	17,500	37,500	—	
1788, *ET LIB* *INDE	175	300	550	1,250	4,000	10,000	—

1788, GEORGIVS III REX/ET•LIB+INDE+

	AG	G	VG	F	VF	EF	AU
1788, GEORGIVS III REX	$300	$500	$900	$2,200	$4,500	$11,000	

Note: This piece should not be confused with the common English halfpence with similar design and reverse legend BRITANNIA.

PRIVATE TOKENS AFTER CONFEDERATION
North American Tokens

This piece was struck in Dublin, Ireland. The obverse shows the seated figure of Hibernia facing left. The date of issue is believed to have been much later than that shown on the token. Like many Irish tokens, this issue found its way to America in limited quantities and was accepted near the Canadian border.

	VG	F	VF	EF	AU
1781, copper or brass	$60	$100	$200	$650	$1,300

Bar Coppers

The Bar copper is undated and of uncertain origin. It has 13 parallel and unconnected bars on one side. On the other side is the large roman-letter USA monogram. The design is virtually identical to that used on a Continental Army uniform button.

The significance of the design is clearly defined by its extreme simplicity. The separate 13 states (bars) unite into a single entity as symbolized by the interlocking letters (USA).

This piece is believed to have first circulated in New York during November 1785, and may have been made in England.

John Adams Bolen (1826–1907), a numismatist and a master diesinker in Springfield, Massachusetts, struck copies of the Bar copper around 1862. On these copies, the letter A passes under, instead of over, the S. Bolen's intent was not to deceive, and he advertised his copies plainly as reproductions. But his skills were such that W. Elliot Woodward, a leading auctioneer of tokens and medals in the 1860s, vacillated between selling Bolen's copies and describing them as "dangerous counterfeits." Bolen copies of the Bar copper are highly collectible in their own right, but they are less valuable than the originals.

	G	VG	F	VF	EF	AU	Unc.
(Undated) (Circa 1785) Bar Copper	$500	$1,900	$3,250	$6,500	$10,000	$14,000	$23,000

Auctori Plebis Tokens

This token is sometimes included with the coins of Connecticut, as it greatly resembles issues of that state. It was struck in England by an unknown maker, possibly for use in America.

	G	VG	F	VF	EF	AU	Unc.
1787, AUCTORI PLEBIS	$90	$110	$225	$450	$900	$1,600	$7,500

Mott Store Cards

This item has long been considered an early token because of its date (1789). Most scholars believe it was produced no earlier than 1807 (possibly in the Hard Times era of the late 1830s) as a commemorative of the founding of the Mott Company, and served as a business card. The firm, operated by Jordan Mott, was located at 240 Water Street, a fashionable section of New York at that time.

	VG	F	VF	EF	AU	Unc.
"1789," Mott Token, Thick Planchet	$80	$175	$300	$450	$600	$1,200
"1789," Mott Token, Thin Planchet	80	200	350	800	1,400	2,500
"1789," Mott Token, Entire Edge Engrailed	80	300	450	1,000	1,800	3,200

Standish Barry Threepence

Standish Barry, of Baltimore, circulated a silver threepence in 1790. He was a watch- and clockmaker, an engraver, and, later, a silversmith. The tokens are believed to have been an advertising venture at a time when small change was scarce. The precise date on this piece may indicate that Barry intended to commemorate Independence Day, but there are no records to prove this. The head on the obverse is probably that of James Calhoun, who was active in Baltimore politics in the 1790s. The legend BALTIMORE TOWN JULY 4, 90, appears in the border. An enigmatic gold doubloon is also attributed to Barry (see page 63).

	VG	F	VF	EF	AU
1790 Threepence	$10,000	$22,500	$50,000	$100,000	$160,000

Albany Church Pennies

The First Presbyterian Church of Albany, New York, authorized an issue of 1,000 copper uniface tokens in 1790. These passed at 12 to a shilling and were used to stop contributions of worn and counterfeit coppers. Two varieties were made, one with the addition of a large D (the British abbreviation for penny) above the word CHURCH.

	VG	F	VF	EF
(Undated) (1790) Without D.	$12,500	$22,500	$40,000	$60,000
(Undated) (1790) With D Added.	12,500	22,500	40,000	60,000

Kentucky Tokens

These tokens were struck in England circa 1792 to 1794. Each star in the triangle represents a state, identified by its initial letter. These pieces are usually called *Kentucky cents* because the letter K (for Kentucky) happens to be at the top. Some of the edges are plain; others are milled with a diagonal reeding; and some have edge lettering that reads PAYABLE IN LANCASTER LONDON OR BRISTOL or PAYABLE AT BEDWORTH NUNEATON OR HINKLEY.

	VF	EF	AU	Unc.
(1792–1794) Copper, Plain Edge	$185	$275	$450	$850
(1792–1794) Copper, Engrailed Edge	500	900	1,350	2,800
(1792–1794) Copper, Lettered Edge, PAYABLE AT BEDWORTH, etc.	—	—	—	—
(1792–1794) Copper, Lettered Edge, PAYABLE IN LANCASTER, etc.	200	300	475	950
(1792–1794) Copper, Lettered Edge, PAYABLE AT I. FIELDING, etc.	—	—	—	—

Franklin Press Tokens

This piece is an English tradesman's token, but, being associated with the Franklin name, has accordingly been included in American collections.

	VG	VF	EF	AU	Unc.
1794 Franklin Press Token	$100	$250	$350	$550	$900
Similar, Edge Reads AN ASYLUM FOR THE OPPRESS'D OF ALL NATIONS *(unique)*					
Similar, Edge Diagonally Reeded *(unique)*.					

Talbot, Allum & Lee Cents

Talbot, Allum & Lee, engaged in the India trade and located at 241 Pearl Street, New York, placed a large quantity of English-made coppers in circulation during 1794 and 1795. ONE CENT appears on the 1794 issue, and the legend PAYABLE AT THE STORE OF on the edge. The denomination is not found on the 1795 reverse but the edge legend was changed to read WE PROMISE TO PAY THE BEARER ONE CENT. Rare plain-edged specimens of both dates exist. Exceptional pieces have edges ornamented or with lettering CAMBRIDGE BEDFORD AND HUNTINGDON.X.X. Many of these tokens were later cut down and used by the U.S. Mint as planchets for coining 1795 and 1797 half cents.

1794 Cent, With NEW YORK

1795 Cent

	VG	F	VF	EF	AU	Unc.
1794 Cent, With NEW YORK	$65	$80	$225	$350	$550	$1,350
1794 Cent, Without NEW YORK	500	850	3,000	6,000	9,500	20,000
1795 Cent	60	80	200	300	400	800

Myddelton Tokens

These tokens were struck at the Soho Mint of Boulton and Watt near Birmingham, England, but they were never actually issued for circulation in Kentucky. They are unsurpassed in beauty and design by any piece of this period.

	PF		PF
1796, Copper	$19,000	1796, Silver	$25,000

Copper Company of Upper Canada Tokens

The obverse of this piece is the same as that of the Myddelton token. The new reverse refers to a Canadian firm and may have been made for numismatic purposes, or as part of the coiner's samples.

	PF
1796, Copper	$7,500

Castorland Medals

These medals, or "jetons," are dated 1796 and allude to a proposed French settlement known as Castorland in Carthage, New York, at the time of the French Revolution. They were given to directors of the colonizing company for their attendance at board meetings.

Copy dies are still available and have been used at the Paris Mint for restriking throughout the years. Restrikes have a more modern look; their metallic content (in French) is impressed on the edge: ARGENT (silver), CUIVRE (copper), or OR (gold).

	EF	AU	Unc.
1796, Original, silver (reeded edge, unbroken dies)	$3,000	$4,400	$7,200
1796, Original, silver (reverse rusted and broken).	300	600	1,500
1796, Original, bronze (reverse rusted and broken)	200	300	700
(1796) Undated, Restrike, silver (Paris Mint edge marks)		30	70
(1796) Undated, Restrike, bronze (Paris Mint edge marks)		20	40

Theatre at New York Tokens

These token pennies were issued by Skidmore of London and illustrate the Park Theatre, New York, circa 1797.

	EF	PF
Penny, THE THEATRE AT NEW YORK AMERICA	—	$26,000

New Spain (Texas) Jola Tokens

In 1817 the Spanish governor of New Spain, Manuel Pardo, authorized Manuel Barrera to coin 8,000 copper tokens known as jolas. These crudely made pieces show the denomination ½ (real), the maker's initials and the date on the obverse, and a star on the reverse.

The 1817 tokens were withdrawn from circulation the following year and replaced by a similar issue of 8,000 pieces bearing the date 1818 and the initials JAG of the maker, José Antonio de la Garza. Several varieties of each issue are known. All are rare.

	F	VF	EF
1817 1/2 Real.	$20,000	$35,000	$50,000
1818 1/2 Real, Large or Small Size	10,000	15,000	20,000

North West Company Tokens

These tokens were probably valued at one beaver skin and struck in Birmingham in 1820 by John Walker & Co. All but two known specimens are holed, and most have been found in the region of the Columbia and Umpqua river valleys.

	AG	G	VG	F	VF
1820, Copper or Brass (with hole)	$375	$800	$2,250	$4,250	$8,500

WASHINGTON PIECES

Medals, tokens, and coinage proposals in this interesting series dated from 1783 to 1795 bear the portrait of George Washington. The likenesses in most instances were faithfully reproduced and were designed to honor the first president. Many of these pieces were of English origin and were made later than their dates indicate.

The legends generally signify a strong unity among the states and the marked display of patriotism that pervaded the new nation during that period. We find among these tokens an employment of what were soon to become the nation's official coin devices, namely, the American eagle, the United States shield, and stars. The denomination ONE CENT is used in several instances, while on some of the English pieces HALFPENNY will be found. Several of these pieces were private patterns for proposed coinage contracts.

Georgivs Triumpho Tokens

Although the head shown on this token bears a strong resemblance to that on some coins of George III, many collectors consider the Georgivs Triumpho ("Triumphant George") a token intended to commemorate America's victory in the Revolutionary War.

The reverse side shows the Goddess of Liberty behind a framework of 13 bars and fleurs-de-lis. Holding an olive branch in her right hand and staff of liberty in her left, she is partially encircled by the words VOCE POPOLI ("By the Voice of the People") 1783.

	VG	F	VF	EF	AU	Unc.
1783, GEORGIVS TRIUMPHO..................	$110	$225	$500	$800	$1,400	$6,000

Washington Portrait Pieces

Large Military Bust, Point of Bust Close to W

	F	VF	EF	AU	Unc.
1783, Large Military Bust............................	$75	$160	$350	$500	$1,750
1783, Small Military Bust, Plain Edge....................	80	175	400	750	2,500
1783, Small Military Bust, Engrailed Edge	100	200	550	1,100	3,000

	F	VF	EF	AU	Unc.	PF
1783, Draped Bust, No Button *(illustrated)*	$80	$160	$300	$500	$1,600	
1783, Draped Bust, With Button (on Drapery at Neck)	125	225	350	700	3,200	
1783, Draped Bust, Copper Restrike, Plain Edge . . .						$900
1783, Draped Bust, Copper Restrike, Engrailed Edge						750
1783, Draped Bust, Silver Restrike, Engrailed Edge						1,800

	VG	VF	EF	AU	Unc.
1783, UNITY STATES	$100	$200	$325	$550	$1,400

	F	VF	EF	AU	Unc.
(Undated) Double-Head Cent.	$100	$250	$425	$725	$2,400

Satirical Medal Presumably of American Origin

	G
1784, Ugly Head, Copper *$20,000, Crude Good, Stack's Bowers auction, December 1983*.	$100,000
1784, Ugly Head, Pewter *(unique)*.	

1791 Cent, Edge Lettered UNITED STATES OF AMERICA

	F	VF	EF	AU	Unc.
1791 Cent, Small Eagle (Date on Reverse)	$475	$650	$800	$1,200	$2,750

1791 Cent, Large Eagle Reverse   **Obverse (Cent and Halfpenny)**   **1791 Halfpenny, Reverse**

	VG	F	VF	EF	AU	Unc.
1791 Cent, Large Eagle (Date on Obverse)	$150	$350	$550	$750	$1,100	$2,400
1791 Liverpool Halfpenny, Lettered Edge	850	1,250	2,100	3,800	7,500	—

1792, Eagle With 13 Stars Reverse

	VG	F	VF	EF
1792, WASHINGTON PRESIDENT, Eagle With 13 Stars Reverse				
PRESIDENT at Side of Bust, copper				—
PRESIDENT, silver.			$125,000	—
PRESIDENT, gold *(unique)*.			—	
PRESIDENT Extends Below Bust, copper *(unique)*.				—

**1792,
WASHINGTON PRESIDENT**

Legend Reverse

**(1792) Undated,
WASHINGTON BORN VIRGINIA**

	VG	F	VF	EF
1792, WASHINGTON PRESIDENT, Legend on Reverse				
Plain Edge, copper	$2,750	$7,500	$18,000	
Lettered Edge, copper	—	—	—	—
(1792) Undated, WASHINGTON BORN VIRGINIA, Eagle With 13 Stars Reverse				
(reverse illustrated on previous page), copper *(3 known)*	—			
(1792) Undated, WASHINGTON BORN VIRGINIA, Legend on Reverse				
Copper	1,250	2,250	4,500	$8,000
Silver	—	—	—	—

Note: Uniface restrike of undated obverse exists, made from transfer dies by Albert Collis, 1959.

Getz Patterns

Dies engraved by Peter Getz of Lancaster, Pennsylvania, are believed to have been made to produce a half dollar and cent as a proposal to Congress for a private contract coinage before the Philadelphia Mint became a reality.

	VG	F	VF	EF	AU	Unc.
1792, Small Eagle, silver	—	—	—	$300,000		
$241,500, AU, Stack's Bowers auction, May 2004						
1792, Small Eagle, copper	$6,000	$12,000	$27,500	45,000	$65,000	$90,000
$299,000, MS-64 BN, Stack's Bowers auction, November 2006						
1792, Small Eagle, Ornamented Edge (Circles and Squares), copper	—	—	—	175,000		
$207,000, AU, Stack's Bowers auction, November 2006						
1792, Small Eagle, Ornamented Edge, silver *(4 known)*	—	—	125,000	200,000		
$391,000, Gem BU PL, Stack's Bowers auction, May 2004						
1792, Large Eagle, silver			—	—		
$34,500, EF, Stack's Bowers auction, May 2004						

1792 Cent, Roman Head, Lettered Edge: UNITED STATES OF AMERICA

	PF
1792 Cent, Roman Head, Lettered Edge UNITED STATES OF AMERICA, Proof.	$90,000

1793 Ship Halfpenny

	VG	F	VF	EF	AU	Unc.
1793 Ship Halfpenny, Lettered Edge.	$100	$200	$400	$600	$850	$3,250
1793 Ship Halfpenny, Plain Edge *(rare)*.		—	—			

1795 Halfpenny, Grate Token
Large Coat Buttons variety shown.

	F	VF	EF	AU	Unc.
1795, Large Buttons, Lettered Edge	$180	$350	$700	$1,500	$2,200
1795, Large Buttons, Reeded Edge.	80	175	300	400	700
1795, Small Buttons, Reeded Edge.	80	200	400	725	1,750

Liberty and Security Tokens

See next page for chart.

	F	VF	EF	AU	Unc.
1795 Halfpenny, Plain Edge	$110	$200	$500	$950	$2,650
1795 Halfpenny, LONDON Edge	100	210	525	750	2,500
1795 Halfpenny, BIRMINGHAM Edge	125	250	550	1,100	2,800
1795 Halfpenny, ASYLUM Edge	200	400	1,100	2,000	5,500
1795 Penny, ASYLUM Edge	2,500	8,500	12,500	18,000	32,500

(1795) Undated, Liberty and Security Penny, ASYLUM Edge

	F	VF	EF	AU	Unc.
(1795) Undated, Liberty and Security Penny	$275	$450	$650	$1,150	$2,250
Same, Corded Outer Rims	600	1,000	2,000	3,250	5,750

North Wales Halfpennies

	G	F	VF	EF	AU
(1795) Undated, NORTH WALES Halfpenny	$90	$200	$500	$1,400	$2,800
(1795) Undated, Lettered Edge	450	1,450	5,000	8,000	—
(1795) Undated, Two Stars at Each Side of Harp	2,200	7,500	13,500		

Success Medals

	F	VF	EF	AU	Unc.
(Undated) SUCCESS Medal, Large, Plain or Reeded Edge	$250	$450	$750	$1,400	$2,750
(Undated) SUCCESS Medal, Small, Plain or Reeded Edge	300	500	800	1,600	3,000

Note: These pieces are struck in copper or brass and are believed to have been made in the mid-19th century. Specimens with original silvering are rare and are valued 20 to 50% higher. Varieties exist.

CONTINENTAL CURRENCY

The Continental Currency pieces were probably made to serve in lieu of a paper dollar, but the exact nature of their monetary role is still unclear. They were the first silver dollar–sized coins ever proposed for the United States, and may have been intended as a substitute for the paper dollar. One obverse die was engraved by someone whose initials were E.G. (undoubtedly Elisha Gallaudet) and is marked EG FECIT ("EG Made It"). Studies of the coinage show that there may have been two separate emissions made at different mints. The link design on the reverse was suggested by Benjamin Franklin.

Varieties result from differences in the spelling of the word CURRENCY and the addition of EG FECIT on the obverse. These coins were struck in pewter, brass, and silver. Pewter pieces probably served as a dollar, substituting for paper currency of this design that was never issued. Brass and silver pieces may have been experimental or patterns. Pewter pieces in original bright Uncirculated condition are worth an additional premium.

Numerous copies and replicas of these coins have been made over the years. Authentication is recommended for all pieces.

CURRENCY   CURENCY

	G	F	VF	EF	AU	Unc.
1776 CURENCY, Pewter *(2 varieties)*.	$7,500	$10,500	$21,000	$32,000	$45,000	$70,000
1776 CURENCY, Brass *(2 varieties)*.	25,000	40,000	75,000	135,000	220,000	—
$299,000, MS-63, Heritage auction, July 2009						
1776 CURENCY, Silver *(2 known)*.		275,000	400,000			
$345,000, VF, Stack's Bowers auction, January 2005						
1776 CURRENCY, Pewter	7,750	12,500	22,000	35,000	47,500	75,000
1776 CURRENCY, EG FECIT, Pewter	8,000	14,000	25,000	37,000	50,000	77,500
$546,250, MS-67, Heritage auction, January 2012						
1776 CURRENCY, EG FECIT, Silver *(2 known)*.		—	—	850,000	—	—
$425,500, EF, Stack's Bowers auction, October 2003						
1776 CURRENCEY, Pewter	—	—	—		125,000	—
1776 CURRENCY, Pewter, Ornamented Date *(3 known)*				—		
$276,000, EF-45, Heritage auction, July 2009						

NOVA CONSTELLATIO PATTERNS

These Nova Constellatio pieces undoubtedly represent the first patterns for a coinage of the United States. They were designed by Benjamin Dudley for Gouverneur Morris to carry out his ideas for a decimal coinage system. The 1,000-unit designation he called a mark, the 500 a quint. These denominations, together with the small 100-unit piece, were designed to standardize the many different coin values among the several states. These pattern pieces represent the first attempt at a decimal ratio, and were the forerunners of our present system of money values. Neither the proposed denominations nor the coins advanced beyond the pattern stage. These unique pieces are all dated 1783. There are two types of the quint. The copper "five" was first brought to the attention of collectors in 1980. Electrotype copies exist.

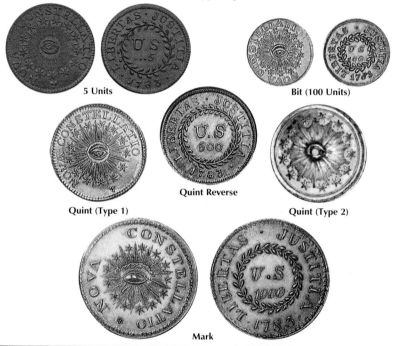

5 Units

Bit (100 Units)

Quint Reverse

Quint (Type 1)

Quint (Type 2)

Mark

1783 (Five) "5," Copper		(unique)
1783 (Bit) "100," Silver, Decorated Edge *$97,500, Unc., B&R auction, November 1979*		(2 known)
1783 (Bit) "100," Silver, Plain Edge		(unique)
1783 (Quint) "500," Silver, Type 1 *$165,000, Unc., B&R auction, November 1979*		(unique)
1783 (Quint) "500," Silver, Type 2 *$55,000, Unc., B&R auction, November 1979*		(unique)
1783 (Mark) "1000," Silver *$190,000, Unc., B&R auction, November 1979*		(unique)

FUGIO COPPERS

The first coins issued by authority of the United States were the "Fugio" pieces. Entries in the *Journal of Congress* supply interesting information about proceedings relating to this coinage. For example, the entry of Saturday, April 21, 1787, reads as follows: "That the board of treasury be authorized to contract for three hundred tons of copper coin of the federal standard, agreeable to the proposition of Mr. James Jarvis. . . . That it be coined at the expense of the contractor, etc."

On Friday, July 6, 1787, it was "[r]esolved, that the board of treasury direct the contractor for the copper coinage to stamp on one side of each piece the following device, viz: thirteen circles linked together, a small circle in the middle, with the words 'United States,' around it; and in the centre, the words 'We are one'; on the other side of the same piece the following device, viz: a dial with the hours expressed on the face of it; a meridian sun above on one side of which is the word 'Fugio,' [the intended meaning is *time flies*] and on the other the year in figures '1787,' below the dial, the words 'Mind Your Business.'"

The legends have been credited to Benjamin Franklin, and the coin, as a consequence, has sometimes been referred to as the Franklin cent.

These pieces were coined in New Haven, Connecticut. Most of the copper used in this coinage came from military stores or salvaged metal. The dies were made by Abel Buell of New Haven.

1787 With Pointed Rays

American Congress Pattern

Cross After Date

Label With Raised Rims

	G	VG	F	VF	EF	AU	Unc.
Obverse Cross After Date, No Cinquefoils							
Reverse Rays and AMERICAN CONGRESS				—	$250,000	$350,000	
Reverse Label with Raised Rims *(extremely rare)*					25,000		
Reverse STATES UNITED	$300	$650	$1,150	$3,000	5,800	12,500	—
Reverse UNITED STATES	275	600	950	2,750	5,500	11,000	—

Cinquefoil After Date

These types, with pointed rays, have regular obverses punctuated with four cinquefoils (five-leafed ornaments).

	G	VG	F	VF	EF	AU	Unc.
STATES UNITED at Sides of Circle, Cinquefoils on Label	$150	$300	$550	$950	$1,500	$2,000	$4,000
STATES UNITED, 1 Over Horizontal 1	225	450	1,000	4,000	8,500		
UNITED STATES, 1 Over Horizontal 1	200	400	900	3,500	7,500		
UNITED STATES at Sides of Circle	150	300	575	900	1,650	2,100	4,500

Chart continued on next page.   **87**

	G	VG	F	VF	EF	AU	Unc.
STATES UNITED, Label With Raised Rims, Large Letters in WE ARE ONE......	$250	$500	$800	$2,500	$5,500	$11,000	$20,000
STATES UNITED, 8-Pointed Star on Label	200	500	700	1,150	2,500	4,400	10,000
UNITED Above, STATES Below	600	1,350	3,000	7,500	10,000	13,500	—

1787 With Club Rays

Rounded Ends   **Concave Ends**

	G	VG	F	VF	EF	AU
Club Rays, Rounded Ends....................	$250	$450	$900	$1,750	$3,500	$7,000
Club Rays, Concave Ends to Rays, FUCIO (C instead of G) *(extremely rare)*...........	1,400	3,250	7,500	20,000	33,000	
Club Rays, Concave Ends, FUGIO, UNITED STATES..	1,900	3,800	8,000	22,000	—	—
Club Rays, Similar, STATES UNITED Reverse	—	—		—	—	

The so-called New Haven "restrikes" were made for Horatio N. Rust from dies recreated in 1859, partially through use of hubs or other devices supposedly (though the story is discredited by modern scholars) obtained by 14-year-old C. Wyllis Betts in 1858 on the site of the Broome & Platt store in New Haven, where the original coins had been made.

New Haven Restrike. *Note narrow rings.*

	EF	AU	Unc.
Gold *(2 known)*..	—	—	
Silver..	$3,000	$4,250	$6,500
Copper or Brass..	400	500	800

1792 PROPOSED COINAGE

Many members of the House favored a representation of the president's head on the obverse of each coin; others considered the idea a monarchical practice. Washington is believed to have expressed disapproval of the use of his portrait on American coins.

The majority considered a figure emblematic of Liberty more appropriate, and the Senate finally concurred in this opinion. Robert Birch was an engraver employed to design proposed devices for American coins. He, perhaps together with others, engraved the dies for the disme and half disme. He also cut the dies for the large copper patterns known today as *Birch cents.*

1792 Silver Center Cent

	F	VF	EF	AU
Cent, Silver Center *(14 known, including one unique specimen without plug)* $414,000, BU, Stack's Bowers auction, January 2002	$250,000	$450,000	$650,000	$750,000
Cent, Without Silver Center *(9 known)*	300,000	600,000	750,000	1,000,000
$603,750, VF-30, Heritage auction, January 2008				

1792 Birch Cent

G★W.Pᴛ.

	F	VF	EF
Copper, Lettered Edge, TO BE ESTEEMED * BE USEFUL* *(8 known)*	$250,000	$650,000	$750,000
Copper, Plain Edge *(2 known)*		700,000	
Copper, Lettered Edge, TO BE ESTEEMED BE USEFUL * *(2 known)*		—	
White Metal, G*W.Pt. (George Washington President) Below Wreath *(unique)*		—	

1792 Half Disme

	Mintage	AG	G	VG	F	VF	EF	AU	Unc.
Silver	1,500	$8,500	$20,000	$27,500	$40,000	$75,000	$110,000	$175,000	$325,000
Copper *(unique)* $1,322,500, SP-67, Heritage auction, April 2006									

1792 Disme

	VF	EF	Unc.
Silver *(3 known)*	$750,000	$1,000,000	$2,000,000
Copper *(about 15 known; illustrated)*	135,000	225,000	500,000
$690,000, PF-62, Heritage auction, July 2008			

1792 Quarter Dollar

Joseph Wright, an accomplished artist in the private sector, designed this pattern intended for the original U.S. coins. He was George Washington's choice for the position of first chief engraver of the Mint, and designed the 1793 Liberty Cap cent in that capacity, but died before being confirmed by Congress. Unique uniface trials of the obverse and reverse also exist.

	EF
1792, Copper *(illustrated) (2 known)*	$750,000
1792, White Metal *(4 known)*	225,000

THE LIBERTAS AMERICANA MEDAL

The Liberty Cap coinage of the fledgling United States was inspired by the famous Libertas Americana medal, whose dies were engraved by Augustin Dupré in Paris in 1782 from a concept and mottoes proposed by Benjamin Franklin. To Franklin (then U.S. minister to France), the infant Hercules symbolized America, strangling two serpents representing the British armies at Saratoga and Yorktown. Minerva, with shield and spear, symbolized France as America's ally, keeping the British Lion at bay. Franklin presented examples of the medal to the French king and queen (in gold) and to their ministers (in silver), "as a monumental acknowledgment, which may go down to future ages, of the obligations we are under to this nation."

Between 100 and 125 original copper medals exist, and two dozen or more silver; the location of the two gold medals is unknown. Over the years the Paris Mint has issued restrikes that have modest value as mementos.

	PF-50	PF-60	PF-65
Libertas Americana medal, copper *(100–125 known)*	$8,000	$12,000	$45,000
Libertas Americana medal, silver *(24+ known)*	30,000	75,000	150,000

The half cent is the lowest face value coin struck by the United States. All half cents are scarce, and this series is beginning to enjoy the popularity of large cents and certain other early series. Prices for the common dates and varieties have remained at reasonable levels for many years.

This denomination was authorized on April 2, 1792. Originally the weight was to have been 132 grains, but this was changed to 104 grains by the Act of January 14, 1793, before coinage commenced. The weight was again changed, to 84 grains, on January 26, 1796, by presidential proclamation in conformity with the Act of March 3, 1795. Coinage was discontinued by the Act of February 21, 1857. All were coined at the Philadelphia Mint.

There were various intermissions in coinage. During the period from 1836 through 1848, coinage consisted entirely of Proofs and in very small quantities, causing a very noticeable lapse in the series for most collectors. While 1796 is the most valuable date, the original and restrike Proofs of 1831, 1836, 1840 through 1848, and 1852, along with other rare varieties, are all difficult to obtain.

LIBERTY CAP, HEAD FACING LEFT (1793)

Designer unknown; engraver Henry Voigt; weight 6.74 grams; composition, copper; approx. diameter 22 mm; edge: TWO HUNDRED FOR A DOLLAR.

AG-3 About Good—Clear enough to identify.
G-4 Good—Outline of bust of Liberty clear, no details. Date readable. Reverse lettering incomplete.
VG-8 Very Good—Some hair details. Reverse lettering complete.
F-12 Fine—Most of hair detail visible. Leaves worn, but all visible.
VF-20 Very Fine—Hair near ear and forehead worn, other areas distinct. Some details in leaves visible.
EF-40 Extremely Fine—Light wear on highest parts of head and wreath.
AU-50 About Uncirculated—Only a trace of wear on Liberty's face.

Values shown are for coins with attractive surfaces and color consistent with the amount of normal wear. Minor imperfections are permissible for grades below Fine. Coins that are porous, corroded, or similarly defective are worth significantly lower prices.

	Mintage	AG-3	G-4	VG-8	F-12	VF-20	EF-40	AU-50
1793	35,334	$1,750	$3,500	$5,500	$9,000	$13,500	$25,000	$38,000

$126,500, MS-61 BN, Heritage auction, January 2009

LIBERTY CAP, HEAD FACING RIGHT (1794–1797)

1794—Designer possibly Joseph Wright; engraver Robert Scot; weight 6.74 grams; composition, copper; approx. diameter 23.5 mm; edge: TWO HUNDRED FOR A DOLLAR. 1795—Designer John Smith Gardner; weight 6.74 grams; composition, copper; approx. diameter 23.5 mm; edge: TWO HUNDRED FOR A DOL-LAR. 1795–1797 (thin planchet)—Weight 5.44 grams; composition, copper; approx. diameter 23.5 mm; edge: plain (some 1797 are either lettered or gripped).

AG-3 About Good—Clear enough to identify.
G-4 Good—Outline of bust of Liberty clear, no details. Date readable. Reverse lettering incomplete.
VG-8 Very Good—Some hair details. Reverse lettering complete.
F-12 Fine—Most of hair detail visible. Leaves worn, but all visible.
VF-20 Very Fine—Hair near ear and forehead worn, other areas distinct. Some details in leaves visible.
EF-40 Extremely Fine—Light wear on highest parts of head and wreath.
AU-50 About Uncirculated—Only a trace of wear on Liberty's face.

Normal Head   **High-Relief Head**

	Mintage	AG-3	G-4	VG-8	F-12	VF-20	EF-40	AU-50
1794, All kinds 81,600								
1794, Normal Head	$300	$575	$800	$1,500	$2,500	$5,500	$13,000
1794, High-Relief Head	325	600	825	1,550	2,750	5,750	13,500

Pole to Cap   **Punctuated Date**   **No Pole to Cap**

	Mintage	AG-3	G-4	VG-8	F-12	VF-20	EF-40	AU-50
1795, All kinds 139,690								
1795, Lettered Edge, With Pole	$295	$570	$800	$1,500	$2,750	$5,750	$10,500
1795, Lettered Edge, Punctuated Date	295	570	800	1,500	2,750	6,000	12,000
1795, Plain Edge, Punctuated Date.	220	475	625	1,100	1,800	4,750	9,000
1795, Plain Edge, No Pole **(a)**.	220	475	625	1,100	1,800	4,750	9,000
1796, With Pole **(b)** 1,390	10,000	18,000	25,000	35,000	56,000	80,000	100,000
$402,500, MS-64 BN, Stack's Bowers auction, August 2012								
1796, No Pole.	*	17,500	35,000	65,000	125,000	175,000	200,000	—
$506,000, MS-65, Stack's Bowers auction, May 1996								

* Included in number above. **a.** Many are struck on cut-down cents, or are on planchets cut from Talbot, Allum & Lee cents (see page 76). **b.** The deceptive "Dr. Edwards" struck copy of this coin has a different head and larger letters.

1797, 1 Above 1   **1797, Low Head**

	Mintage	AG-3	G-4	VG-8	F-12	VF-20	EF-40	AU-50
1797, All kinds **(a)** 127,840								
1797, 1 Above 1, Plain Edge	$235	$425	$625	$1,000	$1,800	$4,000	$7,000
1797, Plain Edge, Low Head.	350	575	900	2,250	3,750	13,500	—
1797, Plain Edge	260	475	650	1,250	3,000	6,000	8,000
1797, Lettered Edge.	700	1,500	3,000	6,000	15,000	30,000	60,000
1797, Gripped Edge	9,000	25,000	55,000	70,000	—	—	—

a. Many are struck on cut-down cents, or are on planchets cut from Talbot, Allum & Lee cents (see page 76).

DRAPED BUST (1800–1808)

Designer probably Gilbert Stuart; engraver Robert Scot; weight 5.44 grams; composition, copper; diameter 23.5 mm; plain edge.

AG-3 About Good—Clear enough to identify.
G-4 Good—Outline of bust of Liberty clear, few details, date readable. Reverse lettering worn and incomplete.
VG-8 Very Good—Some drapery visible. Date and legends complete.
F-12 Fine—Shoulder drapery and hair over brow worn smooth.
VF-20 Very Fine—Only slight wear in previously mentioned areas. Slight wear on reverse.
EF-40 Extremely Fine—Light wear on highest parts of head and wreath.
AU-50 About Uncirculated—Wear slight on hair above forehead.

1st Reverse (Style of 1800)   **2nd Reverse (Style of 1803)**

	Mintage	AG-3	G-4	VG-8	F-12	VF-20	EF-40	AU-50
1800. .202,908		$40	$70	$90	$150	$300	$700	$1,000
1802, 2 Over 0, Reverse of 1800 . . . . . .*	9,000	22,500	35,000	50,000	60,000	90,000	—	
1802, 2 Over 0, Second Reverse . .20,266	350	700	1,700	4,000	12,000	30,000	—	
1803. . . . .*	35	75	100	160	325	975	1,500	
1803, Widely Spaced 3. 92,000	35	75	100	160	325	950	1,500	

* Included in number below.

Plain 4   **Stems to Wreath**

Crosslet 4   **"Spiked Chin"**   **Stemless Wreath**

	Mintage	AG-3	G-4	VG-8	F-12	VF-20	EF-40	AU-50
1804, All kinds 1,055,312								
1804, Plain 4, Stems to Wreath		$40	$75	$120	$200	$475	$1,300	$2,200
1804, Plain 4, Stemless Wreath		35	70	90	120	200	365	675
1804, Crosslet 4, Stemless.		35	70	90	120	200	365	675
1804, Crosslet 4, Stems.		35	70	90	120	200	365	675
1804, "Spiked Chin".		35	85	100	140	250	425	850

Medium 5   **Small 5**   **Large 5**

	Mintage	AG-3	G-4	VG-8	F-12	VF-20	EF-40	AU-50
1805, All kinds 814,464								
1805, Medium 5, Stemless.		$35	$70	$90	$120	$200	$400	$750
1805, Small 5, Stems.		400	900	1,650	4,000	7,750	15,000	30,000
1805, Large 5, Stems.		35	70	90	120	200	400	850

	Small 6		Large 6		1808, 8 Over 7		Normal Date

	Mintage	AG-3	G-4	VG-8	F-12	VF-20	EF-40	AU-50
1806, All kinds	.356,000							
1806, Small 6, Stems.		$90	$235	$425	$750	$1,650	$3,500	$9,000
1806, Small 6, Stemless		35	70	90	120	175	325	675
1806, Large 6, Stems.		35	70	90	120	175	325	675
1807.	.476,000	35	75	90	120	200	500	1,000
1808, All kinds	.400,000							
1808, Normal Date.		35	75	90	120	220	525	1,300
1808, 8 Over 7		80	150	325	650	2,100	4,500	11,000

CLASSIC HEAD (1809–1836)

Designer John Reich. Standards same as for previous issue.

G-4 Good—LIBERTY only partly visible on hair band. Lettering, date, and stars worn but visible.
VG-8 Very Good—LIBERTY entirely visible on hair band. Lower curls worn.
F-12 Fine—Only partial wear on LIBERTY, and hair at top worn in spots.
VF-20 Very Fine—Lettering clear-cut. Hair only slightly worn.
EF-40 Extremely Fine—Light wear on highest points of hair and leaves.
AU-50 About Uncirculated—Sharp hair detail with only a trace of wear on higher points.
MS-60 Uncirculated—Typical brown to red surface. No trace of wear.
MS-63 Choice Uncirculated—Well-defined color, brown to red. No traces of wear.

1809, Small o Inside 0

1809, 9 Over Inverted 9   1809, Normal Date   1811, Wide Date   1811, Close Date

	Mintage	G-4	VG-8	F-12	VF-20	EF-40	AU-50	MS-60BN	MS-63BN
1809, All kinds	1,154,572								
1809, Normal Date.		$55	$65	$80	$100	$150	$300	$850	$1,500
1809, Small o Inside 0		55	75	100	150	385	800	1,400	2,500
1809, 9 Over Inverted 9		55	75	100	150	375	750	1,300	2,500
1810.	215,000	55	75	120	270	575	1,000	2,000	3,250
1811, All kinds	63,140								
1811, Wide Date.		400	800	1,600	2,750	6,500	8,500	12,500	17,000
1811, Close Date		350	700	1,500	2,500	6,200	7,750	10,000	14,000
1811, Reverse of 1802, Unofficial Restrike *(extremely rare)*		—	—	16,000	22,000				
1825.	63,000	55	65	80	100	185	325	900	1,800
1826.	234,000	55	65	80	90	150	300	600	1,000

13 Stars — 12 Stars

	Mintage	G-4	VG-8	F-12	VF-20	EF-40	AU-50	MS-60	MS-63BN
1828, All kinds	606,000								
1828, 13 Stars		$50	$60	$70	$100	$120	$200	$350	$600
1828, 12 Stars		50	60	70	120	250	425	1,300	1,850
1829	487,000	50	60	70	100	140	220	400	700

Beginning in 1831, new coinage equipment and modified dies produced a raised rim on each side of these coins. Proofs and restrikes were made at the Mint for sale to collectors. Restrikes are believed to have been struck circa 1858 through 1861.

Reverse (1831–1836)   **Reverse (1840–1857)**

	Mintage	PF-40	PF-60BN	PF-63BN
1831, Original *(beware of altered date)*	2,200	$50,000	$80,000	—
1831, Restrike, Large Berries (Reverse of 1836)	—	10,000	$15,000
1831, Restrike, Small Berries (Reverse of 1840–1857)	—	14,000	21,000

	Mintage	VG-8	F-12	VF-20	EF-40	AU-50	MS-60	PF-63BN
1832 **(a)** 51,000		$50	$70	$85	$120	$200	$300	$6,000
1833 **(a)** .103,000		50	70	85	120	200	300	6,000
1834 **(a)** .141,000		50	70	85	120	200	300	6,000
1835 **(a)** .398,000		50	70	85	120	200	300	6,000
1836, Original								8,000
1836, Restrike (Reverse of 1840–1857) . .								17,000

a. The figures given here are thought to be correct, although official Mint records report these quantities for 1833 through 1836 rather than 1832 through 1835.

No half cents were struck in 1837. Because of the great need for small change, however, a large number of tokens similar in size to current large cents were issued privately by businessmen who needed them in commerce. Additionally, thousands of half cent tokens were issued of the variety listed and illustrated below.

	G-4	VG-8	F-12	VF-20	EF-40	AU-50	MS-60
1837 Token *(not a coin)*	$40	$60	$70	$110	$200	$375	$650

BRAIDED HAIR (1840–1857)

Both originals and restrikes use the reverse of 1840 to 1857. Most originals have large berries and most restrikes have small berries in the wreath.

Designer Christian Gobrecht; weight 5.44 grams; composition, copper; diameter 23 mm; plain edge.

VG-8 Very Good—Beads in hair uniformly distinct. Hair lines visible in spots.
F-12 Fine—Hair lines above ear worn. Beads sharp.
VF-20 Very Fine—Lowest curl worn; hair otherwise distinct.
EF-40 Extremely Fine—Light wear on highest points of hair and on leaves.
AU-50 About Uncirculated—Very slight trace of wear on hair above Liberty's ear.
MS-60 Uncirculated—No trace of wear. Clear luster.
MS-63 Choice Uncirculated—No trace of wear.
PF-63 Choice Proof—Nearly perfect; only light blemishes.

Large Berries   **Small Berries**

Brilliant red Proof half cents are worth more than the prices shown.

	PF-63BN	PF-65BN
1840, Original.	$6,500	$9,250
1840, Restrike	6,500	9,250
1841, Original.	5,500	8,750
1841, Restrike	5,500	8,750
1842, Original.	7,000	10,000
1842, Restrike	5,500	8,750
1843, Original.	5,500	8,750
1843, Restrike	5,700	8,750
1844, Original.	6,000	9,000
1844, Restrike	5,750	8,750

	PF-63BN	PF-65BN
1845, Original.	$6,000	$9,250
1845, Restrike	5,400	9,000
1846, Original.	6,000	9,000
1846, Restrike	5,750	8,750
1847, Original.	6,000	9,250
1847, Restrike	5,400	8,250
1848, Original.	6,250	9,250
1848, Restrike	5,600	8,250
1849, Original, Small Date	5,500	10,000
1849, Restrike, Small Date	5,750	9,750

1849, Small Date   **1849, Large Date**

Brilliant red Uncirculated half cents are worth more than the prices shown.

	Mintage	VG-8	F-12	VF-20	EF-40	AU-50	MS-60	MS-63BN	PF-63BN
1849, Large Date	39,864	$55	$70	$90	$150	$240	$500	$700	—
1850	39,812	55	70	90	150	240	500	700	$7,000
1851	147,672	50	65	80	100	175	275	550	6,000
1852, Original.									—
1852, Restrike									6,000
1853	129,694	50	65	80	100	175	275	550	
1854	55,358	50	65	80	100	175	275	550	5,000
1855	56,500	50	65	80	100	175	275	550	5,000
1856	40,430	50	75	90	125	185	325	550	5,000
1857	35,180	65	100	135	180	260	400	650	5,000

Cents and half cents were the first coins struck for circulation by the United States Mint. Coinage began in 1793 with laws specifying that the cent should weigh exactly twice as much as the half cent. Large cents were coined every year from 1793 to 1857 with the exception of 1815, when a lack of copper prevented production. All were coined at the Philadelphia Mint. Mintage records in some cases may be inaccurate, as many of the early pieces were struck later than the dates shown on the coins. Varieties listed are those most significant to collectors. Numerous other die varieties may be found because each of the early dies was individually made. Values of varieties not listed in this guide depend on collector interest, rarity, and demand. Proof large cents were first made in 1817; all Proofs are rare, as they were not made available to the general public before the mid-1850s.

FLOWING HAIR

AG-3 About Good—Date and devices clear enough to identify.
G-4 Good—Lettering worn but readable. No detail on bust.
VG-8 Very Good—Date and lettering distinct, some details of head visible.
F-12 Fine—About half of hair and other details visible.
VF-20 Very Fine—Ear visible, most details visible.
EF-40 Extremely Fine—Wear evident on highest points of hair and back of temple.

Chain Reverse (1793)

Designer unknown; engraver Henry Voigt; weight 13.48 grams; composition, copper; approx. diameter 26–27 mm; edge: bars and slender vine with leaves.

| AMERI. Reverse | Obverse | AMERICA Reverse |

Values shown for Fine and better copper coins are for those with attractive surfaces and color consistent with the amount of normal wear. Coins that are porous, corroded, or similarly defective are worth significantly lower prices.

	Mintage	AG-3	G-4	VG-8	F-12	VF-20	EF-40	AU-50
1793, Chain, All kinds. 36,103								
1793, AMERI. in Legend.		$4,500	$10,500	$17,000	$28,000	$45,000	$80,000	$200,000
$368,000, AU-58, Goldberg auction, September 2009								
1793, AMERICA, With Periods.		3,200	8,000	15,000	19,500	37,500	60,000	110,000
1793, AMERICA, Without Periods		3,000	7,500	14,000	18,000	36,000	55,000	100,000
$1,380,000, MS-65 BN, Heritage auction, January 2012								

Wreath Reverse (1793)

The reverse of this type bears a single-bow wreath, as distinguished from the wreath tied with a double bow on the following type. A three-leaf sprig appears above the date on the obverse, and both sides have borders of small beads.

Introduction of this reverse answered criticism of the chain design, which critics saw as symbolic of slavery rather than strength in unity, but the stronger modeling of the face and hair still failed to gain acceptance as representative of Liberty. After three months' production the design was abandoned in favor of the Liberty Cap type.

Instead of the normal sprig above the date, the rare strawberry-leaf variety has a spray of trefoil leaves and a small blossom. The trefoils match those found on the normal wreath reverse. It is not clear why this variety was created. All four known specimens are well worn.

Designer unknown; engraver Henry Voigt; weight 13.48 grams; composition, copper; approx. diameter 26–28 mm; edge: vine and bars, or lettered ONE HUNDRED FOR A DOLLAR followed by either a single or a double leaf.

Wreath Type   **Strawberry Leaf Variety**

	Mintage	AG-3	G-4	VG-8	F-12	VF-20	EF-40	AU-50
1793, Wreath, All kinds 63,353								
1793, Vine/Bars Edge.		$850	$3,000	$4,400	$6,500	$12,500	$24,000	$35,000
$558,125, MS-69 BN, Stack's								
Bowers auction, January 2013								
1793, Lettered Edge.		900	3,200	4,700	7,000	13,500	26,000	37,500
$276,000, MS-64 BN, Heritage								
auction, January 2008								
1793, Strawberry Leaf *(4 known)*		—	450,000	950,000				
$862,500, F-12, Stack's Bowers								
auction, January 2009								

LIBERTY CAP (1793–1796)

Another major change was made in 1793 to satisfy continuing objections to the obverse portrait. This version appears to have been more popular, as it was continued into 1796. The 1793 pieces had beaded borders, but a border of denticles (or "teeth") was adopted in 1794. A famous 1794 variety is the probably whimsical "starred" reverse, with a border of 94 tiny, five-pointed stars among the denticles.

Portrait variations listed for 1794 are the result of several changes of die engravers. The so-called Jefferson Head of 1795 is now thought to be a sample for a proposed coinage contract by a private manufacturer, John Harper.

Planchets became too thin for edge lettering after the weight reduction ordered in late 1795. The variety with reeded edge was probably an experimental substitute, rejected in favor of a plain edge.

1793–1795 (thick planchet)—Designer probably Joseph Wright; engraver Joseph Wright; weight 13.48 grams; composition, copper; approx. diameter 29 mm; edge: ONE HUNDRED FOR A DOLLAR followed by a single leaf. 1795–1796 (thin planchet)—Designer John Smith Gardner; weight 10.89 grams; composition, copper; approx. diameter 29 mm; plain edge.

1793, Vine and Bars Edge   **Lettered Edge (1793–1795)**
Chain and Wreath types only.   **ONE HUNDRED FOR A DOLLAR**

Beaded Border (1793)

"Jefferson" Head

Head of 1793 (1793–1794)
Head in high, rounded relief.

Head of 1794 (1794)
Well-defined hair;
hook on lowest curl. (a)

Head of 1795 (1794–1796)
Head in low relief;
no hook on lowest curl. (a)

1794, Starred Reverse   **Reeded Edge**

	Mintage	AG-3	G-4	VG-8	F-12	VF-20	EF-40
1793, Liberty Cap	11,056	$3,000	$5,000	$11,000	$17,500	$45,000	$77,000
$632,500, AU-55, Heritage auction, February 2008							
1794, All kinds	918,521						
1794, Head of 1793		575	1,500	3,000	4,000	9,000	22,000
1794, Head of 1794		150	370	550	800	1,800	4,000
1794, Head in Low Relief **(a)**		150	370	550	800	1,800	4,000
1794, Exact Head of 1795 **(a)**		175	400	600	1,000	2,200	4,700
$499,375, MS-67 RB, Stack's Bowers auction, January 2013							
1794, Starred Reverse		6,000	12,000	20,000	40,000	80,000	160,000
$632,500, AU-50, Heritage auction, February 2008							
1794, No Fraction Bar		150	375	650	1,100	2,700	6,200
1795, Lettered Edge	37,000	140	340	525	950	2,000	5,250
1795, Plain Edge	501,500	100	325	425	650	1,350	3,000
1795, Reeded Edge *(9 known)*		150,000	300,000	800,000	1,250,000		
$1,265,000, VG-10, Goldberg auction, September 2009							
1795, Jefferson Head *(not a regular Mint issue)*, Plain Edge		8,500	18,000	34,000	55,000	120,000	250,000
1795, Jefferson Head, Lettered Edge *(3 known)*		—	50,000	100,000	250,000		
1796, Liberty Cap	109,825	200	400	600	1,200	2,400	5,500
$690,000, MS-66 RB, Goldberg auction, September 2008							

a. The 1794 coin with Head of 1795 has a hooked curl but is in low relief.

DRAPED BUST (1796–1807)

Designer Robert Scot; weight 10.89 grams; composition, copper; approx. diameter 29 mm; plain edge.

AG-3 About Good—Clear enough to identify.

G-4 Good—Lettering worn, but clear; date clear. Bust lacking in detail.

VG-8 Very Good—Drapery on Liberty partly visible. Less wear in date and lettering.

F-12 Fine—Hair over brow smooth; some detail showing in other parts of hair.

VF-20 Very Fine—Hair lines slightly worn. Hair over brow better defined.

EF-40 Extremely Fine—Hair above forehead and left of eye outlined and detailed. Only slight wear on olive leaves.

1796–1807
*This head was modified
slightly in 1798.
See page 101 for details.*

LIHERTY Error

Reverse of 1794
(1794–1796)
*Note double leaf at top right;
14–16 leaves on left,
16–18 leaves on right.*

Reverse of 1795
(1795–1798)
*Note single leaf at top right;
17–21 leaves on left,
16–20 leaves on right.*

Reverse of 1797
(1796–1807)
*Note double leaf at top right;
16 leaves on left,
19 leaves on right.*

	Mintage	AG-3	G-4	VG-8	F-12	VF-20	EF-40
1796, Draped Bust, All kinds 363,375							
1796, Reverse of 1794.	$120	$250	$600	$900	$2,750	$6,000
1796, Reverse of 1795.	110	175	300	625	2,750	6,000
1796, Reverse of 1797.	110	175	300	625	2,000	4,000
1796, LIHERTY Error.	175	340	750	1,400	4,800	12,000
1796, Stemless Reverse *(3 known)*		25,000					

With Stems

Gripped Edge

Stemless

	Mintage	AG-3	G-4	VG-8	F-12	VF-20	EF-40
1797, All kinds 897,510							
1797, Gripped Edge, 1795-Style Reverse	$60	$140	$250	$425	$1,000	$3,500
1797, Plain Edge, 1795-Style Reverse	60	145	265	435	1,200	4,000
1797, 1797 Reverse, With Stems.	55	110	190	300	950	2,000
1797, 1797 Reverse, Stemless.	60	135	265	550	1,600	6,000

Style 1 Hair
All 1796–1797,
many 1798 varieties,
and on 1800 Over 1798.

Style 2 Hair
1798–1807
(extra curl near shoulder).

1798, 8 Over 7

	Mintage	AG-3	G-4	VG-8	F-12	VF-20	EF-40
1798, All kinds	1,841,745						
1798, 8 Over 7		$60	$135	$275	$550	$3,000	$7,000
1798, Reverse of 1796		50	125	250	500	2,000	6,500
1798, Style 1 Hair		40	95	130	250	600	2,200
1798, Style 2 Hair		40	95	130	250	575	1,950

1799, 9 Over 8

1800, 1800 Over 1798

1800, 80 Over 79

	Mintage	AG-3	G-4	VG-8	F-12	VF-20	EF-40
1799, 9 Over 8 . . . .(a)		$1,500	$3,500	$6,000	$12,500	$30,000	$75,000
$368,000, EF-45, Goldberg auction,							
September 2009							
1799, Normal Date . . . .(a)		1,250	2,750	5,500	10,500	27,000	65,000
1800, All kinds	2,822,175						
1800, 1800 Over 1798, Style 1 Hair		32	75	135	265	1,500	3,850
1800, 80 Over 79, Style 2 Hair		32	75	120	225	600	2,200
1800, Normal Date		32	75	120	225	550	1,900

a. Included in "1798, All kinds" mintage.

Fraction 1/000

Corrected Fraction

1801 Reverse, 3 Errors

Error-fraction dies appear on 1801–1803 cents; all these dies originated in 1801, possibly from same engraver.

	Mintage	AG-3	G-4	VG-8	F-12	VF-20	EF-40
1801, All kinds	1,362,837						
1801, Normal Reverse		$32	$60	$90	$200	$450	$1,250
1801, 3 Errors: 1/000, One Stem,							
and IINITED		75	200	350	800	2,500	7,750
1801, Fraction 1/000		32	70	100	240	600	2,000
1801, 1/100 Over 1/000		32	80	135	275	1,000	2,500
1802, All kinds	3,435,100						
1802, Normal Reverse		32	60	90	190	375	1,000
1802, Fraction 1/000		32	70	110	220	600	1,700
1802, Stemless Wreath		32	60	100	200	450	1,400

**1803, Small Date,
Blunt 1**

**1803, Large Date,
Pointed 1**

Small Fraction

Large Fraction

*All Small Date varieties have blunt 1 in date.
Large Dates have pointed 1 and noticeably larger 3.*

*Values shown for Fine and better copper coins are for those with attractive surfaces and color consistent with the amount of normal wear.
Coins that are porous, corroded, or similarly defective are worth significantly lower prices.*

	Mintage	AG-3	G-4	VG-8	F-12	VF-20	EF-40
1803, All kinds	3,131,691						
1803, Small Date, Small Fraction		$32	$60	$100	$165	$350	$1,000
1803, Small Date, Large Fraction		32	60	100	165	350	1,000
1803, Large Date, Small Fraction		2,400	4,500	8,250	15,000	32,000	75,000
1803, Large Date, Large Fraction		40	90	175	350	1,500	4,000
1803, 1/100 Over 1/000		32	80	120	240	750	2,200
1803, Stemless Wreath		32	80	120	240	750	2,200

Broken Dies

All genuine 1804 cents have crosslet 4 in date and a large fraction. The 0 in date is in line with O in OF on reverse.

	Mintage	AG-3	G-4	VG-8	F-12	VF-20	EF-40
1804 **(a)**	96,500	$700	$1,000	$2,200	$4,000	$7,000	$15,000
$661,250, MS-63 BN, Goldberg auction, September 2009							

a. Values shown are for coins with normal or broken dies.

A "restrike" 1804 was manufactured from discarded Mint dies. An altered 1803 die was used for the obverse and a die of the 1820 cent used for the reverse. They were struck circa 1860 to satisfy the demand for this rare date. Known as the "restrike," the product actually is a combination of two unrelated dies and cannot be confused with the genuine.

Unofficial 1804 "Restrike"

	Mintage	AG-3	G-4	VG-8	F-12	VF-20	EF-40
1804, Unofficial Restrike of 1860 *(Uncirculated)*							$1,000
1805	941,116	$32	$60	$85	$175	$500	1,200
1806	348,000	32	70	115	225	600	2,000

**Small 1807, 7 Over 6
(Blunt 1)**

**Large 1807, 7 Over 6
(Pointed 1)**

"Comet" Variety
Note die break behind head.

	Mintage	AG-3	G-4	VG-8	F-12	VF-20	EF-40
1807, All kinds	829,221						
1807, Small 1807, 7 Over 6, Blunt 1		$1,200	$2,500	$4,500	$9,000	$21,000	$45,000
1807, Large 1807, 7 Over 6, Pointed 1		32	55	80	165	500	1,200
1807, Small Fraction		32	55	80	185	550	1,700
1807, Large Fraction		32	55	80	165	450	1,100
1807, "Comet" Variety		32	60	100	225	850	2,600

CLASSIC HEAD (1808–1814)

This group (1808–1814) does not compare in sharpness and quality to those struck previously (1793–1807) nor to those struck later (from 1816 on). The copper used was softer, having more metallic impurity. This impaired the wearing quality of the series. For this reason, collectors find greater difficulty in obtaining these dates in choice condition.

Designer John Reich; weight 10.89 grams; composition, copper; approx. diameter 29 mm; plain edge.

AG-3 About Good—Details clear enough to identify.
G-4 Good—Legends, stars, and date worn, but plain.
VG-8 Very Good—LIBERTY all readable. Liberty's ear visible. Details worn but plain.
F-12 Fine—Hair on forehead and before ear nearly smooth. Ear and hair under ear sharp.
VF-20 Very Fine—Some detail in all hair lines. Slight wear on leaves on reverse.
EF-40 Extremely Fine—All hair lines sharp. Very slight wear on high points.

	Mintage	AG-3	G-4	VG-8	F-12	VF-20	EF-40
1808	1,007,000	$27	$50	$150	$325	$600	$1,850
1809	222,867	50	120	250	500	1,400	3,750

1810, 10 Over 09   1810, Normal Date

1811, Last 1 Over 0   1811, Normal Date

	Mintage	AG-3	G-4	VG-8	F-12	VF-20	EF-40
1810, All kinds 1,458,500							
1810, 10 Over 09	$27	$50	$125	$250	$600	$1,550
1810, Normal Date	27	50	125	250	600	1,450
1811, All kinds 218,025							
1811, Last 1 Over 0	40	85	135	500	1,750	5,200
1811, Normal Date	45	100	150	400	1,000	2,100

1812, Small Date   1812, Large Date

1814, Plain 4   1814, Crosslet 4

	Mintage	AG-3	G-4	VG-8	F-12	VF-20	EF-40
1812, All kinds 1,075,500							
1812, Small Date	$22	$50	$85	$250	$600	$1,450
1812, Large Date	22	50	85	250	600	1,450
1813 418,000	25	55	120	265	650	1,700
1814, All kinds 357,830							
1814, Plain 4	22	50	85	240	600	1,400
1814, Crosslet 4	22	50	85	240	600	1,400

LIBERTY HEAD (1816–1857)

G-4 Good—Details on Liberty's head partly visible. Even wear in date and legends.
VG-8 Very Good—LIBERTY, date, stars, and legends clear. Part of hair cord visible.
F-12 Fine—All hair lines visible. Hair cords uniformly visible.
VF-20 Very Fine—Hair cords only slightly worn. Hair lines only partly worn, all well defined.
EF-40 Extremely Fine—Both hair cords stand out sharply. All hair lines sharp.
AU-50 About Uncirculated—Only traces of wear on hair and highest points on leaves and bow.
MS-60 Uncirculated—Typical brown surface. No trace of wear.
MS-63 Choice Uncirculated—Some distracting contact marks or blemishes in prime focal areas. Impaired luster possible.

Matron Head (1816–1835)

Designer Robert Scot or John Reich; weight 10.89 grams; composition, copper; approx. diameter 28–29 mm; plain edge.

Standard Design   **15 Stars**

The values shown for all MS-60 and MS-63 Matron Head large cents are for average condition; red to bright red Uncirculated pieces with attractive surfaces (not cleaned) command higher prices. Beware of slightly worn copper coins that have been cleaned and recolored to simulate Uncirculated luster. Cents in VF or better condition with attractive surface and tone may also command higher prices than those listed here.

	Mintage	G-4	VG-8	F-12	VF-20	EF-40	AU-50	MS-60	MS-63BN
1816	2,820,982	$20	$27	$45	$90	$190	$300	$500	$700
1817, All kinds	3,948,400								
1817, 13 Stars		20	25	40	75	140	225	450	600
1817, 15 Stars		26	40	50	150	600	900	2,700	3,600
1818	3,167,000	20	25	40	75	135	225	450	600

1819, 9 Over 8   **1819, Large Date**   **1819, Small Date**

	Mintage	G-4	VG-8	F-12	VF-20	EF-40	AU-50	MS-60	MS-63BN
1819, All kinds	2,671,000								
1819, 9 Over 8		$22	$28	$38	$85	$275	$350	$750	$1,300
1819, Large Date		20	25	32	70	150	300	475	700
1819, Small Date		20	25	32	70	150	300	475	700

1820, 20 Over 19   **1820, Large Date**   **1820, Small Date**
Note 1 under 2.   *Note plain-topped 2.*   *Note curl-topped 2.*

	Mintage	G-4	VG-8	F-12	VF-20	EF-40	AU-50	MS-60	MS-63BN
1820, All kinds	4,407,550								
1820, 20 Over 19		$25	$30	$45	$110	$335	$550	$1,000	$1,600
1820, Large Date		20	24	32	75	175	250	400	600
1820, Small Date		20	24	32	75	250	450	900	1,200
1821	389,000	35	55	135	375	1,300	2,300	7,750	11,000
1822	2,072,339	25	30	45	120	425	700	1,200	1,800

1823, 3 Over 2

Unofficial 1823 "Restrike"

	Mintage	G-4	VG-8	F-12	VF-20	EF-40	AU-50	MS-60	MS-63BN
1823, 3 Over 2 . . . .(a)		$65	$135	$325	$750	$2,400	$4,500	$12,000	—
1823, Normal Date . . . .(a)		65	140	325	900	3,700	7,500	18,000	—
1823, Unofficial Restrike, from broken obverse die					450	550	900	1,250	$1,500

a. Included in "1824, All kinds" mintage.

The 1823 unofficial "restrike" was made at the same time and by the same people as the 1804 "restrike" (see page 102), using a discarded 1823 obverse and an 1813 reverse die. The dies are heavily rusted (producing lumps on the coins) and most examples have both dies cracked across.

1824, 4 Over 2

1826, 6 Over 5

	Mintage	G-4	VG-8	F-12	VF-20	EF-40	AU-50	MS-60	MS-63BN
1824, All kinds 1,262,000									
1824, 4 Over 2		$25	$40	$85	$275	$1,500	$2,500	$6,000	$10,000
1824, Normal Date		20	28	45	165	500	850	2,400	4,000
1825 1,461,100		20	28	35	100	325	650	1,900	2,750
1826, All kinds 1,517,425									
1826, 6 Over 5		24	45	100	275	1,000	1,500	2,800	5,300
1826, Normal Date		20	25	32	100	250	450	900	1,400
1827 2,357,732		20	25	32	100	225	425	775	1,400

Date Size, Through 1828

Date Size, 1828 and Later

	Mintage	G-4	VG-8	F-12	VF-20	EF-40	AU-50	MS-60	MS-63BN
1828, All kinds 2,260,624									
1828, Large Narrow Date		$20	$25	$35	$75	$210	$400	$1,200	$1,750
1828, Small Wide Date		22	30	50	120	275	650	1,950	3,500

Large Letters (1808–1834)
*Note individual
letter size and proximity.*

Medium Letters (1829–1837)
*Note isolation of letters,
especially STATES.*

	Mintage	G-4	VG-8	F-12	VF-20	EF-40	AU-50	MS-60	MS-63BN
1829, All kinds	1,414,500								
1829, Large Letters		$20	$24	$30	$85	$200	$385	$650	$1,500
1829, Medium Letters		20	30	110	340	800	2,500	6,250	10,500
1830, All kinds	1,711,500								
1830, Large Letters		20	24	32	70	190	300	550	1,000
1830, Medium Letters		24	40	160	500	2,000	4,000	13,000	25,000
1831, All kinds	3,359,260								
1831, Large Letters		20	24	30	65	150	250	400	700
1831, Medium Letters		20	24	30	65	200	350	750	1,600
1832, All kinds	2,362,000								
1832, Large Letters		20	24	30	65	150	250	375	650
1832, Medium Letters		20	24	30	85	200	550	900	1,200
1833	2,739,000	20	24	30	65	150	250	375	750

Large 8 and Stars

Large 8, Small Stars

Small 8, Large Stars

	Mintage	G-4	VG-8	F-12	VF-20	EF-40	AU-50	MS-60	MS-63BN
1834, All kinds	1,855,100								
1834, Large 8, Stars, and Reverse Letters		$20	$30	$75	$190	$550	$1,000	$2,200	$4,000
1834, Large 8 and Stars, Medium Letters		160	325	400	1,000	3,200	6,000	9,500	11,000
1834, Large 8, Small Stars, Medium Letters		20	25	32	65	140	240	350	625
1834, Small 8, Large Stars, Medium Letters		20	25	32	65	140	240	350	625

Large 8 and Stars,
Matron Head

Small 8 and Stars,
Matron Head

1835, Head of 1836

	Mintage	G-4	VG-8	F-12	VF-20	EF-40	AU-50	MS-60	MS-63BN
1835, All kinds	3,878,400								
1835, Large 8 and Stars		$20	$25	$32	$75	$225	$400	$750	$1,400
1835, Small 8 and Stars		20	25	32	65	175	375	475	675
1835, Head of 1836		20	25	32	55	125	250	350	550

Matron Head Modified (1835–1839): The "Young Head"

Designer Christian Gobrecht; weight 10.89 grams; composition, copper; diameter 27.5 mm; plain edge.

G-4 Good—Considerably worn. LIBERTY readable.

VG-8 Very Good—Hairlines smooth but visible; outline of ear clearly defined.

F-12 Fine—Hairlines at top of head and behind ear worn but visible. Braid over brow plain; ear clear.

VF-20 Very Fine—All details sharper than for F-12. Only slight wear on hair over brow.

EF-40 Extremely Fine—Hair above ear detailed, but slightly worn.

AU-50 About Uncirculated—Trace of wear on high points of hair above ear and eye and on highest points on leaves and bow.

MS-60 Uncirculated—Typical brown surface. No trace of wear.

MS-63 Choice Uncirculated—Some distracting contact marks or blemishes in prime focal areas. Impaired luster possible.

1829–1837
Medium letters; note letter spacing.

Head of 1838
*Note slim bust
with beaded cords.*

1837–1839
Small letters; note letter spacing.

The values shown for all MS-60 and MS-63 Young Head large cents are for average condition; red to bright red Uncirculated large cents with attractive surfaces (not cleaned) command higher prices. Beware of slightly worn copper coins that have been cleaned and recolored to simulate Uncirculated luster. Cents in VF or better condition with attractive surface and tone may also command higher prices than those listed here.

	Mintage	G-4	VG-8	F-12	VF-20	EF-40	AU-50	MS-60	MS-63BN
1836	2,111,000	$20	$25	$32	$55	$125	$250	$350	$550
1837, All kinds	5,558,300								
1837, Plain Cord, Medium Letters		20	25	32	50	125	250	350	550
1837, Plain Cord, Small Letters		20	25	32	50	125	250	375	600
1837, Head of 1838		20	25	32	45	110	200	325	500
1838	6,370,200	20	25	32	45	120	225	335	575

Silly Head
Note lock at forehead.

1839 Over 1836
Note closed 9, plain cords.

Booby Head
Note shoulder tip.

Mintage	G-4	VG-8	F-12	VF-20	EF-40	AU-50	MS-60	MS-63BN
1839, All kinds 3,128,661								
1839, 1839 Over 1836, Plain Cords	$225	$450	$1,250	$2,600	$9,000	$18,000	$60,000	$90,000
1839, Head of 1838 1838, Beaded Cords	20	25	32	50	110	225	325	550
1839, Silly Head	22	26	35	75	200	400	850	1,200
1839, Booby Head (a)	20	26	35	60	150	300	675	1,100

a. The 1839 Booby Head variety has a modified reverse that omits the line under CENT (see 1837–1839 Small Letters photo on page 108).

Braided Hair (1839–1857)

1840, Large Date

1840, Small Date

1840, Small Date Over Large 18

Mintage	G-4	VG-8	F-12	VF-20	EF-40	AU-50	MS-60	MS-63BN
1839 . . . . (a)	$20	$25	$30	$50	$110	$265	$400	$650
1840, All kinds 2,462,700								
1840, Large Date	19	22	25	35	85	200	300	500
1840, Small Date	19	22	25	35	85	200	300	500
1840, Small Date Over Large 18	20	24	28	50	200	400	900	1,600
1841, Small Date 1,597,367	19	22	25	40	125	250	450	950

a. Included in "1839, All kinds" mintage.

1842, Small Date

1842, Large Date

Small Letters
(1839–1843)

	Mintage	G-4	VG-8	F-12	VF-20	EF-40	AU-50	MS-60	MS-63BN
1842, All kinds 2,383,390									
1842, Small Date		$19	$22	$25	$35	$85	$220	$375	$650
1842, Large Date		19	22	25	35	85	150	300	500

Head of 1840
Petite head (1839–1843)

Head of 1844
Mature head (1843–1857)

Large Letters
(1843–1857)

	Mintage	G-4	VG-8	F-12	VF-20	EF-40	AU-50	MS-60	MS-63BN
1843, All kinds 2,425,342									
1843, Petite, Small Letters		$19	$22	$25	$35	$85	$160	$300	$450
1843, Petite, Large Letters		20	30	45	80	210	320	825	1,500
1843, Mature, Large Letters		19	24	27	45	150	275	550	900
1844, Normal Date 2,398,752		19	22	25	40	85	160	300	500
1844, 44 Over 81 **(b)** . . . .*		32	40	55	100	225	500	1,200	2,600

* Included in number above. **b.** See discussion of date-punch blunders, with images, on the following page.

1846, Small Date
Note squat date,
closed 6.

1846, Medium Date
Note medium height,
ball-top 6.

1846, Tall Date
Note vertically stretched
date, open-mouthed 6.

	Mintage	G-4	VG-8	F-12	VF-20	EF-40	AU-50	MS-60	MS-63BN
1845	3,894,804	$19	$22	$25	$32	$75	$135	$225	$375
1846, All kinds	4,120,800								
1846, Small Date		19	22	25	32	75	135	225	350
1846, Medium Date		19	22	25	35	85	150	250	400
1846, Tall Date		22	28	35	50	150	225	450	900
1847	6,183,669	19	22	25	32	75	135	225	350
1847, 7 Over "Small 7" **(b)**	*	25	35	45	75	175	400	950	1,300

* Included in number above. **b.** See discussion of date-punch blunders, with images, below.

	Mintage	G-4	VG-8	F-12	VF-20	EF-40	AU-50	MS-60	MS-63BN
1848 **(c)**	6,415,799	$19	$22	$25	$32	$75	$130	$225	$350
1849	4,178,500	19	22	25	32	85	150	250	450
1850	4,426,844	19	22	25	32	60	125	180	230

c. The 1848 Small Date cent is a rare contemporary counterfeit.

The following are not true overdates, but are some of the more spectacular of several date-punch blunders of the 1844 through 1854 period. The so-called overdates of 1844 and 1851 each have the date punched upside down, then corrected normally.

1844, 44 Over 81

1847, 7 Over "Small" 7

1851, 51 Over 81

	Mintage	G-4	VG-8	F-12	VF-20	EF-40	AU-50	MS-60	MS-63BN
1851, Normal Date	9,889,707	$19	$22	$25	$32	$60	$125	$180	$230
1851, 51 Over 81	*	25	35	45	65	200	250	500	1,000
1852	5,063,094	19	22	25	32	60	125	180	230
1853	6,641,131	19	22	25	32	60	125	180	230
1854	4,236,156	19	22	25	32	60	125	180	230

* Included in number above.

Original sketches of engraver James B. Longacre's work reveal that the slanting 5's in the following pieces were a peculiarity of his. The figure punch for an upright 5 was probably the work of an apprentice.

1855, Upright 5's   **1855, Slanting 5's**   **Knob on Ear**

	Mintage	G-4	VG-8	F-12	VF-20	EF-40	AU-50	MS-60	MS-63BN
1855, All kinds	1,574,829								
1855, Upright 5's		$19	$24	$25	$32	$60	$125	$180	$230
1855, Slanting 5's		19	24	25	32	65	130	200	275
1855, Slanting 5's, Knob on Ear		20	25	32	50	110	225	360	525
1856, All kinds	2,690,463								
1856, Upright 5		19	22	25	32	65	130	205	270
1856, Slanting 5		19	22	25	32	65	130	205	270

1857, Large Date   **1857, Small Date**

	Mintage	G-4	VG-8	F-12	VF-20	EF-40	AU-50	MS-60	MS-63BN
1857, All kinds	333,546								
1857, Large Date		$60	$80	$100	$125	$200	$300	$400	$750
1857, Small Date		65	85	110	135	200	310	430	800

PASSING OF THE LARGE CENT AND HALF CENT

By 1857, the cost of making and distributing copper coins had risen. Mint Director James Ross Snowden reported that they "barely paid expenses." Both cents and half cents had become unpopular; in fact, they hardly circulated outside the larger cities. The practice of issuing subsidiary silver coins, which began in 1853, brought about a reform of the copper coinage. The half cent was abandoned and a smaller cent was introduced in 1857.

The law of 1857 brought important benefits to the citizens. By its terms, Spanish coins were redeemed and melted at the mint in exchange for new, small cents. The decimal system became popular and official thereafter, and the old method of reckoning in reales, medios, shillings, and so on was gradually given up (although the terms *two bits* and *penny* were still commonly used). The new, convenient small cent won popular favor and soon became a useful instrument of retail trade and a boon to commerce.

The Act of February 21, 1857, provided for the coinage of the new copper-nickel small cent. It also called for Spanish and Mexican coins and old copper cents and half cents in circulation to be brought in and exchanged for U.S. silver coins and the new cents. The cent weighed 72 grains, with a metallic composition of 88% copper and 12% nickel.

The 1856 Flying Eagle cent, a pattern, was made to show Congress how the new cent would look. Additional Proof pieces were struck for sale to collectors. It is believed that between 2,000 and 3,000 pieces were struck in all. These have always been collected along with regular issues because of their early widespread popularity.

Some 1858-dated cents have been deceptively altered to read 1856. They are easy to spot because the shape of the 5 is different on the 1858 than it is on the 1856.

Many varieties are known for 1857 and 1858. In particular, 1858 is found with two major variations. In the Large Letters design, the A and M in AMERICA are joined, while in the Small Letters design they are separated; minor variations of the reverse designs of corn, wheat, cotton, and tobacco also appear. The 1858, 8 Over 7 variety can be identified by a small dot in the field above the first 8—during production, the die was ground down until the 7 was invisible. Coins with the 7 showing are more desirable.

FLYING EAGLE (1856–1858)

Designer James B. Longacre; weight 4.67 grams; composition .880 copper, .120 nickel; diameter 19 mm; plain edge. All coined at Philadelphia Mint.

G-4 Good—All details worn, but readable.
VG-8 Very Good—Details in eagle's feathers and eye evident, but worn.
F-12 Fine—Eagle-head details and feather tips sharp.
VF-20 Very Fine—Considerable detail visible in feathers in right wing and tail.
EF-40 Extremely Fine—Slight wear, all details sharp.
AU-50 About Uncirculated—Slight wear on eagle's left wing and breast.
MS-60 Uncirculated—No trace of wear. Light blemishes.
MS-63 Choice Uncirculated—Some distracting contact marks or blemishes in prime focal areas. Some impairment of luster possible.
PF-63 Choice Proof—Nearly perfect.

Circulation strike.

Proof strike.

| | | 1858, 8 Over 7 | | | Large Letters | | | Small Letters | | |

	Mintage	G-4	VG-8	F-12	VF-20	EF-40	AU-50	MS-60	MS-63	PF-63
1856	2,000	$7,000	$7,500	$9,000	$12,000	$13,500	$14,500	$17,000	$22,000	$17,500
1857	(100) 17,450,000	28	35	45	60	150	200	375	800	8,500
1858, All kinds	24,600,000									
1858, Lg Ltrs (100)		28	35	45	60	150	200	375	800	8,500
1858, 8/7		75	100	200	400	850	1,450	3,400	10,000	
1858, Sm Ltrs (200)		28	35	45	60	150	200	375	800	8,500

INDIAN HEAD (1859–1909)

The "Indian Head" design first issued in 1859 is actually a representation of Liberty wearing an Indian headdress, not an actual Native American. The first year featured a laurel wreath on the reverse. This was changed after one year to the oak wreath with a small shield. Coins of 1859 and early 1860 show a pointed bust. Those made from late 1860 until 1864 have a more rounded bust. Prior to the issuance of nickel five-cent pieces in 1866, these coins were popularly referred to as *nickels* or *nicks*. Later, they were called *white cents*.

G-4 Good—No LIBERTY visible.
VG-8 Very Good—At least some letters of LIBERTY readable on headband.
F-12 Fine—LIBERTY mostly visible.
VF-20 Very Fine—Slight but even wear on LIBERTY.
EF-40 Extremely Fine—LIBERTY sharp. All other details sharp. Only slight wear on ribbon end.
AU-50 About Uncirculated—Very slight trace of wear above the ear and the lowest curl of hair.
MS-60 Uncirculated—No trace of wear. Light blemishes. Values shown are for brown-color coins.
MS-63 Choice Uncirculated—Some distracting contact marks or blemishes in prime focal areas. Impaired luster possible. Values shown are for brown-color coins. Red-brown to red coins are valued higher.

Variety 1 – Copper-Nickel, Laurel Wreath Reverse (1859)

Designer James B. Longacre; weight 4.67 grams; composition .880 copper, .120 nickel; diameter 19 mm; plain edge. All coined at Philadelphia Mint.

Laurel Wreath Reverse, Without Shield
(1859 Only)
Spotted, cleaned, or discolored pieces are worth less than the values shown.

	Mintage	G-4	VG-8	F-12	VF-20	EF-40	AU-50	MS-60	MS-63	PF-63
1859.......(800)...36,400,000		$15	$20	$25	$60	$110	$200	$275	$600	$1,625

Variety 2 – Copper-Nickel, Oak Wreath With Shield (1860–1864)

Standards same as for Variety 1.

Oak Wreath Reverse, With Shield   **Proof strike.**
(1860–1909)
Circulation strike.

	Mintage	G-4	VG-8	F-12	VF-20	EF-40	AU-50	MS-60	MS-63	PF-63
1860......(1,000)..20,566,000		$13	$16	$20	$35	$65	$100	$185	$225	$900
1860, Pointed Bust...........*		18	20	25	50	100	175	300	500	
1861......(1,000)..10,100,000		22	35	45	60	110	175	225	300	1,400
1862........(550)..28,075,000		12	16	20	25	45	70	100	160	725
1863........(460)..49,840,000		12	16	20	25	45	70	100	160	725
1864........(370)..13,740,000		20	30	40	55	100	150	200	225	750

* Included in number above.

Variety 3 – Bronze (1864–1909)

Designer James B. Longacre; weight 3.11 grams; composition .950 copper, .050 tin and zinc; diameter 19 mm; plain edge; mints: Philadelphia, San Francisco.

During the Civil War, nearly all gold and silver, and eventually the copper-nickel cent, disappeared from circulation in the Midwest and East. In larger cities, thin, copper, cent-sized tokens began to be issued by merchants to fill the void left by the missing cents. The government stepped in and with the Act of April 22, 1864, issued its own thin, bronze coin and made the issuance of the merchants' tokens illegal.

The obverse was redesigned near the end of 1864. A slightly sharper portrait included the designer's initial L (for Longacre) on the lower ribbon behind the neck. If the coin is turned slightly (so Indian faces observer) the highlighted details of the L will appear to better advantage. The tip of the bust is pointed on the variety with L, and rounded on the variety without L. This design continued until 1909, when the design was replaced with the Lincoln cent.

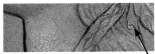

1864, With L on Ribbon　　　　1873, Close 3　　　1873, Open 3

	Mintage	G-4	VG-8	F-12	VF-20	EF-40	AU-50	MS-60	MS-63	PF-63
1864, All kinds 39,233,714										
1864, No L . . . *(150+)*		$14	$20	$25	$45	$70	$90	$115	$150	$1,100
1864, With L . . . *(20+)*		65	95	160	190	280	375	425	600	25,000
$161,000, PF-65 RB, Heritage auction, September 2012										
1865 **(a)** . . . . . . *(500+)* . . 35,429,286		10	15	20	27	45	65	90	150	375
1866 . . . . *(725+)* . . 9,826,500		50	65	80	100	190	250	290	380	400
1867 . . . . *(625+)* . . 9,821,000		50	70	90	135	230	275	300	400	400
1868 . . . . *(600+)* . . 10,266,500		45	50	70	125	170	220	250	360	375
1869 **(a)** . . . . . . *(600+)* . . . 6,420,000		85	120	235	335	445	550	600	700	380
1869, 9 Over 9 . . . . *		125	225	450	575	725	835	975	1,100	
1870, Shallow N **(b)**										
. . . . *(1,000+)* . . . 5,275,000		80	100	220	320	400	500	550	900	425
1870, Bold N **(b)** . . . . *		55	75	200	280	375	450	500	850	325
1871, Shallow N **(b)**										
. . . . *(960+)* . . . 3,929,500		130	180	325	450	575	650	775	950	500
1871, Bold N **(b)** . . . . *		70	85	250	350	475	525	550	800	325
1872, Shallow N **(b)**										
. . . . *(950+)* . . . 4,042,000		100	170	370	425	575	700	950	1,250	
1872, Bold N **(b)** . . . . *		90	140	300	375	500	650	750	1,100	400
1873, All kinds 11,676,500										
1873, Cl 3 . . *(1,100+)*		25	35	65	125	185	235	425	550	265
1873, Doubled LIBERTY		200	350	825	1,750	2,500	5,250	7,500	13,500	
1873, Open 3		22	32	50	85	160	190	250	325	

* Included in number above. **a.** One variety of 1865 appears to show traces of a 4 under the 5 in the date. On other varieties, the tip of the 5 is either plain or curved. The 9 is doubled on some varieties of the 1869; on others it appears to be over an 8, although it is actually a doubled 9. None of these varieties is a true overdate. **b.** Cents dated 1869 and earlier have a shallow N in ONE. Those dated 1870, 1871, or 1872 have either shallow N or bold N. Those dated 1873 to 1876 all have the bold N. Circulation strikes of 1877 have the shallow N, while Proofs have the bold N.

On coins minted from 1859 through mid-1886, the last feather of the headdress points between I and C (Variety 1); on those minted from mid-1886 through 1909, it points between C and A (Variety 2).

| 1875, Dot Reverse | 1886, Variety 1 | 1886, Variety 2 |

	Mintage	G-4	VG-8	F-12	VF-20	EF-40	AU-50	MS-60	MS-63	PF-63
1874........*(700)*	14,187,500	$20.00	$24	$45	$65	$100	$150	$225	$250	$250
1875........*(700)*	13,528,000	22.00	35	60	75	120	160	235	260	250
1875, Dot Reverse **(a)**										—
1876.....*(1,150)*..	7,944,000	35.00	40	70	135	225	240	300	380	250
1877........*(900)*...	852,500	900.00	1,100	1,550	2,000	2,500	3,100	3,800	4,500	2,600
1878......*(2,350)*..	5,797,500	35.00	45	60	110	200	275	325	380	235
1879......*(3,200)*	16,228,000	8.00	12	20	40	70	80	90	140	150
1880......*(3,955)*	38,961,000	5.00	7	9	12	30	60	80	130	150
1881......*(3,575)*	39,208,000	5.00	6	8	11	25	35	60	90	150
1882......*(3,100)*	38,578,000	5.00	6	8	11	25	35	60	90	150
1883......*(6,609)*	45,591,500	5.00	6	8	11	25	35	60	90	150
1884......*(3,942)*	23,257,800	5.50	7	10	14	27	40	75	120	150
1885......*(3,790)*	11,761,594	8.00	9	15	30	65	80	110	200	150
1886, All kinds *(4,290)*	17,650,000									
1886, Var 1		6.00	8	20	50	140	175	200	250	150
1886, Var 2		7.50	12	25	75	175	220	325	500	350

a. This variety has a small, raised dot near the left top of N in ONE. It is believed by some to be a secret mark added to the die in a successful plan to apprehend a Mint employee suspected of stealing coins.

1888, Last 8 Over 7
A less prominent similar variety exists but is valued lower than the clear overdate.

Location of Mintmark S on Reverse of Indian Head Cent (1908 and 1909 Only)

	Mintage	G-4	VG-8	F-12	VF-20	EF-40	AU-50	MS-60	MS-63	PF-63
1887......*(2,960)*..	45,223,523	$3	$4.00	$5	$8.00	$18	$28	$55	$80	$150
1888......*(4,582)*..	37,489,832	3	3.50	5	8.50	22	27	65	125	150
1888, Last 8/7 ....*		1,200	1,500.00	2,000	3,500.00	7,500	16,500	22,500	33,000	
1889......*(3,336)*..	48,866,025	3	3.50	5	7.00	18	27	60	80	150
1890......*(2,740)*..	57,180,114	3	3.50	5	7.00	16	27	60	80	150
1891......*(2,350)*..	47,070,000	3	3.50	5	7.00	16	27	60	80	150
1892......*(2,745)*..	37,647,087	3	3.50	5	8.00	22	27	60	80	150
1893......*(2,195)*..	46,640,000	3	3.50	5	8.00	20	27	60	80	150
1894......*(2,632)*..	16,749,500	5	6.00	12	18.00	50	65	80	115	150
1894, Dbl Date ....*		30	40.00	65	130.00	225	350	575	1,150	
1895......*(2,062)*..	38,341,574	3	3.50	5	8.00	15	25	40	65	160
1896......*(1,862)*..	39,055,431	3	3.50	5	8.00	15	25	40	65	150
1897......*(1,938)*..	50,464,392	3	3.50	5	8.00	15	25	40	65	150

* Included in number above.

	Mintage	G-4	VG-8	F-12	VF-20	EF-40	AU-50	MS-60	MS-63	PF-63
1898......(1,795)...49,821,284		$3	$3.50	$5.00	$8	$15	$25	$40	$65	$150
1899......(2,031)...53,598,000		3	3.50	5.00	8	15	25	40	65	150
1900......(2,262)...66,831,502		2	3.00	4.50	6	10	20	38	55	140
1901......(1,985)...79,609,158		2	3.00	4.50	6	10	20	38	55	140
1902......(2,018)...87,374,704		2	3.00	4.50	6	10	20	38	55	140
1903......(1,790)...85,092,703		2	3.00	4.50	6	10	20	38	55	140
1904......(1,817)...61,326,198		2	3.00	4.50	6	10	20	38	55	140
1905......(2,152)...80,717,011		2	3.00	4.50	6	10	20	38	55	140
1906......(1,725)...96,020,530		2	3.00	4.50	6	10	20	38	55	140
1907......(1,475)...108,137,143		2	3.00	4.50	6	10	20	38	55	140
1908......(1,620)...32,326,367		2	3.00	4.50	6	10	20	38	55	140
1908S...............1,115,000		90	100.00	125.00	145	175	250	290	400	
1909......(2,175)...14,368,470		10	15.00	17.00	20	25	30	45	65	140
1909S...............309,000		550	600.00	675.00	725	825	900	1,000	1,200	

LINCOLN, WHEAT EARS REVERSE (1909–1958)

Victor D. Brenner designed this cent, which was issued to commemorate the 100th anniversary of Abraham Lincoln's birth. The designer's initials (V.D.B.) appear on the reverse of a limited quantity of cents of 1909. The initials were restored, in 1918, to the obverse side on Lincoln's shoulder, as illustrated on page 118. The Lincoln type was the first cent to have the motto IN GOD WE TRUST.

Matte Proof coins were made for collectors from 1909 through 1916, and an exceptional specimen dated 1917 is also reported to exist.

G-4 Good—Date worn but apparent. Lines in wheat heads missing. Full rims.
VG-8 Very Good—Half of lines visible in upper wheat heads.
F-12 Fine—Wheat lines worn but visible.
VF-20 Very Fine—Lincoln's cheekbone and jawbone worn but separated. No worn spots on wheat heads.
EF-40 Extremely Fine—Slight wear. All details sharp.
AU-50 About Uncirculated—Slight wear on cheek and jaw and on wheat stalks.
MS-60 Uncirculated—No trace of wear. Light blemishes. Brown or red-brown color.
MS-63 Uncirculated—No trace of wear. Slight blemishes. Red-brown color.
MS-65 Uncirculated—No trace of wear. Barely noticeable blemishes. Red-brown color.

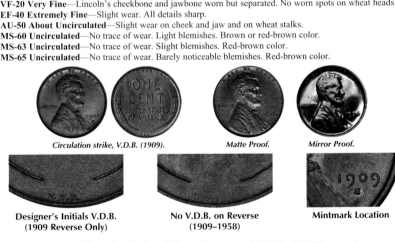

Circulation strike, V.D.B. (1909).   Matte Proof.   Mirror Proof.

Designer's Initials V.D.B.   No V.D.B. on Reverse   Mintmark Location
(1909 Reverse Only)   (1909–1958)

Lincoln, Wheat Ears Reverse (1909–1958)
Variety 1 – Bronze (1909–1942)

Designer Victor D. Brenner; weight 3.11 grams; composition .950 copper, .050 tin and zinc; diameter 19 mm; plain edge; mints: Philadelphia, Denver, San Francisco.

See next page for chart.

Brilliant red Uncirculated cents command higher prices. Discolored or weakly struck pieces are valued lower.

	Mintage	G-4	VG-8	F-12	VF-20	EF-40	AU-50	MS-60	MS-63
1909, V.D.B.	27,995,000	$11.00	$13.00	$15.00	$16.00	$18	$20	$22	$30
1909, V.D.B., Pf (a) (1,194) (b)									2,750
1909S, V.D.B.	484,000	800.00	900.00	1,000.00	1,100.00	1,300	1,500	1,700	2,000
1909	72,702,618	3.50	4.00	4.50	5.00	6	12	17	20
1909, Proof (a) (2,618)									400
1909S	1,825,000	100.00	110.00	125.00	150.00	225	275	325	365
1909S, S Over Horiz S	*	110.00	115.00	135.00	160.00	235	285	340	370
1910	146,801,218	0.35	0.50	0.80	1.40	4	10	18	25
1910, Proof (a) (4,118)									335
1910S	6,045,000	17.00	20.00	22.00	25.00	45	80	100	120
1911	101,177,787	0.45	0.65	1.50	2.50	6	11	21	50
1911, Proof (a) (1,725)									350
1911D	12,672,000	6.00	7.00	10.00	20.00	50	75	95	125
1911S	4,026,000	50.00	55.00	60.00	65.00	85	110	185	235
1912	68,153,060	1.25	1.65	2.25	5.50	13	25	35	50
1912, Proof (a) (2,172)									350
1912D	10,411,000	7.00	8.00	10.00	25.00	65	100	170	240
1912S	4,431,000	24.00	26.00	29.00	40.00	75	110	180	255
1913	76,532,352	0.85	1.00	2.00	4.00	18	27	35	55
1913, Proof (a) (2,983)									375
1913D	15,804,000	3.00	3.50	4.50	10.00	50	70	110	175
1913S	6,101,000	14.00	17.00	20.00	31.00	60	100	175	225
1914	75,238,432	0.75	1.00	2.00	6.00	20	40	55	70
1914, Proof (a) (1,365)									375
1914D (c)	1,193,000	215.00	260.00	385.00	475.00	875	1,500	2,000	3,300
1914S	4,137,000	24.00	28.00	30.00	40.00	85	175	325	460
1915	29,092,120	1.75	2.50	5.00	18.00	60	70	90	105
1915, Proof (a) (1,150)									400
1915D	22,050,000	2.00	3.00	4.00	7.00	22	45	85	120
1915S	4,833,000	20.00	22.00	25.00	30.00	70	135	200	235
1916	131,833,677	0.30	0.50	0.75	2.00	8	13	18	35
1916, Proof (a) (1,050)									1,200
1916D	35,956,000	1.00	1.75	3.00	6.00	15	35	75	150
1916S	22,510,000	1.75	2.25	3.25	8.00	25	50	105	175

* Included in number above. **a.** Matte Proof; valuations are for PF-63 coins. **b.** Reported struck; 400–600 estimated issued. **c.** Beware of altered date or mintmark. No V.D.B. on shoulder of genuine 1914-D cent.

1917, Doubled-Die Obverse

1936, Doubled-Die Obverse

Designer's initials placed on Lincoln's shoulder next to rim, starting 1918.

	Mintage	G-4	VG-8	F-12	VF-20	EF-40	AU-50	MS-60	MS-63
1917	196,429,785	$0.30	$0.40	$0.50	$2.00	$4	$10	$16	$32
1917, Doubled-Die Obverse	*			200.00	425.00	950	1,600	2,750	5,750
1917D	55,120,000	0.80	1.00	1.75	4.50	35	50	80	125
1917S	32,620,000	0.50	0.65	1.00	2.50	10	25	75	160
1918	288,104,634	0.20	0.30	0.50	1.50	3	8	16	27
1918D	47,830,000	0.75	1.25	2.50	4.00	12	35	80	140
1918S	34,680,000	0.50	1.00	2.00	3.00	11	32	80	185

* Included in number above.

SMALL CENTS

	Mintage	G-4	VG-8	F-12	VF-20	EF-40	AU-50	MS-60	MS-63	PF-63
1919	392,021,000	$0.20	$0.30	$0.40	$1.00	$3.25	$5.00	$14	$28	
1919D	57,154,000	0.50	0.75	1.00	4.00	10.00	32.00	65	110	
1919S	139,760,000	0.20	0.40	1.00	2.00	6.00	18.00	50	115	
1920	310,165,000	0.20	0.30	0.35	0.50	2.25	4.00	15	28	
1920D	49,280,000	1.00	1.50	3.00	6.50	19.00	40.00	80	110	
1920S	46,220,000	0.50	0.65	1.50	2.25	10.00	35.00	110	185	
1921	39,157,000	0.50	0.60	1.30	2.10	9.00	22.00	50	80	
1921S	15,274,000	1.50	2.25	3.50	7.00	35.00	75.00	135	190	
1922D	7,160,000	20.00	21.00	25.00	27.00	40.00	75.00	110	165	
1922, No D (d)	*	750.00	850.00	1,200.00	1,650.00	3,100.00	6,250.00	11,000	27,000	
1922, Weak D	*	30.00	40.00	55.00	80.00	190.00	225.00	400	1,000	
1923	74,723,000	0.35	0.45	0.65	1.00	5.00	9.50	15	30	
1923S	8,700,000	4.00	5.25	7.00	10.00	40.00	90.00	220	390	
1924	75,178,000	0.20	0.30	0.40	0.85	5.00	10.00	24	50	
1924D	2,520,000	40.00	45.00	50.00	60.00	125.00	200.00	320	350	
1924S	11,696,000	1.30	1.50	2.75	5.50	20.00	75.00	125	225	
1925	139,949,000	0.20	0.25	0.35	0.60	3.00	6.50	10	20	
1925D	22,580,000	0.85	1.30	2.45	4.00	13.00	30.00	75	90	
1925S	26,380,000	0.75	1.00	1.85	2.75	12.00	30.00	90	200	
1926	157,088,000	0.20	0.25	0.30	0.50	2.00	4.00	8	18	
1926D	28,020,000	1.35	1.75	3.50	5.25	14.00	32.00	85	125	
1926S	4,550,000	9.00	10.00	13.00	17.00	35.00	75.00	155	325	
1927	144,440,000	0.20	0.25	0.30	0.60	2.00	3.50	10	20	
1927D	27,170,000	1.25	1.75	2.75	3.75	7.50	25.00	62	85	
1927S	14,276,000	1.50	2.00	3.00	5.00	15.00	40.00	85	140	
1928	134,116,000	0.20	0.25	0.30	0.60	2.00	3.00	9	13	
1928D	31,170,000	0.75	1.00	1.75	3.00	5.50	17.00	37	80	
1928S (e)	17,266,000	1.00	1.60	2.75	3.75	9.50	30.00	75	100	
1929	185,262,000	0.20	0.25	0.30	0.75	2.00	4.00	8	14	
1929D	41,730,000	0.40	0.85	1.25	2.25	5.50	13.00	25	37	
1929S	50,148,000	0.50	0.90	1.65	2.35	5.80	14.00	21	29	
1930	157,415,000	0.15	0.20	0.25	0.50	1.25	2.00	6	10	
1930D	40,100,000	0.20	0.25	0.30	0.55	2.50	4.00	12	28	
1930S	24,286,000	0.20	0.25	0.30	0.60	1.75	6.00	10	12	
1931	19,396,000	0.50	0.75	1.00	1.50	4.00	9.00	20	35	
1931D	4,480,000	5.25	6.00	7.00	8.50	13.50	37.00	60	70	
1931S	866,000	110.00	120.00	130.00	135.00	150.00	165.00	175	195	
1932	9,062,000	1.50	1.75	2.00	2.50	4.50	12.00	20	28	
1932D	10,500,000	1.50	1.75	2.50	2.75	4.50	11.00	19	28	
1933	14,360,000	1.50	1.75	2.50	3.00	6.25	13.00	20	30	
1933D	6,200,000	3.50	3.75	5.50	7.25	12.00	19.00	26	35	
1934	219,080,000	0.15	0.18	0.20	0.30	1.00	4.00	10	15	
1934D	28,446,000	0.20	0.25	0.50	0.75	2.25	7.50	22	27	
1935	245,388,000	0.15	0.18	0.20	0.25	0.50	1.00	3	6	
1935D	47,000,000	0.15	0.18	0.20	0.25	0.50	2.00	5	8	
1935S	38,702,000	0.15	0.18	0.25	0.50	2.00	5.00	12	17	
1936 (5,569)	309,632,000	0.15	0.18	0.25	0.50	1.50	2.60	5	10	$200
1936, DblDie Obv (f)	*	—	—	72.50	120.00	200.00	350.00	485	2,250	

* Included in number above. **d.** 1922 cents with a weak or missing mintmark were made from extremely worn dies that originally struck normal 1922-D cents. Three different die pairs were involved; two of them produced "Weak D" coins. One die pair (no. 2, identified by a "strong reverse") is acknowledged as striking "No D" coins. Weak D cents are worth considerably less. Beware of removed mintmark. **e.** Large and small mintmark varieties; see page 22. **f.** Values are for pieces with strong doubling, as illustrated on page 118.

Chart continued on next page.

	Mintage	G-4	VG-8	F-12	VF-20	EF-40	AU-50	MS-60	MS-63	PF-63
1936D	40,620,000	$0.15	$0.20	$0.30	$0.50	$1.00	$2.00	$4	$5	
1936S	29,130,000	0.15	0.25	0.40	0.55	1.00	3.00	5	7	
1937	(9,320)	309,170,000	0.15	0.20	0.30	0.50	1.00	2.00	3	4	$65
1937D	50,430,000	0.15	0.20	0.25	0.40	1.00	3.00	5	8	
1937S	34,500,000	0.15	0.20	0.30	0.40	1.00	3.00	5	10	
1938	(14,734)	156,682,000	0.15	0.20	0.30	0.40	1.00	2.00	4	9	60
1938D	20,010,000	0.20	0.30	0.50	0.80	1.25	3.00	4	9	
1938S	15,180,000	0.40	0.50	0.60	0.75	1.10	3.00	4	8	
1939	(13,520)	316,466,000	0.15	0.18	0.20	0.25	0.50	1.00	2	3	55
1939D	15,160,000	0.50	0.60	0.65	0.85	1.25	3.00	4	6	
1939S	52,070,000	0.15	0.20	0.30	0.75	1.00	2.50	3	5	
1940	(15,872)	586,810,000	0.15	0.18	0.20	0.40	0.60	1.00	2	3	45
1940D	81,390,000	0.15	0.18	0.25	0.60	0.75	2.00	3	5	
1940S	112,940,000	0.15	0.18	0.20	0.50	1.00	1.75	3	5	
1941	(21,100)	887,018,000	0.15	0.18	0.20	0.30	0.60	1.50	2	4	40
1941D	128,700,000	0.15	0.18	0.20	0.50	1.00	3.00	4	6	
1941S (g)	92,360,000	0.15	0.18	0.30	0.50	1.00	3.00	4	6	
1942	(32,600)	657,796,000	0.15	0.18	0.20	0.25	0.50	0.75	1	3	41
1942D	206,698,000	0.15	0.18	0.20	0.25	0.50	0.85	1	3	
1942S	85,590,000	0.20	0.25	0.30	0.85	1.25	5.50	7	11	

g. Large and small mintmark varieties; see page 22.

Variety 2 – Zinc-Coated Steel (1943)

Due to a copper shortage during the critical war year 1943, the Treasury used zinc-coated steel to make cents. Although no bronze cents were officially issued that year, a few specimens struck on bronze or silver planchets by error are known to exist; bronze examples have sold for over $200,000 in recent years. Through a similar error, a few 1944 cents were struck on steel planchets. Beware the many regular steel cents of 1943 that were later plated with copper, either as novelties or to deceive; a magnet will reveal their true nature. For more on the 1943 bronze cent, see appendix A.

1943—Weight 2.70 grams; composition, steel coated with zinc; diameter 19 mm; plain edge.

1943-D, Boldly Doubled Mintmark

	Mintage	F-12	VF-20	EF-40	AU-50	MS-63	MS-65
1943	684,628,670	$0.30	$0.35	$0.40	$0.50	$2.50	$8
1943D	217,660,000	0.35	0.40	0.45	0.75	3.00	10
1943D, Boldly Doubled Mintmark	*	40.00	50.00	80.00	110.00	200.00	1,500
1943S	191,550,000	0.40	0.65	0.75	1.00	6.00	20

* Included in number above.

Variety 1 (Bronze) Resumed (1944–1958)

Cartridge cases were salvaged for coinage of 1944 through 1946. Although the color was slightly different for Uncirculated specimens, the coins were satisfactory overall.

1944–1946—Weight, 3.11 grams; composition .950 copper, .050 zinc; diameter 19 mm; plain edge.
1947–1958—Weight 3.11 grams; composition .950 copper, .050 tin and zinc; diameter 19 mm.

1944-D, D Over S

SMALL CENTS

	Mintage	VF-20	EF-40	AU-50	MS-63	MS-65	PF-65
1944	1,435,400,000	$0.10	$0.20	$0.35	$1.00	$5	
1944D	430,578,000	0.10	0.20	0.35	0.85	4	
1944D, D Over S (a)	*	125.00	180.00	235.00	450.00	650	
1944S	282,760,000	0.15	0.20	0.35	0.85	4	
1945	1,040,515,000	0.10	0.20	0.35	0.85	2	
1945D	266,268,000	0.10	0.20	0.35	0.85	2	
1945S	181,770,000	0.15	0.20	0.35	0.85	2	
1946	991,655,000	0.10	0.20	0.35	0.60	2	
1946D	315,690,000	0.10	0.20	0.35	0.60	2	
1946S	198,100,000	0.15	0.20	0.35	0.60	2	
1946S, S Over D	*	35.00	75.00	125.00	250.00		
1947	190,555,000	0.10	0.20	0.40	1.00	3	
1947D	194,750,000	0.10	0.20	0.40	0.60	2	
1947S	99,000,000	0.20	0.25	0.50	0.85	2	
1948	317,570,000	0.10	0.20	0.35	0.85	2	
1948D	172,637,500	0.10	0.20	0.35	0.60	2	
1948S	81,735,000	0.20	0.30	0.35	1.00	3	
1949	217,775,000	0.10	0.20	0.35	1.00	3	
1949D	153,132,500	0.10	0.20	0.35	1.00	3	
1949S	64,290,000	0.25	0.30	0.35	2.00	4	
1950 (51,386)	272,635,000	0.10	0.20	0.35	0.85	2	$70
1950D	334,950,000	0.10	0.20	0.35	0.60	2	
1950S	118,505,000	0.15	0.25	0.35	0.85	2	
1951 (57,500)	284,576,000	0.10	0.25	0.35	0.70	2	65
1951D	625,355,000	0.10	0.12	0.35	0.60	2	
1951S	136,010,000	0.25	0.30	0.50	1.00	3	
1952 (81,980)	186,775,000	0.10	0.15	0.35	1.00	3	55
1952D	746,130,000	0.10	0.15	0.25	0.75	2	
1952S	137,800,004	0.15	0.20	0.35	2.00	4	
1953 (128,800)	256,755,000	0.10	0.15	0.20	0.50	1	30
1953D	700,515,000	0.10	0.15	0.20	0.50	1	
1953S	181,835,000	0.10	0.15	0.20	0.60	2	
1954 (233,300)	71,640,050	0.25	0.35	0.45	0.60	2	20
1954D	251,552,500	0.10	0.12	0.20	0.50	1	
1954S	96,190,000	0.10	0.12	0.20	0.50	1	

* Included in number above. a. Varieties exist.

The popular 1955 doubled-die error coins (illustrated below) were made from improperly prepared dies that show a fully doubled outline of the date and legend. Do not confuse these with less-valuable pieces showing only minor traces of doubling. Counterfeits exist.

1955, Doubled-Die Obverse

	Mintage	VF-20	EF-40	AU-50	MS-63	MS-65	PF-65
1955 (378,200)	330,958,200	$0.10	$0.12	$0.15	$0.35	$1	$18
1955, Doubled-Die Obverse	*	1,750.00	2,000.00	2,100.00	3,500.00 (a)	14,500	
1955D	563,257,500	0.10	0.12	0.15	0.35	1	
1955S	44,610,000	0.20	0.30	0.40	0.85	3	

* Included in number above. a. Value for MS-60 is $2,600.

Chart continued on next page.

	Mintage	VF-20	EF-40	AU-50	MS-63	MS-65	PF-65
1956 . . . . (669,384) . . . 420,745,000		$0.10	$0.12	$0.15	$0.35	$1	$6
1956D 1,098,201,100		0.10	0.12	0.15	0.30	1	
1956D, D Above Shadow D . . . . *		10.00	25.00	30.00	35.00		
1957 . . . . (1,247,952) . . . 282,540,000		0.10	0.12	0.15	0.30	1	6
1957D 1,051,342,000		0.10	0.12	0.15	0.30	1	
1958 . . . . (875,652) . . . 252,525,000		0.10	0.12	0.15	0.30	1	6
1958, DblDie Obv (3 known) . . . . *					—		
1958D 800,953,300		0.10	0.12	0.15	0.30	1	

* Included in number above.

LINCOLN, MEMORIAL REVERSE (1959–2008)

Frank Gasparro designed the Lincoln Memorial reverse, which was introduced in 1959 on the 150th anniversary of Abraham Lincoln's birth.

Copper Alloy (1959–1982)

Designer Victor D. Brenner (obv), Frank Gasparro (rev); mints: Philadelphia, Denver, San Francisco. 1959–1962—Weight 3.11 grams; composition .950 copper, .050 tin and zinc; diameter 19 mm; plain edge. 1962–1982—Weight 3.11 grams; composition .950 copper, .050 zinc. 1982 to date—Weight 2.5 grams; composition copper-plated zinc (core: .992 zinc, .008 copper, with a plating of pure copper; total content .975 zinc, .025 copper).

1960, Small Date   1960, Large Date

	Mintage	MS-63	MS-65	PF-65
1959 . . . . (1,149,291) . . . 609,715,000		$0.20	$0.30	$3.00
1959D 1,279,760,000		0.50	0.55	
1960, Large Date . . . . (1,691,602) . . . 586,405,000		0.20	0.30	2.00
1960, Small Date . . . . *		3.00	7.00	22.00
1960, Large Date Over Small Date . . . . *				—
1960, Small Date Over Large Date . . . . *				—
1960D, Large Date 1,580,884,000		0.20	0.30	
1960D, Small Date . . . . *		0.20	0.30	
1960D, D Over D, Small Date Over Large Date . . . . *		200.00	500.00	
1961 . . . . (3,028,244) . . . 753,345,000		0.15	0.30	1.50
1961D 1,753,266,700		0.15	0.30	
1962 . . . . (3,218,019) . . . 606,045,000		0.15	0.30	1.50
1962D 1,793,148,140		0.15	0.30	
1963 . . . . (3,075,645) . . . 754,110,000		0.15	0.30	1.50
1963D 1,774,020,400		0.15	0.30	
1964 . . . . (3,950,762) . . . 2,648,575,000		0.15	0.30	1.50
1964D 3,799,071,500		0.15	0.30	
1965 1,497,224,900		0.20	0.50	
1966 2,188,147,783		0.20	0.50	
1967 3,048,667,100		0.20	0.50	
1968 1,707,880,970		0.25	0.60	
1968D 2,886,269,600		0.15	0.40	
1968S . . . . (3,041,506) . . . 258,270,001		0.15	0.40	1.00

* Included in number above.

In 1969, the dies were modified to strengthen the design, and Lincoln's head was made slightly smaller. In 1973, dies were further modified and the engraver's initials FG made larger. The initials were reduced slightly in 1974. During 1982 the dies were again modified and the bust, lettering, and date made slightly smaller. One variety of the 1984 cent shows Lincoln's ear doubled. Some 1,579,324 cents dated 1974 were struck in aluminum as experimental pieces. None were placed in circulation, and most were later destroyed. One was preserved for the National Numismatic Collection in the Smithsonian Institution. Other 1974 experimental cents were struck in bronze-clad steel.

1969-S, Doubled-Die Obverse

1970-S, Small Date (High 7)

1970-S, Large Date (Low 7)

1971-S, Proof Doubled-Die Obverse

1972, Doubled-Die Obverse

1982, Large Date

1982, Small Date

	Mintage	MS-65	PF-65
1969	1,136,910,000	$0.70	
1969D	4,002,832,200	0.30	
1969S	(2,934,631)		$1
	544,375,000	0.50	
1969S, DblDie Obv	*	(a)	
1970	1,898,315,000	0.65	
1970D	2,891,438,900	0.30	
1970S, All kinds	(2,632,810)		
	690,560,004		
1970S, Sm Dt (High 7)		55.00	40
1970S, Lg Dt (Low 7)		0.50	1
1970S, DblDie Obv		—	
1971	1,919,490,000	0.60	
1971, DblDie Obv	*	1,000.00	
1971D	2,911,045,600	0.50	
1971S	(3,220,733)		1
	525,133,459	0.50	
1971S, DblDie Obv	*		650
1972	2,933,255,000	0.30	
1972, DblDie Obv (b)	*	625.00	
1972D	2,665,071,400	0.30	
1972S	(3,260,996)		1
	376,939,108	0.75	
1973	3,728,245,000	0.30	
1973D	3,549,576,588	0.30	
1973S	(2,760,339)		1
	317,177,295	0.85	
1974	4,232,140,523	0.30	
1974D	4,235,098,000	0.30	

	Mintage	MS-65	PF-65
1974S	(2,612,568)		$1.00
	409,426,660	$0.75	
1975	5,451,476,142	0.30	
1975D	4,505,275,300	0.30	
1975S	(2,845,450)		3.50
1976	4,674,292,426	0.30	
1976D	4,221,592,455	0.30	
1976S	(4,149,730)		3.20
1977	4,469,930,000	0.30	
1977D	4,194,062,300	0.30	
1977S	(3,251,152)		2.50
1978	5,558,605,000	0.30	
1978D	4,280,233,400	0.30	
1978S	(3,127,781)		2.50
1979	6,018,515,000	0.30	
1979D	4,139,357,254	0.30	
1979S, Type 1 (c)	(3,677,175)		5.00
1979S, Type 2 (c)	*		6.00
1980	7,414,705,000	0.30	
1980D	5,140,098,660	0.30	
1980S	(3,554,806)		2.50
1981	7,491,750,000	0.30	
1981D	5,373,235,677	0.30	
1981S, Type 1 (c)	(4,063,083)		3.00
1981S, Type 2 (c)	*		25.00
1982, Large Date	10,712,525,000	0.35	
1982, Small Date	*	0.50	
1982D	6,012,979,368	0.30	
1982S	(3,857,479)		2.50

* Included in number above. **a.** Value for an MS-63 coin is $50,000. **b.** Other slightly doubled varieties (worth far less) exist. **c.** See page 234 for illustrations of Type 1 and Type 2 varieties.

Copper-Plated Zinc (1982–2008)

The composition for this period changed to copper-plated zinc. The core is 99.2% zinc, 0.8% copper, with a plating of pure copper; the weight is 2.5 grams (approximately 20% lighter than the copper alloy cents).

1983, Doubled-Die Reverse   1984, Doubled Ear Variety   1995, Doubled-Die Obverse

	Mintage	MS-65	PF-65
1982, Large Date . . . . **(a)**		$0.50	
1982, Small Date . . . . **(a)**		0.85	
1982D, Large Date . . . . **(a)**		0.40	
1982D, Small Date . . . . **(a)**		0.30	
1983 7,752,355,000		0.30	
1983, DblDie Rev . . . . *		385.00	
1983D 6,467,199,428		0.30	
1983S . . . . (3,279,126)			$3
1984 8,151,079,000		0.30	
1984, Doubled Ear . . . . *		230.00	
1984D 5,569,238,906		0.30	
1984S . . . . (3,065,110)			4
1985 5,648,489,887		0.30	
1985D 5,287,339,926		0.30	
1985S . . . . (3,362,821)			5
1986 4,491,395,493		0.30	
1986D 4,442,866,698		0.30	
1986S . . . . (3,010,497)			7
1987 4,682,466,931		0.30	
1987D 4,879,389,514		0.30	
1987S . . . . (4,227,728)			5
1988 6,092,810,000		0.30	
1988D 5,253,740,443		0.30	
1988S . . . . (3,262,948)			9
1989 7,261,535,000		0.30	
1989D 5,345,467,111		0.30	
1989S . . . . (3,220,194)			9
1990 6,851,765,000		0.30	
1990D 4,922,894,533		0.30	
1990S . . . . (3,299,559)			5
1990, Proof, No S . . . . *			5,000
1991 5,165,940,000		0.30	
1991D 4,158,446,076		0.30	
1991S . . . . (2,867,787)			12
1992 4,648,905,000		0.30	
1992, Close AM **(b)** . . . . *		—	
1992D 4,448,673,300		0.30	
1992D, Close AM **(b)** . . . . *		—	
1992S . . . . (4,176,560)			5
1993 5,684,705,000		0.30	
1993D 6,426,650,571		0.30	

	Mintage	MS-65	PF-65
1993S . . . . (3,394,792)			$9.00
1994 6,500,850,000		$0.30	
1994D 7,131,765,000		0.30	
1994S . . . . (3,269,923)			9.00
1995 6,411,440,000		0.30	
1995, DblDie Obv . . . . *		50.00	
1995D 7,128,560,000		0.30	
1995S . . . . (2,797,481)			9.00
1996 6,612,465,000		0.30	
1996, Wide AM **(b)** . . . . *		—	
1996D 6,510,795,000		0.30	
1996S . . . . (2,525,265)			4.50
1997 4,622,800,000		0.30	
1997D 4,576,555,000		0.30	
1997S . . . . (2,796,678)			10.00
1998 5,032,155,000		0.30	
1998, Wide AM **(b)** . . . . *		25.00	
1998D 5,225,353,500		0.30	
1998S . . . . (2,086,507)			9.00
1998S, Close AM **(b)** . . . . *		—	
1999 5,237,600,000		0.30	
1999, Wide AM **(b)** . . . . *		500.00	
1999D 6,360,065,000		0.30	
1999S . . . . (3,347,966)			6.00
1999S, Close AM **(b)** . . . . *			90.00
2000 5,503,200,000		0.30	
2000, Wide AM **(b)** . . . . *		20.00	
2000D 8,774,220,000		0.30	
2000S . . . . (4,047,993)			4.00
2001 4,959,600,000		0.30	
2001D 5,374,990,000		0.30	
2001S . . . . (3,184,606)			4.00
2002 3,260,800,000		0.30	
2002D 4,028,055,000		0.30	
2002S . . . . (3,211,995)			4.00
2003 3,300,000,000		0.30	
2003D 3,548,000,000		0.30	
2003S . . . . (3,298,439)			4.00
2004 3,379,600,000		0.30	
2004D 3,456,400,000		0.30	
2004S . . . . (2,965,422)			4.00

* Included in number above. **a.** Included in previous chart. **b.** Varieties were made using Proof dies that have a wide space between A and M in AMERICA. The letters nearly touch on other circulation-strike cents after 1993.

	Mintage	MS-65	PF-65
2005	3,935,600,000	$0.30	
2005D	3,764,450,500	0.30	
2005S	(3,344,679)		$4
2006	4,290,000,000	0.30	
2006D	3,944,000,000	0.30	
2006S	(3,054,436)		4

	Mintage	MS-65	PF-65
2007	3,762,400,000	$0.30	
2007D	3,638,800,000	0.30	
2007S	(2,577,166)		$4
2008	2,558,800,000	0.30	
2008D	2,849,600,000	0.30	
2008S	(2,169,561)		4

Some of the cents minted since 1994 show the faint trace of a mintmark, believed to be the result of the letter's having been removed from the master hub during production of working dies for coinage. So-called phantom mintmark pieces were produced in Philadelphia but show traces of either a D or an S. Values for such pieces vary according to date and condition but are not significantly higher than for normal pieces.

LINCOLN, BICENTENNIAL (2009)

One-cent coins issued during 2009 are a unique tribute to President Abraham Lincoln, recognizing the bicentennial of his birth and the 100th anniversary of the first issuance of the Lincoln cent. These coins use four different design themes on the reverse to represent the four major aspects of President Lincoln's life. The obverse of each of these coins carries the traditional portrait of Lincoln that has been in use since 1909.

The special reverse designs, released as quarterly issues throughout 2009, are as follows. The first, Birth and Early Childhood in Kentucky (designer, Richard Masters; sculptor, Jim Licaretz), depicts a small log cabin like the one in which Lincoln was born. The second, Formative Years in Indiana (designer and sculptor, Charles Vickers), shows a youthful Abe Lincoln taking a break from rail-splitting to read a book. On the third coin, Professional Life in Illinois (designer, Joel Iskowitz; sculptor, Don Everhart), Lincoln stands in front of the state capitol of Illinois. The design commemorates his pre-presidential career in law and politics. Finally, Presidency in Washington (designer, Susan Gamble; sculptor, Joseph Menna), depicts the partially completed U.S. Capitol dome as it appeared when Lincoln held office. The state of the Capitol represents "the unfinished business of a nation torn apart by slavery and the Civil War." Lincoln Bicentennial cents issued for commercial circulation are made of the exact same copper-plated composition used since 1982. Special versions included in satin-finish collector sets are made of the same metallic composition as was used for the original 1909 cents (95% copper, 5% tin and zinc).

The Mint-packaged Abraham Lincoln Coin and Chronicles set of four 2009-S Proof cents and the Lincoln commemorative silver dollar are listed on page 343.

Birth and Early Childhood reverse	**Formative Years reverse**	**Professional Life reverse**	**Presidency reverse**

	Mintage	MS-65	PF-65
2009, Birth and Early Childhood	284,400,000	$0.30	
2009, Birth and Early Childhood, copper, Satin finish		10.00	
2009D, Birth and Early Childhood	350,400,000	0.30	
2009D, Birth and Early Childhood, copper, Satin finish		10.00	
2009S, Birth and Early Childhood, copper	(2,995,615)		$4

Several varieties with minor die doubling exist. Values vary according to the severity of the doubling.

Chart continued on next page.

	Mintage	MS-65	PF-65
2009, Formative Years	376,000,000	$0.30	
2009, Formative Years, copper, Satin finish		10.00	
2009D, Formative Years	363,600,000	0.30	
2009D, Formative Years, copper, Satin finish		10.00	
2009S, Formative Years, copper	(2,995,615)		$4
2009, Professional Life	316,000,000	0.30	
2009, Professional Life, copper, Satin finish		10.00	
2009D, Professional Life	336,000,000	0.30	
2009D, Professional Life, copper, Satin finish		10.00	
2009S, Professional Life, copper	(2,995,615)		4
2009, Presidency	129,600,000	0.30	
2009, Presidency, copper, Satin finish		10.00	
2009D, Presidency	198,000,000	0.30	
2009D, Presidency, copper, Satin finish		10.00	
2009S, Presidency, copper	(2,995,615)		4

Several varieties with minor die doubling exist. Values vary according to the severity of the doubling.

LINCOLN, SHIELD REVERSE (2010 TO DATE)

Since the conclusion of the 2009 Bicentennial One-Cent Program, one-cent coins feature a reverse that has "an image emblematic of President Lincoln's preservation of the United States of America as a single and united country."

Weight 2.5 grams; composition copper-plated zinc (core: .992 zinc, .008 copper, with a plating of pure copper; total content .975 zinc, .025 copper); diameter 19 mm; plain edge; mints: Philadelphia, Denver, San Francisco.

Circulation strike.　　　　*Proof strike.*

	Mintage	MS-65	PF-65
2010	1,963,630,000	$0.30	
2010D	2,047,200,000	0.30	
2010S	(1,689,364)		$4
2011	2,402,400,000	0.30	
2011D	2,536,140,000	0.30	
2011S	(1,453,276)		4
2012	3,132,000,000	0.30	
2012D	2,883,200,000	0.30	
2012S			4
2013		0.30	
2013D		0.30	
2013S			4

The Act of April 22, 1864, which changed the weight and composition of the cent, included a provision for a bronze two-cent piece. The weight was specified as 96 grains, the alloy being the same as for the cent. The two-cent piece is one of the shortest-lived issues of United States coinage. The motto IN GOD WE TRUST appeared for the first time on the new coin, with the personal support of Treasury Secretary Salmon P. Chase. There are two varieties for the first year of issue, 1864: the Small Motto, which is scarce, and the Large Motto. See illustrations at right. On the obverse, the D in GOD is narrow on the Large Motto. The stem to the leaf shows plainly on the Small Motto variety. There is no stem on the Large Motto. The first T in TRUST is very close to the ribbon crease at left on the Small Motto variety; there is a 1 mm gap on the Large Motto variety.

The shield device is very similar to that on the nickel five-cent piece introduced in 1866. Listed Proof mintages are estimates.

Designer James B. Longacre; weight 6.22 grams; composition .950 copper, .050 tin and zinc; diameter 23 mm; plain edge. All coined at Philadelphia Mint.

G-4 Good—At least part of IN GOD visible.
F-12 Fine—Complete motto visible. The word WE weak.
VF-20 Very Fine—WE is clear, but not strong.
EF-40 Extremely Fine—The word WE bold.
AU-50 About Uncirculated—Traces of wear visible on leaf tips, arrow points, and the word WE.
MS-60 Uncirculated—No trace of wear. Light blemishes.
MS-63 Choice Uncirculated—Some distracting contact marks or blemishes in prime focal areas. Some impairment of luster possible.
PF-63 Choice Proof—Attractive, mirrorlike fields. Minimal hairlines. Only a few blemishes in secondary focal areas.

1864, Small Motto

1864, Large Motto

Circulation strike.   Proof strike.

Brilliant red choice Uncirculated and Proof coins command higher prices. Spotted, cleaned, or discolored pieces are valued lower.

	Mintage	G-4	F-12	VF-20	EF-40	AU-50	MS-60	MS-63BN	PF-63BN
1864, Small Motto	*	$215	$375	$500	$750	$950	$1,400	$1,750	$18,500
1864, Large Motto . . *(100+)*	19,822,500	18	25	30	50	80	110	175	535
1865 **(a)** . . . . *(500+)*	13,640,000	18	25	30	50	80	110	175	450
1866 . . . . *(725+)* . .	3,177,000	19	27	32	50	80	120	185	450
1867 . . . . *(625+)* . .	2,938,750	19	28	35	50	80	130	190	450
1867, DblDie Obv . . . . **		100	200	300	600	850	1,350	2,500	
1868 . . . . *(600+)* . .	2,803,750	20	36	50	75	110	150	225	450
1869 . . . . *(600+)* . .	1,546,500	22	38	55	80	125	160	225	450
1870 . . . . *(1,000+)*	861,250	32	55	85	135	200	275	325	450
1871 . . . . *(960+)*	721,250	40	85	110	150	225	300	375	450
1872 . . . . *(950+)*	65,000	375	600	800	1,050	1,650	2,800	3,500	900
1873, Close 3, Proof only . . . . *(600)*	*		1,400	1,500	1,650				3,000
1873, Open 3, Restrike . . . . . *(500)*			1,100	1,300	1,400				2,750

* Included in number below. ** Included in number above. **a.** Varieties show the tip of the 5 either plain or curved.

SILVER THREE-CENT PIECES (TRIMES) (1851–1873)

This smallest of United States silver coins, called the *trime* by the Treasury Department, was authorized by Congress March 3, 1851. The first three-cent silver pieces had no lines bordering the six-pointed star. From 1854 through 1858 there were two lines, while issues of the final 15 years show only one line. Issues from 1854 through 1873 have an olive sprig over the III and a bundle of three arrows beneath. Nearly the entire production of non-Proof coins from 1863 to 1872 was melted in 1873.

Designer James B. Longacre. 1851–1853—Weight .80 gram; composition .750 silver, .250 copper; diameter 14 mm; plain edge; mints: Philadelphia, New Orleans. 1854–1873—Weight .75 gram; composition .900 silver, .100 copper; diameter 14 mm; plain edge.

G-4 Good—Star worn smooth. Legend and date readable.
VG-8 Very Good—Outline of shield defined. Legend and date clear.
F-12 Fine—Only star points worn smooth.
VF-20 Very Fine—Only partial wear on star ridges.
EF-40 Extremely Fine—Ridges on star points (coins of 1854 onward) visible.
AU-50 About Uncirculated—Trace of wear visible at each star point. Center of shield possibly weak.
MS-60 Uncirculated—No trace of wear. Light blemishes.
MS-63 Choice Uncirculated—Some distracting contact marks or blemishes in prime focal areas. Some impairment of luster possible.

Proof strike.

Mintmark location.

| **Variety 1 (1851–1853)** | **Variety 2 (1854–1858)** | **Variety 3 (1859–1873)** | **1862, 2 Over 1** |

Circulation strikes.

Well-struck specimens of Variety 2 command higher prices.

	Mintage	G-4	VG-8	F-12	VF-20	EF-40	AU-50	MS-60	MS-63	PF-63
1851	5,447,400	$27	$35	$50	$60	$80	$150	$175	$275	—
1851O	720,000	38	50	70	100	175	250	400	650	
1852, 1/Inv 2	*				—	775	950	1,150	1,425	
1852	18,663,500	27	35	50	60	80	150	175	275	—
1853	11,400,000	27	35	50	60	80	150	175	275	
1854	671,000	27	35	50	70	120	225	350	675	$13,000
1855	139,000	38	45	60	110	200	350	600	1,100	5,000
1856	1,458,000	27	35	50	70	120	235	360	700	4,300
1857	1,042,000	27	35	50	70	120	235	360	700	3,750
1858	(210)..1,603,700	27	35	50	70	120	235	360	700	2,750
1859	(800)...364,200	27	35	50	60	90	175	215	285	525
1860	(1,000)...286,000	27	35	50	60	90	175	215	285	525
1861	(1,000)...497,000	27	35	50	60	90	175	215	285	525
1862, 2/1	*	27	35	50	60	95	185	225	350	
1862	(550)...343,000	27	35	50	60	90	175	215	285	525
1863, So-called 3 Over 2	*									1,800
1863	(460)....21,000	300	325	350	375	435	550	650	1,000	650
1864	(470)....12,000	300	325	350	375	435	550	650	1,000	650
1865	(500).....8,000	325	350	425	450	475	575	675	1,100	650
1866	(725)....22,000	300	325	350	400	425	480	630	950	650
1867	(625).....4,000	325	350	425	450	475	525	675	1,300	650

* Included in number below.

	Mintage	F-12	VF-20	EF-40	AU-50	MS-60	MS-63	PF-63
1868. . . . . (600) 3,500		$425	$450	$475	$550	$690	$1,400	$650
1869. . . . . (600) 4,500		425	475	525	600	700	1,400	650
1870. . . . .(1,000) 3,000		425	450	475	550	675	1,300	650
1871. . . . . (960) 3,400		425	450	475	500	650	1,000	650
1872. . . . . (950) 1,000		450	475	500	600	1,000	1,800	700
1873 (Close 3, Proof only). . . . . . . (600)					825			2,000

NICKEL THREE-CENT PIECES (1865–1889)

Nickel three-cent pieces were issued because their silver counterpart was hoarded by the public.

Designer James B. Longacre; weight 1.94 grams; composition .750 copper, .250 nickel; diameter 17.9 mm; plain edge. All coined at Philadelphia Mint.

G-4 Good—Date and legends complete though worn. III smooth.
VG-8 Very Good—III half worn. Rims complete.
VF-20 Very Fine—Three-quarters of hair details visible.
EF-40 Extremely Fine—Slight, even wear.
AU-50 About Uncirculated—Slight wear on hair curls, above forehead, and on wreath and numeral III.
MS-60 Uncirculated—No trace of wear. Light blemishes.
MS-63 Choice Uncirculated—Some distracting contact marks or blemishes in prime focal areas. Some impairment of luster possible.

Circulation strike.

Proof strike.

	Mintage	G-4	VG-8	VF-20	EF-40	AU-50	MS-60	MS-63	PF-63
1865. . . . . *(500+)* . .11,382,000		$18	$20	$28	$40	$65	$125	$160	$1,650
1866. . . . . *(725+)* . .4,801,000		18	20	28	40	65	125	160	350
1867. . . . . *(625+)* . . .3,915,000		18	20	28	40	65	125	160	350
1868. . . . . *(600+)* . . .3,252,000		18	20	28	40	65	125	160	350
1869. . . . . *(600+)* . . .1,604,000		18	20	28	40	65	135	185	350
1870. . . . .*(1,000+)* . .1,335,000		18	20	28	40	65	140	195	350
1871. . . . . *(960+)* 604,000		18	20	28	40	65	140	195	350
1872. . . . . *(950+)* 862,000		18	20	28	40	65	150	210	350
1873, Close 3 . . . .*(1,100+)* 390,000		18	20	28	40	65	150	210	350
1873, Open 3 .783,000		18	20	28	40	65	150	210	
1874. . . . . *(700+)* 790,000		18	20	28	40	65	150	210	350
1875. . . . . *(700+)* 228,000		18	20	30	45	80	175	225	350
1876. . . . .*(1,150+)* 162,000		18	20	35	50	110	200	260	350
1877, Proof only . . . . . . (900)				1,250	1,400				2,000
1878, Proof only . . . . . .(2,350)				650	750				1,000
1879. . . . .(3,200) 38,000		60	70	90	125	175	300	400	450
1880. . . . .(3,955) 21,000		90	110	150	200	220	350	410	450
1881. . . . .(3,575) 1,077,000		18	20	28	40	65	125	185	375
1882. . . . .(3,100) 22,200		110	125	180	225	275	400	500	475
1883. . . . .(6,609) 4,000		175	190	275	350	400	550	900	500
1884. . . . .(3,942) 1,700		350	375	510	600	650	900	1,100	550
1885. . . . .(3,790) 1,000		410	435	575	700	800	950	1,200	550
1886, Proof only . . . . . .(4,290)				325	375				500
1887. . . . .(2,960) 5,001		275	325	350	400	500	550	675	500
1887, 7 Over 6 . . . .*				375	425				575
1888. . . . .(4,582) 36,501		50	55	75	90	150	300	400	400
1889. . . . .(3,436) 18,125		80	100	135	220	250	350	450	425

* Included in number above.

SHIELD (1866–1883)

The Shield type nickel was made possible by the Act of May 16, 1866. Its weight was set at 77-16/100 grains (5 grams), with the same composition as the nickel three-cent piece that was authorized in 1865, and an obverse design similar to that of the two-cent coin. In 1866 the coin was designed with rays between the stars on the reverse. Some of the pieces minted in 1867 have the same details, but later the rays were eliminated, creating two varieties for that year. There was no further change in the type until it was replaced by the Liberty Head design in 1883. Only Proof pieces were struck in 1877 and 1878.

Designer James B. Longacre; weight 5 grams; composition .750 copper, .250 nickel; diameter 20.5 mm; plain edge. All coined at Philadelphia Mint.

G-4 Good—All letters in motto readable.

VG-8 Very Good—Motto clear and stands out. Rims slightly worn but even. Part of shield lines visible.

F-12 Fine—Half of each olive leaf worn smooth.

EF-40 Extremely Fine—Slight wear to leaf tips and cross over shield.

AU-50 About Uncirculated—Traces of light wear on only the high points of the design. Half of mint luster present.

MS-60 Uncirculated—No trace of wear. Light blemishes.

MS-63 Choice Uncirculated—Some distracting contact marks or blemishes in prime focal areas. Impaired luster possible.

**Variety 1, Rays Between Stars
(1866–1867)**

1866, Repunched Date   **Example of 1883, 3 Over 2**
*Other varieties exist, as
well as pieces with recut 3.*

**Variety 2, Without Rays
(1867–1883)**

Sharply struck Uncirculated coins are valued higher than the prices shown here.

	Mintage	G-4	VG-8	F-12	EF-40	AU-50	MS-60	MS-63	PF-63
1866, Rays . . . . *(600+)* . .14,742,500		$28	$42	$50	$170	$240	$275	$425	$2,250
1866, Repunched Date . . . .*		55	75	135	260	375	575	900	
1867, Rays . . . . *(25+)* . . .2,019,000		35	50	65	190	285	375	500	35,000
1867, Without Rays . . . . *(600+)* . .28,890,500		20	22	25	65	110	140	225	475
1867, Without Rays, Pattern Reverse									6,000
1868. . . . . *(600+)* . .28,817,000		20	22	25	65	110	140	225	385
1869. . . . . *(600+)* . .16,395,000		20	22	25	65	110	140	225	385
1870. . . . .*(1,000+)* . .4,806,000		25	30	50	85	140	210	300	385
1871. . . . . *(960+)* . . .561,000		75	90	150	270	350	450	625	425
1872. . . . . *(950+)* . .6,036,000		30	40	60	125	175	235	300	385
1873, Close 3 . . . .*(1,100+)* 436,050		28	40	60	140	200	325	585	385
1873, Open 3 4,113,950		28	35	60	100	140	210	300	
1873, Lg Over Sm 3 . . . .*							—		
1874. . . . . *(700+)* . .3,538,000		28	40	65	120	170	250	325	385
1875. . . . . *(700+)* . .2,097,000		40	60	100	150	200	275	360	425
1876. . . . .*(1,150+)* . .2,530,000		35	45	80	130	185	260	325	385
1877, Proof only . . . . (900)					2,200				3,400
1878, Proof only . . . . . .(2,350)					1,200				2,000

* Included in number above.

	Mintage	G-4	VG-8	F-12	EF-40	AU-50	MS-60	MS-63	PF-63
1879 . . . . (3,200) 25,900		$375	$475	$600	$700	$750	$900	$1,000	$500
1879, 9 Over 8 . . . .*									725
1880 . . . . (3,955) 16,000		475	560	675	1,300	1,850	4,000	7,500	500
1881 . . . . (3,575) 68,800		250	300	425	600	775	850	1,000	500
1882 . . . . (3,100) . .11,472,900		20	22	25	60	110	150	225	385
1883 . . . . (5,419) . . .1,451,500		20	22	30	60	110	145	200	385
1883, 3 Over 2 . . . .*		250	325	650	1,250	1,750	2,100	2,700	

* Included in number above.

LIBERTY HEAD (1883–1913)

In early 1883, the nickel design was changed to the Liberty Head. This type first appeared without the word CENTS on the coin, merely a large letter V. Some of these "CENTS-less" coins were gold plated and passed for $5. Later in that year the word CENTS was added to discourage the fraudulent practice.

Liberty Head nickels dated 1913 were first revealed when a former Mint worker showed an example at the 1920 American Numismatic Association convention. Soon after that, five specimens are known to have been in the hands of a Philadelphia coin dealer. The coins were sold in 1924 to another dealer, and thence to Col. E.H.R. Green (son of the famous Hetty Green). These have since been dispersed and are now held in various public and private collections. As they were not a regular issue, they were never placed in circulation.

Designer Charles E. Barber; weight 5 grams; composition .750 copper, .250 nickel; diameter 21.2 mm; plain edge; mints: Philadelphia, Denver, San Francisco.

G-4 Good—No details in head. LIBERTY obliterated
VG-8 Very Good—Some letters in LIBERTY legible.
F-12 Fine—All letters in LIBERTY legible.
VF-20 Very Fine—LIBERTY bold, including letter L.
EF-40 Extremely Fine—LIBERTY sharp. Corn grains at bottom of wreath visible on reverse.
AU-50 About Uncirculated—Traces of light wear on only high points of design. Half of mint luster present.
MS-60 Uncirculated—No trace of wear, but many contact marks possible. Surface may be spotted, or luster faded.
MS-63 Choice Uncirculated—No trace of wear. Light blemishes.

Variety 1, Without CENTS (1883)

Variety 2, With CENTS (1883–1913)

Mintmark Location

Sharply struck Uncirculated coins are valued higher than the prices shown; dull or weakly struck pieces are worth less.

	Mintage	G-4	VG-8	F-12	VF-20	EF-40	AU-50	MS-60	MS-63	PF-63
1883, Without CENTS (5,219) . . .5,474,300		$7	$8	$9	$11	$12	$14	$35	$50	$300
1883, With CENTS (6,783) . .16,026,200		18	27	35	55	85	120	150	200	275
1884 . . . . . . (3,942) . .11,270,000		20	30	35	55	85	130	190	300	250
1885 . . . . . . (3,790) . . .1,472,700		550	600	850	1,000	1,350	1,700	2,000	2,850	1,300
1886 . . . . . . (4,290) . . .3,326,000		275	320	425	500	700	825	1,000	2,200	650
1887 . . . . . . (2,960) . .15,260,692		12	18	32	50	75	110	140	195	250
1888 . . . . . . (4,582) . .10,167,901		26	40	60	120	175	220	275	340	250
1889 . . . . . . (3,336) . .15,878,025		11	16	28	48	75	120	140	175	250
1890 . . . . . . (2,740) . .16,256,532		10	18	27	45	65	110	160	200	250

Chart continued on next page.

	Mintage	G-4	VG-8	F-12	VF-20	EF-40	AU-50	MS-60	MS-63	PF-63
1891..... (2,350)...16,832,000		$7.00	$12.00	$25.00	$45	$65	$110	$160	$200	$250
1892..... (2,745)...11,696,897		6.00	10.00	20.00	40	65	110	140	160	250
1893..... (2,195)...13,368,000		6.00	10.00	20.00	40	65	110	135	160	250
1894..... (2,632)....5,410,500		17.00	34.00	100.00	165	240	300	350	425	250
1895..... (2,062)....9,977,822		6.00	8.00	22.00	45	70	110	140	200	250
1896..... (1,862)....8,841,058		9.00	18.00	35.00	65	90	150	190	265	250
1897..... (1,938)...20,426,797		4.00	5.00	12.00	27	45	70	100	160	250
1898..... (1,795)...12,530,292		4.00	5.00	12.00	27	45	75	150	185	250
1899..... (2,031)...26,027,000		2.25	2.75	8.00	20	30	60	90	130	250
1900..... (2,262)...27,253,733		1.75	2.25	7.50	15	30	60	90	135	250
1901..... (1,985)...26,478,228		1.75	2.25	4.75	13	30	60	75	125	250
1902..... (2,018)...31,487,561		1.75	2.25	4.25	13	30	60	75	125	250
1903..... (1,790)...28,004,935		1.75	2.25	4.25	13	30	60	75	125	250
1904..... (1,817)...21,403,167		1.75	2.25	4.25	13	30	60	75	125	250
1905..... (2,152)...29,825,124		1.75	2.25	4.25	13	30	60	75	125	250
1906..... (1,725)...38,612,000		1.75	2.25	4.25	13	30	60	75	125	250
1907..... (1,475)...39,213,325		1.75	2.25	4.25	13	30	60	75	125	250
1908..... (1,620)...22,684,557		1.75	2.25	4.25	13	30	60	75	125	250
1909..... (4,763)...11,585,763		2.50	3.00	5.00	15	32	75	100	140	250
1910..... (2,405)...30,166,948		1.75	2.25	4.25	13	30	60	75	125	250
1911..... (1,733)...39,557,639		1.75	2.25	4.25	13	30	60	75	125	250
1912..... (2,145)...26,234,569		1.75	2.25	4.25	13	30	60	75	125	250
1912D 8,474,000		3.00	4.00	10.00	38	85	175	300	385	
1912S.............. 238,000		175.00	240.00	285.00	500	850	1,400	1,750	2,000	

1913 Liberty Head *(5 known)* $3,737,500, PF-64, Heritage auction, January 2010   *5,000,000*

INDIAN HEAD OR BUFFALO (1913–1938)

These pieces are known as Buffalo (usually) or Indian Head nickels. In the first year of issue, 1913, there were two distinct varieties, the first showing the bison on a mound, and the second with the base redesigned to a thinner, straight line.

James Earle Fraser designed this nickel, employing three different Native Americans as models. His initial F is beneath the date. The bison was supposedly modeled after "Black Diamond" in the New York Central Park Zoo.

Matte Proof coins were made for collectors from 1913 to 1916.

Designer James Earle Fraser; weight 5 grams; composition .750 copper, .250 nickel; diameter 21.2 mm; plain edge; mints: Philadelphia, Denver, San Francisco.

G-4 Good—Legends and date readable. Buffalo's horn does not show.
VG-8 Very Good—Horn worn nearly flat.
F-12 Fine—Horn and tail smooth but partially visible. Obverse rim intact.
VF-20 Very Fine—Much of horn visible. Indian's cheekbone worn.
EF-40 Extremely Fine—Horn lightly worn. Slight wear on Indian's hair ribbon.
AU-50 About Uncirculated—Traces of light wear on only the high points of the design. Half of mint luster present.
MS-60 Uncirculated—No trace of wear. May have several blemishes.
MS-63 Choice Uncirculated—No trace of wear. Light blemishes.

Circulation strike.   Matte Proof.   Mirror Proof.

Variety 1 – FIVE CENTS on Raised Ground (1913)

	Mintage	G-4	VG-8	F-12	VF-20	EF-40	AU-50	MS-60	MS-63	MATTE PF-63
1913, Variety 1 . . . (1,520) . . .	30,992,000	$11	$14	$16	$20	$25	$35	$45	$60	$1,200
1913D, Variety 1	5,337,000	15	20	24	34	42	60	75	80	
1913S, Variety 1	2,105,000	45	50	60	70	90	110	130	180	

Variety 2 – FIVE CENTS in Recess (1913–1938)

Mintmark Below FIVE CENTS

1916, Doubled-Die Obverse

1918-D, 8 Over 7

	Mintage	G-4	VG-8	F-12	VF-20	EF-40	AU-50	MS-60	MS-63	MATTE PF-63
1913, Var 2 (1,514)	29,857,186	$10.00	$12.00	$14.00	$17	$22	$30	$40	$80	$1,000
1913D, Var 2	4,156,000	120.00	150.00	175.00	200	235	260	300	400	
1913S, Var 2	1,209,000	340.00	400.00	450.00	500	600	750	900	1,100	
1914 . . . . . . (1,275)	20,664,463	20.00	22.00	25.00	30	35	45	60	85	1,000
1914, 4 Over 3 . . . . *			325.00	525	1,000	1,500	2,800	6,250		
1914D 3,912,000		90.00	125.00	160.00	220	325	400	450	550	
1914S 3,470,000		26.00	38.00	45.00	65	90	160	200	450	
1915 . . . . . . (1,050)	20,986,220	6.00	8.00	9.00	12	25	45	60	90	1,000
1915D 7,569,000		20.00	32.00	38.00	70	130	160	270	350	
1915S 1,505,000		50.00	75.00	115.00	200	400	500	650	950	
1916 . . . . . . (600)	63,497,466	6.00	7.00	8.00	10	14	25	50	85	1,200
1916, DblDie Obv . . . . *		2,200.00	4,000.00	7,750.00	11,000	18,500	31,000	60,000	140,000	
$316,250, MS-64, Stack's Bowers auction, November 2007										
1916D 13,333,000		16.00	28.00	30.00	45	90	120	175	260	
1916S 11,860,000		12.00	15.00	20.00	40	90	125	190	275	
1917 51,424,019		6.00	7.00	8.00	10	16	35	60	150	
1917D 9,910,000		18.00	30.00	50.00	85	150	275	350	750	
1917S 4,193,000		22.00	40.00	75.00	115	200	375	450	1,200	
1918 32,086,314		6.00	7.00	8.00	16	32	50	125	325	
1918D, 8 Over 7 . . . . **		1,000.00	1,500.00	2,700.00	5,500	8,500	12,000	34,000	57,500	
$350,750, MS-65, Stack's Bowers auction, August 2006										
1918D 8,362,000		22.00	40.00	65.00	135	225	350	450	1,050	
1918S 4,882,000		14.00	27.00	55.00	110	200	325	585	2,500	
1919 60,868,000		2.25	3.00	3.50	8	15	32	55	125	
1919D (a) 8,006,000		15.00	30.00	75.00	135	260	350	600	1,500	
1919S (a) 7,521,000		9.00	20.00	50.00	125	260	375	625	1,800	
1920 63,093,000		1.50	2.50	3.00	7	14	30	65	140	
1920D (a) 9,418,000		8.00	15.00	32.00	115	275	325	585	1,400	
1920S 9,689,000		4.50	12.00	28.00	100	190	300	575	1,800	
1921 10,663,000		4.00	6.00	8.00	24	50	75	150	320	
1921S 1,557,000		75.00	125.00	200.00	550	950	1,200	1,600	2,100	

*Note: Matte Proof through 1916; mirror Proof thereafter. * Included in number above. ** Included in number below.*
a. Uncirculated pieces with full, sharp details are worth considerably more.

Chart continued on next page.

	Mintage	G-4	VG-8	F-12	VF-20	EF-40	AU-50	MS-60	MS-63	PF-63
1923	35,715,000	$2.00	$3.00	$4.00	$6.00	$13	$35	$65	$160	
1923S **(a)**	6,142,000	8.00	10.00	30.00	135.00	300	400	565	775	
1924	21,620,000	1.50	2.00	5.00	10.00	24	42	75	160	
1924D	5,258,000	8.50	12.00	30.00	85.00	235	325	390	765	
1924S	1,437,000	16.00	32.00	110.00	475.00	1,150	1,600	2,300	3,600	
1925	35,565,100	3.00	3.50	4.00	8.00	15	32	42	100	
1925D **(a)**	4,450,000	10.00	20.00	40.00	95.00	185	265	400	700	
1925S	6,256,000	5.00	9.00	18.00	90.00	180	250	475	1,850	
1926	44,693,000	1.25	1.75	2.50	5.00	10	20	32	75	
1926D **(a)**	5,638,000	10.00	18.00	28.00	110.00	185	300	350	475	
1926S	970,000	22.00	45.00	100.00	375.00	800	2,650	4,500	9,200	
1927	37,981,000	1.25	1.75	2.50	4.00	12	21	35	80	
1927D	5,730,000	2.50	6.00	7.00	32.00	80	135	190	310	
1927S	3,430,000	1.50	3.00	5.00	34.00	95	185	550	2,000	
1928	23,411,000	1.25	1.75	2.50	5.00	13	23	32	80	
1928D	6,436,000	1.50	2.50	5.00	15.00	45	50	60	110	
1928S	6,936,000	1.75	2.00	2.50	11.00	26	110	260	550	
1929	36,446,000	1.25	1.50	2.50	4.00	12	20	40	75	
1929D	8,370,000	1.25	2.00	2.50	7.00	32	45	60	130	
1929S	7,754,000	1.25	1.50	2.00	4.00	12	25	55	80	
1930	22,849,000	1.25	1.50	2.50	4.00	11	20	35	75	
1930S	5,435,000	1.25	1.50	2.50	4.00	14	35	65	120	
1931S	1,200,000	15.00	16.00	19.00	22.00	35	55	65	100	
1934	20,213,003	1.25	1.50	2.50	4.00	10	18	50	65	
1934D **(b)**	7,480,000	1.50	2.50	4.00	9.00	20	45	80	125	
1935	58,264,000	1.00	1.50	1.75	2.00	3	10	22	45	
1935, DblDie Rev	*	45.00	55.00	100.00	160.00	500	1,300	5,250	6,500	
1935D	12,092,000	1.00	1.50	2.50	6.00	15	40	75	85	
1935S	10,300,000	1.00	1.50	2.00	2.50	4	18	55	70	
1936 (4,420)	118,997,000	1.00	1.50	1.75	2.00	3	9	22	40	$1,150
1936D	24,814,000	1.00	1.50	1.75	2.00	4	12	38	45	
1936D, 3-1/2 Legs	*	—	850.00	1,500.00	2,500.00	4,900	8,250	15,000		
1936S	14,930,000	1.00	1.50	1.75	2.00	4	12	38	45	
1937 (5,769)	79,480,000	1.00	1.50	1.75	2.00	3	9	22	40	1,200

Note: Matte Proof through 1916; regular Proof thereafter. * Included in number above. **a.** Uncirculated pieces with full, sharp details are worth considerably more. **b.** Large and small mintmark varieties exist; see page 22.

1937-D, "3-Legged" Variety
A similar variety exists for 1936-D.

1938-D, D Over S

	Mintage	G-4	VG-8	F-12	VF-20	EF-40	AU-50	MS-60	MS-63
1937D	17,826,000	$1.00	$1.50	$1.75	$3.00	$4.00	$10	$32	$42
1937D, 3-Legged	*	550.00	650.00	800.00	900.00	1,200.00	1,300	2,300	5,250
1937S	5,635,000	1.00	1.50	1.75	3.00	3.50	9	32	42
1938D	7,020,000	3.50	4.00	4.50	4.75	5.00	8	22	36
1938D, D Over S	*	5.50	8.00	10.00	14.00	20.00	32	55	80

* Included in number above.

JEFFERSON (1938 TO DATE)

This nickel was originally designed by Felix Schlag, who won an award of $1,000 in a competition with some 390 artists. His design established the definite public approval of portrait and pictorial themes rather than symbolic devices on our coinage.

Designer Felix Schlag; weight 5 grams; composition (1938–1942, 1946 to date), .750 copper, .250 nickel, (1942–1945), .560 copper, .350 silver, .090 manganese, with net weight .05626 oz. pure silver; diameter 21.2 mm; plain edge; mints: Philadelphia, Denver, San Francisco.

VG-8 Very Good—Second porch pillar from right nearly gone, other three still visible but weak.

F-12 Fine—Jefferson's cheekbone worn flat. Hair lines and eyebrow faint. Second pillar weak, especially at bottom.

VF-20 Very Fine—Second pillar plain and complete on both sides.

EF-40 Extremely Fine—Cheekbone, hair lines, eyebrow slightly worn but well defined. Base of triangle above pillars visible but weak.

AU-50 About Uncirculated—Traces of light wear on only high points of design. Half of mint luster present.

MS-60 Uncirculated—No trace of wear. Light blemishes.

MS-65 Gem Uncirculated—No trace of wear. Barely noticeable blemishes.

Circulation strike. *Proof strike.* **1939, Doubled MONTICELLO and FIVE CENTS**

Uncirculated pieces with fully struck steps on Monticello have higher values.

	Mintage	VF-20	EF-40	AU-50	MS-60	MS-63	MS-65	PF-65
1938 . . . . (19,365) . . .	19,496,000	$0.50	$1.00	$1.50	$3.00	$4.00	$18	$125
1938D	5,376,000	1.50	2.00	3.00	7.00	9.00	15	
1938S	4,105,000	2.50	3.00	3.50	4.50	8.00	17	
1939 . . . . (12,535) . .	120,615,000	0.25	0.50	1.00	2.00	2.50	12	125
1939, Doubled MONTICELLO,								
FIVE CENTS . . . . *		75.00	100.00	150.00	200.00	375.00	1,000	
1939D	3,514,000	10.00	13.00	28.00	55.00	85.00	110	
1939S	6,630,000	1.50	5.00	10.00	18.00	35.00	75	
1940 . . . . (14,158) . .	176,485,000	0.25	0.40	0.75	1.00	1.50	10	120
1940D	43,540,000	0.35	0.50	1.00	2.00	2.50	15	
1940S	39,690,000	0.35	0.50	1.00	2.25	3.00	15	
1941 . . . . (18,720) . .	203,265,000	0.20	0.30	0.50	0.75	1.50	12	110
1941D	53,432,000	0.25	0.40	1.50	2.50	3.50	10	
1941S **(a)**	43,445,000	0.30	0.50	1.50	3.00	4.00	12	
1942 . . . . (29,600) . . .	49,789,000	0.30	0.45	1.25	4.00	6.00	15	110
1942D	13,938,000	1.00	2.00	5.00	28.00	38.00	60	
1942D, D Over Horizontal D . . . . *		75.00	200.00	500.00	1,500.00	3,000.00	*10,000*	

* Included in number above. **a.** Large and small mintmark varieties; see page 22.

Wartime Silver Alloy (1942–1945)

On October 8, 1942, the wartime five-cent piece composed of copper (56%), silver (35%), and manganese (9%) was introduced to eliminate nickel, a critical war material. A larger mintmark was placed above the dome of Monticello, indicating the change of alloy. The letter P (Philadelphia) was used for the first time.

| Mintmark Location | 1943-P, 3 Over 2 | 1943-P, Doubled Eye | 1945-P, Doubled-Die Reverse |

	Mintage	VF-20	EF-40	AU-50	MS-60	MS-63	MS-65	PF-65
1942P. . . . . (27,600). . . 57,873,000		$2.50	$2.75	$3.25	$7	$12	$20	$225
1942S. 32,900,000		2.50	2.75	3.25	7	12	25	
1943P, 3 Over 2 . . . . *		50.00	100.00	165.00	225	260	700	
1943P. 271,165,000		2.50	2.75	3.00	5	8	20	
1943P, Doubled Eye . . . . **		25.00	40.00	60.00	90	160	650	
1943D 15,294,000		2.75	3.50	4.00	6	12	20	
1943S. 104,060,000		2.50	2.75	3.00	5	8	20	
1944P. 119,150,000		2.50	2.75	3.25	7	12	25	
1944D 32,309,000		2.50	2.75	3.00	6	12	25	
1944S. 21,640,000		2.50	2.75	3.00	5	10	20	
1945P. 119,408,100		2.50	2.75	3.00	5	8	20	
1945P, DblDie Reverse . . . . **		20.00	30.00	50.00	75	130	800	
1945D 37,158,000		2.50	2.75	3.00	5	8	20	
1945S. 58,939,000		2.50	2.75	3.00	5	8	20	

Note: 1944 nickels without mintmarks are counterfeits. Genuine pieces of other wartime dates struck in nickel by error are known to exist. * Included in number below. ** Included in number above.

Prewar Composition, Mintmark Style Resumed (1946–1967)

	Mintage	VF-20	EF-40	AU-50	MS-60	MS-63	MS-65
1946. 161,116,000		$0.25	$0.30	$0.35	$0.75	$2.00	$10
1946D 45,292,200		0.35	0.40	0.45	1.00	2.00	10
1946S. 13,560,000		0.40	0.45	0.50	1.00	1.50	10
1947. 95,000,000		0.25	0.30	0.35	0.75	1.50	10
1947D 37,822,000		0.30	0.35	0.40	0.90	1.50	10
1947S. 24,720,000		0.40	0.45	0.50	1.00	1.50	10

	Mintage	MS-60	MS-63	MS-65	PF-65
1948. 89,348,000		$1.00	$1.50	$2.75	
1948D 44,734,000		1.60	2.00	3.00	
1948S. 11,300,000		1.50	2.00	4.00	
1949. 60,652,000		2.50	4.00	7.50	
1949D 36,498,000		1.50	2.00	5.50	
1949D, D Over S. . . . . *		150.00	200.00	500.00	
1949S. 9,716,000		1.75	2.50	5.50	
1950. . . . . (51,386) . . 9,796,000		2.00	3.25	6.00	$70
1950D 2,630,030		14.00	16.00	20.00	
1951. . . . . (57,500) . . 28,552,000		3.00	4.00	15.00	60
1951D 20,460,000		4.00	5.00	10.00	
1951S. 7,776,000		1.50	2.00	4.50	
1952. . . . . (81,980) . . 63,988,000		1.00	1.50	3.50	45
1952D 30,638,000		3.50	5.00	9.00	
1952S. 20,572,000		1.00	1.50	3.50	
1953. . . . . (128,800) . . 46,644,000		0.25	0.50	1.50	45
1953D 59,878,600		0.25	0.50	1.50	
1953S. 19,210,900		0.75	1.00	2.00	

* Included in number above.

NICKEL FIVE-CENT PIECES

1954-S, S Over D

1955-D, D Over S

	Mintage	MS-60	MS-63	MS-65	PF-65
1954 . . . . (233,300)	47,684,050	$1.00	$1.50	$3.00	$30
1954D	117,183,060	0.60	1.00	2.00	
1954S	29,384,000	1.75	2.00	3.00	
1954S, S Over D . . . .*		26.00	40.00	100.00	
1955 . . . . (378,200)	7,888,000	0.75	1.00	2.00	25
1955D	74,464,100	0.50	0.75	1.25	
1955D, D Over S (a) . . . .*		36.00	57.50	100.00	
1956 . . . . (669,384)	35,216,000	0.50	0.75	1.00	8
1956D	67,222,940	0.50	0.75	1.00	
1957 . . . . (1,247,952)	38,408,000	0.50	0.75	1.00	6
1957D	136,828,900	0.50	0.70	1.00	
1958 . . . . (875,652)	17,088,000	0.60	0.80	1.50	6
1958D	168,249,120	0.40	0.50	1.00	
1959 . . . . (1,149,291)	27,248,000	0.25	0.50	1.00	5
1959D	160,738,240	0.25	0.50	1.00	
1960 . . . . (1,691,602)	55,416,000	0.25	0.50	1.00	5
1960D	192,582,180	0.25	0.50	2.00	
1961 . . . . (3,028,144)	73,640,100	0.25	0.50	1.00	5
1961D	229,342,760	0.25	0.50	2.00	
1962 . . . . (3,218,019)	97,384,000	0.25	0.50	1.00	5
1962D	280,195,720	0.25	0.50	3.00	
1963 . . . . (3,075,645) . . .	175,776,000	0.25	0.50	1.00	5
1963D	276,829,460	0.25	0.50	1.00	
1964 . . . . (3,950,762) . .	1,024,672,000	0.25	0.50	1.00	5
1964D	1,787,297,160	0.25	0.50	1.00	
1965	136,131,380	0.25	0.50	1.00	

* Included in number above. **a.** Varieties exist; value is for the variety illustrated.

1966 Through 2003

The designer's initials, FS, were added below the bust starting in 1966, and dies were further remodeled to strengthen the design in 1971, 1972, 1977, and 1982. The mintmark position was moved to the obverse starting in 1968.

	Mintage	MS-63	MS-65	PF-65
1966	156,208,283	$0.25	$1	(a)
1967	107,325,800	0.25	1	
1968D	91,227,880	0.25	1	
1968S . . . . (3,041,506)				$1
. . . .	100,396,004	0.25	1	

	Mintage	MS-63	MS-65	PF-65
1969D	202,807,500	$0.25	$1	
1969S . . . . (2,934,631)				$1
. . . .	120,165,000	0.25	1	
1970D	515,485,380	0.25	1	

a. Two presentation pieces were given to the designer.

Chart continued on next page.

	Mintage	MS-63	MS-65	PF-65
1970S . . . . (2,632,810)				$1.00
. 238,832,004	$0.25	$1.00		
1971 106,884,000	0.75	1.50		
1971D 316,144,800	0.30	1.00		
1971, No S (b)				1,000.00
1971S . . . . (3,220,733)				2.00
1972 202,036,000	0.25	1.00		
1972D 351,694,600	0.25	1.00		
1972S . . . . (3,260,996)				2.00
1973 384,396,000	0.25	1.00		
1973D 261,405,000	0.25	1.00		
1973S . . . . (2,760,339)				1.50
1974 601,752,000	0.25	1.00		
1974D 277,373,000	0.25	1.00		
1974S . . . . (2,612,568)				2.00
1975 181,772,000	0.50	1.00		
1975D 401,875,300	0.25	1.00		
1975S . . . . (2,845,450)				2.00
1976 367,124,000	0.45	1.00		
1976D 563,964,147	0.45	1.00		
1976S . . . . (4,149,730)				2.00
1977 585,376,000	0.25	1.00		
1977D 297,313,422	0.50	1.00		
1977S . . . . (3,251,152)				1.50
1978 391,308,000	0.25	1.00		
1978D 313,092,780	0.25	1.00		
1978S . . . . (3,127,781)				1.50
1979 463,188,000	0.25	1.00		
1979D 325,867,672	0.25	1.00		
1979S, All kinds				
. . . . (3,677,175)				
1979S, Type 1 (c)				5.00
1979S, Type 2 (c)				12.00
1980P 593,004,000	0.25	1.00		
1980D 502,323,448	0.25	1.00		
1980S . . . . (3,554,806)				1.50
1981P 657,504,000	0.25	1.00		
1981D 364,801,843	0.25	1.00		
1981S, All kinds (4,063,083)				
1981S, Type 1 (c)				8.00
1981S, Type 2 (c)				15.00
1982P 292,355,000	3.00	8.00		
1982D 373,726,544	2.00	4.00		
1982S . . . . (3,857,479)				3.00
1983P 561,615,000	1.75	6.00		
1983D 536,726,276	1.50	4.00		
1983S . . . . (3,279,126)				3.00
1984P 746,769,000	1.00	2.00		
1984D 517,675,146	0.25	1.00		

	Mintage	MS-63	MS-65	PF-65
1984S . . . . (3,065,110)				$4.00
1985P 647,114,962	$0.50	$1.00		
1985D 459,747,446	0.50	1.00		
1985S . . . . (3,362,821)				3.00
1986P 536,883,483	0.50	1.00		
1986D 361,819,140	1.00	1.75		
1986S . . . . (3,010,497)				7.00
1987P 371,499,481	0.25	1.00		
1987D 410,590,604	0.25	1.00		
1987S . . . . (4,227,728)				3.00
1988P 771,360,000	0.25	1.00		
1988D 663,771,652	0.25	1.00		
1988S . . . . (3,262,948)				5.00
1989P 898,812,000	0.25	1.00		
1989D 570,842,474	0.25	1.00		
1989S . . . . (3,220,194)				4.00
1990P 661,636,000	0.25	1.00		
1990D 663,938,503	0.25	1.00		
1990S . . . . (3,299,559)				4.00
1991P 614,104,000	0.30	1.00		
1991D 436,496,678	0.30	1.00		
1991S . . . . (2,867,787)				4.50
1992P 399,552,000	1.50	2.50		
1992D 450,565,113	0.25	1.00		
1992S . . . . (4,176,560)				3.50
1993P 412,076,000	0.25	1.00		
1993D 406,084,135	0.25	1.00		
1993S . . . . (3,394,792)				4.00
1994P 722,160,000	0.25	2.50		
1994P, Special				
Unc. (d) 167,703	50.00	75.00		
1994D 715,762,110	0.25	1.00		
1994S . . . . (3,269,923)				3.50
1995P 774,156,000	0.25	1.00		
1995D 888,112,000	0.50	1.00		
1995S . . . . (2,797,481)				5.00
1996P 829,332,000	0.25	1.00		
1996D 817,736,000	0.25	1.00		
1996S . . . . (2,525,265)				3.00
1997P 470,972,000	0.50	1.00		
1997P, Special				
Unc. (d) 25,000	200.00	250.00		
1997D 466,640,000	1.00	2.00		
1997S . . . . (2,796,678)				3.00
1998P 688,272,000	0.35	1.00		
1998D 635,360,000	0.35	1.00		
1998S . . . . (2,086,507)				3.00
1999P 1,212,000,000	0.25	1.00		
1999D 1,066,720,000	0.25	1.00		

b. 1971 Proof nickels without mintmark were made in error. See discussion on page 22. **c.** See page 234 for illustrations of Type 1 and Type 2 varieties. **d.** Special "frosted" Uncirculated pieces were included in the 1993 Thomas Jefferson commemorative dollar packaging (sold in 1994) and the 1997 Botanic Garden sets. They resemble Matte Proof coins.

	Mintage	MS-63	MS-65	PF-65
1999S	(3,347,966)			$3.50
2000P	846,240,000	$0.25	$1	
2000D	1,509,520,000	0.25	1	
2000S	(4,047,993)			2.50
2001P	675,704,000	0.25	1	
2001D	627,680,000	0.25	1	
2001S	(3,184,606)			2.50

	Mintage	MS-63	MS-65	PF-65
2002P	539,280,000	$0.25	$1	
2002D	691,200,000	0.25	1	
2002S	(3,211,995)			$2.50
2003P	441,840,000	0.25	1	
2003D	383,040,000	0.25	1	
2003S	(3,298,439)			3.00

"Westward Journey" Nickels

The Westward Journey Nickel Series™ (2004–2005) commemorated the bicentennial of the Louisiana Purchase and the journey of Meriwether Lewis and William Clark to explore that vast territory.

2004: The Louisiana Purchase / Peace Medal reverse, by Mint sculptor Norman E. Nemeth, was adapted from the reverse of certain of the original Indian Peace Medals commissioned for the expedition. These medals bore a portrait of President Thomas Jefferson on one side, and symbols of peace and friendship on the other. They were presented to Native American chiefs and other important leaders as tokens of the goodwill of the United States. The Keelboat reverse, by Mint sculptor Al Maletsky, depicts the boat that transported the Lewis and Clark expedition and their supplies through the rivers of the Louisiana Territory. Built to Captain Lewis's specifications, this 55-foot craft could be sailed, rowed, poled like a raft, or towed from the riverbank.

2005: The new obverse portrait of President Jefferson was inspired by a 1789 marble bust by Jean-Antoine Houdon; the inscription "Liberty" was based on Jefferson's handwriting. Joe Fitzgerald designed the new obverse, which was rendered by Mint sculptor Don Everhart. The American Bison reverse, designed by Jamie Franki and produced by Norman E. Nemeth, features a bison in profile. Described in journals from the expedition, bison held great significance for many American Indian cultures. (The design also recalls the popular Indian Head / Buffalo nickel design of 1913–1938.) The "Ocean in View" reverse, designed by Joe Fitzgerald and produced by Mint sculptor Donna Weaver, depicts cliffs over the Pacific Ocean and an inscription inspired by a November 7, 1805, entry in Clark's journal: "Ocean in view! O! The joy!"

2006: The "Monticello" design shows a facing portrait of Jefferson, designed by Jamie Franki and sculpted by Donna Weaver. This new obverse and the traditional depiction of Monticello are used on this and subsequent nickels.

The Mint also produced Westward Journey Nickel Series™ Coin Sets for 2004 and 2005 (see pages 342–343).

2004 Obverse   2005 Obverse

Peace Medal   **Keelboat**   **American Bison**   **Ocean in View**

Monticello Reverse Resumed (2006 to Date)

2006 Obverse   **Monticello**   *Proof strike.*
Design used from 2006 to date.
Felix Schlag's initials moved to reverse.
Circulation strike.

	Mintage	MS-63	MS-65	PF-65
2004P, Peace Medal.	361,440,000	$0.25	$0.75	
2004D, Peace Medal	372,000,000	0.25	0.75	
2004S, Peace Medal.	(2,992,069)			$8
2004P, Keelboat.	366,720,000	0.25	0.75	
2004D, Keelboat.	344,880,000	0.25	0.75	
2004S, Keelboat.	(2,965,422)			8
2005P, American Bison	448,320,000	0.25	1.00	
2005D, American Bison	487,680,000	0.25	1.00	
2005S, American Bison	(3,344,679)			8
2005P, Ocean in View.	394,080,000	0.25	0.75	
2005D, Ocean in View	411,120,000	0.25	0.75	
2005S, Ocean in View	(3,344,679)			8
2006P, Monticello.	693,120,000	0.25	0.75	
2006D, Monticello	809,280,000	0.25	0.75	
2006S, Monticello.	(3,054,436)			5
2007P.	571,680,000	0.25	0.50	
2007D	626,160,000	0.25	0.50	
2007S.	(2,577,166)			4
2008P.	279,840,000	0.25	0.50	
2008D	345,600,000	0.25	0.50	
2008S.	(2,169,561)			4
2009P.	39,840,000	0.30	0.70	
2009D	468,000,000	0.30	0.70	
2009S.	(2,179,867)			4
2010P.	260,640,000	0.25	0.50	
2010D	229,920,000	0.25	0.50	
2010S.	(1,689,364)			4
2011P.	450,000,000	0.25	0.50	
2011D	540,240,000	0.25	0.50	
2011S.	(1,453,276)			4
2012P.	464,640,000	0.25	0.50	
2012D	558,960,000	0.25	0.50	
2012S.				4
2013P.		0.25	0.50	
2013D		0.25	0.50	
2013S.				4

Half dimes have the same general designs as larger United States silver coins. Authorized by the Act of April 2, 1792, they were not struck until February 1795, although some were dated 1794. At first the weight was 20.8 grains, and fineness .8924. By the Act of January 18, 1837, the weight was reduced to 20-5/8 grains and the fineness changed to .900. The weight was later reduced to 19.2 grains by the Act of February 21, 1853. Half dimes offer many varieties in the early dates.

FLOWING HAIR (1794–1795)

Designer unknown; engraver Robert Scot; weight 1.35 grams; composition .8924 silver, .1076 copper; approx. diameter 16.5 mm; reeded edge. All coined at Philadelphia Mint.

AG-3 About Good—Details clear enough to identify.
G-4 Good—Eagle, wreath, bust outlined but lack details.
VG-8 Very Good—Some details on face. All lettering legible.
F-12 Fine—Hair ends visible. Hair at top smooth.
VF-20 Very Fine—Hair lines at top visible. Hair about ear defined.
EF-40 Extremely Fine—Hair above forehead and at neck well defined but shows some wear.
AU-50 About Uncirculated—Slight wear on high waves of hair, near ear and face, and on head and tips of eagle's wings.
MS-60 Uncirculated—No trace of wear. Light blemishes.
MS-63 Choice Uncirculated—Some distracting marks or blemishes in prime focal areas. Some impairment of luster possible.

	Mintage	AG-3	G-4	VG-8	F-12	VF-20	EF-40	AU-50	MS-60	MS-63
1794	*	$850	$1,500	$1,800	$2,400	$3,750	$7,500	$11,000	$19,000	$35,000
$367,775, SP-67, Heritage auction, October 2012.										
1795	86,416	550	1,200	1,400	1,850	3,000	6,000	8,000	14,000	21,000

* Included in number below.

DRAPED BUST (1796–1805)

Designer probably Gilbert Stuart; engraver Robert Scot; weight 1.35 grams; composition .900 silver, .100 copper; approx. diameter 16.5 mm; reeded edge. All coined at Philadelphia Mint.

AG-3 About Good—Details clear enough to identify.
G-4 Good—Date, stars, LIBERTY readable. Bust of Liberty outlined, but no details.
VG-8 Very Good—Some details visible.
F-12 Fine—Hair and drapery lines worn, but visible.
VF-20 Very Fine—Only left side of drapery indistinct.
EF-40 Extremely Fine—Details visible in all hair lines.
AU-50 About Uncirculated—Slight wear on bust, shoulder, and hair; wear on eagle's head and top of wings.
MS-60 Uncirculated—No trace of wear. Light blemishes.
MS-63 Choice Uncirculated—Some distracting marks or blemishes in prime focal areas. Impaired luster possible.

Small Eagle Reverse (1796–1797)

See next page for chart.

	Mintage	AG-3	G-4	VG-8	F-12	VF-20	EF-40	AU-50	MS-60	MS-63
1796, 6 Over 5	10,230	$650	$1,300	$1,650	$3,100	$4,500	$9,000	$15,000	$26,000	$42,000
$345,000, MS-66, Heritage auction, January 2008										
1796. . . . .*		600	1,300	1,700	3,000	4,200	8,750	12,500	15,250	27,500
1796, LIKERTY . . . .*		600	1,300	1,700	3,000	4,200	8,750	13,500	16,500	35,000
1797, 15 Stars	44,527	600	1,300	1,700	3,000	4,200	8,750	12,500	16,000	25,000
1797, 16 Stars . . . .*		600	1,300	1,700	3,000	4,200	8,750	12,500	16,000	25,000
1797, 13 Stars . . . .*		750	1,800	2,900	4,000	6,000	12,500	24,000	40,000	65,000

* Included in number above.

Heraldic Eagle Reverse (1800–1805)

1800, LIBEKTY

	Mintage	AG-3	G-4	VG-8	F-12	VF-20	EF-40	AU-50	MS-60	MS-63
1800.	24,000	$400	$900	$1,150	$1,800	$2,500	$6,000	$8,000	$12,500	$20,000
1800, LIBEKTY	16,000	400	950	1,200	1,900	2,700	6,200	8,500	13,000	21,000
1801.	27,760	400	1,000	1,300	2,100	3,000	6,500	9,100	16,000	25,500
1802.	3,060	19,800	33,000	44,000	60,500	121,000	220,000	330,000		
1803, Large 8.	37,850	400	950	1,200	2,000	2,800	6,500	9,000	14,000	22,500
1803, Small 8. . . . .*		400	1,000	1,400	2,500	3,200	7,000	10,000	20,000	35,000
1805.	15,600	450	950	1,250	2,000	3,200	9,000	20,000	40,000	

* Included in number above.

CAPPED BUST (1829–1837)

Designer William Kneass, after John Reich; weight 1.35 grams; composition .8924 silver, .1076 copper; approx. diameter 15.5 mm; reeded edge. Changed to 1.34 grams, .900 fine in 1837. All coined at Philadelphia Mint.

G-4 Good—Bust of Liberty outlined, no detail. Date and legend legible.
VG-8 Very Good—Complete legend and date plain. At least three letters of LIBERTY on edge of cap show clearly.
F-12 Fine—All letters in LIBERTY visible.
VF-20 Very Fine—Full rims. Ear and shoulder clasp show plainly.
EF-40 Extremely Fine—Ear very distinct; eyebrow and hair well defined.
AU-50 About Uncirculated—Traces of light wear on many of the high points. At least half of mint luster still present.
MS-60 Uncirculated—No trace of wear. Light blemishes.
MS-63 Choice Uncirculated—No trace of wear. Light blemishes. Attractive mint luster.

	Mintage	G-4	VG-8	F-12	VF-20	EF-40	AU-50	MS-60	MS-63
1829. 1,230,000		$55	$75	$90	$135	$190	$300	$410	$925
1830. 1,240,000		55	75	80	110	165	250	375	850
1831. 1,242,700		55	75	80	110	165	250	375	850
1832. 965,000		55	75	80	110	165	250	375	850

Mintage	G-4	VG-8	F-12	VF-20	EF-40	AU-50	MS-60	MS-63
1833.....................1,370,000	$55	$75	$80	$110	$165	$250	$375	$850
1834.....................1,480,000	55	75	80	110	165	250	375	850
1834, 3 Over Inverted 3 ....*	55	80	90	150	250	450	600	1,200
1835, All kinds.................2,760,000								
1835, Large Date and 5c	55	75	80	110	165	250	375	850
1835, Large Date, Small 5c	55	75	80	110	165	250	375	850
1835, Small Date, Large 5c	55	75	80	110	165	250	375	850
1835, Small Date and 5c	55	75	80	110	165	250	375	850
1836, Small 5c.................1,900,000	55	75	80	110	165	250	375	850
1836, Large 5c.........................*	55	75	80	110	165	250	375	850
1836, 3 Over Inverted 3 ....*	65	85	100	150	250	475	650	1,200
1837, Small 5c................. 871,000	65	85	100	185	300	500	950	2,100
1837, Large 5c.........................*	55	75	80	110	165	250	400	850

* Included in number above.

LIBERTY SEATED (1837–1873)

The Liberty Seated design without stars on the obverse was used on the half dime and dime only at the Philadelphia Mint in 1837 and the New Orleans Mint in 1838. On those coins, Liberty has no drapery fold at her elbow. Starting in 1838 on the Philadelphia coinage, stars were added around the obverse border. During 1840 and thereafter, an additional fold of drapery was added at the elbow of Liberty.

G-4 Good—LIBERTY on shield smooth. Date and letters legible.
VG-8 Very Good—At least three letters in LIBERTY visible.
F-12 Fine—Entire LIBERTY visible, weak spots.
VF-20 Very Fine—Entire LIBERTY strong and even.
EF-40 Extremely Fine—LIBERTY and scroll edges distinct.
AU-50 About Uncirculated—Traces of light wear on many of the high points. At least half of mint luster still present.
MS-60 Uncirculated—No trace of wear. Light blemishes.
MS-63 Choice Uncirculated—No trace of wear. Light blemishes. Attractive mint luster.

Variety 1 – No Stars on Obverse (1837–1838)

Designer Christian Gobrecht; weight 1.34 grams; composition .900 silver, .100 copper; diameter 15.5 mm; reeded edge; mints: Philadelphia, New Orleans.

Mintage	G-4	VG-8	F-12	VF-20	EF-40	AU-50	MS-60	MS-63
1837, Small Date ...1,405,000	$40	$55	$80	$145	$235	$500	$800	$1,200
1837, Large Date ....*	40	55	80	145	235	500	750	1,100
1838O, No Stars...... 70,000	90	150	235	500	800	1,250	2,500	8,500

* Included in number above.

Variety 2 – Stars on Obverse (1838–1853)

From 1838 through 1859, the mintmark was located above the bow on the reverse. Large, medium, or small mintmark varieties occur for several dates.

Designer Christian Gobrecht; weight 1.34 grams; composition .900 silver, .100 copper; diameter 15.5 mm; reeded edge; mints: Philadelphia, New Orleans.

No Drapery From Elbow (1837–1840)   **Drapery From Elbow (Starting 1840)**

	Mintage	G-4	VG-8	F-12	VF-20	EF-40	AU-50	MS-60	MS-63
1838, No Drapery, Large Stars	2,225,000	$18	$21	$28	$35	$75	$160	$250	$420
1838, No Drapery, Small Stars	*	22	30	55	100	185	350	450	1,000
1839, No Drapery	1,069,150	18	21	28	35	75	160	260	420
1839O, No Drapery	1,060,000	22	23	29	38	80	170	525	1,850
1840, No Drapery	1,034,000	18	21	28	35	75	160	260	420
1840O, No Drapery	695,000	20	23	30	40	85	285	725	2,250
1840, Drapery	310,085	22	38	55	120	210	360	460	825
1840O, Drapery	240,000	32	55	110	160	410	1,250	3,100	8,200
1841	1,150,000	16	20	27	32	75	160	210	325
1841O	815,000	18	24	35	50	110	300	665	1,525
1842	815,000	16	20	27	35	75	160	210	325
1842O	350,000	30	40	65	185	525	825	1,275	2,250
1843	1,165,000	16	20	27	35	75	160	210	325
1844	430,000	16	20	27	35	75	160	210	325
1844O	220,000	80	115	200	550	1,100	3,200	5,600	13,000
1845	1,564,000	16	20	27	35	75	160	210	325
1846	27,000	350	525	900	1,250	2,750	4,600	11,000	18,500
1847	1,274,000	16	20	27	35	75	160	275	525
1848, Medium Date	668,000	16	20	27	35	75	160	250	500
1848, Large Date	*	22	32	45	65	130	285	575	1,600
1848O	600,000	22	25	35	60	120	250	410	720
1849, All kinds	1,309,000								
1849, 9 Over 6		24	35	40	60	125	225	500	1,200
1849, 9 Over 8		30	40	60	100	175	260	620	1,400
1849, Normal Date		18	22	28	40	75	150	235	520
1849O	140,000	30	40	85	220	475	1,200	2,500	4,200
1850	955,000	18	22	28	40	75	150	220	350
1850O	690,000	22	30	40	65	120	310	750	1,650
1851	781,000	18	22	28	40	75	150	210	325
1851O	860,000	22	25	30	50	110	235	525	850
1852	1,000,500	18	22	28	40	75	150	210	325
1852O	260,000	30	40	75	135	260	525	865	2,000
1853, No Arrows	135,000	35	45	75	135	250	475	750	1,200
1853O, No Arrows	160,000	190	300	425	750	2,250	3,500	6,200	12,000

* Included in number above.

Variety 3 – Arrows at Date (1853–1855)

As on the dimes, quarters, and halves, arrows were placed at the sides of the date for a short period starting in 1853. They were placed there to denote the reduction of weight under the terms of the Act of February 21, 1853.

Weight 1.24 grams; composition .900 silver, .100 copper; diameter 15.5 mm; reeded edge; mints: Philadelphia, New Orleans.

Circulation strike.   *Proof strike.*

	Mintage	G-4	VG-8	F-12	VF-20	EF-40	AU-50	MS-60	MS-63	PF-63
1853.	13,210,020	$18	$22	$24	$35	$65	$130	$210	$310	$25,000
1853O	2,200,000	20	25	35	50	75	150	275	925	
1854.	5,740,000	18	22	24	35	65	140	230	325	8,500
1854O	1,560,000	20	24	35	45	75	155	285	775	
1855.	1,750,000	18	22	24	35	65	130	210	350	8,500
1855O	600,000	20	25	35	55	175	200	560	1,100	

Variety 2 Resumed, with Weight Standard of Variety 3 (1856–1859)

1858 Over Inverted Date

	Mintage	G-4	VG-8	F-12	VF-20	EF-40	AU-50	MS-60	MS-63	PF-63
1856.	4,880,000	$18	$22	$25	$35	$65	$130	$185	$320	$4,500
1856O	1,100,000	18	22	25	55	110	265	575	1,000	
1857.	7,280,000	18	22	25	35	65	130	185	320	3,000
1857O	1,380,000	18	22	25	45	70	200	375	500	
1858. . . . . *(300)*. . 3,500,000		18	22	25	35	65	130	185	320	1,400
1858, Repunched High Dt. . . . . . *		40	60	100	150	235	350	650	1,200	
1858, Over Inverted Dt . . . . *		40	60	100	150	220	325	625	1,100	
1858O	1,660,000	18	22	30	50	80	155	265	450	
1859. . . . . *(800). . .* 340,000		18	22	30	45	80	130	220	425	1,250
1859O	560,000	20	24	35	50	130	210	285	375	

* Included in number above.

Transitional Patterns

A new die was utilized in 1859 at the Philadelphia Mint, in which the stars are hollow in the center and the arms of Liberty are slimmer. During the years 1859 and 1860 interesting half dime patterns were made which do not bear our nation's identity. These are transitional pieces, not made for circulation, but struck at the time the inscription UNITED STATES OF AMERICA was being transferred from the reverse to the obverse.

	Mintage	MS-60	MS-63	PF-63
1859, Obverse of 1859, Reverse of 1860	20			$35,000
$66,700, PF-65, Stack's Bowers auction, May 2005				
1860, Obverse of 1859 (With Stars), Reverse of 1860	100	$3,750	$5,600	
$9,200, MS-67, Stack's Bowers auction, August 2009				

Variety 4 – Legend on Obverse (1860–1873)

Weight 1.24 grams; composition .900 silver, .100 copper; diameter 15.5 mm; reeded edge; mints: Philadelphia, New Orleans, San Francisco.

Circulation strike.　　　　Proof strike.

1861, So-Called 1 Over 0	Mintmark Below Bow (1860–1869, 1872–1873)	Mintmark Above Bow (1870–1872)

	Mintage	G-4	VG-8	F-12	VF-20	EF-40	AU-50	MS-60	MS-63	PF-63
1860, Legend (1,000)...	798,000	$16	$20	$25	$30	$50	$80	$160	$250	$575
1860O	1,060,000	16	20	25	30	50	100	200	320	
1861 .....(1,000)..	3,360,000	16	20	25	30	50	80	160	250	575
1861, "1 Over 0" ....*		32	45	50	90	250	375	600	900	
1862........ (550)..	1,492,000	22	30	45	55	65	110	180	260	575
1863........ (460)....	18,000	160	185	235	300	475	625	750	950	575
1863S..............	100,000	27	40	45	55	160	320	750	1,000	
1864........ (470)....	48,000	325	440	500	725	925	1,100	1,200	1,350	575
1864S..............	90,000	45	55	100	135	275	440	725	1,400	
1865........ (500)....	13,000	275	340	425	550	675	750	850	1,250	575
1865S..............	120,000	30	40	50	75	175	550	950	2,100	
1866........ (725)....	10,000	320	375	425	550	650	700	825	1,200	575
1866S..............	120,000	27	40	50	65	160	375	475	950	
1867........ (625).....	8,000	450	525	625	750	850	925	1,100	1,400	575
1867S..............	120,000	22	35	50	65	160	325	575	1,200	
1868........ (600)....	88,600	55	65	120	185	325	475	675	900	575
1868S..............	280,000	16	20	30	35	45	130	320	600	
1869........ (600)...	208,000	16	20	30	35	45	160	260	400	575
1869S..............	230,000	16	20	30	35	45	130	320	800	
1870.......(1,000)...	535,000	16	20	25	30	45	80	150	275	575
1870S *(unique)*									1,500,000	
$661,250, MS-63, Stack's Bowers auction, July 2004										
1871........ (960)..	1,873,000	16	20	25	30	45	80	150	275	575
1871S..............	161,000	18	22	32	65	80	180	310	500	
1872........ (950)..	2,947,000	16	20	25	30	45	80	150	275	575
1872S, All kinds	837,000									
1872S, Mmk above bow 16		20	25	30	45	80	150	275		
1872S, Mmk below bow 16		20	25	30	45	80	150	275		
1873 (Close 3 only)..... (600)...	712,000	16	20	25	30	45	80	150	275	575
1873S (Close 3 only)............	324,000	16	20	25	30	45	80	150	275	

* Included in number above.

The designs of the dimes, first coined in 1796, follow closely those of the half dimes up through the Liberty Seated type. The dimes in each instance weigh twice as much as the half dimes.

Note: Values of common-date silver coins have been based on the current bullion price of silver, $40 per ounce, and may vary with the prevailing spot price. To determine the intrinsic value of common silver coins, see page 425.

DRAPED BUST (1796–1807)
Small Eagle Reverse (1796–1797)

Designer probably Gilbert Stuart; engraver Robert Scot; weight 2.70 grams; composition .8924 silver, .1076 copper; approx. diameter 19 mm; reeded edge. All coined at Philadelphia Mint.

AG-3 About Good—Details clear enough to identify.

G-4 Good—Date legible. Bust outlined, but no detail.

VG-8 Very Good—All but deepest drapery folds worn smooth. Hair lines nearly gone and curls lacking in detail.

F-12 Fine—All drapery lines visible. Hair partly worn.

VF-20 Very Fine—Only left side of drapery indistinct.

EF-40 Extremely Fine—Hair well outlined with details visible.

AU-50 About Uncirculated—Traces of light wear on many of the high points. At least half of mint luster still present.

MS-60 Uncirculated—No trace of wear. Light blemishes.

MS-63 Choice Uncirculated—Some distracting marks or blemishes in prime focal areas. Impaired luster possible.

1796

1797, 16 Stars   1797, 13 Stars

	Mintage	AG-3	G-4	VG-8	F-12	VF-20	EF-40	AU-50	MS-60	MS-63
1796	22,135	$1,000	$2,200	$3,200	$4,500	$6,750	$11,000	$16,500	$26,000	$38,000
1797, All kinds	25,261									
1797, 16 Stars		1,100	2,300	3,400	4,800	7,000	11,750	18,000	35,000	47,500
1797, 13 Stars		1,200	2,500	3,500	5,000	7,250	13,500	19,000	45,000	75,000

$402,500, MS-65, Heritage auction, July 2008

Heraldic Eagle Reverse (1798–1807)

	Mintage	AG-3	G-4	VG-8	F-12	VF-20	EF-40	AU-50	MS-60	MS-63
1798, All kinds	27,550									
1798, 8 Over 7, 16 Stars on Reverse		$310	$650	$1,000	$1,250	$2,300	$3,500	$5,000	$9,000	$20,000

Chart continued on next page.

	Mintage	AG-3	G-4	VG-8	F-12	VF-20	EF-40	AU-50	MS-60	MS-63
1798, 8 Over 7, 13 Stars on Reverse		$325	$750	$2,200	$4,000	$7,000	$10,000	$15,000		
1798, Large 8		310	650	900	1,500	2,500	3,750	4,600	$8,000	$20,000
1798, Small 8		350	750	1,000	1,700	3,500	6,000	12,000	20,000	30,000
1800	21,760	310	650	900	1,500	3,000	4,000	8,000	19,000	30,000
1801	34,640	310	675	1,100	2,000	3,750	5,750	10,000	25,000	35,000
1802	10,975	425	1,000	1,400	2,500	5,000	9,000	16,000	35,000	
1803	33,040	310	650	1,000	1,600	3,200	5,500	11,000	46,000	
1804, All kinds	8,265									
1804, 13 Stars on Rev		750	1,800	3,500	8,500	15,000	30,000	60,000	—	
1804, 14 Stars on Rev		800	2,000	3,800	9,000	20,000	40,000	85,000	—	
$632,500, AU-58, Heritage auction, July 2008										
1805, All kinds	120,780									
1805, 4 Berries		250	500	750	1,000	1,800	2,500	3,500	7,500	14,000
1805, 5 Berries		250	500	750	1,000	2,000	3,000	4,000	9,000	20,000
1807	165,000	250	500	750	1,000	1,800	2,500	3,500	6,500	12,500

CAPPED BUST (1809–1837)

Designer John Reich; weight 2.70 grams; composition .8924 silver, .1076 copper; approx. diameter (1809–1827) 18.8 mm, (1828–1837) 18.5 mm; reeded edge. All coined at Philadelphia Mint. Changed to 2.67 grams, .900 fine in 1837.

AG-3 About Good—Details clear enough to identify.

G-4 Good—Date, letters, and stars discernible. Bust outlined, no details.

VG-8 Very Good—Legends and date plain. Some letters in LIBERTY visible.

F-12 Fine—Clear LIBERTY. Ear and shoulder clasp visible. Part of rim visible on both sides.

VF-20 Very Fine—LIBERTY distinct. Full rim. Ear and clasp plain and distinct.

EF-40 Extremely Fine—LIBERTY sharp. Ear distinct. Hair above eye well defined.

AU-50 About Uncirculated—Traces of light wear on only the high points of the design. Half of mint luster present.

MS-60 Uncirculated—No trace of wear. Light blemishes.

MS-63 Choice Uncirculated—Some distracting marks or blemishes in prime focal areas. Impaired luster possible.

Variety 1 – Wide Border (1809–1828)

1811, 11 Over 09

	Mintage	G-4	VG-8	F-12	VF-20	EF-40	AU-50	MS-60	MS-63
1809	51,065	$150	$225	$450	$800	$1,800	$2,100	$4,500	$7,000
1811, 11 Over 09	65,180	120	200	300	625	1,700	2,000	4,000	6,500

1814, Small Date   1814, Large Date

Mintage	G-4	VG-8	F-12	VF-20	EF-40	AU-50	MS-60	MS-63
1814, All kinds 421,500								
1814, Small Date	$55	$85	$110	$225	$600	$1,200	$2,500	$5,000
1814, Large Date	40	50	65	160	500	1,000	2,000	4,000
1814, STATESOFAMERICA . .	60	90	120	300	650	1,250	2,500	4,500

1820, Large 0   1820, Small 0

Mintage	G-4	VG-8	F-12	VF-20	EF-40	AU-50	MS-60	MS-63
1820, All kinds 942,587								
1820, Large 0.	$40	$45	$60	$125	$500	$650	$1,400	$2,750
1820, Small 0.	40	45	60	150	600	700	1,500	3,500
1820, STATESOFAMERICA **(a)**	45	55	100	200	525	1,100	2,000	4,500

a. This is identical to the die used in 1814.

1821, Small Date   1821, Large Date

Mintage	G-4	VG-8	F-12	VF-20	EF-40	AU-50	MS-60	MS-63
1821, All kinds 1,186,512								
1821, Small Date	$35	$50	$75	$150	$525	$850	$1,750	$3,500
1821, Large Date	35	50	60	135	520	800	1,700	3,250
1822. 100,000	600	1,000	2,300	3,500	5,000	9,750	12,000	25,000

1823, 3 Over 2

Small E's   Large E's

Mintage	G-4	VG-8	F-12	VF-20	EF-40	AU-50	MS-60	MS-63
1823, 3 Over 2, All kinds 440,000								
1823, 3 Over 2, Small E's.	$35	$50	$60	$120	$450	$700	$1,400	$3,000
1823, 3 Over 2, Large E's.	35	50	60	120	450	700	1,400	3,000

1824, 4 Over 2

1824 and 1827, Flat Top 1

1824 and 1827, Pointed Top 1

1828, Large Date

1828, Small Date

	Mintage	G-4	VG-8	F-12	VF-20	EF-40	AU-50	MS-60	MS-63
1824, 4 Over 2, Flat Top 1	510,000	$40	$65	$110	$375	$800	$1,400	$2,000	$4,000
1824, 4 Over 2, Pointed Top 1 . . . .*		300	700	1,200	2,500	4,000			
1825. . . . .*		35	50	75	150	500	850	2,000	3,500
1827, Flat Top 1 in 10 C. 1,215,000		225	375	900	1,250	1,500	2,500		
1827, Pointed Top 1 in 10 C. . . . .*		35	50	65	125	450	700	1,500	3,000
1828, Both varieties	125,000								
1828, Large Date, Curl Base 2		50	80	130	300	625	1,000	2,250	5,500

* Included in number above.

Variety 2 – Modified Design (1828–1837)

New Mint equipment was used to make the Small Date 1828 dimes and subsequent issues. Unlike earlier coinage, these have beaded borders and a uniform diameter. Large Date has curl base knob 2; Small Date has square base knob 2.

1829, Curl Base 2

1829, Small 10 C.

1829, Large 10 C.

1830, 30 Over 29

	Mintage	G-4	VG-8	F-12	VF-20	EF-40	AU-50	MS-60	MS-63
1828, Sm Date, Square Base 2 . . . .*		$40	$50	$75	$150	$400	$750	$1,300	$2,500
1829, All kinds	770,000								
1829, Curl Base 2		7,500	10,000	15,000	30,000				
1829, Small 10 C.		32	40	45	100	350	450	1,000	2,000
1829, Medium 10 C.		32	40	45	100	375	500	1,500	2,500
1829, Large 10 C.		35	45	60	125	400	650	1,750	3,500
1830, All kinds	510,000								
1830, 30 Over 29.		40	60	110	200	450	650	1,300	4,000
1830, Large 10 C.		32	40	45	80	325	500	1,200	2,500
1830, Small 10 C.		32	40	45	80	400	650	1,200	2,500
1831.	771,350	32	40	45	80	300	450	1,000	1,800
1832.	522,500	32	40	45	80	300	450	1,000	1,800
1833, All kinds	485,000								
1833		32	40	45	80	300	450	1,000	1,800
1833, Last 3 High.		32	40	45	80	300	450	1,000	1,800
1834, All kinds	635,000								
1834, Small 4.		32	40	45	80	300	450	1,500	2,250
1834, Large 4.		32	40	45	80	300	450	1,000	1,800
1835.	1,410,000	32	40	45	80	300	450	1,000	1,800
1836.	1,190,000	32	40	45	80	300	450	1,000	1,800
1837.	359,500	32	40	45	80	300	450	1,000	1,800

* Included in "1828, Both varieties" mintage.

LIBERTY SEATED (1837–1891)

G-4 Good—LIBERTY on shield not readable. Date and letters legible.
F-12 Fine—LIBERTY visible, weak spots.
VF-20 Very Fine—LIBERTY strong and even.
EF-40 Extremely Fine—LIBERTY and scroll edges distinct.
AU-50 About Uncirculated—Wear on Liberty's shoulder and hair high points.
MS-60 Uncirculated—No trace of wear. Light blemishes.
MS-63 Choice Uncirculated—Some distracting contact marks or blemishes in prime focal areas. Impaired luster possible.

Variety 1 – No Stars on Obverse (1837–1838)

Designer Christian Gobrecht; weight 2.67 grams; composition .900 silver, .100 copper; diameter 17.9 mm; reeded edge; mints: Philadelphia, New Orleans.

No Drapery From Elbow, No Stars on Obverse

Mintmarks on Liberty Seated dimes on reverse, within or below the wreath. Size of mintmark varies on many dates.

	Mintage	G-4	F-12	VF-20	EF-40	AU-50	MS-60	MS-63
1837, All kinds	.682,500							
1837, Large Date		$45	$100	$300	$500	$700	$1,100	$1,800
1837, Small Date		50	120	325	525	725	1,200	2,000
18380	.406,034	60	140	400	750	1,200	3,000	6,750

Variety 2 – Stars on Obverse (1838–1853)

No Drapery From Elbow, Tilted Shield (1838–1840)

1838, Small Stars　　**1838, Large Stars**

Drapery From Elbow, Upright Shield (1840–1891)

	Mintage	G-4	F-12	VF-20	EF-40	AU-50	MS-60	MS-63
1838, All kinds	1,992,500							
1838, Small Stars		$30	$55	$80	$175	$400	$700	$1,350
1838, Large Stars		22	30	40	120	250	350	850
1838, Partial Drapery		30	60	100	200	500	850	2,000
1839, No Drapery	1,053,115	20	30	40	110	250	400	850
18390, No Drapery	1,291,600	24	40	45	135	275	750	1,400
1840, No Drapery	.981,500	20	25	40	110	250	400	850
18400, No Drapery	1,175,000	25	40	55	150	350	2,100	3,000
1840, Drapery	.377,500	35	90	175	300	450	1,200	5,500
1841 **(a)**	1,622,500	20	30	35	60	140	350	650
18410	2,007,500	25	35	50	85	225	900	1,800
1842	1,887,500	20	30	35	50	125	400	650
18420	2,020,000	25	35	70	225	1,300	2,500	5,500
1843	1,370,000	20	30	35	50	125	400	800
18430	.150,000	60	300	600	1,500	6,500	18,000	

a. 1841, Small Stars, No Drapery, Upright Shield: two examples known (one Proof and one VF).

Chart continued on next page.

151

	Mintage	G-4	F-12	VF-20	EF-40	AU-50	MS-60	MS-63
1844.	72,500	$200	$450	$700	$1,200	$1,800	$4,000	$12,000
1845.	1,755,000	20	30	35	50	125	400	800
1845O	230,000	25	75	200	550	1,200	3,500	—
1846.	31,300	200	400	900	2,000	8,000	13,000	35,000
1847.	245,000	20	40	70	125	350	950	2,500
1848.	451,500	20	32	50	85	150	550	850
1849.	839,000	20	30	40	60	125	300	900
1849O	300,000	25	50	125	300	750	2,500	6,000
1850.	1,931,500	20	30	40	60	125	300	700
1850O	510,000	25	40	90	175	375	1,200	2,600
1851.	1,026,500	20	30	40	60	125	350	850
1851O	400,000	25	40	80	175	450	2,250	3,750
1852.	1,535,500	20	30	40	60	125	300	700
1852O	430,000	30	50	140	250	350	1,600	2,750
1853, No Arrows.	95,000	75	175	275	350	475	800	1,250

Variety 3 – Arrows at Date (1853–1855)

Weight 2.49 grams; composition .900 silver, .100 copper; diameter 17.9 mm; reeded edge; mints: Philadelphia, New Orleans.

**Arrows at Date
(1853–1855)**
Circulation strikes.

**Small Date, Arrows Removed
(1856–1860)**

Proof strike.

	Mintage	G-4	F-12	VF-20	EF-40	AU-50	MS-60	MS-63	PF-63
1853, With Arrows	12,078,010	$16	$20	$30	$50	$175	$300	$675	$30,000
1853O	1,100,000	18	25	50	125	350	1,250	3,250	
1854.	4,470,000	16	20	30	50	175	300	675	15,000
1854O	1,770,000	18	22	45	85	200	400	1,100	
1855.	2,075,000	16	20	30	60	185	325	1,000	15,000

Variety 2 Resumed, With Weight Standard of Variety 3 (1856–1860)

Weight 2.49 grams; composition .900 silver, .100 copper; diameter 17.9 mm; reeded edge; mints: Philadelphia, New Orleans, San Francisco.

	Mintage	G-4	F-12	VF-20	EF-40	AU-50	MS-60	MS-63	PF-63
1856, All kinds	5,780,000								
1856, Large Date		$18	$22	$36	$60	$160	$400	$850	
1856, Small Date		16	20	30	50	130	300	700	$4,500
1856O	1,180,000	18	25	35	65	250	800	1,500	
1856S.	70,000	120	375	600	1,250	1,700	3,800	15,000	
1857.	5,580,000	16	20	30	50	130	300	700	3,750
1857O	1,540,000	18	25	35	70	200	425	750	
1858. *(300+)*	1,540,000	16	20	30	50	130	300	700	2,000
1858O	290,000	25	40	85	135	300	600	1,000	
1858S.	60,000	100	225	450	900	1,600	3,800	16,000	
1859. (800)	429,200	20	22	32	60	140	300	700	1,500
1859O	480,000	20	25	60	95	275	400	900	
1859S.	60,000	100	300	650	1,600	4,000	11,000	26,000	
1860S.	140,000	35	60	150	400	950	2,500	5,000	

In 1859 (see the first row of the chart below), an interesting dime pattern was made that does not bear the nation's identity. It is a "transitional" piece, not made for circulation, but struck at the time the inscription UNITED STATES OF AMERICA was being transferred from the reverse to the obverse.

Variety 4 – Legend on Obverse (1860–1873)

Weight 2.49 grams; composition .900 silver, .100 copper; diameter 17.9 mm; reeded edge; mints: Philadelphia, New Orleans, San Francisco, Carson City.

	Mintage	G-4	F-12	VF-20	EF-40	AU-50	MS-60	MS-63	PF-63
1859, Obv of 1859 (With Stars), Rev of 1860							$10,000		$18,500
1860 . . . . (1,000) . . 606,000		$16	$20	$32	$40	$100	200	$500	750
18600 40,000		325	850	1,800	4,000	8,000	15,000	—	
1861 (a) . . . . . (1,000) 1,883,000		16	22	30	40	100	185	300	750
1861S 172,500		40	110	200	450	1,000	2,100	5,500	
1862 . . . . (550) . . 847,000		16	22	25	40	80	185	350	750
1862S 180,750		45	90	200	320	900	2,000	4,000	
1863 . . . . (460) . . . 14,000		310	600	750	900	1,100	1,300	1,800	700
1863S 157,500		40	60	120	200	500	1,500	4,000	
1864 . . . . (470) . . . 11,000		225	425	575	875	1,100	1,200	1,750	700
1864S 230,000		30	45	100	140	325	950	1,500	
1865 . . . . (500) . . . 10,000		250	550	700	800	950	1,200	2,000	750
1865S 175,000		30	60	140	250	800	2,750	6,500	
1866 . . . . (725) 8,000		300	550	750	850	1,200	1,500	2,000	700
1866S 135,000		40	75	135	225	325	1,000	4,500	
1867 . . . . (625) 6,000		400	750	950	1,100	1,300	1,500	2,500	700
1867S 140,000		30	75	135	225	550	1,250	2,500	
1868 . . . . (600) . . 464,000		18	30	40	65	150	300	850	700
1868S 260,000		20	35	70	125	225	400	1,000	
1869 . . . . (600) . . 256,000		18	30	65	100	200	400	900	700
1869S 450,000		18	25	35	65	150	375	800	
1870 . . . . (1,000) . . 470,500		16	22	25	50	100	200	450	700
1870S 50,000		250	400	475	600	850	1,800	2,750	
1871 . . . . (960) . . 906,750		16	22	25	50	150	250	425	700
1871CC 20,100		1,600	4,500	7,500	12,500	22,000	50,000		
1871S 320,000		25	80	140	225	300	500	1,200	
1872 . . . . (950) 2,395,500		18	25	30	40	90	175	300	700
1872, Doubled-Die Reverse *(rare)* . . . . *		50	75	150	250	350	750		
1872CC 35,480		425	1,900	3,750	7,500	18,500	50,000		
1872S 190,000		25	85	140	225	400	1,200	2,500	
1873, Close 3 (1,100) 1,506,900		16	22	25	40	90	150	250	700
1873, Open 3 60,000		20	50	75	130	200	600	1,500	
1873CC *(unique)* (b) 12,400								*1,500,000* (c)	

$1,840,000, MS-65, Stack's Bowers auction, August 2012

* Included in number above. **a.** Dies modified slightly during 1861. First variety with only five vertical lines in top of shield is scarcer than the later variety. **b.** Most of the mintage was melted after the law of 1873 was passed. **c.** Value is for MS-65.

Variety 5 – Arrows at Date (1873–1874)

In 1873 the dime was increased in weight to 2.50 grams. Arrows at the date in 1873 and 1874 indicate this change.

Weight 2.50 grams; composition .900 silver, .100 copper; diameter 17.9 mm; reeded edge; mints: Philadelphia, San Francisco, Carson City.

Circulation strike.

Proof strike.

	Mintage	G-4	F-12	VF-20	EF-40	AU-50	MS-60	MS-63	PF-63
1873 . . . . (800) . . 2,377,700		$18	$26	$55	$140	$300	$550	$900	$1,500
1873, Doubled-Die Obverse . . . .*		65	200	500	1,000	1,500			
1873CC 18,791		1,500	5,000	8,500	17,000	37,000	—	—	
1873S. 455,000		22	35	60	175	450	1,000	2,100	
1874 . . . . (700) . . 2,939,300		18	25	55	140	310	600	1,000	1,500
1874CC 10,817		4,500	12,500	18,000	28,000	48,000	60,000	—	
1874S. 240,000		25	65	110	225	500	900	2,000	

* Included in number above.

Variety 4 Resumed, With Weight Standard of Variety 5 (1875–1891)

Weight 2.50 grams; composition .900 silver, .100 copper; diameter 17.9 mm; reeded edge; mints: Philadelphia, New Orleans, San Francisco, Carson City.

	Mintage	G-4	F-12	VF-20	EF-40	AU-50	MS-60	MS-63	PF-63
1875. . . . . (700) . .10,350,000		$15	$20	$22	$30	$80	$150	$250	$650
1875CC, All kinds. 4,645,000									
1875CC, Above Bow.		16	22	32	65	110	325	500	
1875CC, Below Bow.		20	24	37	70	125	350	550	
1875S, All kinds 9,070,000									
1875S, Below Bow.		15	20	22	30	85	160	250	
1875S, Above Bow.		15	20	22	30	80	150	250	
1876. . . . . (1,150) . .11,450,000		15	20	25	35	80	150	250	650
1876CC .8,270,000		20	24	38	65	100	230	450	
1876S. .10,420,000		15	20	25	35	80	150	250	
1877. . . . . (510) . . .7,310,000		15	20	25	35	80	150	250	650
1877CC .7,700,000		20	24	38	65	100	230	400	
1877S. .2,340,000		15	20	25	35	80	150	250	
1878. . . . . (800) . . .1,677,200		15	20	25	35	80	150	250	650
1878CC 200,000		55	140	200	400	575	1,100	1,750	
1879. . . . . (1,100) 14,000		200	325	400	500	550	625	750	650
1880. . . . .(1,355) 36,000		150	250	350	400	500	650	750	650
1881. . . . . (975) 24,000		160	260	375	425	525	675	775	650
1882. . . . .(1,100) . . .3,910,000		15	20	25	35	80	150	250	650
1883. . . . .(1,039) . . .7,674,673		15	20	25	35	80	150	250	650
1884. . . . . (875) . . .3,365,505		15	20	25	35	80	150	250	650
1884S. 564,969		20	32	60	100	300	750	1,200	
1885. . . . . (930) . . .2,532,497		15	20	25	35	80	150	250	650
1885S. .43,690		400	800	1,400	2,200	4,000	5,500	9,000	
1886. . . . . (886) . . .6,376,684		15	20	25	35	80	150	250	650
1886S. 206,524		30	50	75	135	200	600	1,200	
1887. . . . . (710) . .11,283,229		15	20	25	35	80	150	250	650

Mintage	G-4	F-12	VF-20	EF-40	AU-50	MS-60	MS-63	PF-63
1887S....................4,454,450	$15	$20	$25	$35	$80	$150	$250	
1888............... (832) ...5,495,655	15	20	25	35	80	150	250	$650
1888S....................1,720,000	15	20	25	35	100	250	650	
1889............... (711) ...7,380,000	15	20	25	35	80	150	250	650
1889S....................972,678	20	30	50	80	150	450	900	
1890............... (590) ...9,910,951	15	20	25	35	80	150	250	650
1890S, Large S................1,423,076	18	25	55	85	150	350	700	
1890S, Small S *(rare)*.................*				—	—	—		
1891............... (600) ..15,310,000	15	20	25	35	80	150	250	650
1891O....................4,540,000	15	20	30	60	110	200	400	
1891O, O Over Horizontal O..............*	60	120	150	225	—	—		
1891S....................3,196,116	15	20	25	35	80	175	325	

* Included in number above.

BARBER OR LIBERTY HEAD (1892–1916)

Designed by Charles E. Barber, chief engraver of the Mint, who also designed the twenty-five- and fifty-cent pieces. His initial B is at the truncation of the neck.

Designer Charles E. Barber; weight 2.50 grams; composition .900 silver, .100 copper (net weight: .07234 oz. pure silver); diameter 17.9 mm; reeded edge; mints: Philadelphia, Denver, New Orleans, San Francisco.

G-4 Good—Date and letters plain. LIBERTY obliterated.
VG-8 Very Good—Some letters visible in LIBERTY.
F-12 Fine—Letters in LIBERTY visible, though some weak.
VF-20 Very Fine—Letters of LIBERTY evenly plain.
EF-40 Extremely Fine—All letters in LIBERTY sharp, distinct. Headband edges distinct.
AU-50 About Uncirculated—Slight traces of wear on hair and cheekbone, and on leaf tips in wreath.
MS-60 Uncirculated—No trace of wear. Light blemishes.
MS-63 Choice Uncirculated—Some distracting marks or blemishes in prime focal areas. Impaired luster possible.

Mintmark location is on reverse, below wreath.

Circulation strike.　　　　Proof strike.

Mintage	G-4	VG-8	F-12	VF-20	EF-40	AU-50	MS-60	MS-63	PF-63
1892...... (1,245)..12,120,000	$7	$7.50	$18	$25	$30	$75	$125	$225	$600
1892O.............3,841,700	12	15.00	35	50	75	95	175	300	
1892S.............990,710	65	120.00	190	240	280	330	425	775	
1893, "3 Over 2"............*	140	150.00	160	175	200	300	700	1,800	—
1893.......(792)...3,339,940	8	12.00	20	30	45	75	150	235	600
1893O.............1,760,000	30	45.00	120	150	190	230	325	650	
1893S.............2,491,401	14	25.00	37	60	85	150	290	700	
1894.......(972)...1,330,000	27	42.00	120	160	180	220	325	500	600
1894O.............720,000	70	95.00	200	275	425	600	1,450	2,500	
1894S.................24									1,500,000
$1,552,500, PF-64, Stack's Bowers auction, October 2007									
1895.......(880)...690,000	80	160.00	325	475	550	625	725	1,200	600
1895O.............440,000	375	550.00	850	1,250	2,400	3,500	6,000	9,750	
1895S.............1,120,000	42	60.00	135	190	240	310	500	1,200	
1896.......(762)...2,000,000	10	22.00	50	75	100	120	175	500	600
1896O.............610,000	80	160.00	290	350	450	650	1,000	2,400	

* Included in number below.

Chart continued on next page.

	Mintage	G-4	VG-8	F-12	VF-20	EF-40	AU-50	MS-60	MS-63	PF-63
1896S.	575,056	$80.00	$150.00	$280	$335.00	$400	$550	$850	$1,500	
1897. . . . . (731). .	10,868,533	3.50	4.50	8	15.00	30	70	135	250	$600
1897O	666,000	65.00	115.00	280	375.00	475	600	900	1,700	
1897S.	1,342,844	18.00	35.00	90	120.00	175	260	450	1,000	
1898. . . . . (735). .	16,320,000	3.50	4.50	8	12.00	26	75	115	225	600
1898O	2,130,000	12.00	26.00	85	130.00	190	280	450	1,200	
1898S.	1,702,507	8.00	15.00	32	45.00	80	150	375	1,200	
1899. . . . . (846). .	19,580,000	3.50	4.50	8	12.00	25	70	125	225	600
1899O	2,650,000	10.00	18.00	65	95.00	140	225	400	1,150	
1899S.	1,867,493	8.50	16.00	32	35.00	45	110	300	750	
1900. . . . . (912). .	17,600,000	3.50	4.50	8	12.00	25	70	110	225	600
1900O	2,010,000	18.00	38.00	110	160.00	220	360	650	1,150	
1900S.	5,168,270	5.00	6.00	12	20.00	30	70	175	425	
1901. . . . . (813). .	18,859,665	3.25	4.00	7	10.00	26	70	110	225	600
1901O	5,620,000	4.00	5.50	16	28.00	65	180	450	950	
1901S.	593,022	80.00	150.00	350	450.00	550	675	1,000	1,650	
1902. . . . . (777). .	21,380,000	3.25	4.00	6	8.00	25	70	110	225	600
1902O	4,500,000	4.00	6.00	15	32.00	65	150	400	1,000	
1902S.	2,070,000	9.00	20.00	55	80.00	140	200	400	1,000	
1903. . . . . (755). .	19,500,000	3.25	4.00	5	7.50	25	70	110	225	600
1903O	8,180,000	4.50	6.00	14	25.00	50	110	275	550	
1903S.	613,300	85.00	130.00	350	475.00	725	875	1,250	1,800	
1904. . . . . (670). .	14,600,357	3.25	4.00	6	9.00	25	70	110	225	600
1904S.	800,000	45.00	75.00	160	235.00	325	475	800	1,500	
1905. . . . . (727). .	14,551,623	3.25	4.00	5	7.50	25	70	110	225	600
1905O	3,400,000	4.50	10.00	35	60.00	90	150	300	500	
1905O, Micro O (a). . . . .*		25.00	50.00	110	160.00	200	300	650	3,500	
1905S.	6,855,199	3.25	4.00	9	20.00	40	95	250	325	
1906. . . . . (675). .	19,957,731	3.25	3.50	4	7.00	22	70	110	225	600
1906D	4,060,000	4.00	5.00	8	15.00	35	80	175	400	
1906O	2,610,000	5.50	14.00	45	75.00	95	130	225	325	
1906S.	3,136,640	4.00	6.00	13	25.00	45	110	275	550	
1907. . . . . (575). .	22,220,000	3.25	3.50	4	7.00	22	70	110	225	600
1907D	4,080,000	3.25	4.00	9	18.00	45	110	300	900	
1907O	5,058,000	4.00	7.00	30	45.00	70	110	225	375	
1907S.	3,178,470	4.00	6.00	15	27.00	65	150	400	750	
1908. . . . . (545). .	10,600,000	3.25	3.50	4	7.00	22	75	110	225	600
1908D	7,490,000	3.25	3.50	6	10.00	28	75	130	250	
1908O	1,789,000	6.00	12.00	45	65.00	95	150	300	600	
1908S.	3,220,000	4.00	6.00	12	22.00	45	170	350	750	
1909. . . . . (650). .	10,240,000	3.25	3.50	4	7.00	22	75	110	225	600
1909D	954,000	8.00	20.00	60	90.00	140	225	500	1,000	
1909O	2,287,000	5.00	8.00	13	22.00	50	90	225	550	
1909S.	1,000,000	9.00	20.00	80	130.00	180	310	550	1,400	
1910. . . . . (551). .	11,520,000	3.25	3.50	5	9.00	22	75	110	225	600
1910D	3,490,000	3.25	4.50	9	18.00	45	95	220	450	
1910S.	1,240,000	6.00	9.00	50	70.00	100	180	425	700	
1911. . . . . (543). .	18,870,000	3.25	3.50	4	7.00	22	75	110	225	600
1911D	11,209,000	3.25	3.50	4	7.00	24	75	110	225	
1911S.	3,520,000	3.25	4.00	9	20.00	40	100	225	400	

* Included in number above. **a.** Normal and "microscopic" mintmark varieties; see page 22.

Mintage	G-4	VG-8	F-12	VF-20	EF-40	AU-50	MS-60	MS-63	PF-63
1912.......(700)..19,349,300	$3.25	$3.50	$4	$7.00	$22	$75	$110	$225	$600
1912D 11,760,000	3.25	3.50	4	7.00	22	75	110	225	
1912S..............3,420,000	3.25	3.50	6	12.00	32	90	170	300	
1913.......(622)..19,760,000	3.25	3.50	4	7.00	22	75	110	225	600
1913S.............. 510,000	35.00	55.00	125	190.00	250	320	500	750	
1914.......(425)..17,360,230	3.25	3.50	4	7.00	22	75	110	225	600
1914D 11,908,000	3.25	3.50	4	7.00	22	75	110	225	
1914S..............2,100,000	3.25	4.00	10	18.00	40	80	175	350	
1915.......(450)...5,620,000	3.25	3.50	4	7.00	22	75	110	225	600
1915S.............. 960,000	7.00	12.00	35	50.00	75	140	275	475	
1916..............18,490,000	3.25	3.50	4	7.50	22	75	110	225	
1916S..............5,820,000	3.25	3.50	4	7.50	22	75	110	225	

WINGED LIBERTY HEAD OR "MERCURY" (1916–1945)

Although this coin is commonly called the *Mercury dime,* the main device is in fact a representation of Liberty. The wings crowning her cap are intended to symbolize liberty of thought. The designer's monogram AW is to the right of the neck.

Designer Adolph A. Weinman; weight 2.50 grams; composition .900 silver, .100 copper (net weight: .07234 oz. pure silver); diameter 17.9 mm; reeded edge; mints: Philadelphia, Denver, San Francisco.

G-4 Good—Letters and date clear. Lines and bands in fasces obliterated.
VG-8 Very Good—Half of sticks discernible in fasces.
F-12 Fine—All sticks in fasces defined. Diagonal bands worn nearly flat.
VF-20 Very Fine—Diagonal bands definitely visible.
EF-40 Extremely Fine—Only slight wear on diagonal bands. Braids and hair before ear clearly visible.
AU-50 About Uncirculated—Slight trace of wear. Most mint luster present.
MS-63 Choice Uncirculated—No trace of wear. Light blemishes. Attractive mint luster.
MS-65 Gem Uncirculated—Only light, scattered marks that are not distracting. Strong luster, good eye appeal.

Mintmark location is on reverse, left of fasces.

Circulation strike.   Proof strike.

Uncirculated values shown are for average pieces with minimum blemishes; those with sharp strikes and split horizontal bands on reverse are worth much more.

Mintage	G-4	VG-8	F-12	VF-20	EF-40	AU-50	MS-60	MS-63	MS-65
1916.......22,180,080	$3.50	$5.00	$7.00	$8	$12	$25	$35	$45	$120
1916D 264,000	1,000.00	1,500.00	2,600.00	4,200	6,200	9,200	13,200	17,000	29,000
1916S......10,450,000	4.00	6.00	9.00	12	20	25	42	65	215
1917......55,230,000	3.00	3.25	3.50	6	8	12	30	60	170
1917D 9,402,000	4.50	6.00	11.00	22	45	95	145	350	1,050
1917S......27,330,000	3.00	3.25	4.00	7	12	30	60	180	550
1918......26,680,000	3.00	4.00	6.00	12	25	40	70	125	460
1918D 22,674,800	3.00	4.00	6.00	12	24	50	125	250	600
1918S......19,300,000	3.00	3.25	5.00	10	18	40	120	275	725
1919......35,740,000	3.00	3.25	4.00	6	10	30	45	120	375
1919D 9,939,000	4.00	7.00	12.00	24	35	75	200	450	1,750
1919S......8,850,000	3.50	4.00	8.00	16	35	75	200	450	1,250
1920......59,030,000	3.00	3.25	3.50	5	8	15	35	75	260
1920D 19,171,000	3.00	3.50	4.50	8	20	45	145	350	775
1920S......13,820,000	3.25	4.00	5.00	8	18	45	145	325	1,450
1921........1,230,000	65.00	80.00	130.00	320	600	925	1,200	1,850	3,500

Chart continued on next page.

	Mintage	G-4	VG-8	F-12	VF-20	EF-40	AU-50	MS-60	MS-63	MS-65
1921D	1,080,000	$80.00	$130.00	$210.00	$420	$775	$1,250	$1,500	$2,000	$3,600
1923 **(a)**	50,130,000	3.00	3.25	3.50	5	7	16	30	45	130
1923S	6,440,000	3.00	4.00	8.00	18	65	105	160	400	1,250
1924	24,010,000	3.00	3.25	4.00	6	15	30	45	100	210
1924D	6,810,000	3.25	4.50	8.00	24	70	110	175	500	950
1924S	7,120,000	3.25	4.00	6.00	10	60	110	200	525	1,250
1925	25,610,000	3.00	3.25	4.00	5	10	20	30	85	225
1925D	5,117,000	4.00	5.00	12.00	45	120	200	375	800	1,700
1925S	5,850,000	3.25	4.00	8.00	18	70	110	180	500	1,400
1926	32,160,000	3.00	3.25	3.50	5	7	16	25	65	250
1926D	6,828,000	3.25	4.50	6.00	10	28	50	125	275	600
1926S	1,520,000	13.00	15.00	26.00	60	250	450	825	1,500	2,850
1927	28,080,000	3.00	3.25	3.50	5	7	15	30	60	150
1927D	4,812,000	3.50	5.50	8.00	25	80	100	200	400	1,200
1927S	4,770,000	3.25	4.00	6.00	12	28	50	275	550	1,400
1928	19,480,000	3.00	3.25	3.50	5	7	18	30	55	130
1928D	4,161,000	4.00	5.00	8.00	20	50	95	175	350	850
1928S **(b)**	7,400,000	3.00	3.25	4.00	6	16	45	150	300	400
1929	25,970,000	3.00	3.25	3.50	5	6	12	22	35	75
1929D	5,034,000	3.00	3.50	5.00	8	15	24	30	40	75
1929S	4,730,000	3.00	3.25	3.75	5	10	20	35	45	125
1930 **(a)**	6,770,000	3.00	3.25	3.50	5	8	16	30	50	125
1930S	1,843,000	3.00	4.00	5.00	7	15	45	80	135	210
1931	3,150,000	3.00	3.10	4.00	6	10	22	35	70	140
1931D	1,260,000	8.00	9.00	12.00	20	35	60	90	140	280
1931S	1,800,000	4.00	5.00	6.00	10	16	45	90	150	300

a. Dimes dated 1923-D or 1930-D are counterfeit. **b.** Large and small mintmarks; see page 22.

	Mintage	F-12	VF-20	EF-40	MS-60	MS-63	MS-65	PF-65
1934	24,080,000	$3	$3.10	$3.50	$25	$35	$50	
1934D **(b)**	6,772,000	3	3.10	8.00	50	60	85	
1935	58,830,000	3	3.10	3.25	10	15	35	
1935D	10,477,000	3	3.10	8.00	35	50	90	
1935S	15,840,000	3	3.10	5.00	22	30	40	
1936 . . . . (4,130) . .	87,500,000	3	3.10	3.50	10	18	30	$1,500
1936D	16,132,000	3	3.60	6.00	25	40	55	
1936S	9,210,000	3	3.10	3.50	23	30	35	
1937 . . . . (5,756) . .	56,860,000	3	3.10	3.25	10	15	30	850
1937D	14,146,000	3	3.10	4.00	21	30	45	
1937S	9,740,000	3	3.10	3.50	20	30	40	
1938 . . . . (8,728) . .	22,190,000	3	3.10	3.25	10	15	30	550
1938D	5,537,000	3	3.20	4.00	18	25	35	
1938S	8,090,000	3	3.10	3.50	20	28	40	
1939 . . . . (9,321) . .	67,740,000	3	3.10	3.25	8	12	25	450
1939D	24,394,000	3	3.10	3.25	8	12	28	
1939S	10,540,000	3	3.10	4.00	23	30	42	
1940 . . . . (11,827) . .	65,350,000	3	3.10	3.25	7	12	30	400
1940D	21,198,000	3	3.10	3.25	7	14	35	
1940S	21,560,000	3	3.10	3.25	8	15	35	
1941 . . . . (16,557) . .	175,090,000	3	3.10	3.25	7	12	30	375
1941D	45,634,000	3	3.10	3.25	8	14	25	
1941S **(b)**	43,090,000	3	3.10	3.25	7	12	30	

b. Large and small mintmarks; see page 22.

1942, 42 Over 41 **1942-D, 42 Over 41**

	Mintage	F-12	VF-20	EF-40	MS-60	MS-63	MS-65	PF-65
1942, 42 Over 41 . . . . *		$625.00	$800.00	$1,000.00	$2,500	$4,250	$15,000	
1942 . . . . (22,329) 205,410,000		2.25	3.10	3.25	6	12	30	$385
1942D, 42 Over 41 . . . . *		675.00	850.00	1,100.00	2,600	4,500	9,000	
1942D 60,740,000		3.00	3.10	3.25	6	12	30	
1942S 49,300,000		3.00	3.10	3.25	8	20	35	
1943 191,710,000		3.00	3.10	3.25	6	12	25	
1943D 71,949,000		3.00	3.10	3.25	6	15	30	
1943S 60,400,000		3.00	3.10	3.25	7	16	30	
1944 231,410,000		3.00	3.10	3.25	6	12	25	
1944D 62,224,000		3.00	3.10	3.25	7	15	30	
1944S 49,490,000		3.00	3.10	3.25	7	15	30	
1945 159,130,000		3.00	3.10	3.25	6	12	28	
1945D 40,245,000		3.00	3.10	3.25	6	12	30	
1945S 41,920,000		3.00	3.10	3.25	6	12	30	
1945S, Micro S . . . . **		3.25	3.50	6.00	30	40	100	

* Included in number below. ** Included in number above.

ROOSEVELT (1946 TO DATE)

John R. Sinnock (whose initials, JS, are at the truncation of the neck) designed this dime showing a portrait of Franklin D. Roosevelt. The design has heavier lettering and a more modernistic character than preceding types.

Circulation strike. *Proof strike.*

Mintmark on reverse, 1946–1964. *Mintmark on obverse, starting 1968.*

Silver Coinage (1946–1964)

Designer John R. Sinnock; weight 2.50 grams; composition .900 silver, .100 copper (net weight .07234 oz. pure silver); diameter 17.9 mm; reeded edge; mints: Philadelphia, Denver, San Francisco.

EF-40 Extremely Fine—All lines of torch, flame, and hair very plain.
MS-63 Choice Uncirculated—Some distracting contact marks or blemishes in prime focal areas. Impaired luster possible.
MS-65 Gem Uncirculated—Only light scattered marks that are not distracting. Strong luster, good eye appeal.
PF-65 Gem Proof—Nearly perfect.

See next page for chart.

	Mintage	EF-40	MS-63	MS-65	PF-65
1946	255,250,000	$3.00	$4.50	$12	
1946D	61,043,500	3.00	4.50	14	
1946S	27,900,000	3.00	4.50	20	
1947	121,520,000	3.00	6.00	12	
1947D	46,835,000	3.00	6.50	12	
1947S	34,840,000	3.00	6.00	12	
1948	74,950,000	3.00	4.00	12	
1948D	52,841,000	3.00	6.00	12	
1948S	35,520,000	3.00	5.50	12	
1949	30,940,000	3.75	27.00	38	
1949D	26,034,000	3.00	12.00	20	
1949S	13,510,000	5.00	45.00	70	
1950	(51,386) 50,130,114	3.00	13.00	16	$50
1950D	46,803,000	3.00	6.00	12	
1950S	20,440,000	5.00	38.00	60	
1951	(57,500) 103,880,102	3.00	4.00	10	50
1951D	56,529,000	3.00	4.00	10	
1951S	31,630,000	3.50	15.00	25	
1952	(81,980) 99,040,093	3.00	4.00	10	35
1952D	122,100,000	3.00	4.00	8	
1952S	44,419,500	3.00	8.00	12	
1953	(128,800) 53,490,120	3.00	4.00	8	38
1953D	136,433,000	3.00	4.00	8	
1953S	39,180,000	3.00	4.00	8	
1954	(233,300) 114,010,203	3.00	4.00	8	18
1954D	106,397,000	3.00	4.00	8	
1954S	22,860,000	3.00	4.00	8	
1955	(378,200) 12,450,181	3.00	4.00	8	15
1955D	13,959,000	3.00	4.00	8	
1955S	18,510,000	3.00	4.00	8	
1956	(669,384) 108,640,000	3.00	3.50	7	8
1956D	108,015,100	3.00	3.50	7	
1957	(1,247,952) 160,160,000	3.00	3.50	7	5
1957D	113,354,330	3.00	3.50	7	
1958	(875,652) 31,910,000	3.00	4.00	8	5
1958D	136,564,600	3.00	4.00	8	
1959	(1,149,291) 85,780,000	3.00	3.50	7	4
1959D	164,919,790	3.00	3.50	7	
1960	(1,691,602) 70,390,000	3.00	3.50	7	4
1960, Doubled-Die Obverse	*				150
1960D	200,160,400	3.00	3.25	6	
1961	(3,028,244) 93,730,000	3.00	3.25	6	4
1961D	209,146,550	3.00	3.25	6	
1962	(3,218,019) 72,450,000	3.00	3.25	6	4
1962D	334,948,380	3.00	3.25	6	
1963	(3,075,645) 123,650,000	3.00	3.25	6	4
1963, Doubled-Die Reverse	*			35	150
1963D	421,476,530	3.00	3.25	6	
1964 (a)	(3,950,762) 929,360,000	3.00	3.25	6	4
1964D (a)	1,357,517,180	3.00	3.25	6	
1964D, Doubled-Die Reverse	*	35.00	100.00	150	

* Included in number above. **a.** Variations of 9 in date have pointed or straight tail.

Clad Coinage and Silver Proofs (1965 to Date)

Designer: John R. Sinnock; weight 2.27 grams; composition, outer layers of copper-nickel (.750 copper, .250 nickel) bonded to inner core of pure copper; diameter 17.9 mm; reeded edge; mints: Philadelphia, Denver, San Francisco, West Point. Silver Proofs: pre-1965 standards; mint: San Francisco.

	Mintage	MS-65	PF-65		Mintage	MS-65	PF-65
1965	1,652,140,570	$1.50		1981S, Type 2 **(b)**	*		$25.00
1966	1,382,734,540	1.25		1982, No Mintmark,			
1967	2,244,007,320	1.00		Strong Strike **(a)**		$225.00	
1968	424,470,400	1.00		1982, No Mintmark,			
1968D	480,748,280	1.00		Weak Strike **(a)**		85.00	
1968S **(a)**	(3,041,506)		$2.00	1982P	519,475,000	7.00	
1969	145,790,000	2.00		1982D	542,713,584	1.50	
1969D	563,323,870	1.00		1982S	(3,857,479)		2.50
1969S	(2,394,631)		2.00	1983P	647,025,000	6.00	
1970	345,570,000	1.00		1983D	730,129,224	3.00	
1970D	754,942,100	1.00		1983S **(a)**	(3,279,126)		2.00
1970S **(a)**	(2,632,810)		2.00	1984P	856,669,000	1.00	
1971	162,690,000	1.50		1984D	704,803,976	1.25	
1971D	377,914,240	1.25		1984S	(3,065,110)		2.50
1971S	(3,220,733)		2.00	1985P	705,200,962	1.25	
1972	431,540,000	1.00		1985D	587,979,970	1.25	
1972D	330,290,000	1.00		1985S	(3,362,821)		2.00
1972S	(3,260,996)		2.00	1986P	682,649,693	1.50	
1973	315,670,000	1.00		1986D	473,326,970	1.50	
1973D	455,032,426	1.00		1986S	(3,010,497)		4.00
1973S	(2,760,339)		2.00	1987P	762,709,481	1.00	
1974	470,248,000	1.00		1987D	653,203,402	1.00	
1974D	571,083,000	1.00		1987S	(4,227,728)		3.00
1974S	(2,612,568)		2.00	1988P	1,030,550,000	1.00	
1975	585,673,900	1.00		1988D	962,385,489	1.00	
1975D	313,705,300	1.00		1988S	(3,262,948)		4.00
1975S **(a)**	(2,845,450)		2.50	1989P	1,298,400,000	1.25	
1976	568,760,000	1.00		1989D	896,535,597	1.00	
1976D	695,222,774	1.00		1989S	(3,220,194)		4.00
1976S	(4,149,730)		2.50	1990P	1,034,340,000	1.50	
1977	796,930,000	1.00		1990D	839,995,824	1.00	
1977D	376,607,228	1.00		1990S	(3,299,559)		2.50
1977S	(3,251,152)		2.00	1991P	927,220,000	1.00	
1978	663,980,000	1.00		1991D	601,241,114	1.00	
1978D	282,847,540	1.00		1991S	(2,867,787)		4.00
1978S	(3,127,781)		2.00	1992P	593,500,000	1.00	
1979	315,440,000	1.00		1992D	616,273,932	1.00	
1979D	390,921,184	1.00		1992S	(2,858,981)		3.00
1979S, Type 1 **(b)**	(3,677,175)		6.00	1992S, Silver	(1,317,579)		6.00
1979S, Type 2 **(b)**	*		10.00	1993P	766,180,000	1.00	
1980P	735,170,000	1.00		1993D	750,110,166	1.00	
1980D	719,354,321	1.00		1993S	(2,633,439)		5.00
1980S	(3,554,806)		2.00	1993S, Silver	(761,353)		7.00
1981P	676,650,000	1.00		1994P	1,189,000,000	1.00	
1981D	712,284,143	1.00		1994D	1,303,268,110	1.00	
1981S, Type 1 **(b)**	(4,063,083)		6.00	1994S	(2,484,594)		5.00

* Included in number above. **a.** Some 1968, 1970, 1975, and 1983 Proof dimes without S mintmark were made in error, as were some circulation-strike 1982 dimes. See page 22 for discussion. **b.** See page 234 for illustrations of Type 1 and Type 2 varieties.

Chart continued on next page.

	Mintage	MS-65	PF-65
1994S, Silver	(785,329)		$8.00
1995P	1,125,500,000	$1.00	
1995D	1,274,890,000	1.25	
1995S	(2,117,496)		10.00
1995S, Silver	(679,985)		14.00
1996P	1,421,163,000	1.00	
1996D	1,400,300,000	1.00	
1996W (c)	1,457,000	18.00	
1996S	(1,750,244)		3.00
1996S, Silver	(775,021)		8.00
1997P	991,640,000	1.00	
1997D	979,810,000	1.00	
1997S	(2,055,000)		8.00
1997S, Silver	(741,678)		12.00
1998P	1,163,000,000	1.00	
1998D	1,172,250,000	1.00	
1998S	(2,086,507)		4.00
1998S, Silver	(878,792)		6.00
1999P	2,164,000,000	1.00	
1999D	1,397,750,000	1.00	
1999S	(2,543,401)		4.00
1999S, Silver	(804,565)		7.00
2000P	1,842,500,000	1.00	
2000D	1,818,700,000	1.00	
2000S	(3,082,572)		2.50
2000S, Silver	(965,421)		5.00
2001P	1,369,590,000	1.00	
2001D	1,412,800,000	1.00	
2001S	(2,294,909)		2.50
2001S, Silver	(889,697)		5.00
2002P	1,187,500,000	1.00	
2002D	1,379,500,000	1.00	
2002S	(2,319,766)		2.50
2002S, Silver	(892,229)		5.00
2003P	1,085,500,000	1.00	
2003D	986,500,000	1.00	
2003S	(2,172,684)		2.50
2003S, Silver	(1,125,755)		5.00
2004P	1,328,000,000	1.00	

	Mintage	MS-65	PF-65
2004D	1,159,500,000	$1	
2004S	(1,789,488)		$3.00
2004S, Silver	(1,175,934)		5.00
2005P	1,412,000,000	1	
2005D	1,423,500,000	1	
2005S	(2,275,000)		2.50
2005S, Silver	(1,069,679)		5.00
2006P	1,381,000,000	1	
2006D	1,447,000,000	1	
2006S	(2,000,428)		2.50
2006S, Silver	(1,054,008)		5.00
2007P	1,047,500,000	1	
2007D	1,042,000,000	1	
2007S	(1,702,116)		2.50
2007S, Silver	(875,050)		5.00
2008P	391,000,000	1	
2008D	624,500,000	1	
2008S	(1,405,674)		2.50
2008S, Silver	(763,887)		5.00
2009P	96,500,000	1	
2009D	49,500,000	1	
2009S	(1,482,502)		2.50
2009S, Silver	(697,365)		5.00
2010P	557,000,000	1	
2010D	562,000,000	1	
2010S	(1,103,950)		2.50
2010S, Silver	(585,414)		5.00
2011P	748,000,000	1	
2011D	754,000,000	1	
2011S	(952,881)		2.50
2011S, Silver	(500,395)		5.00
2012P	808,000,000	1	
2012D	868,000,000	1	
2012S			2.50
2012S, Silver			5.00
2013P		1	
2013D		1	
2013S, Proof			2.50
2013S, Silver, Proof			5.00

c. Issued in Mint sets only, to mark the 50th anniversary of the design.

LIBERTY SEATED (1875–1878)

This short-lived coin was authorized by the Act of March 3, 1875. Soon after the appearance of the first twenty-cent pieces, people complained about the similarity in design and size to the quarter dollar. The eagle is very similar to that used on the trade dollar, but the edge of this coin is plain. The mintmark is on the reverse below the eagle.

In the denomination's first year, more than one million pieces were struck at the San Francisco Mint; about 133,000 at the Carson City Mint; and roughly 37,000 at Philadelphia (not including about 2,800 Proofs struck there as well). These numbers dropped sharply in 1876. (Most of the Carson City coins of that year were melted at the mint and never released, a fate likely met by most of the Philadelphia twenty-cent pieces of 1876 as well.) In 1877 and 1878, only Proof examples were minted. None were struck for circulation.

Various factors caused the demise of the twenty-cent piece: the public was confused over the coin's similarity to the quarter dollar, which was better established as a foundation of American commerce; in the eastern United States, small-change transactions were largely satisfied by Fractional Currency notes; and the twenty-cent coin was essentially just a substitute for two dimes.

Designer William Barber; weight 5 grams; composition .900 silver, .100 copper; diameter 22 mm; plain edge; mints: Philadelphia, Carson City, San Francisco.

G-4 Good—LIBERTY on shield obliterated. Letters and date legible.
VG-8 Very Good—One or two letters in LIBERTY barely visible. Other details bold.
F-12 Fine—Some letters of LIBERTY possibly visible.
VF-20 Very Fine—LIBERTY readable, but partly weak.
EF-40 Extremely Fine—LIBERTY mostly sharp. Only slight wear on high points of coin.
AU-50 About Uncirculated—Slight trace of wear on breast, head, and knees.
MS-60 Uncirculated—No trace of wear. Light blemishes.
MS-63 Choice Uncirculated—Some distracting blemishes in prime focal areas. Some impairment of luster possible.

| Circulation strike. | | Proof strike. | Mintmark location is below eagle. |

	Mintage	G-4	VG-8	F-12	VF-20	EF-40	AU-50	MS-60	MS-63	PF-63
1875	(2,790)....36,910	$240	$300	$365	$460	$560	$725	$950	$1,700	$3,000
1875CC	133,290	425	450	550	750	1,100	1,750	2,200	4,500	
1875S	1,155,000	110	120	150	175	250	400	650	1,400	
1876	(1,260)....14,640	210	275	350	420	500	650	950	1,500	3,000
1876CC	10,000						150,000	225,000	325,000	
$564,000, MS-65, Stack's Bowers auction, January 2013										
1877	(510)..........				3,750	4,200				6,000
1878	(600)..........				2,500	3,400				5,250

Authorized in 1792, this denomination was not issued until 1796. The first coinage follows the design of the early half dimes and dimes by the absence of a mark of value. In 1804 the value "25 C." was added to the reverse. Figures were used until 1838, when the term QUAR. DOL. appeared. In 1892 the value was spelled out entirely.

The first type weighed 104 grains, which remained standard until modified to 103-1/8 grains by the Act of January 18, 1837. As with the dime and half dime, the weight was reduced and arrows placed at the date in 1853. Rays were placed in the field of the reverse during that year only. The law of 1873 slightly increased the weight, and arrows were again placed at the date.

Proofs of some dates prior to 1856 are known to exist, and all are rare.

Note: Values of common-date silver coins have been based on the current bullion price of silver, $40 per ounce, and may vary with the prevailing spot price. To determine the intrinsic value of common silver coins, see page 425.

DRAPED BUST (1796–1807)

Designer probably Gilbert Stuart; engraver Robert Scot; weight 6.74 grams; composition .8924 silver, .1076 copper; approx. diameter 27.5 mm; reeded edge. All coined at Philadelphia.

AG-3 About Good—Details clear enough to identify.
G-4 Good—Date readable. Bust outlined, but no detail.
VG-8 Very Good—All but deepest drapery folds worn smooth. Hairlines nearly gone and curls lacking in detail.
F-12 Fine—All drapery lines visible. Hair partly worn.
VF-20 Very Fine—Only left side of drapery indistinct.
EF-40 Extremely Fine—Hair well outlined and detailed.
AU-50 About Uncirculated—Slight trace of wear on shoulder and highest waves of hair.
MS-60 Uncirculated—No trace of wear. Light blemishes.
MS-63 Choice Uncirculated—Some distracting marks or blemishes in focal areas. Impaired luster possible.

Small Eagle Reverse (1796)

	Mintage	AG-3	G-4	VG-8	F-12	VF-20	EF-40	AU-50	MS-60	MS-63
1796	6,146	$7,000	$12,000	$17,000	$26,000	$35,000	$50,000	$55,000	$75,000	$120,000

$322,000, MS-65, Heritage auction, August 2010

Heraldic Eagle Reverse (1804–1807)

1806, 6 Over 5

	Mintage	AG-3	G-4	VG-8	F-12	VF-20	EF-40	AU-50	MS-60	MS-63
1804	6,738	$2,200	$4,250	$6,000	$8,500	$13,000	$28,500	$50,000	$85,000	$165,000
1805	121,394	200	475	600	950	1,600	3,750	5,250	10,000	20,000

	Mintage	AG-3	G-4	VG-8	F-12	VF-20	EF-40	AU-50	MS-60	MS-63
1806, All kinds	206,124									
1806, 6 Over 5		$225	$550	$700	$1,100	$1,725	$4,000	$6,000	$11,000	$28,000
1806		200	450	600	950	1,600	3,600	5,250	10,000	16,500
1807	220,643	200	450	600	950	1,600	3,600	5,250	10,000	16,500

CAPPED BUST (1815–1838)
Variety 1 – Large Diameter (1815–1828)

Designer John Reich; weight 6.74 grams; composition .8924 silver, .1076 copper; approx. diameter 27 mm; reeded edge. All coined at Philadelphia.

AG-3 About Good—Details clear enough to identify.

G-4 Good—Date, letters, stars legible. Hair under Liberty's headband smooth. Cap lines worn smooth.

VG-8 Very Good—Rim well defined. Main details visible. Full LIBERTY on cap. Hair above eye nearly smooth.

F-12 Fine—All hair lines visible, but only partial detail visible in drapery. Shoulder clasp distinct.

VF-20 Very Fine—All details visible, but some wear evident. Clasp and ear sharp.

EF-40 Extremely Fine—All details distinct. Hair well outlined.

AU-50 About Uncirculated—Slight trace of wear on tips of curls and above the eye, and on the wing and claw tips.

MS-60 Uncirculated—No trace of wear. Light blemishes.

MS-63 Choice Uncirculated—Some distracting contact marks or blemishes in prime focal areas. Impaired luster possible.

1818, 8 Over 5   1819, Small 9   1819, Large 9

1820, Small 0   1820, Large 0   1822, 25 Over 50c

1823, 3 Over 2   1824, 4 Over 2   1825, 5 Over 2 (Wide Date)   1825, 5 Over 4 (Close Date)

	Mintage	AG-3	G-4	VG-8	F-12	VF-20	EF-40	AU-50	MS-60	MS-63
1815.	89,235	$65	$135	$200	$300	$550	$1,600	$2,000	$3,500	$7,000
1818, 8 Over 5	361,174	40	100	175	225	450	1,500	2,000	3,450	6,500
1818, Normal Date . . . . *		40	100	150	200	425	1,400	2,000	3,100	6,000
1819, Small 9	144,000	40	100	150	200	425	1,400	2,000	3,200	7,500
1819, Large 9 . . . . *		40	100	150	200	425	1,400	2,000	3,500	11,000

* Included in number above.

Chart continued on next page.

	Mintage	AG-3	G-4	VG-8	F-12	VF-20	EF-40	AU-50	MS-60	MS-63
1820, Small 0 127,444		$40	$100	$150	$200	$425	$1,400	$2,000	$3,100	$6,000
1820, Large 0 . . . . *		40	100	170	225	500	1,550	2,500	3,500	10,000
1821 216,851		40	100	150	200	425	1,400	2,000	3,200	6,500
1822 64,080		55	110	190	265	500	1,550	2,600	3,850	9,000
1822, 25 Over 50c . . . . *		825	2,100	4,750	6,000	8,500	15,000	24,000	40,000	75,000
1823, 3 Over 2 17,800		20,000	32,000	38,000	50,000	65,000	80,000	100,000	—	
1824, 4 Over 2 168,000		300	650	1,000	1,700	3,000	5,500	10,000	25,000	50,000
1825, 5 Over 2 (a) . . . . *		85	175	200	300	750	2,500	8,000	16,000	27,500
1825, 5 Over 4 (a) . . . . *		50	100	150	200	450	1,500	2,000	3,200	6,000
1827, Original (Curl Base 2 in 25c) 4,000							60,000	70,000	85,000	125,000
1827, Restrike (Square Base 2 in 25c)										55,000
1828 102,000		40	100	150	200	425	1,400	2,000	3,250	8,000
1828, 25 Over 50c . . . . *		100	200	350	700	1,600	3,000	4,000	13,000	22,000

* Included in number above. **a.** The date appears to be 5 over 4 over 2. The wide-date variety is the scarcer of the two.

Variety 2 – Reduced Diameter (1831–1838), Motto Removed

Designer William Kneass; weight 6.74 grams; composition .8924 silver, .1076 copper; diameter 24.3 mm; reeded edge. All coined at Philadelphia. Changed to 6.68 grams, .900 fine in 1837.

G-4 Good—Bust of Liberty well defined. Hair under headband smooth. Date, letters, stars legible. Scant rims.

VG-8 Very Good—Details apparent but worn on high spots. Rims strong. Full LIBERTY.

F-12 Fine—All hair lines visible. Drapery partly worn. Shoulder clasp distinct.

VF-20 Very Fine—Only top spots worn. Clasp sharp. Ear distinct.

EF-40 Extremely Fine—Hair details and clasp bold and clear.

AU-50 About Uncirculated—Slight trace of wear on hair around forehead, on cheek, and at top and bottom tips of eagle's wings and left claw.

MS-60 Uncirculated—No trace of wear. Light blemishes.

MS-63 Choice Uncirculated—Some distracting contact marks or blemishes in prime focal areas. Impaired luster possible.

		Small Letters (1831)	Large Letters	O Over F in OF

	Mintage	G-4	VG-8	F-12	VF-20	EF-40	AU-50	MS-60	MS-63
1831, Small Letters . . . 398,000		$70	$100	$125	$150	$400	$750	$1,250	$4,500
1831, Large Letters . . . . *		70	100	125	150	400	750	1,250	4,500
1832 320,000		70	100	125	150	425	750	1,250	5,000
1833 156,000		80	110	135	200	475	850	1,600	5,500
1833, O Over F in OF . . . . . . *		85	120	165	235	500	900	1,750	5,750
1834 286,000		70	100	125	150	400	750	1,250	4,500
1834, O Over F in OF . . . . . . *		80	110	150	200	450	850	1,600	5,000
1835 1,952,000		70	100	125	150	400	750	1,250	4,500
1836 472,000		70	100	125	150	400	750	1,250	4,700
1837 252,400		70	100	125	150	400	750	1,250	4,500
1838 366,000		70	100	125	150	400	750	1,250	4,500

* Included in number above.

LIBERTY SEATED (1838–1891)

Designer Christian Gobrecht.

G-4 Good—Scant rim. LIBERTY on shield worn off. Date and letters legible.
VG-8 Very Good—Rim fairly defined, at least three letters in LIBERTY evident.
F-12 Fine—LIBERTY complete, but partly weak.
VF-20 Very Fine—LIBERTY strong.
EF-40 Extremely Fine—Complete LIBERTY and edges of scroll. Shoulder clasp on Liberty's gown clear.
AU-50 About Uncirculated—Slight wear on Liberty's knees and breast and on eagle's neck, wing tips, and claws.
MS-60 Uncirculated—No trace of wear. Light blemishes.
MS-63 Choice Uncirculated—Some distracting contact marks or blemishes in prime focal areas. Impaired luster possible.

Variety 1 – No Motto Above Eagle (1838–1853)

Weight 6.68 grams; composition .900 silver, .100 copper; diameter 24.3 mm; reeded edge; mints: Philadelphia, New Orleans.

Small Date

Large Date

No Drapery From Elbow   **Drapery From Elbow**
Mintmark location is on reverse, below eagle.

	Mintage	G-4	VG-8	F-12	VF-20	EF-40	AU-50	MS-60	MS-63
1838, No Drapery	466,000	$33	$38	$60	$100	$375	$750	$2,000	$5,750
1839, No Drapery	491,146	31	38	60	95	375	750	1,850	5,500
$517,500, PF-65, Heritage auction, April 2008									
1840O, No Drapery	382,200	38	45	70	120	400	800	1,900	8,200
1840, Drapery	188,127	26	30	55	95	180	300	950	4,500
1840O, Drapery	43,000	28	47	70	110	210	500	1,300	3,900
1841	120,000	45	70	100	150	250	350	900	2,300
1841O	452,000	28	43	60	80	175	320	800	1,900
1842, Sm Date (Pf only)									
1842, Large Date	88,000	75	100	160	250	350	650	1,750	4,500
1842O, All kinds	769,000								
1842O, Small Date		350	550	1,000	1,900	3,750	9,000	18,000	75,000
1842O, Large Date		30	48	70	110	220	600	1,750	4,800
1843	645,600	23	28	33	45	85	175	450	1,250
1843O	968,000	28	43	60	125	250	800	2,500	8,000
1844	421,200	23	28	33	45	85	175	525	1,500
1844O	740,000	28	43	60	85	200	360	1,400	3,700
1845	922,000	23	28	33	45	80	160	550	1,400
1846	510,000	23	28	33	50	85	180	600	1,500
1847	734,000	23	28	33	45	80	160	575	1,200
1847O	368,000	32	48	75	150	350	750	3,500	13,000
1848	146,000	23	35	60	100	175	300	1,150	4,000
1849	340,000	23	28	45	75	160	250	800	1,900
1849O	*	450	600	1,100	2,200	4,000	7,000	13,500	20,000
1850	190,800	28	43	65	95	175	240	1,000	2,800
$460,000, PF-68, Heritage auction, January 2008									
1850O	412,000	28	43	65	95	175	475	1,600	3,400

* Included in 1850-O mintage.

Chart continued on next page.   **167**

	Mintage	G-4	VG-8	F-12	VF-20	EF-40	AU-50	MS-60	MS-63
1851	160,000	$33	$50	$75	$125	$200	$300	$1,000	$2,000
1851O	88,000	150	250	400	750	1,500	3,000	8,000	32,500
1852	177,060	43	55	95	135	225	300	675	2,000
1852O	96,000	175	250	400	1,000	2,250	5,000	9,000	42,500
1853, Recut Dt, No Arrows or Rays (a)	44,200	275	375	600	800	1,500	3,000	4,000	7,800

a. Beware of altered 1858, or removed arrows and rays.

Variety 2 – Arrows at Date, Rays Around Eagle (1853)

The reduction in weight is indicated by the arrows at the date. Rays were added on the reverse side in the field around the eagle. The arrows were retained through 1855, but the rays were omitted after 1853.

Weight 6.22 grams; composition .900 silver, .100 copper; diameter 24.3 mm; reeded edge; mints: Philadelphia, New Orleans.

1853, 3 Over 4

	Mintage	G-4	VG-8	F-12	VF-20	EF-40	AU-50	MS-60	MS-63
1853	15,210,020	$23	$28	$33	$50	$175	$300	$900	$2,000
1853, 3 Over 4	*	35	70	110	225	350	650	2,000	5,500
1853O	1,332,000	23	45	60	75	250	1,100	3,250	11,000

* Included in number above.

Variety 3 – Arrows at Date, No Rays (1854–1855)

Weight 6.22 grams; composition .900 silver, .100 copper; diameter 24.3 mm; reeded edge; mints: Philadelphia, New Orleans, San Francisco.

1854-O, Huge O

	Mintage	G-4	VG-8	F-12	VF-20	EF-40	AU-50	MS-60	MS-63
1854	12,380,000	$23	$28	$33	$45	$75	$225	$500	$1,100
1854O	1,484,000	23	31	40	55	100	250	1,200	2,500
1854O, Huge O	*	900	1,400	2,800	4,500	7,500	12,000	18,000	24,000
1855	2,857,000	23	28	33	45	85	225	575	1,500
1855O	176,000	40	65	110	275	400	2,000	5,000	15,000
1855S	396,400	38	60	85	175	350	1,100	3,000	8,500

* Included in number above.

Variety 1 Resumed, With Weight Standard of Variety 2 (1856–1865)

	Mintage	G-4	VG-8	F-12	VF-20	EF-40	AU-50	MS-60	MS-63	PF-63
1856	7,264,000	$23	$28	$33	$45	$75	$180	$325	$575	$6,500
1856O	968,000	23	42	55	65	80	250	1,100	2,500	
1856S, All kinds	286,000									
1856S		38	60	100	200	1,500	2,250	6,500	15,000	
1856S, S Over Sm S		200	325	750	1,500	2,500	6,000	25,000		
1857	9,644,000	23	28	33	45	75	180	325	575	4,750
1857O	1,180,000	28	40	50	60	150	400	1,200	4,000	
1857S	82,000	60	100	200	375	600	1,200	4,000	8,750	
1858	(300) 7,368,000	23	28	33	45	75	160	325	575	2,500

Mintage	G-4	VG-8	F-12	VF-20	EF-40	AU-50	MS-60	MS-63	PF-63
1858O 520,000	$23	$28	$33	$65	$125	$350	$1,800	$7,500	
1858S 121,000	50	75	250	650	2,000	5,250	15,000	—	
1859 . . . . (800) . . 1,343,200	23	28	33	45	80	180	400	1,100	$2,150
1859O 260,000	23	40	50	65	135	400	1,250	4,000	
1859S 80,000	100	200	350	650	4,200	17,500	55,000	—	
1860 . . . .(1,000) . . . 804,400	23	28	33	45	80	180	400	975	1,200
1860O 388,000	30	45	55	65	95	375	1,000	2,400	
1860S 56,000	500	750	2,000	5,000	13,500	22,500	50,000	—	
1861 . . . .(1,000) . .4,853,600	23	28	33	45	80	180	400	750	1,200
1861S 96,000	150	225	500	1,500	3,500	10,000	40,000	—	
1862 . . . . (550) . . . 932,000	23	28	33	50	85	180	325	750	1,200
1862S 67,000	55	85	150	265	800	1,800	3,800	9,000	
1863 . . . . (460) . . . 191,600	40	50	75	130	240	375	625	1,100	1,200
1864 . . . . (470) 93,600	75	85	120	175	275	425	625	1,700	1,200
1864S 20,000	275	400	800	1,250	3,800	5,500	12,000	30,000	
1865 . . . . (500) 58,800	75	85	130	200	300	500	800	1,400	1,200
1865S 41,000	85	125	175	450	1,000	1,500	3,000	6,000	
1866 *(unique, not a regular issue)*									—

Note: The 1866 Proof quarter, half, and dollar without motto are not mentioned in the Mint director's report, and were not issued for circulation.

Variety 4 – Motto Above Eagle (1866–1873)

The motto IN GOD WE TRUST was added to the reverse side in 1866. As with the half dollar and silver dollar, the motto has been retained since that time.

Circulation strike.

Proof strike.

Mintage	G-4	VG-8	F-12	VF-20	EF-40	AU-50	MS-60	MS-63	PF-63
1866 . . . . (725) . . . 16,800	$350	$500	$625	$950	$1,600	$1,850	$2,200	$2,600	$950
1866S 28,000	200	300	575	1,000	2,500	3,000	4,500	10,000	
1867 . . . . (625) . . . 20,000	200	300	450	650	1,350	1,650	2,600	8,500	950
1867S 48,000	200	310	525	1,000	4,500	8,400	18,000	35,000	
1868 . . . . (600) . . . 29,400	120	150	200	300	525	625	1,200	2,200	950
1868S 96,000	75	100	170	300	900	1,500	3,500	7,750	
1869 . . . . (600) . . . 16,000	250	300	425	550	900	1,100	1,900	3,000	950
1869S 76,000	80	120	190	325	1,000	1,600	4,000	6,500	
1870 . . . .(1,000) . . . 86,400	50	60	110	175	275	450	800	2,200	950
1870CC 8,340	8,500	12,500	18,500	25,000	30,000	52,500		—	
1871 . . . . (960) . . 118,200	28	40	60	115	225	350	600	1,500	950
1871CC 10,890	1,950	4,500	6,500	17,000	28,000	47,500	68,000	—	
1871S 30,900	260	400	800	900	1,500	2,750	5,250	10,000	
1872 . . . . (950) . . 182,000	28	40	60	115	190	300	650	2,100	950
1872CC 22,850	800	1,200	2,000	3,750	10,000	16,000	40,000	—	
1872S 83,000	700	1,000	1,400		6,000	8,000	15,000	25,000	
1873, Close 3 . . (600) . . . 40,000	125	225	300	700	1,500	2,500	18,000	40,000	950
1873, Open 3 172,000	28	45	65	125	200	300	500	1,100	
1873CC *(5 known)* 4,000				—	125,000			550,000	

$460,000, MS-64, Stack's Bowers auction, August 2012

Variety 5 – Arrows at Date (1873–1874)

Arrows were placed at the date in the years 1873 and 1874 to denote the change of weight from 6.22 to 6.25 grams.

Weight 6.25 grams; composition .900 silver, .100 copper; diameter 24.3 mm; reeded edge; mints: Philadelphia, San Francisco, Carson City.

Circulation strike.

Proof strike.

	Mintage	G-4	VG-8	F-12	VF-20	EF-40	AU-50	MS-60	MS-63	PF-63
1873	(540)..1,271,160	$23	$28	$38	$60	$225	$425	$850	$1,650	$1,450
1873CC	12,462	3,000	5,500	11,500	17,000	25,000	35,000	70,000	95,000	
1873S	156,000	35	40	65	125	350	750	2,000	6,000	
1874	(700)... 471,200	25	30	40	65	235	450	900	1,650	1,450
1874S	392,000	25	35	65	115	265	485	950	1,650	

Variety 4 Resumed, With Weight Standard of Variety 5 (1875–1891)

1877-S, S Over Horizontal S

	Mintage	G-4	VG-8	F-12	VF-20	EF-40	AU-50	MS-60	MS-63	PF-63
1875	(700) 4,292,800	$23	$28	$35	$45	$65	$160	$275	$550	$950
1875CC	140,000	75	115	190	300	600	1,000	2,500	6,750	
1875S	680,000	35	45	70	115	200	300	600	1,400	
1876	(1,150) 17,816,000	23	28	35	45	65	160	275	550	950
1876CC	4,944,000	45	65	75	85	120	250	600	1,300	
1876S	8,596,000	23	28	35	45	65	160	275	550	
1877	(510) 10,911,200	23	28	35	45	65	160	275	550	950
1877CC **(a)**	4,192,000	45	65	75	85	120	220	475	900	
1877S	8,996,000	23	28	35	45	65	160	275	550	
1877S, S/Horiz S	*	30	45	85	150	250	400	800	2,200	
1878	(800) 2,260,000	23	28	35	45	65	160	275	550	950
1878CC	996,000	55	70	85	120	200	300	700	1,500	
1878S	140,000	125	230	360	525	800	1,300	2,500	4,750	
1879	(1,100) 13,600	120	140	200	250	325	400	575	800	950
1880	(1,355) 13,600	120	140	200	250	325	400	575	800	950
1881	(975) 12,000	160	180	250	300	375	425	625	850	950
1882	(1,100) 15,200	130	160	210	265	325	425	625	900	950
1883	(1,039) 14,400	130	160	210	265	325	425	625	900	950
1884	(875) 8,000	225	275	350	425	550	600	700	900	950
1885	(930) 13,600	130	160	225	275	325	400	675	1,100	950
1886	(886) 5,000	300	375	475	575	675	750	1,000	1,400	950

* Included in number above. **a.** Variety with fine edge-reeding is scarcer than that with normally spaced reeding.

	Mintage	G-4	VG-8	F-12	VF-20	EF-40	AU-50	MS-60	MS-63	PF-63
1887	(710)....10,000	$225	$250	$325	$385	$475	$525	$750	$1,100	$950
1888	(832)....10,001	200	245	325	425	500	650	700	1,000	950
1888S	1,216,000	23	28	35	45	70	150	300	850	
1889	(711)....12,000	150	175	225	275	325	450	600	750	950
1890	(590)....80,000	60	75	100	125	175	300	525	775	950
1891	(600)..3,920,000	23	28	35	45	65	160	260	550	950
18910	68,000	175	300	500	1,200	1,750	2,500	4,000	8,000	
1891S	2,216,000	23	28	35	45	70	160	260	550	

BARBER OR LIBERTY HEAD (1892–1916)

Like other silver coins of this type, the quarter dollars minted from 1892 to 1916 were designed by Charles E. Barber. His initial B is found at the truncation of the neck of Liberty. There are two varieties of the 1892 reverse: (1) the eagle's wing covers only half of the E in UNITED; (2) the eagle's wing covers most of the E. Coins of the first variety reverse are somewhat scarcer than those of the second variety.

Designer Charles E. Barber; weight 6.25 grams; composition .900 silver, .100 copper (net weight: .18084 oz. pure silver); diameter 24.3 mm; reeded edge; mints: Philadelphia, Denver, New Orleans, San Francisco.

G-4 Good—Date and legends legible. LIBERTY worn off headband.

VG-8 Very Good—Some letters in LIBERTY legible.

F-12 Fine—LIBERTY completely legible but not sharp.

VF-20 Very Fine—All letters in LIBERTY evenly plain.

EF-40 Extremely Fine—LIBERTY bold, and its ribbon distinct.

AU-50 About Uncirculated—Slight trace of wear above forehead, on cheek, and on eagle's head, wings, and tail.

MS-60 Uncirculated—No trace of wear. Light blemishes.

MS-63 Choice Uncirculated—Some distracting contact marks or blemishes in prime focal areas. Impaired luster possible.

PF-63 Choice Proof—Reflective surfaces with only a few blemishes in secondary focal places. No major flaws.

Mintmark location is on reverse, below eagle.

	Mintage	G-4	VG-8	F-12	VF-20	EF-40	AU-50	MS-60	MS-63	PF-63
1892	(1,245)...8,236,000	$8	$10	$26	$45	$75	$125	$235	$425	$800
18920	2,460,000	15	20	45	60	95	160	300	475	
1892S	964,079	30	50	80	130	200	300	475	1,050	
1893	(792)...5,444,023	8	10	26	45	75	125	225	400	800
18930	3,396,000	8	14	30	60	100	170	275	500	
1893S	1,454,535	20	35	60	110	170	300	450	1,100	
1894	(972)...3,432,000	8	10	35	50	95	150	240	450	800
18940	2,852,000	10	20	45	70	130	230	325	725	
1894S	2,648,821	9	15	40	60	120	210	325	725	
1895	(880)...4,440,000	9	14	30	45	80	140	225	500	800
18950	2,816,000	12	20	50	70	140	230	400	900	
1895S	1,764,681	20	32	70	120	170	275	420	1,050	
1896	(762)...3,874,000	9	14	30	45	80	135	250	400	800
18960	1,484,000	55	85	200	320	575	800	1,050	2,000	
1896S	188,039	900	1,500	2,200	3,600	5,000	6,500	9,000	16,000	
1897	(731)...8,140,000	9	14	26	40	70	105	240	400	800
18970	1,414,800	40	65	180	340	400	600	850	1,800	
1897S	542,229	120	150	300	425	575	825	1,250	1,700	
1898	(735)..11,100,000	8	10	26	45	70	125	210	400	800
18980	1,868,000	15	28	70	140	300	390	625	1,500	
1898S	1,020,592	11	25	40	55	90	200	375	1,200	

Chart continued on next page.

171

	Mintage	G-4	VG-8	F-12	VF-20	EF-40	AU-50	MS-60	MS-63	PF-63
1899....(846)....12,624,000		$8	$10	$26	$45	$75	$125	$225	$400	$800
1899O............2,644,000		11	18	35	70	120	250	375	800	
1899S.............708,000		17	30	70	90	140	260	425	1,200	
1900....(912)....10,016,000		8	10	26	45	75	125	225	400	800
1900O............3,416,000		11	26	65	110	140	310	525	850	
1900S............1,858,585		9	15	35	55	80	130	350	1,000	
1901....(813).....8,892,000		8	10	26	45	75	125	225	400	800
1901O............1,612,000		40	60	140	275	450	625	850	1,850	
1901S.............72,664		5,250	10,000	16,000	22,000	28,000	34,000	37,000	46,000	
$550,000, MS-68, Superior auction, May 1990										
1902....(777)....12,196,967		8	10	26	45	70	115	225	400	800
1902O............4,748,000		9	16	50	85	140	225	475	1,300	
1902S............1,524,612		14	22	55	90	160	240	500	950	
1903....(755).....9,759,309		8	10	26	45	70	115	225	450	800
1903O............3,500,000		9	12	40	60	120	275	425	1,200	
1903S............1,036,000		15	25	45	85	150	275	425	850	
1904....(670).....9,588,143		8	10	26	45	70	120	225	400	800
1904O............2,456,000		30	40	85	150	240	450	800	1,300	
1905....(727).....4,967,523		30	35	50	65	75	120	225	420	800
1905O............1,230,000		40	60	120	220	260	350	475	1,250	
1905S............1,884,000		30	40	75	100	115	225	350	1,000	
1906....(675).....3,655,760		8	10	26	45	70	115	225	400	800
1906D............3,280,000		8	10	30	50	70	145	235	450	
1906O............2,056,000		8	10	40	60	100	200	300	550	
1907....(575).....7,132,000		8	10	26	40	70	115	225	400	800
1907D............2,484,000		8	10	26	48	75	175	275	650	
1907O............4,560,000		8	10	26	45	70	135	250	500	
1907S............1,360,000		10	18	45	70	140	280	475	1,000	
1908....(545).....4,232,000		8	10	26	45	70	115	225	400	800
1908D............5,788,000		8	10	26	45	70	115	225	400	
1908O............6,244,000		8	10	26	45	70	115	225	400	
1908S.............784,000		18	38	85	165	325	465	750	1,100	
1909....(650).....9,268,000		8	10	26	45	65	115	225	400	800
1909D............5,114,000		8	10	26	45	85	150	225	400	
1909O.............712,000		40	90	250	400	575	1,000	1,500	2,100	
1909S............1,348,000		8	10	35	55	90	185	285	750	
1910....(551).....2,244,000		8	10	26	45	80	140	225	400	800
1910D............1,500,000		8	11	45	70	125	240	350	900	
1911....(543).....3,720,000		8	10	26	45	70	125	225	400	800
1911D.............933,600		30	40	150	300	425	600	825	1,300	
1911S.............988,000		8	10	55	85	165	280	375	750	
1912....(700).....4,400,000		8	10	26	45	70	115	225	400	800
1912S.............708,000		10	12	50	80	115	220	350	925	
1913....(613)......484,000		15	25	70	180	400	525	900	1,200	850
1913D............1,450,800		12	15	35	60	85	175	275	450	
1913S..............40,000		1,650	2,200	5,000	7,500	10,000	12,750	15,000	20,000	
1914....(380).....6,244,230		8	10	22	40	65	115	225	400	900
1914D............3,046,000		8	10	22	40	65	115	225	400	
1914S.............264,000		125	180	375	550	800	950	1,300	1,550	
1915....(450).....3,480,000		8	10	22	40	65	115	225	400	900
1915D............3,694,000		8	10	22	40	65	115	225	400	
1915S.............704,000		25	40	60	85	115	200	285	475	
1916............1,788,000		8	10	22	40	65	115	225	400	
1916D............6,540,800		8	10	22	40	65	115	225	400	

STANDING LIBERTY (1916–1930)

This type quarter was designed by Hermon A. MacNeil. The left arm of Liberty is upraised, uncovering a shield in the attitude of protection. Her right hand bears the olive branch of peace. MacNeil's initial M is located above and to the right of the date.

There was a modification in 1917 to cover Liberty's exposed breast. The reverse has a new arrangement of the stars, and the eagle is higher.

In 1925 a depression was made in the pedestal on which Liberty stands and that bears the date. On the earlier issues the dates wore off easily because they were too high and were not protected by other features of the coin. The new "recessed" dates proved more durable as a result of this change.

No Proof coins of this type were officially issued, but specimen strikings of the first variety, dated 1917, are known to exist.

Designer Hermon A. MacNeil; standards same as for previous issue; mints: Philadelphia, Denver, San Francisco.

G-4 Good—Date and lettering legible. Top of date worn. Liberty's right leg and toes worn off. Much wear evident on left leg and drapery lines.

VG-8 Very Good—Distinct date. Toes faintly visible. Drapery lines visible above Liberty's left leg.

F-12 Fine—High curve of right leg flat from thigh to ankle. Only slight wear evident on left leg. Drapery lines over right thigh seen only at sides of leg.

VF-20 Very Fine—Garment line across right leg worn, but visible at sides.

EF-40 Extremely Fine—Flattened only at high spots. Liberty's toes are sharp. Drapery lines across right leg evident.

AU-50 About Uncirculated—Slight trace of wear on head, kneecap, shield's center, and highest point on eagle's body.

MS-60 Uncirculated—No trace of wear, but contact marks, surface spots, or faded luster possible.

MS-63 Choice Uncirculated—No trace of wear. Light blemishes. Attractive mint luster.

Some modifications must be made for grading Variety 2.

Variety 1 – No Stars Below Eagle (1916–1917)

Mintmark location is on obverse, to left of date.

Uncirculated pieces with fully struck head of Liberty are worth more than double the values listed below.

	Mintage	G-4	VG-8	F-12	VF-20	EF-40	AU-50	MS-60	MS-63
1916.	52,000	$2,800	$5,500	$7,000	$9,000	$10,000	$11,500	$14,500	$17,500
1917, Variety 1	8,740,000	25	50	70	100	120	210	275	350
1917D, Variety 1	1,509,200	35	60	90	125	200	250	325	425
1917S, Variety 1	1,952,000	40	65	100	150	210	285	350	475

Variety 2 – Stars Below Eagle (1917–1930)
Pedestal Date (1917–1924)

See next page for chart.

1918-S, 8 Over 7

	Mintage	G-4	VG-8	F-12	VF-20	EF-40	AU-50	MS-60	MS-63
1917, Variety 2	13,880,000	$22	$40	$55	$70	$100	$150	$225	$275
1917D, Variety 2	6,224,400	42	55	85	110	150	210	275	350
1917S, Variety 2	5,552,000	42	60	90	120	160	225	300	375
1918	14,240,000	18	20	30	35	55	90	160	225
1918D	7,380,000	25	40	75	90	145	200	300	400
1918S, Normal Date	11,072,000	18	22	35	45	60	120	210	300
1918S, 8 Over 7	*	1,600	2,200	3,600	5,000	8,000	13,000	19,000	32,500
1919	11,324,000	35	45	60	80	100	135	185	250
1919D	1,944,000	85	120	200	400	600	800	1,000	1,500
1919S	1,836,000	80	110	175	350	550	750	925	1,500
1920	27,860,000	15	20	30	35	55	100	175	225
1920D	3,586,400	50	60	80	120	165	225	350	750
1920S	6,380,000	20	25	35	50	65	140	270	750
1921	1,916,000	175	225	475	700	800	1,150	1,650	2,100
1923	9,716,000	15	20	30	38	55	100	175	240
1923S	1,360,000	280	425	740	1,100	1,500	2,000	2,650	3,400
1924	10,920,000	15	20	25	35	55	110	185	275
1924D	3,112,000	55	70	100	140	195	230	320	350
1924S	2,860,000	26	33	45	65	130	250	375	1,000

* Included in number above.

Recessed Date (1925–1930)

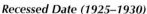

	Mintage	G-4	VG-8	F-12	VF-20	EF-40	AU-50	MS-60	MS-63
1925	12,280,000	$7.50	$8	$10	$20	$45	$100	$160	$250
1926	11,316,000	7.50	8	9	20	45	90	140	250
1926D	1,716,000	7.50	10	22	40	80	140	180	250
1926S	2,700,000	7.50	10	15	28	110	225	375	775
1927	11,912,000	7.50	8	9	17	35	80	140	225
1927D	976,000	15.00	20	30	75	150	220	270	310
1927S	396,000	40.00	50	130	350	1,100	2,800	4,500	7,000
1928	6,336,000	7.50	8	9	17	40	80	140	225
1928D	1,627,600	7.50	8	9	17	35	80	150	235
1928S (a)	2,644,000	7.50	8	9	22	40	90	160	235
1929	11,140,000	7.50	8	9	17	35	80	140	225
1929D	1,358,000	7.50	8	9	17	40	80	160	230
1929S	1,764,000	7.50	8	9	17	35	80	140	230
1930	5,632,000	7.50	8	9	17	35	80	140	225
1930S	1,556,000	7.50	8	9	17	35	80	140	225

a. Large and small mintmark varieties; see page 22.

WASHINGTON (1932 TO DATE)

This type was intended to be a commemorative issue marking the 200th anniversary of George Washington's birth. John Flanagan, a New York sculptor, was the designer; his initials, JF, can be found at the base of Washington's neck. The mintmark is on the reverse below the wreath (1932–1964).

Designer John Flanagan; weight 6.25 grams; composition .900 silver, .100 copper (net weight .18084 oz. pure silver); diameter 24.3 mm; reeded edge; mints: Philadelphia, Denver, San Francisco.

F-12 Fine—Hair lines about Washington's ear visible. Tiny feathers on eagle's breast faintly visible.
VF-20 Very Fine—Most hair details visible. Wing feathers clear.
EF-40 Extremely Fine—Hair lines sharp. Wear spots confined to top of eagle's legs and center of breast.
MS-60 Uncirculated—No trace of wear, but many contact marks, surface spotting, or faded luster possible.
MS-63 Choice Uncirculated—No trace of wear. Light blemishes. Attractive mint luster.
MS-65 Gem Uncirculated—Only light, scattered contact marks that are not distracting. Strong luster, good eye appeal.
PF-65 Gem Proof—Hardly any blemishes, and no flaws.

Circulation strike.
Proof strike.

1934, Doubled Die | **1934, Light Motto** | **1934, Heavy Motto**

Silver Coinage (1932–1964)

	Mintage	VG-8	F-12	VF-20	EF-40	AU-50	MS-60	MS-63	MS-65
1932	5,404,000	$8.00	$9.00	$10	$11.00	$15	$25	$50	$425
1932D	436,800	175.00	190.00	250	300.00	400	1,100	1,900	12,250
1932S	408,000	175.00	190.00	225	275.00	300	450	900	4,900
1934, All kinds	31,912,052								
1934, DblDie		75.00	85.00	200	300.00	600	1,200	1,900	4,350
1934, Light Motto		7.50	7.75	8	10.00	24	50	120	350
1934, Heavy Motto		7.50	7.75	8	10.00	15	30	50	135
1934D **(a)**	3,527,200	7.50	8.00	12	25.00	85	250	340	800
1935	32,484,000	7.50	7.75	8	8.50	10	22	35	150
1935D	5,780,000	7.50	8.00	10	20.00	125	240	275	650
1935S	5,660,000	7.50	8.00	9	15.00	38	100	135	290

a. Large and small mintmark varieties; see page 22.

1937, Doubled-Die Obverse | **1942-D, Doubled-Die Obverse** | **1943, Doubled-Die Obverse**

	Mintage	EF-40	AU-50	MS-60	MS-63	MS-65	PF-65
1936	(3,837) .. 41,300,000	$8	$10	$25	$35	$120	$1,450
1936D	5,374,000	55	250	525	800	1,100	
1936S	3,828,000	15	50	120	140	325	
1937	(5,542) .. 19,696,000	8	12	25	35	90	500
1937, Doubled-Die Obverse	*	700	1,500	2,500	4,000	12,000	
1937D	7,189,600	15	30	70	90	150	
1937S	1,652,000	35	95	150	250	400	

* Included in number above.

Chart continued on next page.

	Mintage	EF-40	AU-50	MS-60	MS-63	MS-65	PF-65
1938 . . . . (8,045)	9,472,000	$15.00	$45.00	$95	$110	$210	$275
1938S	2,832,000	20.00	55.00	105	140	230	
1939 . . . . (8,795) . . .	33,540,000	8.00	12.00	15	25	60	250
1939D	7,092,000	11.00	20.00	40	50	115	
1939S	2,628,000	20.00	60.00	95	135	310	
1940 . . . . (11,246) . . .	35,704,000	8.00	9.00	17	35	60	175
1940D	2,797,600	24.00	65.00	120	165	300	
1940S	8,244,000	9.00	16.00	21	32	65	
1941 . . . . (15,287) . . .	79,032,000	7.50	8.00	10	14	45	140
1941D	16,714,800	8.00	13.00	32	55	70	
1941S (a)	16,080,000	8.00	11.00	28	55	70	
1942 . . . . (21,123) . .	102,096,000	7.50	8.00	9	10	35	135
1942D	17,487,200	8.00	10.00	17	20	40	
1942D, Doubled-Die Obverse . . . .*		350.00	750.00	1,900	4,400	6,600	
1942S	19,384,000	10.00	20.00	70	115	175	
1943	99,700,000	7.50	8.00	9	10	40	
1943, Doubled-Die Obverse . . . .*		300.00	500.00	2,000	3,500	5,500	
1943D	16,095,600	8.00	15.00	28	39	60	
1943S	21,700,000	9.00	13.00	26	42	60	
1943S, Doubled-Die Obverse . . . .*		200.00	350.00	500	1,050	3,150	
1944	104,956,000	7.50	8.00	9	10	35	
1944D	14,600,800	8.00	10.00	17	20	40	
1944S	12,560,000	8.00	10.00	14	20	35	
1945	74,372,000	7.50	8.00	9	10	38	
1945D	12,341,600	8.00	12.00	18	25	42	
1945S	17,004,001	7.50	8.00	9	13	35	
1946	53,436,000	7.50	7.75	9	10	40	
1946D	9,072,800	7.50	7.75	9	10	45	
1946S	4,204,000	7.50	7.75	9	10	40	
1947	22,556,000	7.50	8.00	11	19	45	
1947D	15,338,400	7.50	8.00	11	17	40	
1947S	5,532,000	7.50	7.75	9	15	35	
1948	35,196,000	7.50	7.75	9	10	35	
1948D	16,766,800	7.50	8.00	13	18	55	
1948S	15,960,000	7.50	7.75	9	13	45	
1949	9,312,000	10.00	14.00	35	47	65	
1949D	10,068,400	8.00	9.00	16	38	50	
1950 . . . . (51,386) . . .	24,920,126	7.50	7.75	9	10	35	70
1950D	21,075,600	7.50	7.75	9	10	35	
1950D, D Over S . . . .*		150.00	200.00	300	500	3,000	
1950S	10,284,004	7.50	7.75	9	12	45	
1950S, S Over D . . . .*		150.00	250.00	350	500	1,000	
1951 . . . . (57,500) . . .	43,448,102	7.50	7.75	9	10	25	65
1951D	35,354,800	7.50	7.75	9	10	35	
1951S	9,048,000	7.50	8.00	10	15	40	
1952 . . . . (81,980) . . .	38,780,093	7.50	8.00	10	12	25	45
1952D	49,795,200	7.50	7.75	9	10	30	
1952S	13,707,800	7.50	8.00	12	20	42	
1953 . . . . (128,800) . . .	18,536,120	7.50	7.75	9	10	40	45
1953D	56,112,400	7.50	7.75	9	10	35	

* Included in number above. **a.** Large and small mintmark varieties; see page 22.

	Mintage	EF-40	AU-50	MS-60	MS-63	MS-65	PF-65
1953S	14,016,000	$7.50	$7.75	$9	$10	$34	
1954	(233,300)... 54,412,203	7.50	7.75	9	12	32	$25
1954D	42,305,500	7.50	7.75	9	10	35	
1954S	11,834,722	7.50	7.75	9	10	36	
1955	(378,200)... 18,180,181	7.50	7.75	9	10	27	25
1955D	3,182,400	7.50	7.75	9	10	60	
1956	(669,384)... 44,144,000	7.50	7.75	9	10	21	15
1956D	32,334,500	7.50	7.75	9	10	27	
1957	(1,247,952)... 46,532,000	7.50	7.75	9	10	27	15
1957D	77,924,160	7.50	7.75	9	10	25	
1958	(875,652).... 6,360,000	7.50	7.75	9	10	20	15
1958D	78,124,900	7.50	7.75	9	10	25	
1959	(1,149,291)... 24,384,000	7.50	7.75	9	10	25	12
1959D	62,054,232	7.50	7.75	9	10	25	
1960	(1,691,602)... 29,164,000	7.50	7.75	9	10	20	10
1960D	63,000,324	7.50	7.75	9	10	20	
1961	(3,028,244)... 37,036,000	7.50	7.75	9	10	15	10
1961D	83,656,928	7.50	7.75	9	10	15	
1962	(3,218,019)... 36,156,000	7.50	7.75	9	10	15	10
1962D	127,554,756	7.50	7.75	9	10	15	
1963	(3,075,645)... 74,316,000	7.50	7.75	9	10	15	10
1963D	135,288,184	7.50	7.75	9	10	15	
1964	(3,950,762).. 560,390,585	7.50	7.75	9	10	15	10
1964D	704,135,528	7.50	7.75	9	10	15	

Clad Coinage and Silver Proofs (1965 to Date)

Proof coins from 1937 through 1972 were made from special dies with high relief and minor detail differences. Some of the circulation coins of 1956 through 1964 and 1969-D through 1972-D were also made from reverse dies with these same features. A variety of the 1964-D quarter occurs with the modified reverse normally found only on the clad coins.

Weight 5.67 grams; composition, outer layers of copper-nickel (.750 copper, .250 nickel) bonded to inner core of pure copper; diameter 24.3 mm; reeded edge. Silver Proofs 1992–1998: same as pre-1965 standards.

 **Starting in 1968 mintmark is on obverse, to right of ribbon.**

	Mintage	MS-63	MS-65	PF-65
1965	1,819,717,540	$1.00	$9	
1966	821,101,500	1.00	7	
1967	1,524,031,848	1.00	6	
1968	220,731,500	1.25	8	
1968D	101,534,000	1.10	6	
1968S	(3,041,506)			$4
1969	176,212,000	3.00	10	
1969D	114,372,000	2.50	10	
1969S	(2,934,631)			4
1970	136,420,000	1.00	10	
1970D (a)	417,341,364	1.00	7	
1970S	(2,632,810)			4

	Mintage	MS-63	MS-65	PF-65
1971	109,284,000	$1	$7	
1971D	258,634,428	1	5	
1971S	(3,220,733)			$4
1972	215,048,000	1	5	
1972D	311,067,732	1	5	
1972S	(3,260,996)			4
1973	346,924,000	1	5	
1973D	232,977,400	1	6	
1973S	(2,760,339)			4
1974	801,456,000	1	5	
1974D	353,160,300	1	8	
1974S	(2,612,568)			4

a. Lightweight, thin quarters of 1970-D are errors struck on metal intended for dimes.

Bicentennial (1776–1976)

In October of 1973, the Treasury announced an open contest for the selection of suitable designs for the Bicentennial reverses of the quarter, half dollar, and dollar, with $5,000 to be awarded to each winner. Twelve semifinalists were chosen, and from these the symbolic entry of Jack L. Ahr was selected for the quarter reverse. It features a colonial drummer facing left, with a victory torch encircled by 13 stars at the upper left. Except for the dual dating, "1776–1976," the obverse remained unchanged. Pieces with this dual dating were coined during 1975 and 1976. They were struck for general circulation and included in all the Mint's offerings of Proof and Uncirculated sets.

Designers John Flanagan and Jack L. Ahr; diameter 24.3 mm; reeded edge. Silver issue—Weight 5.75 grams; composition, outer layers of .800 silver, .200 copper bonded to inner core of .209 silver, .791 copper (net weight .0739 oz. pure silver). Copper-nickel issue— Weight 5.67 grams; composition, outer layers of .750 copper, .250 nickel bonded to inner core of pure copper.

	Mintage	MS-63	MS-65	PF-65
1776–1976, Copper-Nickel Clad.	809,784,016	$1.25	$6	
1776–1976D, Copper-Nickel Clad	860,118,839	1.25	6	
1776–1976S, Copper-Nickel Clad.	(7,059,099)			$4
1776–1976S, Silver Clad **(a)**	11,000,000	4.00	7	
1776–1976S, Silver Clad **(a)**	(4,000,000)			8

a. Mintages are approximate. Several million were melted in 1982.

Eagle Reverse Resumed (1977–1998) (Dies Slightly Modified to Lower Relief)

	Mintage	MS-63	MS-65	PF-65		Mintage	MS-63	MS-65	PF-65
1977	468,556,000	$1	$6		1984S	(3,065,110)			$4
1977D	256,524,978	1	6		1985P	775,818,962	$2.00	$14	
1977S	(3,251,152)			$4	1985D	519,962,888	1.00	9	
1978	521,452,000	1	6		1985S	(3,362,821)			4
1978D	287,373,152	1	6		1986P	551,199,333	2.50	12	
1978S	(3,127,781)			4	1986D	504,298,660	6.00	18	
1979	515,708,000	1	6		1986S	(3,010,497)			4
1979D	489,789,780	1	6		1987P	582,499,481	0.50	9	
1979S, T1 **(a)**	(3,677,175)			8	1987D	655,594,696	0.50	6	
1979S, T2 **(a)**	*			12	1987S	(4,227,728)			4
1980P	635,832,000	1	6		1988P	562,052,000	1.25	14	
1980D	518,327,487	1	6		1988D	596,810,688	0.50	10	
1980S	(3,554,806)			4	1988S	(3,262,948)			4
1981P	601,716,000	1	6		1989P	512,868,000	0.75	12	
1981D	575,722,833	1	6		1989D	896,535,597	0.75	4	
1981S, T1 **(a)**	(4,063,083)			12	1989S	(3,220,194)			4
1981S, T2 **(a)**	*			25	1990P	613,792,000	0.75	14	
1982P	500,931,000	7	30		1990D	927,638,181	0.75	14	
1982D	480,042,788	5	20		1990S	(3,299,559)			4
1982S	(3,857,479)			4	1991P	570,968,000	0.75	14	
1983P	673,535,000	24	60		1991D	630,966,693	0.75	12	
1983D	617,806,446	10	42		1991S	(2,867,787)			4
1983S	(3,279,126)			4	1992P	384,764,000	1.50	16	
1984P	676,545,000	1	9		1992D	389,777,107	1.00	17	
1984D	546,483,064	1	9		1992S	(2,858,981)			4

* Included in number above. **a.** See page 234 for illustrations of Type 1 and Type 2 varieties.

	Mintage	MS-63	MS-65	PF-65
1992S, Silver . .	(1,317,579)			$8
1993P	639,276,000	$1.00	$7	
1993D	645,476,128	1.00	7	
1993S	(2,633,439)			4
1993S, Silver . . .	(761,353)			8
1994P	825,600,000	1.00	13	
1994D	880,034,110	1.00	10	
1994S	(2,484,594)			4
1994S, Silver . . .	(785,329)			8
1995P	1,004,336,000	1.25	14	
1995D	1,103,216,000	1.00	13	
1995S	(2,117,496)			8
1995S, Silver . . .	(679,985)			8

	Mintage	MS-63	MS-65	PF-65
1996P	925,040,000	$0.50	$10	
1996D	906,868,000	0.50	10	
1996S	(1,750,244)			$4
1996S, Silver . . .	(775,021)			8
1997P	595,740,000	1.00	11	
1997D	599,680,000	0.75	12	
1997S	(2,055,000)			4
1997S, Silver . . .	(741,678)			8
1998P	896,268,000	0.50	7	
1998D	821,000,000	0.50	7	
1998S	(2,086,507)			4
1998S, Silver . . .	(878,792)			8

State Quarters (1999–2008)

The United States Mint 50 State Quarters® Program begun in 1999 produced a series of 50 quarter dollar coins with special designs honoring each state. Five different designs were issued each year from 1999 through 2008. States were commemorated in the order of their entrance into statehood.

These are all legal tender coins of standard weight and composition. The obverse side depicting President George Washington was modified to include some of the wording previously used on the reverse. The modification was authorized by special legislation, and carried out by Mint sculptor-engraver William Cousins, whose initials were added to the truncation of Washington's neck adjacent to those of the original designer, John Flanagan.

Each state theme was proposed, and approved, by the governor of that state. Final designs were created by Mint personnel.

Circulation coins were made at the Philadelphia and Denver mints. Proof coins were made in San Francisco.

Circulation strike.   Proof strike.

Weight 5.67 grams; composition, outer layers of copper-nickel (.750 copper, .250 nickel) bonded to inner core of pure copper; diameter 24.3 mm; reeded edge. Silver Proof—Pre-1965 standards.

See next page for chart.

179

	Mintage	AU-50	MS-63	MS-65	PF-65
1999P, Delaware	373,400,000	$0.50	$1.25	$3	
1999D, Delaware	401,424,000	0.50	1.25	3	
1999S, Delaware	(3,713,359)				$7
1999S, Delaware, Silver	(804,565)				30
1999P, Pennsylvania	349,000,000	0.50	1.25	3	
1999D, Pennsylvania	358,332,000	0.50	1.25	3	
1999S, Pennsylvania	(3,713,359)				7
1999S, Pennsylvania, Silver	(804,565)				30
1999P, New Jersey	363,200,000	0.50	1.25	3	
1999D, New Jersey	299,028,000	0.50	1.25	3	
1999S, New Jersey	(3,713,359)				7
1999S, New Jersey, Silver	(804,565)				30
1999P, Georgia	451,188,000	0.50	1.25	3	
1999D, Georgia	488,744,000	0.50	1.25	3	
1999S, Georgia	(3,713,359)				7
1999S, Georgia, Silver	(804,565)				30
1999P, Connecticut	688,744,000	0.50	1.25	3	
1999D, Connecticut	657,880,000	0.50	1.25	3	
1999S, Connecticut	(3,713,359)				7
1999S, Connecticut, Silver	(804,565)				30

	Mintage	AU-50	MS-63	MS-65	PF-65
2000P, Massachusetts	628,600,000	$0.35	$1	$2	
2000D, Massachusetts	535,184,000	0.35	1	2	
2000S, Massachusetts	(4,020,172)				$3
2000S, Massachusetts, Silver	(965,421)				8
2000P, Maryland	678,200,000	0.35	1	2	
2000D, Maryland	556,532,000	0.35	1	2	
2000S, Maryland	(4,020,172)				3
2000S, Maryland, Silver	(965,421)				8
2000P, South Carolina	742,576,000	0.35	1	2	
2000D, South Carolina	566,208,000	0.35	1	2	
2000S, South Carolina	(4,020,172)				3
2000S, South Carolina, Silver	(965,421)				8
2000P, New Hampshire	673,040,000	0.35	1	2	
2000D, New Hampshire	495,976,000	0.35	1	2	
2000S, New Hampshire	(4,020,172)				3
2000S, New Hampshire, Silver	(965,421)				8
2000P, Virginia	943,000,000	0.35	1	2	
2000D, Virginia	651,616,000	0.35	1	2	

	Mintage	AU-50	MS-63	MS-65	PF-65
2000S, Virginia	(4,020,172)				$3
2000S, Virginia, Silver	(965,421)				8

	Mintage	AU-50	MS-63	MS-65	PF-65
2001P, New York	655,400,000	$0.35	$1	$1.25	
2001D, New York	619,640,000	0.35	1	1.25	
2001S, New York	(3,094,140)				$3
2001S, New York, Silver	(889,697)				10
2001P, North Carolina	627,600,000	0.35	1	1.25	
2001D, North Carolina	427,876,000	0.35	1	1.25	
2001S, North Carolina	(3,094,140)				3
2001S, North Carolina, Silver	(889,697)				10
2001P, Rhode Island	423,000,000	0.35	1	1.25	
2001D, Rhode Island	447,100,000	0.35	1	1.25	
2001S, Rhode Island	(3,094,140)				3
2001S, Rhode Island, Silver	(889,697)				10
2001P, Vermont	423,400,000	0.35	1	1.25	
2001D, Vermont	459,404,000	0.35	1	1.25	
2001S, Vermont	(3,094,140)				3
2001S, Vermont, Silver	(889,697)				10
2001P, Kentucky	353,000,000	0.35	1	1.25	
2001D, Kentucky	370,564,000	0.35	1	1.25	
2001S, Kentucky	(3,094,140)				3
2001S, Kentucky, Silver	(889,697)				10

	Mintage	AU-50	MS-63	MS-65	PF-65
2002P, Tennessee	361,600,000	$0.75	$1.50	$2	
2002D, Tennessee	286,468,000	0.75	1.50	2	

Chart continued on next page.

181

	Mintage	AU-50	MS-63	MS-65	PF-65
2002S, Tennessee	(3,084,245)				$3
2002S, Tennessee, Silver	(892,229)				8
2002P, Ohio	217,200,000	$0.35	$1	$1.25	
2002D, Ohio	414,832,000	0.35	1	1.25	
2002S, Ohio	(3,084,245)				3
2002S, Ohio, Silver	(892,229)				8
2002P, Louisiana	362,000,000	0.35	1	1.25	
2002D, Louisiana	402,204,000	0.35	1	1.25	
2002S, Louisiana	(3,084,245)				3
2002S, Louisiana, Silver	(892,229)				8
2002P, Indiana	362,600,000	0.35	1	1.25	
2002D, Indiana	327,200,000	0.35	1	1.25	
2002S, Indiana	(3,084,245)				3
2002S, Indiana, Silver	(892,229)				8
2002P, Mississippi	290,000,000	0.35	1	1.25	
2002D, Mississippi	289,600,000	0.35	1	1.25	
2002S, Mississippi	(3,084,245)				3
2002S, Mississippi, Silver	(892,229)				8

	Mintage	AU-50	MS-63	MS-65	PF-65
2003P, Illinois	225,800,000	$0.50	$1.25	$2.00	
2003D, Illinois	237,400,000	0.50	1.25	2.00	
2003S, Illinois	(3,408,516)				$3
2003S, Illinois, Silver	(1,125,755)				8
2003P, Alabama	225,000,000	0.35	1.00	1.25	
2003D, Alabama	232,400,000	0.35	1.00	1.25	
2003S, Alabama	(3,408,516)				3
2003S, Alabama, Silver	(1,125,755)				8
2003P, Maine	217,400,000	0.35	1.00	1.25	
2003D, Maine	231,400,000	0.35	1.00	1.25	
2003S, Maine	(3,408,516)				3
2003S, Maine, Silver	(1,125,755)				8
2003P, Missouri	225,000,000	0.35	1.00	1.25	
2003D, Missouri	228,200,000	0.35	1.00	1.25	
2003S, Missouri	(3,408,516)				3
2003S, Missouri, Silver	(1,125,755)				8
2003P, Arkansas	228,000,000	0.35	1.00	1.25	
2003D, Arkansas	229,800,000	0.40	0.65	1.40	
2003S, Arkansas	(3,408,516)				3
2003S, Arkansas, Silver	(1,125,755)				8

Some 2004-D Wisconsin quarters show one of two different die flaws on the reverse, in the shape of an extra leaf on the corn. On one (middle), the extra leaf extends upward; on the other (right), it bends low. The normal die is shown at left.

	Mintage	AU-50	MS-63	MS-65	PF-65
2004P, Michigan	233,800,000	$0.35	$0.75	$1	
2004D, Michigan	225,800,000	0.35	0.75	1	
2004S, Michigan	(2,740,684)				$3
2004S, Michigan, Silver	(1,769,786)				8
2004P, Florida	240,200,000	0.35	0.75	1	
2004D, Florida	241,600,000	0.35	0.75	1	
2004S, Florida	(2,740,684)				3
2004S, Florida, Silver	(1,769,786)				8
2004P, Texas	278,800,000	0.35	0.75	1	
2004D, Texas	263,000,000	0.35	0.75	1	
2004S, Texas	(2,740,684)				3
2004S, Texas, Silver	(1,769,786)				8
2004P, Iowa	213,800,000	0.35	0.75	1	
2004D, Iowa	251,400,000	0.35	0.75	1	
2004S, Iowa	(2,740,684)				3
2004S, Iowa, Silver	(1,769,786)				8
2004P, Wisconsin	226,400,000	0.35	0.75	1	
2004D, Wisconsin	226,800,000	0.35	0.75	1	
2004D, Wisconsin, Extra Leaf High	*	75.00	125.00	150	
2004D, Wisconsin, Extra Leaf Low	*	50.00	115.00	130	
2004S, Wisconsin	(2,740,684)				3
2004S, Wisconsin, Silver	(1,769,786)				8

* Included in number above.

See next page for chart.

	Mintage	AU-50	MS-63	MS-65	PF-65
2005P, California	257,200,000	$0.30	$0.50	$1	
2005D, California	263,200,000	0.30	0.50	1	
2005S, California	(3,262,960)				$3
2005S, California, Silver	(1,678,649)				8
2005P, Minnesota	239,600,000	0.30	0.50	1	
2005D, Minnesota	248,400,000	0.30	0.50	1	
2005S, Minnesota	(3,262,960)				3
2005S, Minnesota, Silver	(1,678,649)				8
2005P, Oregon	316,200,000	0.30	0.50	1	
2005D, Oregon	404,000,000	0.30	0.50	1	
2005S, Oregon	(3,262,960)				3
2005S, Oregon, Silver	(1,678,649)				8
2005P, Kansas	263,400,000	0.30	0.50	1	
2005D, Kansas	300,000,000	0.30	0.50	1	
2005S, Kansas	(3,262,960)				3
2005S, Kansas, Silver	(1,678,649)				8
2005P, West Virginia	365,400,000	0.30	0.50	1	
2005D, West Virginia	356,200,000	0.30	0.50	1	
2005S, West Virginia	(3,262,960)				3
2005S, West Virginia, Silver	(1,678,649)				8

	Mintage	AU-50	MS-63	MS-65	PF-65
2006P, Nevada	277,000,000	$0.30	$0.50	$1	
2006D, Nevada	312,800,000	0.30	0.50	1	
2006S, Nevada	(2,882,428)				$3
2006S, Nevada, Silver	(1,585,008)				8
2006P, Nebraska	318,000,000	0.30	0.50	1	
2006D, Nebraska	273,000,000	0.30	0.50	1	
2006S, Nebraska	(2,882,428)				3
2006S, Nebraska, Silver	(1,585,008)				8
2006P, Colorado	274,800,000	0.30	0.50	1	
2006D, Colorado	294,200,000	0.30	0.50	1	
2006S, Colorado	(2,882,428)				3
2006S, Colorado, Silver	(1,585,008)				8
2006P, North Dakota	305,800,000	0.30	0.50	1	
2006D, North Dakota	359,000,000	0.30	0.50	1	
2006S, North Dakota	(2,882,428)				3
2006S, North Dakota, Silver	(1,585,008)				8
2006P, South Dakota	245,000,000	0.30	0.50	1	
2006D, South Dakota	265,800,000	0.30	0.50	1	

	Mintage	AU-50	MS-63	MS-65	PF-65
2006S, South Dakota . . . . (2,882,428)					$3
2006S, South Dakota, Silver . . . . (1,585,008)					8

	Mintage	AU-50	MS-63	MS-65	PF-65
2007P, Montana	257,000,000	$0.30	$0.50	$1	
2007D, Montana	256,240,000	0.30	0.50	1	
2007S, Montana . . . . (2,374,778)					$3
2007S, Montana, Silver . . . . (1,313,481)					8
2007P, Washington	265,200,000	0.30	0.50	1	
2007D, Washington	280,000,000	0.30	0.50	1	
2007S, Washington . . . . (2,374,778)					3
2007S, Washington, Silver . . . . (1,313,481)					8
2007P, Idaho	294,600,000	0.30	0.50	1	
2007D, Idaho	286,800,000	0.30	0.50	1	
2007S, Idaho . . . . (2,374,778)					3
2007S, Idaho, Silver . . . . (1,313,481)					8
2007P, Wyoming	243,600,000	0.30	0.50	1	
2007D, Wyoming	320,800,000	0.30	0.50	1	
2007S, Wyoming . . . . (2,374,778)					3
2007S, Wyoming, Silver . . . . (1,313,481)					8
2007P, Utah	255,000,000	0.30	0.50	1	
2007D, Utah	253,200,000	0.30	0.50	1	
2007S, Utah . . . . (2,374,778)					3
2007S, Utah, Silver . . . . (1,313,481)					8

	Mintage	AU-50	MS-63	MS-65	PF-65
2008P, Oklahoma	222,000,000	$0.30	$0.50	$1	
2008D, Oklahoma	194,600,000	0.30	0.50	1	

Chart continued on next page.

	Mintage	AU-50	MS-63	MS-65	PF-65
2008S, Oklahoma	(2,078,112)				$3
2008S, Oklahoma, Silver	(1,192,908)				8
2008P, New Mexico	244,200,000	$0.30	$0.50	$1	
2008D, New Mexico	244,400,000	0.30	0.50	1	
2008S, New Mexico	(2,078,112)				3
2008S, New Mexico, Silver	(1,192,908)				8
2008P, Arizona	244,600,000	0.30	0.50	1	
2008D, Arizona	265,000,000	0.30	0.50	1	
2008S, Arizona	(2,078,112)				3
2008S, Arizona, Silver	(1,192,908)				8
2008P, Alaska	251,800,000	0.30	0.50	1	
2008D, Alaska	254,000,000	0.30	0.50	1	
2008S, Alaska	(2,078,112)				3
2008S, Alaska, Silver	(1,192,908)				8
2008P, Hawaii	254,000,000	0.30	0.50	1	
2008D, Hawaii	263,600,000	0.30	0.50	1	
2008S, Hawaii	(2,078,112)				3
2008S, Hawaii, Silver	(1,192,908)				8

Some statehood quarters were accidentally made with "dis-oriented" dies and are valued higher than ordinary pieces. Normal United States coins have dies oriented in "coin alignment," such that the reverse appears upside down when the coin is rotated from right to left. Values for the rotated-die quarters vary according to the amount of shifting. The most valuable are those that are shifted 180 degrees, so that both sides appear upright when the coin is turned over (called *medal alignment*).

Manufacturing varieties showing die doubling or other minor, unintentional characteristics are of interest to collectors and are often worth premium prices.

District of Columbia and U.S. Territories Quarters (2009)

At the ending of the U.S. Mint 50 State Quarters® Program a new series of quarter-dollar reverse designs was authorized to recognize the District of Columbia and the five U.S. territories: the Commonwealth of Puerto Rico, Guam, American Samoa, the U.S. Virgin Islands, and the Commonwealth of the Northern Mariana Islands. Each of these coins, issued sequentially during 2009, has the portrait of George Washington, as in the past, and is made of the same weight and composition. Each coin commemorates the history, geography, or traditions of the place it represents.

	Mintage	AU-50	MS-63	MS-65	PF-65
2009P, District of Columbia	83,600,000	$0.50	$0.75	$1	
2009D, District of Columbia	88,800,000	0.50	0.75	1	
2009S, District of Columbia	(2,113,478)				$3
2009S, District of Columbia, Silver	(996,548)				8
2009P, Puerto Rico	53,200,000	0.50	0.75	1	
2009D, Puerto Rico	86,000,000	0.50	0.75	1	
2009S, Puerto Rico	(2,113,478)				3
2009S, Puerto Rico, Silver	(996,548)				8
2009P, Guam	45,000,000	0.50	0.75	1	
2009D, Guam	42,600,000	0.50	0.75	1	
2009S, Guam	(2,113,478)				3
2009S, Guam, Silver	(996,548)				8
2009P, American Samoa	42,600,000	0.50	0.75	1	
2009D, American Samoa	39,600,000	0.50	0.75	1	
2009S, American Samoa	(2,113,478)				3
2009S, American Samoa, Silver	(996,548)				8
2009P, U.S. Virgin Islands	41,000,000	0.75	1.00	2	
2009D, U.S. Virgin Islands	41,000,000	0.75	1.00	2	
2009S, U.S. Virgin Islands	(2,113,478)				3
2009S, U.S. Virgin Islands, Silver	(996,548)				8
2009P, Northern Mariana Islands	35,200,000	0.50	0.75	1	
2009D, Northern Mariana Islands	37,600,000	0.50	0.75	1	
2009S, Northern Mariana Islands	(2,113,478)				3
2009S, Northern Mariana Islands, Silver	(996,548)				8

America the Beautiful™ Quarters Program (2010–2021)

Following up on the popularity of the 50 State Quarters® Program, Congress has authorized the production of new circulating commemorative quarters from 2010 to 2021. The coins will honor a site of "natural or historic significance" from each of the 50 states, five U.S. territories, and the District of Columbia. They will continue to bear George Washington's portrait on the obverse.

Five designs will be released each year, in the order the coins' featured locations were designated national parks or national sites. At the discretion of the secretary of the Treasury, this series could be extended an additional 11 years by featuring a second national park or site from each state, district, and territory.

In addition to the circulating quarters, a series of five-ounce silver bullion pieces are being coined each year with designs nearly identical to those of the America the Beautiful™ quarters, with two exceptions: the size, which is three inches in diameter; and the edge, which is marked .999 FINE SILVER 5.0 OUNCE, rather than reeded as on the standard quarters. See pages 352 and 353 for valuation charts.

See next page for chart.

	Mintage	AU-50	MS-63	MS-65	PF-65
2010P, Hot Springs National Park (Arkansas)	35,600,000	$0.50	$0.75	$1	
2010D, Hot Springs National Park (Arkansas)	34,000,000	0.50	0.75	1	
2010S, Hot Springs National Park (Arkansas)	(1,376,671)				$3
2010S, Hot Springs National Park (Arkansas), Silver	(1,162,842)				8
2010P, Yellowstone National Park (Wyoming)	33,600,000	0.50	0.75	1	
2010D, Yellowstone National Park (Wyoming)	34,800,000	0.50	0.75	1	
2010S, Yellowstone National Park (Wyoming)	(1,376,671)				3
2010S, Yellowstone National Park (Wyoming), Silver	(1,162,842)				8
2010P, Yosemite National Park (California)	35,200,000	0.50	0.75	1	
2010D, Yosemite National Park (California)	34,800,000	0.50	0.75	1	
2010S, Yosemite National Park (California)	(1,376,671)				3
2010S, Yosemite National Park (California), Silver	(1,162,842)				8
2010P, Grand Canyon National Park (Arizona)	34,800,000	0.50	0.75	1	
2010D, Grand Canyon National Park (Arizona)	35,400,000	0.50	0.75	1	
2010S, Grand Canyon National Park (Arizona)	(1,376,671)				3
2010S, Grand Canyon National Park (Arizona), Silver	(1,162,842)				8
2010P, Mt. Hood National Forest (Oregon)	34,400,000	0.50	0.75	1	
2010D, Mt. Hood National Forest (Oregon)	34,400,000	0.50	0.75	1	
2010S, Mt. Hood National Forest (Oregon)	(1,376,671)				3
2010S, Mt. Hood National Forest (Oregon), Silver	(1,162,842)				8

	Mintage	AU-50	MS-63	MS-65	PF-65
2011P, Gettysburg National Military Park (Pennsylvania)	30,800,000	$0.50	$0.75	$1	
2011D, Gettysburg National Military Park (Pennsylvania)	30,400,000	0.50	0.75	1	
2011S, Gettysburg National Military Park (Pennsylvania)	(1,077,451)				$3
2011S, Gettysburg National Military Park (Pennsylvania), Silver	(626,002)				8
2011P, Glacier National Park (Montana)	30,400,000	0.50	0.75	1	
2011D, Glacier National Park (Montana)	31,200,000	0.50	0.75	1	
2011S, Glacier National Park (Montana)	(1,077,451)				3
2011S, Glacier National Park (Montana), Silver	(626,002)				8
2011P, Olympic National Park (Washington)	30,400,000	0.50	0.75	1	
2011D, Olympic National Park (Washington)	30,600,000	0.50	0.75	1	
2011S, Olympic National Park (Washington)	(1,077,451)				3
2011S, Olympic National Park (Washington), Silver	(626,002)				8
2011P, Vicksburg National Military Park (Mississippi)	30,800,000	0.50	0.75	1	
2011D, Vicksburg National Military Park (Mississippi)	33,400,000	0.50	0.75	1	
2011S, Vicksburg National Military Park (Mississippi)	(1,077,451)				3
2011S, Vicksburg National Military Park (Mississippi), Silver	(626,002)				8
2011P, Chickasaw National Recreation Area (Oklahoma)	73,800,000	0.45	0.70	1	
2011D, Chickasaw National Recreation Area (Oklahoma)	69,400,000	0.45	0.70	1	

	Mintage	AU-50	MS-63	MS-65	PF-65
2011S, Chickasaw National Recreation Area (Oklahoma) . . . . . (1,077,451)					$3
2011S, Chickasaw National Recreation Area (Oklahoma), Silver (626,002)					8

	Mintage	AU-50	MS-63	MS-65	PF-65
2012P, El Yunque National Forest (Puerto Rico) 25,800,000		$0.50	$0.75	$1	
2012D, El Yunque National Forest (Puerto Rico) 25,000,000		0.50	0.75	1	
2012S, El Yunque National Forest (Puerto Rico) 1,679,240			2.00 (a)		$3
2012S, El Yunque National Forest (Puerto Rico), Silver					8
2012P, Chaco Culture National Historical Park (New Mexico) . . 22,000,000		0.50	0.75	1	
2012D, Chaco Culture National Historical Park (New Mexico) . . 22,000,000		0.50	0.75	1	
2012S, Chaco Culture National Historical Park (New Mexico) . . . 1,389,020			2.00 (a)		3
2012S, Chaco Culture National Historical Park (New Mexico), Silver.					8
2012P, Acadia National Park (Maine) 24,800,000		0.50	0.75		
2012D, Acadia National Park (Maine) 21,606,000		0.50	0.75		
2012S, Acadia National Park (Maine) 1,409,120			2.00 (a)		3
2012S, Acadia National Park (Maine), Silver.					8
2012P, Hawai'i Volcanoes National Park (Hawaii) 46,200,000		0.50	0.75		
2012D, Hawai'i Volcanoes National Park (Hawaii) 78,600,000		0.45	0.70		
2012S, Hawai'i Volcanoes National Park (Hawaii) 1,407,520			2.00 (a)		3
2012S, Hawai'i Volcanoes National Park (Hawaii), Silver.					8
2012P, Denali National Park and Preserve (Alaska). 135,400,000		0.40	0.65		
2012D, Denali National Park and Preserve (Alaska) 166,600,000		0.40	0.65		
2012S, Denali National Park and Preserve (Alaska). 1,401,920			2.00 (a)		3
2012S, Denali National Park and Preserve (Alaska), Silver					8

a. Not issued for circulation.

	Mintage	AU-50	MS-63	MS-65	PF-65
2013P, White Mountain National Forest (New Hampshire)		$0.50	$0.75	$1	
2013D, White Mountain National Forest (New Hampshire)		0.50	0.75	1	

Chart continued on next page.

	Mintage	AU-50	MS-63	MS-65	PF-65
2013S, White Mountain National Forest (New Hampshire)					$3
2013S, White Mountain National Forest (New Hampshire), Silver					8
2013P, Perry's Victory and International Peace Memorial (Ohio)		$0.50	$0.75	$1	
2013D, Perry's Victory and International Peace Memorial (Ohio)		0.50	0.75	1	
2013S, Perry's Victory and International Peace Memorial (Ohio)					3
2013S, Perry's Victory and International Peace Memorial (Ohio), Silver. . . .					8
2013P, Great Basin National Park (Nevada)		0.50	0.75		
2013D, Great Basin National Park (Nevada)		0.50	0.75		
2013S, Great Basin National Park (Nevada)					3
2013S, Great Basin National Park (Nevada), Silver					8
2013P, Fort McHenry Nat'l Monument and Historic Shrine (Maryland)		0.50	0.75		
2013D, Fort McHenry Nat'l Monument and Historic Shrine (Maryland)		0.50	0.75		
2013S, Fort McHenry Nat'l Monument and Historic Shrine (Maryland)					3
2013S, Fort McHenry Nat'l Monument and Historic Shrine (Maryland), Silver					8
2013P, Mount Rushmore National Memorial (South Dakota)		0.50	0.75		
2013D, Mount Rushmore National Memorial (South Dakota)		0.50	0.75		
2013S, Mount Rushmore National Memorial (South Dakota) **(a)**					3
2013S, Mount Rushmore National Memorial (South Dakota), Silver					8

a. Not issued for circulation.

The sites that will be honored on quarters from 2014 through 2021 are as follows:

2014 Great Smoky Mountains Nat'l Park (Tennessee)
Shenandoah Nat'l Park (Virginia)
Arches Nat'l Park (Utah)
Great Sand Dunes Nat'l Park (Colorado)
Everglades Nat'l Park (Florida)

2015 Homestead Nat'l Monument of America (Nebraska)
Kisatchie Nat'l Forest (Louisiana)
Blue Ridge Parkway (North Carolina)
Bombay Hook Nat'l Wildlife Refuge (Delaware)
Saratoga Nat'l Historical Park (New York)

2016 Shawnee Nat'l Forest (Illinois)
Cumberland Gap Nat'l Historical Park (Kentucky)
Harpers Ferry Nat'l Historical Park (West Virginia)
Theodore Roosevelt Nat'l Park (North Dakota)
Fort Moultrie / Fort Sumter Nat'l Monument (South Carolina)

2017 Effigy Mounds Nat'l Monument (Iowa)
Frederick Douglass Nat'l Historic Site (District of Columbia)
Ozark Nat'l Scenic Riverways (Missouri)
Ellis Island Nat'l Monument / Statue of Liberty (New Jersey)
George Rogers Clark Nat'l Historical Park (Indiana)

2018 Pictured Rocks Nat'l Lakeshore (Michigan)
Apostle Islands Nat'l Lakeshore (Wisconsin)
Voyageurs Nat'l Park (Minnesota)
Cumberland Island Nat'l Seashore (Georgia)
Block Island Nat'l Wildlife Refuge (Rhode Island)

2019 Lowell Nat'l Historical Park (Massachusetts)
American Memorial Park (Northern Mariana Islands)
War in the Pacific Nat'l Historical Park (Guam)
San Antonio Missions Nat'l Historical Park (Texas)
Frank Church River of No Return Wilderness (Idaho)

2020 Nat'l Park of American Samoa (American Samoa)
Weir Farm Nat'l Historic Site (Connecticut)
Salt River Bay Nat'l Historical Park and Ecological Preserve (U.S. Virgin Islands)
Marsh-Billings-Rockefeller Nat'l Historical Park (Vermont)
Tallgrass Prairie Nat'l Preserve (Kansas)

2021 Tuskegee Airmen Nat'l Historic Site (Alabama)

The half dollar, authorized by the Act of April 2, 1792, was not minted until December 1794. The early types of this series have been extensively collected by die varieties, of which many exist for most dates. Valuations given below are in each case for the most common variety; scarcer ones as listed by Overton (see the bibliography at the end of the book) generally command higher prices.

When the half dollar was first issued, its weight was 208 grains and its fineness .8924. This standard was not changed until 1837, when the law of January 18, 1837, specified 206-1/4 grains, .900 fine. This fineness continued in use until 1965.

Arrows at the date in 1853 indicate the reduction of weight to 192 grains, in conformity with the Act of February 21, 1853. During that year only, rays were added to the field on the reverse side to identify the lighter coins. Arrows remained in 1854 and 1855.

The 1866 Proof quarter, half, and dollar without motto are not mentioned in the Mint director's report, and were not issued for circulation. In 1873 the weight was raised by law to 192.9 grains and arrows were again placed at the date, to be removed in 1875.

Note: Values of common-date silver coins have been based on the current bullion price of silver, $40 per ounce, and may vary with the prevailing spot price. To determine the intrinsic value of common silver coins, see page 425.

FLOWING HAIR (1794–1795)

Engraver Robert Scot; weight 13.48 grams; composition .8924 silver, .1076 copper; approx. diameter 32.5 mm; edge: FIFTY CENTS OR HALF A DOLLAR with decorations between words.

AG-3 About Good—Clear enough to identify.

G-4 Good—Date and letters sufficient to be legible. Main devices outlined, but lacking in detail.

VG-8 Very Good—Major details discernible. Letters well formed but worn.

F-12 Fine—Hair ends distinguishable. Top hair lines visible, but otherwise worn smooth.

VF-20 Very Fine—Some detail visible in hair in center; other details more bold.

EF-40 Extremely Fine—Hair above head and down neck detailed, with slight wear.

AU-50 About Uncirculated—All hair visible; slight wear on bust of Liberty and on top edges of eagle's wings, head, and breast.

1795, 2 Leaves Under Each Wing　　　**1795, 3 Leaves Under Each Wing**

	Mintage	AG-3	G-4	VG-8	F-12	VF-20	EF-40	AU-50
1794	23,464	$2,500	$4,000	$7,000	$10,000	$21,000	$38,000	$65,000
1795, All kinds	299,680							
1795, Normal Date		640	985	1,450	2,750	3,900	11,000	18,000
1795, Recut Date		640	985	1,450	2,750	3,900	11,000	20,500
1795, 3 Leaves Under Each Wing		1,100	2,200	3,000	4,600	8,500	20,000	37,500

Note: Varieties of 1795 are known with small, or narrow, head, with final S in STATES over D, with A in STATES over E, and with Y in LIBERTY over a star. All are scarce. Some 1795 half dollars were weight-adjusted by insertion of a silver plug in the center of the blank planchet before the coin was struck.

DRAPED BUST (1796–1807)

Designer probably Gilbert Stuart; engraver Robert Scot; weight 13.48 grams; composition .8924 silver, .1076 copper; approx. diameter 32.5 mm; edge: FIFTY CENTS OR HALF A DOLLAR with decorations between words.

AG-3 About Good—Clear enough to identify.
G-4 Good—Date and letters sufficiently clear to be legible. Main devices outlined, but lacking in detail.
VG-8 Very Good—Major details discernible. Letters well formed but worn.
F-12 Fine—Hair ends distinguishable. Top hair lines visible, but otherwise worn smooth.
VF-20 Very Fine—Right side of drapery slightly worn. Left side to curls smooth.
EF-40 Extremely Fine—All lines in drapery on bust distinctly visible around to hair curls.
AU-50 About Uncirculated—Slight trace of wear on cheek, hair, and shoulder.

Small Eagle Reverse (1796–1797)

1796, 16 Stars   **1797, 15 Stars**

	Mintage	AG-3	G-4	VG-8	F-12	VF-20	EF-40	AU-50
1796, 15 Stars 3,918		$23,000	$34,000	$40,000	$52,000	$70,000	$110,000	$185,000
$373,750, MS-63, Heritage auction, February 2008								
1796, 16 Stars . . . . *		23,000	36,500	43,500	56,000	71,000	110,000	185,000
$414,000, MS-64, Goldberg auction, May 2006								
1797, 15 Stars . . . . *		23,000	34,000	40,000	52,000	70,000	110,000	185,000
$1,380,000, MS-63, Stack's Bowers auction, July 2008								

* Included in number above.

Heraldic Eagle Reverse (1801–1807)

	Mintage	G-4	VG-8	F-12	VF-20	EF-40	AU-50	MS-60
1801 30,289		$750	$1,200	$2,400	$3,500	$6,500	$15,000	$40,000
1802 29,890		750	1,200	2,500	3,800	7,750	16,000	40,000
1803, All kinds 188,234								
1803, Small 3		350	475	550	950	2,600	6,000	16,000
1803, Large 3		325	425	500	900	2,050	5,000	14,500

1805, 5 Over 4

1806, 6 Over 5

Branch Stem Not Through Claw

Knobbed-Top 6, Small Stars

Pointed-Top 6

Branch Stem Through Claw

	Mintage	G-4	VG-8	F-12	VF-20	EF-40	AU-50	MS-60
1805, All kinds 211,722								
1805, 5 Over 4		$290	$440	$875	$1,600	$3,500	$7,500	$30,000
1805, Normal Date		260	325	450	850	2,000	5,600	13,500
1806, All kinds 839,576								
1806, 6 Over 5		265	350	450	900	2,000	4,900	10,750
1806, 6 Over Inverted 6		300	450	925	1,450	3,300	6,500	18,500
1806, Knbd 6, Lg Stars (Traces of Overdate) . . .		250	300	350	700	1,800	4,750	9,000
1806, Knbd 6, Sm Stars		250	300	350	700	1,800	4,750	9,000
1806, Knbd 6, Stem Not Through Claw				85,000	115,000	165,000		
1806, Pointed 6, Stem Through Claw		250	300	350	700	1,800	4,500	8,500
1806, E Over A in STATES		400	900	1,600	3,200	6,000		
1806, Pointed 6, Stem Not Through Claw		250	300	350	700	1,800	4,500	8,500
1807 301,076		250	300	350	700	1,800	4,750	9,000

CAPPED BUST, LETTERED EDGE (1807–1836)

John Reich designed this capped-head concept of Liberty. The Capped Bust style was used on most other silver coin denominations for the next 30 years. A German immigrant, Reich became an engraver for the Mint, and served from 1807 to 1817, after having been freed from a bond of servitude by a Mint official. He was the first artist to consistently include the denomination on U.S. gold and silver coins.

Designer John Reich; weight 13.48 grams; composition .8924 silver, .1076 copper; approx. diameter 32.5 mm. 1807–1814—Edge: FIFTY CENTS OR HALF A DOLLAR. 1814–1831—Edge: Star added between DOLLAR and FIFTY. 1832–1836—Edge: Vertical lines added between words.

G-4 Good—Date and letters legible. Bust worn smooth with outline distinct.
VG-8 Very Good—LIBERTY faint. Legends distinguishable. Clasp at shoulder visible; curl above it nearly smooth.
F-12 Fine—Clasp and adjacent curl clearly outlined with slight details.
VF-20 Very Fine—Clasp at shoulder clear. Wear visible on highest point of curl. Hair over brow distinguishable.
EF-40 Extremely Fine—Clasp and adjacent curl fairly sharp. Brow and hair above distinct. Curls well defined.
AU-50 About Uncirculated—Trace of wear on hair over eye and over ear.
MS-60 Uncirculated—No trace of wear. Light blemishes. Possible slide marks from storage handling.
MS-63 Choice Uncirculated—Some distracting contact marks or blemishes in prime focal areas. Impaired luster possible.

First Style (1807–1808)

1807, Small Stars	1807, Large Stars	1807, 50 Over 20

	Mintage	G-4	F-12	VF-20	EF-40	AU-50	MS-60	MS-63
1807, All kinds 750,500								
1807, Small Stars.		$120	$450	$850	$2,400	$4,200	$7,000	$14,000
1807, Large Stars.		100	350	700	1,700	3,400	6,400	12,500
1807, Large Stars, 50 Over 20		100	325	650	1,400	2,700	5,750	10,750
1807, "Bearded" Liberty.		500	975	2,100	4,000	9,000	20,000	—
1808, All kinds 1,368,600								
1808, 8 Over 7.		100	150	275	650	1,350	3,500	9,750
1808		75	110	190	375	725	1,900	4,400

Remodeled Portrait and Eagle (1809–1836)

1809, Experimental Edge, xxxx Between Words	1809, Experimental Edge, IIIII Between Words

	Mintage	G-4	F-12	VF-20	EF-40	AU-50	MS-60	MS-63
1809, All kinds 1,405,810								
1809, Normal Edge.		$75	$110	$190	$375	$625	$2,050	$4,500
1809, xxxx Edge.		90	135	230	475	925	3,250	6,500
1809, IIIII Edge		90	135	230	475	950	3,500	7,300
1810. 1,276,276		75	110	170	315	575	1,900	4,150

"Punctuated" Date 18.11   1811, Small 8   1811, Large 8

1812, 2 Over 1, Small 8   1812, 2 Over 1, Large 8   Single Leaf Below Wing

	Mintage	G-4	F-12	VF-20	EF-40	AU-50	MS-60	MS-63
1811, All kinds 1,203,644								
1811, (18.11), 11 Over 10		$80	$135	$235	$650	$1,025	$2,500	$8,000
1811, Small 8.		75	125	170	325	675	1,850	4,150
1811, Large 8.		75	125	170	325	675	1,850	4,500
1812, All kinds 1,628,059								
1812, 2 Over 1, Small 8		80	150	225	400	800	2,900	5,100
1812, 2 Over 1, Large 8		1,850	4,600	7,400	13,000	25,000	40,000	—
1812		75	110	160	265	525	1,750	3,250
1812, Single Leaf Below Wing		750	1,300	2,400	3,750	6,250	11,500	—

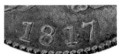

1813, 50 C. Over UNI   1814, 4 Over 3   1814, E Over A in STATES

	Mintage	G-4	F-12	VF-20	EF-40	AU-50	MS-60	MS-63
1813, All kinds 1,241,903								
1813		$70	$110	$160	$265	$525	$1,750	$3,000
1813, 50 C. Over UNI		90	160	235	450	975	2,000	5,500
1814, All kinds 1,039,075								
1814, 4 Over 3		115	200	325	750	1,375	2,600	6,000
1814, E Over A in STATES		95	150	250	475	1,075	2,250	4,000
1814		70	120	175	265	575	1,750	3,250
1814, Single Leaf Below Wing		80	125	225	550	1,400	2,850	5,000

1817, 7 Over 3   1817, 7 Over 4   1817, "Punctuated Date"

	Mintage	G-4	F-12	VF-20	EF-40	AU-50	MS-60	MS-63
1815, 5 Over 2 47,150		$1,250	$2,200	$3,500	$5,150	$8,000	$15,500	$30,000
1817, All kinds 1,215,567								
1817, 7 Over 3		135	275	525	975	2,100	5,000	12,500
1817, 7 Over 4 *(8 known)*.		60,000	150,000	200,000	250,000	350,000		
$356,500, AU-50, Stack's Bowers auction, July 2009								
1817, Dated 181.7		75	125	180	350	750	1,950	3,600
1817		70	100	150	275	525	1,600	3,250
1817, Single Leaf Below Wing		95	135	190	475	1,000	2,750	4,500

1818, First 8 Small, Second 8 Over 7

1818, First 8 Large, Second 8 Over 7

1819, Small 9 Over 8

1819, Large 9 Over 8

	Mintage	G-4	F-12	VF-20	EF-40	AU-50	MS-60	MS-63
1818, All kinds	1,960,322							
1818, 8 Over 7, Small 8		$90	$130	$160	$375	$875	$1,800	$5,750
1818, 8 Over 7, Large 8		90	135	200	425	925	2,100	6,000
1818		70	100	140	235	450	1,500	2,900
1819, All kinds	2,208,000							
1819, Small 9 Over 8		75	120	160	275	550	1,600	3,250
1819, Large 9 Over 8		80	140	200	300	650	1,900	3,600
1819		70	100	140	220	425	1,500	3,000

1820, 20 Over 19,
Square Base 2

1820, 20 Over 19,
Curl Base 2

1820, Curl Base, No
Knob 2, Small Date

	Mintage	G-4	F-12	VF-20	EF-40	AU-50	MS-60	MS-63
1820, All kinds	751,122							
1820, 20 Over 19, Square 2		$100	$140	$230	$475	$1,150	$2,650	$7,000
1820, 20 Over 19, Curl Base 2		90	135	200	450	1,100	2,350	6,000
1820, Curl Base 2, Small Date		85	130	170	340	925	1,850	4,250

Square Base, Knob 2,
Large Date

Square Base, No Knob 2,
Large Date

	Mintage	G-4	F-12	VF-20	EF-40	AU-50	MS-60	MS-63
1820, Sq Base Knob 2, Lg Dt		$80	$125	$150	$300	$850	$1,550	$3,500
1820, Sq Base No Knob 2, Lg Dt		80	125	150	300	850	1,550	3,500
1820, No Serifs on E's		475	725	900	1,400	3,350	6,000	12,000
1821	1,305,797	70	100	130	225	550	1,300	2,950
1822, All kinds	1,559,573							
1822		70	100	130	225	475	1,200	2,850
1822, 2 Over 1		100	140	250	375	800	1,600	3,750

1823, Broken 3

1823, Patched 3

1823, Ugly 3

	Mintage	G-4	F-12	VF-20	EF-40	AU-50	MS-60	MS-63
1823, All kinds	1,694,200							
1823, Broken 3		$80	$135	$225	$550	$1,100	$2,150	$4,400
1823, Patched 3.		75	110	185	425	700	1,500	3,250
1823, Ugly 3.		70	150	250	450	750	1,600	3,350
1823, Normal		70	100	130	180	500	1,250	2,450

"Various Dates"
Probably 4 over 2 over 0.

1824, 4 Over 1

1824, 4 Over 4

1824, 4 Over 4

4 Over 4 varieties are easily mistaken for scarcer 4 Over 1. Note distance between 2's and 4's in each.

1827, 7 Over 6

	Mintage	G-4	F-12	VF-20	EF-40	AU-50	MS-60	MS-63
1824, All kinds	3,504,954							
1824, 4 Over Various Dates		$70	$110	$140	$220	$550	$1,550	$3,100
1824, 4 Over 1.		75	115	150	220	550	1,500	3,100
1824, 4 Over 4 *(2 varieties)*		75	110	140	210	525	1,400	2,950
1824, Normal		75	100	130	200	450	1,150	2,000
1825.	2,943,166	75	100	130	200	400	1,150	2,000
1826.	4,004,180	75	100	130	200	400	1,150	2,000
1827, All kinds	5,493,400							
1827, 7 Over 6.		80	120	160	240	525	1,400	2,550
1827, Square Base 2		75	100	130	200	425	1,200	2,100
1827, Curl Base 2		75	100	130	200	400	1,150	2,000

1828, Curl Base, No Knob 2

1828, Curl Base, Knob 2

1828, Square Base 2, Large 8's

1828, Square Base 2, Small 8's

1828, Large Letters

1828, Small Letters

	Mintage	G-4	F-12	VF-20	EF-40	AU-50	MS-60	MS-63
1828, All kinds	3,075,200							
1828, Curl Base No Knob 2		$70	$95	$130	$200	$410	$1,150	$2,000
1828, Curl Base Knob 2		70	95	130	200	410	1,150	2,000
1828, Square Base 2, Large 8's		70	95	130	200	410	1,150	2,000

Chart continued on next page.

	Mintage	G-4	F-12	VF-20	EF-40	AU-50	MS-60	MS-63
1828, Square Base 2, Small 8's, Large Letters		$65	$90	$120	$200	$400	$1,100	$2,000
1828, Square Base 2, Small 8's and Letters		75	105	150	250	575	1,450	2,850
1829, All kinds	3,712,156							
1829, 9 Over 7		70	110	145	225	450	1,500	3,500
1829		60	80	110	180	375	1,000	2,000
1829, Large Letters		65	90	120	200	400	1,200	2,500

1830, Small 0

1832, Large Letters Reverse

Raised segment lines to right, 1830.

Raised segment lines to left, 1830–1831.

Adopted edge, 1830–1836.

	Mintage	G-4	F-12	VF-20	EF-40	AU-50	MS-60	MS-63
1830, All kinds	4,764,800							
1830, Small 0		$65	$90	$120	$180	$375	$1,100	$2,100
1830, Large 0		65	90	120	180	375	1,100	2,100
1830, Large Letters		1,400	2,950	3,800	4,800	9,000	—	
1831	5,873,660	65	90	120	180	350	1,050	2,000
1832, All kinds	4,797,000							
1832		60	80	110	180	350	1,000	2,000
1832, Large Letters		60	80	110	180	350	1,000	2,000
1833	5,206,000	60	80	110	180	350	1,000	2,000

Slightly Modified Portrait (1834–1836)

1834, Large Date

1834, Small Date

1834, Large Letters Reverse

1834, Small Letters Reverse

1836, 50 Over 00

Proofs of 1833, 1834, and 1835 with crushed edge-lettering use the same reverse die as the 1836 with beaded-border reverse. All are very rare.

	Mintage	G-4	F-12	VF-20	EF-40	AU-50	MS-60	MS-63
1834, All kinds	6,412,004							
1834, Large Dt and Letters		$60	$80	$110	$180	$350	$1,000	$2,000
1834, Large Dt, Small Letters		60	80	110	180	350	1,000	2,000
1834, Small Dt, Stars, Letters		60	80	110	180	350	1,000	2,000

	Mintage	G-4	F-12	VF-20	EF-40	AU-50	MS-60	MS-63
1835	5,352,006	$60	$80	$110	$180	$350	$1,000	$2,000
1836, All kinds	6,545,000							
1836		60	80	110	180	350	1,000	2,000
1836 Over 1336		80	100	130	225	400	1,200	2,250
1836, 50 Over 00		90	130	175	335	925	2,050	3,850
1836, Beaded Border on Reverse		85	120	140	250	500	1,300	2,200

CAPPED BUST, REEDED EDGE (1836–1839)

Designer Christian Gobrecht; weight 13.36 grams; composition .900 silver, .100 copper; diameter 30 mm; reeded edge. All coined at Philadelphia.

G-4 Good—LIBERTY barely discernible on headband.
VG-8 Very Good—Some letters in LIBERTY clear.
F-12 Fine—LIBERTY complete but faint.
VF-20 Very Fine—LIBERTY sharp. Shoulder clasp clear.
EF-40 Extremely Fine—LIBERTY sharp and strong. Hair details visible.
AU-50 About Uncirculated—Slight trace of wear on cap, cheek, and hair above forehead, and on eagle's claws, wing tops, and head.
MS-60 Uncirculated—No trace of wear. Light blemishes.
MS-63 Choice Uncirculated—Some distracting contact marks or blemishes in prime focal areas. Impaired luster possible.

Reverse 50 CENTS (1836–1837)

	Mintage	G-4	VG-8	F-12	VF-20	EF-40	AU-50	MS-60	MS-63
1836	1,200+	$1,000	$1,250	$1,650	$2,000	$3,250	$4,400	$9,000	$19,000
1837	3,629,820	70	80	100	135	215	400	1,200	2,600

Reverse HALF DOL. (1838–1839)

The 1838-O was the first branch mint half dollar, though not mentioned in the Mint director's report. The New Orleans chief coiner stated that only 10 were struck. In 1838 and 1839 the mintmark appears on the obverse, above the date; thereafter, through 1915, all mintmarks are on the reverse.

	Mintage	G-4	VG-8	F-12	VF-20	EF-40	AU-50	MS-60	MS-63
1838	3,546,000	$70	$85	$100	$135	$225	$400	$1,200	$2,600

Chart continued on next page.

	Mintage	G-4	VG-8	F-12	VF-20	EF-40	AU-50	MS-60	MS-63
18380 20						$335,000	$400,000	$500,000	$750,000
$734,375, PF-64, Stack's Bowers auction, January 2013									
1839............ 1,392,976	$65	$85	$100	$145	225	425	1,400	2,900
1839, Sm Ltrs Rev *(ex. rare)*...			40,000	55,000				
18390 116,000	220	300	400	600	900	1,250	3,250	6,500

LIBERTY SEATED (1839–1891)

G-4 Good—Scant rim. LIBERTY on shield worn off. Date and letters legible.
VG-8 Very Good—Rim fairly defined. Some letters in LIBERTY evident.
F-12 Fine—LIBERTY complete, but weak.
VF-20 Very Fine—LIBERTY mostly sharp.
EF-40 Extremely Fine—LIBERTY entirely sharp. Scroll edges and clasp distinct.
AU-50 About Uncirculated—Slight trace of wear on Liberty's breast and knees, and on eagle's head, claws, and wing tops.
MS-60 Uncirculated—No trace of wear. Light blemishes.
MS-63 Choice Uncirculated—Some distracting marks or blemishes in focal areas. Impaired luster possible.

Variety 1 – No Motto Above Eagle (1839–1853)

Designer Christian Gobrecht; weight 13.36 grams; composition .900 silver, .100 copper; diameter 30.6 mm; reeded edge; mints: Philadelphia, New Orleans.

No Drapery From Elbow

	Mintage	G-4	VG-8	F-12	VF-20	EF-40	AU-50	MS-60	MS-63
1839, No Drapery From Elbow .... *	$45	$90	$330	$500	$1,075	$2,500	$6,500	$30,000

* Included in "1839, Drapery From Elbow" mintage.

| **Drapery From Elbow** **(Starting 1839)** | **Small Letters in Legend** **(1839–1841)** | **1840 (Only), Medium** **Letters, Large Eagle** |

	Mintage	G-4	VG-8	F-12	VF-20	EF-40	AU-50	MS-60	MS-63
1839, Drapery From Elbow........ 1,972,400	$40	$55	$65	$100	$175	$290	$850	$2,300
1840, Small Letters 1,435,008	40	55	65	100	175	275	600	1,300
1840, Medium Letters **(a)**............... *	140	190	275	450	800	1,500	3,750	7,500
18400 855,100	40	55	70	115	190	400	850	3,000
1841......................... 310,000	45	60	95	150	275	400	1,300	2,600
18410 401,000	40	55	65	100	215	375	725	2,500

* Included in number below. **a.** Struck at the New Orleans Mint from a reverse die of the previous style without mintmark.

	Mintage	G-4	VG-8	F-12	VF-20	EF-40	AU-50	MS-60	MS-63
1842, Small Date, Small Letters	*					$4,500	$7,500	$17,500	
1842O, Small Date, Small Letters	203,000	$575	$925	$1,400	$2,350	4,500	7,500	18,500	$39,000

* Included in "1842, Medium Date" mintage.

Modified Reverse With Large Letters in Legend (1842–1853)

Small Date

Medium Date

Large Letters in Legend (1842–1853)

1844-O, Doubled Date

	Mintage	G-4	VG-8	F-12	VF-20	EF-40	AU-50	MS-60	MS-63
1842, Medium Date	2,012,764	$40	$55	$65	$100	$150	$325	$875	$1,800
1842, Small Date	*	40	55	65	100	150	350	1,175	3,450
1842O, Medium Date	754,000	40	55	60	100	150	350	1,100	4,250
1843	3,844,000	40	55	65	100	150	225	500	1,100
1843O	2,268,000	60	65	70	100	150	250	575	2,000
1844	1,766,000	40	55	65	100	150	250	500	1,600
1844O	2,005,000	40	55	70	110	175	275	800	2,450
1844O, Doubled Date	*	600	800	1,250	1,600	2,750	6,000	12,000	
1845	589,000	45	70	80	120	240	365	900	3,350
1845O	2,094,000	40	55	65	100	150	300	725	2,000
1845O, No Drapery (a)	*	50	70	80	130	275	450	1,400	4,800

* Included in number above. **a.** Drapery missing because of excessive die polishing.

In 1846 the date size was again enlarged. The 1846 Medium Date is approximately the size of the 1842 Medium Date shown. Tall Date is similar to 1853. See illustrations of large cents on page 110.

	Mintage	G-4	VG-8	F-12	VF-20	EF-40	AU-50	MS-60	MS-63
1846, All kinds	2,210,000								
1846, Medium Date		$40	$50	$55	$85	$150	$325	$750	$1,550
1846, Tall Date		40	50	60	85	140	290	800	2,750
1846, 6 Over Horizontal 6		190	260	300	500	750	1,450	3,500	11,000
1846O, Medium Date	2,304,000	40	50	55	85	140	300	1,050	2,450
1846O, Tall Date	*	175	285	375	600	1,350	1,900	6,500	
1847, 7 Over 6	**	1,800	2,500	3,250	4,500	7,400	17,500	35,000	
1847	1,156,000	40	50	65	85	185	275	485	1,350
1847O	2,584,000	50	65	70	90	195	300	775	2,750
1848	580,000	45	60	100	180	275	500	1,000	1,750
1848O	3,180,000	40	50	65	85	210	360	875	2,450
1849	1,252,000	40	65	75	90	225	400	975	2,450
1849O	2,310,000	40	65	75	90	170	285	850	2,500
1850	227,000	240	325	450	600	775	950	1,750	4,000
1850O	2,456,000	40	50	60	80	175	275	600	1,375
1851	200,750	325	425	500	700	1,250	1,500	2,250	3,900
1851O	402,000	40	50	120	140	200	325	800	1,800

* Included in number above. ** Included in number below.

Chart continued on next page.

	Mintage	G-4	VG-8	F-12	VF-20	EF-40	AU-50	MS-60	MS-63
1852............... 77,130		$350	$475	$600	$850	$975	$1,250	$1,850	$2,500
18520 144,000		70	150	275	400	775	1,400	3,500	10,000
18530 *(4 known)*	200,000	275,000	350,000	500,000					

$368,000, VF-35, Stack's Bowers auction, October 2006

Variety 2 – Arrows at Date, Rays Around Eagle (1853)

Weight 12.44 grams; composition .900 silver, .100 copper; diameter 30.6 mm; reeded edge; mints: Philadelphia, New Orleans, San Francisco, Carson City.

	Mintage	G-4	VG-8	F-12	VF-20	EF-40	AU-50	MS-60	MS-63
1853............3,532,708		$40	$50	$65	$110	$265	$575	$1,450	$3,500
18530 1,328,000		50	60	80	160	350	875	2,750	5,750

Variety 3 – Arrows at Date, No Rays (1854–1855)

Weight 12.44 grams; composition .900 silver, .100 copper; diameter 30.6 mm; reeded edge; mints: Philadelphia, New Orleans, San Francisco.

	Mintage	G-4	VG-8	F-12	VF-20	EF-40	AU-50	MS-60	MS-63
1854............2,982,000		$40	$50	$65	$80	$130	$325	$700	$1,550
18540 5,240,000		40	50	65	80	130	325	700	1,700
1855, All kinds 759,500									
1855 Over 1854...........		75	90	175	300	425	675	2,250	4,600
1855, Normal Date........		40	50	65	80	135	325	750	1,750
18550 3,688,000		40	50	65	80	135	325	750	1,750
1855S............ 129,950		350	550	850	1,750	3,500	7,600	24,000	—

Variety 1 Resumed, With Weight Standard of Variety 2 (1856–1866)

	Mintage	G-4	VG-8	F-12	VF-20	EF-40	AU-50	MS-60	MS-63	PF-63
1856............... 938,000		$40	$50	$65	$85	$130	$225	$550	$1,100	$6,500
18560 2,658,000		40	50	65	100	135	230	500	1,100	
1856S........... 211,000		40	50	175	325	625	1,275	4,250	15,000	
1857............1,988,000		40	50	65	85	125	220	500	1,100	4,500
18570 818,000		40	50	65	90	170	280	1,050	3,500	
1857S............ 158,000		60	90	175	325	775	1,350	4,850	—	
1858....... *(300+)*..4,225,700		40	50	65	85	125	225	450	1,100	2,250
18580 7,294,000		40	50	65	85	130	225	450	1,100	
1858S............ 476,000		45	55	70	120	260	440	1,050	4,000	
1859...... *(800)* 747,200		40	50	65	85	120	250	450	1,100	1,600
18590 2,834,000		40	50	65	85	120	225	450	1,275	
1859S............ 566,000		45	55	70	105	225	350	1,050	3,000	
1860......*(1,000)* 302,700		40	50	65	85	135	275	600	1,100	1,500
18600 1,290,000		40	55	70	100	145	235	450	1,150	
1860S............ 472,000		40	70	75	100	180	290	1,000	3,450	

The 1861-O quantity includes 330,000 struck under the United States government, 1,240,000 for the State of Louisiana after it seceded from the Union, and 962,633 after Louisiana joined the Confederate States of America. As all these 1861-O coins were struck from regular U.S. dies, it is impossible to distinguish one from another, except as noted in footnote (a). They should not be confused with the very rare Confederate half dollar of 1861, which has a distinctive reverse (see page 408).

	Mintage	G-4	VG-8	F-12	VF-20	EF-40	AU-50	MS-60	MS-63	PF-63
1861....... (1,000)..2,887,400		$50	$60	$75	$90	$130	$225	$500	$1,100	$1,500
1861O 2,532,633		55	65	80	100	140	300	650	1,100	
1861O, Cracked Obv (a).......*		200	300	500	800	1,500	2,500	4,500	—	
1861S............ 939,500		50	65	80	95	150	300	775	2,350	
1862.........(550)... 253,000		40	65	85	110	190	335	675	1,150	1,500
1862S............1,352,000		40	60	75	85	150	275	750	2,400	
1863.........(460)... 503,200		40	60	75	90	155	315	650	1,175	1,500
1863S............ 916,000		40	60	75	90	145	265	700	1,975	
1864.........(470)... 379,100		40	60	75	100	175	335	625	1,350	1,500
1864S............ 658,000		40	60	75	100	210	340	900	3,000	
1865.........(500)... 511,400		40	60	75	100	235	375	900	1,350	1,500
1865S............ 675,000		40	60	75	100	210	340	875	2,900	
1866S, No Motto 60,000		450	600	875	1,250	2,300	3,400	6,000	20,000	
1866 *(unique, not a regular issue)*										—

* Included in number above. **a.** Crack from nose to border; same obverse die used to coin pattern Confederate half dollars (see page 408).

Variety 4 – Motto Above Eagle (1866–1873)

Circulation strike.

Proof strike.

	Mintage	G-4	VG-8	F-12	VF-20	EF-40	AU-50	MS-60	MS-63	PF-63
1866.........(725)... 744,900		$50	$70	$80	$100	$145	$235	$500	$1,350	$1,400
1866S............. 994,000		45	55	70	85	180	275	675	2,250	
1867.........(625)... 449,300		40	50	80	130	210	290	550	1,550	1,400
1867S............1,196,000		45	50	65	85	145	260	650	2,300	
1868.........(600)... 417,600		50	60	90	175	275	375	650	1,350	1,400
1868S............1,160,000		45	50	65	85	145	250	650	1,800	
1869.........(600)... 795,300		40	50	65	85	145	250	525	1,300	1,400
1869S............ 656,000		40	50	65	85	165	300	825	2,600	
1870...... (1,000)... 633,900		40	50	65	85	140	210	490	1,150	1,350
1870CC 54,617		1,500	2,750	4,400	8,200	16,000	32,000	85,000	—	
1870S............1,004,000		40	50	65	90	170	325	1,000	3,000	
1871.........(960)..1,203,600		40	50	65	85	130	220	500	1,150	1,300
1871CC 153,950		360	650	850	1,300	3,200	4,750	15,000	52,500	
1871S............2,178,000		45	50	65	85	120	220	600	1,500	
1872.........(950)... 880,600		45	50	65	85	120	235	500	1,400	1,300
1872CC 257,000		180	250	450	850	2,100	4,250	20,000	75,000	
1872S............. 580,000		45	50	65	125	240	350	1,200	2,900	

Chart continued on next page.

Mintage	G-4	VG-8	F-12	VF-20	EF-40	AU-50	MS-60	MS-63	PF-63
1873, Close 3..(600)...587,000	$45	$55	$70	$110	$175	$275	$600	$1,150	$1,300
1873, Open 3.........214,200	3,100	4,250	5,500	6,750	8,000	11,000	19,000	50,000	
1873CC 122,500	240	400	575	1,100	1,750	3,750	10,000	40,000	
1873S, No Arrows 5,000				*(unknown in any collection)*					

Variety 5 – Arrows at Date (1873–1874)

Weight 12.50 grams; composition .900 silver, .100 copper; diameter 30.6 mm; reeded edge; mints: Philadelphia, Carson City, San Francisco.

Arrows placed at date to show change in weight from 12.44 to 12.50 grams.

Mintage	G-4	VG-8	F-12	VF-20	EF-40	AU-50	MS-60	MS-63	PF-63
1873.........(550)..1,815,150	$40	$50	$65	$100	$230	$390	$950	$1,950	$2,650
1873CC 214,560	225	325	475	975	2,000	3,750	7,500	20,000	
1873S..............228,000	55	80	130	250	450	750	2,500	6,000	
1874.........(700)..2,359,600	40	50	65	100	230	390	950	1,875	2,650
1874CC 59,000	550	800	1,600	2,400	4,650	8,250	15,000	28,000	
1874S..............394,000	40	50	80	190	375	700	1,700	3,500	

Variety 4 Resumed, With Weight Standard of Variety 5 (1875–1891)

Mintage	G-4	VG-8	F-12	VF-20	EF-40	AU-50	MS-60	MS-63	PF-63
1875.........(700)..6,026,800	$35	$45	$65	$80	$100	$185	$475	$800	$1,300
1875CC 1,008,000	55	85	120	135	235	335	1,000	2,300	
1875S..............3,200,000	35	45	65	80	100	185	475	800	
1876.......(1,150)..8,418,000	35	45	65	80	100	185	475	800	1,300
1876CC 1,956,000	50	65	90	110	180	300	725	1,500	
1876S..............4,528,000	35	45	65	80	100	185	475	800	
1877.........(510)..8,304,000	35	45	65	80	100	185	475	800	1,300
1877, 7 Over 6..............*		275	450	625	900	1,350			
1877CC 1,420,000	55	65	80	125	200	290	750	1,300	
1877S..............5,356,000	35	45	65	80	100	185	475	800	
1878.........(800)..1,377,600	35	45	65	90	120	200	475	800	1,300
1878CC 62,000	700	1,150	2,200	2,500	3,500	6,000	8,500	22,500	
1878S..............12,000	30,000	40,000	50,000	65,000	75,000	85,000	125,000	160,000	
1879.......(1,100)....4,800	275	315	365	415	525	675	850	1,150	1,300
1880.......(1,355).....8,400	265	300	340	375	525	675	850	1,150	1,300
1881.........(975)....10,000	265	300	340	375	525	675	850	1,150	1,300
1882.......(1,100).....4,400	280	310	350	400	535	675	850	1,150	1,300
1883.......(1,039).....8,000	280	310	350	400	535	675	850	1,225	1,300
1884.........(875).....4,400	325	375	425	525	625	850	950	1,225	1,300
1885.........(930).....5,200	325	375	425	525	625	850	950	1,300	1,300
1886.........(886).....5,000	400	475	575	700	800	875	975	1,300	1,300

* Included in number above.

Mintage	G-4	VG-8	F-12	VF-20	EF-40	AU-50	MS-60	MS-63	PF-63
1887........(710).....5,000	$450	$500	$600	$700	$800	$875	$1,000	$1,400	$1,300
1888........(832)....12,001	250	300	350	400	475	650	800	1,150	1,300
1889........(711)....12,000	250	300	350	400	475	650	800	1,150	1,300
1890........(590)....12,000	250	300	350	400	475	650	800	1,150	1,300
1891........(600)...200,000	50	65	100	125	150	225	450	1,000	1,300

BARBER OR LIBERTY HEAD (1892–1915)

Like the dime and quarter dollar, this type was designed by Charles E. Barber, whose initial B is at the truncation of the neck.

Designer Charles E. Barber; weight 12.50 grams; composition .900 silver, .100 copper; diameter 30.6 mm; reeded edge; mints: Philadelphia, Denver, New Orleans, San Francisco.

G-4 Good—Date and legends legible. LIBERTY worn off headband.

VG-8 Very Good—Some letters legible in LIBERTY.

F-12 Fine—LIBERTY nearly completely legible, but worn.

VF-20 Very Fine—All letters in LIBERTY evenly plain.

EF-40 Extremely Fine—LIBERTY bold, and its ribbon distinct.

AU-50 About Uncirculated—Slight trace of wear above forehead, leaf tips, and cheek, and on eagle's head, tail, and wing tips.

MS-60 Uncirculated—No trace of wear. Light blemishes.

MS-63 Choice Uncirculated—Some distracting contact marks or blemishes in prime focal areas. Impaired luster possible.

PF-63 Choice Proof—Reflective surfaces with only a few blemishes in secondary focal places. No major flaws.

Mintmark location on reverse, below eagle.

Mintage	G-4	VG-8	F-12	VF-20	EF-40	AU-50	MS-60	MS-63	PF-63
1892.......(1,245)...934,000	$27	$40	$70	$115	$210	$335	$525	$1,000	$1,200
1892O.............390,000	300	380	500	600	675	725	900	1,875	
1892O, Micro O **(a)**...........*	2,500	4,250	5,500	7,500	12,000	18,500	28,000		
1892S.............1,029,028	235	340	400	500	575	700	950	2,250	
1893........(792)..1,826,000	20	30	80	160	210	325	550	1,150	1,200
1893O.............1,389,000	35	70	130	220	350	425	675	1,500	
1893S..............740,000	140	210	300	525	600	650	1,200	4,500	
1894........(972)..1,148,000	30	50	110	200	300	375	525	1,100	1,200
1894O.............2,138,000	25	35	90	170	300	375	525	1,000	
1894S.............4,048,690	22	25	70	140	215	365	600	1,400	
1895........(880)..1,834,338	18	25	70	140	210	350	550	1,000	1,200
1895O.............1,766,000	40	60	130	180	260	375	625	1,550	
1895S.............1,108,086	30	55	140	250	300	380	600	1,400	
1896........(762)...950,000	20	25	90	160	240	365	550	1,000	1,200
1896O..............924,000	50	70	210	340	550	825	1,650	6,000	
1896S.............1,140,948	115	165	240	385	575	825	1,550	3,600	
1897........(731)..2,480,000	20	22	45	95	200	360	500	1,000	1,200
1897O..............632,000	160	230	500	750	1,050	1,300	1,750	3,900	

* Included in number above. **a.** Normal and "microscopic" mintmarks; see page 22.

Chart continued on next page.

Mintage	G-4	VG-8	F-12	VF-20	EF-40	AU-50	MS-60	MS-63	PF-63
1897S 933,900	$150	$220	$350	$550	$800	$975	$1,550	$3,650	
1898 . . . . (735) . . 2,956,000	18	20	45	95	200	360	500	1,000	$1,200
18980 874,000	38	90	240	400	540	650	1,200	3,200	
1898S 2,358,550	30	48	90	185	340	440	925	3,500	
1899 . . . . (846) . . 5,538,000	18	20	45	95	200	350	500	1,000	1,175
18990 1,724,000	25	35	80	165	275	390	675	1,600	
1899S 1,686,411	25	40	90	175	300	425	775	2,150	
1900 . . . . (912) . 4,762,000	17	19	45	95	200	350	500	1,000	1,175
19000 2,744,000	17	25	60	170	280	425	850	3,400	
1900S 2,560,322	17	19	45	100	210	365	650	2,350	
1901 . . . . (813) . . 4,268,000	17	18	45	95	200	350	500	950	1,175
19010 1,124,000	17	26	80	230	350	475	1,300	4,850	
1901S 847,044	32	55	165	350	700	1,250	2,250	7,600	
1902 . . . . (777) . 4,922,000	17	18	45	95	200	350	500	950	1,175
19020 2,526,000	17	20	55	105	220	385	775	3,550	
1902S 1,460,670	19	28	65	150	250	425	785	2,800	
1903 . . . . (755) . . 2,278,000	17	18	45	95	200	350	550	1,450	1,175
19030 2,100,000	17	18	55	125	210	375	675	1,550	
1903S 1,920,772	17	19	60	130	230	375	650	1,600	
1904 . . . . (670) . 2,992,000	17	18	35	85	200	350	500	1,050	1,175
19040 1,117,600	22	35	95	235	400	600	1,250	3,750	
1904S 553,038	48	115	340	775	1,500	2,250	9,750	19,500	
1905 . . . . (727) . . . 662,000	25	29	85	185	265	365	550	1,500	1,175
19050 505,000	30	45	125	225	325	450	750	1,650	
1905S 2,494,000	16	19	53	140	240	375	650	1,850	
1906 . . . . (675) . . 2,638,000	16	17	45	95	200	350	500	950	1,175
1906D 4,028,000	16	17	45	95	200	350	500	950	
19060 2,446,000	16	19	42	95	200	350	600	1,400	
1906S 1,740,154	16	19	53	115	210	350	600	1,350	
1907 . . . . (575) . . 2,598,000	16	17	45	95	200	350	500	950	1,175
1907D 3,856,000	16	17	45	95	200	350	500	950	
19070 3,946,600	16	17	45	95	200	350	500	950	
1907S 1,250,000	17	30	85	185	375	625	1,275	5,600	
1908 . . . . (545) . . 1,354,000	16	17	45	95	200	350	500	950	1,175
1908D 3,280,000	16	17	45	95	200	350	500	950	
19080 5,360,000	16	17	45	95	200	350	500	950	
1908S 1,644,828	16	25	75	160	275	420	875	2,400	
1909 . . . . (650) . . 2,368,000	16	17	45	95	200	350	500	950	1,175
19090 925,400	18	22	65	150	315	525	825	1,600	
1909S 1,764,000	16	17	45	95	200	360	600	1,250	
1910 . . . . (551) . . . 418,000	20	30	95	175	320	400	575	1,100	1,175
1910S 1,948,000	18	20	35	95	200	350	625	1,950	
1911 . . . . (543) . . 1,406,000	16	17	45	95	200	350	500	950	1,175
1911D 695,080	16	17	45	95	200	350	500	950	
1911S 1,272,000	18	20	40	100	210	365	650	1,500	
1912 . . . . (700) . . 1,550,000	16	17	45	95	200	350	500	950	1,175
1912D 2,300,800	16	17	45	95	200	350	500	950	
1912S 1,370,000	16	18	45	100	200	390	575	1,100	
1913 . . . . (627) . . . 188,000	75	90	210	425	650	835	1,200	1,800	1,250
1913D 534,000	16	17	45	95	200	350	500	950	
1913S 604,000	16	25	55	120	275	385	600	1,350	
1914 . . . . (380) . . . 124,230	150	170	315	550	775	975	1,350	1,950	1,450

Mintage	G-4	VG-8	F-12	VF-20	EF-40	AU-50	MS-60	MS-63	PF-63
1914S............992,000	$16	$20	$40	$100	$200	$370	$575	$1,150	
1915........(450)...138,000	110	140	285	375	575	850	1,350	2,250	$1,500
1915D.............1,170,400	16	17	45	95	200	350	500	950	
1915S.............1,604,000	16	17	45	95	200	350	500	950	

LIBERTY WALKING (1916–1947)

This type was designed by Adolph A. Weinman, whose monogram, AW, appears under the tips of the tail feathers. On the 1916 coins and some of the 1917 coins the mintmark is located on the obverse below the motto.

Designer Adolph A. Weinman; weight 12.50 grams; composition .900 silver, .100 copper (net weight: .36169 oz. pure silver); diameter 30.6 mm; reeded edge; mints: Philadelphia, Denver, San Francisco.

G-4 Good—Rims defined. Motto IN GOD WE TRUST legible.
VG-8 Very Good—Motto distinct. About half of skirt lines at left clear.
F-12 Fine—All skirt lines evident, but worn in spots. Clear details in sandal below motto.
VF-20 Very Fine—Skirt lines sharp, including leg area. Little wear on breast and right arm.
EF-40 Extremely Fine—All skirt lines bold.
AU-50 About Uncirculated—Slight trace of wear on Liberty's head, knee, and breasts, and on eagle's claws and head.
MS-60 Uncirculated—No trace of wear. Light blemishes.
MS-63 Choice Uncirculated—Some distracting contact marks or blemishes in prime focal areas. Impaired luster possible.
PF-65 Gem Proof—Brilliant surfaces with no noticeable blemishes or flaws. A few scattered, barely noticeable marks or hairlines possible.

1916–1917

1917–1947

Mintmark Locations

Choice Uncirculated, well-struck specimens are worth more than values listed.

Mintage	G-4	VG-8	F-12	VF-20	EF-40	AU-50	MS-60	MS-63
1916.......................608,000	$50	$55	$90	$160	$225	$265	$350	$500
1916D, Obverse Mintmark.......1,014,400	50	60	85	135	215	240	360	600
1916S, Obverse Mintmark.........508,000	100	130	275	435	650	800	1,200	2,100
1917.......................12,292,000	18	19	20	21	40	70	140	210
1917D, Obverse Mintmark.........765,400	25	35	80	150	240	325	600	1,300
1917D, Reverse Mintmark.......1,940,000	18	19	45	145	280	515	950	2,200
1917S, Obverse Mintmark.........952,000	27	50	140	375	750	1,300	2,350	4,750
1917S, Reverse Mintmark.......5,554,000	18	19	20	35	70	170	425	2,000
1918.......................6,634,000	18	19	20	65	155	265	625	975
1918D.......................3,853,040	18	19	38	100	250	475	1,300	3,150
1918S.......................10,282,000	18	19	20	35	80	200	525	2,100
1919.......................962,000	25	32	78	265	515	825	1,350	3,500
1919D.......................1,165,000	26	40	115	345	825	1,675	5,900	18,000
1919S.......................1,552,000	20	30	85	275	815	1,600	3,250	8,750
1920.......................6,372,000	18	19	20	45	80	160	325	700
1920D.......................1,551,000	18	20	75	250	450	925	1,500	3,850
1920S.......................4,624,000	18	19	23	90	230	475	875	3,000

Chart continued on next page.

	Mintage	G-4	VG-8	F-12	VF-20	EF-40	AU-50	MS-60	MS-63	PF-65
1921	246,000	$175	$220	$350	$775.00	$1,700	$2,750	$4,100	$7,750	
1921D	208,000	325	375	525	850.00	2,300	3,300	5,500	14,000	
1921S	548,000	48	80	250	800.00	4,500	8,300	14,750	28,500	
1923S	2,178,000	15	16	30	110.00	365	800	1,500	3,700	
1927S	2,392,000	15	16	18	50.00	160	400	950	2,050	
1928S (a,b)	1,940,000	15	16	19	75.00	180	435	950	2,750	
1929D	1,001,200	15	16	18	30.00	100	190	385	750	
1929S	1,902,000	15	16	18	35.00	115	230	410	950	
1933S	1,786,000	15	16	18	20.00	60	240	635	1,200	
1934	6,964,000	15	16	17	17.50	19	26	75	110	
1934D (b)	2,361,000	15	16	18	20.00	35	85	150	235	
1934S	3,652,000	15	16	17	17.50	30	90	325	800	
1935	9,162,000	15	16	17	17.50	19	25	45	75	
1935D	3,003,800	15	16	17	17.50	30	65	140	300	
1935S	3,854,000	15	16	17	17.50	26	95	250	465	
1936 (3,901)	12,614,000	15	16	17	17.50	18	25	45	75	$4,000
1936D	4,252,400	15	16	17	17.50	20	50	85	120	
1936S	3,884,000	15	16	17	17.50	22	60	130	200	
1937 (5,728)	9,522,000	15	16	17	17.50	18	25	40	70	1,000
1937D	1,676,000	15	16	17	18.00	32	100	215	260	
1937S	2,090,000	15	16	17	17.50	25	60	165	210	
1938 (8,152)	4,110,000	15	16	17	18.00	20	45	70	160	900
1938D	491,600	75	100	110	135.00	175	250	500	625	
1939 (8,808)	6,812,000	15	16	17	17.50	18	26	40	65	700
1939D	4,267,800	15	16	17	17.50	18	25	43	75	
1939S	2,552,000	15	16	17	17.50	26	75	150	190	
1940 (11,279)	9,156,000	15	16	17	17.50	18	20	35	53	625
1940S	4,550,000	15	16	17	17.50	18	22	45	80	
1941 (c) (15,412)	24,192,000	15	16	17	17.50	18	20	35	55	625
1941D	11,248,400	15	16	17	17.50	18	20	38	63	
1941S	8,098,000	15	16	17	17.50	18	20	73	120	
1942 (21,120)	47,818,000	15	16	17	17.50	18	20	38	60	625
1942D	10,973,800	15	16	17	17.50	18	20	38	85	
1942S (b)	12,708,000	15	16	17	17.50	18	20	40	68	
1943	53,190,000	15	16	17	17.50	18	20	35	50	
1943D	11,346,000	15	16	17	17.50	18	24	48	73	
1943S	13,450,000	15	16	17	17.50	18	25	42	60	
1944	28,206,000	15	16	17	17.50	18	20	35	50	
1944D	9,769,000	15	16	17	17.50	18	20	40	58	
1944S	8,904,000	15	16	17	17.50	18	20	40	63	
1945	31,502,000	15	16	17	17.50	18	20	35	50	
1945D	9,966,800	15	16	17	17.50	18	20	35	60	
1945S	10,156,000	15	16	17	17.50	18	20	38	55	
1946	12,118,000	15	16	17	17.50	18	20	37	50	
1946, DblDie Rev	*	20	24	28	40.00	65	125	275	550	
1946D	2,151,000	15	16	17	17.50	22	35	47	60	
1946S	3,724,000	15	16	17	17.50	18	20	43	58	
1947	4,094,000	15	16	17	17.50	18	25	45	60	
1947D	3,900,600	15	16	17	17.50	18	30	45	60	

* Included in number above. **a.** Pieces dated 1928-D are counterfeit. **b.** Large and small mintmark varieties; see page 22. **c.** Proofs struck with and without designer's initials.

FRANKLIN (1948–1963)

The Benjamin Franklin half dollar and the Roosevelt dime were both designed by John R. Sinnock, whose initials appear below the shoulder. The Liberty Bell is similar to that used by Sinnock on the 1926 Sesquicentennial of American Independence commemorative half dollar modeled from a sketch by John Frederick Lewis (see page 292).

Designer John R. Sinnock; weight 12.50 grams; composition .900 silver, .100 copper (net weight .36169 oz. pure silver); diameter 30.6 mm; reeded edge; mints: Philadelphia, Denver, San Francisco.

VF-20 Very Fine—At least half of the lower and upper incused lines on rim of Liberty Bell on reverse visible.
EF-40 Extremely Fine—Wear spots at top of end of Franklin's curls and hair at back of ears. Wear evident at top and on lettering of Liberty Bell.
MS-63 Choice Uncirculated—Some distracting contact marks or blemishes in prime focal areas. Impaired luster possible.
MS-65 Gem Uncirculated—Only light, scattered contact marks that are not distracting. Strong luster, good eye appeal.
PF-65 Gem Proof—Brilliant surfaces with no noticeable blemishes or flaws. A few scattered, barely noticeable marks or hairlines possible.

Mintmark Location

Choice, well-struck Uncirculated halves with full bell lines command higher prices.

	Mintage	VF-20	EF-40	MS-60	MS-63	MS-65	PF-65
1948	3,006,814	$15	$16.00	$20	$27	$80	
1948D	4,028,600	15	16.00	20	24	115	
1949	5,614,000	16	18.00	40	70	130	
1949D	4,120,600	16	18.00	45	70	550	
1949S	3,744,000	16	20.00	65	95	140	
1950 (51,386)	7,742,123	15	15.50	30	40	110	$475
1950D	8,031,600	15	15.50	26	38	250	
1951 (57,500)	16,802,102	15	15.50	16	24	70	375
1951D	9,475,200	15	15.50	30	45	150	
1951S	13,696,000	15	15.50	25	35	70	
1952 (81,980)	21,192,093	15	15.50	16	23	70	230
1952D	25,395,600	15	15.50	16	23	125	
1952S	5,526,000	15	17.00	50	65	100	
1953 (128,800)	2,668,120	15	15.50	16	25	105	190
1953D	20,900,400	15	15.50	16	23	110	
1953S	4,148,000	15	15.50	25	35	70	
1954 (233,300)	13,188,202	15	15.50	16	20	70	85
1954D	25,445,580	15	15.50	16	24	90	
1954S	4,993,400	15	15.50	16	26	55	
1955 (378,200)	2,498,181	18	22.00	25	35	60	75
1956 (669,384)	4,032,000	15	15.50	16	25	48	45
1957 (1,247,952)	5,114,000	15	15.50	16	20	50	28
1957D	19,966,850	15	15.50	16	20	52	
1958 (875,652)	4,042,000	15	15.50	16	20	45	32
1958D	23,962,412	15	15.50	16	20	45	

Chart continued on next page.

	Mintage	VF-20	EF-40	MS-60	MS-63	MS-65	PF-65
1959 . . . . (1,149,291) . . 6,200,000		$15	$15.50	$16	$18	$70	$22
1959D 13,053,750		15	15.50	16	18	90	
1960 . . . . (1,691,602) . . 6,024,000		15	15.50	16	18	100	23
1960D 18,215,812		15	15.50	16	18	200	

1961, Doubled-Die Proof

	Mintage	VF-20	EF-40	MS-60	MS-63	MS-65	PF-65
1961 . . . . (3,028,244) . . . 8,290,000		$15	$15.50	$16	$18	$75	$25
1961, Doubled-Die Proof . . . .*							2,900
1961D 20,276,442		15	15.50	16	18	110	
1962 . . . . (3,218,019) . . . 9,714,000		15	15.50	16	18	90	22
1962D 35,473,281		15	15.50	16	18	120	
1963 . . . . (3,075,645) . . 22,164,000		15	15.50	16	18	40	23
1963D 67,069,292		15	15.50	16	18	45	

* Included in number above.

KENNEDY (1964 TO DATE)

Gilroy Roberts, chief engraver of the Mint from 1948 to 1964, designed the obverse of this coin. His stylized initials are on the truncation of the forceful bust of President John F. Kennedy. The reverse, which uses the presidential coat of arms for the motif, is the work of Frank Gasparro, who was appointed chief engraver in February 1965. A few of the pieces dated 1971-D and 1977-D were struck in silver clad composition by error.

Designers Gilroy Roberts and Frank Gasparro. 1964—Standards same as for previous issue (net weight .36169 oz. pure silver). 1965–1970—Weight 11.50 grams; composition, outer layers of .800 silver and .200 copper bonded to inner core of .209 silver, .791 copper (net weight .1479 oz. pure silver net composition .400 silver, .600 copper). 1971 to date—Weight 11.34 grams; composition, outer layers of copper-nickel (.750 copper, .250 nickel) bonded to inner core of pure copper; diameter 30.6 mm; reeded edge. Mints: Philadelphia, Denver, San Francisco.

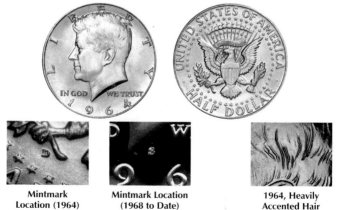

Mintmark Location (1964)

Mintmark Location (1968 to Date)

1964, Heavily Accented Hair

Silver Coinage (1964)

	Mintage	MS-63	PF-65
1964 . . . . (3,950,762) . . 273,304,004		$15	$18
1964, Heavily Accented Hair . . . . *			45
1964D 156,205,446		15	

* Included in number above.

Silver Clad Coinage (1965–1970)

	Mintage	MS-63	PF-65
1965 65,879,366		$8	
1966 108,984,932		8	
1967 295,046,978		8	
1968D 246,951,930		8	
1968S . . . . (3,041,506)			$8
1969D 129,881,800		8	
1969S . . . . (2,934,631)			8
1970D **(a)** 2,150,000		18	
1970S . . . . (2,632,810)			16

a. Issued only in Mint sets.

Clad Coinage and Silver Proofs (1971 to Date)

The design was slightly modified several times between 1971 and the present.

1974-D, Doubled-Die Obverse
Note prominent doubling of RUS.

	Mintage	MS-63	PF-65		Mintage	MS-63	PF-65
1971 155,164,000		$2		1973D 83,171,400		$2	
1971D 302,097,424		2		1973S . . . . (2,760,339)			$4
1971S . . . . (3,220,733)			$4	1974 201,596,000		2	
1972 153,180,000		2		1974D 79,066,300		2	
1972D 141,890,000		2		1974D, DblDie Obverse . . . . *		40	
1972S . . . . (3,260,996)			4	1974S . . . . (2,612,568)			4
1973 64,964,000		2					

* Included in number above.

Bicentennial (1776–1976)

In an open contest for the selection of suitable designs for the special Bicentennial reverses of the quarter, half dollar, and dollar, Seth G. Huntington's winning entry was featured on the half dollar. It shows Independence Hall in Philadelphia as the center device. The obverse was unchanged except for the dual dating 1776–1976. Bicentennial half dollars were struck during 1975 and 1976 and were used for general circulation as well as being included in Proof and Uncirculated sets for 1975 and 1976.

Designers Gilroy Roberts and Seth Huntington; diameter 30.6 mm; reeded edge. Silver clad—Weight 11.50 grams; composition, outer layers of .800 silver, .200 copper bonded to inner core of .209 silver, .791 copper (net weight .14792 oz. pure silver). Copper-nickel clad—Weight 11.34 grams; composition, outer layers of copper-nickel (.750 copper, .250 nickel) bonded to inner core of pure copper.

	Mintage	MS-63	PF-65
1976	234,308,000	$2	
1976D	287,565,248	2	
1976S	(7,059,099)		$4

	Mintage	MS-63	PF-65
1976S, Silver Clad	11,000,000	$8	
1976S, Silver Clad	(4,000,000)		$8

Note: Mintage figures for 1976-S silver coins are approximate; many were melted in 1982.

Eagle Reverse Resumed (1977 to Date)

Copper-nickel clad coinage. Silver Proofs are of pre-1965 standards.

	Mintage	MS-63	PF-65
1977	43,598,000	$2	
1977D	31,449,106	2	
1977S	(3,251,152)		$4
1978	14,350,000	2	
1978D	13,765,799	3	
1978S	(3,127,781)		4
1979	68,312,000	2	
1979D	15,815,422	2	
1979S	(3,677,175)		
1979S, Type 1 **(a)**			4
1979S, Type 2 **(a)**			15
1980P	44,134,000	2	
1980D	33,456,449	2	
1980S	(3,554,806)		4
1981P	29,544,000	2	
1981D	27,839,533	2	
1981S, All kinds	(4,063,083)		
1981S, Type 1 **(a)**			4
1981S, Type 2 **(a)**			17
1982P	10,819,000	5	
1982D	13,140,102	5	
1982S	(3,857,479)		4
1983P	34,139,000	6	
1983D	32,472,244	7	
1983S	(3,279,126)		4
1984P	26,029,000	2	
1984D	26,262,158	2	
1984S	(3,065,110)		4
1985P	18,706,962	5	
1985D	19,814,034	5	
1985S	(3,362,821)		5
1986P	13,107,633	6	
1986D	15,336,145	5	
1986S	(3,010,497)		$5
1987P **(b)**	2,890,758	$5	
1987D **(b)**	2,890,758	5	
1987S	(4,227,728)		4
1988P	13,626,000	5	
1988D	12,000,096	4	
1988S	(3,262,948)		4
1989P	24,542,000	4	
1989D	23,000,216	3	
1989S	(3,220,194)		4
1990P	22,278,000	3	
1990D	20,096,242	3	
1990S	(3,299,559)		4
1991P	14,874,000	4	
1991D	15,054,678	4	
1991S	(2,867,787)		5
1992P	17,628,000	2	
1992D	17,000,106	3	
1992S	(2,858,981)		4
1992S, Silver	(1,317,579)		15
1993P	15,510,000	3	
1993D	15,000,006	3	
1993S	(2,633,439)		5
1993S, Silver	(761,353)		20
1994P	23,718,000	2	
1994D	23,828,110	2	
1994S	(2,484,594)		5
1994S, Silver	(785,329)		20
1995P	26,496,000	2	
1995D	26,288,000	2	
1995S	(2,117,496)		8
1995S, Silver	(679,985)		20
1996P	24,442,000	2	

a. See page 234 for illustrations. **b.** Not issued for circulation; included with Mint and Souvenir sets.

HALF DOLLARS

	Mintage	MS-63	PF-65
1996D 24,744,000		$2	
1996S. . . . .(1,750,244)			$8
1996S, Silver . . . . (775,021)			22
1997P. 20,882,000		2	
1997D 19,876,000		2	
1997S. . . . .(2,055,000)			8
1997S, Silver . . . . (741,678)			22
1998P. 15,646,000		2	
1998D 15,064,000		2	
1998S. . . . .(2,086,507)			8
1998S, Silver . . . . (878,792)			20
1998S, Silver, Matte Finish (b)			125
1999P. 8,900,000		2	
1999D 10,682,000		2	
1999S. . . . .(2,543,401)			9
1999S, Silver . . . . (804,565)			27
2000P. 22,600,000		2	
2000D 19,466,000		2	
2000S. . . . .(3,082,483)			5
2000S, Silver . . . . (965,421)			15
2001P. 21,200,000		2	
2001D 19,504,000		2	
2001S. . . . .(2,294,909)			5
2001S, Silver . . . . (889,697)			18
2002P (c) 3,100,000		2	
2002D (c) 2,500,000		2	
2002S. . . . .(2,319,766)			5
2002S, Silver . . . . (892,229)			15
2003P (c) 2,500,000		2	
2003D (c) 2,500,000		2	
2003S. . . . .(2,172,684)			5
2003S, Silver . . . .(1,125,755)			15
2004P (c) 2,900,000		2	
2004D (c) 2,900,000		2	
2004S. . . . .(1,789,488)			5
2004S, Silver . . . .(1,175,934)			15

	Mintage	MS-63	PF-65
2005P (c) 3,800,000		$3	
2005D (c) 3,500,000		3	
2005S. . . . .(2,275,000)			$5
2005S, Silver . . . .(1,069,679)			15
2006P (c) 2,400,000		2	
2006D (c) 2,000,000		2	
2006S. . . . .(2,000,428)			5
2006S, Silver . . . .(1,054,008)			15
2007P (c) 2,400,000		2	
2007D (c) 2,400,000		2	
2007S. . . . .(1,702,116)			5
2007S, Silver . . . . (875,050)			15
2008P (c) 1,700,000		2	
2008D (c) 1,700,000		2	
2008S. . . . .(1,405,674)			5
2008S, Silver . . . . (763,887)			15
2009P (c) 1,900,000		2	
2009D (c) 1,900,000		2	
2009S. . . . .(1,482,502)			5
2009S, Silver . . . . (697,365)			15
2010P (c) 1,800,000		2	
2010D (c) 1,700,000		2	
2010S. . . . .(1,103,950)			5
2010S, Silver . . . . (585,414)			15
2011P (c) 1,750,000		2	
2011D (c) 1,700,000		2	
2011S. . . . . (952,881)			5
2011S, Silver . . . . (500,395)			15
2012P (c) 1,800,000		2	
2012D (c) 1,700,000		2	
2012S.			5
2012S, Silver			15
2013P (c)		2	
2013D (c)		2	
2013S.			5
2013S, Silver			15

b. Included in commemorative set (see page 342). **c.** Not issued for circulation. The U.S. Mint produces circulation-quality half dollar coins at its Philadelphia and Denver facilities each year. In the years since 2002 these coins have been made available to the public only through direct purchase from the Mint in rolls of 20 coins or bags of 200 coins. These coins are not available through banks for general distribution, and are sold by the Mint for approximately 1.5 to 2 times their face value.

The silver dollar was authorized by Congress on April 2, 1792. Weight and fineness were specified at 416 grains and .8924 fine. The first issues appeared in 1794, and until 1804 all silver dollars had the value stamped on the edge: HUNDRED CENTS, ONE DOLLAR OR UNIT. After a lapse in coinage of the silver dollar during the period 1804 through 1835, in 1836 coins were made with plain edges and the value was placed on the reverse.

The weight was changed by the law of January 18, 1837, to 412-1/2 grains, .900 fineness. The coinage was discontinued by the Act of February 12, 1873, and reauthorized by the Act of February 28, 1878. The silver dollar was again discontinued after 1935, and since then only base-metal pieces have been coined for circulation (also see Silver Bullion on pages 352–355).

ORIGIN OF THE DOLLAR

The word *dollar* evolves from the German *thaler,* the name given to the first large-sized European silver coin. Designed as a substitute for the gold florin, the coin originated in the Tyrol in 1484. So popular did these large silver coins become during the 16th century that many other countries struck similar pieces, giving them names derived from *thaler.* In the Netherlands the coin was called *rijksdaalder,* in Denmark *rigsdaler,* in Italy *tallero,* in Poland *talar,* in France *jocandale,* in Russia *jefimok.* All these names are abbreviations of *joachimsthaler.* Until the discovery of the great silver deposits in Mexico and South America, the mint with the greatest output of large silver coins was that of Joachimsthal in the Bohemian Erzgebirge.

The Spanish dollar, or piece of eight, was widely used and familiar to everyone in the British American colonies. It was only natural, therefore, that the word *dollar* was adopted officially for the standard monetary unit of the United States by Congress on July 6, 1785. The Continental Dollar of 1776 is described on page 85.

Note: Values of common-date silver coins have been based on the current bullion price of silver, $40 per ounce, and may vary with the prevailing spot price. To determine the intrinsic value of common silver coins, see page 425.

FLOWING HAIR (1794–1795)

Varieties listed are those most significant to collectors, but numerous minor variations may be found because each of the early dies was individually made. Blanks were weighed before the dollars were struck and overweight pieces were filed to remove excess silver. Coins with adjustment marks from this process may be worth less than values shown here. Some Flowing Hair type dollars of 1794 and 1795 were weight-adjusted through insertion of a small (8 mm) silver plug in the center of the blank planchet before the coin was struck. Values of varieties not listed in this guide depend on rarity and collector interest.

Engraver Robert Scot; weight 26.96 grams; composition .900 silver, .100 copper; approx. diameter 39–40 mm; edge: HUNDRED CENTS ONE DOLLAR OR UNIT with decorations between words.

AG-3 About Good—Clear enough to identify.
G-4 Good—Date and letters legible. Main devices outlined, but lacking in detail.
VG-8 Very Good—Major details discernible. Letters well formed but worn.
F-12 Fine—Hair ends distinguishable. Top hair lines visible, but otherwise worn smooth.
VF-20 Very Fine—Some detail visible in hair in center. Other details more bold.
EF-40 Extremely Fine—Hair well defined but with some wear.
AU-50 About Uncirculated—Slight trace of wear on tips of highest curls; feathers on eagle's breast usually weak.
MS-60 Uncirculated—No trace of wear. Light blemishes.

Values shown for Uncirculated pieces of this type are for well-struck, attractive coins with minimal surface marks.

	Mintage	AG-3	G-4	VG-8	F-12	VF-20	EF-40	AU-50	MS-60
1794	1,758	$37,500	$65,000	$95,000	$115,000	$160,000	$215,000	$350,000	$675,000
$1,207,500, MS-64, Stack's Bowers auction, August 2010									
1794, Silver Plug *(unique)*	*								
$10,016,875, SP-66, Stack's Bowers auction, January 2013 **(a)**									

* Included in number above. **a.** See appendix E.

Two Leaves Beneath Each Wing

Three Leaves Beneath Each Wing

Silver Plug (1795)

	Mintage	AG-3	G-4	VG-8	F-12	VF-20	EF-40	AU-50	MS-60
1795, All kinds	160,295								
1795, Two Leaves		$1,100	$1,750	$2,400	$4,350	$5,750	$13,500	$20,500	$70,000
$431,250, MS-65, Heritage auction, January 2008									
1795, Three Leaves		1,100	1,750	2,400	4,100	5,500	12,000	19,500	65,000
1795, Silver Plug		1,500	2,800	4,750	8,500	16,000	27,500	47,500	130,000
$1,265,000, V Ch Gem MS, Bullowa auction, December 2005									

DRAPED BUST (1795–1804)
Small Eagle Reverse (1795–1798)

Designer Robert Scot; weight 26.96 grams; composition .8924 silver, .1076 copper; approx. diameter 39–40 mm; edge: HUNDRED CENTS ONE DOLLAR OR UNIT with decorations between words.

AG-3 About Good—Clear enough to identify.

G-4 Good—Bust outlined, no detail. Date legible, some leaves evident.

VG-8 Very Good—Drapery worn except deepest folds. Hair lines smooth.

F-12 Fine—All drapery lines distinguishable. Some detail visible in hair lines near cheek and neck.

VF-20 Very Fine—Left side of drapery worn smooth.

EF-40 Extremely Fine—Drapery distinctly visible. Hair well outlined and detailed.

AU-50 About Uncirculated—Slight trace of wear on the bust shoulder and hair to left of forehead, as well as on eagle's breast and top edges of wings.

MS-60 Uncirculated—No trace of wear. Light blemishes.

	Mintage	AG-3	G-4	VG-8	F-12	VF-20	EF-40	AU-50	MS-60
1795, All kinds	*42,738*								
1795, Off-Center Bust	$960	$1,450	$2,050	$3,500	$5,100	$10,750	$15,500	$60,000
1795, Centered Bust.	960	1,450	2,050	3,500	5,100	10,750	15,500	55,000
$373,750, MS-65, Heritage auction, January 2007									

Small Date

Large Date

Small Letters

Large Letters

	Mintage	AG-3	G-4	VG-8	F-12	VF-20	EF-40	AU-50	MS-60
1796, All kinds	79,920								
1796, Small Date, Small Letters *(3 varieties)*	$825	$1,550	$2,000	$3,800	$5,500	$10,750	$15,000	$62,500
1796, Small Date, Large Letters	825	1,550	2,000	3,800	5,500	10,750	15,000	62,500
1796, Large Date, Small Letters	825	1,550	2,000	3,400	5,100	10,000	15,000	62,500
1797, All kinds	7,776								
1797, 10 Stars Left, 6 Right	850	1,550	1,900	3,000	5,500	10,000	14,500	63,000
1797, 9 Stars Left, 7 Right, Large Letters	850	1,550	1,950	3,100	6,000	10,750	15,300	63,000
1797, 9 Stars Left, 7 Right, Small Letters	1,200	1,750	2,750	3,900	8,200	16,250	32,500	110,000

	Mintage	AG-3	G-4	VG-8	F-12	VF-20	EF-40	AU-50	MS-60
1798, All kinds	327,536								
1798, 15 Stars on Obverse		$1,100	$1,750	$2,650	$3,800	$8,000	$16,000	$27,500	$85,000
1798, 13 Stars on Obverse		1,000	1,700	2,100	3,500	7,750	15,000	26,000	80,000

Heraldic Eagle Reverse (1798–1804)

The two earliest reverse dies of 1798 have five vertical lines in the stripes in the shield. All dollar dies thereafter have four vertical lines.

G-4 Good—Letters and date legible. E PLURIBUS UNUM illegible.
VG-8 Very Good—Motto partially legible. Only deepest drapery details visible. All other lines smooth.
F-12 Fine—All drapery lines distinguishable. Some detail visible in hair lines near cheek and neck.
VF-20 Very Fine—Left side of drapery worn smooth.
EF-40 Extremely Fine—Drapery distinct. Hair well detailed.
AU-50 About Uncirculated—Slight trace of wear on the bust shoulder and hair to left of forehead, as well as on eagle's breast and top edges of wings.
MS-60 Uncirculated—No trace of wear. Light blemishes.

Four Vertical Lines in Shield

	G-4	VG-8	F-12	VF-20	EF-40	AU-50	MS-60
1798, Knob 9, 5 Vertical Lines **(a)**	$900	$1,150	$1,650	$2,900	$4,700	$8,200	$22,000
1798, Knob 9, 4 Vertical Lines	900	1,150	1,650	2,900	4,700	8,800	—
1798, Knob 9, 10 Arrows	900	1,150	1,650	2,900	4,700	8,800	—
1798, Pointed 9, Close Date	900	1,150	1,650	2,800	4,700	8,800	22,000
1798, Pointed 9, Wide Date	900	1,150	1,650	2,800	4,700	8,200	22,000
1798, Pointed 9, 5 Vertical Lines	900	1,150	1,650	2,800	4,700	8,800	25,000
1798, Pointed 9, 10 Arrows	950	1,200	1,750	3,100	4,900	9,250	23,500
1798, Pointed 9, 4 Berries	900	1,150	1,650	2,800	4,700	8,200	21,500

a. 327,536 silver dollars were minted in 1798, but the Mint did not break this figure down by type.

1799 Over 98, Stars 7 and 6   **Stars 8 and 5**

See next page for chart.   **217**

	Mintage	G-4	VG-8	F-12	VF-20	EF-40	AU-50	MS-60
1799, All kinds 423,515								
1799, 99 Over 98, 15-Star Reverse		$960	$1,350	$1,800	$2,850	$5,200	$8,700	$23,000
1799, 99 Over 98, 13-Star Reverse		950	1,250	1,750	2,700	4,700	8,400	22,400
1799, Irregular Date, 15-Star Reverse		950	1,150	1,550	2,550	4,700	8,200	23,000
1799, Irregular Date, 13-Star Reverse		950	1,150	1,550	2,550	4,700	8,200	22,000
1799, Normal Date		900	1,150	1,550	2,550	4,700	8,200	22,400
$379,500, MS-66, Heritage auction, March 2007								
1799, 8 Stars Left, 5 Right		1,000	1,350	1,900	3,100	5,750	13,500	32,500
1800, All kinds 220,920								
1800, Very Wide Date, Low 8		900	1,100	1,600	2,500	4,600	8,100	25,000
1800, "Dotted Date" *(from die breaks)*		900	1,150	1,650	2,600	5,200	8,200	25,000
1800, Only 12 Arrows.		900	1,100	1,600	2,500	4,600	8,100	25,000
1800, Normal Dies		900	1,100	1,600	2,500	4,600	8,100	25,000
1800, AMERICAI		900	1,100	1,600	2,500	4,600	8,100	26,500
1801 54,454		900	1,100	1,600	2,500	4,900	8,350	29,500
1801, Proof Restrike *(reverse struck from first die of 1804 dollar) (2 known)* . .								1,000,000

1802, 2 Over 1, Narrow Date

1802, 2 Over 1, Wide Date

1803, Small 3

1803, Large 3

	Mintage	G-4	VG-8	F-12	VF-20	EF-40	AU-50	MS-60
1802, All kinds 41,650								
1802, 2 Over 1, Narrow Date		$950	$1,200	$1,800	$2,500	$5,000	$9,100	$30,000
1802, 2 Over 1, Wide Date		1,000	1,200	1,900	2,700	5,250	11,100	32,000
1802, Narrow Normal Date		950	1,200	1,700	2,500	4,900	8,100	23,500
1802, Wide Normal Date		1,000	1,200	1,850	2,800	5,000	10,100	36,000
1802, Proof Restrike *(4 known)*								420,000
$920,000, PF-65 Cam, Heritage auction, April 2008								
1803, All kinds 85,634								
1803, Small 3.		1,000	1,200	1,900	2,800	5,000	9,000	27,000
1803, Large 3.		1,000	1,200	1,900	2,800	5,000	9,000	28,000
1803, Proof Restrike *(4 known)*								450,000
$851,875, PF-66, Stack's Bowers auction, January 2013								

1804 DOLLAR

The 1804 dollar is one of the most publicized rarities in the entire series of United States coins. There are specimens known as originals (first reverse), of which eight are known; and restrikes (second reverse), of which seven are known, one of which has a plain edge.

Numismatists have found that the 1804 original dollars were first struck at the Mint in the 1834 through 1835 period, for use in presentation Proof sets. The first coin to be owned by a collector, a Proof, was obtained from a Mint officer by Matthew Stickney on May 9, 1843, in exchange for an Immune Columbia piece in gold. Later, beginning in 1859, the pieces known as *restrikes* and *electrotypes* were made at the Mint to supply the needs of collectors who wanted examples of these dollars.

Evidence that these pieces were struck during the later period is based on the fact that the 1804 dollars differ from issues of 1803 or earlier and conform more closely to those struck after 1836, their edges or borders having beaded segments and raised rims, not elongated denticles such as are found on the earlier dates.

Although the Mint record states that 19,570 dollars were coined in 1804, in no place does it mention that they were dated 1804. It was the practice in those days to use old dies as long as they were serviceable with no regard in the annual reports for the dating of the coins. It is probable that the 1804 total for dollars actually covered coins that were dated 1803.

First Reverse   **Second Reverse**
Note position of words STATES OF in relation to clouds.

1804 First Reverse, Original	*(8 known)*
$4,140,000, PF-68, Stack's Bowers auction, August 1999	
1804 Second Reverse, Restrike	*(6 known)*
$2,300,000, PF-58, Heritage auction, April 2009	
1804 Second Reverse, Restrike With Plain Edge *(Smithsonian Collection)*	*(unique)*
1804 Mint-Made Electrotype of the Unique Plain-Edge Specimen.	*(4 known)*

GOBRECHT DOLLARS (1836–1839)

Suspension of silver dollar coinage was lifted in 1831, but it was not until 1835 that steps were taken to resume coinage. Late in that year the Mint director, R.M. Patterson, ordered engraver Christian Gobrecht to prepare a pair of dies based on designs by Thomas Sully and Titian Peale. The first obverse die, dated 1836, bore the seated figure of Liberty on the obverse with the inscription C. GOBRECHT F. ("F." is an abbreviation for the Latin word *Fecit*, or "made it") in the field above the date. On the reverse was a large eagle flying left, surrounded by 26 stars and the legend UNITED STATES OF AMERICA • ONE DOLLAR •. It is not known whether coins from these dies were struck at that time. A new obverse die with Gobrecht's name on the base of Liberty was prepared, and in December 1836, 1,000 coins were struck for circulation. These coins weighed 416 grains, which was the standard enacted in 1792.

In January 1837 the standard weight for the dollar was lowered to 412-1/2 grains, and 600 pieces were struck in March 1837 using the dies of 1836. Dies were oriented in a "medal" fashion (top to top when rotated on a vertical axis) to distinguish them from those struck in December 1836. Dollars issued for circulation in 1836, 1837, and 1839 are found with different die alignments. The "original" issue of December 1836 has the normal "coin" orientation (reverse upright when coin is turned on a horizontal axis) with the eagle flying upward.

From the late 1850s to the 1870s, the Mint continued to strike Gobrecht dollars to satisfy collector demands. Mules, which had mismatched designs or edge devices, were made in that period and are very rare. Restrikes and mules are seldom seen in worn condition.

Original 1836 die orientation using either "coin" or "medal" turn.

Die alignment of original issues dated 1838 and 1839.

Gobrecht dollars, both original issues and restrikes, were made in either coin-turn orientation ↑↓ (I and III) or medal-turn orientation ↑↑ (II and IV), and were struck in four basic die alignments.

- Die alignment I: ↑↓, head of Liberty opposite DO of DOLLAR, eagle flying upward.
- Die alignment II: ↑↑, head of Liberty opposite ES of STATES, eagle flying upward.
- Die alignment III: ↑↓, head of Liberty opposite N of ONE, eagle flying level.
- Die alignment IV: ↑↑, head of Liberty opposite F of OF, eagle flying level.

Rotated dies are common for original issue and restrike Gobrecht dollars. The 600 coins produced for circulation in March 1837 had dies that rotated from die alignment II to die alignment IV during the striking.

Designer Christian Gobrecht; weight 26.73–26.96 grams; composition .8924 silver, .1076 copper; approx. diameter 39–40 mm; edge: plain or reeded.

Circulation Issues and Patterns

	VF-20	EF-40	AU-50	MS-60
1836, C. GOBRECHT F. on base. Rev as above. Plain edge. Die alignment I, ↑↓. Circulation issue. 1,000 struck..........................	$12,500	$15,500	$19,000	$22,500
1836, As above. Plain edge. Die alignment II and die alignment IV, ↑↑. Circulation issue struck in 1837. 600 struck......................................	13,000	16,000	21,000	24,000

	VF-20	EF-40	AU-50	MS-60
1838, Similar obverse, designer's name omitted, stars added around border. Reverse eagle flying in plain field. Reeded edge. Die alignment IV, ↑↑. Pattern....................				$70,000
1839, As above. Reeded edge. Die alignment IV, ↑↑. Circulation issue. 300 struck..............................	$15,000	$17,500	$22,500	29,000

Restrikes

Restrikes were produced from the late 1850s to the 1870s, and are not official issues. They were all oriented in either die alignment III (coin turn) or die alignment IV (medal turn), with eagle flying level, and almost all were struck from a cracked reverse die.

	PF-60
1836, Name below base; eagle in starry field; plain edge.....................................	$70,000
1836, Name on base; plain edge	23,500
1838, Designer's name omitted; reeded edge	65,000
1839, Designer's name omitted; eagle in plain field; reeded edge	37,500

LIBERTY SEATED (1840–1873)

Starting again in 1840, silver dollars were issued for general circulation. The seated figure of Liberty was adopted for the obverse, but the flying eagle design was rejected in favor of the more familiar form with olive branch and arrows used for certain other silver denominations. By the early 1850s the silver content of these pieces was worth more than their face value, and later issues were not seen in circulation but were used mainly in export trade. This situation continued through 1873.

The 1866 Proof quarter, half, and dollar without motto are not mentioned in the Mint director's report, and were not issued for circulation.

Designer Christian Gobrecht; weight 26.73 grams; composition .900 silver, .100 copper (net weight .77344 oz. pure silver); diameter 38.1 mm; reeded edge; mints: Philadelphia, New Orleans, Carson City, San Francisco.

VG-8 Very Good—Any three letters of LIBERTY at least two-thirds complete.
F-12 Fine—All seven letters of LIBERTY visible, though weak.
VF-20 Very Fine—LIBERTY strong, but slight wear visible on its ribbon.
EF-40 Extremely Fine—Horizontal lines of shield complete. Eagle's eye plain.
AU-50 About Uncirculated—Traces of light wear on only the high points of the design. Half of mint luster present.
MS-60 Uncirculated—No trace of wear. Light marks or blemishes.
PF-60 Proof—Several contact marks, hairlines, or light rubs possible on surface. Luster possibly dull and eye appeal lacking.
PF-63 Choice Proof—Reflective surfaces with few blemishes in secondary focal places. No major flaws.

No Motto (1840–1865)

Location of mintmark, when present, is on reverse, below eagle.

	Mintage	VG-8	F-12	VF-20	EF-40	AU-50	MS-60	PF-60	PF-63
1840	61,005	$300	$375	$450	$700	$1,150	$3,800	$16,000	$30,000
1841	173,000	290	335	375	570	900	2,650	25,000	70,000
$149,500, PF-64, David Lawrence auction, November 2009									
1842	184,618	290	315	375	540	800	2,400	17,500	39,000
1843	165,100	290	315	375	540	800	2,400	17,000	35,000
1844	20,000	290	350	425	725	1,500	5,000	15,000	35,000
1845	24,500	325	375	450	800	1,500	9,000	14,000	30,000
1846	110,600	290	315	400	575	900	2,400	14,000	30,000
1846O	59,000	300	375	450	800	1,400	7,250		
1847	140,750	290	315	375	540	850	2,600	16,000	26,000
1848	15,000	375	500	700	1,100	1,700	4,750	16,000	31,000
1849	62,600	290	315	375	575	950	2,600	19,000	34,000
1850	7,500	550	750	1,100	1,600	2,250	6,900	16,500	28,000
1850O	40,000	350	500	750	1,450	3,200	13,500		
1851, Original, High Date	1,300	7,500	10,000	15,000	20,000	27,500	35,000		
1851, Restrike, Date Centered								21,000	31,000
1852, Original	1,100	6,000	10,000	13,500	17,500	27,500	33,000	35,000	43,500
1852, Restrike					15,000			17,500	30,000

	Mintage	VG-8	F-12	VF-20	EF-40	AU-50	MS-60	PF-60	PF-63
1853.	46,110	$350	$450	$650	$850	$1,350	$3,200	$21,000	$37,000
1854.	33,140	1,500	2,500	3,000	4,150	5,500	8,100	13,500	16,500
1855.	26,000	1,250	1,500	2,250	3,600	4,750	7,500	12,000	16,000
1856.	63,500	425	525	750	1,450	2,250	4,250	6,350	13,500
1857.	94,000	475	575	750	1,550	1,900	3,250	7,000	11,500
1858. . . . . .(300).		4,000	5,000	6,000	7,500	9,000		10,000	14,000

	Mintage	VG-8	F-12	VF-20	EF-40	AU-50	MS-60	MS-63	PF-63
1859. . . . . .(800). . . .	255,700	$325	$425	$525	$700	$1,225	$2,500	$6,000	$4,500
1859O	360,000	280	300	350	500	850	2,050	5,150	
1859S.	20,000	415	550	850	1,700	3,350	13,000	29,000	
1860. . . . (1,330). . . .	217,600	290	400	525	650	900	2,100	5,100	4,750
1860O	515,000	280	300	350	475	785	1,900	3,750	
1861. . . . (1,000). . . .	77,500	775	875	1,050	1,650	2,250	3,450	5,850	4,600
1862. . . . . .(550).	11,540	700	875	1,050	1,650	2,650	3,575	6,300	4,750
1863. . . . . .(460).	27,200	550	600	725	950	1,600	3,575	6,300	4,750
1864. . . . . .(470).	30,700	425	500	700	950	1,600	3,575	6,750	4,750
1865. . . . . .(500).	46,500	400	450	650	850	1,600	3,000	7,500	4,750
1866, No Motto (2 known)									—

$1,207,500, PF-63, Stack's Bowers auction, January 2005

With Motto IN GOD WE TRUST (1866–1873)

	Mintage	VG-8	F-12	VF-20	EF-40	AU-50	MS-60	MS-63	PF-63
1866. . . . . .(725). 48,900		$290	$390	$550	$675	$1,100	$2,300	$5,500	$3,900
1867. . . . . .(625). 46,900		290	365	525	675	1,050	2,300	5,300	3,900
1868. . . . . .(600). . . .162,100		290	350	475	675	1,150	2,400	7,000	3,800
1869. . . . . .(600). . . .423,700		290	340	425	575	1,050	2,300	5,250	3,800
1870. . . . (1,000). . . .415,000		280	325	385	500	950	2,100	4,650	3,800
1870CC 11,758		800	1,000	1,550	3,400	7,000	26,000	50,000	
1870S.		200,000	325,000	600,000	800,000	1,250,000	2,000,000		

$1,092,500, BU PL, Stack's
Bowers auction, May 2003

	Mintage	VG-8	F-12	VF-20	EF-40	AU-50	MS-60	MS-63	PF-63
1871. . . . . .(960). . 1,073,800		280	325	365	500	950	2,000	4,350	3,800
1871CC 1,376		3,500	4,850	7,250	14,000	24,500	75,000	175,000	
1872. . . . . .(950). . 1,105,500		280	325	365	500	950	2,050	4,950	3,850
1872CC 3,150		2,000	3,100	3,850	7,500	13,000	28,000	70,000	
1872S 9,000		500	675	950	1,975	3,500	12,000	37,500	
1873. . . . . .(600). . . .293,000		375	400	450	600	975	2,100	4,850	3,900
1873CC 2,300		7,000	11,000	18,500	28,000	41,500	115,000	190,000	
1873S. 700					*(unknown in any collection)*				

TRADE DOLLARS (1873–1885)

This coin was issued for circulation in Asia to compete with dollar-sized coins of other countries. They were legal tender in the United States, but when silver prices declined, Congress repealed the provision and authorized the Treasury to limit coinage to export demand. Many pieces that circulated in the Orient were counterstamped with Oriental characters, known as *chop marks*. In 1887, the Treasury redeemed trade dollars that were not mutilated. The law authorizing trade dollars was repealed in February 1887. Modifications to the trade dollar design are distinguished as follows:

- **Reverse 1:** Berry under eagle's left (viewer's right) talon; arrowhead ends over 0. Used on all coins from all mints in 1873 and 1874, and occasionally in 1875 and 1876.
- **Reverse 2:** Without extra berry under talon; arrowhead ends over 2. Used occasionally at all mints from 1875 through 1876, and on all coins from all mints 1877 through 1885.
- **Obverse 1:** Ends of scroll point to left; extended hand has only three fingers. Used on coins at all mints 1873 through 1876.
- **Obverse 2:** Ends of scroll point downward; hand has four fingers. Used in combination with Reverse 2 on varieties of 1876 and 1876-S, and on all coins at all mints from 1877 through 1885.

Designer William Barber; weight 27.22 grams; composition .900 silver, .100 copper (net weight .7874 oz. pure silver); diameter 38.1 mm; reeded edge; mints: Philadelphia, Carson City, San Francisco.

VG-8 Very Good—About half of mottoes IN GOD WE TRUST (on Liberty's pedestal) and E PLURIBUS UNUM (on reverse ribbon) visible. Rim on both sides well defined.

F-12 Fine—Mottoes and LIBERTY legible but worn.

VF-20 Very Fine—More than half the details of Liberty's dress visible. Details of wheat sheaf mostly intact.

EF-40 Extremely Fine—Mottoes and LIBERTY sharp. Only slight wear on rims.

AU-50 About Uncirculated—Slight trace of wear on Liberty's left breast and left knee and on hair above ear, as well as on eagle's head, knee, and wing tips.

MS-60 Uncirculated—No trace of wear. Light blemishes.

MS-63 Choice Uncirculated—Some distracting contact marks or blemishes in prime focal areas. Impaired luster possible.

PF-63 Choice Proof—Reflective surfaces with few blemishes in secondary focal places. No major flaws.

Mintmark location on reverse, above D in DOLLAR.   **1875-S, S Over CC**

	Mintage	VG-8	F-12	VF-20	EF-40	AU-50	MS-60	MS-63	PF-63
1873......(865)....	396,635	$145	$165	$200	$250	$350	$1,050	$3,300	$3,300
1873CC	124,500	275	375	450	975	1,700	10,000	22,500	
1873S............	703,000	145	160	200	250	375	1,400	4,000	
1874......(700)....	987,100	145	160	200	250	350	1,100	2,600	3,100
1874CC	1,373,200	280	365	425	600	775	3,200	6,750	
1874S...........	2,549,000	140	160	185	245	325	1,100	2,600	

Mintage	VG-8	F-12	VF-20	EF-40	AU-50	MS-60	MS-63	PF-63
1875 . . . .(700) . . .218,200	$240	$375	$450	$575	$875	$2,450	$4,650	$3,300
1875, Reverse 2 . . . . *	240	375	450	575	875	2,450	4,650	
1875CC, All kinds 1,573,700								
1875CC	265	350	400	475	750	2,300	5,000	
1875CC, Reverse 2.	250	350	400	450	750	2,600	4,750	
1875S, All kinds 4,487,000								
1875S	140	155	165	245	325	1,000	2,000	
1875S, Reverse 2.	145	165	190	250	335	1,025	2,350	
1875S, S Over CC.	265	400	525	975	1,550	4,350	12,500	
1876 . . . . (1,150) . . .455,000	140	155	190	250	335	1,050	2,400	3,100
1876, Obverse 2,								
Reverse 2 *(extremely rare)* . . . . *				—				
1876, Reverse 2 . . . . *	140	155	190	245	325	1,000	2,250	
1876CC, All kinds 509,000								
1876CC	225	300	450	625	1,250	5,750	24,500	
1876CC, Reverse 1.	245	325	485	690	1,550	6,500	26,000	
1876CC, Doubled-Die								
Reverse				850	1,750	10,500	—	
1876S, All kinds 5,227,000								
1876S	140	155	165	245	325	1,000	2,000	
1876S, Reverse 2.	140	155	165	245	325	1,000	2,000	
1876S, Obverse 2,								
Reverse 2.	165	200	225	250	375	1,300	2,650	
1877 . . . .(510) . . 3,039,200	140	155	165	245	325	1,025	2,100	3,250
1877CC 534,000	265	350	450	675	825	2,700	11,500	
1877S. 9,519,000	140	155	165	245	325	1,000	2,050	
1878 . . . .(900)				1,250				3,250
1878CC **(a)**. 97,000	625	950	1,500	2,850	4,750	14,000	25,000	
1878S. 4,162,000	140	155	165	245	325	1,000	2,200	
1879 . . . . (1,541)				1,250				3,200
1880 . . . . (1,987)				1,250				3,200
1881 . . . .(960)				1,250				3,200
1882 . . . . (1,097)				1,250				3,200
1883 . . . .(979)				1,250				3,200
1884 **(b)** . . . .(10)								500,000
1885 **(b)** . . . .(5)								2,000,000

* Included in number above. **a.** 44,148 trade dollars were melted on July 19, 1878. Many of these may have been 1878-CC. **b.** The trade dollars of 1884 and 1885 were unknown to collectors until 1908. None are listed in the Mint director's report, and numismatists believe that they are not a part of the regular Mint issue.

MORGAN (1878–1921)

The coinage law of 1873 made no provision for the standard silver dollar. During the lapse in coinage of this denomination, the gold dollar became the unit coin, and the trade dollar was used for commercial transactions with the Orient.

Resumption of coinage of the silver dollar was authorized by the Act of February 28, 1878, known as the Bland-Allison Act. The weight (412-1/2 grains) and fineness (.900) were to conform with the Act of January 18, 1837.

George T. Morgan, formerly a pupil of William Wyon in the Royal Mint in London, designed the new dollar. His initial M is found at the truncation of the neck, at the last tress. It also appears on the reverse on the left-hand loop of the ribbon.

Coinage of the silver dollar was suspended after 1904, when demand was low and the bullion supply became exhausted. Under provisions of the Pittman Act of 1918,

270,232,722 silver dollars were melted, and later, in 1921, coinage of the silver dollar was resumed. The Morgan design, with some slight refinements, was employed until the new Peace design was adopted later in that year.

Varieties listed are those most significant to collectors. Numerous other variations exist. Values are shown for the most common pieces. Prices of variations not listed in this guide depend on collector interest and rarity.

Sharply struck, prooflike Morgan dollars have highly reflective surfaces and are very scarce, usually commanding substantial premiums.

Designer George T. Morgan; weight 26.73 grams; composition .900 silver, .100 copper (net weight .77344 oz. pure silver); diameter 38.1 mm; reeded edge; mints: Philadelphia, New Orleans, Carson City, Denver, San Francisco.

VF-20 Very Fine—Two thirds of hair lines from top of forehead to ear visible. Ear well defined. Feathers on eagle's breast worn.

EF-40 Extremely Fine—All hair lines strong and ear bold. Eagle's feathers all plain but with slight wear on breast and wing tips.

AU-50 About Uncirculated—Slight trace of wear on the bust shoulder and hair left of forehead, and on eagle's breast and top edges of wings.

MS-60 Uncirculated—No trace of wear. Full mint luster present, but may be noticeably marred by scuff marks or bag abrasions.

MS-63 Choice Uncirculated—No trace of wear; full mint luster; few noticeable surface marks.

MS-64 Uncirculated—A few scattered contact marks. Good eye appeal and attractive luster.

MS-65 Gem Uncirculated—Only light, scattered contact marks that are not distracting. Strong luster, good eye appeal.

PF-63 Choice Proof—Reflective surfaces with only a few blemishes in secondary focal places. No major flaws.

Location of mintmark, when present, is on reverse, below wreath.

First Reverse, 8 Tail Feathers

Second Reverse
Parallel top arrow feather, concave breast.

Third Reverse
Slanted top arrow feather, convex breast.

1878, Doubled Tail Feathers

	Mintage	VF-20	EF-40	AU-50	MS-60	MS-63	MS-64	MS-65	PF-63
1878, 8 Feathers . . . . (500)	749,500	$45	$50	$70	$160	$250	$500	$1,600	$3,500
1878, 7 Feathers, All kinds (250) . . .	9,759,300								
1878, 7 Over 8 Clear									
Doubled Feathers		37	50	73	160	280	500	2,450	
1878, 7 Feathers, 2nd Reverse		37	40	45	68	120	330	1,100	3,450
1878, 7 Feathers, 3rd Reverse		37	40	50	88	185	550	2,300	60,000

	Mintage	VF-20	EF-40	AU-50	MS-60	MS-63	MS-64	MS-65	PF-63
1878CC	2,212,000	$100	$140	$150	$260	$410	$575	$1,750	
1878S	9,774,000	37	40	45	65	85	125	300	
1879	(1,100) . .14,806,000	37	39	40	50	75	150	850	$3,000
1879CC, CC Over CC	756,000	290	770	1,750	3,800	5,900	9,500	44,500	
1879CC, Clear CC	*	290	750	1,850	4,200	6,500	9,000	30,000	
1879O	2,887,000	37	40	47	85	225	525	3,800	
1879S, 2nd Reverse	9,110,000	40	45	58	160	550	1,500	6,500	
1879S, 3rd Reverse	*	37	39	41	50	70	95	175	
1880	(1,355) . .12,600,000	37	39	41	53	78	145	750	3,050
1880, 80 Over 79 (a)	*	37	39	55	100	375	675	3,300	

* Included in number above. **a.** Several die varieties. Values shown are for the most common.

1880-CC, 80 Over 79

1880-CC, 8 Over High 7

1880-CC, 8 Over Low 7

	Mintage	VF-20	EF-40	AU-50	MS-60	MS-63	MS-64	MS-65	PF-63
1880CC, All kinds	495,000								
1880CC, 80 Over 79, 2nd Reverse (b)		$220	$285	$350	$600	$700	$1,700	$3,000	
1880CC, 8 Over 7, 2nd Reverse (a)		210	285	325	550	675	1,100	2,700	
1880CC, 8/High 7, 3rd Reverse (a)		210	275	325	500	600	725	1,300	
1880CC, 8/Low 7, 3rd Reverse (a)		270	365	475	600	640	700	1,400	
1880CC, 3rd Reverse		210	275	325	460	525	675	1,250	
1880O, All kinds	5,305,000								
1880O, 80/79 (a)		37	39	48	150	600	2,500	—	
1880O		37	39	43	75	400	1,800	27,500	
1880S, All kinds	8,900,000								
1880S, 80 Over 79		37	40	47	55	75	120	290	
1880S, 0 Over 9		37	40	45	63	75	120	290	
1880S		37	39	41	50	70	95	175	
1881	(984) . . . 9,163,000	37	39	42	53	75	150	690	$3,050
1881CC	296,000	425	450	475	500	550	600	900	
1881O	5,708,000	37	39	41	50	73	175	1,500	
1881S	12,760,000	37	39	41	50	70	95	175	
1882	(1,100) . .11,100,000	37	39	41	50	70	120	550	2,925
1882CC	1,133,000	120	130	145	220	260	280	500	
1882O	6,090,000	37	39	42	50	75	130	1,200	
1882O, 0 Over S (a)	*	50	70	120	235	800	2,100	50,000	
1882S	9,250,000	37	39	41	50	70	95	175	
1883	(1,039) . .12,290,000	37	39	41	50	70	110	210	2,900
1883CC	1,204,000	120	130	145	210	250	270	475	
1883O	8,725,000	37	39	41	50	70	95	175	
1883S	6,250,000	37	53	180	650	2,500	5,000	47,500	
1884	(875) . .14,070,000	37	39	41	50	70	120	340	2,900
1884CC	1,136,000	120	130	145	210	250	270	475	

* Included in number above. **a.** Several die varieties. Values shown are for the most common. **b.** The 7 and 9 show within the 80; no tip below second 8.

1887, 7 Over 6   **1888-O, Doubled-Die Obverse**

Lips especially prominent ("Hot Lips" variety).

	Mintage	VF-20	EF-40	AU-50	MS-60	MS-63	MS-64	MS-65	PF-63
1884O	9,730,000	$37	$39	$41	$50	$70	$95	$175	
1884S	3,200,000	40	60	290	7,200	35,000	100,000	250,000	
1885 (930)	17,787,000	37	39	41	50	70	95	175	$2,900
1885CC	228,000	475	500	525	600	675	750	1,100	
1885O	9,185,000	37	39	41	50	70	95	175	
1885S	1,497,000	50	63	130	250	350	750	2,000	
1886 (886)	19,963,000	37	39	41	50	70	95	175	2,900
1886O	10,710,000	39	45	95	750	3,500	10,500	185,000	
1886S	750,000	78	93	160	310	525	825	3,250	
1887, 7/6	*	48	70	165	370	550	850	1,800	
1887 (710)	20,290,000	37	39	41	50	70	95	175	2,900
1887O, 7/6	*	48	95	175	450	2,000	5,000	27,000	
1887O	11,550,000	37	42	55	70	130	375	2,400	
1887S	1,771,000	40	48	60	135	275	675	2,600	
1888 (833)	19,183,000	37	39	41	50	70	100	230	2,900
1888O	12,150,000	37	39	41	50	70	110	600	
1888O, DblDie Obv	**	145	290	900	20,000	—	—		
1888S	657,000	165	185	205	300	475	900	3,200	
1889 (811)	21,726,000	37	39	41	50	70	100	365	2,900
1889CC	350,000	1,400	3,000	6,500	24,000	40,000	65,000	325,000	
$531,875, MS-68, Heritage auction, January 2009									
1889O	11,875,000	37	39	55	170	425	950	7,200	
1889S	700,000	60	75	105	250	375	650	2,200	
1890 (590)	16,802,000	37	39	43	53	75	150	2,650	3,000
1890CC	2,309,041	110	165	200	440	800	1,500	5,000	
1890O	10,701,000	37	39	49	75	110	275	2,200	
1890S	8,230,373	37	39	45	70	105	250	1,150	
1891 (650)	8,693,556	38	40	45	65	200	975	8,500	2,900
1891CC	1,618,000	110	155	210	375	700	1,200	4,750	
1891O	7,954,529	37	40	55	175	340	825	8,200	
1891S	5,296,000	38	40	45	70	145	300	1,500	
1892 (1,245)	1,036,000	43	53	90	260	475	1,250	4,850	3,100
1892CC	1,352,000	285	450	690	1,400	2,000	2,600	8,250	
1892O	2,744,000	40	48	70	250	400	1,150	7,500	
1892S	1,200,000	140	325	1,650	40,000	64,000	110,000	190,000	
$460,000, MS-67, Heritage auction, January 2009									
1893 (792)	378,000	225	275	375	725	1,125	2,100	7,500	2,950
1893CC	677,000	625	1,500	2,400	4,000	6,500	11,000	70,000	

* Included in number below. ** Included in number above.

1901, Doubled-Die Reverse
Note tail feathers.

	Mintage	VF-20	EF-40	AU-50	MS-60	MS-63	MS-64	MS-65	PF-63
18930	300,000	$325	$525	$800	$2,600	$6,500	$17,500	$220,000	
1893S **(c)**	100,000	5,200	9,000	20,000	120,000	185,000	330,000	650,000	
$546,250, MS-67, Heritage auction, August 2011									
1894 **(c)** (972)	110,000	1,250	1,500	1,750	3,500	5,250	9,500	44,000	$3,500
18940	1,723,000	60	115	260	750	4,100	10,500	65,000	
1894S	1,260,000	95	165	400	675	1,200	2,000	6,000	
1895, Proof **(d)** (880)		33,500	35,000	38,000	45,000	50,000	55,000	77,500	
18950	450,000	400	600	1,350	14,500	50,000	80,000	170,000	
$575,000, MS-67, Heritage auction, November 2005									
1895S	400,000	900	1,200	1,800	3,900	6,250	8,000	27,500	
1896 (762)	9,976,000	37	39	41	50	70	125	240	2,900
18960	4,900,000	39	43	160	1,400	7,000	42,500	175,000	
1896S	5,000,000	70	240	775	1,800	3,650	5,000	18,000	
$402,500, MS-69, Heritage auction, November 2005									
1897 (731)	2,822,000	37	39	41	50	80	125	325	2,900
18970	4,004,000	37	41	115	750	4,750	17,000	65,000	
1897S	5,825,000	37	39	45	68	130	165	600	
1898 (735)	5,884,000	37	39	41	50	70	100	250	2,900
18980	4,440,000	37	39	41	50	70	95	180	
1898S	4,102,000	40	50	100	275	450	700	2,450	
1899 (846)	330,000	180	200	225	265	350	450	950	2,900
18990	12,290,000	37	39	40	50	70	95	180	
1899S	2,562,000	48	65	120	340	450	850	2,000	
1900 (912)	8,830,000	37	39	41	50	70	95	185	2,900
19000	12,590,000	37	39	41	50	70	95	185	
19000, O/CC **(e)**	*	65	105	190	300	750	950	1,750	
1900S	3,540,000	40	48	100	300	400	650	1,650	
1901 **(c)** (813)	6,962,000	50	115	350	3,000	17,500	50,000	450,000	3,250
1901, DblDie Rev	*	375	1,100	1,900	4,500	—			
19010	13,320,000	37	39	41	50	75	95	190	
1901S	2,284,000	45	65	210	475	750	1,000	3,250	
1902 (777)	7,994,000	37	39	45	55	140	160	485	2,900
19020	8,636,000	37	39	45	55	75	95	200	
1902S	1,530,000	120	175	250	365	600	850	2,800	
1903 (755)	4,652,000	50	55	65	78	90	150	325	2,900
19030	4,450,000	310	340	365	400	425	465	650	
1903S	1,241,000	205	350	1,600	3,900	6,250	7,500	11,500	
1904 (650)	2,788,000	40	47	55	95	260	575	3,000	2,950
19040	3,720,000	37	39	41	50	70	95	175	
1904S	2,304,000	90	215	550	1,800	3,750	5,000	10,500	
1921	44,690,000	36	37	38	45	63	80	175	—
1921D	20,345,000	36	37	38	50	70	130	375	
1921S	21,695,000	36	37	38	50	75	160	1,350	

* Included in number above. **c.** Authentication is recommended. Beware of altered mintmark. **d.** Beware of removed mintmark. Values are for Proofs; circulation strikes are not known to exist. **e.** Several die varieties.

PEACE (1921–1935)

The dollar of new design issued from December 1921 through 1935 was a commemorative peace coin. The Peace dollar was issued without congressional sanction, under the terms of the Pittman Act, which referred to the bullion and in no way affected the design. Anthony de Francisci, a medalist, designed this dollar. His monogram is located in the field of the coin under the neck of Liberty.

The new Peace dollar was placed in circulation on January 3, 1922; 1,006,473 pieces had been struck in December 1921.

The high relief of the 1921 design was found impractical for coinage and was modified to low or shallow relief in 1922, after 35,401 coins had been made and most of them melted at the mint. The rare Matte and Satin Finish Proofs of 1922 are of both the high-relief style of 1921 and the normal-relief style.

Legislation dated August 3, 1964, authorized the coinage of 45 million silver dollars, and 316,076 dollars of the Peace design dated 1964 were struck at the Denver Mint in 1965. Plans for completing this coinage were subsequently abandoned and all of these coins were melted. None were preserved or released for circulation. Many deceptive reproductions exist.

Designer Anthony de Francisci; weight 26.73 grams; composition .900 silver, .100 copper (net weight .77344 oz. pure silver); diameter 38.1 mm; reeded edge; mints: Philadelphia, Denver, San Francisco.

VF-20 Very Fine—Hair over eye well worn. Some strands over ear well defined. Some eagle feathers on top and outside edge of right wing visible.

EF-40 Extremely Fine—Hair lines over brow and ear are strong, though slightly worn. Outside wing feathers at right and those at top visible but faint.

AU-50 About Uncirculated—Slight trace of wear. Most of mint luster present, although marred by contact marks.

MS-60 Uncirculated—No trace of wear. Full mint luster, but possibly noticeably marred by stains, surface marks, or bag abrasions.

MS-63 Choice Uncirculated—Some distracting contact marks or blemishes in prime focal areas. Impaired luster possible.

MS-64 Uncirculated—A few scattered contact marks. Good eye appeal and attractive luster.

MS-65 Gem Uncirculated—Only light, scattered contact marks that are not distracting. Strong luster, good eye appeal.

Location of mintmark, when present, is on reverse, below ONE.

	Mintage	VF-20	EF-40	AU-50	MS-60	MS-63	MS-64	MS-65	MS-66	MATTE PF-65
1921, High Relief	1,006,473	$90	$120	$150	$260	$450	$750	$1,850	$7,500	$75,000
1922, High Relief	35,401			—						125,000
1922, Normal Relief	51,737,000	36	37	38	45	52	75	160	550	75,000

	Mintage	VF-20	EF-40	AU-50	MS-60	MS-63	MS-64	MS-65	MS-66
1922D	15,063,000	$36	$37	$38	$50	$68	$115	$525	$2,550
1922S	17,475,000	36	37	38	50	75	240	2,500	18,500
1923	30,800,000	36	37	38	45	52	75	160	550
1923D	6,811,000	36	37	38	60	140	350	1,250	5,500
1923S	19,020,000	36	37	38	50	100	400	6,500	20,000
1924	11,811,000	36	37	38	45	52	75	160	550
1924S	1,728,000	38	45	70	210	550	1,400	9,750	43,500
1925	10,198,000	36	37	38	45	52	75	160	550
1925S	1,610,000	38	40	45	90	225	1,100	25,000	35,000
1926	1,939,000	37	38	40	55	90	130	450	2,000
1926D	2,348,700	37	38	40	85	175	325	850	2,550
1926S	6,980,000	37	38	40	60	110	250	950	4,950
1927	848,000	39	42	50	80	185	500	2,500	21,000
1927D	1,268,900	39	41	75	180	375	1,000	5,000	25,000
1927S	866,000	39	41	70	180	425	1,200	10,000	40,000
1928	360,649	350	375	425	500	900	1,200	4,400	24,000
1928S	1,632,000	43	48	63	200	475	1,100	23,500	32,000
1934	954,057	40	42	50	115	225	400	750	3,200
1934D (a)	1,569,500	40	42	50	150	400	550	1,650	5,500
1934D, DblDie Obv	*	115	185	375	675	1,650			
1934S	1,011,000	80	175	475	1,850	3,200	4,750	7,750	34,000
1935	1,576,000	40	45	50	70	110	210	650	2,300
1935S (b)	1,964,000	40	50	90	250	375	600	1,250	3,500

* Included in number above. Value is for variety with small mintmark on reverse. A second variety with larger, filled D mintmark is worth only about 20% more than the normal coin. **a.** Large and small mintmark varieties; see page 22. **b.** Varieties exist with either three or four rays below ONE, and are of equal value.

EISENHOWER (1971–1978)
Eagle Reverse (1971–1974)

Honoring both President Dwight D. Eisenhower and the first landing of man on the moon, this design is the work of Chief Engraver Frank Gasparro, whose initials are on the truncation and below the eagle. The reverse is an adaptation of the official *Apollo 11* insignia. Collectors' coins were struck in 40% silver composition, and the circulation issue in copper-nickel.

After 1971, the dies for the Eisenhower dollar were modified several times by changing the relief, strengthening the design, and making Earth above the eagle more clearly defined. Low-relief (Variety I) dies, with flattened Earth and three islands off Florida, were used for all copper-nickel issues of 1971, Uncirculated silver coins of 1971, and most copper-nickel coins of 1972. High-relief (Variety II) dies, with round Earth and weak or indistinct islands, were used for most Proofs of 1971, all silver issues of 1972, and the reverse of some scarce Philadelphia copper-nickel coins of 1972. Improved high-relief reverse dies (Variety III) were used for late 1972 Philadelphia copper-nickel coins and for all subsequent issues. Modified high-relief dies were also used on all issues beginning in 1973.

A few 1974-D and 1977-D dollars in silver clad composition were made in error.

Designer Frank Gasparro; diameter 38.1 mm; reeded edge; mints: Philadelphia, Denver, San Francisco. Silver issue: weight 24.59 grams; composition, outer layers of .800 silver, .200 copper bonded to inner core of .209 silver, .791 copper (net weight .3161 oz. pure silver). Copper-nickel issue: weight 22.68 grams; composition, outer layers of .750 copper, .250 nickel bonded to inner core of pure copper.

Mintmark location is above date.

	Mintage	EF-40	MS-63	PF-65
1971, Copper-Nickel Clad	47,799,000	$2.25	$6	
1971D, Copper-Nickel Clad, Variety I	68,587,424	3.50	20	
1971D, Copper-Nickel Clad, Variety II	*	2.00	5	
1971S, Silver Clad	(4,265,234)...6,868,530		13	$14
1972, Copper-Nickel Clad, Variety I	75,890,000	2.00	5	
1972, Copper-Nickel Clad, Variety II	*	7.00	80	
1972, Copper-Nickel Clad, Variety III	*	2.50	5	
1972D, Copper-Nickel Clad	92,548,511	2.00	5	
1972S, Silver Clad	(1,811,631)...2,193,056		13	14
1973, Copper-Nickel Clad **(a)**	2,000,056		13	
1973D, Copper-Nickel Clad **(a)**	2,000,000		13	
1973S, Copper-Nickel Clad	(2,760,339).........		**(b)**	10
1973S, Silver Clad	(1,013,646)...1,883,140		14	35
1974, Copper-Nickel Clad	27,366,000	2.00	5	
1974D, Copper-Nickel Clad	45,517,000	2.00	5	
1974S, Copper-Nickel Clad	(2,612,568).........			8
1974S, Silver Clad	(1,306,579)...1,900,156		13	15

* Included in number above. **a.** 1,769,258 of each sold only in sets and not released for circulation. Unissued coins destroyed at mint. **b.** Two reported to exist.

Bicentennial (1776–1976)

The national significance of the Bicentennial of the United States was highlighted with the adoption of new reverse designs for the quarter, half dollar, and dollar. Nearly a thousand entries were submitted after the Treasury announced in October 1973 that an open contest was to be held for the selection of the new designs. After the field was narrowed down to 12 semifinalists, the judges chose the rendition of the Liberty Bell superimposed on the moon to appear on the dollar coins. This design is the work of Dennis R. Williams.

The obverse remained unchanged except for the dual date "1776–1976," which appeared on these dollars made during 1975 and 1976. These dual-dated coins were included in the various offerings of Proof and Uncirculated coins made by the Mint. They were also struck for general circulation. The lettering was modified early in 1975 to produce a more attractive design.

Designers Frank Gasparro and Dennis R. Williams; diameter 38.1 mm; reeded edge; mints: Philadelphia, Denver, San Francisco. Silver issue—Weight 24.59 grams; composition, outer layers of .800 silver, .200 copper bonded to inner core of .209 silver, .791 copper (net weight .3161 oz. pure silver). Copper-nickel issue—Weight 22.68 grams; composition, outer layers of .750 copper, .250 nickel bonded to inner core of pure copper.

Variety 1
Design in low relief, bold lettering on reverse.

Variety 2
Sharp design, delicate lettering on reverse.

	Mintage	EF-40	MS-63	PF-65
1776–1976, Copper-Nickel Clad, Variety 1	4,019,000	$2	$8	
1776–1976, Copper-Nickel Clad, Variety 2	113,318,000	2	5	
1776–1976D, Copper-Nickel Clad, Variety 1	21,048,710	2	5	
1776–1976D, Copper-Nickel Clad, Variety 2	82,179,564	2	5	
1776–1976S, Copper-Nickel Clad, Variety 1	(2,845,450)			$10
1776–1976S, Copper-Nickel Clad, Variety 2	(4,149,730)			8
1776–1976, Silver Clad, Variety 2			—	
1776–1976S, Silver Clad, Variety 1 **(a)**	11,000,000		17	
1776–1976S, Silver Clad, Variety 1 **(a)**	(4,000,000)			19

a. Mintage is approximate.

Eagle Reverse Resumed (1977–1978)

	Mintage	EF-40	MS-63	PF-65
1977, Copper-Nickel Clad	12,596,000	$2	$5	
1977D, Copper-Nickel Clad	32,983,006	2	5	
1977S, Copper-Nickel Clad	(3,251,152)			$8
1978, Copper-Nickel Clad	25,702,000	2	5	
1978D, Copper-Nickel Clad	33,012,890	2	5	
1978S, Copper-Nickel Clad	(3,127,781)			8

SUSAN B. ANTHONY (1979–1999)

Intended to honor this pioneer in women's rights, legislation dated October 10, 1978, provided for the issuance of the Susan B. Anthony dollar coin. Both obverse and reverse designs were the work of the chief engraver of the U.S. Mint, Frank Gasparro, whose initials FG are located below the portrait and the eagle.

Placement of Susan B. Anthony's likeness on the dollar represented the first time that a woman other than a model or a mythical figure has appeared on a circulating U.S. coin. The reverse design is the same as that used on the Eisenhower dollar. Mintmarks P, D, or S appear on the obverse, slightly above Anthony's right shoulder.

The size of this coin caused it to be confused with the quarter, and it failed to gain widespread public acceptance. No coins were made for circulation from 1981 to 1998. In 1999 additional pieces were made to meet the needs of vending machines.

Designer Frank Gasparro; weight 8.1 grams; composition, outer layers of copper-nickel (.750 copper, .250 nickel) bonded to inner core of pure copper; diameter 26.5 mm; reeded edge; mints: Philadelphia, Denver, San Francisco.

1979, Narrow Rim (Far Date)

1979, Wide Rim (Near Date)

1979-S, Filled S (Type I)

1979-S, Clear S (Type II, Rounded)
1981-S, First S (Type I, Rounded)

1981-S, Clear S
(Type II, Flat)

	Mintage	MS-63	PF-65
1979P, Narrow Rim **(a)**	360,222,000	$2	
1979P, Wide Rim **(a)**	..........*	60	
1979D	288,015,744	2	
1979S	109,576,000	2	
1979S, Proof, Type 1	...(3,677,175)		$6
1979S, Proof, Type 2	...........*		55
1980P	27,610,000	3	
1980D	41,628,708	3	
1980S	20,422,000	3	

	Mintage	MS-63	PF-65
1980S, Proof	........(3,554,806)		$6
1981P **(b)**	3,000,000	$7	
1981D **(b)**	3,250,000	7	
1981S **(b)**	3,492,000	7	
1981S, Proof, Type 1	...(4,063,083)		6
1981S, Proof, Type 2	...........*		200
1999P	29,592,000	3	
1999P, Proof	...........*(750,000)*		22
1999D	11,776,000	3	

* Included in number above. **a.** The obverse design was modified in 1979 to widen the border rim. Late issues of 1979-P and subsequent issues have the wide rim. Dies for the 1999 coins were further modified to strengthen details on the reverse. **b.** Issued only in Mint Sets.

SACAGAWEA (2000–2008)

The design of this coin was selected in national competition from among 120 submissions that were considered by a panel appointed by Treasury Secretary Robert Rubin. The adopted motif depicts Sacagawea, a young Native American Shoshone, as conceived by artist Glenna Goodacre. On her back she carries Jean Baptiste, her infant son. The reverse shows an eagle in flight designed by Mint engraver Thomas D. Rogers Sr.

The composition exemplifies the spirit of liberty, peace, and freedom shown by Sacagawea in her conduct as interpreter and guide to explorers Meriwether Lewis and William Clark during their famed journey westward from the great northern plains to the Pacific.

These coins have a distinctive golden color and a plain edge to distinguish them from other denominations or coins of a similar size. The change in composition and appearance was mandated under the United States Dollar Coin Act of 1997.

Several distinctive finishes can be identified on the Sacagawea dollars as a result of the Mint's attempts to adjust the dies, blanks, strikes, or finishing to produce coins with minimum spotting and better surface color. One group of 5,000 pieces, dated 2000 and with a special finish, were presented to sculptor Glenna Goodacre in payment for the

obverse design. Unexplained error coins made from mismatched dies (a state quarter obverse combined with a Sacagawea dollar reverse) are extremely rare.

Designers: obv. Glenna Goodacre; rev. Thomas D. Rogers Sr.; weight 8.1 grams; composition, pure copper core with outer layers of manganese brass (.770 copper, .120 zinc, .070 manganese, and .040 nickel); diameter 26.5 mm; plain edge; mints: Philadelphia, Denver, San Francisco; 22-karat gold numismatic specimens dated 2000-W were struck at West Point in 1999 using a prototype reverse design with boldly detailed tail feathers. Some of the early 2000-P circulation strikes were also made using that same prototype design.

	Mintage	MS-65	PF-65
2000P 767,140,000		$3	
2000P, Goodacre			
Presentation Finish 5,000			$600
2000P, Boldly Detailed			
Tail Feathers 5,500		2,500	
2000D 518,916,000		3	
2000S . . . .(4,047,904)			6
2001P 62,468,000		3	
2001D 70,939,500		3	
2001S . . . .(3,183,740)			15
2002P **(a)** 3,865,610		3	
2002D **(a)** 3,732,000		3	
2002S . . . .(3,211,995)			6
2003P **(a)** 3,080,000		3	
2003D **(a)** 3,080,000		3	
2003S . . . .(3,298,439)			6

	Mintage	MS-65	PF-65
2004P **(a)** 2,660,000		$3	
2004D **(a)** 2,660,000		3	
2004S . . . .(2,965,422)			$6
2005P **(a)** 2,520,000		3	
2005D **(a)** 2,520,000		3	
2005S . . . .(3,344,679)			6
2006P **(a)** 4,900,000		3	
2006D **(a)** 2,800,000		3	
2006S . . . .(3,054,436)			6
2007P **(a)** 3,640,000		3	
2007D **(a)** 3,920,000		3	
2007S . . . .(2,577,166)			6
2008P **(a)** 1,820,000		3	
2008D **(a)** 1,820,000		3	
2008S . . . .(2,169,561)			15

a. Not issued for circulation. The U.S. Mint produced circulation-quality Sacagawea dollar coins at its Philadelphia and Denver facilities in 2002, 2007, and 2008. These were never issued for circulation through banks, but were made available to the general public by direct sales from the Mint.

NATIVE AMERICAN (2009 TO DATE)

Since 2009, the reverse of the golden dollar has featured an annually changing design that memorializes Native Americans and, in the words of the authorizing legislation, "the important contributions made by Indian tribes and individual Native Americans to the development [and history] of the United States."

The Native American $1 Coin Act also calls for edge marking on the coins. The year of minting and mintmark are incused on the edge, as is the inscription E PLURIBUS UNUM.

The coins' designs are chosen by the secretary of the Treasury after consultation with the Committee on Indian Affairs of the Senate, the Congressional Native American Caucus of the House of Representatives, the Commision of Fine Arts, and the National Congress of American Indians. They are also reviewed by the Citizens Coinage Advisory Committee.

The original act allowed for the minting of Uncirculated and Proof coins in each design. It also specified that at least 20% of the total mintage of dollar coins in any given year (including Presidential dollars) will be Native American dollars. Production of all dollar coins minted after 2011 is limited to numismatic sales; none will be issued for circulation.

Designers: obv. Glenna Goodacre (date removed); rev. Norm Nemeth (2009), Thomas Cleveland (2010), Richard Masters (2011), Thomas Cleveland (2012), Susan Gamble (2013); lettered edge; weight, composition, diameter, and mints identical to those for the Sacagawea dollar.

Obverse

Three Sisters (2009)

Great Law of Peace (2010)

Wampanoag Treaty (2011)

Trade Routes in the 17th Century (2012)

Treaty With the Delawares (2013)
U.S. Mint artist rendering.

	Mintage	MS-65	PF-65
2009P, Three Sisters	39,200,000	$4	
2009D, Three Sisters	35,700,000	4	
2009S, Three Sisters	(2,179,867)		$10
2010P, Great Law	32,060,000	4	
2010D, Great Law	48,720,000	4	
2010S, Great Law	(1,689,364)		10
2011P, Wampanoag Treaty	29,400,000	4	
2011D, Wampanoag Treaty	48,160,000	4	

	Mintage	MS-65	PF-65
2011S, Wampanoag Treaty	(1,453,276)		$12
2012P, Trade Routes	2,800,000	$5	
2012D, Trade Routes	3,080,000	5	
2012S, Trade Routes			12
2013P, Treaty, Delawares		5	
2013D, Treaty, Delawares		5	
2013S, Treaty, Delawares			12

PRESIDENTIAL (2007–2016)

Former presidents of the United States are honored on this series of one-dollar coins issued for circulation during the period from 2007 through 2011, and only for numismatic sales thereafter. Four different coins are issued each year, in the order that the presidents served. The reverse of each coin has a design featuring the Statue of Liberty. As with the Sacagawea dollars, some coins have been found that lack the usual edge lettering. The motto IN GOD WE TRUST was moved to the obverse starting in 2009.

A companion series of $10 gold bullion coins honors the spouses of each president during that president's term of service. These coins are made of 24-karat gold, and on the obverse have an image of the spouse and a theme symbolic of the spouse's life and work. See pages 358–361 for more information on the First Spouse bullion coins.

Designers: obv. various; rev. Don Everheart; lettered edge; weight, composition, diameter, and mints identical to those for the Sacagawea dollar.

Error coins with wrong or missing edge lettering are valued higher than normal coins.

Presidential Dollars Reverse

Date, Mintmark, and Mottos Incused on Edge

	Mintage	MS-65	PF-65
2007P, Washington. . . .	176,680,000	$2	
2007D, Washington . . .	163,680,000	2	
2007S, Washington	(3,965,989)		$6
2007P, J. Adams	112,420,000	2	
2007D, J. Adams	112,140,000	2	
2007S, J. Adams	(3,965,989)		6

	Mintage	MS-65	PF-65
2007P, Jefferson	100,800,000	$2	
2007D, Jefferson	102,810,000	2	
2007S, Jefferson	(3,965,989)		$6
2007P, Madison	84,560,000	2	
2007D, Madison	87,780,000	2	
2007S, Madison	(3,965,989)		6

	Mintage	MS-65	PF-65
2008P, Monroe.	64,260,000	$2	
2008D, Monroe.	60,230,000	2	
2008S, Monroe.	(3,083,940)		$6
2008P, J.Q. Adams	57,540,000	2	
2008D, J.Q. Adams	57,720,000	2	
2008S, J.Q. Adams.	(3,083,940)		6

	Mintage	MS-65	PF-65
2008P, Jackson	61,180,000	$2	
2008D, Jackson	61,070,000	2	
2008S, Jackson	(3,083,940)		$6
2008P, Van Buren.	51,520,000	2	
2008D, Van Buren	50,960,000	2	
2008S, Van Buren.	(3,083,940)		6

Error coins with wrong or missing edge lettering are valued higher than normal coins.

	Mintage	MS-65	PF-65
2009P, W.H. Harrison	43,260,000	$2	
2009D, W.H. Harrison	55,160,000	2	
2009S, W.H. Harrison	(2,809,452)		$6
2009P, Tyler	43,540,000	2	
2009D, Tyler	43,540,000	2	
2009S, Tyler	(2,809,452)		6

	Mintage	MS-65	PF-65
2009P, Polk	46,620,000	$2	
2009D, Polk	41,720,000	2	
2009S, Polk	(2,809,452)		$6
2009P, Taylor	41,580,000	2	
2009D, Taylor	36,680,000	2	
2009S, Taylor	(2,809,452)		6

	Mintage	MS-65	PF-65
2010P, Fillmore	37,520,000	$2	
2010D, Fillmore	36,960,000	2	
2010S, Fillmore	(2,224,827)		$6
2010P, Pierce	38,220,000	2	
2010D, Pierce	38,360,000	2	
2010S, Pierce	(2,224,827)		6

	Mintage	MS-65	PF-65
2010P, Buchanan	36,820,000	$2	
2010D, Buchanan	36,540,000	2	
2010S, Buchanan	(2,224,827)		$6
2010P, Lincoln	49,000,000	2	
2010D, Lincoln	48,020,000	2	
2010S, Lincoln	(2,224,827)		6

Error coins with wrong or missing edge lettering are valued higher than normal coins.

	Mintage	MS-65	PF-65
2011P, Johnson	35,560,000	$2	
2011D, Johnson	37,100,000	2	
2011S, Johnson	(1,706,916)		$6
2011P, Grant	38,080,000	2	
2011D, Grant	37,940,000	2	
2011S, Grant	(1,706,916)		6

	Mintage	MS-65	PF-65
2011P, Hayes	37,660,000	$2	
2011D, Hayes	36,820,000	2	
2011S, Hayes	(1,706,916)		$6
2011P, Garfield	37,100,000	2	
2011D, Garfield	37,100,000	2	
2011S, Garfield	(1,706,916)		6

	Mintage	MS-65	PF-65
2012P, Arthur **(a)**	6,020,000	$3	
2012D, Arthur **(a)**	4,060,000	3	
2012S, Arthur			$6
2012P, Cleveland, V1 **(a)**	5,460,000	3	
2012D, Cleveland, V1 **(a)**	4,060,000	3	
2012S, Cleveland, V1			6

	Mintage	MS-65	PF-65
2012P, B. Harrison **(a)**	5,640,001	$3	
2012D, B. Harrison **(a)**	4,200,000	3	
2012S, B. Harrison			$6
2012P, Cleveland, V2 **(a)**	10,680,000	3	
2012D, Cleveland, V2 **(a)**	3,920,000	3	
2012S, Cleveland, V2			6

a. Not issued for circulation.

	Mintage	MS-65	PF-65
2013P, McKinley **(a)**		$3	
2013D, McKinley **(a)**		3	
2013S, McKinley			$6
2013P, T. Roosevelt **(a)**		3	
2013D, T. Roosevelt **(a)**		3	
2013S, T. Roosevelt			6

	Mintage	MS-65	PF-65
2013P, Taft **(a)**		$3	
2013D, Taft **(a)**		3	
2013S, Taft			$6
2013P, Wilson **(a)**		3	
2013D, Wilson **(a)**		3	
2013S, Wilson			6

a. Not issued for circulation.

Gold has served as money or established the monetary value of currencies longer than any other material. The use of gold coins was widespread in Europe by 300 B.C. In what became the United States, the earliest coins circulated were foreign, mostly silver and gold, brought from Europe, as well as made in Spanish possessions in the New World. The Coinage Act in 1792 established an independent monetary system with the dollar as the basic U.S. monetary unit containing 24-3/4 grains of fine gold, based on the world price of $19.39 a troy ounce (480 grains). Congress changed the gold specification in 1834 and again in 1837, when it set the dollar price of gold at $20.67 an ounce.

In 1934, U.S. citizens were prohibited from holding monetary gold in the United States; this was extended in 1961 to gold held abroad as well. The dollar price was set at $35 per ounce in 1934. Use of gold in international trade was further restricted as the price rose. The government revalued it at $38 per ounce in 1972, then $42.22 in 1973. It has fluctuated widely over the past few years. All restrictions on holding gold were removed on December 31, 1974.

Coinage of the gold dollar was authorized by the Act of March 3, 1849. The weight was 25.8 grains, .900 fineness. The first type, struck until 1854, is known as the Liberty Head or small-sized type (Type 1). All those made after 1849 have the Close Wreath reverse.

In 1854, the dollar coins were made larger in diameter and thinner. The design was changed to a feather headdress on a female, generally referred to as the Indian Princess Head or large-sized type (Type 2). In 1856, the type was changed slightly by enlarging the size of the head (Type 3).

Note: Values of common gold coins have been based on the current bullion price of gold, $1,900 per ounce, and may vary with the prevailing spot price. The net weight and content listed may be used to recalculate bullion value.

LIBERTY HEAD (1849–1854)

Designer James B. Longacre; weight 1.672 grams; composition .900 gold, .100 copper (net weight .04837 oz. pure gold); diameter 13 mm; reeded edge; mints: Philadelphia, Charlotte, Dahlonega, New Orleans, San Francisco.

VF-20 Very Fine—LIBERTY on headband complete and legible. Knobs on coronet defined.
EF-40 Extremely Fine—Slight wear on hair; knobs on coronet sharp.
AU-50 About Uncirculated—Trace of wear on headband. Nearly full luster.
AU-55 Choice About Uncirculated—Evidence of friction on design high points.
MS-60 Uncirculated—No trace of wear. Light marks and blemishes.
MS-63 Choice Uncirculated—Some distracting contact marks or blemishes in prime focal areas. Impaired luster possible.

Liberty Head (Type 1)
Mintmark is below wreath.

Obverse

**Open Wreath
Reverse**

**Close Wreath
Reverse**

	Mintage	VF-20	EF-40	AU-50	AU-55	MS-60	MS-63
1849, Open Wreath, No L 688,567		$240	$300	$375	$425	$1,050	$2,000
1849, Open Wreath, With L (a). . . . .*		225	250	285	300	1,100	1,850
1849, Close Wreath (Ends Closer to Numeral). . . . . .*		225	250	275	285	600	1,350
1849C, Close Wreath 11,634		1,450	2,000	3,000	3,850	8,250	15,000
1849C, Open Wreath *(extremely rare)*. . . . .*	250,000	325,000	425,000	500,000	600,000	850,000
$690,000, MS-63 PL, DLRC auction,							
July 2004							

* Included in number above. **a.** Liberty's head appears slightly smaller than normal on some variations.

	Mintage	VF-20	EF-40	AU-50	AU-55	MS-60	MS-63
1849D, Open Wreath	21,588	$1,350	$2,100	$3,000	$3,500	$5,000	$13,000
1849O, Open Wreath	215,000	245	325	425	575	1,200	4,000
1850	481,953	225	250	265	285	450	1,350
1850C	6,966	1,300	1,750	2,450	4,500	7,500	32,500
1850D	8,382	1,500	2,000	3,000	4,500	11,000	27,500
1850O	14,000	300	500	950	1,500	3,200	7,000
1851	3,317,671	225	250	265	285	500	1,125
1851C	41,267	1,250	1,550	2,000	2,250	3,200	6,500
1851D	9,882	1,500	1,800	2,450	2,750	5,500	16,500
1851O	290,000	235	285	350	425	850	2,250
1852	2,045,351	225	250	265	285	500	1,125
1852C	9,434	1,500	1,850	2,100	2,600	4,250	11,500
1852D	6,360	1,500	2,000	2,600	3,500	9,500	30,000
1852O	140,000	240	285	450	675	1,400	5,250
1853	4,076,051	225	250	265	285	500	1,125
1853C	11,515	1,350	1,600	2,100	2,500	4,250	12,000
1853D	6,583	1,400	1,850	2,450	3,750	8,500	26,000
1853O	290,000	235	255	335	450	850	2,250
1854	855,502	225	250	265	285	500	1,125
1854D	2,935	1,850	2,450	4,750	6,250	11,500	35,000
1854S	14,632	400	550	950	1,150	2,500	5,750

INDIAN PRINCESS HEAD, SMALL HEAD (1854–1856)

Standards same as for previous issue, except diameter changed to 15 mm.

VF-20 Very Fine—Feather-curl tips on headdress outlined but details worn.
EF-40 Extremely Fine—Slight wear on tips of feather curls on headdress.
AU-50 About Uncirculated—Trace of wear on feathers, nearly full luster.
AU-55 Choice About Uncirculated—Evidence of friction on design high points. Most of original mint luster present.
MS-60 Uncirculated—No trace of wear. Light marks and blemishes.
MS-63 Choice Uncirculated—Some distracting contact marks or blemishes in prime focal areas. Impaired luster possible.

Indian Princess Head, Small Head (Type 2)

PF-63 Choice Proof—Reflective surfaces with only a few blemishes in secondary focal areas. No major flaws.

	Mintage	VF-20	EF-40	AU-50	AU-55	MS-60	MS-63	PF-63
1854	783,943	$350	$500	$625	$875	$1,750	$8,750	*$200,000*
1855	758,269	350	500	625	875	1,750	8,750	*150,000*
$373,750, PF-66 DC, Heritage auction, January 2008								
1855C	9,803	1,750	4,000	8,500	13,000	28,500		
1855D	1,811	8,000	14,500	25,000	30,000	50,000	90,000	
1855O	55,000	575	1,000	1,700	2,350	8,000	28,500	
1856S	24,600	950	1,450	2,350	3,250	8,000	30,000	

INDIAN PRINCESS HEAD, LARGE HEAD (1856–1889)

VF-20 Very Fine—Slight detail in curled feathers in headdress. Details worn smooth at eyebrow, hair below headdress, and behind ear and bottom curl.
EF-40 Extremely Fine—Slight wear above and to right of eye and on top of curled feathers.
AU-50 About Uncirculated—Trace of wear on feathers, nearly full luster.
AU-55 Choice About Uncirculated—Evidence of friction on design high points. Most of original mint luster present.
MS-60 Uncirculated—No trace of wear. Light marks and blemishes.

Indian Princess Head, Large Head (Type 3)

MS-63 Choice Uncirculated—Some distracting contact marks or blemishes in prime focal areas. Impaired luster possible.

PF-63 Choice Proof—Reflective surfaces with few blemishes in secondary focal places. No major flaws.

See next page for chart.

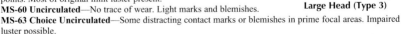

Mintage	VF-20	EF-40	AU-50	AU-55	MS-60	MS-63	PF-63
1856, All kinds 1,762,936							
1856, Upright 5	$250	$275	$325	$400	$650	$1,500	
1856, Slant 5	245	250	260	285	500	1,100	$30,000
1856D 1,460	3,750	6,250	8,500	10,500	29,500	80,000	
1857 774,789	245	250	260	285	500	1,100	17,500
1857C 13,280	1,250	1,750	3,000	4,750	10,000	28,500	
1857D 3,533	1,400	2,400	3,750	4,500	9,500		
1857S 10,000	500	750	1,250	2,000	5,750	18,500	
1858 117,995	245	250	265	300	525	1,150	13,500
1858D 3,477	1,450	2,100	3,750	4,500	8,750	23,000	
1858S 10,000	385	675	1,300	1,750	5,250	16,500	
1859 . . . . (80) 168,244	245	250	255	285	525	1,100	12,000
1859C 5,235	1,400	2,000	3,500	5,750	10,500	26,000	
1859D 4,952	1,500	2,000	3,000	4,500	9,000	21,000	
1859S 15,000	300	575	1,250	1,850	4,750	15,000	
1860 . . . . (154) 36,514	245	250	275	300	525	1,250	8,000
1860D 1,566	3,000	4,250	7,500	9,750	18,000	50,000	
1860S 13,000	350	500	775	1,100	2,650	6,000	
1861 . . . . (349) 527,150	245	250	265	285	525	1,000	8,000
1861D (a) 1,250	20,000	28,000	38,000	47,500	65,000	90,000	
1862 . . . . (35) . . . 1,361,355	245	250	265	285	525	925	8,000
1863 . . . . (50) 6,200	1,350	2,000	3,250	4,750	7,750	13,500	9,000
1864 . . . . (50) 5,900	500	850	1,350	1,750	2,200	4,500	9,000
1865 . . . . (25) 3,725	600	900	1,100	1,500	2,250	5,000	9,000
1866 . . . . (30) 7,100	400	500	750	950	1,100	2,150	9,000
1867 . . . . (50) 5,200	450	525	700	800	1,200	2,000	7,500
1868 . . . . (25) 10,500	285	425	525	600	1,000	2,000	7,500
1869 . . . . (25) 5,900	350	475	700	800	1,150	2,250	7,500
1870 . . . . (35) 6,300	325	450	675	750	1,000	2,000	7,500
1870S 3,000	500	825	1,250	1,750	2,800	8,000	
1871 . . . . (30) 3,900	315	450	575	675	900	1,850	8,000
1872 . . . . (30) 3,500	315	425	575	675	1,100	2,350	8,000
1873, Close 3 . . . . (25) 1,800	425	750	1,100	1,200	1,650	4,250	15,000
1873, Open 3 123,300	245	250	265	285	525	925	
1874 . . . . (20) 198,800	245	250	265	285	525	925	12,000
1875 . . . . (20) 400	2,750	4,500	5,500	6,500	9,000	16,500	18,500
1876 . . . . (45) 3,200	325	375	500	600	800	1,350	7,000
1877 . . . . (20) 3,900	300	375	525	600	850	1,400	8,000
1878 . . . . (20) 3,000	300	350	525	575	750	1,200	7,500
1879 . . . . (30) 3,000	265	300	375	450	650	1,150	6,500
1880 . . . . (36) 1,600	265	300	375	450	650	1,150	5,750
1881 . . . . (87) 7,620	250	285	350	400	650	1,150	5,750
1882 . . . . (125) 5,000	250	285	350	400	650	1,150	5,750
1883 . . . . (207) 10,800	250	285	350	400	625	1,150	5,750
1884 . . . . (1,006) 5,230	250	285	350	400	625	1,150	5,750
1885 . . . . (1,105) 11,156	250	285	350	400	625	1,150	5,750
1886 . . . . (1,016) 5,000	250	285	350	400	625	1,150	5,750
1887 . . . . (1,043) 7,500	250	285	350	400	625	1,150	5,750
1888 . . . . (1,079) 15,501	250	285	350	400	600	925	5,750
1889 . . . . (1,779) 28,950	250	285	350	400	600	900	5,750

a. All were struck under the auspices of the state of Georgia and the Confederate States of America after the Dahlonega Mint had been seized by Rebel troops.

Authorized by the Act of April 2, 1792, quarter eagles weighed 67.5 grains, .9167 fineness, until the weight was changed to 64.5 grains, .8992 fineness, by the Act of June 28, 1834. The Act of January 18, 1837, established fineness at .900. Most dates before 1834 are rare. The first issue was struck in 1796; most of these had no stars on the obverse. Proofs of some dates prior to 1855 are known to exist, and all are rare.

Note: Values of common gold coins have been based on the current bullion price, $1,900 per oz., and may vary with the prevailing spot price. The net weight and content listed may be used to recalculate bullion value.

CAPPED BUST TO RIGHT (1796–1807)

Designer Robert Scot; weight 4.37 grams; composition .9167 gold, .0833 silver and copper; approx. diameter 20 mm; reeded edge.

F-12 Fine—Hair worn smooth on high spots. E PLURIBUS UNUM on ribbon weak but legible.
VF-20 Very Fine—Some wear on high spots.
EF-40 Extremely Fine—Only slight wear on Liberty's hair and cheek.
AU-50 About Uncirculated—Trace of wear on cap, hair, cheek, and drapery.
AU-55 Choice About Uncirculated—Evidence of friction on design high points. Some original mint luster present.
MS-60 Uncirculated—No trace of wear. Light blemishes.

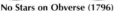

| | No Stars on Obverse (1796) | | Stars on Obverse (1796–1807) | | | |

	Mintage	F-12	VF-20	EF-40	AU-50	AU-55	MS-60
1796, No Stars on Obverse	963	$42,500	$65,000	$90,000	$110,000	$130,000	$225,000
$1,725,000, MS-65, Heritage auction, January 2008							
1796, Stars on Obverse	432	32,500	47,500	70,000	95,000	120,000	185,000
$1,006,250, MS-65, Heritage auction, January 2008							
1797	427	17,500	24,000	37,500	67,500	85,000	137,500
1798	1,094	8,000	10,250	15,500	28,500	39,500	67,500
1802	3,035	6,000	8,500	13,000	17,000	20,000	32,500
1804, 13-Star Reverse	*	75,000	125,000	200,000	275,000	400,000	
1804, 14-Star Reverse	3,327	5,250	9,000	13,500	17,500	22,500	32,500
1805	1,781	5,750	9,250	13,500	17,500	22,500	32,500
1806, 6 Over 4, 8 Stars Left, 5 Right	1,136	5,750	9,250	13,500	17,500	22,500	32,500
1806, 6 Over 5, 7 Stars Left, 6 Right	480	10,000	14,500	18,500	40,000	57,500	95,000
1807	6,812	5,750	8,500	13,250	16,000	20,000	32,500

* Included in number below.

CAPPED BUST TO LEFT, LARGE SIZE (1808)

Designer John Reich; standards same as for previous issue.

F-12 Fine—E PLURIBUS UNUM on reverse, and LIBERTY on headband, legible but weak.
VF-20 Very Fine—Motto and LIBERTY clear.
EF-40 Extremely Fine—All details of hair plain.
AU-50 About Uncirculated—Trace of wear above eye, on top of cap, and on cheek, and hair.
AU-55 Choice About Uncirculated—Evidence of friction on design high points. Some original mint luster present.
MS-60 Uncirculated—No trace of wear. Light blemishes.

	Mintage	F-12	VF-20	EF-40	AU-50	AU-55	MS-60
1808.	2,710	$30,000	$45,000	$60,000	$90,000	$100,000	$150,000

$517,500, MS-63, Stack's Bowers auction, November 2008

CAPPED HEAD TO LEFT (1821–1834)
Large Diameter (1821–1827)

Standards same as for previous issue, except diameter changed to approximately 18.5 mm in 1821.

	Mintage	F-12	VF-20	EF-40	AU-50	AU-55	MS-60
1821.	6,448	$6,250	$8,750	$12,000	$14,000	$17,500	$32,500
1824, 4 Over 1.	2,600	6,250	9,000	13,000	15,500	18,750	32,500
1825.	4,434	6,250	8,000	13,000	15,500	17,500	32,500
1826, 6 Over 6.	760	9,500	11,000	15,000	22,500	32,500	62,500
1827.	2,800	6,500	9,250	13,100	17,500	19,500	30,000

Reduced Diameter (1829–1834)

Quarter eagles dated 1829 through 1834 are smaller in diameter (18.2 mm) than the 1821 through 1827 pieces. They also have smaller letters, dates, and stars.

	Mintage	F-12	VF-20	EF-40	AU-50	AU-55	MS-60
1829.	3,403	$5,500	$7,000	$9,500	$13,000	$17,000	$24,000
1830.	4,540	5,500	7,000	9,500	13,000	17,000	24,000
1831.	4,520	5,500	7,000	9,500	13,000	17,000	24,000
1832.	4,400	5,500	7,000	9,500	13,000	17,000	24,000
1833.	4,160	5,500	7,000	9,500	13,000	17,000	24,000
1834, With Motto	4,000	10,000	15,000	20,000	30,000	37,500	60,000

CLASSIC HEAD, NO MOTTO ON REVERSE (1834–1839)

In 1834, a ribbon binding Liberty's hair, bearing the word LIBERTY, replaced the liberty cap. The motto was omitted from the reverse. In 1840 a coronet and smaller head were designed to conform with the appearance of the larger gold coins.

Designer William Kneass; weight 4.18 grams; composition .8992 gold, .1008 silver and copper (changed to .900 gold in 1837); diameter 18.2 mm; reeded edge; mints: Philadelphia, Charlotte, Dahlonega, New Orleans.

F-12 Fine—LIBERTY on headband legible and complete. Curl under ear outlined but no detail.

VF-20 Very Fine—LIBERTY plain; detail in hair curl.

EF-40 Extremely Fine—Small amount of wear on top of hair and below L in LIBERTY. Wear evident on wing.

AU-50 About Uncirculated—Trace of wear on coronet and hair above ear.

AU-55 Choice About Uncirculated—Evidence of friction on design high points. Some of original mint luster present.

MS-60 Uncirculated—No trace of wear. Light blemishes.

MS-63 Choice Uncirculated—Some distracting contact marks or blemishes in prime focal areas. Impaired luster possible.

Mintmark Location

	Mintage	F-12	VF-20	EF-40	AU-50	AU-55	MS-60	MS-63
1834, No Motto	112,234	$365	$600	$850	$1,350	$1,600	$3,500	$10,500
1835	131,402	365	600	850	1,350	1,600	3,800	10,500
1836, All kinds	547,986							
1836, Script 8		365	600	850	1,350	1,600	3,750	10,500
1836, Block 8		365	600	850	1,350	1,600	3,750	10,500
1837	45,080	385	625	1,200	2,000	2,500	5,250	14,500
1838	47,030	385	625	1,000	1,500	1,850	4,500	11,500
1838C	7,880	1,450	2,500	3,800	8,500	11,750	26,500	47,000
1839	27,021	400	650	1,300	2,250	2,900	6,500	19,500
1839C	18,140	1,400	2,350	3,000	5,000	7,750	25,000	55,000
1839D	13,674	1,500	2,400	4,250	8,500	10,000	28,500	47,500
1839O	17,781	650	950	1,500	2,500	3,800	9,000	25,000

Note: So-called 9 Over 8 varieties for P, C, and D mints are made from defective punches.

LIBERTY HEAD (1840–1907)

Designer Christian Gobrecht; weight 4.18 grams; composition .900 gold, .100 copper (net weight .12094 oz. pure gold); diameter 18 mm; reeded edge; mints: Philadelphia, Charlotte, Dahlonega, New Orleans, San Francisco.

See previous type for grading standards.

Mintmark Location

	Mintage	VF-20	EF-40	AU-50	AU-55	MS-60	MS-63
1840	18,859	$350	$825	$2,400	$3,100	$6,000	$11,000
1840C	12,822	1,500	2,000	3,750	5,250	9,000	23,500
1840D	3,532	3,250	7,500	11,500	17,500	32,500	
1840O	33,580	450	850	1,850	2,450	8,250	24,500
1841 **(a)**	*(unknown)*	65,000	105,000	125,000	150,000	210,000	
1841C	10,281	1,450	2,150	3,150	4,850	14,000	
1841D	4,164	2,100	3,850	8,000	10,900	25,000	46,500
1842	2,823	1,150	2,750	6,000	10,000	19,000	
1842C	6,729	1,750	3,250	6,500	8,500	20,000	

a. Values are for circulated Proofs; recent research suggests circulation strikes were produced.

Chart continued on next page.

	Mintage	VF-20	EF-40	AU-50	AU-55	MS-60	MS-63
1842D	4,643	$2,200	$4,200	$8,750	$14,000	$32,500	
1842O	19,800	525	1,300	2,250	3,850	11,500	$26,000
1843	100,546	360	425	750	1,000	2,500	6,000
1843C, Small Date, Crosslet 4	2,988	2,500	5,000	7,000	9,000	22,500	
1843C, Large Date, Plain 4	23,076	1,300	1,900	2,850	4,500	7,250	16,000
1843D, Small Date, Crosslet 4	36,209	1,300	1,900	2,850	4,500	8,000	26,000
1843O, Small Date, Crosslet 4	288,002	385	400	525	775	1,950	7,250
1843O, Large Date, Plain 4	76,000	425	750	1,600	2,500	6,250	
1844	6,784	475	775	1,700	3,000	6,500	
1844C	11,622	1,375	2,450	5,500	8,000	15,000	40,000
1844D	17,332	1,450	2,350	2,850	4,000	6,750	23,500
1845	91,051	360	375	500	650	1,250	5,000
1845D	19,460	1,450	2,350	3,000	4,250	11,000	32,500
1845O	4,000	1,300	2,350	6,000	8,250	22,500	45,000
1846	21,598	360	450	1,000	1,700	5,000	22,500
1846C	4,808	1,650	2,750	6,000	9,250	17,000	37,500
1846D	19,303	1,550	2,350	3,000	4,250	9,000	28,500
1846O	62,000	400	500	1,200	2,000	5,500	17,500
1847	29,814	360	385	750	1,250	2,800	8,000
1847C	23,226	1,425	2,300	3,000	3,750	5,750	13,500
1847D	15,784	1,550	2,500	3,000	5,250	8,500	22,500
1847O	124,000	385	475	1,000	1,750	3,500	12,500

CAL. Gold Quarter Eagle (1848)

In 1848, about 230 ounces of gold were sent to Secretary of War Marcy by Colonel R.B. Mason, military governor of California. The gold was turned over to the Mint and made into quarter eagles. The distinguishing mark CAL. was punched above the eagle on the reverse side, while the coins were in the die. Several specimens with prooflike surfaces are known.

CAL. Above Eagle on Reverse (1848)

	Mintage	VF-20	EF-40	AU-50	AU-55	MS-60	MS-63
1848	6,500	$550	$900	$1,750	$2,350	$5,000	$13,750
1848, CAL. Above Eagle	1,389	35,000	45,000	55,000	57,500	75,000	105,000
$402,500, MS-68★, Heritage auction, January 2006							
1848C	16,788	1,450	2,350	3,250	4,500	10,500	30,000
1848D	13,771	1,450	2,350	3,250	4,250	8,000	28,500
1849	23,294	375	500	975	1,250	2,350	8,000
1849C	10,220	1,425	2,300	4,500	8,000	18,000	48,500
1849D	10,945	1,450	2,350	3,850	6,000	13,000	34,000
1850	252,923	360	380	400	500	1,050	3,250
1850C	9,148	1,450	2,500	3,500	4,500	11,500	32,500
1850D	12,148	1,500	2,350	3,500	5,500	13,500	42,500
1850O	84,000	400	575	1,350	1,800	4,000	15,000
1851	1,372,748	360	380	390	400	550	1,200
1851C	14,923	1,450	2,450	3,750	6,000	9,500	30,000
1851D	11,264	1,450	2,400	4,000	6,000	10,750	32,000
1851O	148,000	400	475	950	2,000	4,000	12,500
1852	1,159,681	360	380	390	400	550	1,300
1852C	9,772	1,450	2,500	3,850	5,750	12,750	30,000
1852D	4,078	1,850	3,000	6,000	8,000	15,750	40,000
1852O	140,000	400	450	950	1,250	4,750	10,750

QUARTER EAGLES

	Mintage	VF-20	EF-40	AU-50	AU-55	MS-60	MS-63	PF-63
1853.	1,404,668	$360	$375	$385	$400	$550	$1,200	
1853D	.3,178	1,800	3,250	4,850	5,750	15,000	45,000	
1854.	.596,258	360	375	385	400	550	1,250	
1854C.	.7,295	1,500	2,600	4,350	6,250	11,000		
1854D	.1,760	3,500	7,500	12,000	14,500	23,000	67,500	
1854O	.153,000	385	400	575	850	1,450	8,250	
1854S.	246	275,000	400,000	500,000				
$345,000, EF-45, Heritage auction, February 2007								
1855.	.235,480	360	375	385	400	550	1,600	
1855C.	.3,677	1,850	3,250	5,500	10,000	19,500	40,000	
1855D	.1,123	4,500	8,000	14,750	20,000	46,500		
1856.	.384,240	360	365	385	400	550	1,450	$75,000
1856C.	.7,913	1,400	2,600	4,100	6,250	11,500	22,500	
1856D	874	8,000	12,000	28,000	34,000	70,000		
1856O	.21,100	385	700	1,200	2,100	7,000		
1856S.	.72,120	385	450	1,200	1,750	5,500	11,500	
1857.	.214,130	360	365	385	400	550	1,500	57,500
1857D	.2,364	1,600	2,800	4,100	5,500	12,000	27,500	
1857O	.34,000	385	400	1,250	2,000	4,000	12,500	
1857S.	.69,200	385	475	1,275	2,250	6,000	14,000	
1858.	.47,377	375	390	450	575	1,200	3,000	45,000
1858C.	.9,056	1,400	2,250	3,100	4,000	8,000	22,000	

A modified reverse design (with smaller letters and arrowheads) was used on Philadelphia quarter eagles from 1859 through 1907, and on San Francisco issues of 1877 through 1879. A few Philadelphia Mint pieces were made in 1859, 1860, and 1861 with the old Large Letters reverse design.

Old Reverse

New Reverse

	Mintage	VF-20	EF-40	AU-50	AU-55	MS-60	MS-63	PF-63
1859, Old Reverse . . . . (80).	.39,364	$375	$500	$875	$1,175	$2,900	$7,750	$30,000
1859, New Reverse	*	360	370	500	700	1,200	3,200	
1859D	.2,244	2,200	3,250	4,750	6,750	18,500		
1859S.	.15,200	475	950	2,100	2,900	6,250	15,250	
1860, Old Reverse . . . (112).	.22,563	1,400	2,100	3,000	3,750	7,000	13,500	22,500
1860, New Reverse	*	360	370	450	575	1,000	2,750	
1860C.	.7,469	1,575	2,500	4,000	6,000	15,000	37,500	
1860S.	.35,600	425	675	1,150	1,750	3,500	13,500	
1861, Old Reverse . . . . (90). . .	1,283,788	525	1,100	1,800	2,350	4,000	9,000	20,000
1861, New Reverse	*	360	370	385	400	650	1,750	
1861S.	.24,000	400	825	2,500	4,000	7,250		
1862, 2 Over 1	**	1,000	1,850	3,250	4,500	7,500		
1862. . . . . (35).	.98,508	400	600	1,000	2,250	4,750	10,000	20,000
1862S.	.8,000	1,000	1,750	3,250	5,500	16,500	32,500	
1863, Proof only . . . . . . (30).								75,000
1863S.	.10,800	700	1,350	3,500	6,000	13,000	30,000	
1864. . . . . (50).	.2,824	7,500	15,000	27,500	40,000	65,000		25,000
1865. . . . . (25).	.1,520	4,500	8,500	20,000	25,000	37,500	45,000	20,000
1865S.	.23,376	400	650	1,250	2,000	4,500	11,000	
1866. . . . . (30).	.3,080	1,150	3,000	5,250	7,500	12,500	24,000	17,500
1866S.	.38,960	400	750	1,700	3,500	7,500	20,000	
1867. . . . . (50).	.3,200	400	650	1,200	1,700	4,500	12,000	16,000

* Included in number above. ** Included in number below.

Chart continued on next page.

	Mintage	VF-20	EF-40	AU-50	AU-55	MS-60	MS-63	PF-63
1867S. 28,000		$400	$650	$1,250	$1,750	$3,850	$12,000	
1868. . . . .(25). 3,600		385	425	700	850	2,250	7,250	$16,500
1868S. 34,000		360	425	950	1,400	4,000	10,000	
1869. . . . .(25). 4,320		360	425	700	1,100	2,750	8,250	14,000
1869S. 29,500		360	475	1,000	1,500	4,000	9,250	
1870. . . . .(35). 4,520		360	400	600	1,250	3,250	8,000	14,000
1870S. 16,000		360	400	900	1,500	4,000	13,000	
1871. . . . .(30). 5,320		360	400	550	900	2,000	4,000	14,000
1871S. 22,000		360	400	550	900	2,000	4,350	
1872. . . . .(30). 3,000		425	700	1,150	2,000	4,350	13,500	14,000
1872S. 18,000		360	400	950	1,350	4,000	10,500	
1873, Close 3. . . . .(25). 55,200		360	375	385	400	585	1,500	14,000
1873, Open 3 122,800		360	375	385	400	585	1,200	
1873S. 27,000		360	425	975	1,300	2,300	6,500	
1874. . . . .(20). 3,920		360	400	650	950	2,000	6,000	15,000
1875. . . . .(20). 400		4,500	7,500	12,500	17,500	26,500	40,000	35,000
1875S. 11,600		360	400	650	1,050	3,250	7,250	
1876. . . . .(45). 4,176		375	625	950	1,750	2,850	6,500	13,500
1876S. 5,000		360	525	950	1,750	3,000	8,000	
1877. . . . .(20). 1,632		400	750	1,000	1,250	3,000	8,500	13,500
1877S. 35,400		360	365	385	400	700	2,350	
1878. . . . .(20). 286,240		360	365	385	400	585	1,250	13,500
1878S. 178,000		360	365	385	400	585	1,800	
1879. . . . .(30). 88,960		360	365	400	425	585	1,350	13,000
1879S. 43,500		360	365	550	900	1,800	4,800	
1880. . . . .(36). 2,960		375	425	650	800	1,500	3,750	12,500
1881. . . . .(51). 640		2,000	3,000	5,000	6,000	9,750	23,500	13,500
1882. . . . .(67). 4,000		375	425	575	725	925	3,000	9,500
1883. . . . .(82). 1,920		375	450	900	1,250	2,000	6,500	9,500
1884. . . . .(73). 1,950		375	400	700	850	1,650	3,250	9,500
1885. . . . .(87). 800		1,100	2,000	3,000	3,500	5,000	8,500	9,000
1886. . . . .(88). 4,000		375	400	550	750	1,250	3,250	9,500
1887. . . . .(122). 6,160		375	400	450	500	1,000	3,000	9,500
1888. . . . .(97). 16,001		360	375	385	400	585	1,350	8,500
1889. . . . .(48). 17,600		360	375	385	400	585	1,350	8,500
1890. . . . .(93). 8,720		360	375	425	450	650	1,350	8,500
1891. . . . .(80). 10,960		365	400	425	450	500	1,450	8,000
1892. . . . .(105). 2,440		365	400	475	500	900	2,250	8,000
1893. . . . .(106). 30,000		360	375	385	400	585	1,300	7,500
1894. . . . .(122). 4,000		360	365	400	475	750	1,650	7,500
1895. . . . .(119). 6,000		350	360	375	400	625	1,200	7,500
1896. . . . .(132). 19,070		350	360	375	400	585	950	7,500
1897. . . . .(136). 29,768		350	360	375	400	585	900	7,500
1898. . . . .(165). 24,000		350	360	375	400	585	900	7,500
1899. . . . .(150). 27,200		350	360	375	400	585	875	7,500
1900. . . . .(205). 67,000		350	360	375	400	575	700	7,500
1901. . . . .(223). 91,100		350	360	375	400	575	800	7,500
1902. . . . .(193). 133,540		350	360	375	400	575	800	7,500
1903. . . . .(197). 201,060		350	360	375	400	575	800	7,500
1904. . . . .(170). 160,790		350	360	375	400	575	800	7,500
1905 (a) . . . .(144). 217,800		350	360	375	400	575	800	7,500
1906. . . . .(160). 176,330		350	360	375	400	575	800	7,500
1907. . . . .(154). 336,294		350	360	375	400	575	800	7,500

a. Pieces dated 1905-S are counterfeit.

INDIAN HEAD (1908–1929)

This new type represents a departure from all precedents in United States coinage. Its design features no raised edge, and the main devices and legends are in sunken relief below the surface of the coin.

Boston sculptor Bela Lyon Pratt was the designer of this and the similar half eagle piece. A pupil of the famous Augustus Saint-Gaudens, Pratt based his "standing eagle" motif on the reverse of his teacher's gold ten-dollar coin of 1907. (That eagle was itself derived from the reverse of Theodore Roosevelt's 1905 unofficial inaugural medal, designed by Saint-Gaudens and engraved by Adolph A. Weinman, who would later create the Liberty Walking half dollar. The general style had antecedents in coins of the ancient world.)

Among the public, there was some concern that the recessed design of Pratt's quarter eagle would collect germs—an unfounded fear. The artistry of the design was condemned loudly by some numismatists. Few people were interested in saving the coin for their collections. The result is a series with relatively few examples surviving in higher grades. Any initial disfavor has mellowed with time; today Pratt's design is recognized as part of the early 20th-century renaissance of American coinage.

Designer Bela Lyon Pratt; weight 4.18 grams; composition .900 gold, .100 copper (net weight .12094 oz. pure gold); diameter 18 mm; reeded edge; mints: Philadelphia, Denver.

VF-20 Very Fine—Hair-cord knot distinct. Feathers at top of head clear. Cheekbone worn.

EF-40 Extremely Fine—Cheekbone, war bonnet, and headband feathers slightly worn.

AU-50 About Uncirculated—Trace of wear on cheekbone and headdress.

MS-60 Uncirculated—No trace of wear. Light blemishes.

MS-63 Choice Uncirculated—Some distracting contact marks or blemishes in prime focal areas. Impaired luster possible.

MS-64 Uncirculated—A few scattered contact marks visible. Good eye appeal and attractive luster.

MATTE PF-63 Choice Matte Proof—Few blemishes in secondary focal areas. No major flaws.

Mintmark location is on reverse, to left of arrows.

	Mintage	VF-20	EF-40	AU-50	MS-60	MS-63	MS-64	MATTE PF-63
1908 . . . .(236) 564,821		$350	$365	$385	$450	$1,100	$1,750	$9,000
1909 . . . .(139) 441,760		350	365	385	450	1,700	3,000	10,000
1910 . . . .(682) 492,000		350	365	385	450	1,600	2,650	9,500
1911 . . . .(191) 704,000		350	365	385	450	1,100	1,650	9,000
1911D (a) 55,680		2,850	4,000	5,000	10,000	21,000	28,500	
1912 . . . .(197) 616,000		350	365	390	450	1,750	3,000	10,000
1913 . . . .(165) 722,000		350	365	385	450	1,250	1,850	9,000
1914 . . . .(117) 240,000		350	385	400	750	5,750	12,500	10,000
1914D 448,000		350	365	385	450	1,500	4,500	
1915 . . . .(100) 606,000		350	365	385	450	1,100	1,750	12,000
1925D 578,000		350	365	385	450	850	1,350	
1926 446,000		350	365	385	450	850	1,350	
1927 388,000		350	365	385	450	850	1,350	
1928 416,000		350	365	385	450	850	1,350	
1929 532,000		350	365	385	450	850	1,350	

a. Values are for coins with bold mintmark; weak D pieces are worth less. Beware of counterfeits.

INDIAN PRINCESS HEAD (1854–1889)

The three-dollar gold piece was authorized by the Act of February 21, 1853. First struck in 1854, the coin was never popular with the general public and saw very little circulation. Today, some numismatists theorize that the $3 denomination would have been useful for purchasing postage stamps of the day (with their face value of 3¢) or for acquiring 100 silver three-cent pieces ("trimes"), which were also in circulation at the time.

These gold coins changed hands in the East and Midwest until 1861, after which they disappeared from circulation; through the 1860s, fewer than 10,000 were struck annually. In 1874 and 1878, mintages were increased significantly in anticipation of the coins going into broader circulation. On the West Coast, the three-dollar gold piece did see circulation throughout the series' minting, though they probably weren't seen in change very often after the 1860s.

The head on the obverse represents an Indian princess with hair tightly curling over the neck, her head crowned with a circle of feathers (the band of which is inscribed LIBERTY). A wreath of tobacco, wheat, corn, and cotton occupies the field of the reverse, with the denomination and date within it. The coin weighs 77.4 grains, and was struck in .900 fine gold.

In the year 1854 only, the word DOLLARS is in much smaller letters than in later years. The 1856 Proof has DOLLARS in large letters cut over the same word in small letters. Restrikes of some years were made, particularly Proofs of 1865 and 1873.

Although these coins did not see extensive day-to-day circulation, collector interest was high, and many three-dollar gold pieces were saved by speculators beginning about 1879. As a result, Mint State examples are fairly numerous today. The 1870-S coin is unique, currently residing in the Harry W. Bass Jr. Collection on loan to the American Numismatic Association.

Designer James B. Longacre; weight 5.015 grams; composition .900 gold, .100 copper (net weight .14512 oz. pure gold); diameter 20.5 mm; reeded edge; mints: Philadelphia, Dahlonega, New Orleans, San Francisco.

VF-20 Very Fine—Eyebrow, hair about forehead and ear, and bottom curl all worn smooth. Faint details visible on curled feather-ends of headdress.

EF-40 Extremely Fine—Light wear above and to right of eye, and on top of curled feathers.

AU-50 About Uncirculated—Trace of wear on top of curled feathers and in hair above and to right of eye.

AU-55 Choice About Uncirculated—Evidence of friction on design high points. Much of original mint luster present.

MS-60 Uncirculated—No trace of wear. Light blemishes.

MS-63 Choice Uncirculated—Some distracting contact marks or blemishes in prime focal areas. Impaired luster possible.

PF-63 Choice Proof—Reflective surfaces with only a few blemishes in secondary focal places. No major flaws.

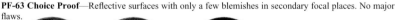

Circulation strike.   Proof strike.   Mintmark location is on reverse, below wreath.

	Mintage	VF-20	EF-40	AU-50	AU-55	MS-60	MS-63	PF-63
1854	138,618	$825	$1,150	$1,400	$1,650	$2,650	$6,000	$95,000
1854D	1,120	17,500	27,500	36,000	45,000	75,000		
1854O	24,000	2,000	3,250	6,000	12,000	27,500	85,000	
1855	50,555	850	1,250	1,600	1,850	3,000	8,500	57,500

	Mintage	VF-20	EF-40	AU-50	AU-55	MS-60	MS-63	PF-63
1855S................6,600		$1,750	$3,250	$7,000	$12,000	$25,000	$95,000	
$1,322,500, PF-64 Cam,								
Heritage auction, August 2011								
1856................26,010		850	1,200	1,600	1,850	3,000	8,500	$45,000
1856S **(a)**..............34,500		1,000	1,750	2,750	4,000	11,500	30,000	
1857................20,891		850	1,200	1,800	2,000	3,500	9,500	30,000
1857S................14,000		1,650	3,500	6,500	12,000	21,500	55,000	
1858................2,133		1,300	2,150	4,000	5,500	12,000	22,500	27,500
1859............(80)......15,558		900	1,300	1,850	2,000	3,250	8,500	20,000
1860............(119)......7,036		950	1,300	1,875	2,250	3,400	9,500	16,000
1860S **(b)**..............7,000		1,300	2,500	8,500	12,500	27,500	72,500	
1861............(113)......5,959		1,000	1,650	2,500	3,750	6,250	11,500	16,000
1862............(35)......5,750		1,000	1,650	2,500	3,750	6,250	12,500	16,000
1863............(39)......5,000		1,050	1,750	2,650	3,800	6,500	13,000	16,000
1864............(50)......2,630		1,200	2,000	3,000	4,000	6,750	13,500	16,000
1865............(25)......1,140		2,250	3,500	7,000	9,500	13,500	30,000	20,000
1866............(30)......4,000		1,100	1,500	2,250	3,000	5,000	11,000	16,500
1867............(50)......2,600		1,100	1,500	2,400	3,000	5,000	11,000	16,500
1868 **(c)**............(25)......4,850		950	1,250	2,000	2,750	4,000	10,000	16,500
1869 **(c)**............(25)......2,500		950	1,250	2,200	2,800	4,500	12,000	16,500
1870............(35)......3,500		1,000	1,350	2,500	3,000	4,500	12,500	16,500
1870S............................		6,000,000		*(unique, in Bass Foundation Collection)*				
$687,500, EF-40, B&R								
auction, October 1982								
1871............(30)......1,300		1,100	1,350	2,250	3,000	4,500	12,500	16,500
1872............(30)......2,000		1,100	1,350	2,250	3,000	4,250	12,500	16,500
1873, Open 3 (Original) (25)...........			18,000	27,500				32,500
$161,000, PF-65 DC, Goldberg								
auction, February 2007								
1873, Close 3....................**(d)**		4,250	7,500	13,500	20,000	32,500	55,000	37,500
1874............(20)......41,800		850	1,150	1,400	1,650	2,500	5,750	28,000
1875, Proof only......(20)...........				80,000				150,000
$218,500, PF-64, Heritage								
auction, January 2012								
1876, Proof only......(45)...........				26,500				45,000
1877............(20)......1,468		3,000	6,000	13,000	20,000	28,500	60,000	30,000
1878 **(c)**............(20)......82,304		850	1,150	1,400	1,650	2,500	5,750	27,500
1879............(30)......3,000		1,000	1,300	2,000	2,750	3,750	9,500	17,000
1880............(36)......1,000		1,200	2,000	3,500	3,850	5,500	11,000	17,000
1881............(54)........500		2,500	4,500	7,500	9,500	12,000	18,500	17,000
1882............(76)......1,500		1,250	1,500	2,350	3,000	4,250	10,500	13,500
1883............(89)........900		1,400	2,000	3,000	3,500	5,500	10,500	13,500
1884............(106)......1,000		1,500	2,000	3,250	4,000	5,500	11,000	13,500
1885............(109)........801		1,650	2,150	3,750	4,500	6,000	17,500	15,000
1886............(142)......1,000		1,500	2,000	2,750	3,750	5,000	10,500	13,500
1887............(160)......6,000		900	1,350	2,250	2,500	3,500	10,500	13,500
1888............(291)......5,000		850	1,150	1,750	2,000	3,000	7,000	12,500
1889............(129)......2,300		850	1,150	1,750	2,000	3,000	7,000	12,500

a. Small S and Medium S varieties exist. **b.** 2,592 melted at mint. **c.** Varieties showing traces of possible overdating include 1868/7, 1869/8, and 1878/7. **d.** The mintage of the 1873, Close 3, coins is unknown. Research suggests that Proofs only may have been struck (none for circulation), and those perhaps as late as 1879. Mint records report 25 Proof coins, with no reference to the style of the 3 (Open or Close); however, the actual mintage may be as high as 100 to 1,000 coins.

STELLA (1879–1880)

These pattern coins were first suggested by John A. Kasson, then U.S. envoy extraordinary and minister plenipotentiary to Austria-Hungary. It was through the efforts of W.W. Hubbell, who patented the alloy *goloid* (used in making another pattern piece, the goloid metric dollar), that we have these beautiful and interesting coins.

The four-dollar Stella—so called because the Latin word for *star* is *stella,* and the coin bears a five-pointed star on the reverse—was envisioned by Kasson as America's answer to various foreign gold coins popular in the international market. The British sovereign, Italy's 20 lire, and the 20 pesetas of Spain were three such coins: each smaller than a U.S. five-dollar gold piece, they were used widely in international trade.

The Stella was one of many proposals made to Congress for an international trade coin, and one of only several that made it to pattern-coin form (others include the 1868 five-dollar piece and 1874 Bickford ten-dollar piece).

Odds were stacked against the Stella from the start. The denomination of four U.S. dollars didn't match any of the coin's European counterparts, and at any rate the U.S. double eagle (twenty-dollar coin)—already used in international commerce—was a more convenient medium of exchange. The Stella was never minted for circulation. Those dated 1879 were struck for congressmen to examine. The 1880 coins were secretly made by Mint officials for sale to private collectors.

There are two distinct types in both years of issue. Charles E. Barber designed the Flowing Hair type, and George T. Morgan the Coiled Hair. They were struck as patterns in gold, aluminum, copper, and white metal. (Only those struck in gold are listed here.)

Precise mintage numbers are unknown. The estimates given below are based on surviving pieces, certified population reports, and auction records.

Some of the finest Stella specimens are housed in the National Numismatic Collection in the Smithsonian Institution. Others are in private collections, and cross the auction block from time to time. Recent auction activity for Stellas certified PF-60 and up:

- 1879 Flowing Hair: $115,000   (PF-62 Cam)   Stack's Bowers   May 2010
- 1879 Coiled Hair: $304,750   (PF-63)   Goldberg   February 2009
- 1880 Flowing Hair: $201,250   (PF-63)   Stack's Bowers   June 2008
- 1880 Coiled Hair: $546,250   (PF-62)   Heritage   August 2009

Flowing Hair Obverse   **Coiled Hair Obverse**   **Reverse**

	Mintage	PF-40	PF-50	PF-60	PF-63	PF-65	PF-66	PF-67
1879, Flowing Hair *(425+)*........		$80,000	$85,000	$100,000	$135,000	$195,000	$240,000	$325,000
$402,500, PF-68UC, Stack's Bowers auction, June 2012								
1879, Coiled Hair *(12 known)*........				275,000	350,000	500,000	650,000	850,000
$655,500, PF-67 Cam, Heritage auction, January 2005								
1880, Flowing Hair *(17 known)*.......				150,000	225,000	300,000	375,000	550,000
$488,750, PF-66 Cam, Heritage auction, March 2008								
1880, Coiled Hair *(8 known)*.........				500,000	600,000	900,000	1,000,000	1,400,000
$977,500, PF-66 Cam, Heritage auction, January 2005								

The half eagle was the first gold coin actually struck for the United States. The five-dollar piece was authorized to be coined by the Act of April 2, 1792, and the first type weighed 135 grains, .9167 fineness. The Act of June 28, 1834, changed the weight to 129 grains, .8992 fineness. Fineness became .900 by the Act of January 18, 1837.

There are many varieties among the early dates, caused by changes in the number of stars and style of eagle, by overdates, and by differences in the size of figures in the dates. Those dated prior to 1807 do not bear any mark of value. The 1822 half eagle is considered one of the most valuable regular-issue coins of the entire United States series. Proofs of some dates prior to 1855 are known to exist, and all are rare. Commemorative and bullion five-dollar coins have been made at West Point since 1986 and 1994, respectively; thus this is the only U.S. denomination made at all eight U.S. mints.

Note: Values of common gold coins have been based on the current bullion price, $1,900 per oz., and may vary with the prevailing spot price. The net weight and content listed may be used to recalculate bullion value.

CAPPED BUST TO RIGHT (1795–1807)

Designer Robert Scot; weight 8.75 grams; composition .9167 gold, .0833 silver and copper; approx. diameter 25 mm; reeded edge.

F-12 Fine—Liberty's hair worn smooth but distinctly outlined. Heraldic type: E PLURIBUS UNUM faint but legible.

VF-20 Very Fine—Slight to noticeable wear on high spots such as hair, turban, and eagle's head and wings.

EF-40 Extremely Fine—Slight wear on hair and highest part of cheek.

AU-50 About Uncirculated—Trace of wear on cap, hair, cheek, and drapery.

MS-60 Uncirculated—No trace of wear. Light blemishes.

MS-63 Choice Uncirculated—Some distracting contact marks or blemishes in prime focal areas. Impaired luster possible.

Small Eagle Reverse (1795–1798)

This type was struck from mid-1795 through early 1798, when the Small Eagle reverse was changed to the Large or "Heraldic" Eagle. Note that the 1795 and 1797 dates exist for both types, but that the Heraldic Eagle reverses of these dates were probably struck in 1798 using serviceable 1795 and 1797 dies.

	Mintage	F-12	VF-20	EF-40	AU-50	AU-55	MS-60	MS-63
1795, Small Eagle	8,707	$18,000	$23,500	$28,500	$40,000	$45,000	$70,000	$155,000

$586,500, MS-65, Stack's Bowers auction, June 2008

Note: One variety has the final S in STATES punched over an erroneous D.

1796, 6 Over 5   **1797, 15 Stars**   **1797, 16 Stars**

See next page for chart.

	Mintage	F-12	VF-20	EF-40	AU-50	AU-55	MS-60	MS-63
1796, 6 Over 5	6,196	$20,000	$25,000	$40,000	$60,000	$75,000	$110,000	$215,000
1797, All kinds	3,609							
1797, 15 Stars		27,000	45,000	65,000	100,000	150,000	275,000	
1797, 16 Stars		25,000	40,000	50,000	80,000	135,000	275,000	
1798, Small Eagle *(7 known)*			375,000	650,000	850,000	1,000,000	—	

Heraldic Eagle Reverse (1795–1807)

	Mintage	F-12	VF-20	EF-40	AU-50	AU-55	MS-60	MS-63
1795, Heraldic Eagle	(a)	$15,000	$22,000	$30,000	$50,000	$60,000	$90,000	$175,000
1797, 7 Over 5	(a)	16,000	27,500	40,000	75,000	115,000	200,000	
1797, 16-Star Obverse	(a)			—	*(unique, in Smithsonian collection)*			
1797, 15-Star Obverse	(a)			—	*(unique, in Smithsonian collection)*			
1798, All kinds	24,867							
1798, Small 8		5,500	7,750	12,500	18,500	21,500	32,500	75,000
1798, Large 8, 13-Star Reverse		4,500	5,750	9,000	14,000	23,000		
1798, Large 8, 14-Star Reverse		4,750	6,750	13,000	23,500	35,000	100,000	
1799	7,451	4,000	5,500	7,500	14,000	18,000	27,500	65,000

a. Thought to have been struck in 1798 and included in the mintage figure for that year.

1802, 2 Over 1   **1803, 3 Over 2**   **1804, Small 8 Over Large 8**

	Mintage	F-12	VF-20	EF-40	AU-50	AU-55	MS-60	MS-63
1800	37,628	$4,000	$5,000	$7,000	$10,000	$12,000	$15,000	$33,500
1802, 2 Over 1	53,176	4,000	5,000	7,000	10,000	12,000	15,000	32,500
1803, 3 Over 2	33,506	4,000	5,000	7,000	10,000	12,000	15,000	32,500
1804, All kinds	30,475							
1804, Small 8		4,000	5,000	7,000	10,000	11,500	15,500	32,500
1804, Small 8 Over Large 8		4,000	5,000	7,000	10,000	12,500	19,500	42,500
1805	33,183	4,000	5,000	7,000	10,000	11,500	15,000	32,500

Pointed-Top 6, Stars 8 and 5   **Round-Top 6, Stars 7 and 6**

	Mintage	F-12	VF-20	EF-40	AU-50	AU-55	MS-60	MS-63
1806, Pointed-Top 6	9,676	$4,000	$5,000	$7,000	$10,000	$12,000	$16,500	$36,500
1806, Round-Top 6	54,417	4,000	5,000	7,000	10,000	11,500	15,500	32,500
1807	32,488	4,000	5,000	7,000	10,000	11,500	15,500	32,500

CAPPED BUST TO LEFT (1807–1812)

Designer John Reich; standards same as for previous issue.

F-12 Fine—LIBERTY on cap legible but partly weak.
VF-20 Very Fine—Headband edges slightly worn. LIBERTY bold.
EF-40 Extremely Fine—Slight wear on highest portions of hair; 80% of major curls plain.
AU-50 About Uncirculated—Trace of wear above eye and on top of cap, cheek, and hair.
AU-55 Choice About Uncirculated—Evidence of friction on design high points. Some mint luster present.
MS-60 Uncirculated—No trace of wear. Light blemishes.
MS-63 Choice Uncirculated—Some distracting contact marks or blemishes in prime focal areas. Impaired luster possible.

1808, 8 Over 7 **1808, Normal Date** **1809, 9 Over 8**

	Mintage	F-12	VF-20	EF-40	AU-50	AU-55	MS-60	MS-63
1807	51,605	$3,000	$4,000	$5,000	$8,000	$9,000	$13,500	$26,500
1808, All kinds	55,578							
1808, 8 Over 7		3,250	5,000	6,500	9,000	11,500	18,500	35,000
1808		3,000	4,000	5,000	8,000	9,000	13,500	28,500
1809, 9 Over 8	33,875	3,000	4,000	5,000	8,000	9,000	13,500	28,500

Small Date **Large Date** **Large 5** **Tall 5**

	Mintage	F-12	VF-20	EF-40	AU-50	AU-55	MS-60	MS-63
1810, All kinds	100,287							
1810, Small Date, Small 5		$20,000	$35,000	$55,000	$90,000	$110,000		
1810, Small Date, Tall 5		3,000	4,000	5,000	8,000	9,000	$14,000	$28,500
1810, Large Date, Small 5		30,000	45,000	75,000	90,000	110,000	175,000	
1810, Large Date, Large 5		3,000	4,000	5,000	8,000	9,000	13,500	28,500

Chart continued on next page.

	Mintage	F-12	VF-20	EF-40	AU-50	AU-55	MS-60	MS-63
1811, All kinds 99,581								
1811, Small 5.		$3,000	$4,000	$5,000	$8,000	$9,000	$13,500	$28,500
1811, Tall 5		3,000	4,000	5,000	8,000	9,000	13,500	28,500
1812. 58,087		3,000	4,000	5,000	8,000	9,000	13,500	28,500

CAPPED HEAD TO LEFT (1813–1834)
Bold Relief (1813–1815), Large Diameter (1813–1829)

	Mintage	F-12	VF-20	EF-40	AU-50	AU-55	MS-60	MS-63
1813. 95,428		$4,750	$5,750	$7,000	$9,500	$10,500	$13,000	$23,500
1814, 4 Over 3 15,454		5,000	6,500	7,750	10,000	12,000	16,500	35,000
1815 *(11 known)* 635				175,000	250,000	300,000	450,000	750,000
$460,000, MS-64, Heritage auction, January 2009								
1818, All kinds 48,588								
1818		5,000	6,000	7,500	15,500	18,500	25,000	45,000
1818, STATESOF one word.		5,000	6,000	7,500	10,500	13,000	21,500	47,500
1818, 5D Over 50.		5,000	6,500	8,000	11,000	15,000	30,000	75,000
1819, All kinds 51,723								
1819				50,000	70,000	90,000	130,000	
1819, 5D Over 50.				45,000	65,000	85,000	125,000	200,000

Curved-Base 2	Square-Base 2	Small Letters	Large Letters

	Mintage	F-12	VF-20	EF-40	AU-50	AU-55	MS-60	MS-63
1820, All kinds 263,806								
1820, Curved-Base 2, Sm Ltrs		$5,250	$7,000	$11,000	$13,250	$15,500	$22,500	$42,500
1820, Curved-Base 2, Lg Ltrs.		5,000	6,750	8,500	10,500	12,500	18,000	37,500
1820, Square-Base 2		5,000	6,750	8,000	10,000	11,500	20,000	40,000
1821. 34,641		18,000	32,500	55,000	85,000	110,000	200,000	275,000
1822 *(3 known)* 17,796				7,500,000				
$687,500, VF-30/EF-40, B&R auction, October 1982								
1823. 14,485		5,500	10,000	15,000	17,500	22,500	30,000	65,000
1824. 17,340		10,000	22,500	30,000	40,000	60,000	85,000	125,000

1825, 5 Over Partial 4	1825, 5 Over 4

	Mintage	F-12	VF-20	EF-40	AU-50	AU-55	MS-60	MS-63
1825, 5 Over Partial 4 29,060		$10,000	$17,500	$27,500	$37,500	$47,500	$67,500	$100,000
1825, 5 Over 4 *(2 known)*. . . . . *				450,000	675,000			
$690,000 AU-50, Heritage auction, July 2008								
1826. 18,069		7,500	15,000	20,000	27,500	37,500	50,000	80,000
1827. 24,913		15,000	20,000	30,000	40,000	50,000	65,000	100,000
$322,000, MS-66, Stack's Bowers auction, January 2008								

* Included in number above.

Large Date

	Mintage	VF-20	EF-40	AU-50	AU-55	MS-60	MS-63
1828, 8 Over 7 *(5 known)* . . . .*		$65,000	$85,000	$100,000	$150,000	$250,000	$500,000
$632,500, MS-64, Heritage auction, January 2012							
1828 28,029		45,000	60,000	75,000	100,000	175,000	300,000
$402,500, MS-64, Heritage auction, January 2012							
1829, Large Date 57,442		—	—			200,000	400,000
$1,380,000, PF-64, Heritage auction, January 2012							

* Included in number below.

Reduced Diameter (1829–1834)

The half eagles dated 1829 (small date) through 1834 are smaller in diameter than the earlier pieces. They also have smaller letters, dates, and stars.

Design modified by William Kneass; standards same as before; diameter 23.8 mm.

1829, Small Date   **1830, Large 5D**   **1830, Small 5D**   **1832, 13 Stars, Square-Base 2**

	Mintage	F-12	VF-20	EF-40	AU-50	AU-55	MS-60	MS-63
1829, Small Date . . . . *			$75,000	$115,000	$165,000	$225,000	$300,000	$450,000
$431,250, MS-61, Heritage auction, January 2012								
1830, Small or Large 5D 126,351	$17,500	27,500	38,500	45,000	52,500	75,000	100,000	
1831, Small or Large 5D 140,594	17,500	27,500	38,500	45,000	52,500	75,000	100,000	
1832, Curved-Base 2,								
12 Stars *(5 known)* . . . .**		200,000	350,000	450,000				
1832, Square-Base 2, 13 Stars . .157,487	17,500	25,000	38,500	45,000	55,000	70,000	100,000	
1833, Large Date 193,630	17,500	25,000	38,500	45,000	52,500	67,500	100,000	
$977,500, PF-67, Heritage auction, January 2005								
1833, Small Date . . . .***	17,500	25,000	38,500	45,000	52,500	70,000	115,000	

* Included in "1829, Large Date" mintage. ** Included in number below. *** Included in number above.

Plain 4   **Crosslet 4**

	Mintage	F-12	VF-20	EF-40	AU-50	AU-55	MS-60	MS-63
1834, All kinds 50,141								
1834, Plain 4	$17,500	$25,000	$38,500	$45,000	$55,000	$70,000	$100,000	
1834, Crosslet 4	21,500	30,000	40,000	47,500	57,000	85,000	125,000	

CLASSIC HEAD (1834–1838)

As on the quarter eagle of 1834, the motto E PLURIBUS UNUM was omitted from the new, reduced-size half eagle in 1834, to distinguish the old coins that had become worth more than face value.

Designer William Kneass; weight 8.36 grams; composition (1834–1836) .8992 gold, .1008 silver and copper, (1837–1838) .900 gold, .100 copper; diameter 22.5 mm; reeded edge; mints: Philadelphia, Charlotte, Dahlonega.

Mintmark is above date (see page 239).

	Mintage	VF-20	EF-40	AU-50	AU-55	MS-60	MS-63
1834, Plain 4 **(a)** 657,460		$675	$900	$1,450	$1,700	$4,500	$10,500
1834, Crosslet 4. . . . .*		2,250	4,000	6,000	9,500	23,500	65,000
1835 **(a)**. 371,534		675	900	1,400	1,650	4,500	11,000
$690,000, PF-67, Heritage auction, January 2005							
1836. 553,147		675	900	1,400	1,650	4,500	11,000
1837 **(a)**. 207,121		675	975	1,550	1,900	4,750	17,500
1838. 286,588		700	975	1,500	1,850	4,500	13,500
1838C. 17,179		3,250	6,750	12,500	17,500	42,500	100,000
1838D. 20,583		3,750	6,500	11,500	15,000	35,000	75,000

* Included in number above. **a.** Varieties have either script 8 or block-style 8 in date.

LIBERTY HEAD (1839–1908)
Variety 1 – No Motto Above Eagle (1839–1866)

Designer Christian Gobrecht; weight 8.359 grams; composition .900 gold, .100 copper (net weight .24187 oz. pure gold); diameter (1839–1840) 22.5 mm, (1840–1866) 21.6 mm; reeded edge; mints: Philadelphia, Charlotte, Dahlonega, New Orleans, San Francisco.

VF-20 Very Fine—LIBERTY on coronet bold. Major lines show in curls on neck.

EF-40 Extremely Fine—Details clear in curls on neck. Slight wear on top and lower part of coronet and on hair.

AU-50 About Uncirculated—Trace of wear on coronet and hair above eye.

AU-55 Choice About Uncirculated—Evidence of friction on design high points. Some original mint luster.

MS-60 Uncirculated—No trace of wear. Light blemishes.

MS-63 Choice Uncirculated—Some distracting contact marks or blemishes in prime focal areas. Impaired luster possible.

PF-63 Choice Proof—Attractive reflective surfaces with only a few blemishes in secondary focal places. No major flaws.

Mintmark: 1839, above date;
1840–1908, below eagle.

	Mintage	VF-20	EF-40	AU-50	AU-55	MS-60	MS-63
1839	118,143	$550	$600	$1,100	$1,300	$3,600	$23,500
1839C	17,205	2,250	3,500	6,000	8,750	20,000	57,500
1839D	18,939	2,500	4,000	7,000	9,750	23,500	
1840 **(a)**	137,382	550	625	1,100	1,600	3,250	10,000
1840C	18,992	2,250	3,250	6,500	7,250	20,000	55,000
1840D	22,896	2,250	3,250	6,250	7,500	14,250	42,500
1840O **(a)**	40,120	600	900	1,600	2,500	9,000	32,500
1841	15,833	550	700	1,250	1,800	4,000	10,250
1841C	21,467	1,750	2,500	3,500	6,500	13,500	40,000
1841D	29,392	2,000	2,500	4,000	6,500	12,500	25,000
1841O *(not known to exist)*	50						

a. Scarce varieties of these 1840 coins have the fine edge-reeding and wide rims of the 1839 issues. These are known as "broad mill."

1842, Large Date	Small Letters	Large Letters	1847, Extra 7 at Border

	Mintage	VF-20	EF-40	AU-50	AU-55	MS-60	MS-63	PF-63
1842, All kinds	27,578							
1842, Small Letters		$550	$1,000	$3,000	$4,000	$11,000		
1842, Large Letters		725	1,600	4,250	6,500	12,500		
1842C, All kinds	27,432							
1842C, Small Letters		7,500	16,500	26,500	32,500	70,000		
1842C, Large Date		1,900	2,500	3,500	4,750	15,000	$30,000	
1842D, All kinds	59,608							
1842D, Small Date		2,000	2,750	3,750	5,000	10,500	30,000	
1842D, Large Date		3,000	5,500	11,500	16,500	37,500		
1842O	16,400	1,000	3,000	8,500	12,500	20,000		
1843	611,205	550	575	600	625	1,650	9,500	
1843C	44,277	1,900	2,500	4,250	6,000	9,500	26,000	
1843D	98,452	1,925	2,650	3,500	4,500	10,000	21,000	
1843O, Small Letters	19,075	800	1,650	2,500	4,000	17,500	35,000	
1843O, Large Letters	82,000	600	1,250	2,000	3,500	9,500	25,000	
1844	340,330	550	575	600	625	1,950	7,500	
1844C	23,631	2,000	3,000	4,500	6,000	13,000	30,000	
1844D	88,982	2,000	2,750	3,750	4,750	9,000	26,000	
1844O	364,600	575	600	875	1,350	4,000	12,500	
1845	417,099	550	575	600	625	2,000	8,500	
1845D	90,629	1,900	2,500	3,500	4,500	10,000	22,500	
1845O	41,000	700	1,000	2,500	4,500	9,750	22,500	
1846, All kinds	395,942							
1846, Large Date		550	575	700	1,300	3,250		
1846, Small Date		550	575	600	750	2,650		
1846C	12,995	1,900	2,750	4,750	7,500	14,500	50,000	
1846D, All kinds	80,294							
1846D		2,000	2,750	3,750	4,750	12,000		
1846D, High 2nd D Over Mmk		2,000	2,750	4,000	5,250	12,500	23,500	
1846O	58,000	675	1,000	2,900	4,500	10,500	25,000	

Chart continued on next page.

	Mintage	VF-20	EF-40	AU-50	AU-55	MS-60	MS-63	PF-63
1847, All kinds	.915,981							
1847		$550	$575	$600	$625	$1,650	$6,500	
1847, Top of Extra 7 Very Low at Border.		575	600	700	1,100	2,150	8,500	
1847C.	.84,151	1,900	2,350	3,500	4,500	9,500	27,500	
1847D	.64,405	2,000	2,600	3,500	4,500	8,750	16,000	
1847O	.12,000	2,350	5,250	10,000	13,500	27,000		
1848.	.260,775	550	575	600	675	1,750	9,000	
1848C.	.64,472	1,900	2,350	3,500	6,750	15,000	42,500	
1848D	.47,465	2,000	2,600	3,500	6,000	10,500	25,000	
1849.	.133,070	550	575	700	1,000	2,750		
1849C.	.64,823	1,900	2,500	3,250	4,500	10,000	23,500	
1849D	.39,036	2,000	2,600	3,250	4,500	10,000	28,500	
1850.	.64,491	550	575	1,000	1,350	3,000	12,500	
1850C.	.63,591	1,900	2,350	3,250	4,000	9,500	17,000	
1850D	.43,984	2,000	2,600	3,450	5,250	21,000		
1851.	.377,505	550	575	600	625	2,750	9,000	
1851C.	.49,176	1,900	2,350	3,250	4,250	11,500	42,500	
1851D	.62,710	2,000	2,500	3,750	5,500	12,000	26,000	
1851O	.41,000	775	1,400	3,250	5,500	9,500	20,500	
1852.	.573,901	550	575	600	625	1,650	8,000	
1852C.	.72,574	1,900	2,500	3,250	4,250	6,000	18,500	
1852D	.91,584	2,000	2,600	3,500	5,000	9,500	21,000	
1853.	.305,770	550	575	600	625	1,700	7,750	
1853C.	.65,571	1,900	2,400	3,250	4,250	7,000	22,500	
1853D	.89,678	2,000	2,600	3,250	4,500	6,500	16,500	
1854.	.160,675	550	575	600	950	2,000	8,250	
1854C.	.39,283	1,900	2,400	3,750	5,000	9,500	28,500	
1854D	.56,413	2,000	2,600	3,500	4,500	9,750	23,500	
1854O	.46,000	600	750	1,450	2,250	6,750	22,500	
1854S (3 known)	268			—	4,000,000	—		
1855.	.117,098	550	575	600	675	1,750	7,500	—
1855C.	.39,788	1,900	2,400	3,500	4,500	12,500	36,000	
1855D	.22,432	2,000	2,600	3,600	5,000	15,000	38,000	
1855O	.11,100	1,000	1,900	4,000	6,000	17,000		
1855S.	.61,000	600	1,300	2,500	4,500	12,500		
1856.	.197,990	550	575	600	625	2,000	10,500	—
1856C.	.28,457	1,900	2,400	3,750	6,000	15,000	45,000	
1856D	.19,786	2,000	2,600	3,750	5,500	9,500	30,000	
1856O	.10,000	1,000	1,850	4,250	6,000	12,500		
1856S.	.105,100	550	700	1,250	2,000	6,000	23,500	—
1857.	.98,188	550	575	600	625	1,800	8,000	
1857C.	.31,360	1,900	2,400	3,500	4,750	7,500	26,000	
1857D	.17,046	2,000	2,600	3,750	5,000	10,000	28,500	
1857O	.13,000	1,000	1,700	3,750	5,500	12,000	42,500	
1857S.	.87,000	600	800	1,500	2,500	10,500	20,000	
1858.	.15,136	550	575	750	1,350	3,000	10,500	—
1858C.	.38,856	1,900	2,400	3,750	4,500	10,000	28,500	
1858D	.15,362	2,000	2,700	3,850	5,250	11,000	32,500	
1858S.	.18,600	1,000	2,600	5,750	9,500	25,000		
1859. . . . . (80)	.16,734	550	575	775	1,350	5,500	11,500	$45,000
1859C.	.31,847	1,900	2,450	3,500	5,250	11,750	32,500	

	Mintage	VF-20	EF-40	AU-50	AU-55	MS-60	MS-63	PF-63
1859D 10,366		$2,000	$2,600	$3,750	$5,500	$12,500	$34,500	
1859S. 13,220		1,500	3,250	4,750	8,500	23,500		
1860. . . . .(62). . .19,763		550	575	975	1,350	3,250	13,500	$37,500
1860C. 14,813		2,000	2,750	4,000	7,000	11,000	27,500	
1860D 14,635		2,200	3,250	4,250	7,250	13,500	40,000	
1860S. 21,200		1,100	2,150	4,750	7,750	21,500		
1861. . . . .(66). . . .688,084		550	575	600	625	1,750	7,500	35,000
1861C. 6,879		3,750	6,000	11,000	16,000	30,000	100,000	
1861D 1,597		15,000	20,000	35,000	42,500	75,000	175,000	
1861S. 18,000		1,100	3,500	6,000	9,250			
1862. . . . .(35). . . .4,430		825	1,650	2,750	3,750	15,000		35,000
1862S. 9,500		2,500	4,500	12,500	20,000	40,000		
1863. . . . .(30). 2,442		1,250	3,500	7,000	10,000	22,500		35,000
1863S. 17,000		1,400	3,750	9,500	13,500	28,500		
1864. . . . .(50). . . .4,170		850	1,750	2,750	6,000	10,500		35,000
1864S. 3,888		6,000	12,000	35,000				
1865. . . . .(25). . . .1,270		1,500	3,500	9,500	12,500	18,500		35,000
1865S. 27,612		1,500	2,500	4,500	7,500	17,500		
1866S, No Motto 9,000		1,700	3,500	10,000	15,000	30,000		

Variety 2 – Motto Above Eagle (1866–1908)

Designer Christian Gobrecht; weight 8.359 grams; composition .900 gold, .100 copper (net weight .24187 oz. pure gold); diameter 21.6 mm; reeded edge; mints: Philadelphia, Carson City, Denver, New Orleans, San Francisco.

VF-20 Very Fine—Half of hair lines above coronet missing. Hair curls under ear evident, but worn. Motto and its ribbon sharp.

EF-40 Extremely Fine—Small amount of wear on top of hair and below L in LIBERTY. Wear evident on wing tips and neck of eagle.

AU-50 About Uncirculated—Trace of wear on tip of coronet and hair above eye.

AU-55 Choice About Uncirculated—Evidence of friction on design high points. Some original mint luster present.

MS-60 Uncirculated—No trace of wear. Light blemishes.

MS-63 Choice Uncirculated—Some distracting contact marks or blemishes in prime focal areas. Impaired luster possible.

PF-63 Choice Proof—Reflective surfaces with only a few blemishes in secondary focal places. No major flaws.

Circulation strike.   *Proof strike.*

	Mintage	VF-20	EF-40	AU-50	AU-55	MS-60	MS-63	PF-63
1866. . . . . (30) 6,700		$750	$1,300	$2,750	$4,500	$13,000		$25,000
1866S. 34,920		925	2,500	7,000	10,000			
1867. . . . . (50) 6,870		600	1,250	3,000	4,000	9,500		25,000
1867S. 29,000		1,100	2,500	8,500	13,000			
1868. . . . . (25) 5,700		600	1,250	2,750	4,750	10,000		25,000
1868S. 52,000		525	1,250	2,750	4,250	15,000		
1869. . . . . (25) 1,760		800	1,800	3,500	4,500	12,500		25,000
1869S. 31,000		575	1,500	3,000	7,000	20,000		

Chart continued on next page.

	Mintage	VF-20	EF-40	AU-50	AU-55	MS-60	MS-63	PF-63
1870. . . . . (35) 4,000		$700	$1,500	$2,750	$4,750	$13,500		$25,000
1870CC 7,675		15,000	25,000	37,500	47,500	115,000		
1870S. 17,000		850	1,850	6,500	9,500	22,500		
1871. . . . . (30) 3,200		750	1,250	2,750	4,500	10,000		25,000
1871CC 20,770		3,000	6,500	15,000	22,500	65,000	$80,000	
1871S. 25,000		525	950	3,250	6,000	11,500		
1872. . . . . (30) 1,660		725	1,350	2,500	4,250	10,500	17,500	22,500
1872CC 16,980		2,250	6,750	13,500	25,000			
1872S. 36,400		575	800	2,500	6,500	12,000		
1873, Close 3 . . . . (25) 112,480		525	535	545	600	1,100	6,500	22,500
1873, Open 3 112,505		525	535	545	565	800	4,000	
1873CC 7,416		4,500	11,500	22,500	30,000	65,000		
1873S. 31,000		600	1,100	2,750	4,500	18,500		
1874. . . . . (20) 3,488		550	1,200	2,250	3,500	10,000	22,500	27,500
1874CC 21,198		1,850	2,750	10,000	14,000	35,000		
1874S. 16,000		800	1,500	4,000	6,000			
1875. . . . . (20) 200		55,000	75,000	105,000	140,000			125,000
1875CC 11,828		2,250	4,500	11,500	20,000	45,000		
1875S. 9,000		775	2,000	5,750	8,000	18,500		
1876. . . . . (45) 1,432		950	2,000	3,750	5,500	10,500	18,500	20,000
1876CC 6,887		2,000	4,750	13,500	20,000	40,000		
$477,250, MS-66, Stack's Bowers auction, August 2012								
1876S. 4,000		1,150	2,850	6,500	8,500			
1877. . . . . (20) 1,132		925	1,800	3,250	4,500	12,500		22,500
1877CC 8,680		1,500	3,750	11,500	15,000	45,000		
1877S. 26,700		525	575	1,500	3,750	6,750		
1878. . . . . (20) 131,720		525	535	545	555	600	2,150	22,500
1878CC 9,054		4,500	10,000	17,500	27,500			
1878S. 144,700		525	535	545	555	900	4,000	
1879. . . . . (30) 301,920		525	535	545	555	600	2,000	21,500
1879CC 17,281		1,100	2,000	3,750	6,000	20,000		
1879S. 426,200		525	535	545	555	900	3,000	
1880. . . . . (36) . . 3,166,400		525	535	545	555	600	850	17,500
1880CC 51,017		850	1,150	1,850	4,500	12,500		
1880S. 1,348,900		525	535	545	555	600	850	
1881, Final 1 Over 0. . . . . *		550	700	850	1,000	1,350	5,000	
1881. . . . . (42) . . 5,708,802		525	535	545	555	600	850	16,500
1881CC 13,886		1,000	2,250	6,500	10,000	22,500	55,000	
1881S. 969,000		525	535	545	555	600	850	
1882. . . . . (48) . . 2,514,520		525	535	545	555	600	850	15,500
1882CC 82,817		750	950	1,250	2,500	10,000		
1882S. 969,000		525	535	545	555	600	850	
1883. . . . . (61) 233,400		525	535	545	555	600	1,650	15,500
1883CC 12,598		800	1,450	3,000	6,000	18,500		
1883S. 83,200		525	535	545	555	825	3,250	
1884. . . . . (48) 191,030		525	535	545	555	800	3,000	15,500
1884CC 16,402		800	1,250	3,250	6,000	20,000		
1884S. 177,000		525	535	545	565	600	1,800	
1885. . . . . (66) 601,440		525	535	545	555	600	950	15,500
1885S. 1,211,500		525	535	545	555	600	850	
1886. . . . . (72) 388,360		525	535	545	555	600	850	15,500

* Included in number below.

HALF EAGLES

	Mintage	VF-20	EF-40	AU-50	AU-55	MS-60	MS-63	PF-63
1886S..................3,268,000		$525	$535	$545	$555	$600	$850	
1887, Proof only.......(87)...........								$65,000
1887S..................1,912,000		525	535	545	555	600	850	
1888............(95)....18,201		525	535	545	555	600	2,250	13,500
1888S...................293,900		525	535	545	675	1,000	4,250	
1889............(45)....7,520		525	535	545	650	975	2,800	14,000
1890............(88)....4,240		525	535	545	900	1,750	7,250	14,500
1890CC...................53,800		750	850	950	1,000	1,650	10,000	
1891............(53)....61,360		525	535	545	555	600	1,750	13,500
1891CC...................208,000		750	850	950	1,100	2,500	4,500	
1892............(92)....753,480		525	535	545	555	600	850	13,500
1892CC...................82,968		750	850	900	1,100	2,200	7,500	
1892O...................10,000		600	875	1,100	1,500	2,750	11,000	
1892S...................298,400		525	535	545	555	600	2,850	
1893............(77)...1,528,120		525	535	545	555	600	850	13,500
1893CC...................60,000		750	850	1,150	1,350	2,250	8,500	
1893O...................110,000		525	535	600	650	1,250	6,000	
1893S...................224,000		525	535	545	555	600	850	
1894............(75)....957,880		525	535	545	555	600	850	13,500
1894O...................16,600		525	535	600	750	1,400	6,500	
1894S...................55,900		525	535	545	800	2,500	7,500	
1895............(81)...1,345,855		525	535	545	555	600	850	12,500
1895S...................112,000		525	535	575	800	2,250	5,500	
1896............(103)....58,960		525	535	545	555	600	850	12,500
1896S...................155,400		525	535	545	555	1,200	5,250	
1897............(83)....867,800		525	535	545	555	600	1,100	12,500
1897S...................354,000		525	535	545	555	800	4,250	
1898............(75)....633,420		525	535	545	555	600	850	12,500
1898S..................1,397,400		525	535	545	555	600	850	
1899............(99)...1,710,630		525	535	545	555	600	850	12,500
1899S..................1,545,000		525	535	545	555	600	850	
1900............(230)...1,405,500		525	535	545	555	600	850	12,500
1900S...................329,000		525	535	545	555	600	1,250	
1901............(140)....615,900		525	535	545	555	600	850	12,500
1901S, All kinds...........3,648,000								
1901S, Final 1/0.................		550	600	650	700	800	1,500	
1901S......................		525	535	545	555	600	850	
1902............(162)....172,400		525	535	545	555	600	850	12,500
1902S...................939,000		525	535	545	555	600	850	
1903............(154)....226,870		525	535	545	555	600	850	12,500
1903S..................1,855,000		525	535	545	555	600	850	
1904............(136)....392,000		525	535	545	555	600	850	12,500
1904S...................97,000		525	535	545	555	1,000	3,000	
1905............(108)....302,200		525	535	545	555	600	850	12,500
1905S...................880,700		525	535	550	575	650	1,800	
1906............(85)....348,735		525	535	545	555	600	850	12,500
1906D...................320,000		525	535	545	555	600	850	
1906S...................598,000		525	535	545	575	650	1,250	
1907............(92)....626,100		525	535	545	555	600	850	12,500
1907D...................888,000		525	535	545	555	600	850	
1908...................421,874		525	535	545	555	600	850	

263

INDIAN HEAD (1908–1929)

This type conforms to the quarter eagle of the same date. The sunken-relief designs and lettering make these two series unique in United States coinage.

Designer Bela Lyon Pratt; weight 8.359 grams; composition .900 gold, .100 copper (net weight .24187 oz. pure gold); diameter 21.6 mm; reeded edge; mints: Philadelphia, Denver, New Orleans, San Francisco.

VF-20 Very Fine—Noticeable wear on large middle feathers and tip of eagle's wing.

EF-40 Extremely Fine—Cheekbone, war bonnet, and headband feathers slightly worn. Feathers on eagle's upper wing show considerable wear.

AU-50 About Uncirculated—Trace of wear on cheekbone and headdress.

AU-55 Choice About Uncirculated—Evidence of friction on design high points. Much of original mint luster present.

MS-60 Uncirculated—No trace of wear. Light blemishes.

MS-63 Choice Uncirculated—Some distracting contact marks or blemishes in prime focal areas. Impaired luster possible.

Mintmark Location

Scarcer coins with well-struck mintmarks command higher prices.

	Mintage	VF-20	EF-40	AU-50	AU-55	MS-60	MS-63	MATTE PF-63
1908 . . . . (167) 577,845		$525	$550	$575	$585	$700	$1,650	$13,000
1908D 148,000		525	550	575	585	800	2,000	
1908S 82,000		600	750	1,000	1,250	1,750	7,500	
1909 . . . . (78) 627,060		525	550	575	585	700	1,700	14,000
1909D 3,423,560		525	550	575	585	700	1,650	
19090 (a) 34,200		4,000	5,000	8,000	12,500	30,000	75,000	
$690,000, MS-66, Heritage auction, January 2011								
1909S 297,200		550	575	600	625	1,500	11,500	
1910 . . . . (250) 604,000		525	550	575	585	700	1,700	13,000
1910D 193,600		525	550	575	585	700	3,750	
1910S 770,200		550	575	600	700	1,750	9,500	
1911 . . . . (139) 915,000		525	550	575	585	700	1,700	13,000
1911D 72,500		750	1,000	1,250	2,000	8,000	45,000	
$299,000, MS-65+, Heritage auction, January 2011								
1911S 1,416,000		550	575	600	650	850	5,750	
1912 . . . . (144) 790,000		525	550	575	585	700	1,700	13,000
1912S 392,000		550	575	600	700	2,500	14,500	
1913 . . . . (99) 915,901		525	550	575	585	700	1,700	13,000
1913S 408,000		550	575	675	825	2,000	14,500	
1914 . . . . (125) 247,000		525	550	575	585	700	2,000	13,000
1914D 247,000		525	550	575	585	700	2,250	
1914S 263,000		550	575	600	650	1,750	14,500	
1915 (b) . . . . (75) 588,000		525	550	575	585	700	1,800	15,000
1915S 164,000		550	575	650	750	2,500	17,000	
1916S 240,000		550	575	625	650	850	6,500	
1929 662,000		15,000	16,500	18,500	21,500	28,500	45,000	

a. Beware spurious "O" mintmark. **b.** Pieces dated 1915-D are counterfeit.

Coinage authority, including weights and fineness, of the eagle is specified by the Act of April 2, 1792. The Small Eagle reverse was used until 1797, when the large Heraldic Eagle replaced it. The early dates vary in the number of stars, the rarest date being 1798. Many of these early pieces show file scratches from the Mint's practice of adjusting planchet weight before coining. No eagles were struck dated 1805 to 1837. Proofs of some dates prior to 1855 are known to exist, and all are rare.

Note: Values of common gold coins have been based on the current bullion price of gold, $1,900 per ounce, and may vary with the prevailing spot price. The net weight and content listed may be used to recalculate bullion value.

CAPPED BUST TO RIGHT (1795–1804)
Small Eagle (1795–1797)

Designer Robert Scot; weight 17.50 grams; composition .9167 gold, .0833 silver and copper; approx. diameter 33 mm; reeded edge.

F-12 Fine—Details on turban and head obliterated.

VF-20 Very Fine—Hair lines in curls on neck and details under turban and over forehead worn but distinguishable.

EF-40 Extremely Fine—Definite wear on hair to left of eye and strand of hair across and around turban, as well as on eagle's wing tips.

AU-50 About Uncirculated—Trace of wear on cap, hair, cheek, and drapery.

AU-55 Choice About Uncirculated—Evidence of friction on design high points. Most of original mint luster present.

MS-60 Uncirculated—No trace of wear. Light blemishes.

MS-63 Choice Uncirculated—Some distracting contact marks or blemishes in prime focal areas. Impaired luster possible.

| | | 13 Leaves | | | 9 Leaves | |

	Mintage	F-12	VF-20	EF-40	AU-50	AU-55	MS-60	MS-63
1795, 13 Leaves Below Eagle	5,583	$27,500	$35,000	$42,500	$50,000	$67,500	$95,000	$250,000
$546,250, MS-64, Stack's Bowers auction, July 2008								
1795, 9 Leaves Below Eagle	*	40,000	55,000	77,500	115,000	137,500	220,000	500,000
1796	4,146	32,500	42,500	50,000	60,000	72,500	100,000	300,000
1797, Small Eagle	3,615	37,500	52,500	65,000	105,000	125,000	215,000	
$448,500, MS-63, Goldberg auction, May 2007								

* Included in number above.

Heraldic Eagle (1797–1804)

1803, Small Reverse Stars

	Mintage	F-12	VF-20	EF-40	AU-50	AU-55	MS-60	MS-63
1797, Large Eagle 10,940		$12,500	$15,000	$20,000	$27,500	$37,500	$52,500	$125,000
1798, 8 Over 7, 9 Stars Left, 4 Right 900		22,500	30,000	39,500	55,000	80,000	125,000	300,000
1798, 8 Over 7, 7 Stars Left, 6 Right 842		40,000	55,000	87,500	165,000	195,000	275,000	
1799, Small Obverse Stars 37,449		8,750	11,000	15,750	20,000	23,500	32,500	65,000
1799, Large Obverse Stars . . . . *		8,750	11,000	15,750	20,000	23,500	32,500	65,000
1800 5,999		9,000	12,000	16,000	21,500	23,500	35,000	85,000
1801 44,344		8,750	11,000	15,000	18,500	21,000	30,000	60,000
1803, Small Reverse Stars 15,017		9,500	12,000	16,000	21,500	23,500	36,000	62,500
1803, Large Reverse Stars **(a)** . . . . *		9,500	12,000	16,000	21,500	23,500	36,000	62,500
1804, Crosslet 4 3,757		19,000	25,000	37,500	52,500	65,000	85,000	155,000
1804, Plain 4, Proof, Restrike *(4 known)*. .								4,000,000

* Included in number above. **a.** Variety without tiny 14th star in cloud is very rare.

LIBERTY HEAD, NO MOTTO ABOVE EAGLE (1838–1866)

In 1838, the weight and diameter of the eagle were reduced and the obverse and reverse were redesigned. Liberty now faces left and the word LIBERTY is placed on the coronet. A more natural-appearing eagle is used on the reverse. The value, TEN D., is shown for the first time on this denomination.

Designer Christian Gobrecht; weight 16.718 grams; composition .900 gold, .100 copper (net weight: .48375 oz. pure gold); diameter 27 mm; reeded edge; mints: Philadelphia, New Orleans, San Francisco.

VF-20 Very Fine—Hair lines above coronet partly worn. Curls under ear worn but defined.
EF-40 Extremely Fine—Small amount of wear on top of hair and below L in LIBERTY. Wear evident on wing tips and neck of eagle.
AU-50 About Uncirculated—Trace of wear on tip of coronet and hair above eye.
AU-55 Choice About Uncirculated—Evidence of friction on design high points. Some of original mint luster present.
MS-60 Uncirculated—No trace of wear. Light blemishes.
MS-63 Choice Uncirculated—Some distracting contact marks or blemishes in prime focal areas. Impaired luster possible.
PF-63 Choice Proof—Attractive reflective surfaces with only a few blemishes in secondary focal places. No major flaws.

Mintmark is on reverse, below eagle.

1853, 3 Over 2

	Mintage	VF-20	EF-40	AU-50	AU-55	MS-60	MS-63
1838 (a)	7,200	$2,750	$6,000	$13,000	$18,000	$45,000	$115,000
$550,000, PF-63, Akers auction, May 1998							
1839, Large Letters (a)	25,801	1,600	3,750	6,500	10,500	35,000	80,000
1839, 9 Over 8, Type of 1838 *$1,610,000,*							
PF-67 UC, Heritage auction, January 2007							
1839, Small Letters	12,447	1,850	3,800	7,000	12,000	45,000	135,000
1840	47,338	1,050	1,100	1,550	2,750	10,000	
1841	63,131	1,050	1,100	1,350	2,500	8,500	
1841O	2,500	5,500	13,500	23,500	40,000		
1842, Small Date, Plain 4	18,623	1,050	1,100	1,800	3,000	13,000	25,000
1842, Large Date, Crosslet 4	62,884	1,050	1,100	1,650	2,750	12,000	22,500
1842O	27,400	1,150	1,250	2,750	7,000	25,000	50,000
1843	75,462	1,050	1,100	1,750	3,500	14,000	
1843O	175,162	1,100	1,200	1,750	3,250	12,500	
1844	6,361	1,350	2,500	4,750	7,500	14,000	37,500
1844O	118,700	1,100	1,200	1,850	3,500	15,000	
1845	26,153	1,050	1,100	1,800	2,750	13,500	
1845O	47,500	1,100	1,250	2,750	5,000	14,500	
1846	20,095	1,150	1,350	3,500	8,000	20,000	
1846O, All kinds	81,780						
1846O		1,100	1,200	4,200	6,000	13,500	
1846O, 6 Over 5		1,150	1,400	4,000	6,750	17,500	
1847	862,258	1,000	1,025	1,075	1,150	3,250	21,500
1847O	571,500	1,000	1,050	1,150	1,350	6,000	21,500
1848	145,484	1,000	1,025	1,075	1,150	4,750	22,500
1848O	35,850	1,100	1,300	3,200	6,750	15,000	27,500
1849	653,618	975	1,000	1,075	1,150	3,250	13,500
1849O	23,900	1,150	2,250	5,000	7,000	23,500	
1850, All kinds	291,451						
1850, Large Date		975	1,000	1,050	1,100	3,750	16,000
1850, Small Date		1,000	1,100	2,250	3,750	8,000	25,000
1850O	57,500	1,100	1,300	3,500	5,000	18,500	
1851	176,328	975	1,000	1,050	1,250	4,000	26,000
1851O	263,000	1,000	1,100	1,600	2,750	6,000	27,500
1852	263,106	975	1,000	1,050	1,200	5,000	
1852O	18,000	1,150	1,600	3,750	7,000	23,500	
1853, All kinds	201,253						
1853, 3 Over 2		1,150	1,500	1,750	3,250		
1853		975	1,000	1,050	1,150	3,250	17,000

a. The Liberty Head style of 1838 and 1839 (Large Letters) differs from that used for subsequent issues.

	Mintage	VF-20	EF-40	AU-50	AU-55	MS-60	MS-63	PF-63
1853O	51,000	$1,050	$1,150	$1,250	$2,500	$13,500		
1854	54,250	975	1,000	1,050	1,250	5,500	$21,500	
1854O, Large or Small Date	52,500	1,000	1,100	1,750	3,250	10,500		
1854S	123,826	1,000	1,050	1,350	1,850	9,500		
1855	121,701	975	1,000	1,050	1,100	4,500	17,500	
1855O	18,000	1,100	1,800	5,000	8,250	23,000		
1855S	9,000	1,400	2,250	5,500	8,750			
1856	60,490	975	1,000	1,050	1,100	4,000	13,500	
1856O	14,500	1,100	1,500	4,250	7,000	16,500		
1856S	68,000	975	1,000	1,400	2,500	9,000	25,000	

Chart continued on next page.

	Mintage	VF-20	EF-40	AU-50	AU-55	MS-60	MS-63	PF-63
1857. 16,606		$975	$1,000	$1,950	$3,750	$12,000		
$396,000, PF-66, Goldberg auction, May 1999								
18570 5,500		1,600	2,500	4,000	6,500	26,000		
1857S. 26,000		1,000	1,250	2,500	4,000	11,500	$23,500	
1858 **(b)**. 2,521		6,000	7,500	12,500	17,500	37,500		
18580 20,000		1,050	1,150	2,000	3,250	9,500	32,500	
1858S. 11,800		1,850	3,250	5,000	12,000			
1859. . . . .(80). 16,013		975	1,000	1,300	2,500	8,500	18,500	$75,000
18590 2,300		4,750	9,000	22,500	37,500			
1859S. 7,000		2,250	5,000	12,500	17,500			
1860. . . . .(50). 15,055		975	1,100	1,750	2,700	7,500	20,000	50,000
18600 11,100		1,050	1,450	2,500	5,000	13,500		
1860S. 5,000		3,000	5,500	13,000	25,000			
1861. . . . .(69). 113,164		975	1,050	1,100	1,250	5,750	13,500	45,000
1861S. 15,500		1,650	3,000	6,750	11,500	45,000		
1862. . . . .(35). 10,960		1,000	1,200	2,000	3,000	11,500		42,500
1862S. 12,500		1,750	3,000	5,000	9,000			
1863. . . . .(30). 1,218		4,250	8,500	15,000	22,500	42,500	75,000	42,500
1863S. 10,000		1,850	3,500	8,000	12,000	25,000		
1864. . . . .(50). 3,530		1,850	3,500	6,500	9,500	17,500		42,500
1864S. 2,500		8,000	18,000	32,500	37,500			
1865. . . . .(25). 3,980		2,250	4,000	7,500	8,500	35,000	60,000	42,500
1865S, All kinds 16,700								
1865S		6,500	10,000	14,500	25,000	55,000		
1865S, 865/Inverted 186		6,500	11,000	18,500	27,500			
1866S. 8,500		2,750	3,750	12,000	17,500	47,500		

b. Beware of fraudulently removed mintmark.

LIBERTY HEAD, MOTTO ABOVE EAGLE (1866–1907)

Designer Christian Gobrecht; weight 16.718 grams; composition .900 gold, .100 copper (net weight: .48375 oz. pure gold); diameter 27 mm; reeded edge; mints: Philadelphia, Carson City, Denver, New Orleans, San Francisco.

VF-20 Very Fine—Half of hair lines over coronet visible. Curls under ear worn but defined. IN GOD WE TRUST and its ribbon sharp.

EF-40 Extremely Fine—Small amount of wear on top of hair and below L in LIBERTY. Wear evident on wing tips and neck of eagle.

AU-50 About Uncirculated—Trace of wear on hair above eye and on coronet.

AU-55 Choice About Uncirculated—Evidence of friction on design high points. Some of original mint luster present.

Mintmark is on reverse, below eagle.

MS-60 Uncirculated—No trace of wear. Light blemishes.

MS-63 Choice Uncirculated—Some distracting contact marks or blemishes in prime focal areas. Impaired luster possible.

PF-63 Choice Proof—Reflective surfaces with only a few blemishes in secondary focal areas. No major flaws.

	Mintage	VF-20	EF-40	AU-50	AU-55	MS-60	MS-63	PF-63
1866. . . . .(30). 3,750		$1,050	$1,800	$4,250	$8,000	$23,500		$32,500
1866S. 11,500		1,500	3,250	7,250	10,000			
1867. . . . .(50). 3,090		1,500	2,500	4,500	7,500	27,000		32,500
1867S. 9,000		2,350	5,500	9,000	14,500			

	Mintage	VF-20	EF-40	AU-50	AU-55	MS-60	MS-63	PF-63
1868 . . . . (25) 10,630		$925	$950	$1,700	$2,750			$32,500
1868S 13,500		1,250	2,250	4,000	5,500			
1869 . . . . (25) 1,830		1,500	2,350	4,750	11,500	$30,000		32,500
1869S 6,430		1,500	2,350	4,750	11,500	30,000		
1870 . . . . (35) 3,990		975	1,250	2,500	6,000	17,500		32,500
1870CC 5,908		22,500	37,500	75,000	115,000			
1870S 8,000		1,200	2,250	5,500	11,000	27,500		
1871 . . . . (30) 1,790		1,400	2,400	3,750	7,500	20,000		32,500
1871CC 8,085		3,250	7,750	16,000	22,500	70,000		
1871S 16,500		1,200	1,850	5,000	9,500			
1872 . . . . (30) 1,620		2,150	3,250	9,000	12,000	16,000		32,500
1872CC 4,600		4,500	11,500	22,500	34,500			
1872S 17,300		925	1,050	1,650	4,250	17,500		
1873 . . . . (25) 800		4,500	9,000	15,000	18,500	40,000		37,500
1873CC 4,543		7,000	14,500	25,000	50,000			
1873S 12,000		1,000	2,250	4,250	7,000	20,000		
1874 . . . . (20) 53,140		925	950	975	985	1,800	$7,500	32,500
1874CC 16,767		1,750	3,000	7,500	13,000			
1874S 10,000		1,100	2,500	5,500	8,500			
1875 . . . . (20) 100		135,000	185,000	250,000	375,000			155,000
$345,000, AU-55+, Stack's Bowers auction, August 2011								
1875CC 7,715		5,500	8,500	15,000	30,000	70,000	125,000	
1876 . . . . (45) 687		3,000	7,000	15,000	20,000			30,000
1876CC 4,696		4,000	7,500	18,500	28,500			
1876S 5,000		1,250	1,750	4,500	8,000			
1877 . . . . (20) 797		2,500	5,000	8,000	10,000	22,500		32,500
1877CC 3,332		4,200	7,250	16,000	25,000			
1877S 17,000		925	975	2,000	4,250	25,000		
1878 . . . . (20) 73,780		925	950	975	985	1,050	6,000	27,500
1878CC 3,244		5,250	9,000	18,000	28,000			
1878S 26,100		925	975	1,750	3,000	12,500	27,500	
1879 . . . . (30) 384,740		925	950	975	985	1,050	3,750	25,000
1879CC 1,762		9,000	14,500	26,000	35,000			
1879O 1,500		3,000	6,000	12,500	16,500	50,000		
1879S 224,000		925	950	975	985	1,150	6,000	
1880 . . . . (36) . . . 1,644,840		925	950	975	985	1,050	3,250	22,500
1880CC 11,190		1,100	1,350	2,200	4,200	15,000		
1880O 9,200		1,000	1,150	2,000	2,750	8,500		
1880S 506,250		925	950	975	985	1,050	4,000	
1881 . . . . (40) . . . 3,877,220		925	950	975	985	1,050	1,500	22,500
1881CC 24,015		1,100	1,250	1,550	1,900	7,500		
1881O 8,350		1,000	1,050	1,650	2,350	8,000		
1881S 970,000		925	950	975	985	1,050	4,250	
1882 . . . . (40) . . . 2,324,440		925	950	975	985	1,050	1,500	20,000
1882CC 6,764		1,100	1,500	3,500	7,000	18,500		
1882O 10,820		950	1,050	1,500	2,250	6,500	23,500	
1882S 132,000		925	950	975	985	1,050	3,000	
1883 . . . . (40) 208,700		925	950	975	985	1,050	2,250	20,000
1883CC 12,000		1,100	1,450	2,500	5,000	16,500		
1883O 800		10,000	18,500	30,000	45,000	80,000		
1883S 38,000		925	950	975	985	1,150	9,000	
1884 . . . . (45) 76,860		925	950	975	985	1,050	3,500	20,000

Chart continued on next page.

	Mintage	VF-20	EF-40	AU-50	AU-55	MS-60	MS-63	PF-63
1884CC	.9,925	$1,100	$1,500	$2,750	$4,750	$12,500	$47,500	
1884S	.124,250	925	950	975	985	1,050	4,750	
1885	(65)....253,462	925	950	975	985	1,050	3,500	$20,000
1885S	.228,000	925	950	975	985	1,050	2,750	
1886	(60)....236,100	925	950	975	985	1,050	3,500	18,500
1886S	.826,000	925	950	975	985	1,050	1,750	
1887	(80).....53,600	925	950	975	985	1,050	5,000	18,500
1887S	.817,000	925	950	975	985	1,050	2,750	
1888	(75)....132,921	925	950	975	985	1,050	6,500	18,500
1888O	.21,335	925	950	1,000	1,050	1,200	5,000	
1888S	.648,700	925	950	975	985	1,050	2,250	
1889	(45).....4,440	925	950	975	1,250	2,500	8,500	18,000
1889S	.425,400	925	950	975	985	1,050	1,750	
1890	(63).....57,980	925	950	975	985	1,050	4,750	16,500
1890CC	.17,500	1,100	1,200	1,300	1,500	2,650	13,500	
1891	(48).....91,820	925	950	975	985	1,050	2,750	16,500
1891CC	.103,732	1,100	1,200	1,300	1,350	1,750	6,250	
1892	(72)....797,480	925	950	975	985	1,050	1,400	16,500
1892CC	.40,000	1,100	1,200	1,350	1,500	3,750	11,000	
1892O	.28,688	925	950	975	985	1,150	6,500	
1892S	.115,500	925	950	975	985	1,050	2,750	
1893	(55)...1,840,840	925	950	975	985	1,050	1,400	16,500
1893CC	.14,000	1,100	1,200	1,750	2,850	10,000		
1893O	.17,000	925	950	975	1,000	1,150	5,000	
1893S	.141,350	925	950	975	985	1,050	3,500	
1894	(43)...2,470,735	925	950	975	985	1,050	1,400	16,500
1894O	.107,500	925	950	975	985	1,200	4,500	
1894S	.25,000	925	950	975	1,100	3,250	14,000	
1895	(56)....567,770	925	950	975	985	1,050	1,400	16,000
1895O	.98,000	925	950	975	1,000	1,150	6,000	
1895S	.49,000	925	950	975	985	2,000	8,000	
1896	(78).....76,270	925	950	975	985	1,050	1,650	16,000
1896S	.123,750	925	950	975	985	2,150	8,500	
1897	(69)...1,000,090	925	950	975	985	1,050	1,400	16,000
1897O	.42,500	925	950	975	985	1,100	5,000	
1897S	.234,750	925	950	975	985	1,050	4,750	
1898	(67)....812,130	925	950	975	985	1,050	1,400	16,000
1898S	.473,600	925	950	975	985	1,050	3,500	
1899	(86)...1,262,219	925	950	975	985	1,050	1,400	15,000
1899O	.37,047	925	950	975	985	1,250	5,000	
1899S	.841,000	925	950	975	985	1,050	2,250	
1900	(120)....293,840	925	950	975	985	1,050	1,400	15,000
1900S	.81,000	925	950	975	985	1,050	5,750	
1901	(85)...1,718,740	925	950	975	985	1,050	1,400	15,000
1901O	.72,041	925	950	975	985	1,200	3,000	
1901S	.2,812,750	925	950	975	985	1,050	1,400	
1902	(113).....82,400	925	950	975	985	1,050	2,000	15,000
1902S	.469,500	925	950	975	985	1,050	1,400	
1903	(96)....125,830	925	950	975	985	1,050	1,400	15,000

	Mintage	VF-20	EF-40	AU-50	AU-55	MS-60	MS-63	PF-63
1903O .112,771		$925	$950	$975	$985	$1,200	$3,000	
1903S. 538,000		925	950	975	985	1,050	1,400	
1904. . . . .(108). 161,930		925	950	975	985	1,050	1,400	$15,000
1904O 108,950		925	950	975	985	1,200	3,000	
1905. . . . .(86). 200,992		925	950	975	985	1,060	1,400	15,000
1905S. 369,250		925	950	975	985	1,200	4,000	
1906. . . . .(77). 165,420		925	950	975	985	1,050	1,900	15,000
1906D 981,000		925	950	975	985	1,050	1,400	
1906O 86,895		925	950	975	985	1,050	4,000	
1906S. 457,000		925	950	975	985	1,050	4,000	
1907. . . . .(74). . . 1,203,899		925	950	975	985	1,050	1,400	15,000
1907D 1,030,000		925	950	975	985	1,050	1,400	
1907S. 210,500		925	950	975	985	1,075	4,750	

INDIAN HEAD (1907–1933)

Augustus Saint-Gaudens, considered by many the greatest of modern sculptors, introduced a new high standard of art in United States coins evidenced by his eagle and double eagle types of 1907. The obverse of the eagle shows the head of Liberty crowned with an Indian war bonnet while an impressively majestic eagle dominates the reverse side. A departure from older standards is found on the edge of the piece, where 46 raised stars (48 stars in 1912 and later) are arranged signifying the states of the Union, instead of there being a lettered or reeded edge.

The first of these coins struck had no motto IN GOD WE TRUST, unlike the later issues, starting in 1908. President Theodore Roosevelt personally objected to the use of the Deity's name on coins. The motto was restored to the coins by an act of Congress in 1908.

Designer Augustus Saint-Gaudens; weight 16.718 grams; composition .900 gold, .100 copper (net weight: .48375 oz. pure gold); diameter 27 mm; edge: (1907–1911) 46 raised stars (one specimen of the 1907 with periods variety with plain edge is known), (1912–1933) 48 raised stars; mints: Philadelphia, Denver, San Francisco.

VF-20 Very Fine—Bonnet feathers worn near band. Wear visible on high points of hair.

EF-40 Extremely Fine—Slight wear on cheekbone and headdress feathers. Slight wear visible on eagle's eye and left wing.

AU-50 About Uncirculated—Trace of wear on hair above eye and on forehead.

AU-55 Choice About Uncirculated—Evidence of friction on design high points. Much of original mint luster present.

MS-60 Uncirculated—No trace of wear. Light blemishes.

MS-63 Choice Uncirculated—Some distracting contact marks or blemishes in prime focal areas. Impaired luster possible.

Variety 1 – No Motto on Reverse (1907–1908)

Mintmark is above left tip of branch on 1908-D, No Motto, and at left of arrow points thereafter.

See next page for chart.

Gem Uncirculated (MS-65) coins are rare and worth substantial premiums.

	Mintage	VF-20	EF-40	AU-50	AU-55	MS-60	MS-63	PF-63
1907, Wire Rim, Periods	500		$22,500	$24,500	$26,000	$30,000	$47,500	
$230,000, MS-67, Stack's Bowers auction, January 2011								
1907, Rounded Rim, Periods Before and After •E•PLURIBUS•UNUM• (a)	50		55,000	60,000	65,000	75,000	115,000	
1907, No Periods	239,406	$975	1,000	1,050	1,075	1,150	3,500	
1908, No Motto	33,500	975	1,000	1,050	1,100	1,250	5,000	
1908D, No Motto	210,000	975	1,000	1,050	1,075	1,275	7,500	

a. 31,500 were minted; all but 50 were melted at the mint.

Variety 2 – Motto on Reverse (1908–1933)

Circulation strike.

Mintmark

Proof strike.

	Mintage	VF-20	EF-40	AU-50	AU-55	MS-60	MS-63	MATTE PF-63
1908 . . . . (116)	341,370	$950	$965	$975	$985	$1,100	$2,500	$16,500
1908D	836,500	950	965	975	985	1,150	7,750	
1908S	59,850	1,000	1,150	1,250	1,350	3,500	13,500	
1909 . . . . (74)	184,789	950	965	975	985	1,100	4,250	16,500
1909D	121,540	950	965	975	1,000	1,200	7,500	
1909S	292,350	950	965	975	985	1,250	8,000	
1910 . . . . (204)	318,500	950	965	975	985	1,100	1,550	16,500
1910D	2,356,640	950	965	975	985	1,100	1,500	
1910S	811,000	950	965	975	985	1,200	10,500	
1911 . . . . (95)	505,500	950	965	975	985	1,100	1,500	16,000
1911D	30,100	1,150	1,250	1,450	2,500	8,000	40,000	
1911S	51,000	950	965	1,000	1,050	1,750	12,500	
1912 . . . . (83)	405,000	950	965	975	985	1,100	1,500	16,000
1912S	300,000	950	965	975	985	1,250	10,000	
1913 . . . . (71)	442,000	950	965	975	985	1,100	1,500	16,000
1913S	66,000	1,000	1,100	1,150	2,000	8,500	37,500	
1914 . . . . (50)	151,000	950	965	975	985	1,100	2,500	16,500
1914D	343,500	950	965	975	985	1,100	2,400	
1914S	208,000	950	965	975	985	1,250	10,000	
1915 . . . . (75)	351,000	950	965	975	985	1,100	2,200	17,500
1915S	59,000	975	1,000	1,050	1,750	4,750	20,000	
1916S	138,500	975	985	1,000	1,025	1,250	8,000	
1920S	126,500	14,500	20,000	25,000	30,000	50,000	110,000	
$1,725,000, MS-67, Heritage auction, March 2007								
1926	1,014,000	950	965	975	985	1,100	1,500	
1930S	96,000	12,500	15,000	21,500	25,000	35,000	55,000	
1932	4,463,000	950	965	975	985	1,100	1,500	
1933 (a)	312,500					275,000	350,000	
$718,750, Gem Unc., Stack's Bowers auction, October 2004								

a. Nearly all were melted at the mint.

Note: Values of common gold coins have been based on the current bullion price of gold, $1,900 per ounce, and may vary with the prevailing spot price. The net weight and content listed may be used to recalculate bullion value.

LIBERTY HEAD (1849–1907)

This largest denomination of all regular United States issues was authorized to be coined by the Act of March 3, 1849. Its weight was 516 grains, .900 fine. The 1849 double eagle is a unique pattern and reposes in the Smithsonian. The 1861 reverse design by Anthony C. Paquet was withdrawn soon after being struck. Very few pieces are known.

Designer James B. Longacre; weight 33.436 grams; composition .900 gold, .100 copper (net weight: .96750 oz. pure gold); diameter 34 mm; reeded edge; mints: Philadelphia, Carson City, Denver, New Orleans, San Francisco.

VF-20 Very Fine—LIBERTY on crown bold; prongs on crown defined; lower half worn flat. Hair worn about ear.
EF-40 Extremely Fine—Trace of wear on rounded prongs of crown and down hair curls. Minor bagmarks.
AU-50 About Uncirculated—Trace of wear on hair over eye and on coronet.
AU-55 Choice About Uncirculated—Evidence of friction on design high points. Some of original mint luster present.
MS-60 Uncirculated—No trace of wear. Light blemishes.
MS-63 Choice Uncirculated—Some distracting contact marks or blemishes in prime focal areas. Impaired luster possible.
PF-63 Choice Proof—Reflective surfaces with only a few blemishes in secondary focal areas. No major flaws.

Without Motto on Reverse (1849–1866)

Mintmark is
below eagle.

1853, "3 Over 2"

	Mintage	VF-20	EF-40	AU-50	AU-55	MS-60	MS-63
1849 *(pattern)*.	1	*(Smithsonian collection)*					
1850.	1,170,261	$2,000	$3,000	$4,500	$7,000	$12,000	$50,000
18500	141,000	2,300	5,500	13,500	22,500	60,000	
1851.	2,087,155	1,900	2,250	2,500	2,750	6,000	22,500
18510	315,000	2,100	4,000	6,500	11,500	26,500	75,000
1852.	2,053,026	1,900	2,250	2,750	3,000	5,500	17,000
18520	190,000	2,350	4,000	5,750	11,500	30,000	65,000
1853, All kinds	1,261,326						
1853, "3 Over 2"		2,750	3,500	5,750	12,000	40,000	
1853		1,900	2,250	2,500	2,750	5,750	24,500
18530	71,000	2,500	3,950	8,500	13,000	37,500	
1854, All kinds	757,899						
1854, Small Date		1,900	2,250	2,500	3,000	8,500	30,000
1854, Large Date		2,250	3,000	6,500	12,500	27,500	
18540	3,250	140,000	265,000	485,000	500,000		

$603,750, AU-55, Heritage auction, October 2008

	Mintage	VF-20	EF-40	AU-50	AU-55	MS-60	MS-63	PF-63
1854S	141,468	$3,000	$4,000	$8,500	$13,000	$20,000	$28,500	
1855	364,666	1,900	2,350	2,850	3,750	11,000	60,000	
1855O	8,000	8,750	25,000	45,000	65,000	105,000		
1855S	879,675	1,900	2,400	2,750	4,000	8,000	19,000	
1856	329,878	1,900	2,250	2,600	3,500	10,000	28,500	
1856O	2,250	140,000	235,000	450,000	575,000			

$1,437,500, SP-63, Heritage
auction, May 2009

	Mintage	VF-20	EF-40	AU-50	AU-55	MS-60	MS-63	PF-63
1856S	1,189,750	1,900	2,250	2,650	3,500	6,500	14,500	
1857	439,375	1,900	2,250	2,500	2,750	4,750	27,500	
1857O	30,000	2,500	5,500	11,000	20,000	45,000	125,000	
1857S	970,500	1,950	2,250	2,650	3,000	6,000	9,500	

$138,000, MS-67, Heritage
auction, January 2012

	Mintage	VF-20	EF-40	AU-50	AU-55	MS-60	MS-63	PF-63
1858	211,714	1,900	2,250	2,650	3,750	8,500	37,500	
1858O	35,250	3,000	6,750	13,500	24,500	50,000		
1858S	846,710	2,000	2,500	3,000	4,000	11,000	45,000	
1859	(80)	43,597	1,900	4,000	7,500	13,500	32,000		$150,000
1859O	9,100	12,500	25,000	42,500	65,000	130,000		
1859S	636,445	1,900	2,400	3,000	4,500	10,500	52,500	
1860	(59)	577,670	1,900	2,250	2,600	3,000	6,750	20,000	100,000
1860O	6,600	12,500	24,500	47,500	65,000			
1860S	544,950	1,900	2,250	3,000	4,250	11,000	30,000	

1861-S, Normal Reverse

1861-S, Paquet Reverse

	Mintage	VF-20	EF-40	AU-50	AU-55	MS-60	MS-63	PF-63
1861	(66)	2,976,453	$1,900	$2,250	$2,600	$3,000	$5,500	$15,000	$95,000
1861O	17,741	12,500	24,000	45,000	67,500	120,000		
1861S	768,000	1,900	2,250	2,750	4,750	13,000	42,500	
1861, Paquet Rev (Tall Ltrs)						2,000,000		

$1,610,000, MS-61, Heritage
auction, August 2006

	Mintage	VF-20	EF-40	AU-50	AU-55	MS-60	MS-63	PF-63
1861S, Paquet Rev (Tall Ltrs)	19,250	32,500	60,000	87,500	135,000	225,000		
1862	(35)	92,133	2,000	5,000	8,750	13,500	22,500	50,000	85,000
1862S	854,173	1,950	2,250	3,000	5,000	13,500	47,500	
1863	(30)	142,790	2,200	2,750	5,250	9,000	20,000	47,500	85,000
1863S	966,570	1,950	2,250	2,750	3,750	8,500	32,000	
1864	(50)	204,235	1,950	2,250	3,250	5,750	16,000	42,500	85,000
1864S	793,660	1,950	2,250	2,750	3,500	9,000	32,500	
1865	(25)	351,175	1,950	2,100	2,600	3,250	7,000	23,500	85,000
1865S	1,042,500	1,950	2,150	2,500	3,000	5,500	11,000	
1866S	120,000	4,750	15,000	35,000	70,000	165,000		

Motto Above Eagle
Value TWENTY D. (1866–1876)

	Mintage	VF-20	EF-40	AU-50	AU-55	MS-60	MS-63	PF-63
1866 . . . . (30) 698,745		$1,875	$1,900	$2,000	$3,500	$10,000	$35,000	$57,500
1866S **(a)** 842,250		1,875	1,900	2,350	8,750	23,500		
1867 . . . . (50) 251,015		1,875	1,900	2,000	2,750	5,250	26,500	57,500
1867S 920,750		1,875	1,900	2,000	4,000	18,000		
1868 . . . . (25) 98,575		1,950	2,000	3,000	7,000	22,500	50,000	57,500
1868S 837,500		1,875	1,900	2,000	3,500	16,000		
1869 . . . . (25) 175,130		1,875	1,900	2,000	3,500	8,000	37,500	57,500
$299,000, MS-65, Heritage auction, January 2008								
1869S 686,750		1,875	1,900	2,000	3,000	10,000	42,500	
1870 . . . . (35) 155,150		1,875	1,900	2,500	5,500	13,500		57,500
1870CC 3,789		225,000	275,000	375,000	450,000			
$414,000, AU-55, Stack's Bowers auction, March 2009								
1870S 982,000		1,875	1,900	1,925	2,750	8,000	40,000	
1871 . . . . (30) 80,120		1,875	1,900	2,250	4,750	9,750	37,500	55,000
1871CC 17,387		11,000	23,500	40,000	60,000	100,000		
$414,000, MS-64, Heritage auction, April 2008								
1871S 928,000		1,875	1,900	1,925	2,750	5,750	27,500	
1872 . . . . (30) 251,850		1,875	1,900	1,925	2,500	6,500	35,000	55,000
1872CC 26,900		3,250	4,500	11,000	17,500	45,000		
1872S 780,000		1,875	1,900	1,925	2,400	4,750	32,500	
1873, Close 3 . . . . (25) . . 1,709,825		1,875	1,950	2,000	2,400	4,250		55,000
1873, Open 3 . . . . *		1,875	1,900	1,925	1,950	2,500	10,500	
1873CC, Close 3 22,410		4,000	6,500	13,000	18,000	43,500		
1873S, Close 3 1,040,600		1,875	1,900	1,925	1,950	2,650	27,500	
1873S, Open 3 . . . . *		1,875	1,900	1,925	2,750	11,000		
1874 . . . . (20) 366,780		1,875	1,900	1,925	1,950	2,750	20,000	57,500
1874CC 115,085		2,750	3,000	4,000	6,500	19,000		
1874S 1,214,000		1,875	1,900	1,925	1,950	3,250	28,500	
1875 . . . . (20) 295,720		1,875	1,900	1,925	1,950	2,750	12,500	100,000
1875CC 111,151		2,750	3,000	3,750	4,250	6,500	34,500	
1875S 1,230,000		1,875	1,900	1,925	1,950	2,750	20,250	
1876 **(b)** . . . . (45) 583,860		1,875	1,900	1,925	1,950	2,750	15,000	55,000
1876CC 138,441		2,750	3,000	4,000	5,500	8,000	37,500	
1876S 1,597,000		1,875	1,900	1,925	1,950	2,500	12,750	

* Included in number above. **a.** The 1866-S was also produced Without Motto; see listing on previous page. **b.** A transitional Proof pattern also exists dated 1876 but of the type of 1877.

Value TWENTY DOLLARS (1877–1907)

	Mintage	VF-20	EF-40	AU-50	AU-55	MS-60	MS-63	PF-63
1877 . . . . (20)	397,650	$1,825	$1,850	$1,875	$1,900	$1,950	$17,500	$37,500
1877CC	42,565	2,000	2,250	3,750	8,500	18,500		
1877S	1,735,000	1,825	1,850	1,875	1,900	1,950	19,500	
1878 . . . . (20)	543,625	1,825	1,850	1,875	1,900	1,950	15,000	40,000
1878CC	13,180	2,850	4,250	7,500	17,500	30,000		
1878S	1,739,000	1,825	1,850	1,875	1,900	1,950	23,500	
1879 . . . . (30)	207,600	1,825	1,850	1,875	1,900	1,950	22,000	40,000
1879CC	10,708	3,000	4,500	10,000	24,000	37,500		
1879O	2,325	15,000	18,500	37,500	60,000	95,000	175,000	
1879S	1,223,800	1,825	1,850	1,875	1,900	2,150	42,500	
1880 . . . . (36)	51,420	1,825	1,850	1,875	1,900	4,000	37,500	35,000
1880S	836,000	1,825	1,850	1,875	1,900	1,950	24,500	
1881 . . . . (61)	2,199	12,500	22,500	37,500	47,500	85,000		38,500
1881S	727,000	1,825	1,850	1,875	1,900	1,950	22,500	
1882 . . . . (59)	571	17,500	37,500	70,000	95,000	135,000	200,000	40,000
1882CC	39,140	2,000	2,250	2,850	5,750	10,000		
1882S	1,125,000	1,825	1,850	1,875	1,900	1,950	18,500	
1883, Proof only . . . . . . (92)								115,000
1883CC	59,962	2,000	2,250	2,850	4,750	7,000	35,000	
1883S	1,189,000	1,825	1,850	1,875	1,900	1,950	8,500	
1884, Proof only . . . . . . (71)								110,000
$264,500, PF-66 Cam, Stack's Bowers auction, August 2006								
1884CC	81,139	2,000	2,250	2,750	4,750	5,750	35,000	
1884S	916,000	1,825	1,850	1,875	1,900	1,950	6,500	
1885 . . . . (77)	751	10,000	15,000	25,000	40,000	75,000	135,000	40,000
1885CC	9,450	3,250	4,250	7,250	15,000	19,000	75,000	
1885S	683,500	1,825	1,850	1,875	1,900	1,950	5,500	
1886 . . . . (106)	1,000	22,500	37,500	60,000	85,000	135,000	195,000	42,500
1887, Proof only . . . . . (121)								67,500
$411,250, PF-67+ Cam, Heritage auction, August 2012								
1887S	283,000	1,825	1,850	1,875	1,900	1,950	16,500	
1888 . . . . (105)	226,161	1,825	1,850	1,875	1,900	1,950	11,500	28,500
1888S	859,600	1,825	1,850	1,875	1,900	1,950	5,250	
1889 . . . . (41)	44,070	1,825	1,850	1,875	1,900	1,950	17,500	27,500
1889CC	30,945	2,000	2,350	3,000	4,750	8,250	35,000	
1889S	774,700	1,825	1,850	1,875	1,900	1,950	6,000	
1890 . . . . (55)	75,940	1,825	1,850	1,875	1,900	1,950	12,500	27,500
1890CC	91,209	2,000	2,250	2,500	4,250	5,750	42,000	
1890S	802,750	1,825	1,850	1,875	1,900	1,950	7,000	
1891 . . . . (52)	1,390	6,500	13,500	22,500	32,500	60,000		27,500
1891CC	5,000	5,500	9,500	13,500	22,500	27,500	60,000	

Mintage	VF-20	EF-40	AU-50	AU-55	MS-60	MS-63	PF-63
1891S.................1,288,125	$1,825	$1,850	$1,875	$1,900	$1,950	$3,000	
1892.............(93).......4,430	2,250	3,500	6,000	8,000	18,000	42,500	$30,000
1892CC 27,265	2,000	2,250	3,000	4,750	10,000	35,000	
1892S.................930,150	1,825	1,850	1,875	1,900	1,950	4,000	
1893.............(59).....344,280	1,825	1,850	1,875	1,900	1,950	3,000	27,500
1893CC 18,402	2,250	2,850	3,250	5,750	9,250	35,000	
1893S.................996,175	1,825	1,850	1,875	1,900	1,950	4,000	
1894.............(50)...1,368,940	1,825	1,850	1,875	1,900	1,950	2,650	27,500
1894S.................1,048,550	1,825	1,850	1,875	1,900	1,950	3,500	
1895.............(51)...1,114,605	1,825	1,850	1,875	1,900	1,950	2,650	27,500
1895S.................1,143,500	1,825	1,850	1,875	1,900	1,950	2,700	
1896.............(128)....792,535	1,825	1,850	1,875	1,900	1,950	2,600	27,500
1896S.................1,403,925	1,825	1,850	1,875	1,900	1,950	2,600	
1897.............(86)...1,383,175	1,825	1,850	1,875	1,900	1,950	2,500	27,500
1897S.................1,470,250	1,825	1,850	1,875	1,900	1,950	2,600	
1898.............(75).....170,395	1,825	1,850	1,875	1,900	2,750	5,500	27,500
1898S.................2,575,175	1,825	1,850	1,875	1,900	1,950	2,750	
1899.............(84)...1,669,300	1,825	1,850	1,875	1,900	1,950	2,500	27,500
1899S.................2,010,300	1,825	1,850	1,875	1,900	1,950	2,850	
1900.............(124)...1,874,460	1,825	1,850	1,875	1,900	1,950	2,500	27,500
1900S.................2,459,500	1,825	1,850	1,875	1,900	1,950	2,800	
1901.............(96).....111,430	1,825	1,850	1,875	1,900	1,950	2,400	27,500
1901S.................1,596,000	1,825	1,850	1,875	1,900	1,950	4,000	
1902.............(114).....31,140	1,825	1,850	1,875	1,900	2,500	22,000	27,500
1902S.................1,753,625	1,825	1,850	1,875	1,900	1,950	3,750	
1903.............(158)....287,270	1,825	1,850	1,875	1,900	1,950	2,400	27,500
1903S.................954,000	1,825	1,850	1,875	1,900	1,950	2,500	
1904.............(98)...6,256,699	1,825	1,850	1,875	1,900	1,950	2,400	27,500
1904S.................5,134,175	1,825	1,850	1,875	1,900	1,950	2,500	
1905.............(92).....58,919	1,825	1,850	1,875	1,900	2,500	15,000	27,500
1905S.................1,813,000	1,825	1,850	1,875	1,900	1,950	3,750	
1906.............(94).....69,596	1,825	1,850	1,875	1,900	1,950	8,500	27,500
1906D 620,250	1,825	1,850	1,875	1,900	1,950	3,500	
1906S.................2,065,750	1,825	1,850	1,875	1,900	1,950	2,600	
1907.............(78)...1,451,786	1,825	1,850	1,875	1,900	1,950	2,500	27,500
1907D 842,250	1,825	1,850	1,875	1,900	1,950	3,250	
1907S.................2,165,800	1,825	1,850	1,875	1,900	1,950	3,000	

SAINT-GAUDENS (1907–1933)

Many consider the twenty-dollar gold piece designed by Augustus Saint-Gaudens to be the most beautiful U.S. coin. The first coins issued were slightly more than 12,000 high-relief pieces struck for general circulation. Their relief is much higher than for later issues, and the date 1907 is in Roman numerals (MCMVII). A few of the Proof coins were made using the lettered-edge collar from the ultra high relief version. These can be distinguished by a pronounced bottom left serif on the N in UNUM, and other minor differences. High-relief Proofs are trial or experimental pieces. Flat-relief double eagles were issued later in 1907 with Arabic numerals, and continued through 1933.

The field of the rare, ultra high relief experimental pieces is exceedingly concave and connects directly with the edge without any border, giving it a sharp, knifelike appearance; Liberty's skirt shows two folds on the side of her right leg; the Capitol building in the background at left is very small; the sun, on the reverse side, has 14 rays, as opposed to the 13 rays on regular high-relief coins.

The Proof finish of 1908 and 1911 through 1915 coins was originally referred to by the Mint as Sand Blast Proof. Proof coins minted in 1909 and 1910 have a different finish described as Satin Proof. In addition, double eagles from 1907 through 1911 have 46 stars on the obverse; and from 1912 through 1933, 48 stars.

Designer Augustus Saint-Gaudens; weight 33.436 grams; composition .900 gold, .100 copper (net weight: .96750 oz. pure gold); diameter 34 mm; edge: E PLURIBUS UNUM with words divided by stars (one specimen of the high-relief variety with plain edge is known); mints: Philadelphia, Denver, San Francisco.

VF-20 Very Fine—Minor wear on Liberty's legs and toes. Eagle's left wing and breast feathers worn.
EF-40 Extremely Fine—Drapery lines on chest visible. Wear on left breast, knee, and below. Eagle's feathers on breast and right wing bold.
AU-50 About Uncirculated—Trace of wear on nose, breast, and knee. Wear visible on eagle's wings.
MS-60 Uncirculated—No trace of wear. Light marks or blemishes.

Ultra High Relief Pattern, MCMVII (1907)

	PF-67
1907, Ultra High Relief, Plain Edge *(unique)*	
1907, Ultra High Relief, Lettered Edge	$2,500,000
$2,990,000, PF-69, Heritage auction, November 2005	

Without Motto IN GOD WE TRUST (1907–1908)
High Relief, MCMVII (1907)

	Mintage	VF-20	EF-40	AU-50	AU-55	MS-60	MS-63
1907, High Relief, Roman Numerals (MCMVII), Wire Rim	12,367	$9,750	$11,000	$12,000	$12,500	$14,500	$24,000
$575,000, MS-69, Heritage auction, November 2005							
1907, Same, Flat Rim . . . .*	9,750	11,000	12,000	12,500	14,500	24,000	
$534,750, PF-69, Heritage auction, November 2005							

* Included in number above.

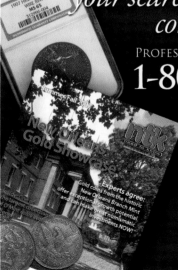

Arabic Numerals, No Motto (1907–1908)

Mintmark is on obverse, above date.

	Mintage	VF-20	EF-40	AU-50	AU-55	MS-60	MS-63
1907, Arabic Numerals..............	361,667	$1,825	$1,850	$1,875	$1,900	$1,950	$2,100
1908.............................	4,271,551	1,825	1,850	1,875	1,900	1,925	2,000
1908D	663,750	1,825	1,850	1,875	1,900	1,950	2,050

With Motto IN GOD WE TRUST (1908–1933)

1909, 9 Over 8

	Mintage	VF-20	EF-40	AU-50	AU-55	MS-60	MS-63	MATTE PF-63
1908.............(101).....156,258		$1,850	$1,900	$1,950	$2,000	$2,100	$2,500	$27,500
1908D 349,500		1,825	1,850	1,875	1,900	1,950	2,000	
1908S......................22,000		2,500	3,750	6,000	7,000	12,500	24,500	
$161,000, MS-67, Heritage auction, January 2012								
1909, All kinds ....(67).....161,282								
1909, 9 Over 8..................		1,850	1,875	1,900	1,950	2,250	6,750	
1909		1,825	1,850	1,875	1,900	2,000	3,500	28,500
1909D 52,500		1,825	1,850	1,900	1,950	3,250	8,000	
1909S...................2,774,925		1,825	1,850	1,875	1,900	1,925	2,000	
1910.............(167).....482,000		1,825	1,850	1,875	1,900	1,950	2,100	28,500
1910D 429,000		1,825	1,850	1,875	1,900	1,925	2,000	
1910S...................2,128,250		1,825	1,850	1,875	1,900	1,925	2,000	
1911.............(100).....197,250		1,825	1,850	1,875	1,900	2,000	2,250	27,500
$184,000, MS-67, Heritage auction, January 2012								
1911D 846,500		1,825	1,850	1,875	1,900	1,925	2,000	
1911S...................775,750		1,825	1,850	1,875	1,900	1,925	2,000	

	Mintage	VF-20	EF-40	AU-50	AU-55	MS-60	MS-63	MATTE PF-63
1912 . . . . (74)	149,750	$1,825	$1,850	$1,875	$1,900	$1,925	$2,300	$27,500
1913 . . . . (58)	168,780	1,825	1,850	1,875	1,900	2,000	2,850	27,500
1913D	393,500	1,825	1,850	1,875	1,900	1,925	2,000	
1913S	34,000	1,825	1,850	1,900	2,100	2,350	5,000	
1914 . . . . (70)	95,250	1,825	1,850	1,875	1,900	2,000	3,500	27,500
1914D	453,000	1,825	1,850	1,875	1,900	1,925	2,000	
1914S	1,498,000	1,825	1,850	1,875	1,900	1,925	2,000	
1915 . . . . (50)	152,000	1,825	1,850	1,875	1,900	2,000	2,500	30,000
1915S	567,500	1,825	1,850	1,875	1,900	1,925	2,000	
1916S	796,000	1,825	1,850	1,875	1,900	1,925	2,000	
1920	228,250	1,825	1,850	1,875	1,900	1,925	2,000	
1920S	558,000	15,000	20,000	25,000	32,500	50,000	85,000	
$575,000, MS-66, Heritage auction, January 2012								
1921	528,500	25,000	37,500	55,000	65,000	125,000	265,000	
$1,495,000, MS-63, Stack's Bowers auction, August 2006								
1922	1,375,500	1,825	1,850	1,875	1,900	1,925	2,000	
1922S	2,658,000	1,850	1,900	2,000	2,150	2,650	5,000	
1923	566,000	1,825	1,850	1,875	1,900	1,925	2,000	
1923D	1,702,250	1,825	1,850	1,875	1,900	1,925	2,000	
1924	4,323,500	1,825	1,850	1,875	1,900	1,925	2,000	
1924D	3,049,500	2,200	2,400	2,650	3,250	4,500	8,750	
1924S	2,927,500	2,200	2,400	2,650	3,250	4,500	10,000	
$172,500, MS-65, Heritage auction, January 2012								
1925	2,831,750	1,825	1,850	1,875	1,900	1,925	2,000	
1925D	2,938,500	2,600	3,200	3,750	4,250	5,500	11,000	
1925S	3,776,500	2,250	3,000	3,750	5,250	9,500	16,500	
1926	816,750	1,825	1,850	1,875	1,900	1,925	2,000	
1926D	481,000	8,000	13,000	14,000	15,500	17,500	25,000	
$402,500, MS-66+, Heritage auction, January 2012								
1926S	2,041,500	2,150	2,450	2,750	2,950	3,500	5,500	
1927	2,946,750	1,825	1,850	1,875	1,900	1,925	2,000	
1927D	180,000			475,000	550,000	750,000	1,200,000	
$1,897,500, MS-67, Heritage auction, November 2005								
1927S	3,107,000			14,000	16,000	26,000	47,500	
$276,000, MS-67, Heritage auction, January 2012								
1928	8,816,000	1,825	1,850	1,875	1,900	1,925	2,000	
1929	1,779,750			13,500	15,500	20,000	35,000	
1930S	74,000			42,000	45,000	65,000	90,000	
1931	2,938,250			20,000	25,000	34,000	63,000	
$322,000, MS-67, Heritage auction, August 2010								
1931D	106,500			20,000	25,000	34,000	65,000	
$230,000, MS-66, Heritage auction, January 2012								
1932	1,101,750			20,000	25,000	34,000	65,000	
1933 *(extremely rare)* **(a)**	445,500							
$7,590,020, Gem BU, Sotheby's/Stack's Bowers auction, July 2002								

Note: From their initial mintages, most of the double eagles of the 1920s were returned to the Mint and melted in the 1930s. Some, however, were unofficially saved by Treasury employees. Estimates of the quantities saved range from a few dozen to several hundred thousand, depending on the date. This explains the high values for coins that, judged only by their initial mintages, should otherwise be more common. **a.** All were to have been melted at the mint. Today at least 13 are known to have survived. Only one, the King Farouk specimen, has ever been sold at auction.

Commemorative coins have been popular since the days of the ancient Greeks and Romans. In the beginning they recorded and honored important events, and passed along the news of the day. Many modern nations have issued commemorative coins, and they are highly esteemed by collectors. No nation has surpassed the United States when it comes to commemorative coins.

The unique position occupied by commemoratives in United States coinage is largely due to the fact that, with few exceptions, all commemorative coins have real historical significance. The progress and advance of people in the New World are presented in an interesting and instructive manner on the commemorative issues. Such a record of facts artistically presented on U.S. gold, silver, and other memorial issues appeals strongly to the collector who favors the historical side of numismatics. It is the historical features of the commemoratives, in fact, that create interest among many people who would otherwise have little interest in coins.

Commemorative issues are considered for coinage by two committees of Congress: the Committee on Banking, Housing, and Urban Affairs; and the Committee on Banking and Financial Services of the House; as well as the Citizens Coinage Advisory Committee. Congress is guided to a great extent by the reports of these committees when passing upon bills authorizing commemorative coins.

These special coins are usually issued either to commemorate events or to help pay for monuments or celebrations that commemorate historical persons, places, or things. Pre-1982 commemorative coins were offered in most instances by a commission in charge of the event to be commemorated, and sold at a premium over face value.

Commemorative coins are popularly collected either by major types or in sets with mintmark varieties. During many years, no special commemorative coins were issued. Some regular coins, such as the Lincoln cent of 1909, quarters of 1999 through 2021, and Bicentennial issues of 1976, are also commemorative in nature.

A note about mintages: Unless otherwise stated, the coinage figures given in each "Distribution" column represent the total released mintage: the original total mintage (including assay coins), minus the quantity of unsold coins. In many cases, larger quantities were minted but not all were sold. The unsold coins were usually returned to the mint and melted, although some were placed in circulation at face value. A limited number of Proof strikings or presentation pieces were made for some of the 1892 through 1954 issues. All are very rare and valuable. For modern commemoratives (1982 to date), this edition of the Red Book has been updated with the latest data as provided by the U.S. Mint. Some of the updated modern mintage figures reflect substantial changes from numbers earlier released by the Mint.

Alphabetical Reference to Dates for Commemoratives and Sets

All commemoratives are of the standard weight and fineness of regular-issue 20th-century gold, silver, or clad coins, and all are legal tender.

Alabama Cent'l, 1921
Albany, NY, Charter, 1936
American Independence, 1926
Antietam, Battle of, 1937
Arkansas Cent'l, 1935–1939
Bald Eagle, 2008*
Bill of Rights, 1993*
Black Revolutionary War Patriots, 1998*

Booker T. Washington. *See* Washington, Booker T.
Boone, Daniel, 1934–1938
Botanic Garden, 1997*
Boy Scouts, 2010
Braille, Louis, 2009
Bridgeport, CT, Cent'l, 1936
Buffalo, American, 2001*
California Diamond Jubilee, 1925

California Pacific International Exposition, 1935–1936
Capitol, U.S., 1994
Capitol Visitor Center, 2001*
Carver, George Washington, 1951–1954
Cincinnati Music Center, 1936
Civil War Battlefields, 1995*
Cleveland / Great Lakes Exposition, 1936

---

* See also in "Government Commemorative Sets."

Columbia, SC, Sesquicent'l, 1936

Columbian Exposition, 1892–1893

Columbus, Christopher, 1992*

Congress Bicent'l, 1989*

Congress, Library of, 2000

Connecticut Tercentenary, 1935

Constitution Bicent'l, 1987*

Delaware Tercentenary, 1936

Disabled Veterans, 2010

Edison, Thomas A., 2004*

Eisenhower Cent'l, 1990

Elgin, IL, Cent'l, 1936

Ericson, Leif, Millennium, 2000*

5-Star Generals, 2013

First Flight Cent'l, 2003

Fort Vancouver Cent'l, 1925

Franklin, Benjamin, 2006*

Gettysburg, Battle of, 1936

Girl Scouts of the U.S.A. Cent'l, 2013

Grant Memorial, 1922

Hawaiian Sesquicent'l, 1928

Hudson, NY, Sesquicent'l, 1935

Huguenot-Walloon Tercentenary, 1924

Illinois Cent'l, 1918

Infantry Soldier, 2012

Iowa Cent'l, 1946

Isabella Quarter Dollar, 1893

Jamestown 400th Anniversary, 2007

Jefferson, Thomas, 1993 (1994)*

Kennedy, Robert F., 1998*

Korean War Memorial, 1991

Lafayette Dollar, 1900

Lewis and Clark Bicent'l, 2004*

Lewis and Clark Exposition, 1904–1905

Lexington-Concord Sesquicent'l, 1925

Library of Congress Bicent'l, 2000

Lincoln, Abraham, Bicent'l, 2009

Little Rock Desegregation, 2007*

Long Island Tercentenary, 1936

Louisiana Purchase Exposition, 1903

Lynchburg, VA, Sesquicent'l, 1936

Madison, Dolley, 1999*

Maine Cent'l, 1920

Marine Corps 230th Anniversary, 2005*

Marshall, John, 2005*

Maryland Tercentenary, 1934

McKinley Memorial, 1916–1917

Medal of Honor, 2011

Missouri Cent'l, 1921

Monroe Doctrine Cent'l, 1923

Mt. Rushmore Golden Anniversary, 1991*

National Law Enforcement Officers, 1997*

National Community Service, 1996*

National Prisoners of War, 1994

New Rochelle, NY, 250th Anniversary, 1938

Norfolk, VA, Bicent'l, 1936

Old Spanish Trail, 1935

Olympics:
1983–1984 (Los Angeles)*
1988 (Seoul)*
1992 (XXV/25th)*
1995 (Centennial)*
2002 (Salt Lake City)*

Oregon Trail Memorial, 1926–1939

Panama-Pacific Exposition, 1915

Pilgrim Tercentenary, 1920–1921

Police Memorial, 1997

P.O.W.s, U.S., 1994

Providence, RI, Tercentenary, 1936

Roanoke Island, NC, 350th Anniversary, 1937

Robinson, Jackie, 1997*

Robinson–Arkansas Cent'l, 1936

Roosevelt, Franklin D., 1997

San Francisco Old Mint Cent'l, 2006*

San Francisco–Oakland Bay Bridge, 1936

Shriver / Special Olympics, 1995*

Smithsonian 150th Anniversary, 1996*

Spanish Trail, Old, 1935

Special Olympics, 1995*

Star-Spangled Banner, 2012

Statue of Liberty Cent'l, 1986*

Stone Mountain Memorial, 1925

Texas Cent'l, 1934–1938

U.S. Army, 2011

U.S. Capitol Bicent'l, 1994

United Service Organizations, 1991

Vermont Sesquicent'l, 1927

Vietnam Veterans, 1994*

Washington, Booker T., 1946–1951; 1951–1954

Washington, George, 1982 Bicentennial of Death, 1999*

West Point Bicent'l, 2002

White House 200th Anniversary, 1992

Wisconsin Territorial Cent'l, 1936

Women in Military Service, 1994

World Cup (Soccer) Tournament, 1994*

World War II 50th Anniversary, 1991–1995

World War II, 1993*

Yellowstone National Park, 1999*

York County, ME, Tercentenary, 1936

* See also in "Government Commemorative Sets."

Price Performance

Few people would ever guess, or even believe, that this country once issued an official half dollar bearing the portrait of P.T. Barnum, the famous impresario to whom the saying "There's a sucker born every minute" was misattributed. He had nothing to do with the coins, which were made in 1936 (long after his death), but the exceptional honor and the fact that the fifty-cent coins were sold to the public for $2 each would have made him smile about bilking the public one last time.

Barnum did not have the last laugh in this matter. Those fortunate enough to buy one of the original coins in 1936, and to save it in Mint State, find that today their treasure is worth more than $150! Only 25,015 of the pieces were made, and at the time they were not very popular even with the few people who ever heard about them.

The Bridgeport commemorative half dollar with P.T. Barnum's portrait is but one of many different designs that have been used on special coins made for collectors since 1892. During that time, commemorative coins have been issued to celebrate the founding of cities, to mark expositions, to honor famous citizens and presidents, and even to promote Olympic contests in recent years. These coins were not normally placed in circulation, and were usually distributed by some agency at a price over face value with the surplus going to fund the event being celebrated. All commemorative coins made since 1982 have been distributed through the Mint with proceeds going directly to the government, and from there, to the various benefiting organizations.

It has mostly been in recent years that the general public has learned about commemorative coins. They have long been popular with coin collectors who enjoy the artistry and history associated with them, as well as the tremendous profit that they have made from owning these rare pieces. Very few ever reached circulation, as all were originally sold above face value, and because they are all so rare. Most early issues were of the half dollar denomination, and were often made in quantities of fewer than 20,000 pieces. This is minuscule when compared to the regular half dollar pieces that are made by the millions each year, and still rarely seen in circulation.

At the beginning of 1988, prices of classic commemoratives in MS-65 condition had risen so high that most collectors had to content themselves with pieces in lower grades. Investors continued to apply pressure to the high-quality pieces, driving prices even higher, while the collector community went after coins in grades from About Uncirculated to MS-63. For several months the pressure from both influences caused prices to rise very rapidly for all issues and grades of commemoratives without even taking the price-adjustment breather that usually goes along with such activity.

By 1990, prices dropped to the point that several of the commemoratives began to look like bargains once again. Many of the MS-65 pieces held firm at price levels above the $3,000 mark, but others were still available at under $500 even for coins of similar mintage. Coins in MS-63 or MS-64 were priced at but a fraction of the MS-65 prices, which would seem to make them reasonably priced because the demand for these pieces is universal, and not keyed simply to grade, rarity, or speculator pressure.

Historically, the entire series of commemorative coins has frequently undergone a roller-coaster cycle of price adjustments. These cycles have usually been of short duration, lasting from months to years, with prices always recovering and eventually exceeding previous levels.

CLASSIC COMMEMORATIVE SILVER AND GOLD
(1892–1893) World's Columbian Exposition Half Dollar

The first United States commemorative coin was the Columbian half dollar designed by Olin Lewis Warner. Charles E. Barber engraved the obverse, showing the bust of Columbus; and George T. Morgan engraved the reverse, a representation of Columbus's flagship the *Santa Maria* above two hemispheres. The coins were sold for $1 each at the World's Columbian Exposition in Chicago during 1893. A great many remained unsold and a substantial quantity was later released for circulation at face value or melted. Approximately 100 brilliant Proofs were struck for each date.

	Distribution	AU-50	MS-60	MS-63	MS-65	MS-66
1892, World's Columbian Exposition.............	950,000	$20	$32	$85	$475	$1,100
1893, Same type	1,550,405	18	30	80	450	1,100

(1893) World's Columbian Exposition, Isabella Quarter

In 1893, the Board of Lady Managers of the World's Columbian Exposition petitioned for a souvenir quarter dollar. Authority was granted March 3, 1893. The coin known as the *Isabella quarter* was designed by Charles E. Barber. These souvenir quarters were sold for $1. The obverse has the crowned bust of Queen Isabella I of Spain. The kneeling female on the reverse with distaff and spindle is emblematic of women's industry.

	Distribution	AU-50	MS-60	MS-63	MS-65	MS-66
1893, World's Columbian Exposition, Chicago	24,214	$450	$500	$600	$2,750	$6,000

(1900) Lafayette Dollar

The heads of George Washington and the marquis de Lafayette appear on this issue, which was the first commemorative coin of one-dollar denomination, and the first authorized United States coin to bear a portrait of a U.S. president. The dies were prepared by Charles E. Barber. The statue on the reverse is similar to the monument of General Lafayette that was later erected in Paris as a gift of the American people. The coins were sold by the Lafayette Memorial Commission for $2 each.

	Distribution	AU-50	MS-60	MS-63	MS-65	MS-66
1900, Lafayette	36,026	$650	$875	$1,800	$10,000	$19,000

(1903) Louisiana Purchase Exposition

The first commemorative U.S. gold coins were authorized for the Louisiana Purchase Exposition, held in St. Louis in 1904. There are two varieties of the gold dollar, each dated 1903—one with the head of Thomas Jefferson, who was president when the Louisiana Territory was purchased from France, and the other with President William McKinley, who sanctioned the exposition. The reverse is the same for each variety. The designs were by Charles E. Barber.

	Distribution	AU-50	MS-60	MS-63	MS-65	MS-66
1903, Louisiana Purchase / Thomas Jefferson	17,500	$500	$665	$850	$1,700	$2,150
1903, Louisiana Purchase / William McKinley	17,500	500	650	800	1,700	2,150

(1904–1905) Lewis and Clark Exposition

The Lewis and Clark Centennial Exposition was held in Portland, Oregon, in 1905. A souvenir issue of gold dollars was struck to mark the event with the dates 1904 and 1905. The two famous explorers are represented on either side of the coin, which was designed by Charles E. Barber. A bronze memorial of the Indian guide, Sacagawea, who assisted in the famous expedition, was erected in Portland, Oregon, and financed by the sale of these coins.

	Distribution	AU-50	MS-60	MS-63	MS-65	MS-66
1904, Lewis and Clark Exposition	10,025	$900	$1,000	$1,575	$7,500	$10,000
1905, Lewis and Clark Exposition	10,041	1,200	1,300	1,800	8,500	15,000

(1915) Panama-Pacific Exposition

This half dollar was designed by Charles E. Barber (obverse) and George T. Morgan (reverse). The exposition held in San Francisco in 1915 celebrated the opening of the Panama Canal. The coins were struck at the San Francisco Mint and were sold at $1 each during the exposition. A representation of Columbia with the golden gate in the background is the principal feature of the obverse. The Panama-Pacific coins were the first commemorative coins to carry the motto IN GOD WE TRUST, which appears above the eagle.

	Distribution	AU-50	MS-60	MS-63	MS-65	MS-66
1915S, Panama-Pacific Exposition	27,134	$475	$515	$725	$2,400	$3,500

Charles Keck designed the gold dollar, the obverse of which has the head of a man, representing a Panama Canal laborer. Two dolphins encircle ONE DOLLAR on the reverse.

The quarter eagle was the work of Charles E. Barber and George T. Morgan. The obverse shows Columbia with a caduceus in her left hand seated on a hippocampus, signifying the use of the Panama Canal. An American eagle with raised wings is shown on the reverse.

	Distribution	AU-50	MS-60	MS-63	MS-65	MS-66
1915S, Panama-Pacific Exposition, gold $1	15,000	$650	$675	$700	$1,250	$1,850
1915S, Panama-Pacific Exposition, $2.50	6,749	1,600	1,850	3,750	6,000	6,750

The fifty-dollar gold piece was designed by Robert Aitken and was issued in both round and octagonal form. The obverse bears a helmeted head of Minerva; the owl, symbol of wisdom, is on the reverse. The octagonal issue has eight dolphins in the angles on both sides. Other devices are smaller on the octagonal variety.

	Distribution	AU-50	MS-60	MS-63	MS-65	MS-66
1915S, Panama-Pacific Exposition, Round	483	$50,000	$53,500	$85,000	$135,000	$185,000
1915S, Panama-Pacific Exposition, Octagonal	645	47,500	50,000	77,500	120,000	180,000

(1916–1917) McKinley Memorial

The sale of the McKinley dollars aided in paying for a memorial building at Niles, Ohio, the martyred president's birthplace. The obverse, showing a profile of McKinley, was designed by Charles E. Barber; the reverse, with the memorial building, was designed by George T. Morgan.

	Distribution	AU-50	MS-60	MS-63	MS-65	MS-66
1916, McKinley Memorial	15,000	$550	$580	$675	$1,350	$1,850
1917, McKinley Memorial	5,000	600	700	875	1,850	3,250

(1918) Illinois Centennial

This coin was authorized to commemorate the 100th anniversary of the admission of Illinois into the Union, and was the first souvenir piece for such an event. The obverse was designed by George T. Morgan and the reverse by J.R. Sinnock. The obverse shows the head of Lincoln taken from the statue by Andrew O'Connor in Springfield, Illinois. The reverse is based on the Illinois State Seal.

	Distribution	AU-50	MS-60	MS-63	MS-65	MS-66
1918, Illinois Centennial	100,058	$130	$150	$165	$535	$800

(1920) Maine Centennial

Congress authorized the Maine Centennial half dollar on May 10, 1920, to be sold at the centennial celebration at Portland. They were received too late for this event and were sold by the state treasurer for many years. Anthony de Francisci modeled this coin from a design by Harry H. Cochrane. The obverse device is the arms of the state of Maine; the Latin word DIRIGO means "I Direct."

	Distribution	AU-50	MS-60	MS-63	MS-65	MS-66
1920, Maine Centennial	50,028	$130	$165	$200	$460	$685

(1920–1921) Pilgrim Tercentenary

To commemorate the landing of the Pilgrims at Plymouth, Massachusetts, in 1620, Congress authorized a special half dollar on May 12, 1920. Cyrus E. Dallin, a Boston sculptor, executed the designs furnished to him by the commission. His initial D is below the elbow of Governor William Bradford, on the obverse. The reverse shows the *Mayflower*. The first issue had no date on the obverse. The coins struck in 1921 show that date in addition to 1620–1920. There was a large coinage of both issues, and not all were sold. A total of 128,000 were returned to the mint and melted.

With 1921 in
Field on Obverse

	Distribution	AU-50	MS-60	MS-63	MS-65	MS-66
1920, Pilgrim Tercentenary	152,112	$85	$110	$125	$350	$850
1921, Same, With Date Added in Field	20,053	180	210	225	425	900

(1921) Missouri Centennial

The 100th anniversary of the admission of Missouri to the Union was celebrated in Sedalia during August 1921. To mark the occasion, Congress authorized the coinage of a fifty-cent piece. Robert Aitken designed the coin, which shows the bust of a frontiersman on the obverse, and a frontiersman and Indian on the reverse. The first coins struck show 2★4 incused, indicating that Missouri was the 24th star in the flag. The type without this marking was struck later, but was the first to be sold.

2★4
in Field

	Distribution	AU-50	MS-60	MS-63	MS-65	MS-66
1921, Missouri Centennial, "2★4" in Field	9,400	$650	$750	$1,100	$3,700	$11,000
1921, Missouri Centennial, Plain	11,400	425	600	850	3,500	10,000

(1921) Alabama Centennial

The Alabama half dollars were authorized in 1920 for the state-hood centennial, which was cele-brated in 1919, but they were not struck until 1921. The coins, designed by Laura Gardin Fraser, were offered first during President Warren Harding's visit to Bir-mingham, October 26, 1921. The St. Andrew's cross, an emblem on

2X2
in Field

the state flag, appears on a part of the issue between the numbers in "2X2," indicating it was the 22nd state of the Union. The obverse has busts of William Wyatt Bibb, first governor of Alabama, and T.E. Kilby, governor at the time of the centennial. This is the first instance of the use of a living person's portrait on a United States coin.

See next page for chart.   **289**

	Distribution	AU-50	MS-60	MS-63	MS-65	MS-66
1921, Alabama Centennial, Plain *35,000*		$200	$230	$450	$1,300	$3,000
1921, Alabama Centennial, With "2X2" in Field of Obverse ... *30,000*		300	325	525	1,400	3,500

(1922) Grant Memorial

This coin was struck during 1922 as a centenary souvenir of Ulysses S. Grant's birth. An incuse (recessed) star that appeared on the first issues was later removed, creating a second variety. The star has no particular significance. The reverse shows the frame house in Point Pleasant, Ohio, where Grant was born on April 27, 1822. Laura Gardin Fraser designed both the Grant half dollar and gold dollar.

Star in Obverse Field
*Fake stars usually have
flattened spot on reverse.*

	Distribution	AU-50	MS-60	MS-63	MS-65	MS-66
1922, Grant Memorial, Star in Obverse Field 4,256		$950	$1,300	$1,900	$7,000	$14,000
1922, Same type, No Star in Field 67,405		110	125	175	750	1,150

Like the half-dollar commemorative coins, the gold dollars were first issued with a star, which was removed for the later issues. The designs by Laura Gardin Fraser are the same as for the half-dollar coinage.

Star ←

	Distribution	AU-50	MS-60	MS-63	MS-65	MS-66
1922, Grant Memorial, With Star 5,016		$1,350	$1,550	$1,850	$2,500	$2,850
1922, Grant Memorial, No Star.................... 5,016		1,350	1,550	1,850	2,500	3,000

(1923) Monroe Doctrine Centennial

The California film industry promoted this issue in conjunction with a motion picture exposition held in June 1923. The obverse shows the heads of James Monroe and John Quincy Adams, who were identified with the Monroe Doctrine. The Western Hemisphere is portrayed on the reverse in forms that suggest two female

figures. Chester Beach prepared the models for this coin. Many unsold coins were released into circulation at face value.

	Distribution	AU-50	MS-60	MS-63	MS-65	MS-66
1923S, Monroe Doctrine Centennial 274,077		$65	$75	$150	$1,800	$5,900

(1924) Huguenot-Walloon Tercentenary

Settling of the Huguenots and Walloons in the New World was the occasion commemorated by this issue. New Netherland, now New York, was founded in 1624 by a group of Dutch colonists. The persons represented on the obverse were not directly concerned with the occasion, however. They are Admiral Coligny and William the Silent. The reverse shows the vessel *Nieuw Nederland.* George T. Morgan prepared the models for this coin.

	Distribution	AU-50	MS-60	MS-63	MS-65	MS-66
1924, Huguenot-Walloon Tercentenary.............	142,080	$135	$160	$175	$400	$800

(1925) Lexington-Concord Sesquicentennial

The two famous battles fought in 1775 are commemorated on this coin. A statue of the familiar Minute Man is depicted on the obverse, and the Old Belfry at Lexington is the reverse device. Chester Beach designed the coin. The famous statue by Daniel Chester French located in Concord was used for the design.

	Distribution	AU-50	MS-60	MS-63	MS-65	MS-66
1925, Lexington-Concord Sesquicentennial	162,013	$100	$120	$150	$500	$1,400

(1925) Stone Mountain Memorial

The models for this coin were prepared by Gutzon Borglum, who would later sculpt Mount Rushmore. The first coins were struck at Philadelphia on January 21, 1925, General Thomas "Stonewall" Jackson's birthday. Generals Robert E. Lee and Jackson, mounted, are shown on the obverse. The funds received from the sale of this large issue of half dollars were devoted to the expense of carving figures of Confederate leaders and soldiers on Stone Mountain in Georgia. The carving was completed and dedicated in 1970. Some of these coins were counterstamped on the reverse by the issuing commission, with letters and numbers for distribution to individual state sales agencies. These are valued much higher than normal coins.

	Distribution	AU-50	MS-60	MS-63	MS-65	MS-66
1925, Stone Mountain Memorial................	1,314,709	$65	$75	$85	$275	$335

(1925) California Diamond Jubilee

The California half dollar was designed by Jo Mora, a noted California sculptor. The obverse bears a kneeling figure of a Forty-Niner. The reverse shows a walking grizzly bear, the state emblem. The celebration for which these coins were struck marked the 75th anniversary of the admission of California into the Union.

	Distribution	AU-50	MS-60	MS-63	MS-65	MS-66
1925S, California Diamond Jubilee	86,594	$200	$225	$300	$950	$1,350

(1925) Fort Vancouver Centennial

John McLoughlin, shown on the obverse of this coin, built Fort Vancouver (Washington) on the Columbia River in 1825. The sale of the coins at $1 each helped to finance the pageant staged for the celebration. Laura Gardin Fraser prepared the models for this coin, which was minted in San Francisco. The S mintmark was omitted. The reverse has a pioneer settler in buckskin suit with a musket in his hands. Fort Vancouver is in the background.

	Distribution	AU-50	MS-60	MS-63	MS-65	MS-66
1925, Fort Vancouver Centennial	14,994	$340	$400	$450	$1,000	$1,300

(1926) Sesquicentennial of American Independence

The 150th anniversary of the signing of the Declaration of Independence was the occasion for an international fair held in Philadelphia in 1926. To help raise funds for financing the fair, special issues of half dollars and quarter eagles were authorized by Congress. For the first time, a portrait of a president appeared on a coin struck during his own lifetime. Presidents Calvin Coolidge and George Washington are depicted on the obverse of the half dollar. The reverse bears an accurate model of the Liberty Bell. John R. Sinnock, chief engraver of the United States Mint, modeled the sesquicentennial coins from designs by John Frederick Lewis. The dies were in very low relief, causing much loss of detail.

	Distribution	AU-50	MS-60	MS-63	MS-65	MS-66
1926, Sesquicentennial of American Independence	141,120	$90	$120	$140	$2,500	$25,000

The obverse of this special gold quarter eagle has a standing female figure symbolic of Liberty, holding in one hand a scroll representing the Declaration of Independence and in the other the Torch of Freedom. The reverse bears a representation of Independence Hall in Philadelphia. The coin was designed by John R. Sinnock.

	Distribution	AU-50	MS-60	MS-63	MS-65	MS-66
1926, Sesquicentennial of American Independence	46,019	$500	$525	$775	$3,000	$9,500

(1926–1939) Oregon Trail Memorial

This memorial coin was struck in commemoration of the Oregon Trail and in memory of the pioneers, many of whom lie buried along the famous 2,000-mile highway of history. James Earle Fraser and his wife, Laura Gardin Fraser, prepared the designs. The original issue was struck at Philadelphia and San Francisco in 1926. Coin-age was resumed in 1928 (released in 1933), and in 1933, 1934, and 1936 through 1939. The 1933 half dollar was the first commemorative coin struck at the Denver Mint.

	Distribution	AU-50	MS-60	MS-63	MS-65	MS-66
1926, Oregon Trail Memorial	47,955	$135	$170	$180	$320	$450
1926S, Same type, S Mint	83,055	135	170	180	320	435
1928, Oregon Trail Memorial (same as 1926)	6,028	215	230	300	380	500
1933D, Oregon Trail Memorial	5,008	360	380	400	500	575
1934D, Oregon Trail Memorial	7,006	200	215	235	350	625
1936, Oregon Trail Memorial	10,006	200	210	220	330	435
1936S, Same type, S Mint	5,006	185	210	230	375	500
1937D, Oregon Trail Memorial	12,008	190	215	250	375	435
1938, Oregon Trail Memorial (same as 1926)	6,006					
1938D, Same type, D Mint	6,005	Set:	500	600	900	1,350
1938S, Same type, S Mint	6,006					
1939, Oregon Trail Memorial (same as 1926)	3,004					
1939D, Same type, D Mint	3,004	Set:	1,600	1,700	2,000	2,850
1939S, Same type, S Mint	3,005					
Oregon Trail Memorial, single type coin		135	170	180	320	435

(1927) Vermont Sesquicentennial

This souvenir issue commemorates the 150th anniversary of the Battle of Bennington and the independence of Vermont. Authorized in 1925, it was not coined until 1927. The models were prepared by Charles Keck. The obverse shows the head of Ira Allen, founder of Vermont. The reverse bears a catamount walking left.

See next page for chart.

	Distribution	AU-50	MS-60	MS-63	MS-65	MS-66
1927, Vermont Sesquicentennial (Battle of Bennington) 28,142		$250	$300	$325	$900	$1,100

(1928) Hawaiian Sesquicentennial

This issue was struck to commemorate the 150th anniversary of the
arrival on the Hawaiian Islands of
Captain James Cook in 1778. The
design was sketched by Juliette
May Fraser of Honolulu and executed by Chester Beach. Captain
Cook is shown on the obverse and
a native chief on the reverse. The
coins were distributed in 1928 and
sold for $2 each, the highest initial sale price up to that time.

	Distribution	AU-50	MS-60	MS-63	MS-65	MS-66
1928, Hawaiian Sesquicentennial 10,008		$1,700	$2,500	$3,300	$5,800	$11,000
1928, Hawaiian Sesquicentennial,						
Sandblast Proof Presentation Piece . . . . (50)				15,000	25,000	100,000

(1934) Maryland Tercentenary

The 300th anniversary of the
founding of the Maryland Colony
by Cecil Calvert (known as Lord
Baltimore) was the occasion for
this special coin. The profits from
the sale of this issue were used to
finance the celebration in Baltimore during 1934. Hans Schuler
designed the coin, which shows
the facing head of Lord Baltimore
on the obverse and the arms of Maryland on the reverse, reminiscent of the Maryland
colonial pieces.

	Distribution	AU-50	MS-60	MS-63	MS-65	MS-66
1934, Maryland Tercentenary 25,015		$150	$165	$190	$385	$550

(1934–1938) Texas Independence Centennial

This issue commemorated the
independence of Texas in 1836.
The first of several dates was
offered in 1934. The later dates
were struck at all three mints. The
models were prepared by Pompeo
Coppini. The reverse shows the
kneeling figure of winged Victory,
and on each side, medallions with
portraits of General Sam Houston
and Stephen Austin, founders of the Republic and State of Texas. The large five-
pointed star behind the eagle on the obverse carries out the Lone Star tradition.

	Distribution	AU-50	MS-60	MS-63	MS-65	MS-66
1934, Texas Independence Centennial 61,463		$140	$155	$165	$300	$425
1935, Texas Independence Centennial (same as 1934) . . 9,996						
1935D, Same type, D Mint 10,007		Set:	450	475	900	1,400
1935S, Same type, S Mint 10,008						
1936, Texas Independence Centennial (same as 1934) . . 8,911						
1936D, Same type, D Mint 9,039		Set:	450	475	900	1,400
1936S, Same type, S Mint 9,055						
1937, Texas Independence Centennial (same as 1934) . . 6,571						
1937D, Same type, D Mint 6,605		Set:	450	475	900	1,400
1937S, Same type, S Mint 6,637						
1938, Texas Independence Centennial (same as 1934) . . 3,780						
1938D, Same type, D Mint 3,775		Set:	650	750	1,350	3,000
1938S, Same type, S Mint 3,814						
Texas Independence Centennial, single type coin		140	155	165	300	425

(1934–1938) Daniel Boone Bicentennial

This coin type, which was minted for five years, was first struck in 1934 to commemorate the 200th anniversary of the famous frontiersman's birth. The change of date to 1935 for the second year's coinage brought about the addition of the commemorative date 1934 above the words PIONEER YEAR. Coinage covered several years, similar to the schedule for the Texas issues. The models for this coin were prepared by Augustus Lukeman. The obverse bears a portrait of Daniel Boone; the reverse shows Boone with Blackfish, war chief of the Chillicothe band of the Shawnee tribe.

Date Added in Field

	Distribution	AU-50	MS-60	MS-63	MS-65	MS-66
1934, Daniel Boone Bicentennial 10,007		$125	$135	$150	$275	$400
1935, Same type 10,010						
1935D, Same type, D Mint 5,005		Set:	410	450	850	1,500
1935S, Same type, S Mint 5,005						
1935, Same as 1934, Small 1934 on Reverse 10,008						
1935D, Same type, D Mint 2,003		Set:	850	975	2,000	3,750
1935S, Same type, S Mint 2,004						
1936, Daniel Boone Bicentennial (same as above) 12,012						
1936D, Same type, D Mint 5,005		Set:	410	450	850	1,500
1936S, Same type, S Mint 5,006						
1937, Daniel Boone Bicentennial (same as above) 9,810						
1937D, Same type, D Mint 2,506		Set:	820	900	1,300	1,800
1937S, Same type, S Mint 2,506						

Chart continued on next page.

	Distribution	AU-50	MS-60	MS-63	MS-65	MS-66
1938, Daniel Boone Bicentennial (same as above) 2,100						
1938D, Same type, D Mint 2,100		*Set:*	$1,000	$1,200	$1,600	$3,000
1938S, Same type, S Mint 2,100						
Daniel Boone Bicentennial, single type coin		$125	135	150	275	400

(1935) Connecticut Tercentenary

In commemoration of the 300th anniversary of the founding of the colony of Connecticut, a souvenir half dollar was struck. Henry Kreis designed the coin. The famous Charter Oak is the main device on the reverse—according to legend, the Royal Charter was secreted in the tree during the reign of James II, who wished to  revoke it. The charter was produced after the king's overthrow in 1688, and the colony continued under its protection.

	Distribution	AU-50	MS-60	MS-63	MS-65	MS-66
1935, Connecticut Tercentenary 25,018		$235	$250	$285	$500	$800

(1935–1939) Arkansas Centennial

This souvenir issue marked the 100th anniversary of the admission of Arkansas into the Union. Edward Everett Burr designed the piece, and models were prepared by Emily Bates of Arkansas. Although 1936 was the centennial year, the first of several issues was brought out in 1935 from all three  mints. The 1936 through 1939 issues were the same as those of 1935 except for the dates. They were sold by the distributors at $8.75 per set of three coins. The reverse shows accolated heads of an Indian chief of 1836 and an American girl of 1935. During 1936, a second design was authorized by Congress. Senator Joseph T. Robinson consented to have his portrait placed on the reverse side of the coins, which were struck at the Philadelphia Mint (see listing on next page).

	Distribution	AU-50	MS-60	MS-63	MS-65	MS-66
1935, Arkansas Centennial 13,012						
1935D, Same type, D Mint 5,505		*Set:*	$290	$335	$700	$2,400
1935S, Same type, S Mint 5,506						
1936, Arkansas Centennial (same as 1935; date 1936 on reverse) 9,660						
1936D, Same type, D Mint 9,660		*Set:*	290	335	750	2,700
1936S, Same type, S Mint 9,662						
1937, Arkansas Centennial (same as 1935) 5,505						
1937D, Same type D mint 5,505		*Set:*	290	365	900	5,250
1937S, Same type S mint 5,506						

	Distribution	AU-50	MS-60	MS-63	MS-65	MS-66
1938, Arkansas Centennial (same as 1935) 3,156						
1938D, Same type, D Mint 3,155		Set:	$500	$550	$1,800	$5,550
1938S, Same type, S Mint 3,156						
1939, Arkansas Centennial (same as 1935) 2,104						
1939D, Same type, D Mint 2,104		Set:	1,000	1,200	2,700	8,850
1939S, Same type, S Mint 2,105						
Arkansas Centennial, single type coin.		$90	100	115	235	800

(1936) Arkansas Centennial – Robinson

A new reverse design for the Arkansas Centennial coin (see prior page) was authorized by the Act of June 26, 1936. Senator Joseph T. Robinson, still living at the time his portrait was used, was the subject for the new issue engraved by Henry Kreis. The obverse, designed by Everett Burr, was unchanged. The law specified a change in the reverse, because of the fact that the obverse side is that which bears the date. From a numismatic viewpoint, however, the side that has the portrait is usually considered the obverse. Thus, in this instance, the side with the eagle device is often considered the reverse.

	Distribution	AU-50	MS-60	MS-63	MS-65	MS-66
1936, Arkansas Centennial (Robinson) 25,265		$150	$175	$200	$385	$700

(1935) Hudson, New York, Sesquicentennial

This souvenir half dollar marked the 150th anniversary of the founding of Hudson, New York, which was named after the explorer Henry Hudson. The designs, by Chester Beach, show Hudson's flagship, the *Half Moon,* on the obverse and the seal of the City of Hudson on the reverse. Details of the seal include representations of Neptune with trident on a spouting whale and a mermaid blowing a conch shell.

	Distribution	AU-50	MS-60	MS-63	MS-65	MS-66
1935, Hudson, New York, Sesquicentennial 10,008		$700	$800	$1,050	$2,000	$3,000

(1935–1936) California Pacific International Exposition

Congress approved the coinage of souvenir half dollars for the exposition on May 3, 1935. Robert Aitken designed the coin, which was struck at the San Francisco Mint. The same type with date 1936 was struck at the Denver Mint, under authority of the special Recoinage Act of May 6, 1936, which specified that 180,000 pieces could be

recoined with the date 1936 irrespective of the year of issue. The obverse displays a seated female with spear and a bear in the left background. The reverse shows the observation tower and the State of California building at the exposition.

	Distribution	AU-50	MS-60	MS-63	MS-65	MS-66
1935S, California Pacific International Exposition	70,132	$100	$110	$120	$160	$200
1936D, California Pacific International Exposition	30,092	100	130	140	190	235

(1935) Old Spanish Trail

This coin commemorated the 400th anniversary of the overland trek of the Cabeza de Vaca Expedition through the Gulf states in 1535. The coin was designed by L.W. Hoffecker, and models were prepared by Edmund J. Senn. The explorer's name literally translated means "head of a cow"; therefore this device was chosen for the

obverse. The reverse bears a yucca tree and a map showing the Old Spanish Trail.

	Distribution	AU-50	MS-60	MS-63	MS-65	MS-66
1935, Old Spanish Trail	10,008	$1,150	$1,300	$1,500	$1,800	$2,100

(1936) Providence, Rhode Island, Tercentenary

The 300th anniversary of Roger Williams's founding of Providence was the occasion for this special half dollar in 1936. The designs were the work of Arthur Graham Carey and John Howard Benson. The obverse shows Roger Williams in a canoe, being welcomed by an Indian. The reverse has the anchor of Hope with a

shield and mantling in the background. Although the founding of Providence was being celebrated, no mention of the city is to be found on the coin.

	Distribution	AU-50	MS-60	MS-63	MS-65	MS-66
1936, Providence, Rhode Island, Tercentenary	20,013					
1936D, Same type, D Mint	15,010	*Set:*	$330	$350	$775	$1,500
1936S, Same type, S Mint	15,011					
Providence, Rhode Island, Tercentenary, single type coin		$100	110	120	225	475

(1936) Cleveland Centennial / Great Lakes Exposition

A special coinage of fifty-cent pieces was authorized in commemoration of the centennial celebration of Cleveland, Ohio, on the occasion of the Great Lakes Exposition held there in 1936. The designs were prepared by Brenda Putnam. Although half the coinage was struck in 1937, all were dated 1936. The obverse has a bust of Moses Cleaveland, and the reverse displays a map of the Great Lakes region with a compass point at the city of Cleveland. Nine Great Lakes cities are marked by stars.

	Distribution	AU-50	MS-60	MS-63	MS-65	MS-66
1936, Cleveland Centennial / Great Lakes Exposition ...	50,030	$120	$130	$140	$200	$390

(1936) Wisconsin Territorial Centennial

The 100th anniversary of the Wisconsin territorial government was the occasion for this issue. The original design was made by David Parsons, a University of Wisconsin student. Benjamin Hawkins, a New York artist, made changes to conform with technical requirements. The reverse has the territorial seal, which includes a forearm holding a pickaxe over a mound of lead ore, and the inscription 4TH DAY OF JULY ANNO DOMINI 1836. The obverse shows a badger on a log, the state emblem, and arrows representing the Black Hawk War of the 1830s.

	Distribution	AU-50	MS-60	MS-63	MS-65	MS-66
1936, Wisconsin Territorial Centennial ...	25,015	$235	$265	$280	$350	$425

(1936) Cincinnati Music Center

Although the head of Stephen Foster, "America's Troubadour," dominates the obverse of this special issue, the anniversary celebrated bears no relation to him. The coins, designed by Constance Ortmayer of Washington, DC, were supposedly struck to commemorate the 50th anniversary in 1936 of Cincinnati as a center of music. The coins were struck at the three mints and were sold only in sets at $7.75, the highest initial cost of a new type at that time.

	Distribution	AU-50	MS-60	MS-63	MS-65	MS-66
1936, Cincinnati Music Center ...	5,005					
1936D, Same type, D Mint ...	5,005	*Set:*	$925	$1,000	$2,175	$5,000
1936S, Same type, S Mint ...	5,006					
Cincinnati Music Center, single type coin ...		$280	310	340	700	1,600

(1936) Long Island Tercentenary

This souvenir issue was authorized to commemorate the 300th anniversary of the first white settlement on Long Island, which was made at Jamaica Bay by Dutch colonists. The design was prepared by Howard Kenneth Weinman, son of the sculptor A.A. Weinman, who designed the regular Liberty Walking type half

dollar. Accolated heads depicting a Dutch settler and an Indian are shown on the obverse, while a Dutch sailing vessel is the reverse device. This was the first issue for which a date was specified (1936) irrespective of the year minted or issued, as a safeguard against extending the coinage over a period of years.

	Distribution	AU-50	MS-60	MS-63	MS-65	MS-66
1936, Long Island Tercentenary	81,826	$95	$100	$125	$350	$840

(1936) York County, Maine, Tercentenary

A souvenir half dollar was authorized by Congress upon the 300th anniversary of the founding of York County, Maine. Brown's Garrison on the Saco River was the site of a town that was settled in 1636. The designs were made by Walter H. Rich of Portland. The obverse design shows a stockade, and the reverse has an adaptation of the York County seal.

	Distribution	AU-50	MS-60	MS-63	MS-65	MS-66
1936, York County, Maine, Tercentenary	25,015	$225	$240	$260	$310	$350

(1936) Bridgeport, Connecticut, Centennial

In commemoration of the 100th anniversary of the incorporation of the city of Bridgeport, a special fifty-cent piece was authorized on May 15, 1936. Henry Kreis designed this coin. The head of P.T. Barnum, Bridgeport's best-known citizen, occupies the obverse. An Art Deco eagle dominates the reverse.

	Distribution	AU-50	MS-60	MS-63	MS-65	MS-66
1936, Bridgeport, Connecticut, Centennial	25,015	$135	$150	$200	$325	$425

(1936) Lynchburg, Virginia, Sesquicentennial

The issuance of a charter to the city of Lynchburg in 1786 was commemorated in 1936 by a special coinage of half dollars. The models for the coin were prepared by Charles Keck. The obverse bears a portrait of Senator Carter Glass, a native of Lynchburg and former secretary of the Treasury, who objected to the idea of using

portraits of living men on coins. Despite his mild protests, his likeness was incorporated on the coin. The reverse shows Liberty standing, with the old Lynchburg courthouse in the background.

	Distribution	AU-50	MS-60	MS-63	MS-65	MS-66
1936, Lynchburg, Virginia, Sesquicentennial.........20,013		$240	$275	$300	$375	$510

(1936) Elgin, Illinois, Centennial

The 100th anniversary of the founding of Elgin was marked by a special issue of half dollars in 1936. The proceeds were devoted to financing a Pioneer Memorial statue, which is depicted on the reverse of the coin. The year 1673 bears no relation to the event but refers to the year in which Louis Joliet and Jacques Marquette

entered Illinois Territory. The designs were prepared by Trygve Rovelstad, who also designed the Pioneer Memorial (which was not dedicated until 2001).

	Distribution	AU-50	MS-60	MS-63	MS-65	MS-66
1936, Elgin, Illinois, Centennial...................20,015		$230	$240	$250	$300	$550

(1936) Albany, New York, Charter

The 250th anniversary of the granting of a charter to the city of Albany was the occasion for this commemorative half dollar. The reverse design shows Governor Thomas Dongan, Peter Schuyler, and Robert Livingston. The obverse depicts a beaver gnawing on a maple branch. Gertrude K. Lathrop of Albany was the designer.

	Distribution	AU-50	MS-60	MS-63	MS-65	MS-66
1936, Albany, New York, Charter 17,671		$310	$340	$360	$450	$535

(1936) San Francisco – Oakland Bay Bridge Opening

The opening of the San Francisco Bay Bridge was the occasion for a special souvenir fifty-cent piece. The designs were the work of Jacques Schnier, a San Francisco artist. A California grizzly bear dominates the obverse. The famous landmark bridge is shown on the reverse. The coins were struck at the San Francisco Mint

in November 1936. The bear depicted was a composite of animals in local zoos.

	Distribution	AU-50	MS-60	MS-63	MS-65	MS-66
1936S, San Francisco–Oakland Bay Bridge Opening . . . 71,424		$170	$180	$210	$350	$475

(1936) Columbia, South Carolina, Sesquicentennial

Souvenir half dollars were authorized to help finance the extensive celebrations marking the sesquicentennial of the founding of Columbia in 1786. A. Wolfe Davidson designed the coin, which was struck at all three mints and sold in sets. The obverse bears the figure of Justice with sword and scales. At the left is the capitol of 1786, and at

the right, the capitol of 1936. A palmetto tree, the state emblem, is the reverse device.

	Distribution	AU-50	MS-60	MS-63	MS-65	MS-66
1936, Columbia, South Carolina, Sesquicentennial 9,007						
1936D, Same type, D Mint 8,009		Set:	$800	$900	$1,000	$1,125
1936S, Same type, S Mint 8,007						
Columbia, South Carolina, Sesquicentennial, single type coin . .		$250	265	300	335	375

(1936) Delaware Tercentenary

The 300th anniversary of the landing of the Swedes in Delaware was the occasion for a souvenir issue of half dollars. The colonists landed on the spot that is now Wilmington and established a church, which is the oldest Protestant church in the United States still used for worship. Their ship, *Kalmar Nyckel,* is shown on the

reverse of the coin, and the Old Swedes Church is on the obverse. Designs were chosen from a competition that was won by Carl L. Schmitz. This coin was authorized in 1936, struck in 1937, and dated 1938 on the reverse and 1936 on the obverse. The anniversary was celebrated in 1938 in both Sweden and the United States. A two-krona coin was issued in Sweden to commemorate the same event.

	Distribution	AU-50	MS-60	MS-63	MS-65	MS-66
1936, Delaware Tercentenary 20,993		$275	$300	$325	$460	$700

(1936) Battle of Gettysburg Anniversary

On June 16, 1936, Congress authorized a coinage of fifty-cent pieces in commemoration of the 1863 Battle of Gettysburg. The models were prepared by Frank Vittor, a Pittsburgh sculptor. Portraits of a Union and a Confederate veteran are shown on the obverse. On the reverse are two shields, representing the Union and Confederate armies, separated by a double-bladed fasces.

	Distribution	AU-50	MS-60	MS-63	MS-65	MS-66
1936, Battle of Gettysburg Anniversary. 26,928		$440	$475	$500	$950	$1,200

(1936) Norfolk, Virginia, Bicentennial

To provide funds for the celebration of Norfolk's anniversary of its growth from a township in 1682 to a royal borough in 1736, Congress first passed a law for the striking of medals. The proponents, however, being dissatisfied, finally succeeded in winning authority for half dollars commemorating the 300th anniversary of the original Norfolk land grant and the 200th anniversary of the establishment of the borough. William Marks Simpson and his wife, Marjorie Emory Simpson, designed the piece. The obverse shows the Seal of the City of Norfolk with a three-masted ship as the central device. The reverse features the Royal Mace of Norfolk, presented by Lieutenant Governor Dinwiddie in 1753.

	Distribution	AU-50	MS-60	MS-63	MS-65	MS-66
1936, Norfolk, Virginia, Bicentennial. 16,936		$450	$460	$475	$575	$650

(1937) Roanoke Island, North Carolina, 350th Anniversary

A celebration was held in Old Fort Raleigh in 1937 to commemorate the 350th anniversary of Sir Walter Raleigh's "Lost Colony" and the birth of Virginia Dare, the first white child born in British North America. A special half dollar for the occasion was designed by William Marks Simpson of Baltimore. The obverse bears a portrait of Sir Walter Raleigh, and the reverse has a figure representing Ellinor Dare holding her child Virginia.

	Distribution	AU-50	MS-60	MS-63	MS-65	MS-66
1937, Roanoke Island, North Carolina, 350th Anniversary. 29,030		$225	$250	$275	$325	$400

(1937) Battle of Antietam Anniversary

A souvenir half dollar was designed by William Marks Simpson and struck in 1937 to commemorate the 75th anniversary of the famous Civil War battle to thwart Lee's invasion of Maryland. The opposing generals McClellan and Lee are featured on the obverse, while the Burnside Bridge, an important tactical  objective, is shown on the reverse. The Battle of Antietam, on September 17, 1862, was one of the bloodiest single-day battles of the war, with more than 23,000 men killed, wounded, or missing.

	Distribution	AU-50	MS-60	MS-63	MS-65	MS-66
1937, Battle of Antietam Anniversary 18,028		$675	$700	$725	$900	$1,100

(1938) New Rochelle, New York, 250th Anniversary

To observe the founding of New Rochelle in 1688 by French Huguenots, a special half dollar was issued in 1938. The title to the land that the Huguenots purchased from John Pell provided that a fattened calf be given away every year on June 20. This is represented by a calf and figure of John Pell on the obverse of the coin.  The fleur-de-lis, which is shown on the reverse, is adapted from the seal of the city. Both sides of the coin were designed by Gertrude K. Lathrop.

	Distribution	AU-50	MS-60	MS-63	MS-65	MS-66
1938, New Rochelle, New York, 250th Anniversary 15,266		$370	$390	$415	$575	$700

(1946) Iowa Centennial

This half dollar, commemorating the 100th anniversary of Iowa's statehood, was designed by Adam Pietz of Philadelphia. The reverse shows the Iowa state seal, and the obverse shows the first stone capitol building at Iowa City. This issue was sold first to the residents of Iowa and only a small remainder to others. Nearly all of the  issue was disposed of quickly, except for 500 that were held back to be distributed in 1996, and another 500 in 2046.

	Distribution	AU-50	MS-60	MS-63	MS-65	MS-66
1946, Iowa Centennial 100,057		$115	$125	$135	$150	$185

(1946–1951) Booker T. Washington Memorial

This commemorative coin was issued to perpetuate the ideals and teachings of Booker T. Washington and to construct memorials to his memory. Issued from all mints, it received wide distribution from the start. The reverse has the legend FROM SLAVE CABIN TO HALL OF FAME. His log-cabin birthplace is shown beneath. This coin was designed by Isaac Scott Hathaway, as was the Carver/Washington half dollar.

	Distribution	AU-50	MS-60	MS-63	MS-65	MS-66
1946, Booker T. Washington Memorial (a) 700,546						
1946D, Same type, D Mint 50,000		*Set:*	$65	$80	$175	$600
1946S, Same type, S Mint 500,279						
1947, Same type as 1946 6,000						
1947D, Same type, D Mint 6,000		*Set:*	125	150	310	2,025
1947S, Same type, S Mint 6,000						
1948, Same type as 1946 8,005						
1948D, Same type, D Mint 8,005		*Set:*	180	235	325	1,200
1948S, Same type, S Mint 8,005						
1949, Same type as 1946 6,004						
1949D, Same type, D Mint 6,004		*Set:*	240	265	350	800
1949S, Same type, S Mint 6,004						
1950, Same type as 1946 6,004						
1950D, Same type, D Mint 6,004		*Set:*	150	170	250	1,500
1950S, Same type, S Mint 62,091						
1951, Same type as 1946 210,082						
1951D, Same type, D Mint 7,004		*Set:*	150	180	230	1,050
1951S, Same type, S Mint 7,004						
Booker T. Washington Memorial, single type coin.		$16	20	25	60	150

a. Minted; quantity melted unknown.

(1951–1954) Carver/Washington Commemorative

Designed by Isaac Scott Hathaway, this coin portrays the conjoined busts of two prominent black Americans. Booker T. Washington was a lecturer, educator, and principal of Tuskegee Institute. He urged training to advance independence and efficiency for his race. George Washington Carver was an agricultural chemist who worked to improve the economy of the South. He spent part of his life teaching crop improvement and new uses for soybeans, peanuts, sweet potatoes, and cotton waste. Money obtained from the sale of these commemoratives was to be used "to oppose the spread of communism among Negroes in the interest of national defense."

See next page for chart.

	Distribution	AU-50	MS-60	MS-63	MS-65	MS-66
1951, Carver/Washington 20,018						
1951D, Same type, D Mint 10,004	*Set:*	$135	$200	$550	$3,750	
1951S, Same type, S Mint 10,004						
1952, Same type as 1951 1,106,292						
1952D, Same type, D Mint 8,006	*Set:*	140	180	385	1,650	
1952S, Same type, S Mint 8,006						
1953, Same type as 1951 8,003						
1953D, Same type, D Mint 8,003	*Set:*	140	210	540	1,650	
1953S, Same type, S Mint 88,020						
1954, Same type as 1951 12,006						
1954D, Same type, D Mint 12,006	*Set:*	135	180	390	1,650	
1954S, Same type, S Mint 42,024						
Carver/Washington, single type coin		$16	21	24	75	320

MODERN COMMEMORATIVES
(1982) George Washington 250th Anniversary of Birth

This coin, the first commemorative half dollar issued since 1954, commemorated the 250th anniversary of the birth of George Washington. It was also the first 90% silver coin produced by the U.S. Mint since 1964. Designed by Elizabeth Jones, chief sculptor and engraver of the United States, the obverse features George Washington astride a horse. The reverse depicts the eastern facade of Washington's home, Mount Vernon. The Uncirculated version was struck at Denver and the Proof at San Francisco.

	Distribution	MS-67	PF-67
1982D, George Washington, 250th Anniversary silver half dollar 2,210,458		$15	
1982S, Same type, Proof . . . . (4,894,044)			$16

(1983–1984) Los Angeles Olympiad

Three distinctive coins were issued to commemorate the 1984 Los Angeles Summer Olympic Games. The silver dollar dated 1983 was designed by Elizabeth Jones, chief engraver of the Mint. On the obverse is a representation of the traditional Greek discus thrower inspired by the ancient work of the sculptor Myron. The reverse depicts the head and upper body of an American eagle.

The 1984 Olympic silver dollar was designed by Robert Graham, an American sculptor who created the controversial headless sculpture placed at the entrance to the Los Angeles Memorial Coliseum. The obverse depicts Graham's sculpture with the coliseum in the background. The reverse features an American eagle.

The commemorative gold coin minted for the 1984 Olympics was the first U.S. gold piece issued in more than 50 years. The weight, size, and fineness are the same as for the previous ten-dollar coin, issued in 1933: weight, 16.718 grams; composition, .900 gold, .100 copper (net weight, .4837 oz. pure gold). It is the first coin ever to bear the W mintmark for West Point. The obverse depicts two runners bearing the Olympic torch aloft, and was designed by John Mercanti from a concept by James Peed, an artist at the Mint. The eagle on the reverse is modeled after that on the Great Seal.

	Distribution	MS-67	PF-67
1983P, Discus Thrower silver dollar 294,543		$36	
1983D, Same type, D Mint 174,014		36	
1983S, Same type, S Mint . . . . (1,577,025) 174,014		36	$37
1984P, Olympic Coliseum silver dollar 217,954		36	
1984D, Same type, D Mint 116,675		36	
1984S, Same type, S Mint . . . . (1,801,210) . . .116,675		36	37
1984P, Olympic Torch Bearers gold $10. . . . .(33,309)			1,025
1984D, Same type, D Mint . . . .(34,533)			1,025
1984S, Same type, S Mint . . . .(48,551)			1,025
1984W, Same type, W Mint . . . .(381,085) 75,886	1,000		1,000

(1986) Statue of Liberty Centennial

The first copper-nickel clad half dollar commemorative depicts the United States' heritage as a nation of immigrants. The obverse, designed by Edgar Steever, pictures a ship of immigrants steaming into New York Harbor, with the Statue of Liberty greeting them in the foreground and the New York skyline in the distance. The reverse, designed by Sherl Joseph Winter, has a scene of an immigrant family with their belongings on the threshold of America.

Designed by Mint artist John Mercanti, the Statue of Liberty silver dollar commemorates Ellis Island as the "Gateway to America." The obverse features a classic pose of Liberty in the foreground, with the Ellis Island Immigration Center behind her. On the reverse is a depiction of Liberty's torch, along with the words GIVE ME YOUR TIRED, YOUR POOR, YOUR HUDDLED MASSES YEARNING TO BREATHE FREE.

The commemorative half eagle was also the first of this denomination to be minted in more than 50 years. Standards for weight and size are the same as for previous half eagle gold coins: weight, 8.539 grams; composition, .900 gold, .100 copper (net weight .2418 oz. pure gold). The design is the creation of the Mint's chief engraver, Elizabeth Jones. The obverse features a compelling close-up view of Liberty's face in sharp relief, with the inscription 1986 LIBERTY. An eagle in flight adorns the reverse. All were minted at West Point and bear the W mintmark.

	Distribution	MS-67	PF-67
1986D, Statue of Liberty Centennial clad half dollar	928,008	$6	
1986S, Same type, S Mint, Proof	(6,925,627)		$6
1986P, Statue of Liberty Centennial silver dollar	723,635	36	
1986S, Same type, S Mint, Proof	(6,414,638)		37
1986W, Statue of Liberty Centennial gold $5	(404,013) 95,248	500	500

(1987) U.S. Constitution Bicentennial

The silver dollar commemorating the 200th anniversary of the United States Constitution was designed by Patricia Lewis Verani using standard weight, size, and fineness. A quill pen, a sheaf of parchment, and the words WE THE PEOPLE are depicted on the obverse. The reverse portrays a cross-section of Americans from various periods representing contrasting lifestyles.

A modernistic design by Marcel Jovine was selected for the five-dollar gold coin of standard weight, size, and fineness. The obverse portrays a stylized eagle holding a massive quill pen. Another large quill pen is featured on the reverse. To the left are nine stars, signifying the first colonies that ratified the Constitution. Four stars to the right represent the remaining original states. Both Uncirculated and Proof versions were minted at West Point.

	Distribution	MS-67	PF-67
1987P, U.S. Constitution Bicentennial silver dollar	451,629	$36	
1987S, Same type, S Mint, Proof	(2,747,116)		$37
1987W, U.S. Constitution Bicentennial gold $5	(651,659) 214,225	500	500

(1988) Seoul Olympiad

The 1988 Olympic silver dollar commemorates U.S. participation in the Seoul Olympiad. Its size and weight are identical to those of other silver dollars. Design of the obverse is by Patricia Lewis Verani. The reverse is by Mint sculptor-engraver Sherl Joseph Winter.

	Distribution	MS-67	PF-67
1988D, Seoul Olympiad silver dollar	191,368	$36	
1988S, Same type, S mint, Proof	(1,359,366)		$37

The 1988 five-dollar gold Olympic coin was designed by Elizabeth Jones, chief sculptor and engraver of the U.S. Mint. The obverse features Nike, goddess of Victory, wearing a crown of olive leaves. The reverse features Marcel Jovine's stylized Olympic flame, evoking the spectacle of the Olympic Games and the renewal of the Olympic spirit every four years.

	Distribution	MS-67	PF-67
1988W, Seoul Olympiad gold $5............................(281,465) 62,913		$500	$500

(1989) Congress Bicentennial

The Bicentennial of the Congress was commemorated on three coins. The obverse of the half dollar was designed by sculptor Patricia L. Verani and features a detailed bust of the Statue of Freedom. The reverse, designed by William Woodward, offers a full view of the Capitol Building accented by a wreath of stars.

Designed by muralist William Woodward, the obverse of the dollar features the Statue of Freedom that towers atop the Capitol dome. The reverse shows the Mace of the House of Representatives, which resides in the House Chamber whenever the House is in session. The mace's staff is topped by an eagle astride a globe. A scarce variety of the 1989-D dollar shows the dies aligned the same way, rather than the normal "coin turn" of 180 degrees.

	Distribution	MS-67	PF-67
1989D, Congress Bicentennial clad half dollar 163,753		$9	
1989S, Same type, S Mint, Proof ....(767,897)			$9
1989D, Congress Bicentennial silver dollar....................................135,203		36	
1989D, Same type, inverted reverse...		1,800	
1989S, Same type, S Mint, Proof ....(762,198)			37

The Capitol dome is depicted on the obverse of the five-dollar gold coin. The design is the work of Mint engraver John Mercanti. The reverse features a majestic eagle atop the canopy overlooking the Old Senate Chamber.

	Distribution	MS-67	PF-67
1989W, Congress Bicentennial gold $5 . . . .(164,690) 46,899		$500	$500

(1990) Eisenhower Centennial

The unusual design on this coin features the profile of President Dwight Eisenhower facing right, superimposed over his own left-facing profile as a five-star general. It is the creation of Mint engraver John Mercanti. The reverse shows the Eisenhower home at Gettysburg, a national historic site, and was designed by Marcel Jovine. The coin was issued to celebrate the 100th anniversary of the birth of the 34th president.

	Distribution	MS-67	PF-67
1990W, Eisenhower Centennial silver dollar 241,669		$36	
1990P, Same type, P Mint, Proof . . . . (1,144,461)			$37

(1991) Mount Rushmore Golden Anniversary

The 50th anniversary of the Mount Rushmore National Memorial was commemorated on three coins. Surcharges from the sale of these pieces were divided between the Treasury Department and the Mount Rushmore National Memorial Society of Black Hills, South Dakota, with money going to finance restoration work on the national landmark.

The obverse of the copper-nickel half dollar was designed by New Jersey artist Marcel Jovine, and features a view of the famous carving by Gutzon Borglum. The reverse, designed by Mint sculptor-engraver James Ferrell, shows an American bison with the words GOLDEN ANNIVERSARY.

The Mount Rushmore Golden Anniversary silver dollar obverse was designed by Marika Somogyi. It displays the traditional portraits of presidents George Washington, Thomas Jefferson, Theodore Roosevelt, and Abraham Lincoln as sculptured on the mountain by Gutzon Borglum, who earlier had modeled the figures shown on the Stone Mountain commemorative coin. The reverse, which was designed by former chief sculptor-engraver of the Mint Frank Gasparro, features a small outline map of the continental United States with the Great Seal above.

311

The five-dollar gold coin commemorating the 50th anniversary of the Mount Rushmore National Memorial features an American eagle flying above the monument with LIBERTY and the date in the field. The obverse was designed by Mint sculptor-engraver John Mercanti, and the reverse was designed by Rhode Island artist Robert Lamb, and engraved by Mint sculptor-engraver William Cousins. The size, weight, and fineness are the same as for all other half eagle coins.

	Distribution	MS-67	PF-67
1991D, Mount Rushmore Golden Anniversary clad half dollar .172,754		$19	
1991S, Same type, S Mint, Proof . . . .(753,257)			$19
1991P, Mount Rushmore Golden Anniversary silver dollar 133,139		47	
1991S, Same type, S Mint, Proof . . . .(738,419)			45
1991W, Mount Rushmore Golden Anniversary gold $5 . . . .(111,991) 31,959		500	500

(1991) Korean War Memorial

The 38th anniversary of the end of the Korean War was the occasion for striking this coin, which honors the end of the conflict and those who served in combat. The design has been criticized as being cluttered, and the occasion no more than a fund-raising opportunity for the creation of a national monument in Washington. The obverse, designed by sculptor-engraver of the U.S. Mint John Mercanti, features an Army infantryman in full gear. On the reverse is an outline map of Korea with North and South divided at the 38th parallel, designed by Mint sculptor-engraver James Ferrell.

	Distribution	MS-67	PF-67
1991D, Korean War Memorial silver dollar 213,049		$36	
1991P, Same type, P Mint, Proof . . . .(618,488)			$37

(1991) United Service Organizations

A special commemorative silver dollar was struck to honor the 50th anniversary of United Service Organizations. The group was founded in 1941 to supply social, recreational, welfare, and spiritual facilities to armed services personnel. Surcharges on sales of the coins were divided equally between the USO and the Department of the Treasury. The coins were launched on Flag Day, June 14, using designs selected in a limited competition between Mint staff and five outside, invited artists. The obverse uses a banner inscribed USO, designed by Rhode Island artist Robert Lamb. On the reverse is a globe with an eagle on top, the work of Mint sculptor-engraver John Mercanti.

	Distribution	MS-67	PF-67
1991D, USO silver dollar. 124,958		$37	
1991S, Same type, S Mint, Proof . . . .(321,275)			$39

(1992) XXV Olympiad

The XXV Olympiad held Winter Olympic games in Albertville and Savoie, France, and Summer Olympic games in Barcelona, Spain. United States commemorative coins were issued to honor the participation of American athletes and to finance their training. Competitive designs were selected from 1,107 entries.

The clad half dollar obverse, designed by Mint sculptor-engraver William Cousins, depicts a gymnast in motion. The reverse, by Steven M. Bieda, has the inscription CITIUS, ALTIUS, FORTIUS (the Olympic motto: "Faster, Higher, Stronger") with an olive branch crossing the Olympic torch.

The 1992 Olympic silver dollar obverse is a rendering by John R. Deecken of a pitcher firing a ball to home plate. The reverse, by sculptor Marcel Jovine, combines the Olympic rings, olive branches, and stars and stripes with a bold USA. Uncirculated dollars minted at Denver have the phrase XXV OLYMPIAD impressed four times around the edge, alternately inverted, on a reeded background.

The obverse of the 1992 Olympic five-dollar gold was designed by James Sharpe, and modeled by T. James Ferrell. It depicts a sprinter in a burst of speed. The reverse, by James Peed, unites two impressive symbols, the Olympic rings and the American bald eagle. **Size and fineness of these coins is the same as for other United States gold and silver issues of these denominations.**

	Distribution	MS-67	PF-67
1992P, XXV Olympiad clad half dollar	161,607	$9	
1992S, Same type, S Mint, Proof	(519,645)		$10
1992D, XXV Olympiad silver dollar	187,552	37	
1992S, Same type, S Mint, Proof	(504,505)		38
1992W, XXV Olympiad gold $5	(77,313) 27,732	500	500

(1992) White House 200th Anniversary

The obverse of this coin, designed by Mint sculptor Edgar Z. Steever IV, depicts the north portico of the White House. The reverse, by Mint sculptor Chester Y. Martin, features a bust of James Hoban, the original architect, and the main entrance he designed.

	Distribution	MS-67	PF-67
1992D, White House 200th Anniversary silver dollar.............................123,803		$38	
1992W, Same type, W Mint, Proof ....(375,851)			$40

(1992) Christopher Columbus Quincentenary

The Columbus quincentenary was honored on U.S. three coins. This copper-nickel half dollar, designed by Mint sculptor T. James Ferrell, depicts Columbus landing in the New World on the obverse, and his three ships on the reverse. Mint sculptor John Mercanti designed the silver dollar obverse, which features a full-length figure of Columbus beside a globe, with his ships above. The reverse, by Mint sculptor Thomas D. Rogers Sr., is a split image of the *Santa Maria* and the U.S. space shuttle *Discovery.*

	Distribution	MS-67	PF-67
1992D, Christopher Columbus Quincentenary clad half dollar.....................135,702		$13	
1992S, Same type, S Mint, Proof ....(390,154)			$12
1992D, Christopher Columbus Quincentenary silver dollar 106,949		40	
1992P, Same type, P Mint, Proof ....(385,241)			39

The five-dollar gold coin obverse, designed by Mint sculptor T. James Ferrell, bears a portrait of Columbus facing a map of the New World. The reverse, by Mint sculptor Thomas D. Rogers Sr., shows the Crest of the Admiral of the Ocean Sea.

	Distribution	MS-67	PF-67
1992W, Christopher Columbus Quincentenary gold $5 . . . .(79,730) 24,329		$500	$500

(1993) Bill of Rights

The silver half dollar in this series depicts James Madison penning the Bill of Rights. It was designed by Mint sculptor T. James Ferrell. The reverse, by Dean McMullen, displays the torch of freedom. Some 9,656 of the Uncirculated version were privately marked on the edge with a serial number and the initials of the Madison Foundation and the American Numismatic Association.

	Distribution	MS-67	PF-67
1993W, Bill of Rights silver half dollar 193,346		$22	
1993S, Same type, S Mint, Proof . . . .(586,315)			$22

A portrait of James Madison is shown on the obverse of this silver dollar, designed by William Krawczewicz. Dean McMullen designed the reverse, which shows Montpelier, the Virginia home of James and Dolley Madison.

	Distribution	MS-67	PF-67
1993D, Bill of Rights silver dollar 98,383		$40	
1993S, Same type, S Mint, Proof . . . .(534,001)			$39

The obverse of the five-dollar gold coin was designed by Scott R. Blazek. It features Madison studying the Bill of Rights. On the reverse, by Joseph D. Peña, is a quotation from Madison, accented by an eagle, torch, and laurel branch.

	Distribution	MS-67	PF-67
1993W, Bill of Rights gold $5.............................(78,651).....23,266		$500	$500

(1991–1995) 50th Anniversary of World War II

Each of the three coins in this series is dated 1991–1995, and commemorates the 50th anniversary of U.S. involvement in World War II, which lasted from 1941 to 1945. Pieces were coined and issued in 1993. The obverse of the clad half dollar was designed by George Klauba. It depicts the faces of three members of the armed services superimposed upon the "V for victory" symbol. The reverse, by Bill J. Leftwich, portrays a Pacific island battle scene.

U.S. Mint sculptor-engraver Thomas D. Rogers Sr. designed the silver dollar showing an American soldier on the beach at Normandy. The reverse depicts the shoulder sleeve insignia of the Supreme Headquarters Allied Expeditionary Force, with a quotation from Dwight D. Eisenhower.

Both Proof and Uncirculated versions of the five-dollar gold coin were struck at the West Point Mint. The obverse, designed by Charles J. Madsen, depicts an American serviceman with rifle raised in victory. The reverse, by Edward Southworth Fisher, features a "V for victory" in the center with Morse code for the letter superimposed.

See next page for chart.

	Distribution	MS-67	PF-67
(1993P) 1991–1995 World War II clad half dollar ....(317,396) 197,072		$25	$24
(1993D) 1991–1995 World War II silver dollar 107,240		40	
(1993W) Same type, W Mint, Proof............................(342,041)			43
(1993W) 1991–1995 World War II gold $5 ....(67,026) 23,672		500	500

(1994) World Cup Tournament

The 1994 World Cup Tournament was the culmination of soccer games among 141 nations. The United States was selected to host the XV FIFA World Cup playoff, and three commemorative coins were issued to celebrate the event. Each of the coins employs a shared design on the reverse.

The obverse of the clad half dollar depicts a soccer player in action. It was designed by Richard T. LaRoche. The reverse, designed by Dean McMullen, features the official World Cup USA 1994 logo flanked by laurel branches.

The obverse of the silver dollar coin features two competing players converging on a soccer ball. It was designed by Dean McMullen, who also executed the reverse design, the official logo that is used on all of the World Cup coins.

Both Proof and Uncirculated versions of the five-dollar gold coin were struck at the West Point Mint. The obverse, designed by William J. Krawczewicz, depicts the modernistic gold World Cup trophy. The reverse was designed by Dean McMullen and shows the same logo used on other World Cup coins.

	Distribution	MS-67	PF-67
1994D, World Cup Tournament clad half dollar..........................168,208		$10	
1994P, Same type, P Mint, Proof ....(609,354)			$10
1994D, World Cup Tournament silver dollar 81,524		40	
1994S, Same type, S Mint, Proof ....(577,090)			42
1994W, World Cup Tournament gold $5........................(89,614) 22,447		500	500

(1993 [1994]) Thomas Jefferson

	Distribution	MS-67	PF-67
1993 (1994) Thomas Jefferson silver dollar, P Mint	266,927	$38	
1993 (1994) Same type, S Mint, Proof	(332,891)		$40

(1994) Vietnam Veterans Memorial

	Distribution	MS-67	PF-67
1994W, Vietnam Veterans Memorial silver dollar	57,290	$85	
1994P, Same type, P Mint, Proof	(227,671)		$70

(1994) U.S. Prisoner of War Museum

	Distribution	MS-67	PF-67
1994W, U.S. Prisoner of War Museum silver dollar	54,893	$95	
1994P, Same type, P Mint, Proof	(224,449)		$50

(1994) Women in Military Service Memorial

	Distribution	MS-67	PF-67
1994W, Women in Military Service Memorial silver dollar.........................69,860		$40	
1994P, Same type, P Mint, Proof ....(241,278)			$40

(1994) U.S. Capitol Bicentennial

	Distribution	MS-67	PF-67
1994D, U.S. Capitol Bicentennial silver dollar..................................68,332		$40	
1994S, Same type, S Mint, Proof ....(279,579)			$42

(1995) Civil War Battlefield Preservation

	Distribution	MS-67	PF-67
1995S, Civil War Battlefield Preservation clad half dollar 119,520		$42	
1995S, Same type, S Mint, Proof ....(330,002)			$40

	Distribution	MS-67	PF-67
1995P, Civil War Battlefield Preservation silver dollar.............................45,866		$70	
1995S, Same type, S Mint, Proof.............................(437,114)...........			$65

	Distribution	MS-67	PF-67
1995W, Civil War Battlefield Preservation gold $5.............................12,735		$800	
1995W, Same type, W Mint, Proof.............................(55,246)...........			$550

(1995) XXVI Olympiad

	Distribution	MS-67	PF-67
1995S, XXVI Olympiad, Basketball clad half dollar.............................171,001		$22	
1995S, Same type, S Mint, Proof.............................(169,655)..........			$20
1995S, XXVI Olympiad, Baseball clad half dollar.............................164,605		24	
1995S, Same type, S Mint, Proof.............................(118,087)..........			22
1996S, XXVI Olympiad, Swimming clad half dollar.............................49,533		160	
1996S, Same type, S Mint, Proof.............................(114,315)..........			40
1996S, XXVI Olympiad, Soccer clad half dollar.............................52,836		130	
1996S, Same type, S Mint, Proof.............................(112,412)..........			100

	Distribution	MS-67	PF-67
1995D, XXVI Olympiad, Gymnastics silver dollar............................42,497		$70	
1995P, Same type, P Mint, Proof............................(182,676).........			$50
1995D, XXVI Olympiad, Paralympics silver dollar............................28,649		80	
1995P, Same type, P Mint, Proof............................(138,337).........			45
1995D, XXVI Olympiad, Track and Field silver dollar............................24,976		100	
1995P, Same type, P mint, Proof............................(136,935).........			50
1995D, XXVI Olympiad, Cycling silver dollar............................19,662		150	
1995P, Same type, P Mint, Proof............................(118,795).........			60
1996D, XXVI Olympiad, Tennis silver dollar............................15,983		275	
1996P, Same type, P Mint, Proof............................(92,016).........			100
1996D, XXVI Olympiad, Paralympics silver dollar............................14,497		280	
1996P, Same type, P Mint, Proof............................(84,280).........			80
1996D, XXVI Olympiad, Rowing silver dollar............................16,258		275	
1996P, Same type, P Mint, Proof............................(151,890).........			60
1996D, XXVI Olympiad, High Jump silver dollar............................15,697		285	
1996P, Same type, P Mint, Proof............................(124,502).........			60

	Distribution	MS-67	PF-67
1995W, XXVI Olympiad, Torch Runner gold $5............................14,675		$950	
1995W, Same type, W Mint, Proof............................(57,442).........			$500
1995W, XXVI Olympiad, Stadium gold $5............................10,579		2,400	
1995W, Same type, W Mint, Proof............................(43,124).........			525
1996W, XXVI Olympiad, Flag Bearer gold $5............................9,174		2,600	
1996W, Same type, W Mint, Proof............................(32,886).........			525
1996W, XXVI Olympiad, Cauldron gold $5............................9,210		2,600	
1996W, Same type, W Mint, Proof............................(38,555).........			525

(1995) Special Olympics World Games

	Distribution	MS-67	PF-67
1995W, Special Olympics World Games silver dollar.	89,301	$36	
1995P, Same type, P Mint, Proof	(351,764)		$37

(1996) National Community Service

	Distribution	MS-67	PF-67
1996S, National Community Service silver dollar	23,500	$185	
1996S, Same type, S Mint, Proof	(101,543)		$65

(1996) Smithsonian Institution 150th Anniversary

	Distribution	MS-67	PF-67
1996D, Smithsonian Institution 150th Anniversary silver dollar.	31,320	$150	
1996P, Same type, P Mint, Proof	(129,152)		$65

	Distribution	MS-67	PF-67
1996W, Smithsonian Institution 150th Anniversary gold $5 9,068		$900	
1996W, Same type, W Mint, Proof ....(21,772)			$500

(1997) U.S. Botanic Garden

	Distribution	MS-67	PF-67
1997P, Botanic Garden silver dollar 58,505		$50	
1997P, Same type, P Mint, Proof ....(189,671)			$50

(1997) Jackie Robinson

	Distribution	MS-67	PF-67
1997S, Jackie Robinson silver dollar 30,180		$80	
1997S, Same type, S Mint, Proof ....(110,002)			$90
1997W, Jackie Robinson gold $5 5,174		3,300	
1997W, Same type, W Mint, Proof ....(24,072)			600

(1997) Franklin D. Roosevelt

	Distribution	MS-67	PF-67
1997W, Franklin D. Roosevelt gold $5	11,894	$1,200	
1997W, Same type, W Mint, Proof	(29,474)		$500

(1997) National Law Enforcement Officers Memorial

	Distribution	MS-67	PF-67
1997P, National Law Enforcement Officers Memorial silver dollar	28,575	$160	
1997P, Same type, P Mint, Proof	(110,428)		$100

(1998) Robert F. Kennedy

	Distribution	MS-67	PF-67
1998S, Robert F. Kennedy silver dollar	106,422	$60	
1998S, Same type, S Mint, Proof	(99,020)		$60

(1998) Black Revolutionary War Patriots

	Distribution	MS-67	PF-67
1998S, Black Revolutionary War Patriots silver dollar	37,210	$160	
1998S, Same type, S Mint, Proof	(75,070)		$105

(1999) Dolley Madison

	Distribution	MS-67	PF-67
1999P, Dolley Madison silver dollar	89,104	$45	
1999P, Same type, P Mint, Proof	(224,403)		$45

(1999) George Washington Death Bicentennial

	Distribution	MS-67	PF-67
1999W, George Washington Death Bicentennial gold $5	22,511	$500	
1999W, Same type, W Mint, Proof	(41,693)		$500

(1999) Yellowstone National Park

	Distribution	MS-67	PF-67
1999P, Yellowstone National Park silver dollar	82,563	$50	
1999S, Same type, S Mint, Proof	(187,595)		$42

(2000) Library of Congress Bicentennial

	Distribution	MS-67	PF-67
2000P, Library of Congress Bicentennial silver dollar	53,264	$45	
2000P, Same type, P Mint, Proof	(198,503)		$42

	Distribution	MS-67	PF-67
2000W, Library of Congress Bicentennial bimetallic (gold/platinum) $10	7,261	$4,200	
2000W, Same type, W Mint, Proof	(27,445)		$1,500

(2000) Leif Ericson Millennium

	Distribution	MS-67	PF-67
2000P, Leif Ericson Millennium silver dollar 28,150		$90	
2000P, Same type, P Mint, Proof . . . . (144,748)			$80

(2001) American Buffalo

	Distribution	MS-67	PF-67
2001D, American Buffalo silver dollar 227,131		$190	
2001P, Same type, P Mint, Proof . . . . (272,869)			$190

(2001) U.S. Capitol Visitor Center

	Distribution	MS-67	PF-67
2001P, U.S. Capitol Visitor Center clad half dollar 99,157		$16	
2001P, Same type, P Mint, Proof . . . . (77,962)			$18

	Distribution	MS-67	PF-67
2001P, U.S. Capitol Visitor Center silver dollar 35,380		$45	
2001P, Same type, P Mint, Proof . . . .(143,793)			$45
2001W, U.S. Capitol Visitor Center gold $5 6,761		2,800	
2001W, Same type, W Mint, Proof . . . .(27,652)			500

(2002) Salt Lake City Olympic Games

	Distribution	MS-67	PF-67
2002P, Salt Lake City Olympics silver dollar 40,257		$45	
2002P, Same type, P Mint, Proof . . . .(166,864)			$42

	Distribution	MS-67	PF-67
2002W, Salt Lake City Olympics gold $5 10,585		$500	
2002W, Same type, W Mint, Proof . . . .(32,877)			$500

(2002) West Point Bicentennial

	Distribution	MS-67	PF-67
2002W, West Point Bicentennial silver dollar	103,201	$37	
2002W, Same type, W Mint, Proof	(288,293)		$38

(2003) First Flight Centennial

	Distribution	MS-67	PF-67
2003P, First Flight Centennial clad half dollar	57,122	$17	
2003P, Same type, P Mint, Proof	(109,710)		$18
2003P, First Flight Centennial silver dollar	53,533	42	
2003P, Same type, P Mint, Proof	(190,240)		48
2003W, First Flight Centennial gold $10	10,009	1,100	
2003W, Same type, W Mint, Proof	(21,676)		1,050

(2004) Thomas Alva Edison

	Distribution	MS-67	PF-67
2004P, Thomas Alva Edison silver dollar.	92,510	$40	
2004P, Same type, P Mint, Proof	(211,055)		$42

(2004) Lewis and Clark Bicentennial

	Distribution	MS-67	PF-67
2004P, Lewis and Clark Bicentennial silver dollar.	142,015	$40	
2004P, Same type, P Mint, Proof	(351,989)		$42

(2005) Chief Justice John Marshall

	Distribution	MS-67	PF-67
2005P, Chief Justice John Marshall silver dollar.	67,096	$42	
2005P, Same type, P Mint, Proof	(196,753)		$40

(2005) Marine Corps 230th Anniversary

	Distribution	MS-67	PF-67
2005P, Marine Corps 230th Anniversary silver dollar 49,671		$53	
2005P, Same type, P Mint, Proof . . . .(548,810)			$53

(2006) Benjamin Franklin Tercentenary

	Distribution	MS-67	PF-67
2006P, Benjamin Franklin "Scientist" silver dollar 58,000		$45	
2006P, Same type, P Mint, Proof . . . .(142,000)			$55

	Distribution	MS-67	PF-67
2006P, Benjamin Franklin "Founding Father" silver dollar 58,000		$50	
2006P, Same type, P Mint, Proof . . . .(142,000)			$50

(2006) San Francisco Old Mint Centennial

	Distribution	MS-67	PF-67
2006S, San Francisco Old Mint Centennial silver dollar 67,100		$45	
2006S, Same type, S Mint, Proof . . . . (160,870)			$45
2006S, San Francisco Old Mint Centennial gold $5 17,500		500	
2006S, Same type, S Mint, Proof . . . . (44,174)			500

(2007) Jamestown 400th Anniversary

	Distribution	MS-67	PF-67
2007P, Jamestown 400th Anniversary silver dollar. 81,034		$40	
2007P, Same type, P Mint, Proof . . . . (260,363)			$40

	Distribution	MS-67	PF-67
2007W, Jamestown 400th Anniversary gold $5 81,623		$500	
2007W, Same type, W Mint, Proof . . . . (47,123)			$500

(2007) Little Rock Central High School Desegregation

	Distribution	MS-67	PF-67
2007P, Little Rock Central High School Desegregation silver dollar 125,678	124,678	$45	
2007S, Same type, S Mint, Proof ....(66,093)			$50

(2008) Bald Eagle

	Distribution	MS-67	PF-67
2008S, Bald Eagle clad half dollar 120,180	120,180	$13	
2008S, Same type, S Mint, Proof ....(220,577)..........			$15
2008P, Bald Eagle silver dollar...................................119,204	119,204	43	
2008P, Same type, P Mint, Proof ....(294,601)..........			45
2008W, Bald Eagle gold $5 15,009	15,009	520	
2008W, Same type, W Mint, Proof ....(59,269)..........			500

(2009) Louis Braille Bicentennial

	Distribution	MS-67	PF-67
2009P, Louis Braille Bicentennial silver dollar.............................82,639		$42	
2009P, Same type, P Mint, Proof ....(135,235)			$42

(2009) Abraham Lincoln Bicentennial

	Distribution	MS-67	PF-67
2009P, Abraham Lincoln Bicentennial silver dollar 125,000		$50	
2009P, Same type, P Mint, Proof ....(325,000)			$50

(2010) American Veterans Disabled for Life

	Distribution	MS-67	PF-67
2010W, American Veterans Disabled for Life silver dollar........................78,101		$42	
2010W, Same type, W Mint, Proof ....(202,970)			$45

(2010) Boy Scouts of America Centennial

	Distribution	MS-67	PF-67
2010P, Boy Scouts Centennial silver dollar	105,020	$45	
2010P, Same type, P Mint, Proof	(244,963)		$45

(2011) Medal of Honor

	Distribution	MS-67	PF-67
2011P, Medal of Honor silver dollar	44,752	$40	
2011P, Same type, P Mint, Proof	(112,833)		$45

	Distribution	MS-67	PF-67
2011P, Medal of Honor gold $5	8,233	$500	
2011P, Same type, P Mint, Proof	(17,999)		$500

(2011) U.S. Army

	Distribution	MS-67	PF-67
2011P, U.S. Army clad half dollar	39,442	$90	
2011S, Same type, S Mint, Proof	(68,332)		$45
2011P, U.S. Army silver dollar	43,512	65	
2011S, Same type, S Mint, Proof	(119,829)		60
2011P, U.S. Army gold $5	8,052	525	
2011S, Same type, S Mint, Proof	(17,148)		525

(2012) Infantry Soldier

	Distribution	MS-67	PF-67
2012W, Infantry Soldier silver dollar		$45	
2012W, Same type, S Mint, Proof			$50

(2012) Star-Spangled Banner

	Distribution	MS-67	PF-67
2012P, Star-Spangled Banner silver dollar		$45	
2012S, Same type, S Mint, Proof			$50
2012W, Star-Spangled Banner gold $5	500		
2012W, Same type, S Mint, Proof			500

(2013) Girl Scouts of the U.S.A. Centennial

U.S. Mint artist renderings.

	Distribution	MS-67	PF-67
2013P, Girl Scouts of the U.S.A. Centennial silver dollar		$45	
2013S, Same type, S Mint, Proof			$50

(2013) 5-Star Generals

U.S. Mint artist renderings.

	Distribution	MS-67	PF-67
2013P, 5-Star Generals clad half dollar		$45	
2013S, Same type, S Mint, Proof			$50

U.S. Mint artist renderings.

	Distribution	MS-67	PF-67
2013P, 5-Star Generals silver dollar		$45	
2013S, Same type, S Mint, Proof			$50
2013P, 5-Star Generals gold $5		45	
2013, Same type, S Mint, Proof			50

GOVERNMENT COMMEMORATIVE SETS

	Value
(1983–1984) Los Angeles Olympiad	
1983 and 1984 Proof dollars	$75
1983 and 1984 6-coin set. One each of 1983 and 1984 dollars,	
both Proof and Uncirculated gold $10 **(a)**	2,250
1983 3-piece collector set. 1983 P, D, and S Uncirculated dollars	110
1984 3-piece collector set. 1984 P, D, and S Uncirculated dollars	110
1983 and 1984 gold and silver Uncirculated set. One each of 1983	
and 1984 Uncirculated dollar and one 1984 Uncirculated gold $10	1,100
1983 and 1984 gold and silver Proof set. One each of 1983 and 1984	
Proof dollars and one 1984 Proof gold $10	1,075
(1986) Statue of Liberty	
2-coin set. Proof silver dollar and clad half dollar	42
3-coin set. Proof silver dollar, clad half dollar, and gold $5	540
2-coin set. Uncirculated silver dollar and clad half dollar	42
2-coin set. Uncirculated and Proof gold $5	1,000
3-coin set. Uncirculated silver dollar, clad half dollar, and gold $5	540
6-coin set. One each of Proof and Uncirculated half dollar, silver dollar, and gold $5 **(a)**	1,080
(1987) Constitution	
2-coin set. Uncirculated silver dollar and gold $5	540
2-coin set. Proof silver dollar and gold $5	540
4-coin set. One each of Proof and Uncirculated silver dollar and gold $5 **(a)**	1,080

a. Packaged in cherrywood box.

	Value
(1988) Seoul Olympiad	
2-coin set. Uncirculated silver dollar and gold $5	$535
2-coin set. Proof silver dollar and gold $5	535
4-coin set. One each of Proof and Uncirculated silver dollar and gold $5 **(a)**	1,075
(1989) Congress	
2-coin set. Proof clad half dollar and silver dollar	45
3-coin set. Proof clad half dollar, silver dollar, and gold $5	540
2-coin set. Uncirculated clad half dollar and silver dollar	45
3-coin set. Uncirculated clad half dollar, silver dollar, and gold $5	540
6-coin set. One each of Proof and Uncirculated clad half dollar, silver dollar, and gold $5 **(a)**	1,080
(1991) Mount Rushmore	
2-coin set. Uncirculated clad half dollar and silver dollar	65
2-coin set. Proof clad half dollar and silver dollar.	65
3-coin set. Uncirculated clad half dollar, silver dollar, and gold $5	570
3-coin set. Proof half dollar, silver dollar, and gold $5	570
6-coin set. One each of Proof and Uncirculated clad half dollar, silver dollar, and gold $5 **(a)**	1,150
(1992) XXV Olympiad	
2-coin set. Uncirculated clad half dollar and silver dollar	50
2-coin set. Proof clad half dollar and silver dollar.	50
3-coin set. Uncirculated clad half dollar, silver dollar, and gold $5	550
3-coin set. Proof half dollar, silver dollar, and gold $5	550
6-coin set. One each of Proof and Uncirculated clad half dollar, silver dollar, and gold $5 **(a)**	1,100
(1992) Christopher Columbus	
2-coin set. Uncirculated clad half dollar and silver dollar	55
2-coin set. Proof clad half dollar and silver dollar.	55
3-coin set. Uncirculated clad half dollar, silver dollar, and gold $5	555
3-coin set. Proof half dollar, silver dollar, and gold $5	555
6-coin set. One each of Proof and Uncirculated clad half dollar, silver dollar, and gold $5 **(a)**	1,110
(1993) Bill of Rights	
2-coin set. Uncirculated silver half dollar and silver dollar	65
2-coin set. Proof silver half dollar and silver dollar	65
3-coin set. Uncirculated silver half dollar, silver dollar, and gold $5	565
3-coin set. Proof silver half dollar, silver dollar, and gold $5	565
6-coin set. One each of Proof and Uncirculated silver half dollar, silver dollar, and gold $5 **(a)**	1,130
"Young Collector" set. Silver half dollar	30
Educational set. Silver half dollar and James Madison medal	35
Proof silver half dollar and 25-cent stamp	25
(1993) World War II	
2-coin set. Uncirculated clad half dollar and silver dollar	65
2-coin set. Proof clad half dollar and silver dollar.	70
3-coin set. Uncirculated clad half dollar, silver dollar, and gold $5	565
3-coin set. Proof clad half dollar, silver dollar, and gold $5	575
6-coin set. One each of Proof and Uncirculated clad half dollar, silver dollar, and gold $5 **(a)**	1,150
"Young Collector" set. Clad half dollar	40
Victory Medal set. Uncirculated clad half dollar and reproduction medal.	42
(1993) Thomas Jefferson	
3-piece set (issued in 1994). Silver dollar, Jefferson nickel, and $2 note	110

a. Packaged in cherrywood box.

COMMEMORATIVES

	Value
(1994) World Cup Soccer	
2-coin set. Uncirculated clad half dollar and silver dollar	$50
2-coin set. Proof clad half dollar and silver dollar.	55
3-coin set. Uncirculated clad half dollar, silver dollar, and gold $5	550
3-coin set. Proof clad half dollar, silver dollar, and gold $5	555
6-coin set. One each of Proof and Uncirculated clad half dollar, silver dollar, and gold $5 **(a)**	1,110
"Young Collector" set. Uncirculated clad half dollar	18
"Special Edition" set. Proof clad half dollar and silver dollar.	60
(1994) U.S. Veterans	
3-coin set. Uncirculated POW, Vietnam, and Women in Military Service silver dollars.	220
3-coin set. Proof POW, Vietnam, and Women in Military Service silver dollars	170
(1995) Special Olympics	
2-coin set. Proof Special Olympics silver dollar, 1995S Kennedy half dollar	125
(1995) Civil War Battlefield Preservation	
2-coin set. Uncirculated clad half dollar and silver dollar	115
2-coin set. Proof clad half dollar and silver dollar.	110
3-coin set. Uncirculated clad half dollar, silver dollar, and gold $5	925
3-coin set. Proof clad half dollar, silver dollar, and gold $5	660
6-coin set. One each of Proof and Uncirculated clad half dollar, silver dollar, and gold $5 **(a)**	1,600
"Young Collector" set. Uncirculated clad half dollar	60
2-coin "Union" set. Clad half dollar and silver dollar.	150
3-coin "Union" set. Clad half dollar, silver dollar, and gold $5	700
(1995–1996) Centennial Olympic Games	
4-coin set #1. Uncirculated half dollar (Basketball), dollars (Gymnastics, Paralympics), gold $5 (Torch Bearer)	1,100
4-coin set #2. Proof half dollar (Basketball), dollars (Gymnastics, Paralympics), gold $5 (Torch Bearer)	700
2-coin set #1: Proof silver dollars (Gymnastics, Paralympics)	110
"Young Collector" set. Uncirculated Basketball half dollar	40
"Young Collector" set. Uncirculated Baseball half dollar	40
"Young Collector" set. Uncirculated Swimming half dollar	200
"Young Collector" set. Uncirculated Soccer half dollar	175
1995–1996 16-coin Uncirculated set. One each of all Uncirculated coins **(a)**	9,400
1995–1996 16-coin Proof set. One each of all Proof coins **(a)**	3,300
1995–1996 8-coin Proof silver dollars set	600
1995–1996 32-coin set. One each of all Uncirculated and Proof coins **(a)**	12,950
(1996) National Community Service	
Proof silver dollar and Saint-Gaudens stamp	100
(1996) Smithsonian Institution 150th Anniversary	
2-coin set. Proof silver dollar and gold $5	575
4-coin set. One each of Proof and Uncirculated silver dollar and gold $5 **(a)**	1,700
"Young Collector" set. Proof silver dollar	90
(1997) U.S. Botanic Garden	
"Coinage and Currency" set. Uncirculated silver dollar, Jefferson nickel, and $1 note	260
(1997) Jackie Robinson	
2-coin set. Proof silver dollar and gold $5	700
4-coin set. One each of Proof and Uncirculated silver dollar and gold $5 **(a)**	4,200
3-piece "Legacy" set. Baseball card, pin, and gold $5 **(a)**	800

a. Packaged in cherrywood box.

	Value

(1997) Franklin D. Roosevelt
2-coin set. One each of Proof and Uncirculated gold $5 . . . . $1,800

(1997) National Law Enforcement Officers Memorial
Insignia set. Silver dollar, lapel pin, and patch 200

(1998) Robert F. Kennedy
2-coin set. RFK silver dollar and JFK silver half dollar 275
2-coin set. Proof and Uncirculated RFK silver dollars 120

(1998) Black Revolutionary War Patriots
2-coin set. Proof and Uncirculated silver dollars 275
"Young Collector" set. Uncirculated silver dollar 175
Black Revolutionary War Patriots set. Silver dollar and four stamps 150

(1999) Dolley Madison
2-coin set. Proof and Uncirculated silver dollars 100

(1999) George Washington Death
2-coin set. One each of Proof and Uncirculated gold $5 1,000

(1999) Yellowstone National Park
2-coin set. One each of Proof and Uncirculated silver dollars 100

(2000) Leif Ericson Millennium
2-coin set. Proof silver dollar and Icelandic 1,000 kronur 110

(2000) Millennium Coin and Currency Set
3-piece set. Uncirculated 2000 Sacagawea dollar; Uncirculated 2000 Silver Eagle;
George Washington $1 note, series 1999 90

(2001) American Buffalo
2-coin set. One each of Proof and Uncirculated silver dollar 400
"Coinage and Currency" set. Uncirculated American Buffalo silver dollar, face reprint of 1899
$5 Indian Chief Silver Certificate, 1987 Chief Red Cloud 10¢ stamp, 2001 Bison 21¢ stamp 225

(2001) U.S. Capitol Visitor Center
3-coin set. Proof clad half dollar, silver dollar, and gold $5 590

(2002) Salt Lake Olympic Games
2-coin set. Proof silver dollar and gold $5 525
4-coin set. One each of Proof and Uncirculated silver dollar and gold $5 1,100

(2003) First Flight Centennial
3-coin set. Proof clad half dollar, silver dollar, and gold $10 1,125

(2003) Legacies of Freedom™
Uncirculated 2003 $1 American Eagle silver bullion coin and an Uncirculated 2002
£2 Silver Britannia coin 75

(2004) Thomas A. Edison
Edison set. Uncirculated silver dollar and light bulb 75

(2004) Lewis and Clark
Coin and Pouch set. Proof silver dollar and beaded pouch 200
"Coinage and Currency" set. Uncirculated silver dollar, Sacagawea golden dollar, two 2005 nickels,
replica 1901 $10 Bison note, silver-plated Peace Medal replica, three stamps, two booklets 100

(2004) Westward Journey Nickel Series™
Westward Journey Nickel Series™ Coin and Medal set. Proof Sacagawea golden dollar,
two 2004 Proof nickels, silver-plated Peace Medal replica 60

COMMEMORATIVES

	Value

(2005) Westward Journey Nickel Series™
Westward Journey Nickel Series™ Coin and Medal set. Proof Sacagawea golden dollar,
two 2005 Proof nickels, silver-plated Peace Medal replica $40

(2005) Chief Justice John Marshall
"Coin and Chronicles" set. Uncirculated silver dollar, booklet, BEP intaglio portrait 65

(2005) American Legacy
American Legacy Collection. Proof Marine Corps dollar, Proof John Marshall dollar, 11-piece Proof set   165

(2005) Marine Corps 230th Anniversary
Marine Corps Uncirculated silver dollar and stamp set 90

(2006) Benjamin Franklin
"Coin and Chronicles" set. Uncirculated "Scientist" silver dollar,
Poor Richard's Almanack replica, intaglio print 75

(2006) American Legacy
American Legacy Collection. Proof 2006P Benjamin Franklin, Founding Father silver dollar;
Proof 2006S San Francisco Old Mint silver dollar; Proof cent, nickel, dime, quarter,
half dollar, and dollar 120

(2007) American Legacy
American Legacy Collection. 16 Proof coins for 2007: five state quarters; four Presidential dollars;
Jamestown and Little Rock Central High School Desegregation silver dollars; Proof cent, nickel,
dime, half dollar, and dollar 150

(2007) Little Rock Central High School Desegregation
Little Rock Coin and Medal set. Proof 2007P silver dollar, bronze medal 165

(2008) Bald Eagle
3-piece set. Proof clad half dollar, silver dollar, and gold $5 635
Bald Eagle Coin and Medal Set. Uncirculated silver dollar, bronze medal 75
"Young Collector" set. Uncirculated clad half dollar 18

(2008) American Legacy
American Legacy Collection. 15 Proof coins for 2008: cent, nickel, dime, half dollar, and dollar;
five state quarters; four Presidential dollars; Bald Eagle dollar 150

(2009) Louis Braille
Uncirculated silver dollar in tri-folded package 50

(2009) Abraham Lincoln Coin and Chronicles
Four Proof 2009S cents and Abraham Lincoln Proof silver dollar 180

(2012) Star-Spangled Banner
2-coin set. Proof silver dollar and gold $5 600

PROOF COINS AND SETS

A Proof is a specimen striking of coinage for presentation, souvenir, exhibition, or numismatic purposes. Pre-1968 Proofs were made only at the Philadelphia Mint, except in a few rare instances in which presentation pieces were struck at branch mints. Current Proofs are made at San Francisco and West Point.

2008 Silver Proof Set

The term *Proof* refers to the method of manufacture and not the condition of a coin. Regular-production coins in Mint State have coruscating, frosty luster; and, often, minor imperfections due to handling during the minting process. A Proof coin can usually be distinguished by its sharpness of detail, high wire edge, and extremely brilliant, mirrorlike surface. All Proofs are originally sold by the Mint at a premium.

Very few Proof coins were made prior to 1856. Because of their rarity and infrequent sales, they are not all listed in this guide book.

Frosted Proofs were issued prior to 1936 and starting again in the late 1970s. These have a brilliant, mirrorlike field with contrasting satiny or frosted letters and motifs.

Matte Proofs have a granular, "sandblast" surface instead of the mirror finish. Matte Proof cents, nickels, and gold coins were issued from 1908 to 1916; a few 1921 and 1922 silver dollars and a 1998-S silver half dollar were also struck in this manner.

Brilliant Proofs have been issued from 1936 to date. These have a uniformly brilliant, mirrorlike surface and sharp, high-relief details.

"Prooflike" coins are occasionally seen. These are examples from dies that have been lightly polished, often inadvertently during the removal of lines, contact marks, or other marks in the fields. In other instances, such as with certain New Orleans gold coins of the 1850s, the dies were polished in the machine shop of the mint. They are not true Proofs, but may have most of the characteristics of a Proof coin and generally command a premium. Collectors should beware of coins that have been buffed to look like Proofs; magnification will reveal polishing lines and lack of detail.

How Modern Proof Coins Are Made

Selected dies are inspected for perfection and are highly polished and cleaned. They are again wiped clean or polished after every 15 to 25 impressions and are replaced frequently to avoid imperfections from worn dies. Coinage blanks are polished and cleaned to assure high quality in striking. They are then hand fed into the coinage press one at a time, each blank receiving two or more blows from the dies to bring up sharp, high-relief details. The coinage operation is done at slow speed with extra pressure. Finished Proofs are individually inspected and are handled with gloves or tongs. They also receive a final inspection by packers before being sonically sealed in special plastic cases.

After a lapse of 20 years, Proof coins were struck at the Philadelphia Mint from 1936 to 1942, inclusive. In 1942, when the composition of the five-cent piece was changed, there were two types of this denomination available to collectors. The striking of Proof coins was temporarily suspended from 1943 through 1949, and again from 1965 through 1967; during the latter period, Special Mint Sets were struck. Proof sets were resumed in 1968.

Sets from 1936 through 1972 include the cent, nickel, dime, quarter, and half; from 1973 through 1981 the dollar was also included, and again from 2000 on. Regular

Proof sets issued from 1982 to 1998 contain the cent through half dollar. Special Prestige sets containing commemorative coins were sold from 1983 through 1997 at an additional premium. From 1999 to 2009, sets contain five different statehood or six territorial quarters. 1999 Proof dollars were sold separately. Four-piece Presidential dollar sets have been issued since 2007. Legacy Collection sets containing Proof and commemorative coins are listed on page 343.

Proof Set Values

Values are for sets in average unspotted condition and after 1955 in original government packaging. Figures in parentheses are the total number of full sets minted.

	Mintage	Issue Price	Current Value
1936.	(3,837)	$1.89	$7,200
1937.	(5,542)	1.89	4,250
1938.	(8,045)	1.89	2,000
1939.	(8,795)	1.89	1,850
1940.	(11,246)	1.89	1,500
1941.	(15,287)	1.89	1,500
1942, Both nickels	(21,120)	1.89	1,400
1942, One nickel	*	1.89	1,300
1950.	(51,386)	2.10	600
1951.	(57,500)	2.10	675
1952.	(81,980)	2.10	250
1953.	(128,800)	2.10	230
1954.	(233,300)	2.10	115
1955, Box pack	(378,200)	2.10	110
1955, Flat pack	*	2.10	135
1956.	(669,384)	2.10	55
1957.	(1,247,952)	2.10	32
1958.	(875,652)	2.10	40
1959.	(1,149,291)	2.10	30
1960, With Large Date cent	(1,691,602)	2.10	30
1960, With Small Date cent	*	2.10	38
1961.	(3,028,244)	2.10	30
1962.	(3,218,019)	2.10	30
1963.	(3,075,645)	2.10	30
1964.	(3,950,762)	2.10	30
1968S.	(3,041,506)	5.00	8
1968S, With No S dime	*	5.00	16,500
1969S.	(2,934,631)	5.00	8
1970S.	(2,632,810)	5.00	10
1970S, With Small Date cent	*	5.00	90
1970S, With No S dime (estimated mintage: 2,200)	*	5.00	950
1971S.	(3,220,733)	5.00	6
1971S, With No S nickel (estimated mintage: 1,655)	*	5.00	1,400
1972S.	(3,260,996)	5.00	7
1973S.	(2,760,339)	7.00	10
1974S.	(2,612,568)	7.00	11
1975S, With 1976 quarter, half, and dollar	(2,845,450)	7.00	10
1975S, With No S dime	*	7.00	—
1976S.	(4,149,730)	7.00	9
1976S, Silver clad, 3-piece set	(3,998,621)	15.00	30
1977S.	(3,251,152)	9.00	9

* Included in number above.

Chart continued on next page.

	Mintage	Issue Price	Current Value
1978S.	(3,127,781)	$9.00	$8
1979S, Type 1 **(a)**	(3,677,175)	9.00	8
1979S, Type 2 **(a)**	*	9.00	85
1980S.	(3,554,806)	10.00	6
1981S, Type 1 **(a)**	(4,063,083)	11.00	7
1981S, Type 2 (all six coins in set) **(a)**	*	11.00	300
1982S.	(3,857,479)	11.00	5
1983S.	(3,138,765)	11.00	5
1983S, With No S dime	*	11.00	850
1983S, Prestige set (Olympic dollar)	(140,361)	59.00	50
1984S.	(2,748,430)	11.00	6
1984S, Prestige set (Olympic dollar)	(316,680)	59.00	45
1985S.	(3,362,821)	11.00	6
1986S.	(2,411,180)	11.00	6
1986S, Prestige set (Statue of Liberty half, dollar)	(599,317)	48.50	45
1987S.	(3,792,233)	11.00	5
1987S, Prestige set (Constitution dollar)	(435,495)	45.00	40
1988S.	(3,031,287)	11.00	7
1988S, Prestige set (Olympic dollar)	(231,661)	45.00	45
1989S.	(3,009,107)	11.00	7
1989S, Prestige set (Congressional half, dollar)	(211,807)	45.00	48
1990S.	(2,793,433)	11.00	7
1990S, With No S cent	(3,555)	11.00	5,500
1990S, With No S cent (Prestige set)	*	45.00	5,500
1990S, Prestige set (Eisenhower dollar)	(506,126)	45.00	45
1991S.	(2,610,833)	11.00	7
1991S, Prestige set (Mt. Rushmore half, dollar)	(256,954)	59.00	50
1992S.	(2,675,618)	11.00	6
1992S, Prestige set (Olympic half, dollar)	(183,293)	56.00	55
1992S, Silver	(1,009,586)	11.00	30
1992S, Silver Premier set.	(308,055)	37.00	32
1993S.	(2,409,394)	12.50	8
1993S, Prestige set (Bill of Rights half, dollar)	(224,045)	57.00	60
1993S, Silver	(570,213)	21.00	35
1993S, Silver Premier set.	(191,140)	37.50	37
1994S.	(2,308,701)	12.50	8
1994S, Prestige set (World Cup half, dollar)	(175,893)	57.00	50
1994S, Silver	(636,009)	21.00	30
1994S, Silver Premier set.	(149,320)	37.50	32
1995S.	(2,010,384)	12.50	12
1995S, Prestige set (Civil War half, dollar)	(107,112)	57.00	90
1995S, Silver	(549,878)	21.00	50
1995S, Silver Premier set.	(130,107)	37.50	65
1996S.	(1,695,244)	12.50	9
1996S, Prestige set (Olympic half, dollar)	(55,000)	57.00	310
1996S, Silver	(623,655)	21.00	30
1996S, Silver Premier set.	(151,366)	37.50	32
1997S.	(1,975,000)	12.50	14
1997S, Prestige set (Botanic dollar)	(80,000)	57.00	85
1997S, Silver	(605,473)	21.00	43

* Included in number above. **a.** See illustrations on page 234 for clarification.

PROOF AND MINT SETS

	Mintage	Issue Price	Current Value
1997S, Silver Premier set	(136,205)	$37.50	$45
1998S	(2,086,507)	12.50	11
1998S, Silver	(638,134)	21.00	30
1998S, Silver Premier set	(240,658)	37.50	30
1999S, 9-piece set	(2,543,401)	19.95	13
1999S, 5-piece quarter set	(1,169,958)	13.95	8
1999S, Silver 9-piece set	(804,565)	31.95	130
2000S, 10-piece set	(3,082,572)	19.95	8
2000S, 5-piece quarter set	(937,600)	13.95	6
2000S, Silver 10-piece set	(965,421)	31.95	60
2001S, 10-piece set	(2,294,909)	19.95	18
2001S, 5-piece quarter set	(799,231)	13.95	12
2001S, Silver 10-piece set	(889,697)	31.95	70
2002S, 10-piece set	(2,319,766)	19.95	13
2002S, 5-piece quarter set	(764,479)	13.95	10
2002S, Silver 10-piece set	(892,229)	31.95	60
2003S, 10-piece set	(2,172,684)	19.95	12
2003S, 5-piece quarter set	(1,235,832)	13.95	6
2003S, Silver 10-piece set	(1,125,755)	31.95	60
2004S, 11-piece set	(1,789,488)	22.95	12
2004S, 5-piece quarter set	(951,196)	15.95	6
2004S, Silver 11-piece set	(1,175,934)	37.95	60
2004S, Silver 5-piece quarter set	(593,852)	23.95	40
2005S, 11-piece set	(2,275,000)	22.95	8
2005S, 5-piece quarter set	(987,960)	15.95	6
2005S, Silver 11-piece set	(1,069,679)	37.95	60
2005S, Silver 5-piece quarter set	(608,970)	23.95	40
2006S, 10-piece set	(2,000,428)	22.95	12
2006S, 5-piece quarter set	(882,000)	15.95	9
2006S, Silver 10-piece set	(1,054,008)	37.95	60
2006S, Silver 5-piece quarter set	(531,000)	23.95	45
2007S, 14-piece set	(1,702,116)	26.95	15
2007S, 5-piece quarter set	(672,662)	13.95	9
2007S, 4-piece Presidential set	(1,285,972)	14.95	10
2007S, Silver 14-piece set	(875,050)	44.95	62
2007S, Silver 5-piece quarter set	(672,662)	25.95	40
2008S, 14-piece set	(1,405,674)	26.95	85
2008S, 5-piece quarter set	(672,438)	13.95	45
2008S, 4-piece Presidential set	(869,202)	14.95	15
2008S, Silver 14-piece set	(763,887)	44.95	75
2008S, Silver 5-piece quarter set	(429,021)	25.95	45
2009S, 18-piece set	(1,482,502)	29.95	25
2009S, 6-piece quarter set	(630,976)	14.95	20
2009S, 4-piece Presidential set	(629,585)	14.95	20
2009S, Silver 18-piece set	(697,365)	52.95	75
2009S, Silver 6-piece quarter set	(299,183)	29.95	50
2009S, 4-piece Lincoln Bicentennial set		7.95	20
2010S, 14-piece set	(1,103,815)	31.95	65
2010S, 5-piece quarter set	(276,296)	14.95	28
2010S, 4-piece Presidential set	(535,397)	15.95	20
2010S, Silver 14-piece set	(585,401)	56.95	75

Chart continued on next page.

	Mintage	Issue Price	Current Value
2010S, Silver 5-piece quarter set	(274,034)	$32.95	$45
2011S, 14-piece set	(952,881)	31.95	40
2011S, 5-piece quarter set	(124,570)	14.95	18
2011S, 4-piece Presidential set	(256,640)	19.95	25
2011S, Silver 14-piece set	(500,395)	67.95	75
2011S, Silver 5-piece quarter set	(125,607)	39.95	45
2012S, 14-piece set		31.95	38
2012S, 5-piece quarter set		14.95	18
2012S, 4-piece Presidential set		18.95	25
2012S, Silver 14-piece set		67.95	75
2012S, Silver 8-piece set		149.95	175
2012S, Silver 5-piece quarter set		41.95	45

UNCIRCULATED MINT SETS

Official Uncirculated Mint sets are specially packaged by the government for sale to collectors. They contain Uncirculated specimens of each year's coins for every denomination issued from each mint. In previous years, the coins were the same as those normally intended for circulation and were not minted with any special consideration for quality. From 2005 through 2010, Mint sets were made with a satin finish rather than the traditional Uncirculated luster. As in the past, coins struck only as Proofs are not included.

Uncirculated Mint sets sold by the Treasury from 1947 through 1958 contained two examples of each regular-issue coin. These were packaged in cardboard holders that did not protect the coins from tarnish. Nicely preserved early sets generally command a 10 to 20% premium above listed values. No official Uncirculated Mint sets were produced in 1950, 1982, or 1983.

Since 1959, sets have been sealed in protective plastic envelopes. In 1965, 1966, and 1967, Special Mint Sets of higher-than-normal quality were made to substitute for Proof sets, which were not made during that period. Similar coins dated 1964 also exist (see page 351). The 1966 and 1967 sets were packaged in hard plastic holders.

Privately assembled Mint sets, and Souvenir sets produced for sale at the Philadelphia or Denver mints or for special occasions, are valued according to the individual pieces they contain. Only the official, government-sealed full sets are included in the following list.

Current-year sets may be ordered by telephoning 1-800-USA-MINT.

Uncirculated Mint Set Values

	Mintage	Issue Price	Face Value	Current Value
1947 P-D-S	5,000	$4.87	$4.46	$1,500
1948 P-D-S	6,000	4.92	4.46	800
1949 P-D-S	5,000	5.45	4.96	1,000
1951 P-D-S	8,654	6.75	5.46	950
1952 P-D-S	11,499	6.14	5.46	850
1953 P-D-S	15,538	6.14	5.46	625
1954 P-D-S	25,599	6.19	5.46	275
1955 P-D-S	49,656	3.57	2.86	190
1956 P-D	45,475	3.34	2.64	175
1957 P-D	34,324	4.40	3.64	285
1958 P-D	50,314	4.43	3.64	160
1959 P-D	187,000	2.40	1.82	70
1960 P-D	260,485	2.40	1.82	60

	Mintage	Issue Price	Face Value	Current Value
1961 P-D	223,704	$2.40	$1.82	$60
1962 P-D	385,285	2.40	1.82	60
1963 P-D	606,612	2.40	1.82	60
1964 P-D	1,008,108	2.40	1.82	60
1968 P-D-S	2,105,128	2.50	1.33	8
1969 P-D-S	1,817,392	2.50	1.33	8
1970 P-D-S, With Large Date cent	2,038,134	2.50	1.33	18
1970 P-D-S, With Small Date cent	*	2.50	1.33	75
1971 P-D-S (no Eisenhower dollar)	2,193,396	3.50	1.83	4
1972 P-D-S (no Eisenhower dollar)	2,750,000	3.50	1.83	4
1973 P-D-S	1,767,691	6.00	3.83	10
1974 P-D-S	1,975,981	6.00	3.83	8
1975 P-D, With 1976 quarter, half, dollar	1,921,488	6.00	3.82	7
1776–1976, Silver clad, 3-piece set	4,908,319	9.00	1.75	27
1976 P-D	1,892,513	6.00	3.82	7
1977 P-D	2,006,869	7.00	3.82	9
1978 P-D	2,162,609	7.00	3.82	7
1979 P-D (a)	2,526,000	8.00	3.82	6
1980 P-D-S	2,815,066	9.00	4.82	8
1981 P-D-S	2,908,145	11.00	4.82	11
1984 P-D	1,832,857	7.00	1.82	5
1985 P-D	1,710,571	7.00	1.82	5
1986 P-D	1,153,536	7.00	1.82	10
1987 P-D	2,890,758	7.00	1.82	6
1988 P-D	1,646,204	7.00	1.82	7
1989 P-D	1,987,915	7.00	1.82	5
1990 P-D	1,809,184	7.00	1.82	5
1991 P-D	1,352,101	7.00	1.82	6
1992 P-D	1,500,143	7.00	1.82	6
1993 P-D	1,297,431	8.00	1.82	8
1994 P-D	1,234,813	8.00	1.82	7
1995 P-D	1,038,787	8.00	1.82	7
1996 P-D, Plus 1996W dime	1,457,949	8.00	1.92	20
1997 P-D	950,473	8.00	1.82	9
1998 P-D	1,187,325	8.00	1.82	5
1999 P-D (18 pieces) (b)	1,243,867	14.95	3.82	10
2000 P-D (20 pieces)	1,490,160	14.95	5.82	10
2001 P-D (20 pieces)	1,116,915	14.95	5.82	13
2002 P-D (20 pieces)	1,139,388	14.95	5.82	15
2003 P-D (20 pieces)	1,001,532	14.95	5.82	12
2004 P-D (22 pieces)	842,507	16.95	5.92	18
2005 P-D (22 pieces)	1,160,000	16.95	5.92	11
2006 P-D (20 pieces)	847,361	16.95	5.82	15
2007 P-D (28 pieces)	895,628	22.95	13.82	20
2008 P-D (28 pieces)	745,464	22.95	13.82	65
2009 P-D (36 pieces)	784,614	27.95	14.38	32
2010 P-D (28 pieces)	*583,897*	31.95	13.82	32
2011 P-D (28 pieces)		31.95	13.82	32
2012 P-D (28 pieces)		27.95	13.82	35

* Included in number above. **a.** S-mint dollar not included. **b.** Dollar not included. *Note:* Sets issued from 2005 through 2010 have a special Satin Finish that is somewhat different from the finish on Uncirculated coins made for general circulation.

Special Mint Sets

In mid-1964 the Treasury Department announced that the Mint would not offer Proof sets or Mint sets the following year. This was prompted by a nationwide shortage of circulating coins, which was wrongly blamed on coin collectors.

In 1966 the San Francisco Assay Office began striking coins dated 1965, for inclusion in so-called United States Special Mint Sets. These were issued in pliofilm packaging similar to that of recent Proof sets. The coins in early 1965 Special Mint Sets are semi-brilliant or satiny (distinctive, but not equal in quality to Proofs); the coins in later 1965 sets feature very brilliant fields (but again not reaching Proof brilliance).

The San Francisco Assay Office started striking 1966-dated coins in August of that year, and its Special Mint Sets were packaged in rigid, sonically sealed plastic holders.

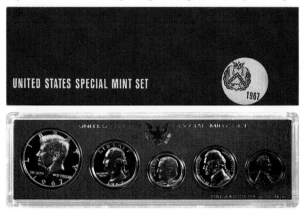

1967 Special Mint Set

The coins were struck once on unpolished planchets, unlike Proof coins (which are struck twice on polished planchets). Also unlike Proofs, the SMS coins were allowed to come into contact with each other during production, which accounts for minor contact marks and abrasions. To achieve a brilliant finish, Mint technicians overpolished the coinage dies. The result was a tradeoff: most of the coins have prooflike brilliance, but many are missing polished-off design details, such as Frank Gasparro's initials on the half dollar.

All 1967-dated coinage was struck in that calendar year. Nearly all SMS coins of 1967 have fully brilliant, prooflike finishes. This brilliance was achieved without overpolishing the dies, resulting in coins that approach the quality of true Proofs. Sales of the 1967 sets were lackluster, however. The popularity of coin collecting had dropped from its peak in 1964. Also, collectors did not anticipate much secondary-market profit from the sets, which had an issue price of $4.00, compared to $2.10 for a 1964 Proof set. As a result, fewer collectors bought multiples of the 1967 sets, and today they are worth more than those of 1966 and 1965.

	Mintage	Issue Price	Face Value	Current Value
1965	2,360,000	$4	$0.91	$12
1966	2,261,583	4	0.91	11
1967	1,863,344	4	0.91	12

1964 Special Strikes

In addition to the normal SMS coins dated 1965–1967, there are other, very similar pieces dated 1964. These coins are unlike ordinary Uncirculated and Proof coins made that year and have characteristics akin to the SMS pieces. Collectors generally refer to the 1964 pieces as *Special Strikes*. All denominations are very rare, whether sold as single pieces or in sets. It is unknown why these pieces rare (whether sold as single pieces or in sets), why they were made, or how they left the Mint.

1964 Special Strike coins. Cent through Half Dollar *10,000*

Souvenir Sets

Uncirculated Souvenir sets were packaged and sold in gift shops at the Philadelphia and Denver mints in 1982 and 1983 in place of the "official Mint sets," which were not made in those years. A bronze Mint medal is packaged with each set. Similar sets were also made in other years.

	Issue Price	Face Value	Current Value
1982P	$4	$0.91	$70
1982D	4	0.91	70
1983P	4	0.91	120
1983D	4	0.91	100

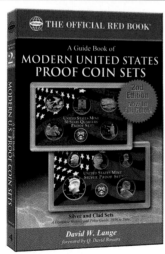

AMERICA THE BEAUTIFUL™ SILVER BULLION COINS

In conjunction with the America the Beautiful™ quarter dollar circulating coins, the Mint also produces a companion series of bullion pieces with matching designs. Five different sites of "natural or historic significance" are being honored each year from 2010 through 2021.

The bullion coins contain five ounces of pure silver and have designs nearly identical to those of the America the Beautiful™ quarters, with the exceptions of their size (3 inches in diameter) and their edge (marked .999 FINE SILVER 5.0 OUNCE, instead of being reeded like the standard quarters). Although all are coined at the Philadelphia Mint, the bullion pieces do not have a mintmark. These coins are not intended for circulation and are sold by the Mint and to authorized distributors.

The obverse of the ATB bullion coin was reworked to more closely resemble John Flanagan's original design. (Compare to the modern quarter-dollar obverse shown on page 179.)

Weight and purity incused on edge.
Actual size 3 inches.

	Mintage	MS	SP
25c, 2010(P), Hot Springs National Park (Arkansas)	26,788	$240	
25c, 2010P, Hot Springs National Park (Arkansas)	(33,000)		$300
25c 2010(P), Yellowstone National Park (Wyoming)	26,711	240	
25c 2010P, Yellowstone National Park (Wyoming)	(33,000)		275
25c 2010(P), Yosemite National Park (California)	26,716	240	
25c 2010P, Yosemite National Park (California)	(33,000)		275
25c, 2010(P), Grand Canyon National Park (Arizona)	25,967	240	
25c, 2010P, Grand Canyon National Park (Arizona)	(33,000)		275
25c, 2010(P), Mount Hood National Park (Oregon)	26,637	240	
25c, 2010P, Mount Hood National Park (Oregon)	(33,000)		275
25c, 2011(P), Gettysburg National Military Park (Pennsylvania)		240	
25c, 2011P, Gettysburg National Military Park (Pennsylvania)	(126,700)		260

	Mintage	MS	SP
25c, 2011(P), Glacier National Park (Montana)		$240	
25c, 2011P, Glacier National Park (Montana)	(126,700)		$260
25c, 2011(P), Olympic National Park (Washington)		240	
25c, 2011P, Olympic National Park (Washington)	(95,600)		260
25c, 2011(P), Vicksburg National Military Park (Mississippi)		240	
25c, 2011P, Vicksburg National Military Park (Mississippi)	(41,200)		260
25c, 2011(P), Chickasaw National Recreation Area (Oklahoma)		240	
25c, 2011P, Chickasaw National Recreation Area (Oklahoma)	(31,400)		260
25¢, 2012(P), El Yunque National Forest (Puerto Rico)		240	
25¢, 2012P, El Yunque National Forest (Puerto Rico)	(21,900)		260
25¢, 2012(P), Chaco Culture National Historical Park (New Mexico)		240	
25¢, 2012P, Chaco Culture National Historical Park (New Mexico)	(20,000)		260
25¢, 2012P, Acadia National Park (Maine)		240	
25¢, 2012P, Acadia National Park (Maine)	(25,400)		260
25¢, 2012(P), Hawai'i Volcanoes National Park (Hawaii)		240	
25¢, 2012P, Hawai'i Volcanoes National Park (Hawaii)	(20,000)		260
25¢, 2012(P), Denali National Park and Preserve (Alaska)		240	
25¢, 2012P, Denali National Park and Preserve (Alaska)	(20,000)		260
25¢, 2013(P), White Mountain National Forest (New Hampshire)		240	
25¢, 2013P, White Mountain National Forest (New Hampshire)			260
25¢, 2013(P), Perry's Victory and International Peace Memorial (Ohio)		240	
25¢, 2013P, Perry's Victory and International Peace Memorial (Ohio)			260
25¢, 2013(P), Great Basin National Park (Nevada)		240	
25¢, 2013P, Great Basin National Park (Nevada)			260
25¢, 2013(P), Fort McHenry National Monument and Historic Shrine (Maryland)		240	
25¢, 2013P, Fort McHenry National Monument and Historic Shrine (Maryland)			260
25¢, 2013(P), Mount Rushmore National Memorial (South Dakota)		240	
25¢, 2013P, Mount Rushmore National Memorial (South Dakota)			260

Note: The U.S. Mint produces the America the Beautiful™ 5-oz. silver coins in bullion and numismatic versions. The bullion version, which lacks the P mintmark, has a brilliant Uncirculated finish and is sold only through dealers. The numismatic version, with the mintmark, has a matte or burnished finish (although it is not marketed by the Mint as "Burnished"). These coins, designated Specimens (SP) by grading services, are sold directly to the public.

$1 SILVER EAGLES

The silver eagle is a one-ounce bullion coin with a face value of one dollar. The obverse has Adolph A. Weinman's Liberty Walking design used on the half dollar coins from 1916 through 1947. His initials are on the hem of the gown. The reverse design is a rendition of a heraldic eagle by John Mercanti.

Since 2001, the U.S. Mint's West Point facility has been the exclusive producer of regular-strike (without mintmark) and Proof (with mintmark) silver eagles; Reverse Proofs were produced in Philadelphia in 2006 and 2011. The U.S. Mint does not release bullion mintage data on a regular basis; the numbers below are the most recent official mintages.

Designers Adolph A. Weinman (obv) and John Mercanti (rev); composition .9993 silver, .0007 copper (net weight 1 oz. pure silver); weight 31.101 grams; diameter 40.6 mm; reeded edge; mints: Philadelphia, San Francisco, West Point.

	Mintage	Unc.	PF
$1 1986	5,393,005	$46	
$1 1986S	(1,446,778)		$80
$1 1987	11,442,335	43	
$1 1987S	(904,732)		80
$1 1988	5,004,646	43	
$1 1988S	(557,370)		80
$1 1989	5,203,327	43	
$1 1989S	(617,694)		80
$1 1990	5,840,210	43	
$1 1990S	(695,510)		80
$1 1991	7,191,066	43	
$1 1991S	(511,925)		80
$1 1992	5,540,068	43	
$1 1992S	(498,654)		80
$1 1993	6,763,762	43	
$1 1993P	(405,913)		90
$1 1994	4,227,319	45	
$1 1994P	(372,168)		100
$1 1995	4,672,051	45	
$1 1995P	(438,511)		95
$1 1995W	(30,125)		3,200
$1 1996	3,603,386	65	
$1 1996P	(500,000)		85
$1 1997	4,295,004	47	
$1 1997P	(435,368)		85
$1 1998	4,847,549	45	
$1 1998P	(450,000)		80
$1 1999	7,408,640	43	
$1 1999P	(549,769)		80
$1 2000(W)	9,239,132	43	
$1 2000P	(600,000)		80
$1 2001(W)	9,001,711	43	
$1 2001W	(746,398)		80
$1 2002(W)	10,539,026	43	
$1 2002W	(647,342)		80
$1 2003(W)	8,495,008	43	
$1 2003W	(747,831)		80
$1 2004(W)	8,882,754	43	

	Mintage	Unc.	PF
$1 2004W. . . . .(801,602)			$80
$1 2005(W). 8,891,025	8,891,025	$43	
$1 2005W. . . . .(816,663)			80
$1 2006(W). 10,676,522	10,676,522	43	
$1 2006W, Burnished (a) 468,020	.468,020	85	
$1 2006W. . . . .(1,092,477)			80
$1 2006P, Reverse Proof (b) . . . .(248,875)			300
$1 2007(W). 9,028,036	9,028,036	43	
$1 2007W, Burnished. 621,333	.621,333	45	
$1 2007W. . . . .(821,759)			80
$1 2008(W). 20,583,000	20,583,000	43	
$1 2008W, Burnished. 533,757	.533,757	65	
$1 2008W, Burnished, Reverse of 2007 (c). 47,000	47,000	450	
$1 2008W. . . . .(700,979)			80
$1 2009(W) (d) 30,459,000	30,459,000	43	
$1 2010W. . . . .(860,000)			80
$1 2010(W). 374,764,500	374,764,500	43	
$1 2011(W)(S) 39,768,000	39,768,000	43	
$1 2011W, Burnished.		55	
$1 2011S, Burnished 100,000	100,000	450	
$1 2011W. . . . .(849,861)			80
$1 2011P, Reverse Proof . . . .(100,000)			300
$1 2012(W).		43	
$1 2012W, Burnished.		50	
$1 2012W.			80
$1 2012S, Reverse Proof			100

a. In celebration of the 20th anniversary of the Bullion Coinage Program, in 2006 the W mintmark was used on bullion coins produced in sets except for the Reverse Proof, which was struck at the Philadelphia Mint. **b.** Reverse Proof coins have brilliant devices, and frosted fields in the background. **c.** Reverse dies of 2007 and earlier have a plain U in UNITED. Modified dies of 2008 and later have a small serif at the bottom right of the U. **d.** No Proof dollars were made in 2009. Beware of alterations made privately outside the Mint.

From 2006 to 2011, special American Eagle Uncirculated coins in silver, gold, and platinum were sold directly from the United States Mint. The term "Uncirculated-burnished" refers to the specialized minting process used to create these coins. Although they are similar in appearance to the ordinary Uncirculated American Eagle bullion coins, the Uncirculated-burnished coins can be distinguished by the addition of a mintmark and by the use of burnished coin blanks. Proof coins, which also have a mintmark, have a highly reflective, mirrorlike surface.

Anniversary Sets

1997 Impressions of Liberty Set (a)	
2006 20th Anniversary Silver Coin Set. Uncirculated, Proof, Reverse Proof.	$450
2006W 20th Anniversary 1-oz. Gold- and Silver-Dollar Set. Uncirculated	2,000
2011 25th Anniversary Five-Coin Set. 2011W Uncirculated, Proof; 2011P Reverse Proof; 2011S Uncirculated; 2011 Bullion	700
2012 75th Anniversary of San Francisco Mint Two-Piece Set. S-Mint Proof and Reverse Proof silver dollars	185

a. See page 359.

AMERICAN EAGLE GOLD BULLION COINS

The American Eagle gold bullion coins are made in four denominations that contain 1 oz., 1/2 oz., 1/4 oz., and 1/10 oz. of gold. The obverse features a modified rendition of the Augustus Saint-Gaudens design used on U.S. twenty-dollar gold pieces from 1907 until 1933. The reverse displays a "family of eagles" motif designed by Miley Busiek.

Uncirculated American Eagles, unlike their Proof counterparts, are sold not directly to the general public, but to a series of authorized buyers. These buyers obtain the Uncirculated bullion coins from the Mint based on the current spot price of the metal plus a small premium. The coins are then sold to secondary distributors for sale to other dealers and the general public. From 2006 to 2008, the Mint issued a collectors' version of the Uncirculated bullion coins, available directly from the Mint.

$5 Tenth-Ounce Gold

Designers Augustus Saint-Gaudens (obv), Miley Busiek (rev); weight 3.393 grams; composition .9167 gold, .03 silver, .0533 copper (net weight 1/10 oz. pure gold); diameter 16.5 mm; reeded edge; mints: Philadelphia, West Point.

All modern Proof Eagles and sets must contain complete original U.S. Mint packaging for these values.

	Mintage	Unc.	PF		Mintage	Unc.	PF
$5 MCMLXXXVI (1986)	912,609	$200		$5 2000	569,153	$200	
$5 MCMLXXXVII (1987)	580,266	200		$5 2000W	(49,971)		$225
$5 MCMLXXXVIII (1988)	159,500	230		$5 2001	269,147	200	
$5 MCMLXXXVIII (1988)P	(143,881)		$225	$5 2001W	(37,530)		225
$5 MCMLXXXIX (1989)	264,790	200		$5 2002	230,027	210	
$5 MCMLXXXIX (1989)P	(84,647)		225	$5 2002W	(40,864)		225
$5 MCMXC (1990)	210,210	210		$5 2003	245,029	200	
$5 MCMXC (1990)P	(99,349)		225	$5 2003W	(40,027)		225
$5 MCMXCI (1991)	165,200	230		$5 2004	250,016		
$5 MCMXCI (1991)P	(70,334)		225	$5 2004W	(35,131)		235
$5 1992	209,300	200		$5 2005	300,043	200	
$5 1992P	(64,874)		225	$5 2005W	(49,265)		235
$5 1993	210,709	200		$5 2006	285,006	200	
$5 1993P	(58,649)		225	$5 2006W, Burnished	20,643	230	
$5 1994	206,380	200		$5 2006W	(47,277)		225
$5 1994W	(62,849)		225	$5 2007	190,010	200	
$5 1995	223,025	200		$5 2007W, Burnished	22,501	230	
$5 1995W	(62,667)		225	$5 2007W	(58,553)		225
$5 1996	401,964	200		$5 2008	305,000	200	
$5 1996W	(57,047)		225	$5 2008W, Burnished	12,657	350	
$5 1997	528,266	200		$5 2008W	(28,116)		225
$5 1997W	(34,977)		225	$5 2009	270,000	200	
$5 1998	1,344,520	200		$5 2010	*380,000*	200	
$5 1998W	(39,395)		225	$5 2010W	(19,704)		225
$5 1999	2,750,338	200		$5 2011		200	
$5 1999W	(48,428)		225	$5 2011W			225
$5 1999W, Unc. made from unpolished Proof dies	*14,500*	800		$5 2012		200	
				$5 2012W			225

$10 Quarter-Ounce Gold

Designers Augustus Saint-Gaudens (obv), Miley Busiek (rev); weight 8.483 grams; composition .9167 gold, .03 silver, .0533 copper (net weight 1/4 oz. pure gold); diameter 22 mm; reeded edge; mints: Philadelphia, West Point.

	Mintage	Unc.	PF			Mintage	Unc.	PF
$10 MCMLXXXVI (1986)	726,031	$525			$10 2000	128,964	$475	
$10 MCMLXXXVII (1987)	269,255	525			$10 2000W	(36,036)		$500
$10 MCMLXXXVIII (1988)	49,000	525			$10 2001	71,280	475	
$10 MCMLXXXVIII (1988)P	(98,028)		$500		$10 2001W	(25,613)		500
$10 MCMLXXXIX (1989)	81,789	525			$10 2002	62,027	475	
$10 MCMLXXXIX (1989)P	(54,170)		500		$10 2002W	(29,242)		500
$10 MCMXC (1990)	41,000	525			$10 2003	74,029	475	
$10 MCMXC (1990)P	(62,674)		500		$10 2003W	(30,292)		500
$10 MCMXCI (1991)	36,100	525			$10 2004	72,014	475	
$10 MCMXCI (1991)P	(50,839)		500		$10 2004W	(28,839)		500
$10 1992	59,546	485			$10 2005	72,015	475	
$10 1992P	(46,269)		500		$10 2005W	(37,207)		500
$10 1993	71,864	475			$10 2006	60,004	475	
$10 1993P	(46,464)		500		$10 2006W, Burnished	15,188	900	
$10 1994	72,650	475			$10 2006W	(36,127)		500
$10 1994W	(48,172)		500		$10 2007	34,004	475	
$10 1995	83,752	475			$10 2007W, Burnished	12,766	900	
$10 1995W	(47,526)		500		$10 2007W	(46,189)		500
$10 1996	60,318	475			$10 2008	70,000	475	
$10 1996W	(38,219)		500		$10 2008W, Burnished	8,883	1,600	
$10 1997	108,805	475			$10 2008W	(18,877)		500
$10 1997W	(29,805)		500		$10 2009	110,000	475	
$10 1998	309,829	475			$10 2010	58,000	475	
$10 1998W	(29,503)		500		$10 2010W	(9,926)		500
$10 1999	564,232	475			$10 2011		475	
$10 1999W	(34,417)		500		$10 2011W			500
$10 1999W, Unc. made from unpolished Proof dies	10,000	1,500			$10 2012		475	
					$10 2012W			500

$25 Half-Ounce Gold

Designers Augustus Saint-Gaudens (obv), Miley Busiek (rev); weight 16.966 grams; composition .9167 gold, .03 silver, .0533 copper (net weight 1/2 oz. pure gold); diameter 27 mm; reeded edge; mints: Philadelphia, West Point.

	Mintage	Unc.	PF			Mintage	Unc.	PF
$25 MCMLXXXVI (1986)	599,566	$1,000			$25 MCMLXXXIX (1989)	44,829	$1,500	
$25 MCMLXXXVII (1987)	131,255	1,000			$25 MCMLXXXIX (1989)P	(44,798)		$1,000
$25 MCMLXXXVII (1987)P	(143,398)		$1,000		$25 MCMXC (1990)	31,000	1,800	
$25 MCMLXXXVIII (1988)	45,000	1,425			$25 MCMXC (1990)P	(51,636)		1,000
$25 MCMLXXXVIII (1988)P	(76,528)		1,000		$25 MCMXCI (1991)	24,100	2,500	

Chart continued on next page. 357

	Mintage	Unc	PF
$25 MCMXCI (1991)P	(53,125)		$1,000
$25 1992	54,404	$1,125	
$25 1992P	(40,976)		1,000
$25 1993	73,324	975	
$25 1993P	(43,819)		1,000
$25 1994	62,400	975	
$25 1994W	(44,584)		1,000
$25 1995	53,474	1,200	
$25 1995W	(45,388)		1,000
$25 1996	39,287	1,275	
$25 1996W	(35,058)		1,000
$25 1997	79,605	975	
$25 1997W	(26,344)		1,000
$25 1998	169,029	920	
$25 1998W	(25,374)		1,000
$25 1999	263,013	920	
$25 1999W	(30,427)		1,000
$25 2000	79,287	920	
$25 2000W	(32,028)		1,000
$25 2001	48,047	1,150	
$25 2001W	(23,240)		1,000
$25 2002	70,027	920	
$25 2002W	(26,646)		1,000

	Mintage	Unc	PF
$25 2003	79,029	$920	
$25 2003W	(28,270)		$1,000
$25 2004	98,040	920	
$25 2004W	(27,330)		1,000
$25 2005	80,023	920	
$25 2005W	(34,311)		1,000
$25 2006	66,005	920	
$25 2006W, Burnished	15,164	1,800	
$25 2006W	(34,322)		1,000
$25 2007	47,002	920	
$25 2007W, Burnished	11,455	1,950	
$25 2007W	(44,025)		1,000
$25 2008	61,000	920	
$25 2008W, Burnished	15,682	1,920	
$25 2008W	(22,602)		1,000
$25 2009	110,000	920	
$25 2010	40,000	920	
$25 2010W	(9,946)		1,000
$25 2011		920	
$25 2011W			1,000
$25 2012		920	
$25 2012W			1,000

$50 One-Ounce Gold

Designers Augustus Saint-Gaudens (obv), Miley Busiek (rev); weight 33.931 grams; composition .9167 gold, .03 silver, .0533 copper (net weight 1 oz. pure gold); diameter 32.7 mm; reeded edge; mints: Philadelphia, West Point.

	Mintage	Unc.	PF
$50 MCMLXXXVI (1986)	1,362,650	$1,850	
$50 MCMLXXXVI (1986)W	(446,290)		$2,100
$50 MCMLXXXVII (1987)	1,045,500	1,850	
$50 MCMLXXXVII (1987)W	(147,498)		2,100
$50 MCMLXXXVIII (1988)	465,000	1,850	
$50 MCMLXXXVIII (1988)W	(87,133)		2,100
$50 MCMLXXXIX (1989)	415,790	1,850	
$50 MCMLXXXIX (1989)W	(54,570)		2,100
$50 MCMXC (1990)	373,210	1,850	
$50 MCMXC (1990)W	(62,401)		2,100
$50 MCMXCI (1991)	243,100	1,850	
$50 MCMXCI (1991)W	(50,411)		2,100
$50 1992	275,000	1,850	
$50 1992W	(44,826)		2,100
$50 1993	480,192	1,850	
$50 1993W	(34,369)		2,100

	Mintage	Unc.	PF
$50 1994	221,633	$1,850	
$50 1994W	(46,674)		$2,100
$50 1995	200,636	1,850	
$50 1995W	(46,368)		2,100
$50 1996	189,148	1,850	
$50 1996W	(36,153)		2,100
$50 1997	664,508	1,850	
$50 1997W	(32,999)		2,100
$50 1998	1,468,530	1,850	
$50 1998W	(25,886)		2,100
$50 1999	1,505,026	1,850	
$50 1999W	(31,427)		2,100
$50 2000	433,319	1,850	
$50 2000W	(33,007)		2,100
$50 2001	143,605	1,850	
$50 2001W	(24,555)		2,100

	Mintage	Unc	PF		Mintage	Unc	PF
$50 2002	222,029	$1,850		$50 2007W	(51,810)		$2,100
$50 2002W	(27,499)		$2,100	$50 2008	710,000	$1,850	
$50 2003	416,032	1,850		$50 2008W, Burnished	11,908	2,200	
$50 2003W	(28,344)		2,100	$50 2008W	(30,237)		2,100
$50 2004	417,019	1,850		$50 2009	1,493,000	1,850	
$50 2004W	(28,215)		2,100	$50 2010	988,500	1,850	
$50 2005	356,555	1,850		$50 2010W	(24,899)		2,100
$50 2005W	(35,246)		2,100	$50 2011		1,850	
$50 2006	237,510	1,850		$50 2011W, Burnished		2,400	
$50 2006W, Burnished	45,053	2,000		$50 2011W			2,100
$50 2006W	(47,092)		2,100	$50 2012		1,850	
$50 2006W, Reverse Proof	(9,996)		2,500	$50 2012W, Burnished		2,500	
$50 2007	140,016	1,850		$50 2012W			2,100
$50 2007W, Burnished	18,066	2,000					

Gold Bullion Sets

	PF		PF
1987 Gold Set. $50, $25	$3,200	1997 Impressions of Liberty Set. $100	
1988 Gold Set. $50, $25, $10, $5	3,900	platinum, $50 gold, $1 silver	$4,050
1989 Gold Set. $50, $25, $10, $5	3,900	1998 Gold Set. $50, $25, $10, $5	3,900
1990 Gold Set. $50, $25, $10, $5	3,900	1999 Gold Set. $50, $25, $10, $5	3,900
1991 Gold Set. $50, $25, $10, $5	3,900	2000 Gold Set. $50, $25, $10, $5	3,900
1992 Gold Set. $50, $25, $10, $5	3,900	2001 Gold Set. $50, $25, $10, $5	3,900
1993 Gold Set. $50, $25, $10, $5	3,900	2002 Gold Set. $50, $25, $10, $5	3,900
1993 Bicentennial Gold Set. $25, $10,		2003 Gold Set. $50, $25, $10, $5	3,900
$5, $1 silver eagle, and medal	1,800	2004 Gold Set. $50, $25, $10, $5	3,900
1994 Gold Set. $50, $25, $10, $5	3,900	2005 Gold Set. $50, $25, $10, $5	3,900
1995 Gold Set. $50, $25, $10, $5	3,900	2006 Gold Set. $50, $25, $10, $5	3,900
1995 Anniversary Gold Set. $50, $25,		2007 Gold Set. $50, $25, $10, $5	3,900
$10, $5, and $1 silver eagle	6,700	2008 Gold Set. $50, $25, $10, $5	3,900
1996 Gold Set. $50, $25, $10, $5	3,900	2010 Gold Set. $50, $25, $10, $5 (a)	3,900
1997 Gold Set. $50, $25, $10, $5	3,900	2011 Gold Set. $50, $25, $10, $5	3,900

a. The U.S. Mint did not issue a 2009 gold set.

2006 20th Anniversary Sets

2006W $50 Gold Set. Uncirculated, Proof, Reverse Proof	$6,750
2006W 1-oz. Gold- and Silver-Dollar Set. Uncirculated	2,000

Gold Bullion Burnished Sets 2006–2008

	Unc.
2006W Burnished Gold Set. $50, $25, $10, $5	$4,900
2007W Burnished Gold Set. $50, $25, $10, $5	5,000
2008W Burnished Gold Set. $50, $25, $10, $5	5,500

AMERICAN BUFFALO .9999 FINE GOLD BULLION COINS

American Buffalo gold bullion coins were the first .9999 fine (24-karat) gold coins made by the U.S. Mint. They are struck at the West Point facility and distributed in the same manner as American Eagle gold bullion coins. In 2006 and 2007, only one-ounce coins (with a $50 face value) were minted. In 2008 the Mint also produced half-ounce ($25 face value), quarter-ounce ($10), and tenth-ounce ($5) pieces in Proof and Uncirculated, individually and in sets.

Values change frequently and are based on prevailing bullion and fabrication costs relative to the weight of each denomination.

	Mintage	Unc.	PF
$5 2008W, Burnished	17,429	$550	
$5 2008W	(18,884)		$600
$10 2008W, Burnished	9,949	1,400	
$10 2008W	(13,125)		1,500
$25 2008W, Burnished	16,908	1,350	
$25 2008W	(12,169)		1,650
$50 2006	337,012	1,900	
$50 2006W	(246,267)		2,000
$50 2007	136,503	1,900	
$50 2007W	(58,998)		2,000
$50 2008	189,500	1,900	

	Mintage	Unc.	PF
$50 2008W	(18,863)		$3,750
$50 2008W, Burnished	9,074	$3,100	
$50 2009	200,000	1,900	
$50 2009W	(49,306)		2,000
$50 2010	209,000	1,900	
$50 2010W	(49,263)		2,000
$50 2011	174,500	1,900	
$50 2011W			2,000
$50 2012	132,000	1,900	
$50 2012W			2,000

American Buffalo Gold Bullion Sets

	Unc.	PF
2008W Four-coin set ($5, $10, $25, $50)		$7,500
2008W Four-coin set ($5, $10, $25, $50), Burnished	$6,500	
2008W Double Prosperity set. Uncirculated $25 Buffalo gold and $25 American Eagle coins	3,000	

FIRST SPOUSE $10 GOLD BULLION COINS

The U.S. Mint's First Spouse gold bullion coins are struck in .9999 fine (24-karat) gold. They weigh one-half ounce and have a $10 face value. The coins honor the nation's first spouses on the same schedule as the Mint's Presidential dollars program. Each features a portrait on the obverse, and on the reverse a unique design symbolic of the spouse's life and work. In instances where a president held office without a first spouse, the coin bears "an obverse image emblematic of Liberty as depicted on a circulating coin of that era and a reverse image emblematic of themes of that president's life."

The U.S. Mint has also issued a series of bronze medals with designs similar to those on the First Spouse bullion gold coins, available directly from the Mint.

Martha Washington   **Abigail Adams**

Jefferson's Liberty

Dolley Madison

	Mintage	Unc.	PF
$10 2007W, Martha Washington	(19,169)	17,661	$925	$950
$10 2007W, Abigail Adams	(17,149)	17,142	925	950
$10 2007W, Thomas Jefferson's Liberty	(19,815)	19,823	925	950
$10 2007W, Dolley Madison	(17,661)	11,813	925	950

Elizabeth Monroe

Louisa Adams

Jackson's Liberty

Van Buren's Liberty

	Mintage	Unc.	PF
$10 2008W, Elizabeth Monroe	(7,933)	4,519	$1,200	$1,300
$10 2008W, Louisa Adams	(7,454)	4,223	1,200	1,300
$10 2008W, Andrew Jackson's Liberty	(7,454)	4,281	1,700	1,650
$10 2008W, Martin Van Buren's Liberty	(6,187)	3,443	1,800	1,750

Anna Harrison

Letitia Tyler

Julia Tyler

Entry continued on next page.

361

Sarah Polk   **Margaret Taylor**

	Mintage	Unc.	PF
$10 2009W, Anna Harrison.	(5,801) 2,993	$1,400	$1,300
$10 2009W, Letitia Tyler	(4,341) 2,381	1,550	1,350
$10 2009W, Julia Tyler.	(3,878) 2,188	1,900	1,850
$10 2009W, Sarah Polk.	(3,512) 1,893	1,450	1,250
$10 2009W, Margaret Taylor		1,250	1,300

Abigail Fillmore   **Jane Pierce**

Buchanan's Liberty   **Mary Lincoln**

	Mintage	Unc.	PF
$10 2010W, Abigail Fillmore.		$1,200	$1,100
$10 2010W, Jane Pierce		1,000	1,250
$10 2010W, James Buchanan's Liberty		1,100	1,150
$10 2010W, Mary Lincoln.		1,000	1,025

Eliza Johnson   **Julia Grant**

Lucy Hayes   **Lucretia Garfield**

	Mintage	Unc.	PF
$10 2011W, Eliza Johnson		$1,000	$1,025
$10 2011W, Julia Grant		1,000	1,025
$10 2011W, Lucy Hayes		1,000	1,025
$10 2011W, Lucretia Garfield		1,000	1,025

Alice Paul

Frances Cleveland (Variety 1)

Caroline Harrison

Frances Cleveland (Variety 2)

	Mintage	Unc.	PF
$10 2012W, Alice Paul		$1,000	$1,025
$10 2012W, Frances Cleveland, Variety 1		1,000	1,025
$10 2012W, Caroline Harrison		1,000	1,025
$10 2012W, Frances Cleveland, Variety 2		1,000	1,025

Images for 2013 First Spouse bullion issues were unavailable at press time.

	Mintage	Unc.	PF
$10 2013W, Ida McKinley		$1,000	$1,025
$10 2013W, Edith Roosevelt		1,000	1,025
$10 2013W, Helen Taft		1,000	1,025
$10 2013W, Ellen Wilson / Edith Wilson		1,000	1,025

MMIX ULTRA HIGH RELIEF GOLD COIN

A modern version of the famous United States 1907 Ultra High Relief double eagle gold pattern was produced in 2009 at the Philadelphia Mint. It was made as a tour de force to demonstrate how technical advances in minting techniques can now accommodate manufacturing such a coin. The original design was never made for commercial use because it was at that time impossible to make it in sufficient quantities.

The original striding-Liberty design used on these coins was the artistry of Augustus Saint-Gaudens. A version of it in much lower relief was used on double eagle coins minted from 1907 to 1933. In recreating the artist's attempt to mint a stunning coin in ultra high relief, the 2009 version was made in a slightly smaller diameter, and composed of 24-karat gold, thus making it easier to strike and maintain the fidelity of the design. Through 21st-century technology the original Saint-Gaudens plasters were digitally mapped by the Mint and used in the die-making process. The date was changed to 2009, and four additional stars were added to represent the current 50 states. Also included was the inscription "In God We Trust," which was not used on the 1907 version.

The MMIX Ultra High Relief gold coins are 4 mm thick and contain one ounce of .999 fine gold. All are Uncirculated (business strikes). All were made at the U.S. Mint's West Point facility, and were packaged in a special mahogany box.

MMIX Ultra High Relief Gold Coin
Photographed at an angle to show the edge, lettered E PLURIBUS UNUM, and the depth of relief.

	Mintage	Unc.
MMIX Ultra High Relief $20 Gold Coin	114,427	$2,500

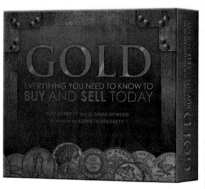

AMERICAN EAGLE PLATINUM BULLION COINS

American Eagle platinum coins are made in four denominations different from the similar gold coins. The $100 coin contains one ounce of pure platinum. Fractional denominations containing 1/2 oz., 1/4 oz., and 1/10 oz. are denominated fifty, twenty-five, and ten dollars, respectively. In 1997, Proof platinum coins had the same reverse design as regular strikes. Since then, regular strikes have continued with the 1997 reverse design, while the Proof one-ounce coins have featured a different reverse design each year. From 1998 through 2002, these special Proof designs displayed American eagles flying through various "Vistas of Liberty."

Vistas of Liberty Reverse Designs

1998
Eagle Over
New England

1999
Eagle Above
Southeastern
Wetlands

2000
Eagle Above
America's
Heartland

2001
Eagle Above
America's Southwest

2002
Eagle Fishing in
America's Northwest

$10 Tenth-Ounce Platinum

Designers John M. Mercanti (obv), Thomas D. Rogers Sr. (orig rev); weight 0.10005 oz.; composition .9995 platinum; diameter 16.5 mm; reeded edge; mints: Philadelphia, West Point.

	Mintage	Unc.	PF		Mintage	Unc.	PF
$10 1997	70,250	$190		$10 2000	34,027	$190	
$10 1997W	(36,993)		$215	$10 2000W	(15,651)		$215
$10 1998	39,525	190		$10 2001	52,017	190	
$10 1998W	(19,847)		215	$10 2001W	(12,174)		215
$10 1999	55,955	190		$10 2002	23,005	190	
$10 1999W	(19,133)		215	$10 2002W	(12,365)		215

Chart continued on next page.

	Mintage	Unc	PF
$10 2003 22,007	$190	
$10 2003W. . . . . (9,534)		$265
$10 2004 15,010	190	
$10 2004W. . . . . (7,161)		450
$10 2005 14,013	190	
$10 2005W. . . . . (8,104)		290
$10 2006 11,001	190	
$10 2006W, Burnished 3,544	450	

	Mintage	Un	PF
$10 2006W. . . . . (10,205)		$215
$10 2007 13,003	$265	
$10 2007W, Burnished 5,556	275	
$10 2007W. . . . . (8,176)		215
$10 2008 17,000	190	
$10 2008W, Burnished 3,706	300	
$10 2008W. . . . . (5,138)		500

$25 Quarter-Ounce Platinum

Designers John M. Mercanti (obv), Thomas D. Rogers Sr. (orig rev); weight 0.2501 oz.; composition .9995 platinum; diameter 22 mm; reeded edge; mints: Philadelphia, West Point.

	Mintage	Unc.	PF
$25 1997 27,100	$450	
$25 1997W. . . . . (18,628)		$475
$25 1998 38,887	450	
$25 1998W. . . . . (14,873)		475
$25 1999 39,734	450	
$25 1999W. . . . . (13,507)		475
$25 2000 20,054	450	
$25 2000W. . . . . (11,995)		475
$25 2001 21,815	450	
$25 2001W. . . . . (8,847)		475
$25 2002 27,405	450	
$25 2002W. . . . . (9,282)		475
$25 2003 25,207	450	
$25 2003W. . . . . (7,044)		475

	Mintage	Unc.	PF
$25 2004 18,010	$450	
$25 2004W. . . . . (5,193)		$1,000
$25 2005 12,013	450	
$25 2005W. . . . . (6,592)		600
$25 2006 12,001	450	
$25 2006W, Burnished 2,676	600	
$25 2006W. . . . . (7,813)		475
$25 2007 8,402	450	
$25 2007W, Burnished 3,690	600	
$25 2007W. . . . . (6,017)		475
$25 2007W, Frosted FREEDOM . . . (21)		—
$25 2008 22,800	450	
$25 2008W, Burnished 2,481	650	
$25 2008W. . . . . (4,153)		850

$50 Half-Ounce Platinum

Designers John M. Mercanti (obv), Thomas D. Rogers Sr. (orig rev); weight 0.5003 oz.; composition .9995 platinum; diameter 27 mm; reeded edge; mints: Philadelphia, West Point.

	Mintage	Unc.	PF
$50 1997 20,500	$900	
$50 1997W. . . . . (15,431)		$950
$50 1998 32,415	900	
$50 1998W. . . . . (13,836)		950

	Mintage	Unc.	PF
$50 1999 32,309	$900	
$50 1999W. . . . . (11,103)		$950
$50 2000 18,892	900	
$50 2000W. . . . . (11,049)		950

	Mintage	Unc	PF
$50 2001	12,815	$900	
$50 2001W	(8,254)		$950
$50 2002	24,005	900	
$50 2002W	(8,772)		950
$50 2003	17,409	900	
$50 2003W	(7,131)		950
$50 2004	13,236	900	
$50 2004W	(5,063)		1,500
$50 2005	9,013	900	
$50 2005W	(5,942)		1,100

	Mintage	Unc	PF
$50 2006	9,602	$900	
$50 2006W, Burnished	2,577	1,050	
$50 2006W	(7,649)		$950
$50 2007	7,001	900	
$50 2007W, Burnished	3,635	1,000	
$50 2007W	(25,519)		950
$50 2007W, Frosted FREEDOM	(21)		—
$50 2008	14,000	900	
$50 2008W, Burnished	2,253	1,200	
$50 2008W	(4,020)		1,400

$100 One-Ounce Platinum

Designers John M. Mercanti (obv), Thomas D. Rogers Sr. (orig rev); weight 1.0005 oz.; composition .9995 platinum; diameter 32.7 mm; reeded edge; mints: Philadelphia, West Point.

	Mintage	Unc.	PF
$100 1997	56,000	$1,800	
$100 1997W	(20,851)		$2,000
$100 1998	133,002	1,800	
$100 1998W	(14,912)		2,000
$100 1999	56,707	1,800	
$100 1999W	(12,363)		2,000
$100 2000	10,003	1,800	
$100 2000W	(12,453)		2,000
$100 2001	14,070	1,800	
$100 2001W	(8,969)		2,000
$100 2002	11,502	1,800	
$100 2002W	(9,834)		2,000
$100 2003	8,007	1,800	
$100 2003W	(8,246)		2,000
$100 2004	7,009	1,800	
$100 2004W	(6,007)		2,200

	Mintage	Unc.	PF
$100 2005	6,310	$1,800	
$100 2005W	(6,602)		$2,400
$100 2006	6,000	1,800	
$100 2006W, Burnished	3,068	2,200	
$100 2006W	(9,152)		2,000
$100 2007	7,202	1,800	
$100 2007W, Burnished	4,177	2,000	
$100 2007W	(8,363)		2,000
$100 2007W, Frosted FREEDOM	(21)		—
$100 2008	21,800	1,850	
$100 2008W, Burnished	2,876	2,200	
$100 2008W	(4,769)		2,900
$100 2009W	(9,871)		2,200
$100 2010W			2,100
$100 2011W			2,000
$100 2012W			2,000

2003 Proof Design   2004 Proof Design

2005 Proof Design   2006 Proof Design   2007 Proof Design

2008 Proof Design   2009 Proof Design   2010 Proof Design

2011 Proof Design

2012 Proof Design

Designs for Proofs 1998 through 2002 appear on page 362.

Platinum Bullion Sets

	PF
1997 Platinum Set. $100, $50, $25, $10	$3,750
1998 Platinum Set. $100, $50, $25, $10	3,750
1999 Platinum Set. $100, $50, $25, $10	3,750
2000 Platinum Set. $100, $50, $25, $10	3,750
2001 Platinum Set. $100, $50, $25, $10	3,750
2002 Platinum Set. $100, $50, $25, $10	3,750
2003 Platinum Set. $100, $50, $25, $10	3,750
2004 Platinum Set. $100, $50, $25, $10	5,200
2005 Platinum Set. $100, $50, $25, $10	4,300
2006W Platinum Set. $100, $50, $25, $10.	3,750
2006W Platinum Burnished Set. $100, $50, $25, $10	4,500
2007W Platinum Set. $100, $50, $25, $10.	3,750
2007W Platinum Burnished Set. $100, $50, $25, $10	4,000
2008W Platinum Set. $100, $50, $25, $10.	5,250
2008W Platinum Burnished Set. $100, $50, $25, $10	5,000

American Eagle 10th Anniversary Platinum Set

	Proof
Two-coin set containing one Proof platinum half-ounce and one Enhanced Reverse Proof half-ounce dated 2007W. Housed in hardwood box with mahogany finish	$2,300

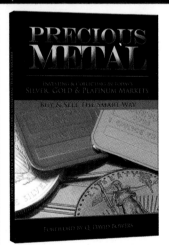

United States patterns are a fascinating part of numismatics that encompass a myriad of designs and experimental pieces made by the U.S. Mint to test new concepts and motifs, to provide coins for numismatists, and for other reasons. The book *United States Pattern Coins,* by J. Hewitt Judd, gives extensive details of the history and characteristics of more than 2,000 different pattern varieties from 1792 to the present era.

Patterns provide students and collectors a chronology of the continuing efforts of engravers and artists to present their work for approval. Throughout the 200+ years of federal coinage production, concepts meant to improve various aspects of circulating coins have been proposed and incorporated into representative patterns. In some instances, changes have been prompted by an outcry for higher aesthetics, a call for a more convenient denomination, or a need to overcome striking deficiencies. In many other instances, the Mint simply created special coins for the numismatic trade—often controversial in their time, but enthusiastically collected today. Certain patterns, bearing particular proposed designs or innovations, provided tangible examples for Mint and Treasury Department officials or members of Congress to evaluate. If adopted, the pattern design became a familiar regular-issue motif; those that were rejected have become part of American numismatic history.

The patterns listed and illustrated in this section are representative of a much larger group. Such pieces generally include die and hub trials, off-metal Proof strikings of regular issues, and various combinations of dies that were sometimes struck at a later date. Certain well-known members of this extended pattern family historically have been included with regular issues in many popular, general-circulation numismatic reference books. The four-dollar gold Stellas of 1879 and 1880; certain Gobrecht dollars of 1836, 1838, and 1839; and the Flying Eagle cents of 1856 are such examples. No official mintage figures of patterns and related pieces were recorded in most instances, and the number extant of each can usually only be estimated from auction appearances and from those found in museum holdings and important private collections. Although most patterns are very rare, the 2,000+ distinct varieties make them unexpectedly collectible—not by one of each, but by selected available examples from favorite types or categories.

Unlike regular coin issues that were emitted through the usual channels of commerce, and Proofs of regular issues that were struck expressly for sale to collectors, patterns were not intended to be officially sold. Yet as a matter of Mint policy in accordance with certain previously established restrictions, countless patterns were secretly and unofficially sold and traded to favorite dealers and collectors, disseminated to government officials, and occasionally made available to numismatic societies. Not until mid-1887 did the Mint enforce stringent regulations prohibiting their sale and distribution, although there had been several misleading statements to this effect earlier. In succeeding decades the Mint, while not making patterns available to numismatists, did place certain examples in the Mint Collection, now called the National Numismatic Collection, in the Smithsonian Institution. On other occasions, selected patterns were obtained by Mint and Treasury officials, or otherwise spared from destruction. Today, with the exception of certain cents and five-cent pieces of 1896, all pattern coins dated after 1885 are extremely rare.

The private possession of patterns has not been without its controversy. Most significant was the 1910 seizure by government agents of a parcel containing some 23 pattern pieces belonging to John W. Haseltine, a leading Philadelphia coin dealer with undisclosed private ties to Mint officials. The government asserted that the patterns had been removed from the Mint without authority, and that they remained the property of the United States. Haseltine's attorney successfully used the Mint's pre-1887 policies in his defense, and recovered the patterns a year after their confiscation.

This set precedent for ownership, at least for the patterns minted prior to 1887, as all of the pieces in question predated that year. Today, pattern coins can be legally held.

Among the grandest impressions ever produced at the U.S. Mint are the two varieties of pattern fifty-dollar gold pieces of 1877. Officially titled *half unions,* these large patterns were created at the request of certain politicians with interests tied to the gold-producing state of California. Specimens were struck in copper, and one of each variety was struck in gold. Both of the gold pieces were purchased around 1908 by numismatist William H. Woodin (who, years later, in 1933, served as President Franklin D. Roosevelt's first secretary of the Treasury). The Mint desired to re-obtain the pieces for its own collection, and through a complex trade deal for quantities of other patterns, did so, adding them to the Mint Collection. Now preserved in the Smithsonian Institution, these half unions are regarded as national treasures.

Special credit is due to the following individuals for contributing to this feature: Q. David Bowers, Marc Crane, Robert Hughes, Julian Leidman, Andy Lustig, Saul Teichman, and Eddie Wilson. The following sources are recommended for additional information, descriptions, and complete listings:

- *United States Pattern Coins,* 10th ed., J. Hewitt Judd, ed. by Q. David Bowers, 2009.
- *United States Patterns and Related Issues,* Andrew W. Pollock III, 1994. (Out of print)
- www.harrybassfoundation.org
- www.uspatterns.com

Judd-52   J-67

	PF-60	PF-63	PF-65
1836 Two-cent piece (J-52, billon) This proposal for a two-cent coin is one of the earliest collectible patterns. It was designed by Christian Gobrecht. *(21–30 known). .* *$8,625, PF-65, Heritage auction, January 2009*	$2,500	$4,500	$8,500
1836 Gold dollar (J-67, gold) Gobrecht styled the first gold dollar pattern after the familiar Mexican "cap and rays" design, then legal tender in this country. *(31–75 known) $24,725, PF-65, Stack's Bowers auction, November 2010*	10,000	17,500	22,500

J-164   J-177

	PF-60	PF-63	PF-65
1854 Cent (J-164, bronze) Beginning in 1850, the Mint produced patterns for a reduced-weight cent. Among the designs were ring-style, Liberty Head, and Flying Eagle motifs. These experiments culminated with the 1856 Flying Eagle cent. *(31–75 known) $16,100, PF-67 BN, Stack's Bowers auction, March 2005*	$2,000	$4,000	$6,750
1856 Half cent (J-177, copper-nickel) Before producing copper-nickel small-size cents in 1856, the Mint experimented with that alloy using half-cent dies. *(31–75 known) $6,038, PF-64, Stack's Bowers auction, January 2006*	3,000	4,750	8,500

Note: Red examples of J-164 are worth more than the prices listed here.

J-486

J-611

	PF-60	PF-63	PF-65

1866 Lincoln five-cent piece (J-486, nickel) A number of pattern nickels were produced in 1866, including one designed to depict the recently assassinated president. *(7–12 known) $8,740, Ch PF, Stack's Bowers auction, October 2003*. . . . | $5,750 | $10,000 | $18,000

1868 Cent (J-611, copper) There is no known reason for the minting of this unusual piece, which mimics the original large cents that had last been made in 1857. There was no intent to resume the coinage of old-style copper "large" cents in 1868. Accordingly, this variety is regarded as a rarity created for collectors. Fewer than 15 are believed to exist. *$36,800, PF-66 BN, Stack's Bowers auction, March 2005* | 19,000 | 26,000 | 36,000

J-1195

J-1235

	PF-60	PF-63	PF-65

1872 Amazonian quarter (J-1195, silver) Many of the most popular patterns have been given colorful nicknames by collectors in appreciation of their artistry. This design is by Chief Engraver William Barber. *(7–12 known)*. . . . . | $28,000 | $50,000 | $85,000
$80,500, PF-66 Cam, Heritage auction, January 2009

1872 Amazonian gold $3 (J-1235, gold) This unique piece was contained in the Mint's only uniform gold set using the same design from the gold dollar to the double eagle. . . . . | — | — | 1,250,000

J-1373

	PF-60	PF-63	PF-65

1874 Bickford eagle (J-1373, gold) Dana Bickford, a manufacturer, proposed a ten-dollar gold coin that would be exchangeable at set rates with other world currencies. Patterns were made, but the idea proved impractical. *(2 known)*. . . . . . . | — | $500,000 | $1,250,000
$1,265,000, PF-65 DC, Heritage auction, January 2010

J-1548

	PF-60	PF-63	PF-65

1877 Half union (J-1548, gold) This famous fifty-dollar pattern by William Barber
would have been the highest denomination ever issued by the Mint up to that time.
The gold impression is unique (residing in the Smithsonian), but copper specimens
(J-1549, which are priced here), sometimes gilt, occasionally come to the market.
Varieties exist with a somewhat larger or smaller head. $125,000 $200,000 $500,000
 $575,000, PF-67 BN, Heritage auction, January 2009

J-1590

	PF-60	PF-63	PF-65

1879 Quarter dollar (J-1590, silver) Referred to as the "Washlady" design, this
was Charles Barber's first attempt at a uniform silver design. *(13–20 known)* $7,500 $15,000 $25,000
 $34,500, PF-68, Heritage auction, January 2007

J-1609

	PF-60	PF-63	PF-65

1879 Dollar (J-1609, copper) The "Schoolgirl" design by George T. Morgan is
a widespread favorite among pattern collectors, although examples are rare.
(7–12 known) $74,750, PF-66 RB, Heritage auction, September 2006 . . . . $25,000 $45,000 $85,000

373

J-1905

	PF-60	PF-63	PF-65

1907 Indian Head double eagle (J-1905, gold) Designed by Augustus
Saint-Gaudens, this pattern is unique and extremely valuable. A variation
of the reverse of this design was used on the twenty-dollar gold coins of
1907 through 1933. . . . . *$7,500,000*

J-1992

	PF-60	PF-63	PF-65

1916 Liberty Walking half dollar (J-1992, silver) Various pattern Mercury dimes,
Standing Liberty quarters, and Liberty Walking half dollars were struck, all dated
1916. All are extremely rare, but a few found their way into circulation $60,000 $100,000 $165,000
  $115,000, PF-65, Heritage auction, July 2008

J-2063

	PF-60	PF-63	PF-65

**1942 Experimental cent (J-2051 through J-2069) Several metallic and other
compositions, including various colors of plastic.** Before settling on the zinc-coated
steel composition used for the Lincoln cents of 1943, the Mint considered various
alternative compositions, including plastics. Most were struck by outside contractors using
specially prepared dies provided by the Mint. *(7–12 known of most types and colors)* $1,500 $2,750 $4,750

The expression *private gold,* used with reference to coins struck outside the United States Mint, is a general term. In the sense that no state or territory had authority to coin money, *private gold* simply refers to those interesting necessity pieces of various shapes, denominations, and degrees of intrinsic worth that were circulated in isolated areas of the United States by individuals, assayers, bankers, and so on. Some numismatists use the words *territorial* and *state* to cover certain issues because they were coined and circulated in a territory or state. While the state of California properly sanctioned the ingots stamped by F.D. Kohler as state assayer, in no instance were any of the gold pieces struck by authority of any of the territorial governments.

The stamped fifty-dollar and other gold coins, sometimes called *ingots,* but in coin form, were made by Augustus Humbert, the United States Assayer of Gold, but were not receivable at face value for government payments, despite the fact that Humbert was an official agent. However, such pieces circulated widely in commerce.

Usually, private coins were circulated due to a shortage of regular coinage. In the Western states particularly, money became so scarce that the very commodity the pioneers had come so far to acquire was converted into a local medium of exchange.

Ephraim Brasher's New York doubloon of 1787 is also a private American gold issue and is described on page 63.

TEMPLETON REID
Georgia Gold 1830

The first private gold coinage in the 19th century was struck by Templeton Reid, a jeweler and gunsmith, in Milledgeville, Georgia, in July 1830. To be closer to the mines, he moved to Gainesville, where most of his coins were made. Although weights were accurate, Reid's assays were not and his coins were slightly short of claimed value. He was severely attacked in the newspapers and soon lost the public's confidence. He closed his mint before the end of October in 1830; his output had amounted to only about 1,600 coins. Denominations struck were $2.50, $5, and $10.

	VF	EF	AU
1830 $2.50.......	$110,000	$165,000	$275,000

	VF	EF	AU
1830 $5 *(7 known)*	$275,000	$400,000	$550,000

	VF	EF
1830 TEN DOLLARS		
(6 known)............	$600,000	$850,000

	VF	EF
(No Date) TEN DOLLARS		
(3 known)...........	$700,000	$1,000,000

California Gold 1849

The enigmatic later issues of Templeton Reid were probably made from California gold. Reid, who never went to California, was then a cotton-gin maker in Columbus, Georgia, where he died in 1851. The coins were in denominations of ten and twenty-five dollars. Struck copies of both exist in various metals.

The only example known of the twenty-five-dollar piece was stolen from the cabinet of the U.S. Mint on August 16, 1858. It was never recovered.

1849 TEN DOLLAR CALIFORNIA GOLD	*(unique, in Smithsonian collection)*
1849 TWENTY-FIVE DOLLARS CALIFORNIA GOLD	*(unknown)*

THE BECHTLERS
RUTHERFORD COUNTY, NC, 1831–1852

A skilled German metallurgist, Christopher Bechtler, assisted by his son August and his nephew, also named Christopher, operated a private mint in Rutherford County, North Carolina. Rutherford County and other areas in the Piedmont region of North Carolina and Georgia were the principal sources of the nation's gold supply from 1790 until the California gold strikes in 1848.

The coins minted by the Bechtlers were of only three denominations, but they covered a wide variety of weights and sizes. Rotated dies are common throughout the series. In 1831, the Bechtlers produced the first gold dollar in the United States. (The U.S. Mint struck its first circulating gold dollar in 1849.) Bechtler coins were well accepted by the public and circulated widely in the Southeast.

The inscription AUGUST 1. 1834 on several varieties of five-dollar pieces has a special significance. The secretary of the Treasury recommended to the Mint director that gold coins of the reduced weight bear the authorization date. This was not done on federal gold coinage, but the elder Christopher Bechtler evidently acted on the recommendation to avoid potential difficulty with Treasury authorities.

Christopher Bechtler

	VF	EF	AU	Unc.
ONE GOLD DOLLAR N. CAROLINA, 30.G., Star.	$2,600	$4,000	$6,000	$13,000
ONE GOLD DOLLAR N. CAROLINA, 28.G Centered, No Star.	4,000	5,000	10,000	24,500
ONE GOLD DOLLAR N. CAROLINA, 28.G High, No Star	8,500	13,000	21,500	35,000

	VF	EF	AU	Unc.
ONE DOLLAR CAROLINA, 28.G, N Reversed	$2,250	$2,800	$4,000	$7,500
2.50 CAROLINA, 67.G., 21 CARATS.	5,750	9,500	13,000	24,000

	VF	EF	AU	Unc.
2.50 CAROLINA, 70.G, 20 CARATS	$6,000	$11,000	$13,500	$28,000
2.50 GEORGIA, 64.G, 22 CARATS (Uneven "22").	6,500	11,500	14,000	29,000
2.50 GEORGIA, 64.G, 22 CARATS (Even "22").	8,300	13,000	18,000	37,000

	VF	EF	AU	Unc.
2.50 NORTH CAROLINA, 75.G., 20 C. RUTHERFORD in a Circle.				
Border of Large Beads	$22,000	$32,500	$45,000	$80,000
2.50 NORTH CAROLINA, 20 C. Without 75.G.	21,000	34,500	47,500	87,500
2.50 NORTH CAROLINA, 20 C. Without 75.G., CAROLINA above 250				
instead of gold *(unique)*				—
2.50 NORTH CAROLINA, 20 C. on Obverse, 75.G. and Star on Reverse.				
Border Finely Serrated	—	—	—	

	VF	EF	AU	Unc.
5 DOLLARS NORTH CAROLINA GOLD, 150.G., 20.CARATS	$22,500	$35,000	$50,000	$95,000
Similar, Without 150.G. *(1 or 2 known)*.	—	—		

Christopher Bechtler – Carolina

	VF	EF	AU	Unc.
5 DOLLARS CAROLINA, RUTHERFORD, 140.G., 20 CARATS, Plain Edge ...	$5,250	$7,750	$11,000	$24,000
5 DOLLARS CAROLINA, RUTHERFORD, 140.G., 20 CARATS, Reeded Edge	17,000	27,500	40,000	63,000
5 DOLLARS CAROLINA GOLD, RUTHER., 140.G., 20 CARATS,				
AUGUST 1, 1834	10,000	17,000	30,000	50,000
Similar, but "20" Distant From CARATS	6,000	9,500	14,000	24,000
5 DOLLARS CAROLINA GOLD, 134.G., 21 CARATS, With Star	5,000	7,000	10,000	19,000

Georgia

	VF	EF	AU	Unc.
5 DOLLARS GEORGIA GOLD, RUTHERFORD, 128.G., 22 CARATS.........	$7,000	$10,000	$13,000	$28,000
5 DOLLARS GEORGIA GOLD, RUTHERFORD, 128.G:, 22 CARATS,				
With Colon After G	15,000	25,000	37,500	
5 DOLLARS GEORGIA GOLD, RUTHERF, 128.G., 22 CARATS	7,000	9,500	13,000	28,000

August Bechtler

	VF	EF	AU	Unc.
1 DOL:, CAROLINA GOLD, 27.G., 21.C.	$1,500	$2,000	$3,000	$5,000
5 DOLLARS, CAROLINA GOLD, 134.G:, 21 CARATS..................	5,000	7,500	12,500	32,500
5 DOLLARS, CAROLINA GOLD, 134 G: 21 CARATS,				
Reverse of C. Bechtler as Shown Above......................	—	—		

	VF	EF	AU	Unc.
5 DOLLARS, CAROLINA GOLD, 128.G., 22 CARATS	$13,000	$16,500	$27,500	$42,500
5 DOLLARS, CAROLINA GOLD, 141.G., 20 CARATS	11,000	15,000	22,500	38,000

Note: Restrikes in "Proof" of this type using original dies were made about 1920.

NORRIS, GREGG & NORRIS
SAN FRANCISCO 1849

Collectors consider this piece the first of the California private gold coins. A newspaper account dated May 31, 1849, described a five-dollar gold coin, struck at Benicia City, though with the imprint San Francisco. It mentioned the private stamp of Norris, Gregg & Norris. The initials N.G.&N. were not interpreted until 1902, when the coins of Augustus Humbert were sold.

	F	VF	EF	AU	Unc.
1849 Half Eagle, Plain Edge	$4,500	$6,750	$11,500	$16,000	$33,000
1849 Half Eagle, Reeded Edge	4,500	6,500	11,000	14,500	30,000
1850 Half Eagle, With STOCKTON Beneath Date *(unique, in Smithsonian collection)*	—				

MOFFAT & CO.
SAN FRANCISCO 1849–1853

The firm of Moffat & Co. was perhaps the most important of the California private coiners. The assay office they conducted was semi-official in character. The successors to this firm, Curtis, Perry, and Ward, later sold their coining facility to the Treasury Department, which in March 1854 reopened it as the branch mint of San Francisco.

In June or July 1849, Moffat & Co. began to issue small, rectangular ingots of gold owing to lack of coin in the locality, in values from $9.43 to $264. The $9.43, $14.25, and $16.00 varieties are the only types known today.

$9.43 Ingot *(unique, in Smithsonian collection)*	—
$14.25 Ingot *(unique, in Smithsonian collection)*	—
$16.00 Ingot	$150,000

The dies for the ten-dollar piece were cut by a Bavarian, Albert Kuner. On the coronet of Liberty appear the words MOFFAT & CO., instead of the word LIBERTY as in regular United States issues.

	F	VF	EF	AU	Unc.
1849 FIVE DOL. *(all varieties)*	$1,650	$2,750	$4,000	$6,500	$13,500
1850 FIVE DOL. *(all varieties)*	1,650	2,850	4,250	6,000	15,000
1849 TEN DOL.	3,750	6,000	11,000	20,000	36,000
1849 TEN D.	3,900	6,500	12,500	23,000	42,500

UNITED STATES ASSAY OFFICE
Augustus Humbert
United States Assayer of Gold, 1851

Augustus Humbert, a New York watchcase maker, was appointed United States assayer, and he placed his name and the government stamp on the ingots of gold issued by Moffat & Co. The assay office, a provisional government mint, was a temporary expedient to accommodate the Californians until the establishment of a permanent branch mint.

The fifty-dollar gold piece was accepted by most banks and merchants as legal tender on a par with standard U.S. gold coins and was known variously as a *slug, quintuple eagle,* or *five-eagle piece.* It was officially termed an *ingot.*

Lettered-Edge Varieties

	F	VF	EF	AU	Unc.
1851 50 D C 880 THOUS., No 50 on Reverse. Sunk in Edge: AUGUSTUS HUMBERT UNITED STATES ASSAYER OF GOLD, CALIFORNIA 1851	$22,500	$32,500	$55,000	$77,500	$150,000
$546,250, MS-63, Heritage auction, August 2010					

	F	VF	EF	AU	Unc.
1851 50 D C 880 THOUS, Similar to Last Variety, but 50 on Reverse	$30,000	$50,000	$80,000	$130,000	$250,000
1851 50 D C, 887 THOUS., With 50 on Reverse	25,000	40,000	65,000	95,000	185,000

Reeded-Edge Varieties

	F	VF	EF	AU	Unc.
1851 FIFTY DOLLS, 880 THOUS., "Target" Reverse	$16,500	$25,000	$35,000	$50,000	$85,000
$460,000, MS-65, Stack's Bowers auction, September 2008					
1851 FIFTY DOLLS, 887 THOUS., "Target" Reverse	16,500	25,000	35,000	50,000	85,000
$500,000, Proof, B&R auction, March 1980					
1852 FIFTY DOLLS, 887 THOUS., "Target" Reverse	16,500	25,000	35,000	52,500	87,500

Moffat-Humbert

In 1851, certain issues of the Miners' Bank, Baldwin, Pacific Company, and others were discredited by newspaper accounts stating they were of reduced gold value. This provided an enhanced opportunity for Moffat and the U.S. Assay Office of Gold. Fractional-currency coins of almost every nation were being pressed into service by the Californians, but the supply was too small to help to any extent. Moffat & Co. proceeded in January 1852 to issue a new ten-dollar gold piece bearing the stamp MOFFAT & CO.

Close Date   **Wide Date**

	F	VF	EF	AU	Unc.
1852 TEN D. MOFFAT & CO. (Close Date)	$4,200	$6,500	$12,500	$30,000	$72,500
1852 TEN D. MOFFAT & CO. (Wide Date)	4,200	6,500	12,500	30,000	72,500

1852, Normal Date   **1852, 2 Over 1**

	F	VF	EF	AU	Unc.
1852 TEN DOLS.	$2,750	$4,250	$6,500	$11,000	$25,000
1852 TEN DOLS. 1852, 2 Over 1	2,850	5,250	8,750	15,000	30,000

	F	VF	EF	AU	Unc.
1852 TWENTY DOLS., 1852, 2 Over 1	$7,250	$11,500	$24,000	$37,500	$95,000

$434,500, PF-64, Superior auction, October 1990

United States Assay Office of Gold – 1852

The firm of Moffat & Co. was dissolved in 1852 and a newly reorganized company known as the United States Assay Office of Gold took over the contract. Principals were Curtis, Perry, and Ward.

	F	VF	EF	AU	Unc.
1852 FIFTY DOLLS., 887 THOUS.	$16,500	$25,000	$35,000	$50,000	$90,000
1852 FIFTY DOLLS., 900 THOUS.	16,500	26,000	37,500	52,500	92,500

	F	VF	EF	AU	Unc.
1852 TEN DOLS., 884 THOUS.	$1,800	$3,200	$4,800	$7,000	$17,000
1853 TEN D., 884 THOUS.	7,000	14,000	25,000	35,000	72,500
1853 TEN D., 900 THOUS.	4,000	6,000	9,500	15,000	22,500

	F	VF	EF	AU	Unc.
1853 TWENTY D., 884 THOUS.	$7,000	$10,000	$17,000	$27,000	$47,500

	F	VF	EF	AU	Unc.
1853 TWENTY D., 900 THOUS.	$2,200	$3,200	$4,500	$6,250	$12,000

Note: Modern prooflike forgeries exist.

Moffat & Co. Gold

The last Moffat issue, an 1853 twenty-dollar piece, is very similar to the U.S. double eagle of that period. It was struck after John L. Moffat retired from the Assay Office.

	F	VF	EF	AU	Unc.
1853 TWENTY D.	$4,500	$6,000	$9,500	$15,000	$32,500

J.H. BOWIE

Joseph H. Bowie joined his cousins in San Francisco in 1849 and possibly produced a limited coinage of gold pieces. A trial piece of the dollar denomination is known in copper, but may never have reached the coinage stage. Little is known about the company or the reason for considering these pieces.

1849 1 DOL. (copper pattern)		—
1849 5 DOL.		—

CINCINNATI MINING & TRADING CO. (1849)

The origin and location of this company are unknown.

	EF	Unc.
1849 FIVE DOLLARS *(unique)*		
1849 TEN DOLLARS *(5 known)* $431,250, EF, Stack's Bowers auction, May 2004	$750,000	—

Note: Beware of spurious specimens cast in base metal with the word TRACING in place of TRADING.

MASSACHUSETTS AND CALIFORNIA COMPANY

This company was believed to have been organized in Northampton, Massachusetts, in May 1849. Pieces with 5D are not genuine.

	VF	EF
1849 FIVE D. *(5–7 known)*	$175,000	$275,000

MINERS' BANK
SAN FRANCISCO 1849

The institution of Wright & Co., exchange brokers located in Portsmouth Square, San Francisco, was known as the Miners' Bank.

A ten-dollar piece was issued in the autumn of 1849, but the coins were not readily accepted because they were worth less than face value. The firm was dissolved on January 14, 1850. Unlike the gold in most California issues, the gold in these coins was alloyed with copper.

Dentelated Border **Crimped Border**

	VF	EF	AU	Unc.
(1849) TEN D., Dentelated Border, Raised Rim	$17,500	$30,000	$45,000	$85,000
(1849) TEN D., Crimped Border, Crushed Rim.	17,500	30,000	45,000	85,000

J.S. ORMSBY
SACRAMENTO 1849

The initials J.S.O., which appear on certain issues of California privately coined gold pieces, represent the firm of J.S. Ormsby & Co. They struck both five- and ten-dollar denominations, all undated.

	VF
(1849) 5 DOLLS, Plain Edge *(possibly unique)*	—
(1849) 5 DOLLS, Reeded Edge *(unique, in Smithsonian collection)*	—
(1849) 10 DOLLS *(4 known)*	$400,000

PACIFIC COMPANY, SAN FRANCISCO 1849

The origin of the Pacific Company is very uncertain. All data regarding the firm are based on conjecture.

Edgar H. Adams wrote that he believed that the coins bearing the stamp of the Pacific Company were produced by the coining firm of Broderick and Kohler. The coins were probably hand struck with the aid of a sledgehammer.

	EF	AU
1849 1 DOLLAR *(2 known)*	$275,000	$400,000
1849 5 DOLLARS *(4 known)*	350,000	500,000
1849 10 DOLLARS *(4 known)*	600,000	750,000

F.D. KOHLER
CALIFORNIA STATE ASSAYER 1850

The State Assay Office was authorized on April 12, 1850. That year, Governor Peter Burnett appointed F.D. Kohler, who thereupon sold his assaying business to Baldwin & Co. He served at both the San Francisco and Sacramento offices. The State Assay Offices were discontinued at the time the U.S. Assay Office was established, on February 1, 1851.

Ingots issued ranged from $36.55 to $150. An Extremely Fine specimen sold in the Garrett Sale, 1980, for $200,000. Each is unique.

$36.55 Sacramento	—		$45.34 San Francisco	—
$37.31 San Francisco	—		$50.00 San Francisco	—
$40.07 San Francisco	—		$54.09 San Francisco	—

Note: A $40.07 ingot was stolen from the Mint Cabinet in 1858 and never recovered.

DUBOSQ & COMPANY
SAN FRANCISCO 1850

Theodore Dubosq, a Philadelphia jeweler, took melting and coining machinery to San Francisco in 1849.

	VF			VF
1850 FIVE D. *(3–5 known)*	$275,000	1850 TEN D. *(8–10 known)*		$275,000

BALDWIN & CO.
SAN FRANCISCO 1850

George C. Baldwin and Thomas S. Holman were in the jewelry business in San Francisco and were known as Baldwin & Co. They were the successors to F.D. Kohler & Co., taking over its machinery and other equipment in May 1850.

	F	VF	EF	AU	Unc.
1850 FIVE DOL.	$7,000	$12,500	$22,500	$30,000	$47,500
1850 TEN DOLLARS, Horseman Type	40,000	67,500	110,000	140,000	225,000

	F	VF	EF	AU	Unc.
1851 TEN D.	$15,000	$30,000	$45,000	$70,000	$150,000

    The Baldwin & Co. twenty-dollar piece was the first of that denomination issued in California. Baldwin coins are believed to have contained about 2% copper alloy.

	EF	Unc.
1851 TWENTY D. *(4–6 known)*	$400,000	—

SCHULTZ & COMPANY
SAN FRANCISCO 1851

The firm of Schultz & Co., a brass foundry, was operated by Judge G.W. Schultz and William T. Garratt. The surname is misspelled Shultz on the coins.

	F	VF	EF	AU
1851 FIVE D.	$30,000	$52,500	$80,000	$135,000

DUNBAR & COMPANY
SAN FRANCISCO 1851

Edward E. Dunbar operated the California Bank in San Francisco. Dunbar later returned to New York City and organized the famous Continental Bank Note Co.

	EF
1851 FIVE D. *(4–6 known)*	$400,000

WASS, MOLITOR & CO.
SAN FRANCISCO 1852–1855

The gold-smelting and assaying plant of Wass, Molitor & Co. was operated by two Hungarian patriots, Count S.C. Wass and A.P. Molitor. They maintained an excellent laboratory and complete apparatus for analysis and coinage of gold.

The company struck five-, ten-, twenty-, and fifty-dollar coins. In 1852 they produced a ten-dollar piece similar in design to the five-dollar denomination. The difference is in the reverse legend, which reads: S.M.V. [Standard Mint Value] CALIFORNIA GOLD TEN D.

No pieces were coined in 1853 or 1854, but they brought out the twenty- and fiftydollar pieces in 1855. A considerable number of the fifty-dollar coins were made. There was a ten-dollar piece issued in 1855 also, with the Liberty head and small close date.

Small Head, Rounded Bust

Large Head, Pointed Bust

	F	VF	EF	AU	Unc.
1852 FIVE DOLLARS, Small Head, With Rounded Bust	$5,000	$10,000	$21,000	$37,500	$75,000
1852 FIVE DOLLARS, Large Head, With Pointed Bust	4,500	9,000	17,500	32,500	62,500

Large Head

Small Head	Small Date	1855

	F	VF	EF	AU	Unc.
1852 TEN D., Large Head	$2,750	$4,200	$7,000	$12,000	$24,000
1852 TEN D., Small Head	6,200	8,000	18,000	30,000	77,000
1852 TEN D., Small Close Date	12,500	27,500	45,000	86,000	
1855 TEN D	9,000	15,000	20,000	27,500	50,000

Large Head   Small Head

	F	VF	EF	AU	Unc.
1855 TWENTY DOL., Large Head *(4–6 known)*	—	—	$425,000	—	—
1855 TWENTY DOL., Small Head	$12,000	$25,000	35,000	$52,500	$110,000

	F	VF	EF	AU	Unc.
1855 50 DOLLARS	$25,000	$35,000	$50,000	$80,000	$175,000

KELLOGG & CO.
SAN FRANCISCO 1854–1855

John G. Kellogg went to San Francisco on October 12, 1849, from Auburn, New York. At first he was employed by Moffat & Co., and remained with that organization when control passed to Curtis, Perry, and Ward. When the U.S. Assay Office was discontinued, December 14, 1853, Kellogg became associated with G.F. Richter, who had been an assayer in the government assay office. These two set up business as Kellogg & Richter on December 19, 1853.

When the U.S. Assay Office ceased operations, a period ensued during which no private firm was striking gold. The new San Francisco branch mint did not produce coins for some months after Curtis & Perry took the contract for the government (Ward having died). The lack of coin was again keenly felt by businessmen, who petitioned Kellogg & Richter to "supply the vacuum" by issuing private coin. Their plea was soon answered: on February 9, 1854, Kellogg & Co. placed their first twenty-dollar piece in circulation.

The firm dissolved late in 1854 and reorganized as Kellogg & Humbert. The latter partner was Augustus Humbert, for some time identified as U.S. assayer of gold in California. Regardless of the fact that the branch mint was then producing coins, Kellogg & Humbert issued twenty-dollar coins in 1855 in a quantity greater than before.

	F	VF	EF	AU	Unc.
1854 TWENTY D.	$3,250	$4,250	$6,000	$8,750	$22,500

The 1855 twenty-dollar piece is similar to that of 1854. The letters on the reverse are larger and the arrows longer on one 1854 variety. There are die varieties of both.

	F	VF	EF	AU	Unc.
1855 TWENTY D.	$3,500	$4,500	$6,750	$9,500	$25,000

In 1855, Ferdinand Grüner cut the dies for a round-format fifty-dollar gold coin for Kellogg & Co., but coinage seems to have been limited to presentation pieces. Only 10 to 12 pieces are known to exist. A "commemorative restrike" was made in 2001 using transfer dies made from the original and gold recovered from the SS *Central America*. These pieces have the inscription S.S. CENTRAL AMERICA GOLD, C.H.S. on the reverse ribbon.

	PF
1855 FIFTY DOLLS. *(13–15 known) $747,500, PF-64, Heritage auction, January 2007.*	$500,000

OREGON EXCHANGE COMPANY
OREGON CITY 1849
The Beaver Coins of Oregon

Upon the discovery of gold in California, a great exodus of Oregonians joined in the hunt for the precious metal. Soon, returning gold seekers offered their gold dust, which became the accepted medium of exchange. As in other Western areas at that time, the uncertain qualities of the gold and weighing devices tended to irk the tradespeople, and petitions were made to the legislature for a standard gold coin issue.

On February 16, 1849, the territorial legislature passed an act providing for a mint and specified five- and ten-dollar gold coins without alloy. Oregon City, the largest city in the territory with a population of about 1,000, was designated as the location for the mint. At the time this act was passed, Oregon had been brought into the United States as a territory by act of Congress. When the new governor arrived on March 2, he declared the coinage act unconstitutional.

The public-spirited people, however, continued to work for a convenient medium of exchange and soon took matters into their own hands by starting a private mint. Eight men of affairs, whose names were Kilborne, Magruder, Taylor, Abernethy, Willson, Rector, Campbell, and Smith, set up the Oregon Exchange Company.

The coins struck were of virgin gold as specified in the original act. Ten-dollar dies were made slightly later, and were of finer design and workmanship.

	F	VF	EF	AU	Unc.
1849 5 D.	$30,000	$45,000	$65,000	$110,000	—

	F	VF	EF	AU	Unc.
1849 TEN.D	$75,000	$140,000	$250,000	$325,000	—

MORMON GOLD PIECES
SALT LAKE CITY, UTAH, 1849–1860

The first name given to the organized Mormon Territory was the "State of Deseret," the last word meaning "honeybee." The beehive, which is shown on the reverse of the five-dollar 1860 piece, was a favorite device of the followers of Joseph Smith and Brigham Young. The clasped hands appear on most Mormon coins and exemplify strength in unity. HOLINESS TO THE LORD was an inscription frequently used.

Brigham Young was the instigator of the coinage system and personally supervised the mint, which was housed in a little adobe building in Salt Lake City. The mint was inaugurated late in 1848 as a public convenience.

	F	VF	EF	AU	Unc.
1849 TWO.AND.HALF.DO.	$12,000	$22,000	$32,500	$55,000	$85,000
1849 FIVE.DOLLARS	9,500	17,500	27,500	35,000	77,500

	F	VF	EF	AU	Unc.
1849 TEN.DOLLARS	$225,000	$400,000	$500,000	$700,000	$900,000

The first coin of the twenty-dollar denomination to be struck in the United States.

	F	VF	EF	AU	Unc.
1849 TWENTY.DOLLARS.	$92,500	$165,000	$250,000	$350,000	$500,000

	F	VF	EF	AU	Unc.
1850 FIVE DOLLARS	$11,000	$21,500	$30,000	$47,500	$80,000

	F	VF	EF	AU	Unc.
1860 5.D.	$20,000	$30,000	$40,000	$65,000	$80,000

COLORADO GOLD PIECES
Clark, Gruber & Co.
Denver 1860–1861

Clark, Gruber & Co. was a well-known private minting firm in Denver, Colorado, in the early 1860s.

	F	VF	EF	AU	Unc.
1860 2 1/2 D	$1,800	$2,750	$3,750	$5,250	$13,500
1860 FIVE D	2,100	3,250	4,500	6,000	14,500

	F	VF	EF	AU	Unc.
1860 TEN D	$8,500	$12,500	$17,500	$27,500	$50,000
1860 TWENTY D					
$690,000, MS-64, Heritage auction, January 2006	65,000	125,000	200,000	375,000	650,000

The $2.50 and $5 pieces of 1861 follow closely the designs of the 1860 issues. The main difference is found in the legends. The reverse side now has CLARK GRUBER & CO. DENVER. PIKES PEAK now appears on the coronet of Liberty.

	F	VF	EF	AU	Unc.
1861 2 1/2 D	$1,900	$2,900	$4,300	$7,500	$14,000
1861 FIVE D	2,300	3,500	5,600	9,250	37,500
1861 TEN D	2,400	3,600	6,000	10,000	25,000

	VF	EF	AU	Unc.
1861 TWENTY D	$35,000	$75,000	$85,000	$200,000

John Parsons & Company
Tarryall Mines – Colorado, 1861

Very little is known regarding the mint of John Parsons and Co., although it is reasonably certain that it operated in the South Park section of Park County, Colorado, near the original town of Tarryall, in the summer of 1861.

Pikes Peak Gold

	VF	EF
(1861) Undated 2 1/2 D. *(6–8 known)*	$200,000	$300,000
(1861) Undated FIVE D. *(5–6 known)*	275,000	375,000

J.J. Conway & Co.
Georgia Gulch, Colorado, 1861

Records show that the Conway mint operated for a short while in 1861. As in all gold-mining areas the value of gold dust caused disagreement among the merchants and the miners. The firm of J.J. Conway & Co. solved this difficulty by bringing out its gold pieces in August 1861.

	VF	EF
(1861) Undated 2 1/2 DOLL'S *(8–12 known)*	$155,000	$200,000
(1861) Undated FIVE DOLLARS *(5–8 known)*	225,000	300,000

(1861) Undated TEN DOLLARS *(3 known)* . . . .   —

CALIFORNIA SMALL-DENOMINATION GOLD

There was a scarcity of small coins during the California gold rush. Starting in 1852, quarter, half, and dollar coins were privately minted from native gold to alleviate the shortage. The acceptability of these hard-to-handle, underweight coins was always limited, but they soon became popular as souvenirs. Early coins contained up to 85% of face value in gold. The amount and quality of gold in the coins soon decreased, and some are merely gold plated.

The Coinage Act of April 22, 1864, made private coinage illegal, but the law was not fully enforced until 1883. In compliance with the law, non-denominated tokens were made, and from 1872 until 1883 both coins and tokens were produced. After 1883, most of the production was tokens. To circumvent the law, and to make them more acceptable, some pieces made after 1881 were backdated to the 1850s or 1860s.

Early issues have Liberty heads; later issues have Indian heads and often are proof-like. Most have a wreath on the reverse, but some have original designs. About 35,000 pieces are believed to exist. More than 570 different varieties have been identified, many of them very rare. The quality of strike and edge treatment is inconsistent. Many bear their makers' initials: D, DERI, DERIB, DN, FD, G, GG, GL, H, L, N, or NR. Major denominated coins are listed below; values are for the most common variety of each type. Non-denominated tokens are not included in these listings. They are much less valuable. *Beware of extremely common modern replicas* (often having a bear in the design), which have little numismatic value.

The values in the following charts are only for coins made before 1883 with the denomination on the reverse expressed as CENTS, DOL., DOLL., or DOLLAR.

Quarter Dollar – Octagonal

	EF	AU	Unc.
Large Liberty Head / Value and Date in Wreath.	$175	$250	$450
Large Liberty Head / Value and Date in Beaded Circle	175	275	470
Large Liberty Head / Value and CAL in Wreath	175	230	350
Small Liberty Head / Value and Date in Wreath.	170	230	320
Small Liberty Head / Value and Date in Beaded Circle	175	250	340
Small Liberty Head / Value in Shield, Date in Wreath	175	250	375
Small Liberty Head / Value and CAL in Wreath	175	250	425
Small Liberty Head, date below / Value in Wreath.	175	230	320
Large Indian Head / Value in Wreath.	215	310	475
Large Indian Head / Value and CAL in Wreath.	195	280	450
Small Indian Head / Value and CAL in Wreath.	500	625	975
Washington Head 1872 / Value and CAL in Wreath.	775	1,350	2,000

Quarter Dollar – Round

	EF	AU	Unc.
Liberty Head / Value in Wreath	$150	$250	$425
Large Liberty Head / Value and Date in Wreath	190	310	450
Large Liberty Head / Value and CAL in Wreath	150	250	400
Small Liberty Head / 25 CENTS in Wreath	320	500	800
Small Liberty Head / Value and Date in Wreath	180	300	435
Small Liberty Head / Value in Shield, Date in Wreath	180	315	550
Small Liberty Head / Value and CAL in Wreath	180	225	400
Large Indian Head / Value in Wreath	350	520	825
Large Indian Head / Value and CAL in Wreath	300	400	675
Small Indian Head / Value and CAL in Wreath	375	525	850
Washington Head 1872 / Value and CAL in Wreath	725	1,000	1,600

Half Dollar – Octagonal

	EF	AU	Unc.
Large Liberty Head / Value and Date in Wreath	$300	$370	$690
Large Liberty Head / Value and Date in Beaded Circle	170	210	450
Large Liberty Head / Value and CAL in Wreath	210	425	650
Large Liberty Head / Legend Surrounds Wreath	400	600	1,000
Small Liberty Head / Value and Date in Wreath	200	375	575
Small Liberty Head / Value and CAL in Wreath	185	320	475
Small Liberty Head / Small Eagle With Rays	1,300	2,000	3,250
Small Liberty Head / Large Eagle With Raised Wings	1,500	2,200	3,250
Large Indian Head / Value in Wreath	210	400	675
Large Indian Head / Value and CAL in Wreath	235	350	575
Small Indian Head / Value in Wreath	250	425	700
Small Indian Head / Value and CAL in Wreath	450	585	975

Half Dollar – Round

	EF	AU	Unc.
Liberty Head / Value in Wreath	$180	$325	$500
Liberty Head / Value and Date in Wreath	180	325	500
Liberty Head / Value and CAL in Wreath	225	350	575
Liberty Head / CALIFORNIA GOLD Around Wreath	225	375	600
Large Indian Head / Value in Wreath	210	325	525
Large Indian Head / Value and CAL in Wreath	200	300	465
Small Indian Head / Value and CAL in Wreath	200	330	525

Dollar – Octagonal

	EF	AU	Unc.
Liberty Head / Value and Date in Wreath	$500	$750	$1,350
Liberty Head / Value and Date in Beaded Circle	500	800	1,500
Liberty Head / Legend Around Wreath	500	825	1,550
Liberty Head / Large Eagle	2,150	3,150	5,250
Large Indian Head / Value in Wreath	725	1,150	2,100
Small Indian Head / Value and CAL in Wreath	725	1,150	2,100

Dollar – Round

	EF	AU	Unc.
Liberty Head / CALIFORNIA GOLD. Value and Date in Wreath	$1,750	$2,600	$4,500
Liberty Head / Date Beneath Head	2,300	3,200	5,100
Indian Head / Date Beneath Head	2,000	3,100	5,000

COINS OF THE GOLDEN WEST

Small souvenir California gold pieces were made by several manufacturers in the early 20th century. A series of 36 pieces, in the size of 25¢, 50¢, and $1 coins, was made by the M.E. Hart Company of San Francisco to honor Alaska and various Western states. The Hart Company also marketed the official commemorative Panama-Pacific gold coins from the 1915 Exposition and manufactured plush copper cases for them. Similar cases were acquired by Farran Zerbe, who mounted 15 complete sets of what he termed "Coins of the Golden West." Intact, framed 36-piece sets are rare; individual specimens are among the most popular of all souvenir pieces of that era.

	AU	MS-63
Alaska Pinch, 25c, octagonal, 1902	$350	$650
Alaska Pinch, 50c, octagonal, 1900	400	700
Alaska Pinch, $1, octagonal, 1898 .	500	850
Alaska Pinch, 25c, round, 1901 ...	350	650
Alaska Pinch, 50c, round, 1899 ...	400	700
Alaska Pinch, $1, round, 1897	500	850
Alaska Parka, 25c, round, 1911 ...	1,200	1,900
Alaska Parka, 50c, round, 1911 ...	1,300	2,250
Alaska Parka, $1, round, 1911	1,500	2,650
Alaska AYPE, 25c, round, 1909 ...	175	300
Alaska AYPE, 50c, round, 1909 ...	200	350
Alaska AYPE, $1, round, 1909	250	400
California Minerva, 25c, octag, 1915	200	350
California Minerva, 50c, octag, 1915	250	400
California Minerva, $1, octag, 1915	300	500
California Minerva, 25c, round, 1915	200	350
California Minerva, 50c, round, 1915	250	400
California Minerva, $1, round, 1915	300	500

	AU	MS-63
California 25c, octag, 1860 or 1902	$ 500	$1,200
California 50c, octag, 1900.......	600	1,350
California $1, octag, 1898	700	1,600
California 25c, round, 1849, 1860, 1871, or 1901	550	1,250
California 50c, round, 1849 or 1899	650	1,500
California $1, round, 1849	800	1,750
Idaho, 25c, round, 1914.........	650	1,150
Idaho, 50c, round, 1914.........	750	1,250
Idaho, $1, round, 1914..........	850	1,500
Montana, 25c, round, 1914	650	1,150
Montana, 50c, round, 1914	750	1,250
Montana, $1, round, 1914	850	1,500
Oregon, 25c, round, 1914........	600	1,100
Oregon, 50c, round, 1914........	700	1,200
Oregon, $1, round, 1914	800	1,400
Washington, 25c, round, 1914	600	1,100
Washington, 50c, round, 1914	700	1,200
Washington, $1, round, 1914	800	1,400

CALIFORNIA GOLD INGOT BARS

During the Gold Rush era, gold coins, ingots, and "dust" were sent by steamship from San Francisco to other ports, most importantly to New York City and London, where the gold was sold or, in some instances, sent to mints for conversion into coins. The typical procedure in the mid-1850s was to send the gold by steamship from San Francisco to Panama, where it was sent across 48 miles of land on the Panama Railroad, then loaded aboard another ship at the town of Aspinwall on the Atlantic side. On September 12, 1857, the SS *Central America,* en route from Aspinwall to New York City with more than 475 passengers, over 100 crew members, and an estimated $2.6 million in gold (in an era in which pure gold was valued at $20.67 per ounce) was lost at sea. Miraculously, more than 150 people, including all but one of the women and children, were rescued by passing ships. The SS *Central America* went to the bottom of the Atlantic Ocean off the Carolina coast.

In the 1980s a group of researchers in Ohio formed the Columbus-America Discovery Group and secured financing to search for the long-lost ship. After much study and many explorations, they discovered the wreck of the SS *Central America* 7,200 feet below the surface. Tommy Thompson, Bob Evans, and others from C-ADG used the robotic *Nemo,* a sophisticated device weighing several tons, to photograph the wreck and to carefully bring to the surface many artifacts. A king's ransom in gold ingots was found, along with more than 7,500 coins, the latter mostly consisting of Mint State 1857-S double eagles.

The 500-plus gold ingots furnished a unique opportunity to study specimens that, after conservation, were essentially in the same condition as they had been in 1857. These bore the imprints of five different California assayers, who operated seven offices. With few exceptions, each ingot bears individual stamps, indicating its maker, a serial number, the weight in ounces, the fineness (expressed in thousandths, e.g., .784 indicating 784/1000 pure gold), and the 1857 value in dollars. The smallest bar found was issued by Blake & Co., weighed 4.95 ounces, was .795 fine, and was stamped with a value of $81.34. The largest ingot, dubbed the Eureka bar, bore the imprint of Kellogg & Humbert, and was stamped with a weight of 933.94 ounces, .903 fine, and a value of $17,433.57.

Blake & Co., Sacramento, California: From December 28, 1855, to May 1858, Blake & Co. was operated by Gorham Blake and W.R. Waters. • 34 ingots recovered. Serial numbers in the 5,100 and 5,200 series. Lowest weight and value: 4.95 ounces, $81.34. Highest weight and value: 157.40 ounces, $2,655.05. These bars have beveled or "dressed" edges and may have seen limited use in California commerce.

Harris, Marchand & Co., Sacramento and Marysville: Founded in Sacramento in 1855 by Harvey Harris and Desiré Marchand, with Charles L. Farrington as the "& Co." The Marysville office was opened in January 1856. Serial numbers in the 6,000 series are attributed to Sacramento, comprising 36 bars; a single bar in the 7,000 series (7095) is attributed to Marysville. The Marchand bars each have a circular coin-style counterstamp on the face. Lowest weight and value (Sacramento): 9.87 ounces, $158.53. Highest weight and value (Sacramento): 295.20 ounces, $5,351.73. • Unique Marysville bar: 174.04 ounces, $3,389.06.

Henry Hentsch, San Francisco: Henstch, a Swiss, was an entrepreneur involved in banking, real estate, assaying, and other ventures. In February 1856, he opened an assay office as an annex to his bank. It is likely that many of his ingots were exported to Europe, where he had extensive banking connections. • 33 ingots recovered.

Lowest weight and value: 12.52 ounces, $251.82. Highest weight and value: 238.84 ounces, $4,458.35.

Justh & Hunter, San Francisco and Marysville: Emanuel Justh, a Hungarian, was a lithographer in San Francisco in the early 1850s. In 1854 and 1855 he worked as assistant assayer at the San Francisco Mint. Solomon Hillen Hunter came to California from Baltimore. The Justh & Hunter partnership was announced in May 1855. • Although study is continuing, the 60 ingots in the 4,000 series are tentatively attributed to San Francisco, and the 26 ingots in the 9,000 series are attributed to Marysville. • San Francisco—Lowest weight and value: 5.24 ounces, $92.18. Highest weight and value: 866.19 ounces, $15,971.93. • Marysville—Lowest weight and value: 19.34 ounces, $356.21. Highest weight and value: 464.65 ounces, $8,759.90.

Kellogg & Humbert, San Francisco: John Glover Kellogg and Augustus Humbert, two of the most famous names in the minting of California gold coins, formed the partnership of Kellogg & Humbert in spring 1855. The firm was one of the most active of all California assayers during the mid-1850s. • 346 ingots recovered, constituting the majority of those found. • Lowest weight and value: 5.71 ounces, $101.03. Highest weight and value: 933.94 ounces, $17,433.57.

A selection of gold ingots from the SS *Central America* treasure (with an 1857S-S $20 double eagle shown for scale, near lower left). (1) Harris, Marchand & Co., Marysville office, serial number 7095, 174.04 ounces, .942 fine, $3,389.06 (all values as stamped in 1857). (2) Henry Henstch, San Francisco, serial number 3120, 61.93 ounces, .886 fine, $1,134.26. (3) Kellogg & Humbert, San Francisco, serial number 215, .944 fine, $1,045.96. (4) Blake & Co., Sacramento, 19.30 ounces, .946 fine, $297.42. (5) Another Blake & Co. ingot, serial number 5216, .915 fine, $266.12. (6) Justh & Hunter, Marysville office, serial number 9440, 41.79 ounces, $761.07. (7) Justh & Hunter, San Francisco office, serial number 4243, 51.98 ounces, .916 fine, $984.27. (8) Harris, Marchand & Co., Sacramento office, serial number 6514, 35.33 ounces, .807 fine, $589.38. (9) Harris, Marchand & Co., Sacramento office, serial number 6486, 12.64 ounces, .950 fine, $245.00.

HARD TIMES TOKENS (1832–1844)

Hard Times tokens, as they are called, are mostly the size of a contemporary large copper cent. Privately minted from 1832 to 1844, they display diverse motifs reflecting political campaigns and satire of the era as well as carrying advertisements for merchants, products, and services. For many years these have been a popular specialty within numismatics, helped along with the publication of *Hard Times Tokens* by Lyman H. Low (1899; revised edition, 1906) and later works, continuing to the present day. In 1899 Low commented (adapted) that "the issues commonly called Hard Times tokens . . . had no semblance of authority behind them. They combine the character of political pieces with the catch-words of party cries; of satirical pieces with sarcastic allusions to the sentiments or speeches of the leaders of opposing parties; and in some degree also of necessity pieces, in a time when, to use one of the phrases of the day, 'money was a cash article,' hard to get for daily needs."

Although these are designated as Hard Times tokens, the true Hard Times period began in a serious way on May 10, 1837, when banks began suspending specie payments and would no longer exchange paper currency for coins. This date is memorialized on some of the token inscriptions. Difficult economic conditions continued through 1843; the first full year of recovery was 1844. From March 1837 to March 1841, President Martin Van Buren vowed to "follow in the steps of my illustrious predecessor," President Andrew Jackson, who had been in office from March 1829 until Van Buren's inauguration. Jackson was perhaps the most controversial president up to that time. His veto in 1832 of the impending (1836) recharter of the Bank of the United States set off a political firestorm, made no calmer when his administration shifted deposits to favored institutions, derisively called "pet banks."

The Jackson era was one of unbridled prosperity. Due to sales of land in the West, the expansion of railroads, and a robust economy, so much money piled up in the Treasury that distributions were made in 1835 to all of the states. Seeking to end wild speculation, Jackson issued the "Specie Circular" on July 11, 1836, mandating that purchases of Western land, often done on credit or by other non-cash means, had to be paid in silver or gold coins. Almost immediately, the land boom settled and prices stabilized. A chill began to spread across the economy, which finally warmed in early 1837. Finally, many banks ran short of ready cash, causing the specie suspension.

After May 10, 1837, silver and gold coins completely disappeared from circulation. Copper cents remained, but were in short supply. Various diesinkers and others produced a flood of copper tokens. These were sold at discounts to merchants and banks, with $6 for 1,000 tokens being typical. Afterward, they were paid out in commerce and circulated for the value of one cent.

The actions of Jackson, the financial tribulations that many thought he precipitated, and the policies of Van Buren inspired motifs for the Hard Times tokens known as "politicals." Several hundred other varieties were made with the advertisements of merchants, services, and products and are known as "store cards" or "merchants' tokens." Many of these were illustrated with elements such as a shoe, umbrella, comb, coal stove, storefront, hotel, or carriage.

One of the more famous issues depicts a slave kneeling in chains, with the motto "Am I Not a Woman & a Sister?" This token was issued in 1838, when abolition was a major rallying point for many Americans in the North. The curious small-size Feuchtwanger cents of 1837, made in Feuchtwanger's Composition (a type of German silver), were proposed to Congress as a cheap substitute for copper cents, but no action was taken. Lewis Feuchtwanger produced large quantities on his own account and circulated them extensively. (See page 404.)

As the political and commercial motifs of Hard Times tokens are so diverse, and reflect the American economy and political scene of their era, numismatists have found them fascinating to collect and study. Although there are major rarities in the series, most of the issues are very affordable. Expanded information concerning more than 500 varieties of Hard Times tokens can be found in Russell Rulau's *Standard Catalog of United States Tokens, 1700–1900* (fourth edition). A representative selection is illustrated here.

L1, HT1   L57, HT76

L4, HT6   L56, HT75

L66, HT24   L54, HT81

L55, HT63   L31, HT46

	VF	EF	AU
L1, HT1. Andrew Jackson. Copper	$5,750	$9,000	—
L57, HT76. Van Buren, facing left. Brass	2,500	3,500	$4,500
L4, HT6. Jackson President of the U.S. Brass	150	300	800
L56, HT75. Van Buren facing left. Copper	85	175	400
L66, HT24. Agriculture. Copper	250	375	700
L54, HT81. A Woman & A Sister. Copper	200	300	500
L55, HT63. Loco Foco, 1838. Copper	60	150	250
L31, HT46. Not One Cent, Motto. Copper	50	100	200

L8, HT9

L18, HT32

L51, HT70

L47, HT66

L60, HT18

L44, HT69

L59, HT17

L65, HT23

	VF	EF	AU
L8, HT9. My Victory / Jackson. Copper	$35	$100	$225
L18, HT32. Executive Experiment. Copper	30	80	125
L51, HT70. Roman Firmness. Copper	40	110	170
L47, HT66. Phoenix / May Tenth. Copper	30	75	135
L60, HT18. Ship/Lightning. Copper	30	75	135
L44, HT69. Ship/Jackson. Copper	30	90	150
L59, HT17. Ship / Wreath Border	26	65	125
L65, HT23. Ship / Liberty Head. Copper	120	200	300

FEUCHTWANGER TOKENS (1837–1864)

Lewis Feuchtwanger produced a metal that was really a variety of German silver consisting of nickel, copper, and some zinc. He suggested to Congress as early as 1837 that his metal be substituted for copper, and he made one-cent and three-cent trial pieces that circulated freely during the coin shortage of 1836 through 1844.

	VF	EF	AU	Unc.
1837 One Cent, Eagle	$140	$210	$300	$510
1837 Three-Cent, New York Coat of Arms	750	1,600	2,750	5,250
1837 Three-Cent, Eagle	1,300	3,600	5,500	13,000
1864 Three-Cent, Eagle	1,700	2,800	3,800	7,500

LESHER REFERENDUM DOLLARS (1900–1901)

Distributed in 1900 and 1901 by Joseph Lesher of Victor, Colorado, these private tokens were used in trade to some extent, and stocked by various merchants who redeemed them in goods. Coins were numbered and a blank space left at bottom of 1901 issues, in which were stamped names of businessmen who bought them. All are quite rare; many varieties are extremely rare. Composition is .950 fine silver (alloyed with copper).

	EF	AU	Unc.
1900 First type, no business name	$2,600	$3,700	$5,600
1900 A.B. Bumstead, with or without scrolls (Victor)	1,400	1,950	3,200
1900 Bank type	14,500	21,000	—
1901 Imprint type, no name	1,400	2,200	3,500
1901 Imprint type, Boyd Park. Denver	1,500	2,300	3,750
1901 Imprint type, Slusher. Cripple Creek	2,100	3,000	4,300
1901 Imprint type, Mullen. Victor	3,500	5,500	9,100
1901 Imprint type, Cohen. Victor	6,500	8,500	12,000
1901 Imprint type, Klein. Pueblo	3,750	9,000	13,000
1901 Imprint type, Alexander. Salida	7,800	10,000	15,000
1901 Imprint type, White. Grand Junction	14,000	19,000	—
1901 Imprint type, Goodspeeds. Colorado Springs	20,000	26,000	—
1901 Imprint type, Nelson. Holdrige, Nebrask.	20,000	27,000	—
1901 Imprint type, A.W. Clark (Denver) (unique)		34,000	

CIVIL WAR TOKENS (1860s)

Civil War tokens are generally divided into two groups: tradesmen's tokens (also called store cards), and anonymously issued pieces with political or patriotic themes. These were struck during the Civil War, mostly in 1863. In July of that year federal cents disappeared from circulation and were hoarded. Various substitutes appeared, including tokens. Most production ended after bronze federal cents again became plentiful in circulation in the summer of 1864.

The tradesmen's tokens were purchased at a discount by various firms, who distributed them with advertising messages. Some of these were redeemable in goods. Political and patriotic tokens were produced at a profit by private maufacturers and put into circulation, with no identification as to the issuer. As there was no provision to redeem these, tokens of both types remained in circulation for many years, until they gradually disappeared.

These tokens are of great variety in composition and design. A number were more or less faithful imitations of the copper-nickel cent. A few of this type have the word NOT in very small letters above the words ONE CENT.

Many pieces, especially tradesmen's tokens, were individual in device and size, representing any caprice of design or slogan that appealed to the maker. Some were political or patriotic in character, carrying the likeness of some military leader such as McClellan or bearing such inscriptions as "Millions for contractors, not one cent for the widows." An estimated 50,000,000 or more of these pieces were issued. Approximately 10,000 different varieties have been recorded. Among these tokens are many issues made for numismatists of the era, including overstrikes on Indian Head and Flying Eagle cents and silver dimes, and strikings in white metal and silver. These are highly prized today.

The legal status of the Civil War tokens was uncertain. Mint Director James Pollock thought they were illegal; however, there was no law prohibiting the issue of tradesmen's tokens or of private coins not in imitation of United States coins. A law was passed April 22, 1864, prohibiting the issue of any one- or two-cent coins, tokens, or devices for use as money, and on June 8 another law was passed that abolished private coinage of every kind.

Values shown are for the most common tokens in each composition.

	F	VF	EF	MS-63
Copper or brass	$15	$25	$50	$120
Nickel or German silver	60	75	130	290
White metal	80	125	175	250
Copper-nickel	75	125	225	325
Silver	200	500	725	1,200

Patriotic Civil War Tokens

Patriotic Civil War tokens feature leaders such as Abraham Lincoln; military images such as cannons or ships; and sociopolitical themes popular in the North, such as flags and slogans. Thousands of varieties are known.

	F	VF	AU	MS-63
Lincoln	$35	$70	$150	$300
Monitor	23	50	125	225
"Wealth of the South" **(a)**	170	400	600	850
Various common types	15	20	50	100

a. Dated 1860, but sometimes collected along with Civil War tokens.

Civil War Store Cards

Tradesmen's tokens of the Civil War era are often called *store cards*. These are typically collected by geographical location or by topic. The Fuld text (see bibliography) catalogs store cards by state, city, merchant, die combination, and metal. Values shown below are for the most common tokens for each state.

	VG	VF	AU	MS-63		VG	VF	AU	MS-63
Alabama	$1,500	$3,000	$4,000	$5,500	Minnesota	$150	$450	$550	$750
Connecticut	10	25	50	75	Missouri	40	100	150	250
Washington, DC	—	1,000	1,400	2,000	New Hampshire	80	130	175	275
Idaho	400	700	1,300	—	New Jersey	10	25	50	100
Illinois	10	25	50	75	New York	10	20	45	100
Indiana	10	25	40	100	Ohio	10	20	45	85
Iowa	150	400	500	1,100	Pennsylvania	10	25	50	85
Kansas	900	2,500	3,500	5,000	Rhode Island	10	25	50	100
Kentucky	50	125	200	350	Tennessee	300	650	1,200	1,750
Louisiana	2,000	3,500	4,500	—	Virginia	250	500	1,000	—
Maine	50	100	175	275	West Virginia	45	90	165	350
Maryland	150	350	550	1,000	Wisconsin	15	30	60	100
Massachusetts	15	30	60	90	Sutlers' **(a)**	185	375	500	700
Michigan	10	20	40	75					

a. Sutlers' tokens were issued by registered contractors who operated camp stores that traveled with the military.

DC500A-1h   IN190D-3a

	VG	VF	AU	MS-63
DC500a-1h. H.A. Hall, Washington, DC	—	$1,000	$1,400	$2,000
IN190D-3a. J.L. & G.F. Rowe, Corunna, IN, 1863	$15	40	75	175

MI865A-1a   MN980A-1a

MO910A-2a   NY630AQ-4a

NY630Z-1a   OH165M-1a

NY630BJ-1a   WI510M-1a

PA750F-1a   WV890D-4a

	VG	VF	AU	MS-63
MI865A-1a, W. Darling, Saranac, MI, 1864.	$7,500	$12,000	$15,000	—
MN980A-1a. C. Benson, Druggist, Winona, MN	300	700	900	$1,500
MO910A-4a. Drovers Hotel, St. Louis, MO, 1863	125	300	600	1,250
NY630AQ-4a. Gustavus Lindenmueller, New York, 1863	15	20	45	75
NY630Z-1a. Fr. Freise, Undertaker, New York, 1863	20	35	85	125
OH165M-1a. B.P. Belknp., "Teeth Extracted Without Pain"	125	250	400	600
NY630BJ-1a. Sanitary Commission, New York, 1864	400	850	1,100	1,750
WI510M-1a. Goes & Falk Malt House & Brewery, Milwaukee, WI, 1863	25	65	100	175
PA750F-1a. M.C. Campbell's Dancing Academy, Philadelphia, PA	16	35	50	100
WV890D-4a. R.C. Graves, News Dealer, Wheeling, WV, 1863	45	90	165	350

CONFEDERATE CENTS

An order to make cents for the Confederacy was placed with Robert Lovett Jr., an engraver and diesinker of Philadelphia, through a jewelry firm of that city. Fearing arrest by the United States government for assisting the enemy, Lovett decided instead to hide the coins and the dies in his cellar. Captain John W. Haseltine later purchased the original dies and made restrikes with them in 1874. Circa 1961, the dies were copied and additional pieces made by New York City coin dealer Robert Bashlow. These show die cracks and rust marks that distinguish them from earlier copies.

	Mintage	Unc.	PF
1861 Cent, Original, Copper-Nickel, Unc. *12–15*		$120,000	
1861 Cent, Haseltine Restrike, Copper, Proof .... (55)			$15,000
1861 Cent, Haseltine Restrike, Gold, Proof .... (7)			42,500
1861 Cent, Haseltine Restrike, Silver, Proof .... (12)			12,500

CONFEDERATE HALF DOLLARS

According to records, only four original Confederate half dollars were struck (on a hand press). Regular silver planchets were used, as well as a regular federal obverse die. One of the coins was given to Secretary of the Treasury Christopher G. Memminger, who passed it on to President Jefferson Davis for his approval. Another was given to Professor J.L. Riddell of the University of Louisiana. E. Ames of New Orleans received a third specimen. The last was kept by chief coiner B.F. Taylor. Lack of bullion prevented the Confederacy from coining more pieces.

The Confederate half dollar was unknown to collectors until 1879, when a specimen and its reverse die were found in Taylor's possession in New Orleans. E. Mason Jr., of Philadelphia, purchased both and later sold them to J.W. Scott and Company of New York. J.W. Scott acquired 500 genuine 1861 half dollars, smoothed the reverses, and then restamped them with the Confederate die. Known as restrikes, these usually have slightly flattened obverses. Scott also struck some medals in white metal using the Confederate reverse die and an obverse die bearing this inscription: 4 ORIGINALS STRUCK BY ORDER OF C.S.A. IN NEW ORLEANS 1861 / ******* / REV. SAME AS U.S. (FROM ORIGINAL DIE•SCOTT)

Confederate Reverse

Scott Obverse

	Mintage	VF-20	EF-40	Unc.
1861 HALF DOL. *(4 known) $632,500, VF, Stack's Bowers auction, October 2003*		—	—	—
1861 HALF DOL., Restrike 500		$6,000	$7,000	$12,000
1861 Scott Obverse, Confederate Reverse 500		2,200	3,250	5,000

HAWAIIAN ISSUES

Five official coins were issued for the Kingdom of Hawaii. These include the 1847 cent issued by King Kamehameha III and the 1883 silver dimes, quarters, halves, and dollars of King Kalakaua I, which bear his portrait. The silver pieces were all designed by Charles Barber and struck at the San Francisco Mint. After Hawaii became a U.S. territory in 1900, the legal-tender status of these coins was removed and most were withdrawn and melted. The 1883 eighth-dollar piece is a pattern. The 1881 five-cent piece is an unofficial issue.

One Cent, 1847   Ten Cents, 1883

	Mintage	F-12	VF-20	EF-40	AU-50	MS-60	MS-63	PF-63
1847 Cent	100,000	$350	$450	$675	$900	$1,250	$2,100	
1881 Five Cents*	7,000	10,000	15,000	18,000	22,000	30,000	$7,500
1883 Ten Cents . . . . . . (26)	249,974	70	120	275	450	1,200	2,800	13,000
1883 Eighth Dollar . . . . (20)								46,000
1883 Quarter Dollar . . . (26)	499,974	65	90	150	175	250	400	15,000
1883 Half Dollar . . . . . . (26)	699,974	120	175	325	500	1,200	2,800	18,000
1883 Dollar. . . . . (26)	499,974	350	450	700	1,250	4,000	10,000	25,000

* All Proofs are later restrikes c. 1900.

Plantation Tokens

During the 19th century, several private firms issued tokens for use as money in Hawaiian company stores. These are often referred to as Plantation tokens. The unusual denomination of 12-1/2 cents was equivalent to a day's wages in the sugar plantations, and was related to the fractional part of the Spanish eight-real coin.

Kahului Railroad, 1891

Waterhouse Token (1860)   Haiku Plantation, 1882

Wailuku Plantation (1871)	Wailuku Plantation, 1880

	F-12	VF-20	EF-40	AU-50
Waterhouse / Kamehameha IV, ca. 1860	$1,500	$3,000	$4,500	$6,000
Wailuku Plantation, 12-1/2 (cents), (1871), narrow starfish	600	1,700	3,000	4,500
Similar, broad starfish	600	1,800	3,400	5,200
Wailuku Plantation, VI (6-1/4 cents), (1871), narrow starfish	1,600	3,750	5,500	7,250
Similar, broad starfish	1,800	4,000	6,000	7,500
Wailuku Plantation, 1 Real, 1880	600	1,200	2,000	4,000
Wailuku Plantation, Half Real, 1880	1,800	4,200	6,000	8,000
Thomas H. Hobron, 12-1/2 (cents), 1879	550	750	1,100	1,500
Similar, two stars on both sides	1,200	2,000	3,000	4,750
Thomas H. Hobron, 25 (cents), 1879 *(3 known)*			32,000	
Haiku Plantation, 1 Real, 1882	700	1,200	1,700	2,400
Grove Ranch Plantation, 12-1/2 (cents), 1886	1,200	2,200	4,000	5,500
Grove Ranch Plantation, 12-1/2 (cents), 1887	1,800	3,500	6,000	7,750
Kahului Railroad, 10 cents, 1891	1,400	2,750	4,200	6,000
Kahului Railroad, 15 cents, 1891	1,400	2,750	4,200	6,000
Kahului Railroad, 20 cents, 1891	1,400	2,750	4,200	6,000
Kahului Railroad, 25 cents, 1891	1,400	2,750	4,200	6,000
Kahului Railroad, 35 cents, 1891	1,400	2,750	4,200	6,000
Kahului Railroad, 75 cents, 1891	1,400	2,750	4,200	6,000

PUERTO RICAN ISSUES

Puerto Rico, the farthest east of the Greater Antilles, lies about 1,000 miles southeast of Florida between the Atlantic Ocean and the Caribbean Sea. Settled by Spain in 1508, the island was ceded to the United States after the Spanish-American War in 1898. Puerto Ricans were granted U.S. citizenship in 1917. Today Puerto Rico is a self-governing territory of the United States with commonwealth status.

Collectors of United States coins often include Puerto Rican coins in their collections, even though they are not U.S. issues. After the Spanish-American War, exchange rates were set for these coins relative to the U.S. dollar, and the island transitioned to a dollar-based currency. Today in Puerto Rico the dollar is still popularly referred to as a "peso."

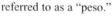   

Puerto Rico 5 Centavos, 1896	Puerto Rico 20 Centavos, 1895

	Mintage	F	VF	EF	AU	Unc.
1896 5 Centavos	600,000	$30	$50	$100	$150	$200
1896 10 Centavos	700,000	40	85	135	200	300
1895 20 Centavos	3,350,000	45	100	150	250	400
1896 40 Centavos	725,002	180	300	875	1,500	2,500
1895 1 Peso	8,500,021	200	400	900	1,600	2,750

The Philippine Islands were acquired by the United States in 1899 as part of a treaty with Spain ending the Spanish-American War of the previous year. A military government was replaced with a civil administration in 1901, and one of its first tasks was to sponsor a new coinage that was compatible with the old Spanish issues, yet was also legally exchangeable for American money at the rate of two Philippine pesos to the U.S. dollar.

The resulting coins were introduced in 1903 and bear the identities of both the Philippines (*Filipinas* in Spanish) and the United States of America. Following Spanish custom, the peso was divided into 100 centavos. A dollar-size coin valued at one peso was the principal issue in this series, but silver fractions were also minted in values of 50, 20, and 10 centavos. Minor coins included the copper-nickel five-cent piece, as well as one-centavo and half-centavo coins of bronze.

A rise in the price of silver forced the reduction of the fineness and weight for each silver denomination beginning in 1907, and subsequent issues are smaller in diameter. The smaller size of the new silver issues led to confusion between the silver 20-centavo piece and the copper-nickel five-centavo piece, resulting in a mismatching of dies for these two denominations in 1918 and again in 1928. A solution was found by reducing the diameter of the five-centavo piece beginning in 1930.

In 1935, the Commonwealth of the Philippines was established by an act of Congress, and a three-piece set of commemorative coins was issued the following year to mark this transition. Despite the popularity of United States commemoratives at that time, these sets sold poorly, and thousands remained within the Philippine Treasury at the onset of World War II. The commonwealth arms were adapted to all circulating issues beginning in 1937.

The advance on the Philippines by Japanese forces in 1942 prompted removal of much of the Treasury's bullion to the United States. More than 15 million pesos' worth of silver remained, mostly in the form of one-peso pieces of 1907 through 1912 and the ill-fated 1936 commemoratives. These coins were hastily crated and dumped into Manila's Caballo Bay to prevent their capture. Partially recovered after the war, these coins were badly corroded from their exposure to saltwater, adding further to the scarcity of high-grade prewar silver coins.

The Philippines became an independent republic on July 4, 1946, ending a historic and colorful chapter in U.S. history and numismatics.

Basic Design for Half-, One-,
and Five-Centavos Pieces
(Large-size five centavos shown.)

Basic Design for Ten-, Twenty-, and
Fifty-Centavo and 1-Peso Pieces
(Reduced-size twenty centavos shown.)

PHILIPPINES UNDER U.S. SOVEREIGNTY
Bronze Coinage

Philippine coins dated from 1903 to 1919 were struck at the Philadelphia and San Francisco mints. Those dated after 1920 were made in Manila. During World War II, coins of 1944 and 1945 were made at Philadelphia, Denver, and San Francisco.

Half Centavo (17.5 mm)

Mintage	EF	MS-60	MS-63	PF-65
1903.....12,084,000	$2.25	$20	$40	
1903, Pf.....(2,558)		50	100	$150
1904......5,654,000	3.50	30	70	
1904, Pf.....(1,355)		75	125	200

Mintage	EF	MS-60	MS-63	PF-65
1905, Pf only......(471)		$200	$300	$525
1906, Pf only......(500)		175	250	500
1908, Pf only......(500)		175	250	500

One Centavo (24 mm)

Mintage	VF	EF	MS-60	MS-63
1903.....10,790,000	$1.25	$2.50	$15	$40
1903, Pf.....(2,558)			100	150
1904.....17,040,400	1.25	2.75	30	60
1904, Pf.....(1,355)			100	150
1905.....10,000,000	1.25	3.50	30	60
1905, Pf.......(471)			200	275
1906, Pf only ...(500)			175	250
1908, Pf only ...(500)			150	325
1908S.....2,187,000	4.00	7.00	50	100
1909S.....1,737,612	16.00	25.00	100	225
1910S.....2,700,000	4.50	8.00	50	65
1911S.....4,803,000	2.50	5.00	20	60
1912S.....3,001,000	7.50	18.00	75	150
1913S.....5,000,000	4.00	7.00	40	85
1914S.....5,000,500	3.50	7.00	45	95
1915S.....2,500,000	40.00	90.00	750	1,500
1916S.....4,330,000	12.50	20.00	100	200
1917S.....7,070,000	3.00	5.50	60	125

Mintage	VF	EF	MS-60	MS-63
1918S....11,660,000	$4.50	$7.50	$75	$150
1918S, Lg S.......*	150.00	250.00	1,000	1,800
1919S.....4,540,000	4.00	7.50	75	175
1920S.....2,500,000	8.00	20.00	125	225
1920.....3,552,259	2.50	5.00	35	175
1921.....7,282,673	2.50	5.00	40	75
1922.....3,519,100	3.00	7.50	55	100
1925M 9,325,000	2.50	5.00	35	75
1926M 9,000,000	2.50	6.00	30	75
1927M 9,279,000	2.50	6.00	30	50
1928M 9,150,000	2.00	5.00	35	65
1929M 5,657,161	3.00	6.00	35	75
1930M 5,577,000	2.00	4.50	20	60
1931M 5,659,355	2.25	5.00	20	60
1932M 4,000,000	3.00	6.00	30	85
1933M 8,392,692	1.00	2.50	17	25
1934M 3,179,000	2.50	4.50	50	70
1936M ...17,455,463	2.50	4.00	30	65

* Included in number above.

Copper-Nickel Coinage
Five Centavos
(Large-Size [1903–1928]: 20.5 mm; Reduced-Size [1930–1935]: 19 mm)

Mintage	VF	EF	MS-60	MS-63
1903.....8,910,000	$1.25	$2.50	$20	$35
1903, Pf.....(2,558)			80	145
1904.....1,075,000	2.50	4.00	20	40
1904, Pf.....(1,355)			85	150
1905, Pf only .. (471)			300	600
1906, Pf only .. (500)			225	300
1908, Pf only .. (500)			300	500
1916S......300,000	75.00	150.00	800	1,250
1917S.... 2,300,000	4.00	10.00	125	300
1918S.... 2,780,000	8.00	14.00	125	275
1918S, Mule*........	550.00	1,300.00	4,500	9,500

Mintage	VF	EF	MS-60	MS-63
1919S.....1,220,000	$10.00	$20.00	$175	$400
1920......1,421,078	8.50	35.00	175	300
1921......2,131,529	10.00	20.00	110	200
1925M 1,000,000	12.00	25.00	175	300
1926M 1,200,000	6.00	18.00	120	225
1927M 1,000,000	6.00	12.50	85	150
1928M 1,000,000	8.00	15.00	85	125
1930M 2,905,182	2.50	4.50	40	85
1931M 3,476,790	2.50	4.50	65	150
1932M 3,955,861	2.00	4.00	50	140
1934M 2,153,729	3.50	9.00	60	150
1935M 2,754,000	2.50	8.00	80	220

* Small-Date Reverse of 20 centavos.

Silver Coinage
Ten Centavos
(Large-Size [1903–1906]: 17.5 mm; Reduced-Size [1907–1935]: 16.5 mm)

Mintage	VF	EF	MS-60	MS-63		Mintage	VF	EF	MS-60	MS-63
1903......5,102,658	$4	$5	$35	$75	1911S.....1,000,505	$4.50	$12.50	$150	$500
1903, Pf.....(2,558)			100	200	1912S.....1,010,000	4.50	12.00	125	300
1903S.....1,200,000	25	50	350	900	1913S.....1,360,693	6.00	12.00	85	150
1904........10,000	20	35	80	140	1914S.....1,180,000	7.50	20.00	175	300
1904, Pf.....(1,355)			110	250	1915S.....450,000	25.00	35.00	225	750
1904S.....5,040,000	4	7	60	130	1917S.....5,991,148	2.50	5.00	50	125
1905, Pf only ...(471)			200	275	1918S.....8,420,000	1.50	2.50	20	65
1906, Pf only ...(500)			150	225	1919S.....1,630,000	2.50	4.00	30	110
1907......1,500,781	4	5	50	125	1920........520,000	5.00	15.00	95	200
1907S.....4,930,000	2	3	40	90	1921......3,863,038	2.00	3.00	20	45
1908, Pf only ...(500)			175	225	1929M....1,000,000	2.00	3.25	22	50
1908S.....3,363,911	2	5	40	75	1935M....1,280,000	2.00	4.00	20	45
1909S......312,199	35	65	450	1,200					

Twenty Centavos
(Large-Size [1903–1906]: 23 mm; Reduced-Size [1907–1929]: 20 mm)

Mintage	VF	EF	MS-60	MS-63		Mintage	VF	EF	MS-60	MS-63
1903......5,350,231	$5.00	$8.00	$40	$100	1911S......505,000	$25	$50	$300	$800
1903, Pf.....(2,558)			100	150	1912S......750,000	14	30	200	350
1903S......150,080	35.00	75.00	600	1,750	1913S......795,000	10	15	175	250
1904........10,000	30.00	40.00	100	200	1914S......795,000	8	40	250	450
1904, Pf.....(1,355)			100	200	1915S......655,000	22	75	600	1,750
1904S.....2,060,000	6.50	11.00	100	200	1916S.....1,435,000	10	25	190	575
1905, Pf only ...(471)			225	375	1917S.....3,150,655	3	5	80	175
1905S......420,000	15.00	35.00	500	1,000	1918S.....5,560,000	3	5	50	120
1906, Pf only ...(500)			175	275	1919S......850,000	5	15	100	200
1907......1,250,651	6.00	13.50	200	325	1920......1,045,415	8	20	135	225
1907S.....3,165,000	4.00	5.50	70	175	1921......1,842,631	3	5	70	125
1908, Pf only ...(500)			200	300	1928M,				
1908S.....1,535,000	4.50	10.00	75	200	Mule*.. 100,000	18	70	900	1,800
1909S......450,000	25.00	50.00	400	1,000	1929M....1,970,000	3	4	25	75
1910S......500,259	30.00	100.00	400	1,000					

* Reverse of 1903–1928 5 centavos.

Fifty Centavos
(Large-Size [1903–1906]: 30 mm; Reduced-Size [1907–1921]: 27 mm)

Mintage	VF	EF	MS-60	MS-63		Mintage	VF	EF	MS-60	MS-63
1903......3,099,061	$15	$20	$70	$125	1907......1,200,625	$15.00	$40	$150	$300
1903, Pf.....(2,558)			125	200	1907S.....2,112,000	10.00	20	135	300
1903S					1908, Pf only ...(500)			200	350
(2 known)......		22,000			1908S.....1,601,000	10.00	35	325	1,250
1904........10,000	40	75	150	300	1909S......528,000	20.00	45	350	800
1904, Pf.....(1,355)			150	225	1917S......674,369	11.00	25	200	500
1904S......216,000	12	20	125	225	1918S.....2,202,000	7.50	15	90	150
1905, Pf only ...(471)			250	425	1919S.....1,200,000	7.50	15	100	200
1905S......852,000	15	40	750	2,000	1920........420,000	7.50	10	50	100
1906, Pf only ...(500)			225	375	1921......2,316,763	7.50	10	35	75

413

One Peso
(Large-Size [1903–1906]: 38 mm; Reduced-Size [1907–1912]: 35 mm)

	Mintage	VF	EF	MS-60	MS-63
1903	2,788,901	$35	$40	$175	$450
1903, Proof	(2,558)			200	325
1903S	11,361,000	28	35	125	200
1904	11,355	80	125	250	450
1904, Proof	(1,355)			200	375
1904S	6,600,000	30	40	175	400
1905, Proof only	(471)			750	1,500
1905S, Curved Serif on "1"	6,056,000	35	50	300	750
1905S, Straight Serif on "1"	*	50	65	850	2,500
1906, Proof only	(500)			700	1,400
1906S	201,000	1,400	2,600	17,500	30,000
1907, Proof only *(2 known)*					100,000
1907S	10,278,000	16	20	75	200
1908, Proof only	(500)			650	1,000
1908S	20,954,944	16	20	75	200
1909S	7,578,000	18	22	125	300
1910S	3,153,559	20	25	225	550
1911S	463,000	40	75	750	3,500
1912S	680,000	50	100	2,000	5,500

* Included in number above.

COMMONWEALTH ISSUES
Bronze Coinage
One Centavo (24 mm)

	Mintage	VF	EF	MS-60	MS-63		Mintage	VF	EF	MS-60	MS-63
1937M	15,790,492	$2.00	$3.00	$20.00	$40	1940M	4,000,000	$1.25	$2.50	$12	$25
1938M	10,000,000	1.50	2.50	17.50	35	1941M	5,000,000	1.25	3.50	17	35
1939M	6,500,000	2.50	3.50	17.50	45	1944S	58,000,000	0.25	0.50	2	7

Copper-Nickel Coinage
Five Centavos (19 mm)

	Mintage	VF	EF	MS-60	MS-63		Mintage	VF	EF	MS-60	MS-63
1937M	2,493,872	$5	$7.00	$50	$150	1944*	21,198,000	$0.50	$1.00	$2	$4
1938M	4,000,000	1	2.25	20	50	1944S*	14,040,000	0.25	0.50	1	2
1941M	2,750,000	3	7.00	55	150	1945S*	72,796,000	0.25	0.50	1	2

* Copper-nickel-zinc alloy.

Silver Coinage
Ten Centavos (16.5 mm)

	Mintage	VF	EF	MS-60	MS-63		Mintage	VF	EF	MS-60	MS-63
1937M	3,500,000	$2.25	$3.50	$20	$40	1944D	31,592,000	$1.25	$2	$2.50	$5
1938M	3,750,000	1.75	2.25	10	15	1945D	137,208,000	1.25	2	2.50	5
1941M	2,500,000	1.75	2.50	10	15	1945D, D/D	*	8.50	15	28.00	50

* Included in number above.

Twenty Centavos (20 mm)

	Mintage	VF	EF	MS-60	MS-63		Mintage	VF	EF	MS-60	MS-63
1937M	2,665,000	$3	$5.00	$25.00	$50	1944D	28,596,000	$1.00	$2.75	$3	$4
1938M	3,000,000	3	3.50	15.00	30	1944D, D/S	*	7.50	10.00	35	50
1941M	1,500,000	3	3.50	12.50	25	1945D	82,804,000	1.00	2.75	3	4

* Included in number above.

Fifty Centavos (27 mm)

	Mintage	VF	EF	MS-60	MS-63
1944S.	19,187,000	$7	$8	$10	$15
1945S.	18,120,000	7	8	10	12
1945S, S/S.	*	10	15	35	45

* Included in number above.

COMMEMORATIVE ISSUES

Silver Fifty Centavos

Silver One Peso, Busts of Murphy and Quezon

Silver One Peso, Busts of Roosevelt and Quezon

	Mintage	VF	EF	MS-60	MS-63
1936M, Silver fifty centavos	20,000	$25	$50	$125	$175
1936M, Silver one peso, busts of Murphy and Quezon	10,000	60	85	200	250
1936M, Silver one peso, busts of Roosevelt and Quezon	10,000	60	85	200	250

ALASKA RURAL REHABILITATION
CORPORATION TOKENS OF 1935

These tokens were issued by the U.S. government for the use of the Midwestern-ers who relocated to Alaska as part of the Matanuska Valley Colonization Project, to supply them with much-needed federal aid. They were redeemable only at the ARRC stores. The "Bingles," as they were called, were in use only about six months during 1935 and 1936, after which they were redeemed for regular U.S. money and destroyed. They were issued on a basis of family dependents. Each token is similar in size to the corresponding U.S. coin, with the exception of the one-cent piece, which is octagonal. The design is the same on both sides of each denomination.

Aluminum

	Mintage	EF	Unc.		Mintage	EF	Unc.
One Cent	5,000	$100	$185	Twenty-Five Cents	3,000	$150	$275
Five Cents	5,000	100	185	Fifty Cents	2,500	150	275
Ten Cents	5,000	100	185	One Dollar	2,500	250	325

Brass

	Mintage	EF	Unc.		Mintage	EF	Unc.
Five Dollars	1,000	$250	$375	Ten Dollars	1,000	$275	$450

With the production of millions of coins each year, it is natural that a few abnormal pieces escape inspection and are inadvertently released for circulation, usually in original bags or rolls of new coins. These are not considered regular issues because they were not made intentionally. They are all eagerly sought by collectors for the information they shed on minting techniques, and as a variation from normal date and mint series collecting.

Nearly every misstruck or error coin is unique in some way, and prices may vary from coin to coin. They may all be classified in general groups related to the kinds of errors or manufacturing malfunctions involved. Collectors value these pieces according to the scarcity of each kind of error for each type of coin. Non-collectors usually view them as curios, and often believe that they must be worth much more than normal coins because they look so strange. In reality, the value assigned to various types of errors by collectors and dealers reflects both supply and demand, and is based on recurring transactions between willing buyers and sellers.

The following listings show current average values for the most frequently encountered kinds of error coins. In each case, the values shown are for coins that are unmarred by serious marks or scratches, and in Uncirculated condition for modern issues, and Extremely Fine condition for obsolete types. Exceptions are valued higher or lower. Error coins of rare date issues generally do not command a premium beyond their normal values. In most cases each of these coins is unique in some respect and must be valued according to its individual appearance, quality, and eye appeal.

There are many other kinds of errors and misstruck coins beyond those listed in this guide book. Some are more valuable, and others less valuable, than the most popular pieces that are listed here as examples of what this interesting field contains. The pieces illustrated are general examples of the types described.

Early in 2002 the mints changed their production methods to a new system designed to eliminate deformed planchets, off-center strikes, and similar errors. They also changed the delivery system of bulk coinage, and no longer shipped loose coins in sewn bags to be counted and wrapped by banks or counting rooms, where error coins were often found and sold to collectors. Under the new system, coins are packaged in large quantities and go directly to automated counters that filter out deformed coins. The result has been that very few error coins have entered the market since late 2002, and almost none after that date. The values shown in these listings are for pre-2002 coins; those dated after that, with but a few exceptions, are valued considerably higher.

For additional details and information about these coins, the following books are recommended:

- Margolis, Arnold, and Weinberg, Fred. *The Error Coin Encyclopedia* (4th ed.), 2004.
- Herbert, Alan. *Official Price Guide to Minting Varieties and Errors,* New York, 1991.
- Fivaz, Bill, and Stanton, J.T. *The Cherrypickers' Guide to Rare Die Varieties* (5th ed.), vol. 1, Atlanta, GA, 2009; vol. 2, Atlanta, GA, 2012.

The coins discussed in this section must not be confused with others that have been mutilated or damaged after leaving the mint. Examples of such pieces include coins that have been scratched, hammered, engraved, impressed, acid etched, or plated by individuals to simulate something other than a normal coin. Those pieces have no numismatic value, and can only be considered as altered coins not suitable for a collection.

TYPES OF ERROR COINS

Clipped Planchet—**An incomplete coin, missing 10 to 25% of the metal.** Incomplete planchets result from accidents when the steel rods used to punch out blanks from the metal strip overlap a portion of the strip already punched. There are curved, straight, ragged, incomplete, and elliptical clips. Values may be greater or less depending on the nature and size of the clip. Coins with more than one clip usually command higher values.

Multiple Strike—**A coin with at least one additional image from being struck again off center.** Value increases with the number of strikes. These minting errors occur when a finished coin goes back into the press and is struck again with the same dies. The presence of a date can bring a higher value.

Blank or Planchet—**A blank disc of metal intended for coinage but not struck with dies.** In the process of preparation for coinage, the blanks are first punched from a strip of metal and then milled to upset the rim. In most instances, first-process pieces (blanks without upset rims) are slightly more valuable than the finished planchets. Values shown are for the most common pieces.

No Rim　　　　With Rim

Defective Die—**A coin showing raised metal from a large die crack, or small rim break.** Coins that show evidence of light die cracks, polishing, or very minor die damage are generally of little or no value. Prices shown here are for coins with very noticeable, raised die-crack lines, or those for which the die broke away, producing an unstruck area known as a *cud*.

Off Center—**A coin that has been struck out of collar and incorrectly centered, with part of the design missing.** Values are for coins with approximately 10 to 20% of design missing from obsolete coins, or 20 to 60% missing from modern coins. These are misstruck coins that were made when the planchet did not enter the coinage press properly.

Coins that are struck only slightly off center, with none of the design missing, are called broadstrikes (see the next category). Those with nearly all of the impression missing are generally worth more, but those with a readable date and mint are the most valuable.

Broadstrike—**A coin that was struck outside the retaining collar.** When coins are struck without being contained in the collar die, they spread out larger than normal pieces. All denominations have a plain edge.

Lamination—**A flaw whereby a fragment of metal has peeled off the coin's surface.** This defect occurs when a foreign substance, such as gas oxides or dirt, becomes trapped in the strip as it is rolled out to the proper thickness. Lamination flaws may be missing or still attached to the coin's surface. Minor flaws may only decrease a coin's value, while a clad coin that is missing the full surface of one or both sides is worth more than the values listed here.

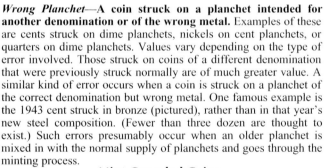

Brockage—**A mirror image of the design impressed on the opposite side of the same coin.** These errors are caused when a struck coin remains on either die after striking, and impresses its image into the next blank planchet as it is struck, leaving a negative or mirror image. Off-center and partial brockage coins are worth less than those with full impression. Coins with negative impressions on both sides are usually mutilated pieces made outside the mint by the pressing together of coins.

Wrong Planchet—**A coin struck on a planchet intended for another denomination or of the wrong metal.** Examples of these are cents struck on dime planchets, nickels on cent planchets, or quarters on dime planchets. Values vary depending on the type of error involved. Those struck on coins of a different denomination that were previously struck normally are of much greater value. A similar kind of error occurs when a coin is struck on a planchet of the correct denomination but wrong metal. One famous example is the 1943 cent struck in bronze (pictured), rather than in that year's new steel composition. (Fewer than three dozen are thought to exist.) Such errors presumably occur when an older planchet is mixed in with the normal supply of planchets and goes through the minting process.

Mint-Canceled Coins

In mid-2003, the U.S. Mint acquired machines to eliminate security concerns and the cost associated with providing Mint police escorts to private vendors for the melting of scrap, substandard struck coins, planchets, and blanks. Under high pressure, the rollers and blades of these machines cancel the coins and blanks in a manner similar in appearance to the surface of a waffle, and they are popularly known by that term. This process has effectively kept most misstruck coins produced after 2003 from becoming available to collectors. Waffled examples are known for all six 2003-dated coin denominations, from the Lincoln cent through the Sacagawea dollar. The Mint has not objected to these pieces' trading in the open market because they are not considered coins with legal tender status.

419

Misstruck and Error Pieces

	Clipped Planchet	Multiple Strike	Blank, No Raised Rim	Planchet, Raised Rim	Defective Die	Off Center	Broadstrike	Lamination	Brockage
Large Cent	$60	$900	$200.00	$200.00	$25	$500	$100	$25	$850
Indian 1¢	15	700	—	—	25	150	60	15	400
Lincoln 1¢ (95% Copper)	3	65	4.00	3.00	12	10	8	3	35
Steel 1¢	45	250	30.00	40.00	15	75	35	15	200
Lincoln 1¢ (Zinc)	4	50	3.00	2.00	15	8	5	15	40
Liberty 5¢	25	700	45.00	50.00	35	200	110	25	400
Buffalo 5¢	35	2,500	15.00	30.00	40	450	250	35	1,000
Jefferson 5¢	3	60	15.00	10.00	15	12	10	15	50
Wartime 5¢	15	400	400.00	350.00	25	175	70	15	250
Barber 10¢	60	750	—	—	75	300	100	15	400
Mercury 10¢	20	800	—	—	35	175	75	15	275
Roosevelt 10¢ (Silver) . . .	15	250	50.00	50.00	35	125	60	12	110
Roosevelt 10¢ (Clad)	3	50	2.50	3.50	15	10	10	16	50
Washington 25¢ (Silver)	20	400	175.00	150.00	25	350	200	15	300
Washington 25¢ (Clad) . .	5	150	7.00	5.00	12	70	20	25	50
Bicentennial 25¢	35	350	—	—	65	150	50	50	250
Statehood 25¢	35	500	—	—	25	110	40	400	350
Franklin 50¢	40	1,800	—	—	150	1,500	450	25	650
Kennedy 50¢ (40% Silver)	30	1,100	185.00	135.00	70	450	250	40	450
Kennedy 50¢ (Clad)	25	600	150.00	100.00	50	275	100	25	300
Bicentennial 50¢	45	700	—	—	90	300	75	40	750
Silver $1	50	5,000	1,600.00	1,500.00	950	2,500	1,000	50	—
Eisenhower $1	40	1,350	200.00	100.00	500	600	150	50	1,200
Bicentennial $1	50	2,000	—	—	750	850	200	50	1,500
Anthony $1	30	750	160.00	120.00	100	275	75	30	300
Sacagawea $1	85	1,800	275.00	85.00	50	1,500	350	50	700

Wrong Planchets

	1¢ ZN	1¢ CU	1¢ Steel	5¢	10¢ (S)	10¢ (C)	25¢ (S)	25¢ (C)	50¢ (C)
Indian 1¢	np	—	np	np	$8,500	np	np	np	np
Lincoln 1¢	—	—	—	np	1,250	$350	np	np	np
Buffalo 5¢	np	$4,000	np	—	11,000	np	np	np	np
Jefferson 5¢	$300	250	$2,500	—	450	400	np	np	np
Wartime 5¢	np	2,000	3,500	—	2,250	np	np	np	np
Washington 25¢ (Silver) . . .	np	950	7,000	$550	1,800	—	—	—	np
Washington 25¢ (Clad)	—	850	np	225	—	350	—	—	np
Bicentennial 25¢	np	2,750	np	2,000	—	3,500	—	—	np
Statehood 25¢	—	4,500	np	900	np	4,000	np	—	np
Walking Liberty 50¢	np	—	—	—	—	np	$25,000	np	np
Franklin 50¢	np	5,200	np	5,500	6,750	np	1,500	np	np
Kennedy 50¢	np	3,500	np	1,250	—	2,250	—	$650	—
Bicentennial 50¢	np	4,000	np	2,750	—	—	—	1,200	—
Eisenhower $1	np	12,500	np	9,500	—	11,000	—	6,000	$3,500
Anthony $1	np	3,500	np	5,000	np	—	—	1,500	np
Sacagawea $1	10,000	np	np	10,000	np	10,000	np	3,000	np

Note: ZN = Zinc; CU = Copper; S = Silver; C = Copper-Nickel Clad; np = not possible.

The Kennedy fifty-cent piece struck on an Anthony one-dollar planchet is very rare. Coins struck over other coins of different denominations are usually valued three to five times higher than these prices. Values for statehood quarter errors vary with each type and state, and are generally much higher than for other quarters. Coins made from mismatched dies (statehood quarter obverse combined with Sacagawea dollar reverse) are extremely rare.

THE RED BOOK AS A COLLECTIBLE

The *Guide Book of United States Coins* has long held the record for being the longest-running annual retail coin-price guide. It has passed its 65th anniversary, and collectors seem to be almost as interested in assembling sets of old Red Books as of old coins. The demand for old Red Books has created a solid market. Some who collect these old editions maintain reference libraries of all kinds of coin publications. To them, having one of each edition is essential, because that is the way old books are collected. Others are speculators who believe that the value of old editions will go up as interest and demand increase. Many people who save old Red Books do so to maintain a record of coin prices going back further than any other source.

Following price trends in old Red Books is a good indicator of how well individual coins are doing in comparison to each other. The price information published in this book each year is an average of what collectors are paying for each coin. It is a valuable benchmark, showing how prices have gone up or down over the years. Information like this often gives investors an edge in predicting what the future may hold.

Old Red Books are also a handy resource on collecting trends. They show graphically how grading has changed over the years, what new coins have been discovered and added to the listings, and which areas are growing in popularity. Studying these old books can be educational as well as nostalgic. It's great fun to see what your favorite coins sold for 15 or 25 years ago or more—and a bit frustrating to realize what might have been if we had only bought the right coins at the right time in years past.

Many collectors have asked about the quantities printed of each edition. That information has never been published, and now no company records exist specifying how many were made. The original author, R.S. Yeoman, told inquirers that the first press run in November 1946 was for 9,000 copies. In February 1947 an additional 9,000 copies were printed to satisfy the unexpected demand.

There was a slight difference between the first and second printings. The wording in the first printing, at the bottom of page 135, reads, "which probably accounts for the scarcity of *this* date." Those last few words were changed to "the scarcity of *1903 O*" in the second printing.

The second edition had a press run of 22,000. The printing of each edition thereafter gradually increased, with the highest number ever being reached with the 18th edition, dated 1965. In that year, at the top of a booming coin market, a whopping 1,200,000 copies were produced. Since that time the numbers have decreased, but the Red Book still maintains a record of being the world's largest-selling coin publication each year.

In some years a very limited number of Red Books were made for use by price contributors. Those were interleaved with blank pages. No more than 50 copies were ever made for any one year. Perhaps fewer than 20 were made in the first few years. Three of these of the first edition, and one of the second edition, are currently known. Their value is now in four figures. Those made in the 1960s sell for about $300–$500 today.

There are other unusual Red Books that command exceptional prices. One of the most popular is the 1987 special edition that was made for, and distributed only to, people who attended the 1986 American Numismatic Association banquet in Milwaukee. Only 500 of those were printed with a special commemorative cover.

Error books are also popular with collectors. The most common is one with double-stamped printing on the cover. The second most frequently seen are those with an upside-down cover. Probably the best known of the error books is the 1963 16th edition with a missing page. For some uncanny reason, page 239 is duplicated in some of those books, and page 237 is missing. The error was corrected on most of the printing.

The terminology used to describe book condition differs from that utilized in grading coins. A "Very Fine" book is one that is nearly new, with minimal signs of use. Early editions of the Red Book are rarely if ever found in anything approaching "New" condition. Exceptionally well-preserved older editions command a substantial premium and are in great demand. Nice used copies that are still clean and in good shape, but slightly worn from use, are also desirable. Only the early editions are worth a premium in badly worn condition.

For a more detailed history and edition-by-edition study of the Red Book, see *A Guide Book of The Official Red Book of United States Coins* (Whitman, 2009).

Valuation Guide for Past Editions of the Red Book

CLASSIC HARDCOVER BINDING

See pages 423 and 424 for special editions in the classic hardcover binding.

Year/Edition	Issue Price	VG	F	VF	New
1947 (1st ed.), 1st Printing	$1.50	$350	$650	$1,000	$1,700(a)
1947 (1st ed.), 2nd Printing	1.50	300	600	1,000	1,600(a)
1948 (2nd ed.)	1.50	80	150	225	350(a)
1949 (3rd ed.)	1.50	80	150	350	500(a)
1951/52 (4th ed.)	1.50	55	110	175	225(a)
1952/53 (5th ed.)	1.50	150	300	500	1,500(a)
1953/54 (6th ed.)	1.75	45	65	100	150
1954/55 (7th ed.)	1.75	40	50	100	120
1955 (8th ed.)	1.75	30	45	90	115
1956 (9th ed.)	1.75	25	40	70	110
1957 (10th ed.)	1.75	15	20	35	50
1958 (11th ed.)	1.75		8	12	25
1959 (12th ed.)	1.75		8	12	25
1960 (13th ed.)	1.75		7	9	20
1961 (14th ed.)	1.75		4	6	17
1962 (15th ed.)	1.75		4	6	10
1963 (16th ed.)	1.75		4	6	10
1964 (17th ed.)	1.75		4	5	7
1965 (18th ed.)	1.75		3	4	7
1966 (19th ed.)	1.75		3	4	7
1967 (20th ed.)	1.75		3	5	8
1968 (21st ed.)	2.00		3	5	10
1969 (22nd ed.)	2.00		3	5	10
1970 (23rd ed.)	2.50		3	6	11
1971 (24th ed.)	2.50		3	4	7
1972 (25th ed.)	2.50		5	8	10
1973 (26th ed.)	2.50		4	5	7
1974 (27th ed.)	2.50		3	4	7
1975 (28th ed.)	3.00			4	6
1976 (29th ed.)	3.95			4	7
1977 (30th ed.)	3.95			4	6
1978 (31st ed.)	3.95			4	6
1979 (32nd ed.)	3.95			4	7

Year/Edition	Issue Price	VF	New
1980 (33rd ed.)	$3.95	$4	$9
1981 (34th ed.)	4.95	2	5
1982 (35th ed.)	4.95	2	5
1983 (36th ed.)	5.95	2	5
1984 (37th ed.)	5.95	2	5
1985 (38th ed.)	5.95	2	5
1986 (39th ed.)	5.95	2	5
1987 (40th ed.)	6.95	2	5
1988 (41st ed.)	6.95	2	5
1989 (42nd ed.)	6.95	3	7
1990 (43rd ed.)	7.95	2	6
1991 (44th ed.)	8.95	2	5
1992 (45th ed.)	8.95	2	5
1993 (46th ed.)	9.95	2	5
1994 (47th ed.)	9.95	1	4
1995 (48th ed.)	10.95	1	4
1996 (49th ed.)	10.95	1	4
1997 (50th ed.)	11.95	1	4
1998 (51st ed.)	11.95		3
1999 (52nd ed.)	11.95		3
2000 (53rd ed.)	12.95		3
2001 (54th ed.)	13.95		3
2002 (55th ed.)	14.95		3
2003 (56th ed.)	15.95		2
2004 (57th ed.)	15.95		2
2005 (58th ed.)	15.95		2
2006 (59th ed.)	16.95		3
2007 (60th ed.)	16.95		3
2008 (61st ed.)	16.95		3
2009 (62nd ed.)	16.95		3
2010 (63rd ed.)	16.95		3
2011 (64th ed.)	16.95		2
2012 (65th ed.)	16.95		
2013 (66th ed.)	16.95		

Note: Values are for unsigned books. Those signed by R.S. Yeoman are worth substantially more. **a.** Values are for books in Near Mint condition, as truly New copies are effectively nonexistent.

SOFTCOVERS (1993–2007)

The first softcover (trade paperback) Red Book was the 1993 (46th) edition. The softcover binding was offered (alongside other formats) in the 1993, 1994, 1995, and 1996 editions; again in the 1998 edition; and from 2003 through 2007. All are fairly common and easily collectible today. Values in New condition range from $2 up to $3–$4 for the earlier editions.

SPIRALBOUND SOFTCOVERS (1997 TO DATE)

The first spiralbound softcover Red Book was the 1997 (50th) edition. The spiralbound softcover format was next available in the 1999 edition, and it has been an annually offered format every edition since then. Today the spiralbound softcovers all are easily collectible. The 1997 edition is worth $4 in New condition, and later editions are valued around $2.

SPIRALBOUND HARDCOVERS (2008 TO DATE)

The first spiralbound hardcover Red Book was the 2008 (61st) edition. The format has been available (alongside other formats) every edition since. All spiralbound hardcovers are readily available to collectors, and are valued from $2 to $4.

JOURNAL EDITION (2009)

The large-sized Journal Edition, featuring a three-ring binder, color-coded tabbed dividers, and removable pages, was issued only for the 2009 (62nd) edition. Today it is valued at $5 in VF and $30 in New condition.

LARGE PRINT EDITIONS (2010 TO DATE)

The oversized Large Print format of the Red Book has been offered annually since the 2010 (63rd) edition. All editions are readily available to collectors and are valued at $5 in New condition.

LEATHER LIMITED EDITIONS (2005 TO DATE)

Year/Edition	Issue Price	Print Run	New	Year/Edition	Issue Price	Print Run	New
2005 (58th ed.)	$69.95	3,000	$75	2008 (61st ed.), American			
2006 (59th ed.)	69.95	3,000	75	Numismatic Society **(b)**		250*	$700
2007 (60th ed.)	69.95	3,000	100	2009 (62nd ed.)	$69.95	3,000	75
2007 1947 Tribute Edition	49.95	500	135	2010 (63rd ed.)	69.95	1,500	75
2008 (61st ed.)	69.95	3,000	60	2011 (64th ed.)	69.95	1,500	75
2008 (61st ed.), Numismatic				2012 (65th ed.)	69.95	1,000	80
Literary Guild **(a)**		135*	1,000	2013 (66th ed.)	69.95	1,000	75

* Included in total print-run quantity. **a.** One hundred thirty-five imprinted copies of the 2008 leather Limited Edition were created. Of these, 125 were distributed to members of the NLG at its 2007 literary awards ceremony; the remaining 10 were distributed from Whitman Publishing headquarters in Atlanta. **b.** Two hundred fifty copies of the 2008 leather Limited Edition were issued with a special bookplate honoring the 150th anniversary of the ANS. They were distributed to attendees of the January 2008 celebratory banquet in New York.

SPECIAL EDITIONS

Year/Edition	Issue Price	VF	New
1987 (40th ed.), Special ANA Cover		$700	$1,400
1992 (45th ed.), Special ANA Cover		150	250
1997 (50th ed.), Special Anniversary Cover	$24.95	50	100
2002 (55th ed.), Special ANA Cover	100.00	50	90
2002 SS *Central America* Cover	35.00	25	35
2005 (58th ed.), F.U.N. Special Edition		45	100
2007 (60th ed.), Special ANA Cover		50	125
2007 (60th ed.), Michigan Special Edition		50	125
2007 (1st ed.), 1947 Tribute Edition	17.95	5	20
2008 (61st ed.), Special ANA Edition		30	50

Year/Edition	Issue Price	VF	New
2008 (61st ed.), Stack's Rare Coins Edition		$4	$20
2010 (63rd ed.), Hardcover, Philadelphia Expo Edition **(a)**	$50.00	18	35
2011 (64th ed.), Boston Numismatic Society Special Edition	85.00	60	100
2012 (65th ed.), Special ANA Cover		30	100
2013 (66th ed.), American Numismatic Society **(b)**			

a. Two thousand and nine copies of a special 2010 edition were made for distribution to dealers at the premiere Whitman Coin and Collectibles Philadelphia Expo (September 2009). Extra copies were sold at $50 apiece with proceeds benefiting the National Federation for the Blind. **b.** Two hundred fifty copies of the 2013 hardcover were issued with a special bookplate honoring ANS Trustees' Award recipient (and Red Book contributor) Roger Siboni.

THE BLUE BOOK AS A COLLECTIBLE

The precursor to the Red Book was *The Handbook of United States Coins With Premium List,* popularly known as the "Blue Book" because of its cover color. The mastermind behind the Blue Book was R.S. Yeoman, who had been hired by Western Publishing Company as a commercial artist in 1932. He distributed Western's Whitman line of "penny boards" to coin collectors, promoting them through department stores, along with children's books and games. He eventually arranged for Whitman to expand the line of penny boards into other denominations, giving them the reputation of a more serious numismatic endeavor rather than a "game" of filling holes with missing coins. He also developed these flat boards into a line of popular folders.

Soon Yeoman realized that coin collectors needed other resources and supplies, and he began to compile coin mintage data and market values. This research grew into the Blue Book: now collectors had a coin-by-coin, grade-by-grade guide to the average prices dealers would pay for U.S. coins. The first and second editions were both published in 1942, indicating the strong demand for this kind of information.

In the first edition of the Red Book, Whitman Publishing would describe the Blue Book as "a low-priced standard reference book of United States coins and kindred issues" for which there had been "a long-felt need among American collectors."

The Blue Book has been published annually (except in 1944 and 1950) since its debut. Past editions offer valuable information about the hobby of yesteryear as well as developments in numismatic research and the marketplace. Old Blue Books are collectible, but they are not yet as avidly sought as the Red Book, and most editions after the 12th can be found for a few dollars in VF or better condition. Major variants were produced for the third, fourth, and ninth editions, including perhaps the only "overdate" books in American numismatic publishing. Either to conserve the previous years' covers or to correct an error in binding, the cloth on some third-edition covers was overstamped "Fourth Edition," and a number of eighth-edition covers were overstamped "Ninth Edition." The third edition was produced in several shades of blue ranging from light to dark. Some copies of the fourth edition were also produced in black cloth—the only time the Blue Book was bound in other than blue.

Valuation Guide for Select Past Editions of the Blue Book

Edition	Date* Title-Page	Copyright	VF	New	Edition	Date* Title-Page	Copyright	VF	New
1st	1942	1942	$100	$160	7th	1949	1948	$12	$25
2nd	1943	1942	45	75	8th	1950	1949	10	20
3rd	1944	1943	35	65	9th	1952	1951	5	10
4th	*None*	1945	40	60	10th	1953	1952	5	8
5th	*None*	1946	20	35	11th	1954	1953	3	7
6th	1948	1947	15	30	12th	1955	1954	3	7

* During its early years of production, the Blue Book's date presentation was not standardized. Full information is given here to aid in precise identification of early editions.

BULLION VALUES

These charts show the bullion values of silver and gold U.S. coins. These are intrinsic values and do not reflect any numismatic premium a coin might have. The weight listed under each denomination is its actual silver weight (ASW) or actual gold weight (AGW).

In recent years, the bullion price of silver has fluctuated considerably. You can use the following chart to determine the approximate bullion value of many 19th- and 20th-century silver coins at various price levels—or you can calculate the approximate value by multiplying the current spot price of silver by the ASW for each coin, as indicated. Dealers generally purchase common silver coins at around 15% below bullion value, and sell them at around 15% above bullion value.

Nearly all U.S. gold coins have an additional premium value beyond their bullion content, and thus are not subject to minor bullion-price variations. The premium amount is not necessarily tied to the bullion price of gold, but is usually determined by supply and demand levels in the numismatic marketplace. Because these factors can vary significantly, there is no reliable formula for calculating "percentage below and above bullion" prices that would remain accurate over time. The gold chart on the next page lists bullion values based on AGW only; consult a coin dealer to ascertain current buy and sell prices.

Bullion Values of Silver Coins

Silver Price Per Ounce	Wartime Nickel .05626 oz.	Dime .07234 oz.	Quarter .18084 oz.	Half Dollar .36169 oz.	Silver Clad Half Dollar .14792 oz.	Silver Dollar .77344 oz.
$20	$1.13	$1.45	$3.62	$7.23	$2.96	$15.47
21	1.18	1.52	3.80	7.60	3.11	16.24
22	1.24	1.59	3.98	7.96	3.25	17.02
23	1.29	1.66	4.16	8.32	3.40	17.79
24	1.35	1.74	4.34	8.68	3.55	18.56
25	1.41	1.81	4.52	9.04	3.70	19.34
26	1.46	1.88	4.70	9.40	3.85	20.11
27	1.52	1.95	4.88	9.77	3.99	20.88
28	1.58	2.03	5.06	10.13	4.14	21.66
29	1.63	2.10	5.24	10.49	4.29	22.43
30	1.69	2.17	5.43	10.85	4.44	23.20
31	1.74	2.24	5.61	11.21	4.59	23.98
32	1.80	2.31	5.79	11.57	4.73	24.75
33	1.86	2.39	5.97	11.94	4.88	25.52
34	1.91	2.46	6.15	12.30	5.03	26.30
35	1.97	2.53	6.33	12.66	5.18	27.07
36	2.03	2.60	6.51	13.02	5.33	27.84
37	2.08	2.68	6.69	13.38	5.47	28.62
38	2.14	2.75	6.87	13.74	5.62	29.39
39	2.19	2.82	7.05	14.11	5.77	30.16
40	2.25	2.89	7.23	14.47	5.92	30.94
41	2.31	2.97	7.41	14.83	6.06	31.71
42	2.36	3.04	7.60	15.19	6.21	32.48
43	2.42	3.11	7.78	15.55	6.36	33.26
44	2.48	3.18	7.96	15.91	6.51	34.03
45	2.53	3.26	8.14	16.28	6.66	34.80
46	2.59	3.33	8.32	16.64	6.80	35.58
47	2.64	3.40	8.50	17.00	6.95	36.35

Bullion Values of Gold Coins

Gold Price Per Ounce	$5.00 Liberty Head 1839–1908 Indian Head 1908–1929 .24187 oz.	$10.00 Liberty Head 1838–1907 Indian Head 1907–1933 .48375 oz.	$20.00 1849–1933 .96750 oz.
$1,200	$290.24	$580.50	$1,161.00
1,225	296.29	592.59	1,185.19
1,250	302.34	604.69	1,209.38
1,275	308.38	616.78	1,233.56
1,300	314.43	628.88	1,257.75
1,325	320.48	640.97	1,281.94
1,350	326.52	653.06	1,306.13
1,375	332.57	665.16	1,330.31
1,400	338.62	677.25	1,354.50
1,425	344.66	689.34	1,378.69
1,450	350.71	701.44	1,402.88
1,475	356.76	713.53	1,427.06
1,500	362.81	725.63	1,451.25
1,525	368.85	737.72	1,475.44
1,550	374.90	749.81	1,499.63
1,575	380.95	761.91	1,523.81
1,600	386.99	774.00	1,548.00
1,625	393.04	786.09	1,572.19
1,650	399.09	798.19	1,596.38
1,675	405.13	810.28	1,620.56
1,700	411.18	822.38	1,644.75
1,725	417.23	834.47	1,668.94
1,750	423.27	846.56	1,693.13
1,775	429.32	858.66	1,717.31
1,800	435.37	870.75	1,741.50
1,825	441.41	882.84	1,765.69
1,850	447.46	894.94	1,789.88
1,875	453.51	907.03	1,814.06
1,900	459.55	919.13	1,838.25
1,925	465.60	931.22	1,862.44
1,950	471.65	943.31	1,886.63
1,975	477.69	955.41	1,910.81
2,000	483.74	967.50	1,935.00
2,025	489.79	979.59	1,959.19
2,050	495.83	991.69	1,983.38
2,075	501.88	1,003.78	2,007.56
2,100	507.93	1,015.88	2,031.75
2,125	513.97	1,027.97	2,055.94
2,150	520.02	1,040.06	2,080.13
2,175	526.07	1,052.16	2,104.31
2,200	532.11	1,064.25	2,128.50
2,225	538.16	1,076.34	2,152.69
2,250	544.21	1,088.44	2,176.88
2,275	550.25	1,100.53	2,201.06

Note: The U.S. bullion coins first issued in 1986 are unlike the older regular issues. They contain the following amounts of pure metal: silver $1, 1 oz.; gold $50, 1 oz.; gold $25, 1/2 oz.; gold $10, 1/4 oz.; gold $5, 1/10 oz.

TOP 250 U.S. COIN PRICES REALIZED AT AUCTION

Rank	Price	Coin	Grade	Firm	Date
1	$10,016,875	$1(s), 1794, Silver Plug **(X)**	PCGS SP-66	Stack's Bowers	Jan-13
2	7,590,020	$20, 1933	Gem BU	Soth/Stack's Bowers	Jul-02
3	4,140,000	$1(s), 1804, Class I	PCGS PF-68	B&M	Aug-99
4	3,737,500	5¢, 1913, Liberty Head	NGC PF-64	Heritage	Jan-10
5	3,737,500	$1(s), 1804, Class I	NGC PF-62	Heritage	Apr-08
6	2,990,000	Prefed, 1787, Brasher dbln, EB-Breast **(A)**	NGC EF-45	Heritage	Jan-05
7	2,990,000	$20, MCMVII, Ultra HR, LE **(U)**	PCGS PF-69	Heritage	Nov-05
8	2,760,000	$20, MCMVII, Ultra HR, LE **(U)**	PCGS PF-69	Stack's Bowers	Jun-12
9	2,415,000	Prefed, 1787, Brasher dbln, EB on Wing	NGC AU-55	Heritage	Jan-05
10	2,300,000	$1(s), 1804, Class III	PCGS PF-58	Heritage	Apr-09
11	2,185,000	$10, 1907, Rounded Rim	NGC Satin PF-67	Heritage	Jan-11
12	1,897,500	$20, 1927-D **(I)**	PCGS MS-67	Heritage	Nov-05
13	1,840,000	10¢, 1873-CC, No Arrows	PCGS MS-65	Stack's Bowers	Aug-12
14	1,840,000	5¢, 1913, Liberty Head	NGC PF-66	Superior	Mar-08
15	1,840,000	$20, MCMVII, Ultra HR, LE	PCGS PF-68	Heritage	Jan-07
16	1,840,000	$1(s), 1804, Class I **(B)**	PCGS PF-64	Stack's Bowers	Oct-00
17	1,815,000	$1(s), 1804, Class I	PF-63	B&M/Stack's Bowers	Apr-97
18	1,725,000	$2.5, 1796, No Stars **(O)**	PCGS MS-65	Heritage	Jan-08
19	1,725,000	$10, 1920-S	PCGS MS-67	Heritage	Mar-07
20	1,610,000	$10, 1839/8, Type of 1838, Lg Letters **(K)**	NGC PF-67 UC	Heritage	Jan-07
21	1,610,000	$20, 1861, Paquet Reverse	PCGS MS-61	Heritage	Aug-06
22	1,552,500	10¢, 1894-S	PCGS PF-64	Stack's Bowers	Oct-07
23	1,495,000	$20, 1927-D	PCGS MS-66	Heritage	Jan-10
24	1,495,000	$20, 1921	PCGS MS-63	B&M	Aug-06
25	1,485,000	5¢, 1913, Liberty Head	Gem PF-66	B&M/Stack's Bowers	May-96
26	1,437,500	$20, 1856-O	NGC SP-63	Heritage	May-09
27	1,410,000	Pattern half disme, 1792, J-7 **(W)**	PCGS SP-67	Heritage	Jan-13
28	1,380,000	$5, 1829, Large Date	PCGS PF-64	Heritage	Jan-12
29	1,380,000	1¢, 1793, Chain AMERICA, S-4	PCGS MS-65 BN	Heritage	Jan-12
30	1,380,000	50¢, 1797, O-101a **(N)**	NGC MS-66	Stack's	Jul-08
31	1,380,000	$2.5, 1796, No Stars **(O)**	PCGS MS-65	Stack's Bowers	Jun-05
32	1,322,500	$3, 1855-S	NGC PF-64 Cam	Heritage	Aug-11
33	1,322,500	Pattern half disme, 1792, J-7 **(W)**	PCGS SP-67	Heritage	Apr-06
34	1,322,500	$20, 1927-D	NGC MS-65	Heritage	Jan-06
35	1,322,500	10¢, 1894-S	NGC PF-66	DLRC	Mar-05
36	1,265,000	Pattern $10, 1874, Bickford, J-1373	PCGS PF-65 DC	Heritage	Jan-10
37	1,265,000	1¢, 1795, Reeded Edge, S-79	PCGS VG-10	Goldberg	Sep-09
38	1,265,000	$1(s), 1795, Flowing Hair, B-7, BB-18	V Ch Gem MS	Bullowa	Dec-05
39	1,210,000	$20, MCMVII, Ultra HR, LE **(J)**	PCGS PF-67	Goldberg	May-99
40	1,207,500	$1(s), 1794	NGC MS-64	B&M	Aug-10
41	1,207,500	$1(s), 1866, No Motto	NGC PF-63	Stack's Bowers	Jan-05
42	1,207,500	$1(s), 1804, Class III **(C)**	PCGS PF-58	B&M	Jul-03
43	1,150,000	Pattern 1¢, 1792, Silver Center, J-1	PCGS MS-61 BN	Heritage	Apr-12
44	1,150,000	$1(s), 1794	NGC MS-64	Stack's Bowers	Jun-05
45	1,145,625	Pattern half disme, 1792, J-7	NGC MS-68	Stack's Bowers	Jan-13
46	1,092,500	$20, 1921	PCGS MS-66	Heritage	Nov-05
47	1,092,500	$1(s), 1870-S	BU PL	Stack's Bowers	May-03
48	1,057,500	$20, MCMVII, Ultra HR, LE of 06	PCGS PF-58	Heritage	Aug-12
49	1,035,000	10¢, 1894-S	PCGS PF-65	Heritage	Jan-05
50	1,012,000	$20, 1921 **(L)**	PCGS MS-65 PQ	Goldberg	Sep-07
51	1,006,250	$2.5, 1796, Stars, Bass-3003, BD-3 **(P)**	NGC MS-65	Heritage	Jan-08
52	1,006,250	$1 Trade, 1885	NGC PF-62	DLRC	Nov-04
53	998,750	1¢, 1793, Chain, S-2	PCGS MS-65 BN	Stack's Bowers	Jan-13
54	990,000	$1(s), 1804, Class I **(B)**	Choice Proof	Rarcoa	Jul-89

Rank	Price	Coin	Grade	Firm	Date
55	$881,250	1¢, 1794, Head of 93, S-18b	PCGS MS-64 BN	Stack's Bowers	Jan-13
56	977,500	1¢, 1799, S-189	NGC MS-62 BN	Goldberg	Sep-09
57	977,500	$4, 1880, Coiled Hair	NGC PF-66 Cam	Heritage	Jan-05
58	977,500	$5, 1833, Large Date (G)	PCGS PF-67	Heritage	Jan-05
59	966,000	50¢, 1797, O-101a (N)	NGC MS-66	Stack's Bowers	Mar-04
60	962,500	5¢, 1913, Liberty Head	Proof	Stack's Bowers	Oct-93
61	948,750	Terr, 1852 Moffat & Co., $10, Wide Dt, K-9	PCGS SP-67	Stack's Bowers	Aug-06
62	920,000	$1(s), 1802, Restrike	PCGS PF-65 Cam	Heritage	Apr-08
63	920,000	$20, 1907, Small Edge Letters	PCGS PF-68	Heritage	Nov-05
64	920,000	$1 Trade, 1885	NGC PF-61	Stack's Bowers	May-03
65	907,500	$1 Trade, 1885	Gem PF-65	B&M/Stack's Bowers	Apr-97
66	891,250	10¢, 1873-CC, No Arrows (D)	NGC MS-65	B&M	Jul-04
67	874,000	$1(s), 1804, Class III (C)	PCGS PF-58	B&M	Nov-01
68	862,500	1¢, 1793, Strawberry Leaf, NC-3	NGC F-12	Stack's Bowers	Jan-09
69	862,500	Pattern $20, 1879, J-1643, P-1843	PCGS PF-62	Heritage	Jan-07
70	862,500	$2.5, 1796, Stars, Bass-3003, BD-3 (P)	NGC MS-65	Heritage	Jan-07
71	851,875	$1(s), 1803, Restrike	PCGS PF-66	Heritage	Jan-13
72	851,875	$1(s), 1802, Restrike	PCGS PF-65 Cam	Heritage	Aug-12
73	825,000	$20, MCMVII Ultra HR, LE	Proof	Sotheby's	Dec-96
74	805,000	$1(s), 1870-S	NGC EF-40	Heritage	Apr-08
75	805,000	$20, 1921	PCGS MS-65	Heritage	Nov-05
76	747,500	1¢, 1793, Chain, S-3	NGC MS-66 BN	Stack's Bowers	Aug-12
77	747,500	$20, 1921	PCGS MS-66	Heritage	Jan-12
78	747,500	Terr, 1855, Kellogg & Co. $50	PCGS PF-64	Heritage	Jan-07
79	747,500	$1(s), 1794	NGC MS-61	Heritage	Jun-05
80	734,375	50¢, 1838-O	PCGS PF-64	Heritage	Jan-13
81	725,000	Prefed, 1787, Brasher dbln, EB on Wing	MS-63	B&R	Nov-79
82	718,750	$10, 1933	Unc.	Stack's Bowers	Oct-04
83	705,698	$1(s), 1870-S	Very Fine (25)	B&M	Feb-08
84	690,000	$5, 1909-O	PCGS MS-66	Heritage	Jan-11
85	690,000	1¢, 1796, Liberty Cap, S-84	PCGS MS-66 RB	Goldberg	Sep-08
86	690,000	Pattern disme, 1792, copper, RE, J-10 (V)	NGC PF-62 BN	Heritage	Jul-08
87	690,000	$5, 1825, Over 4	NGC AU-50	Heritage	Jul-08
88	690,000	$20, MCMVII, Ultra HR, LE of 06 (H)	NGC PF-58	Stack's Bowers	Jul-08
89	690,000	Terr, 1860, Clark, Gruber & Co. $20	NGC MS-64	Heritage	Jan-06
90	690,000	Prefed, 1742 (1786), Lima Brasher dbln	NGC EF-40	Heritage	Jan-05
91	690,000	$5, 1835	PCGS PF-67	Heritage	Jan-05
92	690,000	Gold $1, 1849-C, Open Wreath	NGC MS-63 PL	DLRC	Jul-04
93	690,000	$20, MCMVII, Ultra HR, LE	Proof	Soth/Stack's Bowers	Oct-01
94	690,000	$10, 1839/8, Type of 1838 Lg Letters (K)	NGC PF-67	Goldberg	Sep-99
95	687,500	$3, 1870-S	EF-40	B&R	Oct-82
96	687,500	$5, 1822	VF-30/EF-40	B&R	Oct-82
97	672,750	$1(s), 1803, Restrike	PF-66	B&M	Feb-07
98	661,250	1¢, 1804, S-266c	PCGS MS-63 BN	Goldberg	Sep-09
99	661,250	1/2 10¢, 1870-S	NGC MS-63 PL	B&M	Jul-04
100	660,000	$20, MCMVII, Ultra HR, LE (J)	PF-67	B&M	Jan-97
101	660,000	$20, 1861, Paquet Reverse	MS-67	B&M	Nov-88
102	655,500	$4, 1879, Coiled Hair	NGC PF-67 Cam	Heritage	Jan-05
103	632,500	$5, 1828 Over 7	NGC MS-64	Heritage	Jan-12
104	632,500	$1(s), 1870-S	PCGS EF-40	B&M	Aug-10
105	632,500	10¢, 1804, 14-Star Reverse, JR-2	NGC AU58	Heritage	Jul-08
106	632,500	1¢, 1793, Liberty Cap, S-13, B-20	PCGS AU-55	Heritage	Feb-08
107	632,500	1¢, 1794, Starred Reverse, S-48, B-38	PCGS AU-50	Heritage	Feb-08
108	632,500	50¢, 1838-O	PCGS PF-63 BM	Heritage	Feb-08
109	632,500	Prefed, 1652, Willow Tree 3-pence, N-1A	VF	Stack's Bowers	Oct-05

Rank	Price	Coin	Grade	Firm	Date
110	$632,500	Confed, 1861, Original 50¢	VF	Stack's Bowers	Oct-03
111	632,500	10¢, 1873-CC, No Arrows (D)	PCGS MS-64	Heritage	Apr-99
112	632,500	50¢, 1838-O	PCGS PF-64 BM	Heritage	Jun-05
113	625,000	Prefed, 1787 Brasher dbln, EB on Breast (A)	VF	B&R	Mar-81
114	618,125	$4, 1880, Coiled Hair	NGC PF-63	Superior	Jul-05
115	605,000	$2.5, 1796, No Stars	Choice BU	Stack's Bowers	Nov-95
116	603,750	$20, 1854-O	PCGS AU-55	Heritage	Oct-08
117	603,750	Pattern 1¢, 1792, No Silver Center, J-2 (Q)	PCGS VF-30	Heritage	Jan-08
118	603,750	$1 Trade, 1884	PCGS PF-65	Heritage	Nov-05
119	587,500	Pattern disme, 1792, copper, RE, J-10 (V)	NGC PF-62 BN	Heritage	Oct-12
120	587,500	$20, 1921 (L)	PCGS MS-65	Heritage	Aug-12
121	586,500	$5, 1795, Small Eagle, BD-1	PCGS MS-65	Stack's	Jun-08
122	583,000	$5, 1795, Small Eagle	NGC MS-65 PL	Bullowa	Jan-07
123	577,500	$20, 1927-D	PCGS MS-65	Akers	May-98
124	577,500	$1(s), 1794	Gem BU	Stack's Bowers	Nov-95
125	576,150	$20, 1856-O	NGC AU-58	Heritage	Oct-08
126	575,000	$20, 1920-S	PCGS MS-66	Heritage	Jan-12
127	575,000	$1(s), 1794	PCGS AU-58 PQ	Goldberg	May-11
128	575,000	$4, 1880, Coiled Hair	NGC PF-62	Heritage	Jan-09
129	575,000	Pattern $50, 1877, copper, J-1549	NGC PF-67 BN	Heritage	Jan-09
130	575,000	$1(s), 1895-O	PCGS MS-67	Heritage	Nov-05
131	575,000	$20, MCMVII, HR, WR (M)	PCGS MS-69	Heritage	Nov-05
132	575,000	$20, 1927-D	NGC MS-62	DLRC	Jul-04
133	564,000	20¢, 1876-CC	PCGS MS-65	Stack's Bowers	Jan-13
134	558,125	1¢, 1793, Wreath, S-9	PCGS MS-69 BN	Stack's Bowers	Jan-13
135	552,000	$10, 1933	PCGS MS-65	Heritage	Jan-08
136	552,000	$1(s), 1870-S	VF-20	Stack's Bowers	Oct-07
137	550,000	$10, 1838	Ch Proof	Akers	May-98
138	550,000	10¢, 1873-CC, No Arrows (D)	Gem MS-65	B&M/Stack's Bowers	May-96
139	550,000	25¢, 1901-S	NGC MS-68	Superior	May-90
140	546,250	Prefed, 1776, Cont. $1, pewter, N-3D	NGC MS-67	Heritage	Jan-12
141	546,250	$1(s), 1893-S	NGC MS-67	Heritage	Aug-11
142	546,250	Terr, 1851 Humb't $50, 880 Thous., No 50 Rev.	PCGS MS-63	Heritage	Aug-10
143	546,250	$4, 1880, Coiled Hair	NGC PF-62	Heritage	Jul-09
144	546,250	$10, 1795, 13 Leaves, BD-1, T-1	PCGS MS-64	Stack's Bowers	Jul-08
145	546,250	$10, 1933	PCGS MS-65	Heritage	Jan-07
146	546,250	$20, MCMVII, HR, WR (M)	PCGS MS-69	Heritage	Jan-07
147	542,800	$20, 1856-O	NGC SP-63	Heritage	Jun-04
148	534,750	$20, MCMVII, HR, FR	NGC PF-69	Heritage	Nov-05
149	531,875	$1(s), 1889-CC (T)	PCGS MS-68	Heritage	Jan-09
150	529,000	Pattern $1, 1838, copper, J-87, P-96	PCGS PF-63 RB	Stack's Bowers	Jan-08
151	529,000	$1(s), 1889-CC	PCGS MS-68	B&M	Jan-01
152	528,750	Pattern half disme, 1792, J-7	PCGS MS-64	Heritage	Jan-13
153	522,500	$20, 1927-D (I)	Gem BU	Stack's Bowers	Mar-91
154	517,500	$2.5, 1808, BD-1	PCGS MS-63	Stack's Bowers	Nov-08
155	517,500	25¢, 1839, No Drapery	NGC PF-65	Heritage	Apr-08
156	517,500	$20, MCMVII, HR, WR (M)	PCGS MS-69	Heritage	Mar-08
157	517,500	$10, 1933	PCGS MS-65 PQ	Goldberg	Feb-09
158	517,500	$10, 1933	PCGS MS-65	Heritage	Nov-05
159	517,500	$20, 1920-S	PCGS MS-66	Heritage	Nov-05
160	517,000	50¢, 1797, O-102a	Gem BU	Stack's Bowers	Nov-95
161	510,600	$1 Trade, 1884	PCGS PF-67	Goldberg	Oct-00
162	506,000	1¢, 1794, Liberty Cap, Bisected Obv., S-14	PCGS AU-53	Goldberg	Sep-09
163	506,000	$10, 1795, 13 Leaves, T-1	PCGS MS-65	B&M	Jul-03
164	506,000	1/2¢, 1796, No Pole	MS-65 RB PL	B&M/Stack's Bowers	May-96

Rank	Price	Coin	Grade	Firm	Date
165	$506,000	$1(s), 1794 **(X)**	PCGS MS-65	Superior	May-91
166	503,125	$1(s), 1794	NGC MS-61	Heritage	Apr-09
167	503,125	$1(s), 1870-S	PCGS EF-40	Heritage	Apr-09
168	503,125	Pattern half dime, 1792, J-7, P-7	PCGS MS-63	Heritage	Jan-08
169	500,000	Terr, 1851 Humbert $50	Proof	B&R	Mar-80
170	499,375	1¢, 1794, Head of 95, S-67	PCGS MS-67 RB	Stack's Bowers	Jan-13
171	494,500	$20, 1854-O	AU-55	B&M	Aug-07
172	494,500	$10, 1795, 13 Leaves, T-1	NGC MS-65	B&M	Aug-06
173	488,750	$20, 1854-O	PCGS AU-55	B&M	Aug-10
174	488,750	$10, 1933	PCGS MS-65	Heritage	Jan-09
175	488,750	$2.5, 1796, No Stars, BD-2, B-1	PCGS MS-62	Stack's Bowers	Jul-08
176	488,750	$1(s), 1794	NGC AU-58	Heritage	Apr-08
177	488,750	$4, 1880, Flowing Hair	NGC PF-66 Cam	Heritage	Mar-08
178	488,750	1¢, 1794, Head of 95, S-67, B-59	PCGS MS-67 RB	Heritage	Feb-08
179	488,750	$20, MCMVII, Ultra HR, LE of 06 **(H)**	Proof Ch EF	Stack's Bowers	Mar-05
180	477,250	$5, 1876-CC	PCGS MS-66	Stack's Bowers	Aug-12
181	475,000	$1(s), 1804, Class I	AU	Stack's Bowers	Oct-93
182	475,000	Pattern $20, 1907, J-1776 **(F)**	Proof	B&R	Jul-81
183	474,375	$20, 1921	PCGS MS-64	Heritage	Jul-08
184	467,500	$5, 1833, Large Date **(G)**	Gem Proof	Akers	Oct-97
185	467,500	Pattern $20, 1907, J-1776 **(F)**	PF-67	Paramount	Jul-84
186	462,000	$1(s), 1889-CC **(T)**	MS-66 PL	B&M/Stack's Bowers	Apr-97
187	462,000	$1(s), 1870-S	Unc	Stack's Bowers	Mar-95
188	460,000	25¢, 1873-CC, No Arrows	PCGS MS-64	Stack's Bowers	Aug-12
189	460,000	20¢, 1876-CC	PCGS MS-64	Stack's Bowers	Aug-12
190	460,000	$20, 1854-O	PCGS AU-55	Heritage	Jan-11
191	460,000	Pattern 50¢, 1915, No S, Pan-Pac, J-1960	NGC PF-64	Heritage	Aug-10
192	460,000	$10, 1933	PCGS MS-65	Heritage	Jul-09
193	460,000	$20, 1856-O	NGC AU-58	Heritage	Jul-09
194	460,000	20¢, 1876-CC	PCGS MS-66	Heritage	Apr-09
195	460,000	$1(s), 1892-S	PCGS MS-67	Heritage	Jan-09
196	460,000	$5, 1815	NGC MS-64	Heritage	Jan-09
197	460,000	Terr, 1851, A. Humb't $50, 880 Thous., RE	NGC MS-65	B&M	Sep-08
198	460,000	$10, 1795, 13 Leaves, T-5	NGC MS-64	Goldberg	Feb-08
199	460,000	$10, 1907, Rounded Rim **(R)**	PCGS MS-67	Heritage	Jan-08
200	460,000	25¢, 1850	NGC PF-68	Heritage	Jan-08
201	460,000	Terr, 1855, Kellogg & Co. $50	PCGS PF-62	Stack's Bowers	Oct-07
202	460,000	$10, 1933	NGC MS-65	Goldberg	May-05
203	460,000	$10, 1795, 13 Leaves, T-1	PCGS MS-64	Heritage	Jan-05
204	460,000	50¢, 1796, 16 Stars, O-102	SP-66	Stack's Bowers	May-99
205	451,000	10¢, 1894-S	Gem PF-64	B&M/Stack's Bowers	May-96
206	448,500	$10, 1795, 13 Leaves, T-1	NGC-64	Goldberg	Sep-07
207	448,500	$10, 1797, Small Eagle	NGC MS-63	Goldberg	May-07
208	440,625	$4, 1880, Flowing Hair	NGC PF-66	Heritage	Jan-13
209	440,000	$4, 1880, Coiled Hair	PCGS PF-66	Superior	Aug-91
210	437,000	$10, 1933	PCGS MS-64 PQ	Goldberg	Sep-07
211	437,000	Pattern 1¢, 1792, No Silver Center, J-2 **(Q)**	PCGS VF-30 PQ	Goldberg	Feb-05
212	434,500	Terr, 1852/1, Humbert $20	NGC PF-64	Superior	Oct-90
213	431,250	Prefed, Undated (1652), NE 6-pence, N-1A	PCGS VF Damage	Stack's Bowers	Nov-12
214	431,250	$5, 1829, Small Date	PCGS MS-66	Heritage	Jan-12
215	431,250	$20, 1854-O	PCGS AU-55	Heritage	Oct-11
216	431,250	1¢, 1795, Reeded Edge, S-79	NGC Details Fine G-5	Heritage	Jan-11
217	431,250	$10, 1920-S	PCGS MS-66	Heritage	Jan-09
218	431,250	25¢, 1873-CC, No Arrows	PCGS MS-63	Stack's Bowers	Jan-09
219	431,250	$4, 1880, Flowing Hair	PCGS PF-64	Heritage	Jul-08

Rank	Price	Coin	Grade	Firm	Date
220	$431,250	$1(s), 1795, Flowing Hair, B-1, BB-21	NGC MS-65	Heritage	Jan-08
221	431,250	$1(s), 1794	NGC AU-55	Heritage	Nov-05
222	431,250	$20, 1854-O	NGC AU-58	Heritage	Jul-05
223	431,250	$20, 1856-O	PCGS AU-55	Heritage	Jul-05
224	431,250	1¢, 1793, Chain, AMERICA, S-2	PCGS MS-65 BN	Stack's Bowers	Jan-05
225	431,250	Terr, 1849, Cincinnati Mining & Trading $10	EF	Stack's Bowers	May-04
226	431,250	10¢, 1894-S	Gem Proof	Stack's Bowers	Oct-00
227	430,000	Prefed, 1787, Brasher dbln, EB on Wing	AU	Rarcoa	Jul-79
228	425,500	$2.5, 1808, BD-1	PCGS MS-63	Stack's Bowers	Mar-07
229	425,500	Prefed, 1776, Cont. $1, silver, N-3D	EF	Stack's Bowers	Oct-03
230	416,875	Prefed, Undated (1652) NE shilling, Noe-III-C	PCGS AU-50	Heritage	Aug-10
231	414,000	$20, 1870-CC	NGC AU-55	B&M	Mar-09
232	414,000	$20, 1871-CC	NGC MS-64	Heritage	Apr-08
233	414,000	$4, 1879, Coiled Hair	NGC PF-63	Goldberg	May-07
234	414,000	Prefed, Undated (1652), NE shilling, N-2A	EF-40	Stack's Bowers	May-07
235	414,000	50¢, 1796, 16 Stars, O-102	PCGS MS-64	Goldbergs	May-06
236	414,000	$10, 1795, 13 Leaves, B-1A, T-1	PCGS MS-64	Stack's Bowers	Jun-05
237	414,000	1¢, 1793, Strawberry Leaf, NC-3	NGC F-12	Stack's Bowers	Nov-04
238	414,000	$1(s), 1870-S	NGC EF-40	DLRC	Nov-04
239	414,000	Pattern 1¢, 1792, Silver Center, J-1	BU	Stack's Bowers	Jan-02
240	414,000	$1(s), 1893-S	Superb Gem BU	Stack's Bowers	Nov-01
241	411,250	$1(s), 1895-O	NGC SP-65	Stack's Bowers	Jan-13
242	411,250	$1(s), 1802, Restrike	PCGS PF-64	Heritage	Oct-12
243	411,250	$20, 1887 **(E)**	NGC PF-67+ê Cam	Heritage	Aug-12
244	402,500	1/2¢, 1796, With Pole	PCGS MS-64 BN	Stack's Bowers	Aug-12
245	402,500	$2.5, 1796, No Stars	PCGS MS-61	Stack's Bowers	Aug-12
246	402,500	$4, 1879, Flowing Hair	NGC PF-68 UC	Stack's Bowers	Jun-12
247	402,500	$10, 1933	PCGS MS-64+	Heritage	Jan-12
248	402,500	$5, 1828	PCGS MS-64	Heritage	Jan-12
249	402,500	$20, 1926-D	PCGS MS-66+	Heritage	Jan-12
250	402,500	$20, 1887 **(E)**	PCGS PF-67+ê	Heritage	Jan-11

Key

Price: The sale price of the coin, including the appropriate buyer's fee.

Class: The denomination or classification of the coin. Confed = Confederate States of America issue; Pattern = a pattern, experimental, or trial piece; Prefed = pre-federal issue; Terr = territorial issue.

Coin: The date and description of the coin, along with pertinent catalog or reference numbers. B = Baker (for pre-federal), Bolender (for silver dollars), Breen (for gold), Browning (for quarter dollars); BB = Bowers/Borckardt; BD = Bass-Dannreuther; Brasher = Brasher doubloon; J = Judd; JR = John Reich Society; N = Newman; NC = Non-Collectible; O = Overton; P = Pollock; S = Sheldon; T = Taraskza; HR = High Relief; LE = Lettered Edge. Letters in parentheses, **(A)** through **(X)**, note instances in which multiple sales of the same coin rank within the Top 250.

Grade: The grade of the coin, plus the name of the grading firm (if independently graded). BM = branch mint; NGC = Numismatic Guaranty Corporation of America; PCGS = Professional Coin Grading Service; PQ = premium quality.

Firm: The auction firm (or firms) that sold the coin. ANR = American Numismatic Rarities; B&M = Bowers & Merena; B&R = Bowers & Ruddy; DLRC = David Lawrence Rare Coins; Soth = Sotheby's; Stack's Bowers = Stack's Bowers Galleries (name under which Stack's and B&M merged in 2010; also encompasses the merger of Stack's and ANR in 2006).

Date: The month and year of the auction.

Auction records compiled and edited by P. Scott Rubin.

For more than ten years one magnificent twenty-dollar gold piece stood at the top of the charts as the single most valuable coin ever sold at auction. This was the 1933 double eagle once owned by King Farouk of Egypt. The coin sold for $7,590,020 in July 2002. In January 2013 that record was shattered when another famous coin—this time a 1794 silver dollar—broke through the $10 million barrier.

The story of the 1933 double eagle starts in mid-March of that year, when the Philadelphia Mint began striking the gold coins in a normal production run. Through May 19 the Mint struck 445,000 pieces. President Franklin Roosevelt's Executive Order 6102, which prohibited the hoarding of gold in an attempt to heal the country's financial depression, sealed the fate of the 1933 double eagles. The coins were never monetized or released into circulation. Two specimens were sent to the Smithsonian Institution's National Numismatic Collection in 1934; the rest were kept by the Treasury and slated for melting. However, nearly two dozen of the coins, originally set aside for assay purposes, escaped the mint and made their way into private hands. Over the years several of the coins came to light in the marketplace. The U.S. government seized them when it could (and presumably had them melted), declaring private ownership illegal.

In 1952 Farouk, the king of Egypt (and a famous collector of coins, automobiles, jewelry, Fabergé eggs, and other treasures), was overthrown in a military coup. Two years later Egypt's ruling junta sold off the deposed king's massive coin collection in a fire-sale auction in Cairo. One of the coins offered was a 1933 double eagle, which was withdrawn from the sale at the request of the U.S. government. The coin resurfaced more than 40 years later, in 1996, when a London dealer tried to sell it in New York City for around $1 million. The "buyers" were actually federal agents, who confiscated the double eagle and arrested its sellers. Criminal charges were later dropped, but the government insisted the coin was against the law to own. This resulted in a legal battle wherein it was shown that the Treasury Department had actually issued an export license for King Farouk's coin when he bought it from dealer B. Max Mehl in February 1944. This changed the equation. In 2001 the government and the coin's sellers agreed to settle the ownership question by selling the coin and splitting the proceeds. The Farouk specimen was declared to be the only 1933 double eagle that is legal to own, and the Treasury officially monetized the coin—which is why a sum of $20 was added to its phenomenal $7-million-plus price when it was sold on July 30, 2002.

That record—nearly double the next-highest auction sale (of an 1804 silver dollar for $4,140,000 in August 1999)—was untouchable until January 24, 2013. It took another silver dollar to knock the double eagle off its lofty perch.

The new record-holder is a 1794 dollar, one of only 1,758 dollar coins that were released by the U.S. Mint from its press run of October 15 that year. (Another 242 of the coins failed to pass inspection, being too poorly struck, and were melted for recoining.) These were the first silver dollars ever struck by the Mint. On top of that historical significance and the issue's low mintage and survivorship (only about 135 are known to have survived the centuries since being minted), this particular coin is considered by many numismatic experts, after careful study of its characteristics, to be the very first one struck on that groundbreaking October day. It has been graded Specimen-66, the finest of its kind, and shows strong details—unusual for these dollar coins. The Mint's largest coin press at the time was the one used to make cents and half dollars, and most 1794 dollars were weakly struck. (The dollar's coinage dies were not parallel in the press, which also contributed to the weak strike.)

The record-setting coin's surfaces are prooflike, with high reflectivity and minimal handling marks. The planchet used to make it has a silver plug in its center. (Such plugs were added to underweight planchets to bring them up to the Mint's precise specification of 26.96 grams' weight.) The coin also shows light adjustment marks from where a Mint worker filed the planchet down to the correct weight. (The planchet probably started out too light, then a plug was added to increase its weight, then it was filed down to the proper specification, after which the coin was struck.) This is the only 1794 dollar known with a silver plug, which suggests that the planchet was specially prepared for a coin intended to be set aside as an important specimen of America's minting technology.

The 1794 dollar was sold for $10,016,875 by Stack's Bowers Galleries in its New York Americana Sales, as part of the Cardinal Collection. How long will this new world record hold? What effect will it have on the broader rare-coin market? How many new collectors will enter the hobby after learning about this extraordinary transaction—their imaginations fired by the history, romance, and artistry of America's coins? Time will answer these questions. For now, collectors worldwide can appreciate the significance of this record-setting event.

The 1933 double eagle once owned by King Farouk of Egypt—
one of the most expensive rare coins ever sold at auction.

The new record-holder as the world's most valuable coin:
the 1794 silver dollar that sold for more than $10 million.

The American Numismatic Association, headquartered in Colorado Springs, Colorado, is the national congressionally chartered group that promotes the hobby and science of numismatics. Membership in the ANA is one of the best values in numismatics; the organization is devoted to education and consumer protection. Its web site is at www.money.org; you can also call 1-800-367-9723 or email ana@money.org for more information. Scores of smaller, local groups are member clubs of the ANA. To learn more about coins, and to connect with fellow collectors in your community, join a local ANA club. The following clubs are either statewide, or else the largest/oldest in their states. *Contact information can change over time; check the ANA web site at money.org for the most current web-site and email information.*

Alaska: Anchorage Coin Club (www.alaska.net/~nakata/coin_club.htm)

Alabama: Madison County Coin Club (http://mccc.anaclubs.org)

Arkansas: Border Town Coin Club (http://www.bordertowncoinclub.org)

Arizona: Tucson Coin Club Inc (http://www.tucsoncoinclub.org/)

California: California State Numismatic Association (CSNA; http://www.calcoin.org)

Colorado: Colorado Springs Numismatic Society (http://csns.anaclubs.org)

Connecticut: Mansfield Numismatic Society
(http://www.MansfieldNumismaticSociety.org)

District of Columbia: Washington Numismatic Society Inc
(http://wns.anaclubs.org)

Delaware: Wilmington Coin Club (http://www.wilmingtoncoinclub.org)

Florida: Florida United Numismatists (FUN; http://www.funtopics.com)

Georgia: Georgia Numismatic Association (GNA; http://www.gamoney.org)

Hawaii: Hawaii State Numismatic Association (www.hawaiicollectibles.org/)

Iowa: Iowa Numismatic Association (http://ina.anaclubs.org)

Idaho: Eagle Rock Numismatic Society (paz@sbcglobal.net)

Illinois: Illinois Numismatic Association (http://www.ilnaclub.info)

Indiana: Indiana State Numismatic Association
(http://www.indianastatenumismatics.org)

Kansas: Kansas Numismatic Association
(http://www.kansasnumismaticassociation.org)

Kentucky: Louisville and Kentucky State Numismatic Association, Inc.
(puifox@aol.com)

Louisiana: Crescent City Coin Club (www.crescentcitycoinclub.org/)

Massachusetts: New England Numismatic Association
(NENA; www.nenacoin.org)

Maryland: Maryland State Numismatic Association
(http://www.mdstatenumisassn.org)

Maine: Maine Numismatic Association

Michigan: Michigan State Numismatic Society (http://www.michigancoinclub.org)

Minnesota: Minnesota Organization of Numismatists (jerryswanson@hotmail.com)

Missouri: Missouri Numismatic Society (www.missourinumismaticsociety.org)

Mississippi: Mississippi Numismatic Association (epsor@teleclipse.net)

North Carolina: North Carolina Numismatic Association (NCNA; www.ncnaonline.org)

North Dakota: Capital City Coin Club (ND; capitalcitycoinclub@bis.midco.net)

Nebraska: Nebraska Numismatic Association (nna_journal@msn.com)

New Hampshire: Nashua Coin Club (www.nashuacoinclub.org)

New Jersey: Garden State Numismatic Association (GSNA; http://www.gsna.org/)

New Mexico: Albuquerque Coin Club (http://albuquerquecoinclub.org)

Nevada: Reno Coin Club (www.renocoinclub.org)

New York: Rochester Numismatic Association (www.the-rna.com)

Ohio: Ohio State Numismatic Association (http://www.eosna.org)

Oklahoma: Oklahoma Numismatic Association (smcornell@cox.net)

Oregon: Salem Numismatic Society (http://www.oregoncoinclubs.org)

Pennsylvania: Pennsylvania Association Of Numismatists (PAN; www.pancoins.org)

Rhode Island: Newport County Coin Club (carltonrj@aol.com)

South Carolina: South Carolina Numismatic Association Inc (http://www.sc-na.org)

South Dakota: Great Plains Coin Club (Sioux Falls)

Tennessee: Tennessee State Numismatic Society (www.tsns.org)

Texas: Texas Numismatic Association (TNA; www.tna.org)

Virginia: Virginia Numismatic Association (www.vnaonline.org)

Washington: Seattle Numismatic Society (http://www.seattlenumismaticsociety.org)

Wisconsin: Milwaukee Numismatic Society (http://www.milwaukeenumismaticsociety.com)

West Virginia: Kanawha Valley Coin Club (http://www.kvcc.eznetway.com)

Wyoming: Cheyenne Coin Club (wfa1972@aol.com)

Canada: Sherwood Park (Royal Canadian Numismatic Association Library (www.canadian-numismatic.org/)

Over the years coin collectors have developed a special jargon to describe their coins. The following list includes terms that are used frequently by coin collectors or that have a special meaning other than their ordinary dictionary definitions. You will find them useful when you want to discuss or describe your coins.

alloy—A combination of two or more metals.

altered date—A false date on a coin; a date altered to make a coin appear to be one of a rarer or more valuable issue.

bag mark—A surface mark, usually a small nick, acquired by a coin through contact with others in a mint bag.

billon—A low-grade alloy of silver (usually less than 50%) mixed with another metal, typically copper.

blank—The formed piece of metal on which a coin design will be stamped.

bronze—An alloy of copper, zinc, and tin.

bullion—Uncoined gold or silver in the form of bars, ingots, or plate.

cast coins—Coins that are made by pouring molten metal into a mold, instead of in the usual manner of striking blanks with dies.

cent—One one-hundredth of the standard monetary unit. Also known as a *centavo*, *centimo*, or *centesimo* in some Central American and South American countries; *centime* in France and various former colonies in Africa; and other variations.

certified coin—A coin that has been graded, authenticated, and encapsulated in plastic by an independent (neither buyer nor seller) grading service.

cherrypicker—A collector who finds scarce and unusual coins by carefully searching through unattributed items in old accumulations or dealers' stocks.

circulation strike—An Uncirculated coin intended for eventual use in commerce, as opposed to a Proof coin.

clad coinage—Issues of the United States dimes, quarters, halves, and some dollars made since 1965. Each coin has a center core of pure copper and a layer of copper-nickel or silver on both sides.

collar—The outer ring, or die chamber, that holds a blank in place in the coinage press while the coin is impressed by the obverse and reverse dies.

contact marks—Minor abrasions on an Uncirculated coin, made by contact with other coins in a bag or roll.

countermark—A stamp or mark impressed on a coin to verify its use by another government or to indicate revaluation.

crack-out—A coin that has been removed from a grading service holder.

crown—Any dollar-size coin (c. 38 mm in diameter) in general, often struck in silver; specifically, one from the United Kingdom and some Commonwealth countries.

cud—An area of raised metal at the rim of a coin where a portion of the die broke off, leaving a void in the design.

designer—The artist who creates a coin's design. An engraver is the person who cuts a design into a coinage die.

die—A piece of metal engraved with a design and used for stamping coins.

die crack—A fine, raised line on a coin, caused by a broken die.

die defect—An imperfection on a coin, caused by a damaged die.

die variety—Any minor alteration in the basic design of a coin.

dipped, dipping—Refers to chemical cleaning of a coin to remove oxidation or foreign matter.

double eagle—The United States twenty-dollar gold coin.

doubled die—A die that has been given two misaligned impressions from a hub; also, a coin made from such a die.

doubloon—Popular name for a Spanish gold coin originally valued at $16.

eagle—A United States ten-dollar gold coin; also refers to U.S. silver, gold, and platinum bullion pieces made from 1986 to the present.

edge—Periphery of a coin, often with reeding, lettering, or other decoration.

electrotype—A reproduction of a coin or medal made by the electrodeposition process. Electrotypes are frequently used in museum displays.

electrum—A naturally occurring mixture of gold and silver. Some of the world's first coins were made of this alloy.

encapsulated coins—Coins that have been authenticated, graded, and sealed in plastic by a professional service.

engraver—The person who engraves or sculpts a model for use in translating to a coin die.

error—A mismade coin not intended for circulation.

exergue—That portion of a coin beneath the main design, often separated from it by a line, and typically bearing the date.

field—The background portion of a coin's surface not used for a design or inscription.

filler—A coin in worn condition but rare enough to be included in a collection.

fineness—The purity of gold, silver, or any other precious metal, expressed in terms of one thousand parts. A coin of 90% pure silver is expressed as .900 fine.

flan—A blank piece of metal in the size and shape of a coin; also called a *planchet*.

gem—A coin of exceptionally high quality, typically considered MS-65 or PF-65 or better.

half eagle—The United States five-dollar gold coin minted from 1795 to 1929.

hub—A positive-image punch to impress the coin's design into a die for coinage.

incuse—The design of a coin that has been impressed below the coin's surface. A design raised above the coin's surface is in relief.

inscription—The legend or lettering on a coin.

intrinsic value—Bullion or "melt" value of the actual precious metal in a numismatic item.

investment grade—Promotional term; generally, a coin in grade MS-65 or better.

junk silver—Common-date silver coins taken from circulation; worth only bullion value.

key coin—One of the scarcer or more valuable coins in a series.

laureate—Head crowned with a laurel wreath.

legal tender—Money that is officially issued and recognized for redemption by an authorized agency or government.

legend—A principal inscription on a coin.

lettered edge—The edge of a coin bearing an inscription, found on some foreign and some older United States coins, modern Presidential dollars, and the MMIX Ultra High Relief gold coin.

luster—The brilliant or "frosty" surface quality of an Uncirculated (Mint State) coin.

milled edge—The raised rim around the outer surface of a coin, not to be confused with the reeded or serrated narrow edge of a coin.

mint error—Any mismade or defective coin produced by a mint.

mint luster—Shiny "frost" or brilliance on the surface of an Uncirculated or Mint State coin.

mintmark—A small letter or other mark on a coin, indicating the mint at which it was struck.

Mint set—A set of Uncirculated coins packaged and sold by the Mint. Each set contains one of each of the coins made for circulation at each of the mints that year.

motto—An inspirational word or phrase used on a coin.

mule—A coin struck from two dies not originally intended to be used together.

obverse—The front or face side of a coin.

overdate—Date made by superimposing one or more numerals on a previously dated die.

overgraded—A coin in poorer condition than stated.

overstrike—An impression made with new dies on a previously struck coin.

patina—The green or brown surface film found on ancient copper and bronze coins, caused by oxidation over a long period of time.

pattern—Experimental or trial coin, generally of a new design, denomination, or metal.

pedigree—The record of previous owners of a rare coin.

planchet—The blank piece of metal on which a coin design is stamped.

Proof—Coins struck for collectors by the Mint using specially polished dies and planchets.

Proof set—A set of each of the Proof coins made during a given year, packaged by the Mint and sold to collectors.

quarter eagle—The United States $2.50 gold coin.

raw—A coin that has not been encapsulated by an independent grading service.

reeded edge—The edge of a coin with grooved lines that run vertically around its perimeter, as seen on modern United States silver and clad coins.

relief—Any part of a coin's design that is raised above the coin's field is said to be in relief. The opposite of relief is incuse, meaning sunk into the field.

restrike—A coin struck from genuine dies at a later date than the original issue.

reverse—The back side of a coin.

rim—The raised portion of a coin that protects the design from wear.

round—A round one-ounce silver medal or bullion piece.

series—A set of one coin of each year of a specific design and denomination issued from each mint. For example, Lincoln cents from 1909 to 1959.

slab—A hard plastic case containing a coin that has been graded and encapsulated by a professional service.

spot price—The daily quoted market value of precious metals in bullion form.

token—A privately issued piece, typically with an exchange value for goods or services, but not an official government coin.

trade dollar—Silver dollar issued especially for trade with a foreign country. In the United States, trade dollars were first issued in 1873 to stimulate commerce with the Orient. Many other countries have also issued trade dollars.

truncation—The sharply cut-off bottom edge of a bust or portrait.

type—A series of coins defined by a shared distinguishing design, composition, denomination, and other elements. For example, Barber dimes or Franklin half dollars.

type set—A collection consisting of one representative coin of each type, of a particular series or period.

Uncirculated—A circulation-strike coin that has never been used in commerce, and has retained its original surface and luster; also called Mint State.

unique—An item of which only one specimen is known to exist.

variety—A coin's design that sets it apart from the normal issue of that type.

wheaties—Lincoln cents with the wheat ears reverse, issued from 1909 to 1958.

year set—A set of coins for any given year, consisting of one of each denomination issued that year.

COLONIAL ISSUES

Bowers, Q. David. *Whitman Encyclopedia of Colonial and Early American Coins,* Atlanta, GA, 2009.

Breen, Walter. *Walter Breen's Complete Encyclopedia of U.S. and Colonial Coins,* New York, 1988.

Carlotto, Tony. *The Copper Coins of Vermont,* Chelsea, MI, 1998.

Crosby, S.S. *The Early Coins of America,* Boston, 1875 (reprinted 1945, 1965, 1974, 1983).

Demling, Michael. *New Jersey Coppers.* 2011.

Kessler, Alan. *The Fugio Cents,* Newtonville, MA, 1976.

Maris, Edward. *A Historic Sketch of the Coins of New Jersey,* Philadelphia, 1881 (reprinted 1965, 1974, 1987).

Martin, Syd. *The Hibernia Coinage of William Wood (1722–1724),* n.p., 2007.

Miller, Henry C., and Hillyer, Ryder. *The State Coinages of New England,* New York, 1920.

Nelson, Philip. *The Coinage of William Wood 1722–1733,* London, 1903 (reprinted 1959).

Newman, Eric P. *Coinage for Colonial Virginia,* New York, 1956.

Newman, Eric P. *The United States Fugio Copper Coinage of 1787,* Ypsilanti, MI, 2007.

Newman, Eric P., and Doty, Richard G. *Studies on Money in Early America,* New York, 1976.

Noe, Sydney P. *The New England and Willow Tree Coinage of Massachusetts,* New York, 1943; *The Oak Tree Coinage of Massachusetts,* New York, 1947; and *The Pine Tree Coinage of Massachusetts,* New York, 1952 (combined reprint as *The Silver Coins of Massachusetts,* 1973).

Rulau, Russell, and Fuld, George. *Medallic Portraits of Washington,* Iola, WI, 1999.

Salmon, Christopher J. *The Silver Coins of Massachusetts.* New York, 2010.

Vlack, Robert. *An Illustrated Catalogue of the French Billon Coinage in the Americas,* Boston, 2004.

HISTORY OF THE U.S. MINT

Augsburger, Leonard D., and Orosz, Joel J. *The Secret History of the First U.S. Mint.* Atlanta, GA, 2011.

Evans, George. *Illustrated History of the U.S. Mint* (various eds.), Philadelphia, 1885–1901.

Lange, David W. *History of the United States Mint and Its Coinage*, Atlanta, GA, 2005.

HALF CENTS

Breen, Walter. *Walter Breen's Encyclopedia of United States Half Cents 1793–1857,* South Gate, CA, 1983.

Cohen, Roger S., Jr. *American Half Cents—The "Little Half Sisters"* (2nd ed.), 1982.

Manley, Ronald P. *The Half Cent Die State Book, 1793–1857,* United States, 1998.

LARGE CENTS

Breen, Walter. *Walter Breen's Encyclopedia of Early United States Cents 1793–1814,* Wolfeboro, NH, 2001.

Grellman, J.R. *Attribution Guide for United States Large Cents 1840–1857* (3rd ed.), Bloomington, MN, 2002.

Newcomb, H.R. *United States Copper Cents 1816–1857,* New York, 1944 (reprinted 1983).

Noyes, William C. *United States Large Cents 1793–1794,* Ypsilanti, MI, 2006.

Noyes, William C. *United States Large Cents 1793–1814,* Bloomington, MN, 1991.

Noyes, William C. *United States Large Cents 1795–1797,* Ypsilanti, MI, 2007.

Noyes, William C. *United States Large Cents 1816–1839,* Bloomington, MN, 1991.

PENNY-WISE, official publication of Early American Coppers, Inc.

Sheldon, William H. *Penny Whimsy (1793–1814),* New York, 1958 (reprinted 1965, 1976).

Wright, John D. *The Cent Book 1816–1839,* Bloomington, MN, 1992.

SMALL CENTS

Bowers, Q. David. *A Guide Book of Lincoln Cents*, Atlanta, GA, 2008.

Lange, David W. *The Complete Guide to Lincoln Cents*, Wolfeboro, NH, 1996.

Snow, Richard. *A Guide Book of Flying Eagle and Indian Head Cents* (2nd ed.), Atlanta, GA, 2009.

Steve, Larry, and Flynn, Kevin. *Flying Eagle and Indian Cent Die Varieties*, Jarretteville, MD, 1995.

Wexler, John, and Flynn, Kevin. *The Authoritative Reference on Lincoln Cents*, Rancocas, NJ, 2009.

TWO-CENT PIECES

Flynn, Kevin. *Getting Your Two Cents Worth*, Rancocas, NJ, 1994.

NICKEL FIVE-CENT PIECES

Bowers, Q. David. *A Guide Book of Buffalo and Jefferson Nickels*, Atlanta, GA, 2007.

Bowers, Q. David. *A Guide Book of Shield and Liberty Head Nickels*, Atlanta, GA, 2006.

Fivaz, Bill, and Stanton, J.T. *The Cherrypickers' Guide to Rare Die Varieties*, Atlanta, GA, 2009.

Fletcher, Edward L., Jr. *The Shield Five Cent Series*, Ormond Beach, FL, 1994.

Lange, David W. *The Complete Guide to Buffalo Nickels*, Virginia Beach, VA, 2006.

Nagengast, Bernard. *The Jefferson Nickel Analyst* (2nd ed.), Sidney, OH, 1979.

Peters, Gloria, and Mahon, Cynthia. *The Complete Guide to Shield and Liberty Head Nickels*, Virginia Beach, VA, 1995.

HALF DIMES

Blythe, Al. *The Complete Guide to Liberty Seated Half Dimes*, Virginia Beach, VA, 1992.

Breen, Walter. *United States Half Dimes: A Supplement*, New York, 1958.

Logan, Russell, and McClosky, John. *Federal Half Dimes 1792–1837*, Manchester, MI, 1998.

Newlin, H.P. *The Early Half-Dimes of the United States*, Philadelphia, 1883 (reprinted 1933).

Valentine, D.W. *The United States Half Dimes*, New York, 1931 (reprinted 1975).

DIMES

Ahwash, Kamal M. *Encyclopedia of United States Liberty Seated Dimes 1837–1891*, Kamal Press, 1977.

Davis, David; Logan, Russell; Lovejoy, Allen; McCloskey, John; and Subjack, William. *Early United States Dimes 1796–1837*, Ypsilanti, MI, 1984.

Flynn, Kevin. *The 1894-S Dime: A Mystery Unraveled*, Rancocas, NJ, 2005.

Flynn, Kevin. *The Authoritative Reference on Roosevelt Dimes*, Brooklyn, NY, 2001.

Greer, Brian. *The Complete Guide to Liberty Seated Dimes*, Virginia Beach, VA, 2005.

Lange, David W. *The Complete Guide to Mercury Dimes* (2nd ed.), Virginia Beach, VA, 2005.

Lawrence, David. *The Complete Guide to Barber Dimes*, Virginia Beach, VA, 1991.

QUARTER DOLLARS

Bowers, Q. David. *A Guide Book of Washington and State Quarters*, Atlanta, GA, 2006.

Bressett, Kenneth. *The Official Whitman Statehood Quarters Collector's Handbook*, New York, 2000.

Briggs, Larry. *The Comprehensive Encyclopedia of United States Seated Quarters*, Lima, OH, 1991.

Browning, A.W. *The Early Quarter Dollars of the United States 1796–1838*. New York, 1925 (reprinted 1992).

Cline, J.H. *Standing Liberty Quarters* (3rd ed.), 1996.

Duphorne, R. *The Early Quarter Dollars of the United States*, 1975.

Fivaz, Bill, and Stanton, J.T. *The Cherrypickers' Guide to Rare Die Varieties*, Atlanta, GA, 2012.

Lawrence, David. *The Complete Guide to Barber Quarters*, Virginia Beach, VA, 1989.

Rea, Rory, Peterson, Glenn, Karoleff, Bradley, and Kovach, John. *Early Quarter Dollars of the U.S. Mint, 1796–1838*. 2010.

Tompkins, Steve M. *Early United States Quarters, 1796–1838*. 2008.

HALF DOLLARS

Flynn, Kevin. *The Authoritative Reference on Barber Half Dollars,* Brooklyn, NY, 2005.

Fox, Bruce. *The Complete Guide to Walking Liberty Half Dollars*, Virginia Beach, VA, 1993.

Lawrence, David. *The Complete Guide to Barber Halves*, Virginia Beach, VA, 1991.

Overton, Al C. *Early Half Dollar Die Varieties 1794–1836,* Colorado Springs, CO, 1967 (3rd ed., 1990, edited by Donald Parsley).

Peterson, Glenn R. *The Ultimate Guide to Attributing Bust Half Dollars*, Rocky River, OH, 2000.

Tomaska, Rick. *A Guide Book of Franklin and Kennedy Half Dollars* (2nd ed.), Atlanta, GA, 2012.

Wiley, Randy, and Bugert, Bill. *The Complete Guide to Liberty Seated Half Dollars*, Virginia Beach, VA, 1993.

SILVER DOLLARS

Bolender, M.H. *The United States Early Silver Dollars From 1794 to 1803* (5th ed.), Iola, WI, 1987.

Bowers, Q. David. *The Rare Silver Dollars Dated 1804*, Wolfeboro, NH, 1999.

Bowers, Q. David. *Silver Dollars and Trade Dollars of the United States: A Complete Encyclopedia*, Wolfeboro, NH, 1993.

Bowers, Q. David. *A Guide Book of Morgan Silver Dollars: A Complete History and Price Guide* (4th ed.), Atlanta, GA, 2012.

Burdette, Roger W. *A Guide Book of Peace Dollars* (2nd ed.), Atlanta, GA, 2012.

Fey, Michael S., and Oxman, Jeff. *The Top 100 Morgan Dollar Varieties*, Morris Planes, NJ, 1997.

Fivaz, Bill, and Stanton, J.T. *Cherrypickers' Guide to Rare Die Varieties of United States Coins* (5th ed., vol. II), Atlanta, GA.

Logies, Martin A. *The Flowing Hair Silver Dollars of 1794,* 2004.

Newman, Eric P., and Bressett, Kenneth E. *The Fantastic 1804 Dollar*, Racine, WI, 1962.

Van Allen, Leroy C., and Mallis, A. George. *Comprehensive Catalogue and Encyclopedia of U.S. Morgan and Peace Silver Dollars*, New York, 1997.

Willem, John M. *The United States Trade Dollar* (2nd ed.), Racine, WI, 1965.

GOLD PIECES ($1 THROUGH $20)

Akers, David W. *Gold Dollars (and Other Gold Denominations),* Englewood, OH, 1975–1982.

Bowers, Q. David. *A Guide Book of Double Eagle Gold Coins*, Atlanta, GA, 2004.

Bowers, Q. David. *A Guide Book of Gold Dollars,* Atlanta, GA, 2008.

Bowers, Q. David. *United States Gold Coins: An Illustrated History*, Wolfeboro, NH, 1982.

Breen, Walter. *Major Varieties of U.S. Gold Dollars (and Other Gold Denominations),* Chicago, 1964.

Dannreuther, John W., and Bass, Harry W. *Early U.S. Gold Coin Varieties*, Atlanta, GA, 2006.

Fivaz, Bill. *United States Gold Counterfeit Detection Guide*, Atlanta, GA, 2005.

Garrett, Jeff, and Guth, Ron. *Encyclopedia of U.S. Gold Coins, 1795–1933* (2nd ed.), Atlanta, GA, 2008.

COMMEMORATIVES

Bowers, Q. David. *A Guide Book of United States Commemorative Coins*, Atlanta, GA, 2008.

Bullowa, David M. *The Commemorative Coinage of the United States 1892–1938,* New York, 1938.

Flynn, Kevin. *The Authoritative Reference on Commemorative Coins 1892–1954,* Roswell, GA, 2008.

Swiatek, Anthony J. *Encyclopedia of the Commemorative Coins of the United States,* Chicago, IL, 2012.

Swiatek, Anthony, and Breen, Walter. *The Encyclopedia of United States Silver and Gold Commemorative Coins 1892–1954*, New York, 1981.

Taxay, Don. *An Illustrated History of U.S. Commemorative Coinage*, New York, 1967.

TOKENS AND MEDALS

Fuld, George, and Fuld, Melvin. *U.S. Civil War Store Cards*, Lawrence, MA, 1975.

Fuld, George, and Fuld, Melvin. *Patriotic Civil War Tokens,* Ypsilanti, MI, 1982.

Jaeger, Katherine, and Bowers, Q. David. *100 Greatest American Medals and Tokens*, Atlanta, GA, 2007.

Jaeger, Katherine. *A Guide Book of United States Tokens and Medals*, Atlanta, GA, 2008.

Rulau, Russell. *Standard Catalog of United States Tokens 1700–1900*, Iola, WI, 1997.

PATTERNS

Judd, J. Hewitt. *United States Pattern Coins* (10th ed., edited by Q. David Bowers), Atlanta, GA, 2008.

PRIVATE AND TERRITORIAL GOLD

Adams, Edgar H. *Official Premium Lists of Private and Territorial Gold Coins*, Brooklyn, NY, 1909.

Adams, Edgar H. *Private Gold Coinage of California 1849–1855*, Brooklyn, NY, 1913.

Bowers, Q. David. *A California Gold Rush History Featuring Treasure from the S.S.* Central America, Wolfeboro, NH, 2001.

Bowers, Q. David. *The History of United States Coinage as Illustrated by the Garrett Collection*, Los Angeles, 1979.

Breen, Walter, and Gillio, Ronald. *California Pioneer Fractional Gold* (2nd ed.), Santa Barbara, CA, 1983.

Clifford, Henry H. "Pioneer Gold Coinage in the West—1848–1861," reprint from *The Westerners Brand Book—Book Nine*, Los Angeles, 1961.

Griffin, Clarence. *The Bechtlers and Bechtler Coinage and Gold Mining in North Carolina 1814–1830*, Spindale, NC, 1929.

Kagin, Donald H. *Private Gold Coins and Patterns of the United States*, New York, 1981.

Lee, Kenneth W. *California Gold—Dollars, Half Dollars, Quarter Dollars*, Santa Ana, CA, 1979.

Leonard, Robert D., Jr., et al. *California Pioneer Fractional Gold by Walter Breen and Ronald J. Gillio* (2nd ed.), Wolfeboro, NH, 2003.

Owens, Dan. *California Coiners and Assayers*, Wolfeboro, NH, and New York, 2000.

Seymour, Dexter C. *The 1830 Coinage of Templeton Reid*, American Numismatic Society Museum Notes No. 22, New York, 1977.

WORLD ISSUES

Allen, Lyman L. *U.S. Philippine Coins*, Lyman Allen Numismatic Services, Oakland Park, FL, 1998.

Medcalf, Donald, and Russell, Ronald. *Hawaiian Money Standard Catalog* (2nd ed.), Mill Creek, WA, 1991.

Shafer, Neil. *United States Territorial Coinage for the Philippine Islands*, Whitman Publishing, 1961.

PROOF COINS AND PROOF SETS

Lange, David W. *A Guide Book of Modern United States Proof Coin Sets* (2nd ed.), Atlanta, GA, 2010.

TYPE COINS

Bowers, Q. David. *A Guide Book of United States Type Coins* (2nd ed.), Atlanta, GA, 2008.

Garrett, Jeff, and Guth, Ron. *100 Greatest U.S. Coins* (3rd ed.), Atlanta, GA, 2008.

Guth, Ron, and Garrett, Jeff. *United States Coinage: A Study by Type*, Atlanta, GA, 2005.

SEE THE OTHER SIDE FOR A SPECIAL FREE OFFER!

El Yunque   Chaco Culture   Acadia   Hawaiʻi   Denali

Starting in 2012, the U.S. Mint has issued special versions of the National Park quarters, struck at the San Francisco Mint and featuring an "S" mintmark. *These are the first circulation-strike coins to be produced at San Francisco in more than 30 years.* Not released into general circulation, they're available directly from the Mint in 40-coin rolls and 100-coin bags. For more information, visit Whitman.com.

FREE gift for readers of THE OFFICIAL RED BOOK®

Complete and mail this card to receive one free folder to collect and display your National Park quarters.

An $8⁹⁹ Value FREE!

National Park Cushioned Folder

120 openings, for every Philadelphia and Denver Mint quarter, 2010–2021

Which format of the Red Book do you most prefer?

☐ Red Book Professional Edition

☐ Large Print Red Book

☐ Spiralbound Red Book

☐ Red Book Bookazine

☐ Other

Have you tried the **RED BOOK Online** two-week free trial offer? ☐ Yes ☐ No

Are you collecting the new 2010–2021 America the Beautiful™ National Park quarters? ☐ Yes ☐ No

Before reading the Insider Tip at far right, were you aware of the new non-circulating 2012 America the Beautiful™ National Park S-mintmark quarters?
☐ Yes ☐ No

PLEASE PRINT

Name _____

Address _____

City _____

State _____ Zip _____

Email _____

Phone _____

Offer good in USA only. Postcard must be fully completed to receive a free folder. Limit one offer per address. Please allow 4–6 weeks for delivery. Offer expires 4/6/2014. No cash value. Void where prohibited by law.

SEE THE OTHER SIDE FOR A SPECIAL FREE OFFER!

El Yunque   Chaco Culture   Acadia   Hawai'i   Denali